总主编 张西平 〔美〕费乐仁

理雅各文集
第 1 卷

中国圣书（一）

书经、诗经、孝经

〔英〕理雅各 译注

丁大刚 潘琳 主编

商务印书馆
创于1897 The Commercial Press

THE SACRED BOOKS OF THE EAST   VOL. III
THE SACRED BOOKS OF CHINA   PART I
The Shû King
The Shih King
The Hsiâo King
Translated by James Legge

根据英国 Clarendon 出版社 1879 年版译出

北京外国语大学"双一流"建设重大标志性项目
"文明互鉴：中国文化与世界"
（2021SYLZD020）
研究成果

北京外国语大学比较文明与人文交流高等研究院
中国文化走出去协同创新中心
中华文化国际传播研究院
资助出版

总　序

张西平

　　1873 年，欧洲的首届国际东方学家大会在巴黎召开，这是对法国从雷慕沙到儒莲汉学成就的肯定。就大学体制内推进汉学发展而言，法国的首创之功受到欧洲东方学界的尊重是很自然的。1874 年，第二届国际东方学家大会在英国召开，理雅各（James Legge，1815—1897）已从中国回到了英国，这次会议在欧洲东方学史上同样具有重要的意义。"伦敦大会的召开，标志着东方学、比较科学以及汉学研究成就的火炬，已经从欧洲大陆传递到英国。这是汉学研究的一段进程，也可以说从儒莲时代，进入理雅各的新时代。理雅各最终返回英国的 1873 年，也是伟大的儒莲在巴黎辞世的那一年。"①

　　理雅各 1840 年抵达马六甲，1873 年从伦敦会退休，1897 年去世，无论是在中国身兼传教士和汉学家于一身的时候，还是返回英国开创牛津汉学时代期间，他都是一个极其勤奋的人。每日四点起床开始写作，直到晚年这个习惯都未改变。理雅各一生著作等身，从 1861 年开始，先后在香港出版五卷本《中国经典》，其中包含了《论语》《大学》《中庸》《孟子》《尚书》《诗经》《春秋》《左传》等中国古代文化的经典著作。1875 年他与马克斯·缪勒（Fredrich Max

---

① 〔美〕吉瑞德：《朝觐东方：理雅各评传》，段怀清、周俐玲译，广西师范大学出版社 2011 年版，第 125 页；另参见胡优静《英国 19 世纪的汉学史研究》，学苑出版社 2009 年版。

Müller，1823—1900）合作，为其主编的《东方圣书》贡献了六卷本的《中国圣书》，先后译注了《书经》《诗经》《孝经》《易经》《礼记》《道德经》《庄子》《太上感应篇》等中国重要典籍。在牛津期间他不仅先后翻译和写出了《佛国记》《景教碑》《中国的宗教：儒教、道教与基督教的对比》等著作，开展了一系列汉学讲座，而且对其早年在香港出版的《中国经典》进行修订，完善了自己对儒家文化的看法。理雅各一生笔耕不辍，在学术上取得了巨大的成就。

理雅各作为 19 世纪西方汉学的大师，作为中国经典英语翻译的实践者，在整个西方汉学史上，在中国经典外译史上都有着不可动摇的学术地位。[①]

首先，理雅各翻译的中国经典的数量是前无古人的。在西方汉学史上对中国经典的翻译是从来华的天主教传教士和基督新教传教士开始的。就明清之际来华的耶稣会士来说，对中国典籍翻译的集大成者是卫方济（Francois Noel，1651—1721）。他的翻译代表作是《中国六部古典文学：大学、中庸、论语、孟子、孝经、小学》，显然，他在翻译的数量上是无法和理雅各相比的。而在理雅各之前来华的新教传教士的中国典籍翻译则是零星展开的。

尽管雷慕沙和儒莲在翻译中国经典的种类上大大开拓了以往传教士所不注意的领域，但他们在翻译的数量上依然无法和理雅各相比。在对中国经典的翻译上理雅各所达到的高度无人可以企及。其实，即便将其放到整个 17—20 世纪的西方汉学史中，他的学术地位也是举足轻重，有人将他和卫礼贤（Richard Wilhelm，1873—1930）、顾赛芬（Couvreur Seraphin，1835—1919）并称为西方汉学的中国古代经典的三大翻译家。在这三位翻译家中，就翻译的数量

---

① 参见 Helen Edith Legge, *James Legge: Missionary and Scholar*, London: The Religious Tract Society, 1905。

来说，理雅各仍居于首位，这点在下面的研究中我们还会涉及。①

其次，理雅各译本的学术质量和影响力至今仍有重要的地位。②1875 年，理雅各获得了首届儒莲奖（Prix Stanislas Julien），说明他的汉学研究得到了欧洲汉学界的认可。③理雅各翻译的《中国经典》出版后在西方汉学界获得了好评，这些评论是对其长年从事中国典籍翻译的一种认可。最有代表性的是汉学家欧德理（Ernst Johann Eitel，1838—1908）在《中国评论》（*The China Review*）上发表的评论，这实际上是学术界第一次对理雅各译作的学术评论。他说："无论是在中国国内抑或国外，没有一个外国人对这个文明古国的经典之花的熟悉，无论是在广度、深度还是在可靠性上，能够与理雅各博士相匹敌。"④ 显然，在欧德理看来，理雅各在汉学翻译和研究上的水平已经超越了儒莲等法国汉学家。

最后，理雅各开创了英国汉学的新时期。19 世纪的英国汉学处于起步阶段，理雅各来到牛津大学任教。他在就职演讲中说道："牛津大学每次首立一个教授位置，就标志着一门新学科史上一个重要时代的开始"。⑤ 他的到来使汉学成为"英国学术界第一次在东方学的学科海洋中出现的一门新学科"，而理雅各从传教士到职业汉学家这个身份的转变也"从远在巴黎的儒莲和其他第一流的专门从事汉学研究的东方学家那里得到了肯定"。⑥ 同时，在理雅各时代，他

① 参见黄文江《理雅各：中西十字路口的先驱》（Wong Man Kong, *James Legge: A Pioneer at the Crossrads of East and West*, Hong Kong Educational Publishing Co., 1996）。

② 参见岳峰《架设东西方的桥梁——英国汉学家理雅各研究》，福建人民出版社 2004 年版。

③ 参见 T. H. Barrett, *Singular Listlessness, Short History of Chinese Books and British Scholars*, Wellsweep, 1989, p.76。

④ 转引自〔美〕吉瑞德《朝觐东方：理雅各评传》，段怀清、周俐玲译，第 64—65 页。

⑤ James Legge, *Inaugural Lecture on the Constituting of a Chinese Chair in the University of Oxford*, London: Trübner & co., 1876.

⑥ 〔美〕吉瑞德：《朝觐东方：理雅各评传》，段怀清、周俐玲译，第 64 页。

和欧洲汉学界保持着密切的联系，从而使英国汉学获得了良好的声誉。他对德国汉学家甲柏连孜教授（Georg Conon von der Gabelentz，1840—1893）代表作《汉文经纬》（*Chinesische Grammatik*）的热情赞扬，对青年汉学家们的帮助都显示出一位长者的大度与宽容，这些都提高了英国汉学的地位。1893 年，荷兰皇家科学院授予他荣誉研究员头衔，足见他在欧洲汉学界的地位。[①] 在理雅各生前与其有过争论的翟理斯（Herbert Allen Giles，1845—1935）在理雅各去世后写道："理雅各的著作对中国研究是最伟大的贡献，在今后的汉学研究中，人们将铭记他的贡献。"[②]

作为 19 世纪的西方汉学家，理雅各通过对中国经典的翻译，表达了他对中国历史文化的看法。这些观点与他广泛阅读中国历代的经典注释著作，特别是清代学者的训诂著作，是分不开的。在这些研究中，理雅各也表达了他的学术见解，一旦将其置于中国 19 至 20 世纪的学术史中，就会发现他的不少研究与观点是相当有价值的，值得我们深入思考。

例如，他对《春秋》真实性的评论和中国近代史学界的疑古思潮有异曲同工之处，正如刘家和先生所说，理雅各翻译的《春秋》出版以后，"在中国学术界首先出现了以康有为为代表的经今文公羊学派，他们对于《春秋》、《左传》的态度与理氏正好相反。可是，康氏所倡导的维新运动失败了。到了本世纪五四运动开始的时候，传统儒家意识形态已对知识界失去了号召力，'打倒孔家店'的口号直入云霄，在史学界随即也兴起了疑古的思潮。《春秋》被看作'最不成东西'的东西，《左传》也被视为刘歆之伪作，一切儒家经典都

---

① 参见潘琳《理雅各牛津时代思想研究》，北京外国语大学 2012 年博士论文。

② Lindsay Ride, "Biographical Note", *The Chinese Classics*, Hong Kong University, 1960, p. 21.

被视为过时的历史垃圾，激烈抨击的程度不知要比理氏高多少倍。尽管疑古学者与理氏在正面的方向指引上有所不同，但是二者同视中国文化不能再按老路走下去了，在这一点上双方则完全是一致的。也正是在这一点上，我们不妨把理氏对于《春秋》的见解看作是一种有意义的远见，他竟然先于当时中国学者而有见于此。当然，那也并非理氏个人的见识高于当时中国学者的问题，差别在于他和中国学者身历的是不同的文化背景和历史环境。"①

汉学家们对中国历史文化的研究大大开拓了中国学术研究的疆域，与中国学者同行的汉学家们展示了中国文化研究走向世界后，所呈现的多样性和复杂性。② 如何将他们的研究纳入中国学术研究的整体思考之中，如何了解他们的研究成果，熟悉他们的研究路数和话语，如何在与其对话中合理吸收其研究成果，推进本土研究的发展，如何在与其对话中，坚守中国本土立场，纠正其知识与观点上的不足。这都是中国传统文化国际化发展中必须解决的问题。自说自话已经不再可能，随汉学家起舞显然也不是一个真正的学术立场。从陈寅恪提出的"预流"到清华国学院的"汉学之国学"，前辈学者都有所尝试。今日的中国学术界在整体上仍显准备不足，十分可喜的是继刘家和先生之后，葛兆光的《宅兹中国：重建有关"中国"的历史论述》在这方面迈出了坚实的一步。③

---

① 刘家和:《理雅各〈中国经典〉第五卷引言》，见《中国经典》第 5 卷，华东师范大学出版社 2011 年版，第 11—12 页。

② 从瑞典汉学家高本汉（Klas Bernhard Johannes Karlgren，1889—1978）对中国近代语言学研究的影响，法国汉学家伯希和（Paul Pelliot，1878—1945）的敦煌研究和历史研究对中国近代的历史学界的冲击便可略窥一斑。参见桑兵《国学与汉学：近代中外学界交往录》，中国人民大学出版社 2010 年版。

③ 葛兆光《宅兹中国：重建有关"中国"的历史论述》表现出作者开阔的学术视野，将国外汉学家的研究纳入自己的研究之中，并给予独立而有见地的回答。这本书对中国历史的研究令我们耳目一新。

理雅各在汉学研究上所取得的成就与其生活的经历有直接的关系，如果同法国儒莲所代表的欧洲汉学界相比，中国的实际经验，尤其他 1873 年的华北之行对他的思想产生了重要的影响。另一个重要的原因是他与中国文人的密切合作。关于理雅各与中国文人的合作，费乐仁（Lauren F. Pfister）教授有一系列的论文，说明了他和这些文人之间的交往与互动。①

晚清学者王韬撰有《春秋左氏传集释》《春秋朔闰日至考》《春秋日食辨正》《春秋朔至表》等著作。他 1862 年到港之后，对理雅各翻译后三卷《中国经典》都有所帮助，尤其是《诗经》的翻译。理雅各在谈到王韬时说："有时候我根本用不着他，因为一整个星期我都不需要咨询他。不过，可能有时候又会出现这样的需要，而此时他对我又有巨大帮助，而且，当我着手撰写学术绪论的时候，他的作用就更大了。"② 王韬对理雅各也十分欣赏，他说："先生独不惮其难，注全力于十三经，贯串考核，讨流溯源，别具见解，不随凡俗。其言经也，不主一家，不专一说，博采旁涉，务极其通，大抵取材于孔、郑而折衷于程、朱。于汉、宋之学，两无偏袒。译有四

---

① 〔美〕费乐仁：《重认路径：对何进善著作的若干看法》（"Reconfirming the Way: Perspectives from the Writings of Rev. Ho Tsun-sheen", *Ching Feng*, Vol. 36, No. 4 [December 1993], pp. 218–259.）；《述而不作：近代中国第一位新教神学家何进善（1817—1871）》，载〔以色列〕伊爱莲等：《圣经与近代中国》，蔡锦图编译，香港汉语圣经协会 2003 年版，第 133—162 页；《一神论的探讨：理雅各和罗仲藩的解经学思考》（"Discovering Monotheistic Metaphysics: The Exegetical Reflections of James Legge [1815–1897] and Lo Chung-fan [d. circa 1850]", in Ng On-cho, et al., eds., *Imagining Boundaries: Changing Confucian Doctrines, Texts and Hermeneutics*, Albany: SUNY Press, 1999, pp. 213–254）；〔美〕费乐仁《王韬与理雅各对新儒家忧患意识的回应》（"The Response of Wang Tao and James Legge to the Modern Ruist Melancholy", *History and Culture* [Hong Kong] 2 [2001], pp. 1–20, 38）；或参见林启彦、黄文江主编《王韬与近代世界》，香港教育图书公司 2000 年版，第 117—147 页。

② 转引自〔美〕吉瑞德《朝觐东方：理雅各评传》，段怀清、周俐玲译，第 520 页。

子书、尚书两种。书出，西儒见之，咸叹其详明该洽，奉为南针。"①
理雅各在香港布道，王韬则因太平天国关系逃到香港，两人在香港
的合作促成了《中国经典》翻译事业的继续。这种合作如余英时所
说："理雅各如果不到香港，他便不可能直接接触到当时中国经学研
究的最新成果，他的译注的学术价值将不免大为减色。另一方面，
王韬到香港以后，接受了西方算学和天文学的新知识，这对于他研
究春秋时代的历法和日蚀有莫大的帮助。"②

理雅各在 19 世纪西方汉学史上的特殊性在于他是一个介乎传
教士汉学家和专业汉学家之间的人物，或者说从传教士汉学家转换
成为专业汉学家的代表。这样一种身份使他对中国经典有着自己的
独特理解，这种理解直接反映在他对中国经典的翻译之中。因此，
认真梳理理雅各思想的特点是我们全面把握他的汉学成就的一个基
本点。

理雅各在香港期间所从事的《中国经典》翻译的立足点是认为
在中国古代思想中有着一神论的信仰，在中国的《五经》中有着和
四福音书相类似的信仰。这是一个重要的观点，这个看法可以将他
对《中国经典》的翻译、对中国古代文化的崇敬与其每日所做的布
道工作有机结合起来。如他所说："传教士们应当祝贺他们自己，因
为在儒家思想中有那么多关于上帝的内容。"这样的一个立足点自然
使他对孔子、孟子的评价不高。在对《春秋》一书的翻译中，他对
孔子的看法表明了他的文化立场。最初理雅各是相信此书为孔子所
作的，后来又否认是孔子所作。在《中国经典》第五卷的绪论中，

① 王韬：《弢园文录外编》卷 8，1959 年，第 218 页。参见〔美〕费乐仁《王韬与理雅
各对新儒家忧患意识的回应》。
② 余英时：《香港与中国学术研究——从理雅各和王韬的汉学合作说起》，见《余英时
文集·第五卷·现代学人与学术》，广西师范大学出版社 2006 年版，第 457 页。

他用了大量篇幅来证明《春秋》非孔子所作，并且说道："如果他们不再赞同《春秋》中所记载的这些和长期以来他们已经接受与保持的信仰，那么，对中国人来说将是比任何帝国的衰落都要巨大的灾难性结果。当孔子的著作对他们来说已经完全不能再作为行为的指南时，中国人便将陷入危急的境地。如果我的《春秋》研究对他们确信这一点有帮助，并能促使他们离开孔子而另寻一位导师，那么我就实现了我终生的一个重大目标。"[①]

熟悉西方汉学史的人可以清楚地看到，理雅各的中国古代文化观并非他的发明创造，明末来华的意大利耶稣会士利玛窦（Matteo Ricci，1552—1610），所采取的"适应政策"的基点就是承认中国古代有着和西方一样的"上帝信仰"，只是被中国的后儒们遗忘了，传教士的任务就是唤醒中国人的这种信仰。所以，崇先儒而批后儒成为利玛窦的基本文化策略。在他的《天主实义》上卷第二篇中有段很有名的话："夫至尊无两，惟一焉耳。曰天曰地，是二之也……吾天主，乃古经书所称上帝也。《中庸》引孔子曰：'郊社之礼，以事上帝也。'……《商颂》云：'圣敬日跻，昭假迟迟，上帝是祗。'《雅》云：'维此文王，小心翼翼，昭事上帝。'《易》曰：'帝出乎震。'夫帝也者，非天之谓，苍天者抱八方，何能出于一乎'。……《汤誓》曰：'夏氏有罪，予畏上帝，不敢不正。'又曰：'惟皇上帝，降衷于下民，若有恒性，克绥厥猷惟后。'《金縢》周公曰：'乃命于帝庭，敷佑四方。'上帝有庭，则不以苍天为上帝，可知。历观古书，而知上帝与天主，特异以名也。"这些话全部都是引自《中庸》《诗》

---

① *The Chinese Classics*, Vol. 5, "prolegomena", p. 53. 理雅各这样的学术立场很自然会遭到中国学术界的批评，辜鸿铭在他的《中国学》《春秋大义》中就直接点名批评了理雅各，尤其不赞同他的《论语》翻译。参见岳峰《架设东西方的桥梁——英国汉学家理雅各研究》，第183—185页；黄兴涛《文化怪杰辜鸿铭》，中华书局1995年版，第61页。

《书》《易》《礼》这些中国古代经典。[①]理雅各在华期间在译名问题上坚持用"上帝"译名就和他的这一理解有关。理雅各晚年翻译《景教碑》（*The Nestorian Monument of Hsî-an Fû in Shen-hsî, China*）时，"毫不犹豫地站在了伟大的利玛窦的'自由'方法一边，这种方法试图调和对中国的一些'宗教术语'和'祭祀习惯'的使用。"[②]

理雅各离华前的华北之行对其以后的思想产生了重要的影响，特别是回到牛津后与比较宗教学家缪勒的共事，他在《东方圣书》中开始重新修订出版中国的古代文化经典，缪勒的比较思想为他提供了重新理解中国思想的角度和方法。缪勒在第二届国际东方学家大会上的发言很经典，他说："首先，东方研究曾经被当作同北方民族在罗马和雅典所学的课程一样来学习，那就是，在我们的世界之外，还有别的世界，还有别的宗教、别的神话、别的法则，而且从泰利斯到黑格尔的哲学史，并非人类思想的所有历史。在所有这些主题上，东方都为我们提供了平行的相似性，即在所有包含在平行的相似性之中的比较的、检测的和理解的可能性。"[③]显然，这和维多利亚时代的自由主义思潮是连在一起的，尽管在这种对异文化的宽容中仍是以西方固有的文化价值为尺度来比较的，但已经承认了文化的多元性，承认了"还有别的世界，还有别的宗教、别的神话、别的法则"。这已经走出了基督教思想具有唯一性的狭隘理解。

如何看待理雅各这样的文化立场呢？吉瑞德将"理雅各主义"说成是一种"汉学东方主义"，其实用"东方主义"是不足以解释西方汉学历史的，理雅各思想的复杂性和多面性是很难用一个后现代

---

① 关于利玛窦的研究参见朱维铮《利玛窦中文著译集》，复旦大学出版社 2001 年版；张西平《跟随利玛窦来中国：1500—1800 年中西文化交流史》，中国社会科学出版社 2020 年版；林金水《利玛窦与中国》，中国社会科学出版社 1996 年版。

② 〔美〕吉瑞德：《朝觐东方：理雅各评传》，段怀清、周俐玲译，第 351 页。

③ 转引自〔美〕吉瑞德《朝觐东方：理雅各评传》，段怀清、周俐玲译，第 124 页。

思潮和方法来解释的。在中国学术研究和中国思想史的研究者看来，理雅各直到晚年仍未完全透彻地理解中国思想中的上古思想和孔子代表的儒家思想的关联，以及这种转变所形成的原因，仍坚持认为上古的思想更为纯洁。他也一直未全面理解中国文化的"大传统"与"小传统"之间复杂和多元的关系，从而无法解释儒家所代表的知识阶层和民间信仰之间的关系。① 对孔子地位的起伏与变迁，他很难从中国政治思想史的角度给予合理的说明。② 同时，他的翻译也有许多可以讨论的地方。

尽管"理雅各将自己整个生命用来发现、理解和评价这个古老的中国世界"，但作为中国文化的一个"他者"，他在苏格兰时期所奠定的世界观，"苏格兰常识哲学学派，特别是此流派与福音教会形式的新教世界观之间的关联，业已成为了理雅各的强大理智全副武器。"③ 理雅各永远不可能像一个中国学者那样来理解中国文化。在理雅各对孔子的解释中所呈现出来的文化本色是很正常的、很自然的。"他者"作为"异文化"的阅读者和批评者，永远是其所阅读和观察的文化，反思自身和确立自身的对话者。跨文化之间的"误读"是文化交流与思想移动的正常现象，对于这种"误读"既不能将其看成毫无意义的解释，或者将这种"误读"作为西方帝国主义对中国文化的扭曲的铁证；同样，也不能因为这些架起东西文化桥梁的人的辛劳和对中国文化的尊敬而忽视他们的"误读"。简单地用西方学术界创造出来的"乌托邦"和"意识形态"这样的概念来对待文化之间的交流与理解，来解释这些文化间的"转移者"的复杂性格与

---

① 参见 1893 年《中国经典》第一卷绪论部分第 97—101 页对孔子宗教观的解释。

② 参见 1893 年《中国经典》第一卷绪论部分第 92 页对孔子历史地位变化的评价。

③ 参见张西平、〔美〕费乐仁《理雅各〈中国经典〉绪论》，《中国经典》第 1 卷，第 16—18 页。

特点是远远不够的。对西方汉学的研究，在方法论上必须有一种新的理论创新，不加批判地移植西方时髦的理论，来解释西方汉学历史中的复杂人物和复杂过程是远远不够的。①

西方汉学史上对理雅各的评价是复杂的，他的立场始终受到来自保守主义和自由主义两方面的批评。②无论理雅各坚信中国古代文化所具有的宗教性，还是当代汉学家已经完全抛弃了理雅各所认同的中国古代思想宗教性的论述，中国文化的独特性、中国文化与西方文化的巨大差异性都困扰着西方汉学家。用"东方主义"是说不清这种文化间移动的复杂状态的，我们必须看到理雅各作为文化之间的传播者，作为中国古代文化典籍的最有影响的翻译者，他所表现出来的矛盾与变化，所最终呈现出来的对原有文化底色的坚持与对东方文化的重新理解都是文化间移动的必然产物，这些都必须从跨文化的角度给予理解和解释。③

因此，要将西方对中国经典的翻译研究放入西方近代的思想

---

① 问题在于中国学界一些人看不到西方汉学作为不同的知识和思想体系的学术产物所具有的"异质性"，特别是在当下中国文化走向世界之时，简单将西方汉学的一些经典译本拿来就用，而没有考虑其"异质性"。在这些学者眼中"汉学"或者说"中国学"就是关于中国的知识，它和"国学"以及中国本土学者的研究没有太大的区别。这其实是很复杂的问题。一般而言，在知识系统上，汉学家们的研究是可取的，在这点上是无中外之分的，但在知识的评价系统上，就十分复杂，要做跨文化的分析，例如理雅各。因此，在中国经典的翻译上不加批判和分析地采用西方汉学家的翻译须格外谨慎。湖南出版社出版的"汉英对照中国古典学术名著丛书"采用的是理雅各的《四书》译本，中国学者刘重德、罗志野校注。这本书将理雅各有价值的译注全部删去了，而对理雅各的译文并未做实质性的修改。

② 参见〔美〕吉瑞德《朝觐东方：理雅各评传》，段怀清、周俐玲译，第341页。

③ 这对我们当下中国文化走出去的理论研究来说是一个亟待解决的文化理论问题。这里表现出两种倾向：一种观点认为，外国人很难准确理解和翻译中国的文化典籍，故主张中国典籍的外译应以中国学者为主；另一种观点认为，中国典籍的外译最终是给外国人看的，外语再好也好不过母语，而且从翻译的数量上也基本应由汉学家来翻译。如果以汉学家为主来进行翻译，理雅各的问题自然就会出现，如果中国典籍的外译都由中国人来翻译，这几乎是不可能做到的。

史中考察，这样的翻译研究绝不仅仅是一个翻译技能问题，而是西方对东方思想的理解问题。但这只是我们考察中国经典外译的一个维度，如果从中西文化交流的角度，从将中国介绍给世界，推动西方世界对中国理解的角度看，理雅各的工作是伟大的，是前无古人的。他是 19 世纪后半叶西方汉学的真正领袖。英国汉学家艾约瑟（Joseph Edkins，1823—1905）在理雅各去世后曾这样评价道：

> 如今，甚至即便在理雅各已经离开了我们，不再与我们一起的时候，他殚精竭虑经年累月的付出，那些卷帙浩繁的译著，依然包含着丰富的事实，通过这些事实，欧洲和美国的观察者可以如此正确地判断中国人，因为这是他们生活的箴言，在他们的生活当中流行，这里所包含、所阐明的思想观点，规范着他们的学者和人民的思想。这里所包含的原则，打破了区域性的界限，将整个民族连接在一起。想想《圣经》对于基督徒意味着什么；想想莎士比亚对于学习英国诗歌的学生意味着什么；想想《可兰经》对于穆罕默德的信徒意味着什么，这些儒家经典通往普遍的中国思想。将这些书置放在那些绝望地看着《孟子》或者《书经》某一页的人手上，就是一种最坚实的服务，一个最为有用的成就。①

《理雅各文集》对于理雅各的作品进行了翻译和整理，由张西平、费乐仁任总主编，潘琳、丁大刚任分卷主编并承担主要的整理、翻译、审校工作。文集共 15 卷，具体内容如下：

---

① Helen Edith Legge, *James Legge: Missionary and Scholar*, pp. 38-39. 译文参考了段怀清《晚清英国新教传教士"适应"中国策略的三种形态及其评价》，《世界宗教研究》2006 年第 4 期。

第1—6卷影印了理雅各翻译的《中国圣书》，包括《书经》《诗经》《孝经》《易经》《礼记》《道德经》《庄子》等。并辅以费乐仁为各卷所撰"导读""索引"。赵倞、刘霁、顾庆瑞等人参与了翻译工作。

第7卷编译了理雅各为《中国经典》五卷撰写的"序言""导论"。因《中国经典》已影印出版，故文集不再收入。

第8卷包括理雅各在牛津大学的讲稿，以及在期刊上发表的有关中国历史、典籍研究的论文。杨慧玲、程熙旭等人参与了翻译工作。

第9卷整理出版理雅各指导何进善翻译的《正德皇帝游江南》，此外，本卷还收录了理雅各翻译的《河南奇荒铁泪图》《佛国记》《景教碑》等。其中，《佛国记》的序言、导论和注释由法显研究专家张梁（笔名东夷）翻译。

第10卷收录了理雅各的游记、自传、他传等。

第11卷辑录了理雅各晚年的未刊翻译手稿，以中国文史经典作品为主；并附上两份藏书目录。

第12卷收录理雅各自1830年代至1890年代所写的信件，另附部分回信，以便于读者了解某些重要事件的前因后果。

第13—15卷收录理雅各的宗教研究论著及手稿。

本文集是世界范围内第一次系统整理和翻译理雅各的译作、著作、手稿和档案文献，从开始筹备到正式立项出版，历经十余年时间。在此过程中，得到了诸多前辈、学者、同仁出版界人士的帮助。如早期在牛津大学进行档案复制时，获得了理雅各的重孙克里斯托弗·理雅各（Christopher Legge）的授权，他也出席了在香港和北京举行的学术会议。费乐仁一直以来为文集的出版倾注了很多心血，这次更是为文集出版撰写了35万字的导读。潘琳在伦敦大学亚非学院进行文献复制时，曾得到傅熊教授（Prof. Bernhard Fuehrer）及夫人的热心帮助。中国社会科学院的辛岩老师翻译了《中国的宗教》以及《中国人的鬼神观》初稿，如今辛岩老师已经仙逝，他所留下的遗产我们会将其发扬光大。北京外国语大学海外汉学中心（现名中国文化研究院）的杨慧玲、康太一等师生都曾参与了翻译工作。上海师范大学外国语学院张斌老师在纽约公共图书馆拍摄了《理雅各牧师书房存书目录》。上海师范大学的多位硕士研究生参与了文献录入和整理工作。还有商务印书馆的各位编辑也为文集的顺利出版做了大量工作。曾经为这套多达15卷，筹备长达十年的文集提供帮助的人无法在此一一列举，在此一并向他们表示衷心的感谢。最重要的是，我们应当感谢北京外国语大学，没有来自北京外国语大学的慷慨资助，本文集将不会有机会问世。

在世界范围内展开中华文明的研究，当以学术史的梳理、文献的整理与出版为基础，唯此才能展现文明互鉴的波澜壮阔的历史。

本卷说明

　　《理雅各文集》第 1 卷辑录了由理雅各译注的《中国圣书》第 1 卷《书经》《诗经》《孝经》。该书采用英国学者马克斯·缪勒主编的《东方圣书》第 3 卷的英文影印本，于 1879 年出版。其中理雅各所撰序言和导论及费乐仁撰写的导读，均译成中文，收入本卷。

目　录

理雅各《中国圣书》总论

费乐仁

一、《中国圣书》实现了理雅各的愿景

　　1875 年初，缪勒邀请理雅各参加他主持的一个宗教学项目，那是 19 世纪晚期最大的翻译工程。[①] 在这项特别的工程中，理雅各负责中国两大宗教传统（儒教和道教）"圣书"的译注。这一邀请还与理雅各被提名任职牛津大学首位中国语言文学教授一事有关，缪勒在促成这件事的过程中发挥了重要作用。缪勒希望实现的是让理雅各与众多学者一起参与计划中的一大套丛书《东方圣书》。重要的是，为什么缪勒会在 1875 年选择理雅各参与如此重大的出版工程？其中有非常充分的理由。当时，理雅各因其在"儒学"领域的学术贡献——以《中国经典》（*The Chinese Classics*）为名翻译的八部儒经——在欧洲汉学界可谓声名显赫。理雅各 1861 年出版《中国经典》第一卷后，缪勒不仅知晓这一工程，而且还在其出版不久之后写了一个书评；因为缪勒对中文感兴趣，也一直在促进东方宗教经典的研究。[②] 事实上，在较短时间内（1861—1872）完成了五卷八册

[①] 根据吉瑞德的研究，缪勒给理雅各写的第一封信的日期是 1875 年 2 月 13 日，此后他们之间有大量的通信。参见〔美〕吉瑞德《维多利亚时代翻译中国：理雅各的东方朝圣之旅》（Norman J. Girardot, *The Victorian Translation of China: James Legge's Oriental Pilgrimage*, Berkeley: The University of California Press, 2002），第 161 页。

[②] 同上书，第 138 页。

《中国经典》丛书的翻译出版之后，1875 年的理雅各已年近花甲，这充分证明了他在阅读海量中国文献方面的学术能力。这使缪勒等人非常自然地认为，理雅各很有可能继续从事中国典籍研究工作至少一二十年。

让理雅各获得声誉的另外两件事，缪勒也完全知晓。1873 年，享誉国际的汉学家儒莲去世，享年 74 岁。为了纪念他卓绝的汉学成就，汉学界创立了儒莲奖，用于奖励年度最佳著作。理雅各是这个奖项的第一位获得者，① 但是这个奖不是仅仅颁给其《中国经典》的最后一卷，而是颁给这一整套从 1861 到 1872 年出版的丛书。② 那么，从这个角度讲，就像吉瑞德用睿智之言概括的那样，这开启了"汉学的理雅各时代"（the Leggian Epoch of Sinology），③ 直到1897年理雅各去世。

由于本文的读者都能读到理雅各修订的《中国经典》第二版（1893—1895），以及他为缪勒翻译工程贡献的六卷本《中国圣书》（1879—1891）；因此有必要花点时间描述这两者之间的互文关系，以及这一互文关系在《中国圣书》中如何进一步地得到表现。这样

---

① 参见 Girardot, *The Victorian Translation of China*, p. 100，吉瑞德提到了儒莲的逝世日期，也提到了儒莲奖。1875 年 12 月 14 日，缪勒在写给理雅各的信中说："失去儒莲之后，我想你将成为我了解中国的新向导。"（同上书，第 164 页）

② 吉瑞德起初认为这个奖只是颁给理雅各《中国经典》的最后一部著作（即第五卷《春秋左传》的翻译），但后来他说这是颁给这套丛书所有卷册的。参见 Girardot, *The Victorian Translation of China*, pp. 100, 142。法文官方文件称是颁给理雅各《中国经典》所有八册书的，法文原文是 "Receuil des classiques chinois avec traduction et commentaires en anglaise"（英文译注《中国经典》丛书）。参见 *Comptes rendus des séances de l'Académie des Inscriptions et Belles Lettre*, Vol. 19, issue 4 (1875), p. 376。

③ 这个短语是吉瑞德描述这一时期所用的一个小标题，参见 Girardot, *The Victorian Translation of China*, pp. 142-144。

的关系出现在《中国圣书》每卷的"导论"①和通常②以脚注形式呈现的评注性阐释中。纵观理雅各对欧洲汉学的两大学术贡献——儒家经典和道家经典的翻译，不难明白理雅各为什么认为《中国圣书》实现了他长久以来的学术愿景。事实上，这六卷书中的前四卷是1850年代理雅各在香港时就憧憬要完成的译本，那时他是伦敦会（London Missionary Society）的传教士。③（参见文后附录）他最初的愿景是译注重要的儒家经典，并在1872年出版的《中国经典》第五卷"序言"中重申了这一愿景。他说："现在只剩下《礼记》和《易经》要翻译和注解了。"如他所预见的那样，到那时他将"全部完成"他1850年代中期的设想。④事实上，他最终承诺缪勒翻译《中

①　这些"导论"通常都在每卷的"序言"之后，但并非全部如此。例如，《中国圣书》第四卷（《东方圣书》第二十八卷）和《中国圣书》第六卷（《东方圣书》第四十卷）开篇就没有"导论"，因为它们是两卷译本的下卷（前者是《礼记》译本，后者是《庄子》译本）。而且，在第一卷和第六卷，特别分开介绍了一些"小经"。例如，《中国圣书》第一卷（《东方圣书》第三卷）介绍了选自《诗经》的宗教诗歌和《孝经》；《中国圣书》第六卷（《东方圣书》第四十卷）介绍了《太上感应篇》这部较小且后出的"道教文本"。因此，读者要特别注意这些"导论"的位置。

②　我在这里之所以附加"通常"一词，是因为在最后两卷《中国圣书》中，理雅各用了另一种评注方式。对于《中国圣书》第五卷中《道德经》的翻译，以及《中国圣书》第六卷前四个附录所呈现的四个后期道教小册子的翻译，理雅各没有采取脚注，而是将阐释性讨论和其他评注信息融入了正文，放在正文每个章节之后。他在《中国经典》第五卷《左传》的翻译中也采用了这种形式，这样做的原因是，可以将《左传》的译文与评注文字以同样小号的英文单词和汉字来呈现。

③　根据我对理雅各早期作为伦敦会传教士生涯的研究——这时理雅各成就了他"传教士-学者"的生活方式，我发现他第一次提出翻译和研究中国经典的愿景是在他1848年写的一篇日记中；但《中国经典》的大部分实际工作成形于1858年，一直持续到1872年。拙著《为完成"人所当尽的本分"而奋斗：苏格兰新教传教士理雅各与中国的遭遇》（*Striving for "The Whole Duty of Man": James Legge and the Scottish Protestant Encounter with China*, Frankfurt am Main: Peter Lang, 2004）第二卷 重点解读了他的《中国经典》。我在该书第一卷第185页描述了他最初的愿景，直接讨论《中国经典》各卷的篇章，参见第二卷第62、63、75、76、150—165、173—191、208—218页。

④　引文参见 James Legge, trans. and comm., *The Chinese Classics: The Ch'un Ts'ew with The Tso Chuen*, Vol. S, Hong Kong: Anglo-Chinese Press, 1872, p. v。

国圣书》，这把他最初的愿景又向前推进了一步，这不仅使他进入了新的儒经翻译领域，也使他后来进入了道家经典的翻译和阐释领域。那时的理雅各显然没有忘记他最初的愿景，所以他在《中国圣书》第三卷（《东方圣书》第二十七卷）的"序言"中说：

> 请容许我表达我的欣慰之情，随着《礼记》两卷本的出版，我已经完成而且超额完成了 25 年前我开始承担的《中国经典》的翻译工作。1861 年第一卷［《中国经典》］出版之后，我的朋友、已故的儒莲写信问我是否会考虑翻译卷帙浩繁的《礼记》，并且对我是否能完成它表示怀疑。然而，我开始了这项工作并最终完成了，尽管中间不得不被打断好几次，并且还要完成许多其他工作。①

为什么理雅各会在 1885 年说他"已经完成而且超额完成了"那一愿景？敏锐的读者也许已经注意到理雅各为《东方圣书》添加的众多内容中的其中一项，即放弃不甚完善的马礼逊汉语拼音体系，改用比较完善的威妥玛拼音体系，*这是自 1873 或 1874 年后理雅各所研究和刻意应用的拼音体系。然而，理雅各做得更多的是互文注释和阐释（参见附录）。理雅各不仅翻译了八部儒经，甚至 1861 年《中国经典》第一卷出版之前，就广泛阅读了中国的经书和其他古代文本。正如我们所看见的那样，为了翻译和解释"四书"（《论语》《大学》《中庸》《孟子》），理雅各此前已经研读了部分《书经》

---

① 理雅各译注：《中国圣书》（James Legge, trans. and comm., *The Sacred Books of China: The Texts of Confu-cianism,* Part IV, Oxford: Oxford University Press, 1882），第三卷，第 xi 页（即《理雅各文集》第 3 卷边码，余同。——译者）。

* 理雅各在《中国圣书》中使用的不是威妥玛拼音体系，而是缪勒制定的东方字母表拼音方案。参见《中国圣书》第一卷，第 xxx 页（指原书页码，即本书边码，余同。——译者）。——译者

《诗经》《礼记》《易经》和《春秋》。尤其需要注意的是，这五部经典中，有些作品纷繁复杂，浩大广博。总的来讲，这些经典涵盖了大量的跨学科研究话题，包括中国古代史、文化、诗歌、占卜、形而上学、祭祀，以及其他文化和宗教仪式。到理雅各 1871 年开始翻译《诗经》和 1872 年开始翻译《春秋左传》之时，为了以学术的方式解释那些儒经，他参考了 17 部其他儒家经典和古代作品（参见我为本书制作的"索引"）。另外，需要强调的是，这还不包括他参阅的众多中国评注作品，而且有时候还在注释中翻译部分评注。① 在那个没有电脑和互联网档案可供检索的年代，理雅各经过艰苦卓绝的努力，最终完成了中国古典文学的研究工作，这是东亚、东南亚、欧洲、北美、南美等世界各地鲜有人能完成的工作。

然而，对于 19 世纪晚期及当代的汉学研究而言，关于理雅各卓越的成就，有待我们理解的东西还有很多。仔细阅读附录，读者将发现理雅各在《中国圣书》中"重复"了他在《中国经典》中译注过的四部书。② 在《中国圣书》第一卷，他又完整地呈现了《书经》（这是理雅各偏爱的书名，通常被称为《尚书》）和近三分之一的《诗经》。③ 另外，在《中国圣书》第四卷，他还呈现了《中庸》和《大学》的另一个译本。这次理雅各没有接受朱熹重构和解释的"今本"，而是翻译了《礼记》的"古本"。④ 这一翻译选择的历史意义和诠释

---

① 在五卷八册的《中国经典》丛书中，理雅各为了完成翻译和相关的阐释性工作，参考了三百多部中文作品，包括注疏、史书、阐释性和语言学性质的工具书。

② 我之所以为"重复"一词加了双引号，是因为理雅各非常谦虚地说自己"只是"呈现了之前所做的工作；但如我在《中国圣书》第一卷"导读"中所言，他显然是重译了那卷书中的《书经》和《诗经》。

③ 即《诗经》305 篇诗中的 100 多篇。

④ 在我最近的工作中，尤其是近期在中国大学的几次讲座和拙著《后世俗视角下的中国哲学问题》(*Vital Post-Secular Perspectives on Chinese Philosophical Issues*) 中，我强调了今天围绕朱熹"今本"《大学》《中庸》所产生的哲学争论的意义。中国的读者知道，这一争论是由台湾学者傅佩荣所著《朱熹错了》（东方出版社，2013 年）一

意义突出表现在理雅各重译《中庸》标题为 *The State of Equilibrium and Harmony*，我们不可低估这一意义。① 在下文中，我将说明理雅各参与 19 世纪晚期欧洲"汉学东方主义"，② 与他译注《中国圣书》时所做的许多根本性变化有重要关系。这其中的一个选择是，他关注如何解释和反映中国儒家和道家经典主要注疏传统之间的既复杂又多面的种种亚传统（subtraditions），而他的关注是有着自己原则的。从这一更为宽广的阐释视角出发，理雅各不仅没有被欧洲思潮限制住他的阐释视野，而且通过参考他精心挑选的中国标准文本和评注传统，证明其翻译和阐释选择合理性的同时，为欧洲思潮提供了信息和知识，也向其发起了挑战，纠正和克服了欧洲思潮所存在的问题。③

（接上页）书引起的。在英语世界，引发对《大学》《中庸》的"今本"和"古本"阐释性差异关注的是艾乔恩、王平对《大学》《中庸》的专业翻译和阐释。（Ian Johnston and Wang Ping, trans. and comm., *Daxue and Zhongyong: Bilingual Edition*, Hong Kong: The Chinese University Press, 2012.）我在《后世俗视角下的中国哲学问题》第四章《〈大学〉〈中庸〉的后世俗启示"（Post-Secular Revelations regarding the *Dàxué* and the *Zhōngyōng*）详细探讨了从 12 世纪到 21 世纪儒家知识分子围绕这两个文本进行争论的哲学意义。参见 Lauren Pfister, *Vital Post-Secular Perspectives on Chinese Philosophical Issues*, New York: Lexington Books, 2020, pp. 133-168。

① 理雅各 1861 年把这个标题译为 *The Doctrine of the Mean*，但他当时也明白这一翻译不能充分表达"中庸"的意义。1885 年，随着理雅各理解的加深，他决定改变这一译名，但之前的译名由于有亚里士多德哲学的意味，已经深入人心，因此在英语中仍被用于指称这个文本，尽管已经出现了许多其他的译法，包括他自己偏爱的新译名。参见理雅各对这一问题的说明：*The Chinese Classics*, Vol. 1, 1893, p. 383。

② 这是吉瑞德在《维多利亚时代翻译中国：理雅各的东方朝圣之旅》中不断提及的主要阐释视角，我欣赏这一视角在欧洲背景下的文化和历史广度。但吉瑞德的这一视角忽略了理雅各在文化转化方面所采取的谨慎态度；在翻译和阐释儒家和道家著作时，理雅各始终坚持给出中国众多评注者注疏的理据。

③ 我最初在试图论述理雅各跨文化翻译研究的诸多标准时，发明了"翻译中的正典"（canon-in-translation）一词，即翻译作品在目标语中成为了经典。参见 Lauren Pfister, "Classics or Sacred Books? Grammatological and Interpretive Problems of Ruist and Daoist Scriptures in the Translation Corpora of James Legge (1815-1897) and

　　因此，从理雅各自己的思想和精神历程来看，他在 1885 年完成了他早在 30 年前所许下的思想挑战和跨文化翻译的愿景：以学术评注的方式翻译所有的儒家经典。[①] 不过，有几部重要的儒经，理雅各并未翻译。这包括《仪礼》，还有《春秋》的另两传——《穀梁传》《公羊传》，理雅各虽然经常引用这两部著作，但没有提供全译本。[②] 即便如此，理雅各所完成的知识壮举也是后来的传教士很少能够在其他欧洲语言中完成的。[③] 我们都知道，理雅各继续用了五年多时间

　　（接上页）Richard Wilhelm (1873-1930)", in Max Deeg, Oliver Frieberger, and Christoph Kline, eds., *Kanonizierung und Kanon-bildung in der asiatischen Religionsgeschichte*, Vienna: Austrian Academy of Sciences, 2011, pp. 421-463。在这篇文章中，我列举了理雅各汉学翻译的 15 条标准（同上书，第 437—452 页），并且比较了中国儒家和道家经典理雅各的英语翻译和卫礼贤的德语翻译（同上书，第 455 页）。我发明的"翻译中的正典"一语及其详尽解释，还有阿斯曼（Jan and Alexia Assmann）所说的"正典症候群"的六个特征，参见我的上述文章（同上书，第 424 页）。

① 这是拙著《为完成"人所当尽的本分"而奋斗：苏格兰新教传教士理雅各与中国的相遇》第二卷研究的主题。详见前文注释。

② 考虑到《左传》的巨大篇幅，这本身就是一项艰巨的工作。理雅各选译了《公羊传》和《穀梁传》的部分内容，但他说："它们真的没有什么值得我认真思考的。"（《中国经典》第五卷，第 36 页）尽管有这样的看法，理雅各还是为英语读者选译了这两传（《中国经典》第五卷，第 54—81 页）。理雅各在翻译《左传》时，仍不时地在注释中引用这两部书。许多情况下，它们的主张相同，因此理雅各就在注释中简单地称"Kung and Kuh"或"Kuh and Kung"（参见《中国经典》第五卷，第 6 页右、28 页左、34 页右、48 页左、115 页右、171 页左、214 页左、420 页右、517 页左、579 页右 2 次、681 页右、759 页左）。有时候为了指出异文、阐释的差异或不同的主张，理雅各也会单独提及某一传或称其全名（参见《中国经典》第五卷，第 274 页右、322 页左、388 页左、472 页左、606 页左、681 页右、737 页右、807 页右）。两传所涵盖年份结束之时，理雅各也指出了这两传的全名（第 834 页右），尽管《左传》的记载还持续了数年。这一切说明理雅各是比照着阅读这三传的，在译注《中国经典》第五卷的整个过程中，他都认真地思考了这三传。

③ 我这里想到的是当时住在徐家汇的意大利耶稣会士晁德莅（Angelo Zottoli, 1826—1902）于 1879—1882 年用拉丁文翻译的部分儒家著作；住在中国东北的法国耶稣会士顾赛芬（Séraphin Couvreur, 1835—1919）于 1895—1916 年用教会拉丁文和法文翻译了多部儒经；在青岛（1910—1920）和北京（1922—1924）工作的德国路德会传教士卫礼贤（Richard Wilhelm, 1873—1930）用德语翻译了少量儒经；还有住在澳门（1979—1988）的葡萄牙耶稣会士戈振东（Joaquim Guerra, 1908—1993）用葡萄牙语翻译了多部儒经。

研读中国经典，最终翻译出版了代表道教传统的最后两卷《中国圣书》。从这两卷书的"导论"和评注中可以明显看出来，理雅各这样做更多是为了满足缪勒的喜好，而非他自己的。但理雅各仍然以一贯的严谨和批判的眼光来对待这两卷书，包括他认为无论从哪个方面来讲这两部道教经典都是非常了不起的；还有出自后来道教的五份小册子，他认为它们远远够不上圣书的标准。另外，他还翻译了为老子和庄子写的两个赞辞。一个是6世纪晚期薛道衡写的《老子庙碑》，这是一篇杰作，理雅各非常欣赏。另一个是11世纪中国著名的文学家苏轼写的《庄子祠堂记》，但理雅各觉得这篇文章没有真正显示出苏轼敏锐的思维。

二、理雅各将《中国经典》编织进《中国圣书》的其他方式

我这里进一步指出这两套皇皇译著之间的关联，目的是说明理雅各为了突出《中国圣书》不同篇章的内容，常常在"导论"和评注中参照《中国经典》。我们已经在《中国圣书》第一卷的"导论"和注释中发现了这样的关联。《中国圣书》第一卷所包含的三部经典，全部引用和参考了《中国经典》中的"四书"和其他"三经"。我们可以在理雅各这卷书的评注中找到这些引用，在他后期翻译的其他儒经中也可以找到这样的引用。另外，他还参考了许多古代的历史类和训诂类的书。他在其他五卷《中国圣书》（包括两卷"道教文本"）的注释中参阅的儒经有《论语》《中庸》《孟子》《诗经》《春秋》以及《左传》。也就是说，理雅各继续通过互文讨论，以及对儒家和道家"圣书"的跨文化理解，增进其文本的深度，而这多半都是通过参阅他已经翻译过的儒经实现的。那么，从这个意义上讲，理雅各为儒家和道家传统提供的是儒学视角下的阐释，这一视角主

要是受到了元代和清代儒家学者批判道家宗教主张的影响。缪勒为理雅各提供了阐释的契机，但他大概不知道理雅各是这样做的。从这个方面来看，理雅各的阐释方法不仅参考了许多儒家经典文献，而且通过引用儒家学者的评注突出其重要意义，还常常直接批评古代的道家和后来的道教主张。当然，理雅各还引用了许多解释《孝经》《易经》《礼记》的儒家注疏，但这些经书都不在《中国经典》丛书中。今天的读者也许没想到的是，理雅各不仅阅读和翻译道家经典以及后来出现的道教小册子，而且依靠之前不知名的儒家评注者挑战这些著作中的世界观和宗教主张。事实上，理雅各在《中国圣书》评注中所表现出来的这些阐释偏好被忽略了，这很不应该；结果，人们基本上都误解了最后两卷书中他所做工作的争议性，即19世纪晚期他对道教主张进行汉学评价所引发的争议。

三、理雅各对《东方圣书》的巨大贡献

从理雅各参与《东方圣书》这一大型翻译工程的角度讲，也许还有一些重要的成就是读者不曾认识到的。这套大型丛书代表了19世纪晚期英语世界对东方宗教研究的新发展，理雅各的贡献是巨大的。自1879年到1910年，这套致力于宗教研究的大型丛书共出版了50卷，包括七大宗教传统。大多数翻译（49卷中的31卷）[①]是源自印度教和佛教的"圣书"。琐罗亚斯德教（Zoroastrianism）"圣书"占了八卷。除了这三个宗教传统，其他四个宗教传统"圣书"的卷数相对较少。理雅各贡献的儒教传统有四卷；道教、耆那教（Jainism）、伊斯兰教各有两卷。从更广阔的视角来看，只有两位学

---

① 1910年出版的第50卷是"索引"，因此不算在这个翻译工程之内。

者（译者和阐释者）触及了一个以上的"东方"宗教传统，理雅各就是其中之一。这意义重大。毫无疑问，理雅各是唯一一位独自翻译和阐释两个传统（儒教和道教）的学者。另一个做了类似工作的学者是缪勒。作为一名印度教专家，缪勒也为第 10 卷做了与佛教文本相关的翻译工作，但他只做了其中一部分工作。因此，就这一点而言，理雅各是独一无二的。再者，理雅各是唯一一位独立完成 6 卷《东方圣书》的译者。虽然也有译者和阐释者完成了多达 5 卷的《东方圣书》，但不是独立完成的。① 因此，理雅各对这套丛书的贡献确实巨大。

为了准确说明那些来自中国的文本，还需要附加一点。理雅各以《中国圣书》之名完成的 6 卷，可能会让人自然地认为他是这套丛书中唯一一位把中国文本翻译为英文的学者，但事实并非如此。这套丛书的第 19 卷是关于中国佛教的作品，由英国汉学家和后来成为伦敦大学学院（University College，London）中文教授的毕尔（Samuel Beal，1825—1889）翻译。不过，这是毕尔为《东方圣书》贡献的唯一一卷。

理雅各之所以更适合被纳入《东方圣书》众多著名的译者-学者之列，是因为他自 1843 年至 1865 年在香港传教期间就已经关注古代儒家传统的宗教性。早在 1850 年代，他就明确主张古代儒家传统是建立在上帝一神论的基础之上的。② 只不过理雅各认为那些古代的一神论主张在后来被模糊的有神论世界观所取代了，取而代之的是多神崇拜，包括祖先崇拜，尤其是《礼记》《左传》记载的各种神

---

① 韦斯特（E. W. West）完成了五卷巴拉维语文本（第 5、18、24、37、47 卷），艾格林（Julius Eggeling）完成了印度教的一部长篇巨著《百道梵书》（*Śatapatha-Brāhmaṇa*）（第 12、26、41、43、44 卷）。另外，达梅斯特泰（James Darmesteter）和米尔斯（L. H. Mills）完成了三卷《阿维斯陀的诠释》（*Zend-Avesta*）（第 4、23、31 卷），戴维斯（T. W. Rhys Davids）和奥尔登堡（Hermann Oldenberg）完成了三卷佛教戒律文本（第 13、17、20 卷）。

② 参见 Pfister, *Striving for "The Whole Duty of Man"*, Vol. 1, pp. 187-196。

灵。① 为了突出说明春秋时期的宗教特征，理雅各引用了法国耶稣会
士嘉略利（Joseph-Marie Callery，1810—1862）对这一主题的论述：

> 《礼记》作为一"经"，理应深入探讨诸如祭天、祭祖、祭
> 祀守护神等宗教问题。然而，它却将那些纯粹的玄想轻轻地一
> 笔带过，以极度冷静的态度谈论这些严肃的问题。这对我而言
> 证明了两点：第一，中国古代最伟大的天才头脑中没有明确的
> 造物主概念，也没有思考过灵魂的本质及其归宿，只有一些模
> 糊不清和相互矛盾的观念；第二，（《礼记》所描述的那个时期）
> 中国人的宗教情感体验非常肤浅，没有像同时期的西方人那样
> 迫切地要去探求无形世界的奥秘。②

　　嘉略利的论述过于简化，理雅各在《中国圣书》其他部分的评
注中表现出他不愿接受嘉略利的主张。但是，嘉略利揭示了春秋时
期中国人宗教思想和宗教实践的复杂性、多样性和矛盾性；对此，
理雅各并不否认。

四、走向神圣：理雅各的思想和存在性困惑

　　更为重要的是，理雅各虽然主张选用"上帝"翻译《圣经》中
的"God"（他是持此主张的几个重要人物之一）；但要接受这一术

---

① 动荡不安的时代常常会出现各种宗教表达。关于对春秋时期动荡局势的描写，参见
Legge, *CC5, Prolegomena*, pp. 112–122。理雅各刻画了各个诸侯国不同宗教表达的诸多
方面，特别强调后来的中国古代社会不同于上古的中国古代社会。理雅各在文本中发
现那一时期儒家有强烈的有神论主张。关于这些有神论的表述，参见陈来《古代思想
文化的世界：春秋时代的宗教、伦理与社会思想》，台北允晨文化 2006 年版。
② 参见《中国圣书》第三卷，第 13 页。

语还有一个文化障碍，这一文化障碍是由反清的太平天国运动引发的。理雅各撰写了许多"上帝"论作品，最为完整的是 1850 年出版的《中国人关于上帝和神的观念》。[①] 在他书写这些作品之后的几年里，他注意到 1850 年代，太平军是如何使用这一术语来称呼神的，同时他们还主张其他一些世界观，在此基础上创立了拜上帝教——中国文化和国际背景下几千年来最具军事化和宗派化的表达之一。[②] 从理解晚清文化转型的角度考虑，理雅各等传教士不得不重新思考为什么本来能够与清朝文化融合的基督教宗教生活会出现问题。[③] 抛开 19 世纪清帝国内部这场毁灭性的大动荡不谈，从更广泛的意义上讲，应该如何看待各色中国人所认识且崇拜的"神圣"，而且他们愿意顺从那种实在观（vision of reality），甚至愿意献出自己的生命？[④] 人类有能力构

---

① 参见 James Legge, *The Notions of the Chinese Concerning God and Spirits: With an Examination of the Defense of an Essay, on the Proper Rendering of the Words Elohim and Theos, Into the Chinese Language by William J. Boone*, Hong Kong: The Hongkong [sic] Register Office, 1850。

② 英语世界有许多关于太平天国运动的著作，包括我的一些反思，参见 *Striving for "The Whole Duty of Man"*, Vol. 2。我读到这个领域最好的研究是赖利的著作，参见 Thomas H. Reilly, *The Taiping Heavenly Kingdom: Rebellion and Blasphemy of Empire*, Seattle: University of Washington Press, 2004。

③ 请思考理雅各与洪仁玕的关系。洪仁玕曾接受过理雅各和何进善（1817—1871）的福音宣讲训练，后来成了太平天国最重要的一个王。理雅各与洪仁玕的这一关系促使我提出了以上问题，尤其是理雅各等人当时密切关注着洪仁玕这位曾经非常虔诚的基督教福音宣教师如何堕落和最终被毁灭。参见 Lauren F. Pfister, "Plucking the Plank Out of One's Own Eye: Reflective Moments of Transformation Gained from James Legge's Christian Engagement with Four Notable Chinese Persons", in Alexander Chow, ed., *Scottish Missions to China: Commemorating the Legacy of James Legge (1815–1897)*, Leiden and Boston: Brill, 2022, pp. 28–35。

④ 这种反思是理雅各切身体验过的。这关系到另一个广东基督徒车锦光，他在 1861 年的一场教案中被排外的中国暴徒杀害，成为中国第一位基督教殉道者。关于这个事件的简单叙述，参见 *Striving for "The Whole Duty of Man"*, Vol. 2, pp. 114–124；更详尽的研究，参见 Lauren F. Pfister, "The Proto-martyr of Chinese Protestants: Reconstructing the Story of Ch'ëa Kam-Kwong", *Journal of the Hong Kong Branch of the Royal Asiatic Society*, Vol. 42 (2002/2003), pp. 187–244。

建他们所认为的神圣的世界观；① 但理雅各是一位苏格兰公理会信徒和思想开放的福音派新教传教士，他所偏爱的世界观可能会与此大不相同。因此，从理论和文化的视角看，理雅各及其他传教士和基督教同道不仅要辨别中国人所谓的神圣，还要明白为什么有时所谓的神圣会成为精神和文化破坏者的借口。

　　这就是理雅各翻译阐释儒家和道家经典之时所面临的宗教和哲学挑战。其中有没有可看作是神圣的东西？如果有，在与儒家和道家学说极为不同的传统中，它是如何将中国人和其他群体区分开，并且代代相传？作为基督教知识分子和传教士-学者，理雅各不仅从自身关于现实本质的基督教信仰出发，而且也从中国古代圣贤、宗教人物和著名思想家所奠定的中国文献出发，于此他可以确认何种形式的中国神圣性？他又应该如何认识和评价那些误入歧途的神圣形式？这是指那些潜在的或已经表现出来的宗教生活形式，但这样的形式被扭曲了，有时还有点迷信，甚至发展成了罪行，具有破坏性。这些问题在理雅各阅读和翻译最后一卷《中国经典》的时候被再次提了出来，而且异常鲜活；那是在1864年太平天国运动结束后，仍然被战争的乌云笼罩着的年代。理雅各研读的《春秋》及其三传（《左传》《公羊传》《穀梁传》）中记载了大量伦理问题、道德问题、政治阴谋和战争创伤；以上问题是在他研读这四部书的过程中浮现出来的。从这个意义上讲，且多少有点令人惊讶的是，理雅各对最后一卷《中国经典》的翻译和阐释为更多问题的提出奠定了基础；这些问题关系到古代中国人的宗教表达，他们的实在观，以及他们对

① 我从文化转变和神圣空间制造的角度谈论过这一问题，参见 Lauren F. Pfister, "Philosophical Explorations of the Transformative Dimension in Chinese Culture", *Journal of Chinese Philosophy*, Vol. 35, No. 4 (December 2008), pp. 663–682; "Ubication: A Phenomenological Study about Making Spaces Sacred," *International Communication of Chinese Culture* [Beijing and Heidelberg], Vol. 4, No. 3 (August 2017), pp. 393–411.

于人类精神无论是积极变革、中立性抑或是邪恶的破坏性表达所具有的相对性的优点。这些问题在《圣经》传统中也存在，尤其是在希伯来《圣经》中，犹太教的神耶和华（Yahweh）被卷入了多场与不同文化和军队之间的战争，那些文化中对神和对现实的观念非常不同，于是就誓死要摧毁犹太人的一神论者（犹太人的军队也常常还之以暴）。理雅各为了寻找表达基督教信仰的原则，曾经阅读、传授和研究过希伯来《圣经》的先知书。这些先知书中还记录了一些发人深省的问题，甚至记载了犹太人如何忽视了耶和华教导中的精神、思想和道德基础等问题。在他们自身历史的各个时期，他们也会变得反叛、自私、邪恶。这些记录还提到了一些精神文化遗产，既包括对神圣性正面转化的表达，也有负面转化的表达。用《圣经》的话来说，耶和华会审判那些不义之人，赞扬那些有义之人，即先知弥迦所说"行公义，好怜悯，存谦卑的心，与你的神同行"[①]的人。从这个角度看，许多人民、许多宗教和许多文化之间都有很大的相似性，理雅各在中国古代儒家和道家的作品中也能发现这些问题。

在缪勒邀请理雅各参与《东方圣书》这个项目之时，理雅各仍面临着这些问题。从历史的、理论的和宗教的角度理解这些问题，有助于我们大概了解理雅各在他将要翻译和阐释的中国古代作品中能够发现什么"神圣"内容。另外，这样的理解为理雅各的解释判断提供了理性原则，即在那些文本中辨别出正面的转化、世俗的日常和令人恐惧的残酷，以及应该谴责的邪恶。因此，在处理《书经》《诗经》《孝经》里与古代儒家有神论相关的宗教篇章时，总的来说，理雅各对其中的主张持非常正面的态度，但他也发现需要质疑有些篇章所表达的精神见解和世界观。具体而言，理雅各发现与《易经》

---

① 引自《弥迦书》6: 8，参见 Robert Alter, trans. and comm., *Prophets: Nevi'im*, *The Hebrew Bible*, Vol.2, New York and London: W. W. Norton and Company, 2019, p. 1314.

有关的占卜，及其在《易传》里的解释，应该算是迷信，而且关于占卜的大多数基础性断言都是在误导人。《礼记》是一部相对晚出的作品，其中的祭祀和其他宗教仪式涉及大量的宗教行为和制度，这考验着理雅各是否能够分辨其内容的相对价值。相对道家而言，理雅各一直偏向儒家。他一直用"Tàoistic"这一贬称来描述道家的宗教实践，而且一直认为其宗教性不如儒家。他认为儒家的宗教实践有崇尚某种一神论的倾向。有趣的是，理雅各发现《道德经》对终极实在的探寻无论从哪个方面来讲都值得敬佩；但理雅各认为《庄子》中关于成仙（即至人、真人、神人、圣人、大人）的主张在理性上令人不可思议，显得很虚幻、不切实际。这一切都离不开理雅各对古代儒家和道家作品中各种神圣内容的性质和价值方面日益清晰的认知。

　　我们不可能从理雅各《中国圣书》的"索引"里寻得"神圣"（sacred）一词的确切含义。通过这些"索引"，我们无法直接找到可以让我们确定何谓"神圣"的条目或信息。在理雅各为六卷《中国圣书》制作的三个索引中，没有一个专名或字词是"sacred"。（这三个索引分别在第四卷末和第六卷末；第四卷末有两个"儒教文本"索引，① 第六卷末有一个"道教文本"索引。②）但是，理雅各在这套丛书的总序中说："儒教是中国的正统宗教……"③ 因此我们期待前两个索引会为何谓"神圣"提供进一步的提示。虽然有两个"敬"（respect 和 reverence）的条目，④ 四个关于不同种类的"祭祀"（sacrifices）的条目，⑤ 以及一个与"神"和"鬼神"有关的条

----

① 这是理雅各为前四卷《中国圣书》制作的两个索引，其中一个是"主题索引"（Index of Subjects）(《中国圣书》第四卷，第471—485页)，另一个是"专名索引"（Index of Proper Names）(《中国圣书》第四卷，第485—491页)。

② 这是理雅各为两卷"道教文本"制作的"索引"(《中国圣书》第六卷，第325—336页)。

③ 参见《中国圣书》第一卷，第 xiv 页。

④ 参见《中国圣书》第四卷，第 480 页左栏。

⑤ 同上书，第 481 页。

目（spirit, spirits, spirit-like and cognate words），[1] 但没有一个条目明确地界定理雅各所使用的"神圣"一词的意义。另外，出乎意料也非常有趣的是，这两个索引中也没有"圣人"（sage）这个条目，更不用说"异教"（cult）、"宗教"（religion）或"崇拜"（worship）了，但有"祝"或"祈祷"（prayer）这个条目，且出处有二。[2] 后两卷"道教文本"索引中类似的条目就更少了，甚至没有一个上面提到过的条目。

然而，有两个文化和宗教范畴表明了理雅各对中国古代儒教和道教传统内神圣性的思考。有趣的是，这两个范畴与理雅各的苏格兰身份和新教信仰密切相关。这两个范畴就是英雄和先知。意味深长的是，这两个范畴在苏格兰思想家卡莱尔（Thomas Carlyle，1795—1881）的作品中，被统一在了"宗教英雄"（religious hero）这一标题下。不过，再次让人感到奇怪的是，"英雄"（hero）和"先知"（prophet）两个词都没有被收录进《中国圣书》的三个索引中。但是理雅各很为这两个范畴所感动和吸引。而且附带说明一点，理雅各自己被一些人看作是苏格兰福音派英雄，甚至被他同时代的一些人看作是先知。[3] 就理雅各在中国的经历而论，他期望洪仁玕成为太平天国领导层中一股英雄的基督教反击力量，但洪仁玕辜负了理雅各的期望。在他心目中，最接近英雄先知的人是他的合作牧师何进善（1817—1871）和来自广东博罗的中国殉道者车锦光。确切地说，经过研究《春秋》中那些他认为隐讳、歪曲和不诚的评判原则，理雅各得出了下面的评价，也证实了他非常严肃和系统地对待这些问题的态度：

---

[1] 参见《中国圣书》第四卷，第482—483页。
[2] 同上书，第480页右栏，分别是周宣王的祈祷和周公的祝辞。
[3] 关于这一主题的阐释详见拙著：Pfister, *Striving for "The Whole Duty of Man"*, Vol. 2, pp. 3—6. 有趣的是，吉瑞德也在其著作《维多利亚时代翻译中国》的多个地方提到了卡莱尔的著作，但他的索引中没有"hero"和"prophet"两个条目。

　　我很不情愿写下这些有关孔子的评论，但出于一种责任感我不得不把它写下来。已有人批评我对他不公，待他很残酷。有人说我偏袒他，太过赞许他的品格和教义。这些相互矛盾的控诉使我认为我已经追求了"中道"，已公正地对待我的对象。对于有些批评说我是在有意寻找机会贬低孔子，我的良心是不会对这样的控诉做出回应的。相反，我知道我一直期待大大地赞赏他和他的教义。但我不能把他当作英雄。①

　　理雅各一直在研究和思考这个问题。事实上，经过深入研究，理雅各发现清代学者袁枚曾以同样的脉络批判过《春秋》，在此基础上袁枚认为孔子不可能是这样一部问题重重的文献的编纂者。理雅各发现这样的主张之后感到很惊讶，但在当时（1872）他并没有肯定袁枚如此大胆的判断。理雅各总结说："袁枚很想否认孔子与编纂这部编年体史书有任何关系。我也说过，我会很乐意这么做。但是，对立面的证据太过充分……"② 尽管如此，即使理雅各在1872年根据他对《春秋》的研究发现，孔子并没有做正义的事，因为孔子实际上是《春秋》的编纂者，但孔子品格中的其他要素仍然影响着理雅各的心灵：总的来说，孔子是一个仁人，他在被自己称作"天"的神灵面前仍然表现得很谦卑。在发表对孔子品格的这些评判后的一年之内，理雅各的立场就发生了变化；到1877年，他称孔子是"上帝派来教导中国人的"。③ 理雅各的这一心路历程详细记录在他1880

---

① 参见《中国经典》第五卷，第 51 页。

② 同上书，第 83 页。

③ 参见 James Legge, *Confucianism in Relation to Christianity*, London: Trubner & Co; Shanghai: Kelly and Walsh, 1877, p. 10。关于理雅各这一转变的过程，详见拙文："From Derision to Respect: The Hermeneutic Passage within James Legge's (1815–1897) Ameliorated Evaluation of Master Kong (Confucius)", *Bochumer Jahrbuch zur Ostasienforschung*, Vol. 26 (2002), pp. 53–88.

年出版的演讲集《中国宗教：儒教、道教与基督教的比较》(*The Religions of China: Confucianism and Tâoism Described and Compared with Christianity*) 中。① 在公开演讲中，理雅各探讨了孔子的地位和品格，重复了他在《春秋》中发现的不忠于事实的保留意见。孔子这位中国先师的影响在理雅各心中留下了污点，一直令理雅各内心感到痛楚，即使在《中国经典》第五卷出版八年后，理雅各仍然对此耿耿于怀。但是，经过对"儒教"更广泛的研究和深入反思之后，理雅各回忆起了一幕让他感动的场景，促使他重新思考之前对孔子品格的负面评价。理雅各说他 1873 年 5 月"朝拜孔子墓"之时，"想了很多事情"。然后他描述了自己冥想的心态和一种特别的意象：

> 我绕着走了一圈又一圈，然后爬上了土丘，那大大的土丘里一定有孔子的骨灰，上面植被茂盛，长满了可用于卜筮的蓍草。②

他在想什么？理雅各的女儿海伦·伊迪丝·理雅各（Helen Edith Legge）总结了理雅各那段旅行的文献，③ 后来吉瑞德又补充了一些资料；④ 这些材料告诉我们，理雅各当时曾花费了一些时间自问法国大革命时期的拿破仑和中国古代哲学家孔子哪个更伟大。这是卡莱尔式的发问，比较的是两大文明中两个典范人物的伟大性——一个是革命天才，一个是至圣先师，两人最终都没有实现自己的目标；理

---

① 参见我在《中国圣书》第三卷"导读"开篇几页对这部书的详细讨论。

② 参见 Legge, *The Religions of China*, p. 135。

③ 参见 Helen Edith Legge, *James Legge, Missionary and Scholar*, London: Religious Tract Society, 1905, pp. 196–197。

④ 参见 Girardot, *The Victorian Translation of China*, pp. 94–95。

雅各正是在这样一个卡莱尔时刻重新思考、重新确定这两位伟人谁更伟大的问题。在那一时刻，理雅各在日记中给远在苏格兰的妻子和儿女写道："我倾向于认为是中国的这位圣人。没有谁能像他那样对自己的同胞有如此持久和深远的影响，他所阐发的许多道德和社会原则永远不会丧失其价值。"① 在绕行和爬上孔子墓 12 年后，在最后一卷"儒教文本"（《中国圣书》第四卷）中，理雅各为那转化性的时刻又添加了非凡的一笔。重译《中庸》之时，其中有一章说"至诚"之人有预知文化和政治命运的能力，这让理雅各想起他曾经做过的另一个象征行为。1873 年他在孔子的坟丘上发现了许多用于卜筮的蓍草，他以自己一向好学的习惯准确地用植物学名称"ptarmica sibirica"称之，他当时还采集了一束蓍草带回了苏格兰。② 这补充了理雅各在拜访孔子墓时经历的冥想和反思，而且很有启发意义。然而，理雅各对孔子墓地所发生之事的描述，其意义还不止于此。在《中国宗教》第二章结尾，理雅各附加了一条评论，把他对孔子的研究和对儒教的评价与他所认为的神圣的成就联系在了一起：

> 这一皇家的祝辞（理雅各在前一页翻译的《大清通礼》里的一段祝辞）可以充分为我对名之为儒教的中国古代信仰的态

---

① 转引自 Girardot, *The Victorian Translation of China*, p. 94。海伦·理雅各的如下文字，显然是编自原日记："我站在这位圣人坟地的山顶上，思绪回到了圣赫勒拿岛上的那个露天坟墓，拿破仑的遗体就是从那里运到法国。这两位谁是更伟大的人呢？我倾向于中国的这位圣人。"参见：Helen Edith Legge, *James Legge: Missionary and Scholar*, London: The Religious Tract Society, 1905, p. 197。我没有读过理雅各 1873 年当时写的日记，但接下来我会根据其他出版的资料补充更多的见解。

② 理雅各对此有两种表述。在早期的一个文本中，他说的是"两束"（two bundles）；在后期的一个文本中，他说的是"一束"。参见《中国圣书》第一卷，第 145 页注释 1；《中国圣书》第四卷，第 320 页注释 1。

度做出辩护。孔子是一位杰出的伟人；但是，我认为，他所发现（found）并努力传之后世的宗教更加伟大和不同凡响。①

我们应该先消除这段话可能引起的一个误解。理雅各不是说孔子"建立"（founded）或创立了儒家有神论，而是说他在中国古代圣王的文字中"发现"了有神论并将其作为真正的知识遗产传诸后世。因此，古代儒家有神论以及后来孔子倡导的相关祭祀，将成为儒家神圣性的检验标准。而这些都是理雅各在古代儒家经典中所研究和阐发过的，尤其是他在《中国圣书》第一卷中所凸显的那些儒经。在此基础上，理雅各还可以权衡和评价儒家和道家精神性及其实践的其他表述。这包括权衡和评价与《易经》有关的占卜行为；从这个角度讲，理雅各在孔子坟墓上采集蓍草就象征着那样的一种权衡和评价。这一标准还可以用于权衡后期产生的复杂的儒家祭祀制度，包括祭祀各种精神实在和祖先的神灵，以及《礼记》中详细描述的繁复的丧葬仪式。另外，这一标准还可让理雅各在概念的层面上评价《道德经》中描述的形而上的"道"，挑战《庄子》中提出的人能成神或向其他精神层面转化。因此，理雅各将会把这些另类的精神性全部评价为逊于儒家有神论及其相关制度构成的神圣性。

理雅各通过比较典范人物的伟大性，并对之进行反思，从中认识到儒家的神圣性；我们现在从这个视角回到理雅各对中国英雄人物的讨论，了解他最终是如何重新评价孔子的。在理雅各最后一次离开香港之前，他发表了一场公开演讲，题为《中国历史上的两位英雄》（Two Heroes of Chinese History）。这两位英雄是理雅各在研读《左传》中大量叙事文本的基础上辨别和挑选出来的。香港初创

---

① 参见 Legge, *The Religions of China*, p. 149。

的一份汉学杂志《中国评论》第一卷收录了这份讲稿，足以见得这场讲座的重要性。理雅各聚焦的是春秋时期的两位国君——齐桓公（约前685—前643年在位）和晋文公（约前635—前628年在位）。他们试图在各个诸侯国之间创造一个永久和平的条约，相互之间永远不再有武力征伐；虽然他们的努力失败了，但理雅各仍尊崇他们为有远见卓识的英雄人物，值得赞扬。[1]演讲发表之后，理雅各离开了香港，并有机会在1873年初的几个月，游历了中国北方，先是到上海，然后在4月份到达北京。在北京天坛，理雅各与其他传教士合唱基督教颂歌。5月份在艾约瑟的陪同下到了山东，参观了几处与孔子相关的景点，包括孔子的家乡曲阜。[2]如上所述，就在曲阜孔子墓前，理雅各对于这位先师品格的评价发生了根本转变，并且让他在内心深处和思想上做好了谈论"儒教"神圣性的准备。到了1880年，他能够更为全面地公开欣赏孔子。他最后对孔子的修正性评价是在1893年，在他的《中国经典》修订本中。这一评价不仅是他谨慎的学术和思想历程的回响，也是他内心不断反思的结果：

> 我现在必须得离开这位圣人了。我希望没有对他不公；越深入研究他的人格和学说，我就越尊重他。他是一个伟大的人，总体而言他对中国人发生了极为有益的影响，他的学说也为信仰基督的我们提供了重要的教诲。[3]

---

① 参见 James Legge, "Two Heroes of Chinese History," *China Review*, Vol. 1, Issue 6 (1872-1873), pp. 370-381。

② 吉瑞德按时间顺序详细讨论了这一复杂有趣的旅行。参见 Girardot, *The Victorian Translation of China*, pp. 83-95。

③ 参见 James Legge, *The Chinese Classics*, Vol. 1, Oxford: Clarendon Press, 1893。

五、如何有效地阅读《中国圣书》？

谈完了理雅各如何看待儒家和道家传统中的"神圣"这个话题之后，我提出七个导引问题，鼓励读者彻底地探寻和认真地研究《中国圣书》文本。提出问题之后，我会额外做些评论并提供一些例子，但我的主要目的是突出读者最初不太能辨识出来的一些特征，尤其是对中国读者而言。

问题 1. 理雅各用了什么样的版式凸显他翻译的各种"儒教文本"和"道教文本"？

这个问题在上文已经有所回答，但这里我要从手稿学的视角讲述三种不同的版式。也就是说，打开《中国圣书》（一页在左，一页在右），通读六卷各个不同部分，观察每个页面的布局，我们能从中学到什么？若打开《中国经典》（第一版，1861—1872）前四卷的任何一卷，拿它与《中国圣书》前四卷的任何一卷相比，最重要的差异便凸显出来。最明显的是，理雅各没有或者说没有机会在《中国圣书》每个页面的上半部分附上标准的中文文本。同样重要的是，《中国经典》中的脚注一般都很长，包括大量中文及其翻译，这在《中国圣书》各卷中并不多见。

《中国圣书》的版式相对比较简单，注释中的汉字也很少。大多数正文页面只有清晰的两个部分：上面是标准字号的英文译文，底部是较小字号的简短脚注。注释很少占去半个页面。在《中国圣书》第二卷介绍六十四卦卦爻辞的部分，每个页面的上部分有很大不同。[1] 其中，除了英文译文之外，每卦之始有卦画。

---

[1] 参见《中国圣书》第二卷，第57—210页。

　　《中国圣书》中的注释包含了不止一种语言。一般而言，这些注释是理雅各写的英文，有时会附加少量汉字，但偶尔也会见他引用来自拉丁文、法文、德文的翻译或评注，德语只见于《中国圣书》第五、六卷。还有一项不同寻常的内容，《中国圣书》第三、四卷（《礼记》）的注释中有时会有一些插图。但需要说明的是，这些插图的数量非常少，尤其是与《中国圣书》第二卷里的六十四卦卦画相比。

　　《中国圣书》的正文部分还有两种版式需要注意。

　　第一种是把评注放在正文里。也就是说，读者不会看到页面被分隔成"上""下"两个部分，而是看到紧跟在英文翻译之后的评论，而且评论的字号与译文的字号一样大。许多情况下那些评论部分会有明显的注释，而且有数字编号，好像脚注一样，但它们并不出现在页面底端。有时候，译文之后的评论甚至没有数字编号使之区别于正文，主要是因为所评论的译文太短。

　　第二种是页面上没有任何形式的评注。这种情况很少，据我观察，只有《中国圣书》第六卷附录五、六是这种版式。

　　另外需要注意的是，理雅各的"序言""导论"通常采用的是上面说到的主要版式。导论的末尾还会有几张折叠起来的大幅插图，但并非每个导论都有，其版式会因主题的不同而有差别。还有两卷的末尾附有索引，字号较小，分两栏。

问题 2. 理雅各是如何翻译每部经书的关键术语的？他在什么时候选择不译，而只是采用拼音？他是如何解释如此选择的？

　　这些问题我在每个分卷的"导读"中已经作了部分解答；但没有哪卷中有一个关键术语列表。若读者在每卷末记录关键术语，或在笔记本上写出那些关键术语的翻译和页码，我相信那将是一份宝贵的资料。我之所以这样建议，是因为理雅各没有用统一的方式翻译关键术语。他认为这些关键术语的意义会根据其上下文的不同而有所变化。因此，他会根据上下文的需要而改变一个关键术语的译文，并且在脚注或评论中指出其意义的变化。难怪他会反对翟理斯主张用"严格的英文对等词"翻译中文术语。理雅各认为把许多中文术语翻译为英文时是不能应用"严格对等"这个标准的。① 许多当代翻译学者都认同理雅各的主张。

因此，研究大量的术语是值得的，因为它表明理雅各能够敏感地注意到每个术语在不同上下文意义的细微差别。例如，儒家经典和道家经典中"道"这个术语就尤其应该以这样的方法处理。尽管理雅各喜欢用"the superior man"翻译儒家的"君子"这个概念，但有时候他会根据上下文的需要用"gentleman"或"prince"。还有许多其他术语的英文翻译都可揭示理雅各翻译敏感性的微妙之处；我们可以用这一研究方法记录理雅各翻译的多样性。② 这样的术语有很多，我不便提供那么多，但有些关键术语还是值得我们注意理雅各是如何将其翻译成英文的。这些术语（除了上面提到的两个以外）

---

① 参见《中国圣书》第五卷，第 17 页。理雅各引用翟理斯的原文，认为这是翟理斯处理译文的原则。

② 对理雅各翻译诠释学感兴趣的读者，可参阅我撰写的如下文章 "Chinese: Translation of Theological Terms," in J. M. Y. Simpson and J. F. A. Sawyer, eds., *Concise Encyclopedia of Language and Religion*, Amsterdam: Elsevier, May 2001, pp. 118–122; "Translation and its Problems," in Antonio Cua, ed., *Encyclopedia of Chinese Philosophy*, New York: Routledge, 2003, pp. 734–739; "Bible Translations and the Protestant 'Term Question'," in R. G. Tiedemann, ed., *Handbook of Christianity in China*, Volume Two, *1800 to the Present*, Leiden and Boston: E. J. Brill, 2010, pp. 361–370; "The Mengzian Matrix for Accommodationist Missionary Apologetics: Identifying the Cross-cultural Linkage in Evangelical Protestant Discourse within the Chinese writings of James Legge (1815–1897), He Jinshan (1817–1871), and Ernst Faber (1839–1899)," *Monumenta Serica* 50 (2002), pp. 391–416; "Nineteenth Century Ruist Metaphysical Terminology and the Sino-Scottish Connection in James Legge's *Chinese Classics*" in Michael Lackner and Natascha Vittinghoff, eds. *Mapping Meanings: The Field of New Learning in Late Qing China*, Leiden: Brill, 2004, pp. 615–638。

包括儒经中的宗教价值观和宗教制度：祭、敬、命、天命、孝；文化美德和典范：诚、德、礼、仁、圣人、义；以及各种形而上学术语：帝、鬼神、上帝、神、圣、天、天德，等等。道家经典中的关键术语除了无处不在的"道"之外，还有德、神人、圣、生、天、天道、无为、阴、真人、至人、自得、自然，等等。值得注意的是，理雅各给这些术语的英文翻译相对多样化。事实上，在21世纪的今天，这些文本在其他语言中的翻译也呈现出了这种多样化，包括东亚和东南亚语境中的日语、韩语、越南语；西欧语境中的法语、德语、意大利语、葡萄牙语、西班牙语，还有东欧语境中的克罗地亚语、捷克语、匈牙利语、俄语等。在20世纪末和21世纪的前20年，一些流传很广的中国古代经典又有了许多语言的新译本。①

如果理雅各选择不译一个关键术语，而是用拼音，那么他这样做是有非常重要的理由的。找出这样的地方，看理雅各如何解释他为什么不译那些术语，你是否认同他的解释？

问题3. 基督教和苏格兰实在主义哲学对理雅各翻译和阐释《中国圣书》的15个文本（9个主要文本和6个次要文本）有多大影响？

有些读者也许会认为这是一个"令人困惑的问题"，因为许多读者觉得很难立即从翻译和评注中感觉出基督教的影子。再者，要回答这个问题的后半部分，对于那些从未学习过苏格兰实在主义哲学或苏格兰常识哲学的读者来说根本就不可能。我们怎么才能够辨别那些受到影响的术语、段落或阐释倾向呢？虽然很难看出这些影响，但我在这里给读者一些提示，教读者如何辨别，以及在哪里可以发现这些影响。下面有些内容非常明显，但有些内容会出乎读者的意

---

① 这些语言的种类远比大多数人知道的要多。郎宓榭（Michael Lackner）等人研究过《论语》译本，发现它被翻译成37种语言（包括东亚和东南亚的语言），共有120个译本。

料，因此会令人震惊。

理雅各的儒经翻译（《中国圣书》前四卷）最显著的一个方面是，他坚持认为这些最古老儒经中的"帝"就对等于英语中的"God"。他用了较长的篇幅来讨论这个问题，援引了经文中大量的例子，包括"帝"的各种含义，然后拿它与"天"和"神"比较。这些内容都在《中国圣书》第一卷的"序言"中，该"序言"也基本上是四卷"儒教文本"的"序言"。①然而，读者需要明白的是，除了"God"这个术语本身之外，这并不是直接的"基督教影响"，因为"God"是指代终极存在的总称。也就是说，理雅各没有说儒经中有一个清晰可辨的指代"三一神"（Trinitarian Deity）的术语，只是指任何理性的人都可以认识的终极实在。这说法揭示了苏格兰常识哲学的影响。凡是在译文或评注中有"God"出现的地方，都是受了苏格兰常识哲学的影响，很少与明显的基督教（尤其是《圣经》的）主张有关联。

就这些与神有关的形而上学问题而言，值得注意的是，理雅各在诠释学的意义上怀疑他读到的每一种译本，因为这些翻译采用的都是明显的神学术语，理雅各认为这不符合中国经典的性质。例如，他原则上拒绝接受翟理斯在翻译《庄子》时把"道"译为"God"，②尽管理雅各自己有充足的理由认为《道德经》有一章在他看来似乎是在寻找上帝的概念。③这在理雅各对道家经典的阐释中并不是一个矛盾，而是微妙的概念辨析，他区分了翻译对等和思想探索，其目的是揭示终极实在的特征。所有这些讨论都与他希望描述的翻译问题和阐释性见解有关，讨论所依赖的原理是他阅读过的苏格兰常识

① 参见《中国圣书》第一卷，第 xxiii—xxix 页。
② 理雅各对翟理斯这一翻译选择的批评，参见《中国圣书》第五卷，第17页。
③ 理雅各对《道德经》第二十五章的评注参见《中国圣书》第五卷，第68—69页。

哲学著作所阐述的关于实在的原则。①

苏格兰实在主义对理雅各的影响，可从如下的总结中窥见一斑：

根据里德的说法，"道德感"（moral sense）或"良知"
（conscience）的体验涉及"必然真理"（necessary truths）的
直觉原理。这是可以用主张的方式表达的"第一原理"（first
principles），一旦听明白了，就会相信，无需进一步解释。……
［这需要］发现"知识与信仰的法则或条件"（laws or conditions
of knowledge and belief），因为它拥有超越任何依据经验总结的
"天生的普遍性"（native universality）。②

里德认为直觉的道德感在人类当中发展，形成更普遍和更
清晰的道德观念和道德判断。……最初自然的"道德判断或良
知"发展到我们可以"冷静地"判断我们人类的方法，并且更
清晰地感受和表达合适的情感。里德在这个语境中使用了一个
神学词语："我们的道德判断或良知从我们造物主种下的一颗小
小种子发展成熟。"这与《孟子》人性论中的道德隐喻"四端"
（four seeds 或 four germs）产生了共鸣。③

正因为道德判断会因不同的成长和教育环境而发生改变，
里德认为人类很可能会为道德原则提出不同的解说。但是这些
分歧……可以在评价和争论原则的指引下，通过对立双方真正
的对话，得以化解。……由于这些规定不仅适用于道德问题，

---

① 理雅各研读的是第二代苏格兰常识哲学家斯图尔特（Dugald Stewart, 1753—1828）
的作品，而斯图尔特的作品基本上发展自第一代苏格兰常识哲学家里德（Thomas
Reid, 1710—1796）的作品。我曾经概述了这些关键人物的著作、哲学主张和独特
之处，以及他们的哲学方法将为理雅各后来的汉学著作开启文化比较的大门，参见
Pfister, *Striving for "The Whole Duty of Man,"* Vol. 1, pp. 73-82, 224-230。

② 同上书，p. 79.

③ 同上书，p. 81.

也适用于自然科学、逻辑学、政治学、美学和形而上学的"第一原理"，因此里德哲学描述了真诚地理解各种不同思想体系的方法。……尽管人类各种生命形式的发展不尽相同，但［他相信苏格兰实在论者］发现的直觉原则是人类的基本天性。①

因此，每当理雅各强调他在中国古代经典中发现的"原则"或"责任"，他都是在肯定苏格兰实在主义哲学所宣称的价值观。值得注意的是，可以用这种方式探讨的问题包括人性、人伦道德、科学发现、政治制度，以及对各种实在层次的形而上的解释。

理雅各把这一跨文化的概念比较看作是自己实际生活的一部分，这从他敬爱自己三个哥哥的表现方式可以看出来。毫无疑问，他是个守悌的苏格兰人，完全认同这一美德以及由此发展出来的各种人伦道德。理雅各在晚年——三个哥哥都去世之后——跟自己的孩子们讲述他的三个哥哥，"品格和成就超越普通人之上"，是最高意义上的"君子"。② 也就是说，理雅各认为"君子"是一种文化修养，既适用于儒家，也适用于西方人。同样，他发现许多其他价值观和美德在人类社会中都是共通的，这是苏格兰常识哲学的人性主张。

理雅各对《中国圣书》中的诸多说法，尤其是道家经典文本和后来的道教文本中的许多主张，都提出了批判，他拒绝接受与物化有关的主张，认为它们不可信，"不切实际"或"荒谬"。另外，理雅各还批评那些文本中记录的不人道的行为和邪恶残忍的行为，他批评的依据是"道德反感"（moral revulsion），他认为这是人类在不同文化中的普遍经历。

---

① 参见 Pfister, *Striving for "The Whole Duty of Man,"* Vol. 1, p. 82。
② 参见理雅各未刊稿《吾生漫录》（"Notes of My Life"），这份 140 页自传性质的手稿现藏于牛津大学博德莱安图书馆。但不幸的是，我没有记下这些话的确切页码。此处引文转引自 Pfister, *Striving for "The Whole Duty of Man,"* Vol. 1, p. 43。

关于各种价值观和制度的跨文化冲突，理雅各也从苏格兰实在主义那里获得了重要的支持。当对这些"人类的普遍经验"的性质和地位产生分歧时，18和19世纪的苏格兰哲学家认为，有一些逻辑的和对话的原则可指引人们化解冲突。目标不仅是化解冲突，而且还要达成一致意见。读者应该细读理雅各《中国圣书》各卷导论和较长的评注，辨别和评价理雅各依据这些苏格兰实在主义哲学原则讨论中国经典的方法。

在这六卷书中，理雅各还运用了以《圣经》为信仰基础的新教原则，这有助于我们辨别中国和苏格兰宗教文化的异同。令人略感意外的是，它们的数量相对较少，而且牵涉到更为复杂的问题和文本；因此，我要在结论中讨论这些问题。

问题4. 都有哪些欧洲译本可供理雅各参考？

我为六卷本《中国圣书》制作了特殊的"索引"，包括主要的中文典籍和中国评注者，还有一些重要的西文作品和外国研究者。认真阅读这些"索引"，读者会很容易辨认出理雅各在每卷的评注、序言和导论中参考的英文、法文、拉丁文和德文译本。我之所以把这个导引问题的重点放在欧洲译本上，是因为这些译本表明理雅各如何努力阅读、评价、阐释和挑战与自己英文译本相关的欧洲汉学成果。这些欧洲译本中有一多半都出版于19世纪，少数出版于17和18世纪（主要是拉丁文和法文，还有几部欧洲其他语言的译本）。

问题5. 理雅各在翻译这9部主要作品和6部次要作品之时主要依赖的中国评注者有哪些？

我相信，我为每卷《中国圣书》制作的"索引"有助于读者回答这个问题，其中提供了大量关于这个问题的基本信息。我统计出了理雅各在每卷书中引用一个中国评注者的次数，虽然这能够大概揭示理雅各的阐释重点（我也在导读文章中指出了这些重点），但这不能取代对那些参考文献做文本研究。只有研读了那些文本，才能够理解理雅各利用那些注疏的方法。需要注意的是，理雅各如果特别钟情于某个评注者，他会在脚注中说明他为什么觉得那个评注者的注解特别有用。当然，有时候理雅各也会明确指出这个评注者的注解有问题。我之所以指出这一点，是因为理雅各非常严肃地对待他的阐释责任，因此有时会在他的评注中非常直接地评价他所参考的文献。

后来有一些英国和美国的汉学家说理雅各翻译《中国经典》时太过追随朱熹，理雅各在《中国圣书》中对宋儒的参考之少应该会对持这一主张的人有所启发。另外，考察他欣赏的其他儒家学者也是很有趣的一件事，这些学者包括自汉代至清代许多著名的评注者。① 这也在某种程度上说明理雅各的汉学研究反映了晚清的学术状况，晚清学者并不惟朱熹之注是从。

问题 6. 理雅各对某些文本的阐释还受到了哪些其他影响，包括他在中国香港和内地的经历，以及他对现代实证科学新趋势的关注？

我试图在每卷的导读文章中竭力强调了某些历史、文化和存在主义的影响，尤其是与道教经典作品相关的影响。然而，我做得不到位的地方是，没有强调在理雅各的评注和阐释中发现的现代科学主张和概念。其中有大量与中国古代天文学、生物学、动物学有关的材料。这里有必要强调理雅各面对实证科学的一个困境，即如何阐释"五行"。

---

① 这只是一个总体的说法，理雅各参考的学者也包括唐之前、唐、宋、元、明的儒家学者。其中许多学者在他的注释中并不明显。但也有一些例外，尤其是在"道教文本"中，理雅各多次参考了元代大儒吴澄（1249—1333）和明代道家学者焦竑（1541—1620）的著作。在翻译《礼记》时，唐代学者孔颖达（574—648）和元代学者陈澔（1260—1341）也非常显著。

问题 7. 为了让英语读者理解儒家和道家传统，理雅各在《中国圣书》中使用了哪些跨文化阐释（至少包括《圣经》、地中海古典作者、现代欧洲著作）？

理雅各引用最多的是《圣经》，他认为这是 19 世纪英语读者大都非常熟悉的文本。因此，我要在这篇总论的结论中探讨理雅各是如何利用《圣经》的。但是，与汉学研究不相关的著作，理雅各参考得很少。他在《中国圣书》中引用的著名诗人包括莎士比亚、弥尔顿、詹姆斯·汤姆逊。① 理雅各参考的古典希腊语和拉丁语作者包括古罗马讽刺作家尤韦纳尔（Juvenal，约 55—127），② 古罗马文学大师塞涅卡（Seneca，前 4—65）③ 和著名的古希腊哲学家柏拉图④。理雅各提到和引用的其他重要的欧洲文学家有法国剧作家和哲学家伏尔泰⑤，苏格兰文学家和历史学家司各特（Walter Scott，1771—1832）⑥，以及更著名的英国浸信会文学家约翰·班扬（John Bunyan，1628—1688），理雅各借助班扬的作品描述了《庄子》文学风格的不同方面。⑦

结论：理雅各《中国圣书》的三大变革性影响

这六卷《中国圣书》是理雅各晚年对英国和欧洲汉学的主要贡献，通过对这六卷书的研究，我对理雅各解读儒家和道家经典的能力有了一个全新的认识。这包括我从他精心准备的导论和内容丰富

---

① 参见《中国圣书》第二卷注释，引用莎士比亚见第 xvi、38、221 页，引用弥尔顿见第 54 页，引用汤姆逊见第 52 页。
② 参见《中国圣书》第三卷，第 70 页。
③ 参见《中国圣书》第五卷，第 13、14、35 页。
④ 同上书，第 xiii、65 页。
⑤ 参见《中国圣书》第六卷，第 5 页。
⑥ 参见《中国圣书》第三卷，第 100 页。
⑦ 参见《中国圣书》第五卷，第 3、33、124 页。

的评注中发现他在阐释文本时参考的新文献。阅读理雅各参考的这些众多中外著作，尤其是脚注中提到的那些著作，能够产生许多新的见解；另外，我现在更能体会他所着手解决的那些极具争议的阐释意见。毫无疑问，理雅各最纠结的是理解和阐释《易经》及《易传》（《中国圣书》第二卷）；还有，阅读古典的和后来的道教文本（《中国圣书》第五、六卷）时，他显然会遇到许多尖锐的世界观冲突，从而触发他的对立情绪。

为什么之前我在研究理雅各的汉学著作时没有意识到这些问题？原因其实很简单。我想许多理雅各的读者也像我一样。大多数情况下，我在参阅理雅各著作的时候，我只是为了研究某一特定的篇章；我查阅他如何翻译那一篇章，有时候（但并非总是如此）我会查看他的注释，看理雅各如何为他的翻译辩解，希望从中得到一些新的见解。事实上，在这些年中，我查阅的大多是《中国经典》，而非《中国圣书》，因为我在 1980 年代在美国学习中国哲学时，人们认为中国哲学传统的基础文本是《中国经典》前两卷中包含的那些文本（即"四书"，但并非其全部）。① 1980 年代，在研究中国哲学传统的背景下研读《易经》和道家经典时，甚至没有人提起理雅各的翻译，所以我几乎完全不知道理雅各的译本。一旦有人提及理雅各的译本，立马就会被一些哲学学者否定，他们认为理雅各的译本对于那些学习哲学的人来说是"不再相关"的文本。现在，40 年后，教授和学习了更多儒家和道家的经典之后，我更深刻地意识到，我在 1980 年代学习的"中国哲学传统"形成于中国"文革"的背景下，② 我的老师们

① 重点是《论语》和《孟子》，所以更多与《大学》和《中庸》有关的难题几乎没有被触及过。我很晚的时候才认识到这两个文本涉及哲学问题的重要性质。参见 Lauren Pfister, *Vital Post-Secular Perspectives on Chinese Philosophical Issues*, pp. 133-168。

② 然而需要注意的是，革命哲学及其文本不是我们那个时候学习"中国哲学"的哲学素材。

的思想也受到了强烈的后传统世俗主义（post-traditional secularism）的影响。当然，这也影响了他们选择用于学习中国哲学的合适的英译本，最终也影响了他们对那些经典的阐释方法。① 理雅各为我开启了跨文化阐释的大门，让我了解了晚清传统儒家对"四书""五经"及道家经典的解释。结果，我越是系统地研究理雅各的翻译和评注，我就越是钦佩晚清传统儒家知识分子多样的阐释视角。这些视角向我揭示了晚清出现的充满活力的文化挑战和机遇，这些都是之前我所没有学过的；而且还启发我用许多新的方法去评价"中国哲学"后传统的发展，这样的发展在中国 20 世纪上半叶，在欧美尤其是在二战之后才开始得到重视。结果，随着我记录和评价理雅各翻译和阐释的各个方面——既包括《中国经典》也包括《中国圣书》，我意识到我需要重新思考为什么这些卷册后来会被一代一代中国传统文化学者所阅读和参考。我越来越相信，也越来越清晰地认识到《中国圣书》在英语世界产生的三大变革性影响。这三大变革性影响源于理雅各的三大学术和精神贡献，鲜有读者能够理解。因此，我要在这个篇幅相对较长的结论部分揭示我在《中国圣书》中发现的这三大变革力量，并说明为什么我认为这三大变革性影响可以指引 21 世纪的读者对理雅各的巨大成就有一个全新的理解。读者将在我为各分卷写的导读文章中发现，我对理雅各汉学成就欣赏的同时，也批判了他犯的技术性错误和有问题的主张，以及他所经历的翻译难点和阐释冲突，尤其是在上面提到的三卷书中，他经历了巨大的阐

---

① 鉴于这个原因，作为在香港从事教学工作的比较哲学家和宗教学学者，研究 21 世纪早期中国的中国哲学研究的"后世俗"（post-secular）环境对我来说才会显得尤为重要。我把这一阐释视角主要应用到了儒家哲学传统和在当代中国更广泛的文化体验上了，其哲学思考主要表现在我 2020 年出版的一卷著作中，我希望接下来还会有更多卷出版。参见 Lauren F. Pfister, *Vital Post-Secular Perspectives on Chinese Philosophical Issues*, Lanham, et al.: Lexington Press, 2020。

释挑战和世界观冲突。

我下面要讨论的三大变革性影响涉及以下问题。第一，《圣经》诠释学和其他《圣经》主张影响了理雅各处理中国古代文本的方法，以及以《中国圣书》为媒介预先回应英语世界的读者。第二个影响是理雅各对中国注疏文献的阅读，这使他的回应超越了限制英国和欧洲汉学的话语问题，最终使其翻译和阐释能够被后代研究中国传统文化的学者所欣赏。第三个影响涉及创造儒家和道家经典在英语世界"翻译中的正典"的学术标准的广度、深度和一贯性，再加上30年精益求精的汉学翻译和阐释，成功地克服了存在于理雅各生命和著作中非常具体的文化和诠释局限。这有助于回答为什么他的作品仍然被后代研究中国的国内外学者所重视，以及为什么这些作品对于中国传统文化的后传统研究有重要的贡献。

1.《圣经》基督教与儒家、道家经典文本和文化之间的关联性

我们在《中国圣书》中可以发现三个方面的《圣经》基督教影响。① 我将以如下顺序讨论这些影响：直接和间接引用《圣经》中的特定章节；新教《圣经》诠释学不甚明显但无处不在的影响；理雅各通过另一种创造性努力表达了他对《中国圣书》的预期，这一努力与特定的《圣经》文本有关。

（1）对《圣经》一般意义上的引用和某些特别章节的引用

在六卷《中国圣书》中，有直接引用《圣经》经文，也有间接引用《圣经》经文和短语，但不是很明晰。若是不甚熟悉《圣经》，很难辨别出后一种情况；但理雅各认为他那个时代英文世界的读者大多数都能理解他的话语，也能辨别出那些源自《圣经》的文字。

---

① 我用"《圣经》基督教影响"一语是想说明，不一定要像犹太教、伊斯兰教或其他宗教传统那样阅读《圣经》，并以某种方式将之融入自己的宗教阐释历史。用这个表达，我主要关注的是理雅各参考和利用《圣经》文本的新教方式。

　　然而，这里还有一些其他问题需要解决。一些批评传教士的世俗学者（包括传教士-学者）强调传教士的著作引用《圣经》，目的是说明跨文化和宗教阐释的偏见扭曲了他们著作的意义。[①] 也就是说，因为理雅各引用《圣经》批评儒家和道家的主张，所以要想真正理解中国古代经典，理雅各一定要克服这些几乎不可逾越的障碍。然而，我要表明的是，为什么应该反思如此严厉地批评理雅各的翻译和阐释，至少应该反思这种批评的刻薄性。那些泛泛的批评是否有证据可循，这是我想在本结论部分强调的问题。

　　首先我们应该明白，在与中国古代经典的翻译和阐释有关的英文学术著作中，引用《圣经》的方法有多种。有时候，引用《圣经》经文有助于 19 世纪晚期英语世界的学者型读者进行跨文化类比，因为这些读者大多熟悉《圣经》经文和阐释传统，而不了解中文文本。另外，因为理雅各的许多观念源自苏格兰实在主义哲学——通过类比不仅可以强调普遍的智慧，而且可以确认《圣经》和中国古代经典中存在相同的原则或真理——这一发现再次证明人性相近，来自不同文化背景的人也可以拥有相同的德行，也可以对幸福充实的生活具有相同的看法。有时候，引用《圣经》经文的目的是批评在中国古代经典中发现的与《圣经》相冲突的主张。在这种情况下，可能会经历世界观的冲突，因此理雅各及其英语世界的读者必须在权衡之后才能明白这样的冲突是否可以接受。接下来，我先对理雅各

---

① 大约 25 年前，面对欧阳祯（Eugene Chen Eoyang）对理雅各的严厉批评，我讨论过这个问题。我那时非常清楚地表明欧阳祯的批评过于泛化，而且在很大程度上是没有道理的；但我那时的观念是建立在对理雅各五卷本《中国经典》阅读基础上的，并以更为"开放的""汉学东方主义"视角对之进行阐释。在这篇文章里，我要依据六卷本《中国圣书》来回应这些批评，而且使论述的视角超越"汉学东方主义"这一早期的观念。关于我早期的论述，参见 Pfister, *Striving for "The Whole Duty of Man"*, Vol. 2, pp. 160–165。

引用《圣经》的情况做量化分析，然后说明《中国圣书》中《圣经》
经文及思想的各种利用情况。

　　从汉学的角度看，有很重要的一点需要注意，理雅各在参考中
外著作时，会根据翻译和阐释儒家和道家经典的具体情况改变他参
考的文本。有时候他发现参考非汉学文献也有助于他把中国古代经
典里的各种问题向英语世界的读者解释清楚。结果，大多数非汉学
文献在一卷书中只被引用过一次，而且只出现在这六卷书中的其中
一卷中。[①] 只有少数情况下，这些著作才会在一卷书中被参考一次
以上。[②] 从这个角度讲，《圣经》无疑是《中国圣书》中引用的一个
与众不同的非汉学文本，每卷书都有引用。六卷《中国圣书》引用
《圣经》的总次数大约为 60 次；但并非均衡地分布于每卷书中。例
如，《中国圣书》第四卷和第六卷只有 2 页引用了《圣经》，而这
两卷书分别有 491 页和 336 页。若按页数计，其引用频率远远低于
1%。[③] 相比之下，《中国圣书》第二卷和第五卷都有 13 页引用了《圣
经》（这两卷书分别有 444 页和 392 页）。[④] 引用频率多达 3%，这在
统计意义上是很重要的。对于这些数据，我想做进一步的定性和定
量分析，从而更深入地揭示理雅各《中国圣书》的汉学性质。

　　就理雅各引用的汉学翻译与阐释文献而言，必须认识到理雅各
最常引用的汉学文献还是儒家和道家经典作品在欧洲语言中的各个
译本。然而，这些译本只与其中的一两卷有关，尽管它们在某一卷
中被引的次数比《圣经》多，但在整部丛书中被引的总次数可能不

---

① 读者可参考我为每卷《中国圣书》制作的索引中列举的理雅各参考的中外文献（以
　及中外人物）。
② 莎士比亚的著作在《中国圣书》第二卷被引用了 3 次，班扬的著作（尤其是《天路
　历程》和《圣战》）在《中国圣书》第五卷被引用了 3 次。
③ 前者的频率只有 0.4%，后者的频率只有 0.6%。
④ 前者的频率为 2.9%，后者的频率为 3.3%。

到 60 次。例如,《中国圣书》第二卷引用最多的是 18 世纪雷孝思
（Jean Baptiste Régis，1663—1738）等耶稣会士的拉丁文本《易经》,
总计有 29 页引用,而只有 13 页引用《圣经》。[①] 对比更强的是理雅
各《礼记》译本对嘉略利（Joseph-Marie Callery，1810—1862）《礼
记》法语译本的引用;《中国圣书》第三卷有 63 页引用嘉略利,第四
卷有 31 页引用嘉略利,而这两卷书对《圣经》的引用分别只有 8 页
和 2 页。两卷书引用嘉略利的总页数是 94,实际次数是 105 次,远
远超越整部《中国圣书》丛书引用《圣经》的页数（45 页）和次数
（57 次）。引用《圣经》的页数还不到引用嘉略利《礼记》页数的一
半,次数也只是刚过一半。从更广泛的引用范围来讲,与《圣经》
在非汉学外国作品中独特地位形成对比的是,其中三卷《中国圣书》
引用的外国汉学作品至少有 20 种,[②] 另外两卷引用的外国汉学作品
有 10 余种,[③] 还有一卷引用的外国汉学作品相对比较少,只有 7 种。[④]
在我看来,这些数据说明,尽管理雅各对《圣经》的引用有时很显
著,但他对汉学著作的重视是不容争辩的。

　　虽然我要在下面说明理雅各如何以多种方式引用《圣经》和其
他文献,但我坚决认为,理雅各是利用这些文本来说明他不同意在
中国经典文本中发现的主张,他是用这些文本来表达他最决然的反
对态度。哪怕一卷书中有一句此类的话,我们也应该把它看作是对
整卷书中要解决问题的最重要的判断。从性质上来说,理雅各这位
基督教知识分子和牛津大学教授如此引用《圣经》是他能够表达的

① 　有时一页会有多次引用的情况,《中国圣书》第二卷那 29 页引用雷孝思拉丁文《易
　　经》译本的次数为 33 次,那 13 页引用《圣经》的次数为 19 次。
② 　《中国圣书》第一卷引用的外国汉学作品有 19 种,《中国圣书》第五、六卷引用的外
　　国汉学作品有 21 种。
③ 　《中国圣书》第二卷引用的外国汉学作品有 17 种,《中国圣书》第三卷引用的外国汉
　　学作品只有 14 种。
④ 　这一卷是《中国圣书》第四卷。

最强烈的批评形式。

　　然而，为英语世界读者着想，理雅各还是用了许多其他方式引用《圣经》。例如，他把《道德经》的篇幅比作"最短的福音书"，那便是《马可福音》。① 有一处，理雅各比较了西安碑林石碑上刻的儒经长度和整部《圣经》的长度，说两者很接近。② 他还说《孝经》流传过程中文本变化很小，与《新约》差不多，而且都是些无足轻重的变化。③ 还有，理雅各注意到《礼记》和《庄子》每篇的篇名常常取自开篇的一个词，这也是希伯来文《摩西五经》的做法。④ 为了说明和确证《易经》文本已有至少 3000 年的历史，理雅各拿它与《摩西五经》《约书亚书》《士师记》写作的时期相比较。⑤ 理雅各还

---

① 参见《中国圣书》第五卷，第 6 页。

② 理雅各在一个脚注中提及佛教学者戴维斯（T. W. Rhys Davids）说到《圣经》的大概长度，戴维斯显然是拿它与佛经相比的。参见《中国圣书》第一卷，第 457 页注释 1。

③ 参见《中国圣书》第一卷，第 458—459 页注释。阅读过吉瑞德《维多利亚时代翻译中国》的读者，看到理雅各注释中这一比较会感到惊讶且出乎意料，因为吉瑞德对《新约》通用古希腊语（Koiné Greek）文献的可靠性高度怀疑，这与理雅各的看法形成鲜明对照。出人意料的是，吉瑞德显然不知道理雅各曾以当时流行的《新约》研究方式研究过这些文本问题；令人惊讶的是，吉瑞德竟然利用这些信息质疑《圣经》的主张，但理雅各作为基督教知识分子觉得这个问题根本不值得担忧，因为他认为经文的变化事实上无足轻重。21 世纪福音派新教对这些问题有了更深入的研究，备受尊重的《新约》学者布隆贝格（Craig Blomberg）和寇斯藤博格（Andreas J. Köstenberger）的研究完全确证了理雅各 140 年前对《新约》可靠性的肯定。参见 Craig L. Blomberg and Robert B. Stewart, *The Historical Reliability of the New Testament: Countering the Challenges to Evangelical Christian Beliefs*, Nashville: B & H Academic, 2016; Andreas Köstenberger, Benjamin L. Merkle and Robert L. Plummer, *Going Deeper with New Testament Greek: An Intermediate Study of the Grammar and Syntax of the New Testament*, Nashville: B & H Academic, 2016［尤其是 "希腊语与文本校勘"（The Greek Language and Textual Criticism）章，第 17—48 页］。

④ 《圣经》的现代欧洲语言译本没有遵循这样的命名法；因此理雅各比较的是古希伯来和中国古代为文本命名的做法。参见《中国圣书》第三卷，第 25 页;《中国圣书》第五卷，第 11 页。

⑤ 值得注意的是，理雅各是在批评有人认为《易经》是儒经中 "最古老的书"，他指出《书经》《诗经》中的某些部分更古老。在这个背景下，他做出了这一比较。参见《中国圣书》第二卷，第 7 页。

以同样的方式从整体上对比了中国古代经典和《圣经》文本。例如，《圣经》许多篇章都断言，耶和华的一个特别启示是通过《旧约》和《新约》的先知和见证者呈现出来的；因此，理雅各开始翻译和阐释《中国圣书》时，先就其宗教地位做了一个原则性声明："中国的古籍并不自称受到了启发，也不包含我们所说的启示。历史学家、诗人等撰写这些作品，只是有感而发。"① 然而，这个声明需要根据理雅各在六卷本《中国圣书》中实际呈现的内容来判断。就理雅各翻译和阐释的所有儒经而言，他所说为实；这些儒经是"中国的正统宗教"② 的经典。但就某些后来的道教文本而言，事实并非如此。理雅各不仅没有把"特别启示"的主张融入《太上感应篇》开篇，反而认为第一句话的意思不是来自被奉为神明的老子的启示性宣言，而是借用了《左传》中一段相当模糊的文本，且指出《太上感应篇》是道家智慧的代表。③ 另外，在《中国圣书》第六卷的附录中介绍后来的小篇幅道教文本时，理雅各在原则上拒不接受其中三篇是神仙所作，认为这种说法"难以置信""不可接受"。④ 这是世界观冲突的一个显例，但理雅各在这些地方没有附加《圣经》引文来强化他的评断。

中国古代经典与《圣经》文本之间形成鲜明对比的另一组例子与《礼记》中的古代祭祀有关。理雅各多次强调，那些祭祀，即使是献

---

① 参见《中国圣书》第一卷，第 xv 页。

② 引文见《中国圣书》第一卷，第 xiv 页。这个短语意味着这一"宗教"是中国一切精神性表达的标准，这一主张与晚清某些儒家学者对其传统的看法一致。理雅各同意并采用了这个观点，尤其表现在他对古典的和后来的道教文本的批评中。

③ 关于理雅各对这些主张的论证，参见《中国圣书》第五卷，第 40 页；《中国圣书》第六卷，第 235 页注释 2。他认为《太上感应篇》开篇的措辞"取自一部不能被认为是道教的文献"。事实上，理雅各要说的是，因为儒教是"中国的正统宗教"，后来的道教作者采用了这个措辞，目的是增强其文本的可信性。我不同意理雅各的这一阐释，更愿意认为"太上"这一称号就指被奉为神明的老子。

④ 参见《中国圣书》第六卷，第 248—249、255—256、265 页。

给上帝的最高层次的祭祀，也不涉及罪的代价（"赎罪"〈atonement〉
或"挽回祭"〈propitiation〉），而且一般都是感恩的行为，而不是寻
求矫正做过的不可接受的事（"祈求免罪"〈deprecation〉）。① 除了这
些总体性的评论，理雅各还强调了另一种祭祀情形，即祭祀用的动
物（牲）必须"纯一"（guileless simplicity）；然后理雅各指出这
类似于希伯来的献祭制度，要求献祭的羔羊"毫无瑕疵"（without
blemish），而且比希伯来要求的祭品更"进一步"（refinement）。②
通过这些例子，我们可以明显看出，理雅各是用各种各样的比较教
育英语世界的读者了解《礼记》中所载的中国古代文化的方方面面。

　　理雅各在这六卷书中有两次提到了当时流行的《圣经》中文译
本，目的也是教育英语世界的读者了解《圣经》翻译。在比较中国
古代经典和《圣经》经文长度时，理雅各说委办本《诗篇》第一篇
有 100 个汉字，而"钦定本"（我们的英文版本）则有 130 个单词。
理雅各还说中文译文"典雅、精炼"。③ 理雅各以这种方式很直观
地表明，在表现一篇著名的《圣经》经文方面，文雅的中文可以比
标准的英文更简练。这一注释出现在《中国圣书》第一卷接近结尾
处，它也表明理雅各在翻译《书经》《诗经》《孝经》的过程中，这
种比较经学思维令他非常耗神。而且这样美妙的比较在第一卷中并
非仅有这一次，但我要稍后谈论其他比较。理雅各有意识地保持这
种比较经学思维，最出人意料的一个例子是他给《庄子》"达生篇"
做的一个注释。理雅各在翻译和注释中对其中的一个词语"更生"
做了不同的跨文化阐释。④ 整个句子的中文原文 ⑤ 和理雅各的翻译

---

① 关于这些与祭祀有关的比较性言论，参见《中国圣书》第三卷，第 35—37 页；《中
　国圣书》第四卷，第 201 页注释 1。
② 详见《中国圣书》第三卷，第 417 页注释 1。
③ 参见《中国圣书》第一卷，第 457 页注释 1。
④ 下面的一句话及其英文翻译和注释参见《中国圣书》第六卷，第 12 页。
⑤ 参见黄锦鋐《新译庄子读本》，台北三民书局 1983 年版，第 218 页。

如下：

> 弃世则无累，无累则正平，正平则与彼更生，更生则几矣。
>
> Abandoning the world, they are free from its entanglements. Free from its entanglements, their (minds) are correct and their (temperament) is equable. Thus correct and equable, they succeed in securing a renewal of life, as some have done.

理雅各在脚注中说：

> 我想我已经捕捉到了它的意义。这个词语的意思是"生命的更新"（the renewal of life），在《约翰福音》第三章被用来翻译"being born again"*。

理雅各完全明白这个词语在两部经中的意义差别，但他仍然试图表明一个中国基督徒的生命转化观与道家所理解的生命转化有相同的地方，尽管不完全对等。理雅各没有回避这个词语意义的多样性和复杂性，而是向英语世界的读者突出了这些复杂性，并揭示了中文《圣经》翻译所面临的跨文化挑战。

　　根据我对理雅各在《中国圣书》中利用《圣经》文本情况的总结和评价，我们已经看到理雅各恰当地展现了他对人类共有智慧的讨论。理雅各在此肯定了苏格兰实在主义哲学（或"苏格兰常识哲学"）的主张：人类可以共享同样的"第一原理"，包括逻辑、道德、自然科学、形而上学等人类经验的许多方面。在古希伯来和古

---

* 委办本《圣经》译文用的是"更生"，和合本译文用的是"重生"。参见《约翰福音》3:3—4。——译者

中国社会更人道的规定中，有一条法则允许新婚丈夫与妻子同住，无需上战场或履行威胁其婚姻生活或家庭发展的义务。有趣的是，理雅各发现《礼记》和《庄子》都引述了这条法则，因此古代儒家和道家经典都支持这条法则。[1] 另一条人道的规定是收获过后要留下一些谷穗给贫穷的人；在《诗经》中，这些谷穗是留给寡妇的，在《申命记》中，这些谷穗是留给"外乡人、孤儿、寡妇"[2]。在理雅各看来，对于这两种文化中边缘化和贫穷的人，有可比较的共同原则。在第十七卦随卦的象传中，理雅各注意到中国评注者从中得出了高贵者能"看别人比自己强"（esteem others as higher than themselves）[*]的原则，这一原则在《新约》很多处都提及了。[3]

中国古代经典和《圣经》中也可找到许多类同的悖论式名言，表达的都是关于如何明智生活的洞见。《道德经》第六十一章所提倡的谦德在《圣经》中也有类似的悖论式表达："自卑的，必升为高。"[4]《庄子》和《福音书》都讽刺世俗的成功者和社会名流，认为他们在上天的眼里只不过是乞丐和流浪儿。[5] 理雅各向英语世界读者指出这两大经典传统中类似的名言还有很多：关于人必有一死更为冷静的

---

[1] 参见《中国圣书》第三卷，第 374 页注释 4；《中国圣书》第五卷，第 231 页注释 2。这些规定的细节不尽相同，但它们都类似于《申命记》24：5 里的一条法则。

[2] 参见《中国圣书》第一卷，第 373 页注释 1。理雅各把《诗经·小雅·大田》一诗与《申命记》24：19—22 联系了起来。

[*] "看别人比自己强"是理雅各对王宗传之注"以上下下，以贵下贱"的解释。王宗传之言，参见［清］李光地撰，刘大钧整理，《周易折中》第 3 版，巴蜀书社 2008 年版第 263 页。——译者

[3] 参见《中国圣书》第二卷，第 228 页。理雅各没有给出他参考的《新约》引文，但《罗马书》12：10、《腓立比书》2：3 都有这条原则（理雅各参考的是钦定本《圣经》）。

[4] 参见《中国圣书》第五卷，第 105 页。理雅各引用了这句话，但没有标明出处，因为他认为英语世界的读者能看出它出自《路加福音》14：11。

[5] 《庄子·大宗师》有这样一个非常精彩的悖论句（"天之小人，人之君子；人之君子，天之小人也。"）；《马太福音》7：28—29 刻画了耶稣与当时犹太教名士的关系。参见《中国圣书》第五卷，第 253 页注释 2。

真理，^①乍看上去如此稳定的世界的不稳定性，^②父母的罪恶会深深影响子女的生命，^③统治者有权裁决作恶的人。^④

关于人类经验和我们的生命世界，还有更多言论可供比较，反映在生命的方方面面。古代中国语境中的生命世界的三个维度——天、地、人"三才"——如果"和谐运行"，就会造就"幸福繁荣的世界"。《礼记》卷十七《乐记》就是如此表达的，这与先知何西阿的愿景中耶和华赐福于天、地、人可以相类比。^⑤有时，人类的苦难源自人类的自大傲慢或残酷无情；傲慢、残酷之人必将受到正义的审判，但有时候不易辨别其间的关联。《道德经》第七十三章和《诗篇》第九十七章揭示了其中隐藏的关联性。^⑥有时候，政府做不了该做的事，因为有更大的生命条件影响了它的决策。在这种情况下，如果统治者不懂得三思而后行，那么其行动的结果只能是毁灭性的。《礼记》有这样的记载，《圣经》也有这样的箴言："愚昧人不宜得尊荣。"^⑦因此，在那些遭受苦难的生命条件下，有时候人必须相信更高的力量终有解决的办法，所以理雅各就比较了在面对相冲突的"事实"（facts）的情况下道家和基督徒的"信仰"（faith）态度。^⑧

---

① 文见《道德经》第 50 章，理雅各让读者比较《约伯记》1: 21。参见《中国圣书》第五卷，第 93 页。

② 这是理雅各在《易经》译本中对《序卦》主题的总结，参见《中国圣书》第二卷，第 55 页。

③ 这是理雅各在《易经》译本中根据《文言》得出的结论，他在"导论"中有详细讨论，参见《中国圣书》第二卷，第 47—48、417 页。

④ 这是《易经》之《象传》讨论的一个原则，《罗马书》13: 4 对此也有表述。参见《中国圣书》第二卷，第 287 页。

⑤ 参见《中国圣书》第四卷，第 115 页注释 1。理雅各参照的《圣经》经文是《何西阿书》2: 21—22。

⑥ 那么，"谁能知天意？"《道德经》说只有圣人。参见《中国圣书》第五卷，第 116 页。

⑦ 参见《中国圣书》第三卷，第 257 页注释 2。

⑧ 理雅各把《庄子》里的一段话与《约伯记》和《诗篇》第七十三章联系了起来。参见《中国圣书》第五卷，第 237 页。对于外国基督教知识分子而言，在道家经典与

虽然《道德经》中的许多篇章都令理雅各感到值得敬佩，但他认为"老子学说的最大荣耀"是他主张"报怨以德"。① 这位苏格兰汉学家以其敏锐的眼光指出，这一爱之伦理甚至连孔子也不能完全接受；② 因此他认为《道德经》清晰地说出了中国古代文化中这一伟大的道德原则，也是明智生活的原则。虽然如此，理雅各对后期道家传统做出了悲观的评价，他认为这一高尚的道德原则没有在后来的道家作品中发现，无论是《庄子》还是其他汉代道家学者的作品。③ 理雅各认为这只能看作是后期道家作品的文化缺陷，并且相信中国最早的新教徒身上体现了"报怨以德"的典范价值观。④ 看出这一点之后，理雅各直接、冷静地指出了道家文化和宗教中的这一缺陷："［这一原则］的果实还没有最终结成"，⑤ 真诚地肯定了这一伦理原则的文化转化力量。因为理雅各尊崇老子的这一道德洞见，所以

（接上页）《圣经》文本之间做出正面的比较，是很难得的。理雅各不仅做了大量这样的比较，而且进一步指出《庄子》里的这段话有与"信仰实践"相类似的东西，这是一个非凡的比较宗教立场。

① 参见《中国圣书》第五卷，第 107 页；《道德经》引文在第六十三章。理雅各对其意义更直接的肯定在《中国圣书》第五卷第 31 页。

② 参见《中国圣书》第五卷，第 31 页。理雅各在论述这一问题的时候，参考了《论语·宪问》第十六章描述的情形。这一点在理雅各的评价中非常重要，所以他在《道德经》第四十九章的评注中详细引用了《论语》这一章的内容，参见《中国圣书》第五卷，第 92 页。

③ 理雅各在一条长长的注释中讨论了这个问题，即后来的道家作品中没有传承和发扬这一仁德原则。理雅各说《庄子》《韩非子》或《淮南子》没有申述这一原则，但是他发现刘向（前 77—前 6）的著作中提到了两次。理雅各如此彻底地追踪这一原则的发展，说明了他对道家传统最终的总结性评价的合理性。详见《中国圣书》第五卷，第 107 页。

④ 例如何进善牧师和车锦光生命中就有这样的价值观。关于他们的生平以及与理雅各的交往，参见 Lauren F. Pfister, "Plucking the Plank Out of One's Own Eye: Reflective Moments of Transformation Gained from James Legge's Christian Engagement with Four Notable Chinese Persons", in Alexander Chow, ed., *Scottish Missions to China: Commemorating the Legacy of James Legge (1815–1897)*, Leiden and Boston: Brill, 2022, pp. 13–49.

⑤ 参见《中国圣书》第五卷，第 31 页。

他批评福斐礼误解了《庄子》里的一句话：福斐礼错误地认为爱之伦理原则，即所谓的"金律"是庄子的主张。①

　　毫无疑问，这里非常突出的一个问题是，理雅各认同中国古代传统的"神圣性"，还把它上升到对实在性和伴之而生的形而上学哲学反思的高度，这是一个概念化和理解神性（nature of divine）这一终极主体的问题。②在不同传统中这一终极主体或神（deity）也不尽相同；神如何与现象世界存在相关联，甚至神是否与世界的产生有关，都揭示了对终极实在及其与物质世界的关系的多种表述。某些有神论认为世界是神通过说话的方式创造的，因此在神之前没有物质的存在（例如犹太教、基督教、伊斯兰教）；③另一些有神论认为世界的基本要素呈现出一种或另一种形式——有些选择具体的元素，有些选择混沌的混合体，神从中塑造出现象世界。④某些古希腊学者提出了"第一因"（first cause）主张，认为那是创世神的一个独特的功能，尽管神创世的方式不同。⑤还有一些有神论设定的终极实在与物质秩序或有秩序的宇宙（cosmos）没有直接关系，自然秩序好像

---

①　参见《中国圣书》第六卷，第 240 页注释 1。《马太福音》7: 12 记载了这条"金律"："你们希望［别人］怎样对待你们，你们也应当怎样对待别人。"

②　为了说明终极实在与现象世界关系的各种表述，我这里参考了马兰（Solomon Caesar Malan, 1812—1894）的三卷本著作《箴言书新注》（*Original Notes on the Book of Proverbs*）。《箴言》3: 19 说耶和华以智慧创造了天地。马兰在第一卷对这条箴言用了很长的篇幅进行注解，引用了 20 多种语言的智慧文本（包括汉语）。马兰注意到这些智慧文本对天地创生（production 或 creation）的描述至少有十种不同的方式。参见 Solomon Caesar Malan, *Original Notes on the Book of Proverbs*, London: William and Norgate, 1889, Vol. 1, pp. 141–171。

③　参见 Malan, *Original Notes on the Book of Proverbs*, Vol. 1, pp. 142, 169–171。

④　包括蒙古、阿尔泰鞑靼文献，以及拜火教《亚斯纳》篇和赫西奥德的诗句。参见 Malan, *Original Notes on the Book of Proverbs*, Vol. 1, pp. 159–164。可能还包括儒家的主张，因为马兰还引用了理雅各的相关译文，同上书，第 154—157 页。

⑤　参见马兰引自柏拉图（Plato）、西塞罗（Cicero）、品达（Pindar）、普罗提诺（Plotinus）的著作：Malan, *Original Notes on the Book of Proverbs*, Vol. 1, pp. 165–168。

是自发形成的一样。① 还有人对终极实在的描述不属于有神论，认为它不是独一无二或有位格的存在（personal being），他们声称这一终极存在没有创造现象世界。② 还有一些更独特的，尤其是佛教的许多说法，因为他们否认任何的终极神，认为现在现象世界的性质是由复杂的"佛陀世界"（Buddha worlds）决定的，而佛陀世界之前就存在，而且在现在的秩序被破坏后还会继续存在。③

面对这些处理终极实在和现象世界之间关系的世界观，理雅各坚持基督教的表述，把终极实在看作是万能之神的创造；无论是作为基督徒，还是传教士和学者，理雅各都接受这一《圣经》中的说法。但是，像马兰一样，④ 理雅各明白不同宗教和形而上传统中对神的理解不尽相同。理雅各接触中国文化之前，就曾在古希腊和古罗马著作中学习过那些不同的世界观，那是与犹太一神教不同的地中海文化，而且是能够理解基督教三一神的文化。

让每种文化都在其自有作品的范围内思考终极神，这是理雅各所能肯定的最高层次的哲学和宗教意识。理雅各明白这一形而上概念有许多表述，所以他就区分了古代儒家文献中发现的神和后期儒家和古典道家文献中发现的神。只要儒家或道家古典文献中有什么

---

① 持有这个世界观的一个具体的例子是卢克莱修（Lucretius），参见 Malan, *Original Notes on the Book of Proverbs*, Vol. 1, p. 166。

② 某些印度、埃及、希腊和拉丁传统所称的"神"（gods）和"灵"（spirits）是这样的；但马兰发现他们在独一无二的神与复数的神之间游移，并没有一致的表述，因此不想严肃地对待他们的观点。参见 Malan, *Original Notes on the Book of Proverbs*, Vol. 1, p. 167。

③ 参见 Malan, *Original Notes on the Book of Proverbs*, Vol. 1, pp. 157-159。

④ 对马兰生平和著作各个方面感兴趣的读者，可参阅最新出版的研究 Lauren F. Pfister, ed., *Polyglot from the Far Side of the Moon: The Life and Works of Solomon Caesar Malan (1812-1894)*, Sankt Augustin: Monumenta Serica Institute, 2022。值得注意的是，理雅各在牛津大学期间曾与马兰有联系，因此他们了解彼此针对中国经典中的问题和主张所采取的阐释立场。

篇章暗示了"寻求上帝"（search for God）的内容，或是有渴望了解
终极实在的内容，都会引起理雅各的关注。孝子之情，一种深深触
动内心的情感，难道也是一种圣言，是"接近""在你口中，在你心
里"之言？理雅各想到了使徒保罗谈到这种情感，深深地被服丧的
孝子该如何做的主张感动了。[①] 同样，《道德经》第25章"有物混成，
先天地生"[②] 表现了道家对"无因之因"（the Uncaused Cause）的探
寻，虽然那是无位格的"道"，但也是对实在深刻的探求，理雅各觉
得这一点非常了不起。[③] 老子把"道"描述作"自发行为，而非出自
个人意志"，理雅各从中感觉到与约伯的寻求很相似，约伯认为很难
寻得上帝。[④] 读到《易经》的一个传注说"帝不可见，即物见之"，
理雅各想到《罗马书》中非常类似的说法。[⑤] 在理雅各看来，这些共
有的智慧不是偶然的巧合，而是说明人类文化中随时随地都可能出
现更高层次的成就。

　　因此，理雅各发现《书经》《诗经》中有用表示"上帝"之意的
"帝"和"天"表达终极存在、终极神的概念时，他无疑会强烈地断
定中国古代文化中是有"神圣"的。[⑥] 从概念上讲，理雅各认为中文

---

① 他的评论针对的是《礼记·问丧》结尾一章，《中国圣书》第三卷"导论"第48页
有对这一章的总结，理雅各于此引用了《罗马书》10:6—8。《礼记》原文参见《中
国圣书》第四卷，第379页。
② 参见《中国圣书》第五卷，第67页。
③ 此处及下面的引文，参见《中国圣书》第五卷，第69页。此处理雅各引用了《使徒
行传》17:27，但没有注明出处，说明他认为英语世界的读者能够辨识出来。
④ 参见《中国圣书》第五卷，第69页。理雅各这次引用的是《约伯记》11:7，也没有
注明出处。
⑤ 参见《中国圣书》第二卷，第52页。理雅各所引出自万充宗（万斯大）父子所辑
《辨志堂新辑易经集解》。类比之言出自《罗马书》1:20。
⑥ 关于理雅各对这一断言的详细论述，以及这三个术语是如何进入古代中国的宗教生
活，主要在第一卷序言部分，对此我会稍后补充一些细节。参见《中国圣书》第一
卷，第xxiii—xxix页。

"天"是神的模糊表达，① 因此"天"被用于指神时，他常常用大写的"Heaven"翻译。② 他然后说，"帝"和"上帝"用于指古代儒家的神时，是"God"的"人格名"（personal names），③ 因此给人一种强烈的亲切感，相当于"我们在天上的父"（our Father in heaven）。④

　　理雅各知道，翻译这些形而上的术语，还有其他选择，他引用了之前宋君荣（Antoine Gaubil，1689—1759）的法语翻译、麦都思（Walter Henry Medhurst，1796—1857）的英文翻译，而且他自己还提出了一些可能的翻译，但认为都不充分。⑤ 理雅各说，有人认为这两个术语在某些语境下不对等于"God"，因为"帝"这一称号后来被用于早期儒家的圣王尧和舜。后儒使用这一谥号神化尧舜，⑥ 其根

---

① 　理雅各说"天"表达的是"绝对至高无上权力的概念"（the idea of Supreme Power in the absolute）。这是根据宋儒陈祥道的主张而做出的断言，并且解释陈氏的主张说"天类似于绝对神之名"（Heaven would approximate to the name for Deity in the absolute），还说它相当于《摩西五经》中把"耶和华"（Jehovah）很戏剧性地定义为"我是自有永有的"（《出埃及记》3:14，理雅各误把此章标为了"Exodus xv 14"）。参见《中国圣书》第一卷，第 xxv 页，第 478 页。理雅各在这两处书写的英文无论是语法还是逻辑上都不是 21 世纪英语的用法和意义，因此需要进一步说明。我认为理雅各所用的"in the absolute"表示作为"独一无二"（unique）的术语，不能用于其他概念。"天"也是那样的一个"名"，被特定用来指神。另外，理雅各这里用的"名"（name）现在应该称"概念"（concept），并不真正指名字或姓名。还有，现在常用更接近希伯来发音的"Yahweh"来指称上帝之名，而不是"Jehovah"。

② 　阅读《中国圣书》第一卷译文部分，读者会很快发现许多地方都有"Heaven"这个英文单词。（例如，第 98 页有一个，第 99 页有两个。）在《诗经·小雅》部分，出现得更频繁（几乎每页都有），但在《大雅》和《国风》部分出现得不是那么频繁。在《中国圣书》第一卷注释部分，"Heaven"出现了 60 次。读者从此可领略"Heaven"一词在《中国圣书》第一卷三部经典中出现的频繁程度了。

③ 　理雅各用的是单数"personal name"，参见《中国圣书》第一卷，第 xxv 页。我理解他的意思是，这两个中文词语本身包含了与宇宙中的其他人和物之间的关系，而"绝对的"（absolute）或被抽离出来的"天"（Heaven）的内涵则不一定包含那样的关系维度。

④ 　参见《中国圣书》第一卷，第 478 页。

⑤ 　同上书，第 xxiii—xxiv 页。

⑥ 　值得注意的是，理雅各指出孔子没有用这个神化的称号指这两位圣王，但孟子有。这是让这位先师在理雅各心目中占据突出位置的另一个因素。参见《中国圣书》第一卷，第 xxviii 页。

据是这一称号早期的意义，指儒家的真神，还是说仅仅是后来的捏造，随之而来的仅仅是一种神化英雄人物的形式，催生了多神论或多精气论（polypneumatisms）——存在众神但无至高无上神的世界观？[①] 理雅各认为，儒家的真神是通过这些术语认定和命名的，后来被用于神化那些圣王，后来发展出多神的世界观，又导致所谓的"自然崇拜"，以及"对古代英雄和圣贤的崇拜"，这一切都被他认为是古代儒家一神论的堕落。[②] 结果，凡是《书经》和其他书中"帝"被用作神圣化的称号时，理雅各都对其作不译处理。[③]

最重要的是，"God"在《书经》《诗经》的译文中仍占有主要地位，尽管没有"Heaven"那么突出，数量上也不及"Heaven"。[④] 在《中国圣书》第一卷的评注中，有30页出现了"God"，虽然不到总页数的6%，但也足以支持这套丛书中古代儒家一神论"神圣性"的

---

① 理雅各依据四个文本接合文化原因对这一问题做了充分论证，参见《中国圣书》第一卷，第 xxvi—xxix 页。

② 理雅各发现，古代儒家一神论这些后期的发展在《礼记·月令》中表现得最为突出。理雅各对此做了详细说明。我引用的"自然崇拜"以及与"英雄和圣贤"有关的宗教实践也出自这个上下文。这是理雅各为什么坚持用"God"翻译"帝"和"上帝"的第四个原因。参见《中国圣书》第一卷，第 xxviii—xxix 页。

③ 读者几乎可在《尧典》《舜典》的每页译文都能发现不译的"Ti"，参见《中国圣书》第一卷，第 32—36、38—52、53—62 页。

④ 我说"最重要"，因为《中国圣书》第一卷有三部儒经，但《书经》《诗经》包含儒家传统里最古老的文本，而《孝经》（其中有一处有"God"）是很晚出现的一个文本。《书经》译文中有30页出现了"God"，《诗经》有24页，《孝经》有1页。总计55页，82例。值得注意的是，在这卷书中"Heaven"出现的次数大概是"God"的三倍，因此"天"是中国最古老文本中儒家神更为重要的称谓，后来的儒家文本《论语》《孟子》中也主要用"天"称呼儒家神，尽管《论语》用得较少，《孟子》用得也不多。参见《中国圣书》第一卷，第 39、58、87、91、95、99、111、126、130、139、144、153、159、161、166、184、185、196、197、198、206—208、214、215、221、222、245、259、266、307、309、310、319—321、341、343、354、378、379、381、382、389、390、391、392、397、399、408、410、412、420、422、477 页。

主张。^①在评注中，理雅各强调古代儒家文本承认人类和自然秩序中存在一个主宰的神，^②并且指出《诗经》中有两处用诗性的语言清晰地表明了儒家神人格化的维度。^③

不过，应该注意的是，理雅各感觉道家说的"神人"的品质只能让他联想到终极神，于是他就引用了一连串的《圣经》经文强调他反对道家的这一说法。^④这是理雅各在《中国圣书》中表达得最强烈的反对意见。因为在理雅各看来，凡是常人成神的说法都是错误的，这样只能试图用一个低下得多的、前身是人的存在取代他所崇拜的上帝（而他相信古代儒家的圣王也崇拜和祭祀上帝）的荣耀。然而，根据理雅各在整部《中国圣书》中利用《圣经》经文的其他方式，我认为这一世界观冲突没有在根本上影响理雅各对道家和儒家经典文本的正确理解。尽管如此，在理雅各对《庄子》的评注中，我们还是发现了明显的负面语气，出现的频率远远高于他对《道德经》和其他众多儒经的评注。

（2）《中国圣书》中隐藏的《圣经》诠释学之维

不甚明显的是，理雅各翻译《中国圣书》中的五部儒家经典和

---

① 这些例子不仅出现在脚注中，而且也出现在《书经》《诗经》不同部分译文之间的评注和导言性介绍中。参见《中国圣书》第一卷，第 99 页注释 1、138、302、317、317 页注释 1、320、321、323、325 页注释 1、343 页注释 2、354、354 页注释 4、377、378 页注释 1、379 页注释 3、390 页注释 1、391 页注释 1、392 页注释 3、396 页注释 3、397 页注释 1、405 页注释 1、408 页注释 1、411 页注释 1、419、420 注释 2、422 页注释 1、476 页注释 2、477 注释 1、484 页注释 3。

② 理雅各用了"providence"（天意）这个词来说明他的这一认识。参见《中国圣书》第一卷，第 376 页注释 3、434 页注释 1。

③ 参见《中国圣书》第一卷，第 378 页注释 1、391 页注释 1。理雅各注意到许多中国评注者试图规避这个问题，但他还是根据中国的经典文本证明儒家有人格神的主张。

④ 理雅各反对的是他认为的那些"亵渎神明"（blasphemous）之言，虽然他没有用这个词。理雅各为了否定那些道家的言论，一连引用了五处《圣经》经文（分别是《约翰福音》4：24，《提摩太前书》6：15，《诗篇》104：2—3；《诗篇》18：10，《以赛亚书》57：15）。参见《中国圣书》第五卷，第 127、128 页。

三部道家"经典"，① 以及第二卷和第六卷附录，② 他用了著名的新教诠释原则及其推论来研究和阐释这些中国的"神圣文本"。主要的原则就是通常所谓的"以经解经"，不是依赖其他传统或后来解经家的著作确定某一章节的意义。这一基本原则的推论有许多，读者可参考陈终道牧师的论述；③ 这一原则及其推论被广泛用于许多宗教和经典传统，至于在儒教、基督教、犹太教和伊斯兰教传统里的应用，读者可参考亨德森（John B. Henderson）的论述。④ 在《中国圣书》第一卷"导读"中，我提到了两部 21 世纪的"研读本《圣经》"，指出了他们阐释《圣经》经文的方法，因为其中的大部分特征都能在这套 19 世纪的《中国圣书》中找到。我这里重点讨论陈终道牧师论述的《圣经》诠释原则，这有助于说明理雅各对《中国圣书》的阐释。

　　"以经解经"的基本原则意味着译者或阐释者理雅各在全部六卷《中国圣书》中都是这样做的，而且还把儒经的诠释权威应用到他所处理的道教文本中，尽管他也确实大量参考了其他古代的道教文本。事实上，如我在最后两卷的导读文章中所讲的那样，那些文本包括他翻译和阐释的道家经典文本，理雅各采用的是清代儒家学者阐释道家经典的传统，对道家的主张充满了蔑视和否定。从本总论的附录可以看出，在评注道家经典和道教文本时，理雅各参考了许多儒家经典。

---

① 五部儒家经典是《中国圣书》第一卷的《书经》《诗经》《孝经》，《中国圣书》第二卷的《易经》和《中国圣书》第三、四卷的《礼记》。三个道教文本包括不是古代"经典"的《太上感应篇》，所以我为"经典"一词加了双引号。另外两部道家经典是《道德经》和《庄子》。
② 即《易经》的传"十翼"（理雅各在《中国圣书》第二卷中将之缩为七个"附录"），以及《中国圣书》第六卷末所附的来自后期道教传统的八个译文中的六个。这样来看，加上理雅各对这些文本的编辑，总共多了 13 个文本。不过，应该注意的是，理雅各把《易传》和《易经》分开了，区别于他认为是那卷书中"神圣文本"的经文（六十四卦卦文），所以我在这里将它们区别对待。
③ 参见陈终道《以经解经》（第二版），香港金灯台出版社 1997 年版。
④ 参见 John B. Henderson, *Scripture, Canon, and Commentary: A Comparison of Confucian and Western Exegesis*, Princeton: Princeton University Press, 1991。

那么，理雅各在《中国圣书》中还利用了什么次要的《圣经》诠释原则？

如果对某一特定传统的经典文本有高度的阐释兴趣，那么这些经典——指儒家和道家经典——所用的任何一个独特的术语都应该受到特别关注和重视。[①] 这就是为什么理雅各经常强调儒家或道家经典独特的用语，并且认真解释它在那个篇章和其他语境中的意义，帮助英语世界的读者理解那些独特的术语在中文里的用法。

理雅各在《中国圣书》中经常用的另一个阐释原则是，为儒家和道家经典的某一章节提供历史和文化背景信息。[②] 因此，经常出现的情况是，《诗经》某篇诗提到一个人物或仪式，需要参考《书经》中的那个人物来说明，或是参考其他历史作品（例如《礼记》或《左传》）来描述那一仪式。[③] 这在理雅各对《庄子》的评注中也特别重要，他会拿《庄子》中那些嘲讽和反对儒家的言论与早期儒家著作中的主张做对比。通过这种方式，理雅各表明道家是在用虚假的历史记录故意曲解某些人物，同时也强调《庄子》为了维护道家的世界观主张而创造出一个虚构的人物，并且在历史人物和虚构人物之间虚构一场讨论。[④]

---

① 陈牧师著作的第十八章主要讲《圣经》独特的用语（希伯来语、阿拉姆语和希腊语）。参见陈终道《以经解经》，第 297—306 页。

② 陈牧师著作的第十章讲到了解经的背景问题。参见陈终道《以经解经》，第 155—170 页。

③ 这是对这一诠释原则的正面应用，经常出现在《中国圣书》第一卷每篇诗的评注中。理雅各常常会首先参考《诗经》中提到那一人物或仪式的其他诗，然后有必要时再根据其他资料附加历史解释。他常常参考之前评注中已经讨论过的历史文化著作，目的是为这样的阐释提供文本内互文的证据。当然，这样做也是为了节省篇幅，不用每次都重复那些说过的话。

④ 这是对这一诠释原则的反面应用，被理雅各用来表达他强烈反对《庄子》中的各种主张。这是理雅各利用儒家的阐释立场阐释道家作品的偏见，这个问题我将稍后处理，因为它也是理雅各接受的《圣经》诠释学训练的一个部分，并且用在了他的翻译和阐释工作中。

还有一个阐释原则是理雅各引自《孟子》的说《诗》原则。^① 理雅各非常重视这个原则，把它印在了《中国经典》每卷本的扉页。^② 其原文和理雅各的译文如下：^③

故说《诗》者，不以文害辞，不以辞害志，以意逆志，是为得之。

Those who explain the odes, may not insist on one term so as to do violence to a sentence, nor on a sentence so as to do violence to the general scope. They must try with their thoughts to meet that scope, and then we shall apprehend it.

因此，无论是用《圣经》诠释学还是用《孟子》的话讲，这里都有一个关乎阐释的问题：不容许偏执的阐释，因为它不符合词语或句子所处的语境。理雅各常常用这个阐释原则批评其他译本，包括英语、法语、德语或拉丁语译本。基于这个原则，他对19世纪两位汉学家福斐礼和翟理斯的《庄子》译本中某些术语的翻译进行了激烈批评。^④

从跨宗教（inter-religious）和跨文化的视角出发，理雅各强调

---

① 陈牧师著作的第七章讲到了这个问题。参见陈终道《以经解经》，第113—124页。
② 我在下面的一篇文章中论述了孟子的这个原则及其对理雅各的意义："Mediating Word, Sentence and Scope without Violence: James Legge's Understanding of 'Classical Confucian' Hermeneutics", in Tu Ching-i, ed., *Classics and Interpretations: The Hermeneutic Traditions in Chinese Culture*, New Brunswick, New Jersey: Transaction Publishers, 2000, pp. 371-382。
③ 参见 Legge, *CC2, The Mencius* 5A: 4, Oxford: Clarendon Press, 1893, p. 353。
④ 这涉及理雅各批评福斐礼对《庄子》中"道"的翻译和翟理斯对《庄子》中"天"的翻译。理雅各的基本主张是，这两位英国汉学家只是用了每个术语的一个特定的意义，这样做明显扭曲了它们在《庄子》其他句子和段落中的意义。理雅各通过引用不同的篇章表明他们是如何"害意"的。参见《中国圣书》第五卷，第14—18页。

儒家经典没有获得任何来自神启的特殊地位，但他认为其中所阐述的生命原则、态度、圣人的行为都是人类共同的智慧。理雅各根据《圣经》发展出了特定的属灵观，儒经中有些篇章影响了他对《圣经》传统和儒家传统之间重大差异的看法。这样的重大差异虽然不多，但只要遇到这种情形，理雅各都会认为《圣经》的主张优于儒家。[①] 我们已经说过，理雅各发现儒家的注解者否认某些古代诗歌中"天"具有任何人格属性，但在那些地方"天"明显地表现出了决定性的选择、带有情感的态度和无法否认的思虑。在这种情况下，理雅各设法使英语世界的读者相信，有一种文化的偏见限制了那些儒家学者思考古代文本的方式，虽然理雅各并没有用我的术语来表达这些问题。理雅各基本认为，古代文本提供的信息比后来注解者承认或肯定的信息要多，所以他优先考虑经文，而不是那些深深影响儒家注疏传统上千年的理性化阐释。同样，但更频繁的是，理雅各在《易传》（《中国圣书》第二卷）和后来的道教文本（《中国圣书》第六卷）中面对着更多与《圣经》主题和主张相冲突的世界观。理雅各会用"模糊"（obscure）、"荒谬"（ridiculous）、"怪诞"（fantastic）"难以置信"（fabulous）或"荒诞"（absurd）来评论他认为不正确的说法或主张。[②] 这里有阐释的"偏见"问题，不仅适用于理雅各的翻译和阐释，也适用于古代儒家和道家的主张。这也是《圣经》诠释学所关注的问题，陈牧师的著作也非常直接地给予了回

---

① 陈终道著作的许多章都讨论了这些问题，第五章、第六章讨论了《圣经》"启示的渐次显明"问题，第十三章讨论了《圣经》的属灵观。参见陈终道《以经解经》，第77—110 页，第 209—224 页。

② 这里应该指出，在 21 世纪的英语中，"fantastic"和"fabulous"的意义已经发生了改变，通常用于描述特别令人羡慕和具有非凡价值的事物。但在 19 世纪的英语中，它们通常具有强烈的负面含义。"fantastic"用于描写"不真实""不正当"因而"难以置信"的事物，而"fabulous"表达的则是更强烈的"难以置信"之意，与人类经验相抵触。理雅各常常用"fabulous"这个词描述道家所说的仙人的能力或"物化"。

答。^①换句话说，"偏见"是通过有原则地反对不同主张而形成的看法，那些看法有时候是依据主观判断而表达出来的，而那些判断被批判的旁观者听到或看到时则被认为没有充足的理由。理雅各常常在注释中说中国评注者和外国译者的说法不充分，因为他们的主张不合理或没能说明白他们要阐释的内容。^②有时，理雅各的批评专门针对一位中国评注者^③或一位欧洲译者^④；有时，他会引用一位中国评注者的言论反对另一个中国评注者，^⑤或者反对所有的阐释者（无论中外）。^⑥有

---

① 参见陈终道《以经解经》（第 16 章），第 261—278 页。这里介绍了产生偏见的七种方式，其中五种与理雅各正在研究和经历的有关。

② 参见以下几例：《中国圣书》第一卷，第 131 页注释 1 [理雅各挑战某些中国评注者关于"西夷"（barbarous people from the west）的说法]，第 154 页注释 2（反对"许多学者"的说法，理雅各认为他们的说法也有可能，但他提出了一个他感觉更合理的说法），第 255 页注释 1（理雅各反对宋君荣的翻译，说它"超出了中文文本的内容"），第 319 页注释 1（理雅各反对给一句诗"强加的观点"和朱熹的观点）；《中国圣书》第二卷，第 69 页（理雅各反对雷孝思为需卦上六爻爻辞中"三人"一语赋予的具体意义），第 134 页（理雅各反对麦格基把晋卦六二爻爻辞中的"王母"认作"帝天之妻（朱诺）"，说它是毫无根据的解读，扭曲了原爻辞的意思），第 190 页（理雅各批评中国评注者的阐释太随意），第 281 页（理雅各反对宋儒程颐的象征主义阐释太"牵强"）；《中国圣书》第三卷，第 141 页注释 1（理雅各倾向于乾隆朝《钦定礼记义疏》编纂者的意见，不赞同"某些"其他评注者的意见，并说明了原因），第 240 页注释 1（理雅各反对孔颖达和嘉略利的阐释，因为孔颖达所征引的证据不足以证明他的主张）；《中国圣书》第四卷，第 143 页注释 1（理雅各反对关于一位中国古人身份的"普遍认为"的阐释，并引用一位不知名的中国评注者的解释为证），第 265 页注释 1（理雅各反对郑玄的注）；《中国圣书》第五卷，第 115 页（反对"中国评注者和外国译者"对《道德经》第 72 章的解释，因为他们似乎谁也不同意谁的解释），第 248 页注释 3（理雅各反对福斐礼和翟理斯的翻译，并说明了原因）；《中国圣书》第六卷，第 177 页（理雅各反对一个道家人物说孔子腐败，并引用《论语》说"没有证据"支持那一控诉）。

③ 例如他在《中国圣书》第二卷第 281 页对程颐的批评，在《中国圣书》第四卷第 265 页注释 1 对郑玄的批评。

④ 例如他否定法语译者宋君荣、拉丁语译者雷孝思、爱尔兰圣公会传教士麦格基、英国汉学家福斐礼和翟理斯的翻译和阐释。分别参见《中国圣书》第一卷，第 255 页；《中国圣书》第二卷，第 69、134 页；《中国圣书》第六卷，第 248 页注释 3。

⑤ 参见《中国圣书》第三卷，第 141 页注释 1；《中国圣书》第四卷，第 143 页注释 1。

⑥ 参见《中国圣书》第一卷，第 319 页；《中国圣书》第五卷，第 115 页。

时，那些因偏见而形成的不可接受的阐释与某一特定的阐释学派有关，或与评注者独特的形而上思想有关。然而，有时不是偏见的问题，而是无知，因为有时候评注者或译者没办法理解中国古代文本讲的是什么意思。在这种情况下，如果评注者仍然说他知道文本讲的是什么意思，那么很可能就有某种偏见，再加上任性以及思想上的大胆妄为，就很难把道理说得清了。理雅各有时也发现，《庄子》中关于"物化"的主张与他在 19 世纪苏格兰大学接受的科学教育相违背，因此他就会反对那些古典道家的主张。[①] 如果提出了否定意见，但没有提供任何推理或证据，那么那样的否定意见（无论是来自理雅各还是任何其他人）本身就有偏见的嫌疑。[②] 但是，如果那些否定意见是根据经验提出的，而且这样的经验是许多其他 19 世纪的中国或英语世界读者所认同的，那么理雅各和他人的判断就可被看作不仅合理，而且正确。

这里附加一点，以便让我们对理雅各阐释中国古代文本的方法多一层了解，那就是理雅各在《中国圣书》的评论文章或脚注中几乎从来没有提到一位基督教神学家。我们从他大量的布道文稿可以看出，他阅读了许多神学家的著作，而且能够引用这些著作；但他

---

① 参见《中国圣书》第五卷，第 361 页注释 1。理雅各为一段文字附注了一个嘲讽性的问题。那段话是假托老子之口讲出来的，从科学上讲显得很荒谬。那段文字的原话是："夫白鶂之相视，眸子不运而风化；虫，雄鸣于上风，雌应于下风而风化。类自为雌雄，故风化。"理雅各用冷嘲的语气反问这些说法："老子或作者是从哪里学的动物学？"

② 老子和庄子为了提倡史前的"小国寡民"（paradisiacal state），反对儒家的圣人和圣王，理雅各认为这是古典道家的偏见扭曲了他们的主张，因为没有古代历史文献可证明他们的主张。参见《中国圣书》第五卷，第 62 页。读者也可挑战理雅各反对占卜的主张——理雅各认为占卜不能达成"上天的意志"（the will of Heaven）。参见《中国圣书》第四卷，第 215 页。还有，理雅各说中国评注者对"灶神"（the spirit of the fire place）之名的解释实际上增添了"许多荒谬的细节"（many absurd details），但他自己并没有提供任何相关的例子，这可令人怀疑是偏见在作祟。参见《中国圣书》第六卷，第 236 页。

书写那些布道文是讲给基督徒听众的，包括中国基督徒和英国基督徒。① 相比之下，理雅各在《中国圣书》中几乎把它对基督教和《圣经》的思考仅仅限制在引用和解释《圣经》经文。当然，理雅各也提到过"天意"（providence）这个加尔文教义突出的思想范畴，但他仅仅提到了这个概念并引用《圣经》支持他的主张，而没有提到哪位加尔文主义神学家的著作。理雅各这是在实践一种跨文化比较的经文阐释，类似于当代中国学者石衡潭② 的做法，只是模式不同，或者说理雅各是在做一种类似于"经文辩读"的比较研究，③ 其中一些包括佛教 ④、道教 ⑤、儒教文本和传统的比较。⑥

　　任何一位译者和阐释者所写的著作都有可能受到各种偏见的影

---

① 在研究理雅各的生平时，我阅读了收藏在伦敦基督教世界宣道会（Christian World Missions）档案馆中理雅各的四百余册布道笔记中的一百多册。后来，我在关于理雅各早期生平及传教生涯著作的第二卷中引用了其中的 15 篇布道文。对这些细节感兴趣的读者，可查阅索引部分的 "sermons" 词条，参见 Pfister, *Striving for "The Whole Duty of Man"*, Vol. 2, p. 437。理雅各一生受到了许多苏格兰和英国牧师、神学院教授的影响，他阅读过许多人发表的布道文和神学著作。当时对其基督教思想影响最大的著名神学家是他的哥哥乔治·理雅格（约 1803—1861），他是一位公理会神学家。对其神学思想有影响的有加尔文主义神学家约翰·诺克斯（John Knox，约 1514—1572），历史学家和基督教人文主义学者乔治·布坎南（George Buchanan，1506—1582），清教牧师和作家约翰·班扬（John Bunyan，1628—1688），英国国教神学家和哲学家约瑟夫·巴特勒（Joseph Butler，1692—1752），公理会牧师、神学家，同时也是理雅各的岳父、伦敦会的董事约翰·莫里森（John Morison，1791—1859）。在理雅各任牛津大学教职期间，他时常与牛津大学一位年轻、有声望的非国教哲学家和神学家费尔贝恩（Andrew Martin Fairbairn，1838—1912）一起工作。

② 参见石衡潭《中西元典对读》，中国社会科学出版社 2018 年版。

③ 参见 You Bin, "Scriptural Reasoning in China", in K. K. Yeo, ed., *The Oxford Handbook of The Bible in China*, Oxford: Oxford University Press, 2021, pp. 527–539。

④ 参见 Liu Boyun, "Chinese Buddhist Writings and the Bible", in Yeo, ed., *The Oxford Handbook of The Bible in China*, pp. 235–249。

⑤ 参见 Archie C. C. Lee, "The Bible and Daoist Writings", in Yeo, ed., *The Oxford Handbook of The Bible in China*, pp. 219–233。

⑥ 参见 Paulos Huang and K. K. Yeo, "Confucian Classics and the Bible", in Yeo, ed., *The Oxford Handbook of The Bible in China*, pp. 251–265。

响——无论是中国人、苏格兰人、德国人、法国人，还是天主教徒、儒教徒、新教教徒、道教徒，以上所引例子都说明了这一点。问题是，他们的主张和判断是由未被证明的偏好形成的，还是经过高度理性的评价形成的。正是这个原因，理雅各的主要主张——最古老的儒家经典文本中有明显的证据表明古代儒家是一神论——才会被今天的许多人认为非常合理，尽管当时有一些外国传教士和许多中国士人不同意他的意见。这样的评价也是理雅各在《中国圣书》中利用《圣经》诠释学的一部分内容。

（3）理雅各对《中国圣书》做的创造性预备活动

理雅各 1876 年任牛津大学基督圣体学院教授之前，已经翻译出版了《诗经》韵律体译本。这是一项不同寻常的美学创举，我在 1997 年用翻译诠释学的方法评价了这个译本的特色。[①] 然而，许多人不知道的是，理雅各后来还用韵律体翻译了希伯来《诗篇》，大约完成于 1875 年，但没有发表。[②] 这些翻译手稿——包括全部 150 章《诗篇》的韵律体英译文，以及一篇导论文章和一些脚注——现收藏于爱丁堡大学新学院图书馆。[③] 我感觉这件工作最有趣的是，它完全是

---

① 参见 Lauren F. Pfister, "James Legge's Metrical Book of Poetry," *Bulletin of the School of Oriental and African Studies*, Vol. 60, No. 1 (February 1997), pp. 64–85.

② 许多人不知道理雅各做的这一独特的创造性工作，其中一个原因是，吉瑞德在叙述他任牛津教职前几年做的准备工作时，根本没有提到这一点。虽然吉瑞德确实提到了理雅各的《诗经》韵律体译本，也意识到理雅各与"希伯来诗篇传统"（the Hebrew Psalmist tradition）及著名的苏格兰诗人彭斯（Robert Burns, 1759—1796）有天然的"联系"（connections），但他不知道这段时间内理雅各有意在希—汉之间做的比较性"串联工作"（working in tandem）。事实上，理雅各做的儒耶比较研究工作远比吉瑞德所意识到的丰富和训练有素。参见 Girardot, *The Victorian Translation of China*, p. 103.

③ 据我所知，还没有哪位学者对理雅各这些手稿做过独立研究。但有趣的是，理雅各在人生的这一关键时刻做了一件与众不同的诗歌创作工作，同时它也确证了理雅各在有意识地做跨文化比较研究，这是他早在 1861 年出版《中国经典》第二卷时就明确用过的研究方法，那时他比较的是孟子的教义和英国国教基督徒哲学家巴特勒的著作。吉瑞德说，理雅各任牛津教职之前有"原始比较学者的倾向"（protocomparativist

理雅各进行自我精神修炼的一项活动，[①] 做这项活动的同时，他还在编辑《诗经》韵律体译本的终稿。[②] 这使我认为，虽然理雅各积极从事基督教活动，包括布道、演讲、接受在华传教工作相关问题的咨询，[③] 但与此同时他不仅继续从事与中国古典文学相关的创造性的汉学工作，而且以自己的审美情趣翻译《诗篇》为韵文。这与他在香港做的事情是一致的，当时他作为传教士，每天凌晨便开始汉学研究。然而，到了1874年他已经不再隶属于伦敦会，[④] 所以他做这件事完全是为了修炼自己的精神。事实上，这是一个调整阶段，在某种

（接上页）inclinations），但这一说法完全忽略了理雅各比较研究方法论的许多方面。理雅各在1850年代参与"译名之争"时开始用这一方法，然后在《中国经典》"导论"中开始大量使用，尤其是1861年出版的《中国经典》第二卷和1865年出版的《中国经典》第三卷。关于吉瑞德的说法，参见 Girardot, *The Victorian Translation of China*, p. 109；关于孟子与巴特勒的比较研究，参见《中国经典》第二卷，第56—64页。

① 这里有一个有趣的问题需要研究：为什么理雅各最终没有发表这部手稿？从这部手稿的书写方式来看，它是为印刷准备的，因此理雅各最初似乎是想发表的。我在理雅各的"导论"中看出他内心有挣扎，试图把他关于特别启示的观念融入他在诅咒诗中发现的问题。也许他最终感觉，发表他对这些问题的质疑，对基督徒读者而言坏处大于好处。（译者按：爱丁堡大学新学院图书馆收藏的这份《诗篇》译稿信封封面标注的时间是1887年。实际上，理雅各1884和1885年在《福音杂志》上发表过他翻译的部分《诗篇》，参见 Metrical Versions of Psalms, *The Evangelical Magazine and Missionary Chronicle*, Vol.14，1884, pp. 73-74, 166-167, 265-266; Metrical Versions of Psalms, *The Evangelical Magazine and Missionary Chronicle*, Vol.15，1885, pp. 73、74、165、166、265、266、259-261、366-368、458、459。理雅各在1885年8月31日写给朋友尼尔先生的信中，提到了他翻译并发表《诗篇》的事，参见牛津大学图书馆藏理雅各手稿 MS. Eng. c. 7124。）

② 理雅各早年学习过布坎南（George Buchanan, 1506—1582）用拉丁文释译的希伯来《诗篇》。布坎南是苏格兰著名的拉丁语学者和人文主义学者，后来成了16世纪苏格兰宗教改革运动的主要人物。关于他对理雅各的影响，参见 Pfister, *Striving for "The Whole Duty of Man"*, Vol. 1, pp. 48、49。理雅各决定用韵律体翻译《诗篇》似乎是一个有意识的行为，似乎是要同时裁定和翻译这部古希伯来文诗歌集和中国古代诗歌集，从而继续了解如此艰难的工作始终需要的跨语言挑战和翻译诠释学。

③ 参见 Girardot, *The Victorian Translation of China*, p. 101。

④ 同上书，pp. 99-100。吉瑞德说理雅各从伦敦会退休的正式日期是1874年1月9日。这就是说，即使1866—1869年理雅各在英国休假期间，以及1870年到1873年初再次回到香港担任佑宁堂（Union Church）牧职期间，仍与伦敦会保持着联系。

程度上是为他 1876 年在牛津大学开始新的学术岗位做准备。最终，它也预示了理雅各在《中国圣书》后几卷中表现出来的审美创造力，下面我将解释这一点。

值得注意的是，1876 年出版了《诗经》韵律体译本之后，在 1879 年《中国圣书》第一卷的《诗经》选译本中他没有收录 1876 年版中的任何一篇。无论理雅各在《中国圣书》第一卷中让"诗歌翻译"退回到非诗歌形式背后的原因是什么，从《中国圣书》第二卷《易传》开始，理雅各的翻译发生了非常大的变化。其中有四个片段，理雅各翻译成了韵律体诗的形式；[①] 另外，最后一传（《杂卦》）的 51 行全部押韵。[②]《礼记》中杂糅了更多中国古代的诗行，而且押韵的诗行比不押韵的诗行多。《中国圣书》第三卷只有 6 个押韵诗行，[③] 3 个不押韵的诗行。[④] 相比之下，《中国圣书》第四卷有大量的诗行，90 行不押韵，占篇幅 33 页，214 行押韵，占篇幅 39 页。令人惊奇的是，理雅各押韵诗的韵法多样。然而，《中国圣书》这一审美维度的真正典范则表现在第五卷：在《道德经》81 章中，有 24 章理雅各都用了押韵诗的形式翻译，总计 181 行，而且韵法多样，[⑤] 这是我在其他任何《道德经》英译本中所未曾见过的。[⑥]

这一诗体翻译活动对理雅各而言说明了什么？我认为，他翻译的韵律体《诗经》和韵律体《诗篇》最终使他有勇气主动采用英诗的形式翻译许多类型的中国古诗。虽然结果不是很漂亮，但一般都

---

① 参见《中国圣书》第二卷，第 248 页（14 行）、280 页（2 行）、361 页（4 行）、362 页（9 行）。因此，前六传总计 29 个诗行。

② 同上书，第 441—444 页。

③ 参见《中国圣书》第三卷，第 432 页（4 行）和 433 页（2 行）。

④ 同上书，第 138 页。

⑤ 关于理雅各《道德经》译文的这一审美维度，详见我为《中国圣书》第五卷写的导读文章的附录。

⑥ 我必须得为我的这一断言做些补充说明，我没有阅读《道德经》的所有英译本，所以也有可能存在像理雅各那样处理的译本。

比较雅致，有时甚至很吸引人。至少，这项特别的尝试为理雅各翻译的六卷《中国圣书》增添了文学附加值。

2. 超越汉学东方主义：源自理雅各方法论的洞见

萨义德（Edward Said）构想了欧洲学科"东方主义"这一颇具决定论的概念之后，后期虽然他的批评有所缓和，但这一概念已经开始了它自己的生命历程。大约 20 年前，我论证了为什么理雅各没有"'只是'东方化"（"merely" orientalizing）一个"他者中国"（Chinese other），没有不断坚持"把某些伟大的原创思想伪化身成与基督、欧洲和西方"同质的东西。① 如本文所示，理雅各非常敏感也非常了解他所研究的复杂的中文文献，所以他不会提倡这样一种被扭曲的儒家或道家传统的形象；儒家和道家传统都体现在古代经典之中，然后在中国各个朝代的历史进程中以各种各样的方式发展着。他在《中国经典》中也是这样做的，不过程度稍逊一点，因为 1861 年理雅各开始研究儒家传统之时强烈否认孔子的地位和影响；这一看法随着时间的流逝逐渐在改变，而且 20 年后由最初的嘲讽批评转变成了欣赏尊敬。② 我在 2004 年说理雅各通过《中国经典》对汉学的贡献阐明了"汉学东方主义"（sinological Orientalism）这个更为"开明的"（open-minded）表达 ③，这里我要说他最终通过《中国圣

---

① 这是引自萨义德的著作《东方主义》的文字。参见我当初对"重新定位汉学东方主义"的讨论：Pfister, *Striving for "The Whole Duty of Man"*, Vol. 2, p. 236。萨义德原文参见 Edward W. Said, *Orientalism*, New York: Vintage Books, 1979, p. 72。

② 这里我主要想到的是理雅各在《中国宗教》第二章结尾极为欣赏地评价了孔子的生平、教义和影响，其中有一些注释非常有启发意义，涵盖了孔子生平许多有争议的方面。参见 *The Religions of China: Confucianism and Tâoism Described and Compared with Christianity*, London: Hodder and Stoughton, 1880, pp. 124-149, 150-156。我对理雅各的这一转变做过详细研究，涵盖了从 1861 年到 1893 年较长的历史时期，参见 "From Derision to Respect: The Hermeneutic Passage within James Legge's (1815-1897) Ameliorated Evaluation of Master Kong ('Confucius')", *Bochumer Jahrbuch zur Ostasienforschungs*, Vol. 26 (2002), pp. 53-88。

③ 参见 Pfister, *Striving for "The Whole Duty of Man"*, Vol. 2, pp. 236-239。

书》所取得的成就不仅表现了更加人道的汉学东方主义，而且最终超越了汉学东方主义这一学科话语的限制。对于 21 世纪一些知识分子而言，无论是在中国、欧洲、北美，还是其他什么地方，只要是研究和讨论学术正典的，我的这一说法是非常大胆的，所以我要给出四个原因，说明我为什么认为理雅各后期的汉学翻译成功克服了汉学东方主义话语的限制。

首先，为了理解"东方主义"的主张，我们应该描述和澄清这一颇具决定论的概念。作为形成于 19 世纪晚期的一个学术话语，它在制度和概念上都与大英帝国内高度发达的帝国主义时期紧密相连。也就是说，理雅各的《中国经典》翻译依赖的是"英国盘根错节的商业和传教利益"，[①] 如果用萨义德想要强调的方式说，就是一些非中立制度滋生出的"分类、综合和专注的细节追求"扭曲的方式。[②] 然而，萨义德的"东方主义"概念以其学术话语的决定论特征所不能预见的是，理雅各能够成为"不从国教的先知"（Nonconformist prophet）。[③] 作为苏格兰福音派先知（Scottish Evangelical prophet），[④] 理雅各批评和警告英国军事和商业侵略，[⑤] 反对鸦片贸易。[⑥] 作为传教

---

① 参见 *Striving for "The Whole Duty of Man"*, Vol. 2, p. 56。

② 参见 Pfister, *Striving for "The Whole Duty of Man"*, Vol. 2, p. 165。

③ Ibid., p. 56。

④ 这在许多方面都不同于卡莱尔的先知，参见 Pfister, *Striving for "The Whole Duty of Man"*, Vol. 2, pp. 3–6。

⑤ 1861 年他在《中国经典》第一卷"导论"中首次表达了这一点，也就是在第二次鸦片战争结束后的次年。参见 Legge, *CC*1, pp. 105, 107–108。我在这里选择引用其中的一些话："在我看来，在西方社会的发展过程中，我们很少去想（其实理应多想）政府部门的示范力量。对陆军、海军的示范力量想的更少。……目前，大英帝国统治着印度民众，我们也越来越多地接触到数以万计的中国人，掌权者尤其是那些负责处理具体事务的官员应当认真思考我们的圣人的至理名言。"（同上书，第 105 页）注意，这里理雅各用"我们的圣人"来称呼孔子，试图把孔子明智的忠告包含进英语世界读者应该拥护的智慧领域。

⑥ 参见 Girardot, *The Victorian Translation of China*, pp. 196–197。吉瑞德精彩的洞察部分源自理雅各与郭嵩焘的一次会面，尤其是理雅各在《中国宗教》中勇敢地记述了郭大使反对鸦片的立场（理雅各表示赞同），参见 *Religions of China*, p. 310。

士–学者（missionary-scholar），^①理雅各能够发展出融合儒耶世界观
的新的学术阐释主张，这使他明白了对待儒家和道家两大文化传统
内复杂、多样的附属传统的方法。^②一种更具决定性的"东方主义"
表述没有想到在其思想领域内会有这样一种反主流文化的学术生产
模式，即使理雅各在"汉学东方主义"学术圈的限制之内，所表达
的东西不仅出乎意料，而且最终还超出了它扭曲的影响范围。

　　理雅各在《中国圣书》里的翻译和阐释之所以能够超越汉学东
方主义的限制，一个原因是他优先考虑中国儒家（Chinese Ruist）^③的
阐释动态，而不是 19 世纪晚期英语世界和欧洲汉学圈内流行的东方
学理论。虽然理雅各在六卷本《中国圣书》中也参考儒家和道家经
典的英语、法语、拉丁语和德语翻译和阐释，但他评价那些作品的
方式不是依据当时欧美关于那些文本及其意义的理论，而是根据中
国著名的儒家学者的注疏。理雅各以这样的方法参与评价了那些外
国作品，但没有把他的阐释局限于他们的某些主张和理论倾向。因
而他在方法论上应用中国的评注传统，帮助他批判理解了儒家和道
家的经典，也从中获得了批判阐释的优势以挑战那些英语世界和欧
洲汉学家流行的或古怪的主张。这不仅使他有了诠释学的支撑，得
以逃离英语世界汉学圈时兴的学术话语的不良影响——例如金斯密
（Kingsmill）、拉克伯里（Lacouperie）、麦格基（McClatchie）、道格
拉斯（Douglas）、福斐礼（Balfour）和翟理斯（Giles）所提倡的那

① 关于吉瑞德发明的这个短语的意义，详见 Lauren F. Pfister, "China's Missionary-Scholars",
in R. G. Tiedemann, ed., *Handbook of Christianity in China. Volume Two: 1800 to the
Present*, Leiden and Boston: E. J. Brill, 2010, pp. 742–765。
② 关于这一融合儒耶的阐释视角，我结合理雅各所依赖的儒家文献对其做了解释，也
说明了它在某些阐释语境中的应用，参见 Pfister, *Striving for "The Whole Duty of
Man"*, Vol. 2, pp. 154–155。
③ 我用 "Chinese Ruist"，是有意区别日本、韩国、越南的儒家，理雅各基本上不了解
他们。

些，而且能够为英语世界一代又一代的读者呈现来自晚清儒家学术圈的阐释视角，并加上自己的评判意见，从而使其翻译和阐释成为一座历史的丰碑，发挥着儒家和道家学术在中国和欧美之间跨文化交流的价值。

第二，毫无疑问，理雅各的阐释原则主要是在英语世界的背景下形成的，包括他学习的苏格兰常识哲学尤其是斯图尔特（Dugald Stewart）的著作，还有他在海布里神学院（Highbury College）接受的《圣经》诠释学训练。然而，这些苏格兰实在论者认为人类根本上具有相同的心灵和本性，所以他们能够在人类经验和智慧的许多方面达成一致。正是因为他们的这些主张，理雅各到中国儒家学者那里寻找关于阐释原则的主张，以增进对他之前所学知识的认识。而且他找到了这样的主张。早在翻译《中国经典》时，他就发现《孟子》里的一段文字非常重要，于是就把它印在了《中国经典》每卷书扉页的背面。① 同样，理雅各在《中国圣书》第一卷也强调了朱熹的解诗原则。他把朱熹的主张放在了一个跨文化比较诠释的语境中，值得在这里引用：

> 我想，西方的汉学家几乎没有人会不同意我所认同的朱熹的解诗原则，即我们必须在诗歌本身中发现诗歌的意义，而不是接受我们所不认识的那些人的阐释，循着这样的阐释只会把许多诗化为荒谬的谜。②

同样，理雅各发现元代儒家学者吴澄对他阐释《道德经》和部分《礼

---

① 在吉瑞德《维多利亚时代翻译中国》一书的扉页上也印有这段话的中英文。但吉瑞德选的中文并非标准的全文，不能完全与他提供的英文形成对照。
② 参见《中国圣书》第一卷，第297—298页。

记》的篇章时非常有帮助，他如此评价吴澄的作品：

> 在 1865 年的《书经》导论（第 36 页）中，我曾提到过吴澄，称他是"无畏的思想者和有胆魄的批评家，其作品体现出的自由，在中国作者中是仅见的"。对吴澄作品后续的研读，让我对此更为确信。或许他更应被划归为一个独立的思想者，而不仅仅是勇敢无畏的思想者，其评论所体现的胆识，是经过深思熟虑的。[1]

如此满怀欣赏和字斟句酌的称赞，能说是萨义德批评的那类"只是东方化的"汉学家所为吗？我想不能。理雅各在这里表现出的是对这位元代大儒作品卓越性真正、人道的崇敬，那是理雅各对其阐释广泛阅读而得来的感受，满是同情和欣赏。给一个中国注疏家最高的褒奖莫过于把他对《庄子》诸篇的阐释都翻译成英文，否则英语世界的读者就不可能接触到这位注疏家的中文原作。理雅各就是如此厚待清初儒家学者林西仲（即林云铭，1658 年进士及第）的。在《中国圣书》第六卷的附录五中翻译了林云铭评注《庄子》三十三篇的九篇。[2]注意，这个附录是这卷书八个附录中篇幅最长的。在我看来，所有这些亮点都是理雅各对有着丰富诠释意义的中国学术的跨文化追寻，是任何形式的东方主义批评家所完全想不到的。

　　第三，我看不出理雅各对《道德经》"仁德"原则的认同是萨义德所谓文本中实际上不存在之物的"伪化身"（pseudo-incarnation）。《道德经》第六十三章说的是"报怨以德"（to recompense injury with

---

① 参见《中国圣书》第五卷，第 xvii—xviii 页。
② 参见《中国圣书》第六卷，第 273—297 页。

kindness）。[1] 理雅各在这里看到了一条勇敢的"以善胜恶"（overco-
mes evil with good）[2] 的伦理原则；这个概念对等的表达出现在《圣
经·罗马书》中。这绝非在译文中"强加"这一概念，说了没有要
传递的意思。另外，关于这条仁德原则，理雅各还进行了一个勇敢
的比较：关于《道德经》和《论语》中对这个原则的表述，他觉得
《道德经》的表述更值得尊敬和提倡。[3] 对于像理雅各这样的儒家学
者而言，这确实是一个很高的赞誉。理雅各对道家这一原则的公开
肯定，表明他已超越了汉学东方主义的话语限制，进入了对共同智
慧进行真正的跨文化比较研究的领域。

　　第四，理雅各对《庄子》各个部分所呈现的古典道家世界观的
许多方面，都从儒耶的视角进行了批评。没有采用缪勒或其他欧美
汉学家所提倡的理论主张，理雅各到中国评注者当中寻找，并且找
到了两位儒家学者批评道家经典的方式与他自己的阐释原则一致。
这是理雅各作为译者和阐释者有意识的内在辩证——首先阅读标准
文本，思考其内容，然后阅读评注者的注疏，思考他们的评价，最
终以更丰富的知识重新思考自己的翻译和对标准中文文本的评价。
这在理雅各评论两位清儒批评《庄子》的文字中表达得很清楚：

　　　　在读林西仲和陆树芝的注本时，读者会惊讶于他们频繁
　　地将"旧注"视为"不完整、不令人满意"，有时还是"荒
　　诞""滑稽"的，参验核实之后，读者会发现他们所说不无道

---

① 译文参见《中国圣书》第五卷，第106页。理雅各对其意义和重要性的讨论参见
　《中国圣书》第五卷，第31页。中文标准文本采自许渊冲译解，《道德经》，五洲传
　播出版社2011年版，第259页。
② 参见《罗马书》21：21："你不可为恶所胜，反要以善胜恶。"
③ 关于理雅各对于两者的评价，详见《中国圣书》第五卷，第92页。

理。于是读者马上就会明白，翻译《庄子》既需要个人的判断，还要广泛借鉴一些解读外文文献的关键程序。①

如果理雅各"只是汉学东方学家"，他批评《庄子》只需要根据他的19世纪苏格兰新教世界观就可以轻松做到；他为什么还要称赞这两位清儒的思想？我想是因为他想通过他们的著作说明，如果认真阅读和评价《庄子》，尽管要跨越"浓重的"文化差异，但总能达成共识。

正因为理雅各对待儒家和道家经典方法论上的这四重特点，他能够真正突破当时汉学东方主义制度和意识形态的诸多方面。因此，当时其他许多汉学家的作品现在都被认为不合时宜或早就过时了，但理雅各翻译和阐释的儒家和道家经典仍然吸引着世界上有真知灼见的读者，尽管它们也有缺陷。理雅各的翻译和阐释为什么有如此持久的生命力？这是我要在结论部分探讨的最后一个问题。

3. 理雅各译著生命力持久的原因

阅读这篇总论的某些读者也许知道，2015年，为庆祝理雅各诞辰200周年和研讨理雅各的生平及著作，先后在香港浸会大学、北京外国语大学和爱丁堡大学举办了三场学术研讨会。2022年，爱丁堡会议论文集出版。② 当然，在这些会议上免不了有人会问：为什么理雅各的著作会被不断重印，不断吸引那些对中国古代经典感兴趣者的注意？

就我而言，这三场会议给了我一个契机，丰富了我对理雅各的认识。虽然我之前一直在研究理雅各的生平和著作，但主要聚焦于

---

① 参见《中国圣书》第五卷，第 xx—xxi 页。
② 参见 Alexander Chow, ed., *Scottish Missions to China: Commemorating the Legacy of James Legge (1815–1897)*, Leiden and Boston: Brill, 2022。

《中国经典》。所以，在为北京会议做准备的时候，我认真总结了理雅各翻译和阐释儒经的各种局限，写出了九大诠释局限，并在会议上做了报告，在报告前我意识到自己忘记了一条诠释局限，并把它加了上去。① 现在，我完成了六卷本《中国圣书》的研究，要修改其中的一些诠释局限。

然而，我提起这些事的目的，不仅是要回忆我在 2015 年讲过的内容以及现在要讲的理雅各汉学译著的诠释局限，而且要为此提供一个背景，这是 2015 年北京师范大学著名的历史学家刘家和教授对我讲的内容的回应。下面首先列举我修改和更新过的关于理雅各译著的诠释局限，现在主要聚焦于《中国经典》和《中国圣书》，然后叙述刘教授 2015 年 4 月回应我的意见。

在讲之前，我首先指出理雅各是"开创性地翻译儒家和道家经典"的五位传教士-学者之一。现在，我要指出六位这样的学者，且让理雅各排在第二位。这六位非常著名的传教士-学者是俄国东正教修士雅金夫（Iakinf），俗名比丘林（Nikita Y. Bichurin，1777—1852）；② 然后是理雅各；继而是意大利耶稣会士晁德莅（Antonio Zottoli，1825—1902）；③ 法国耶稣会士顾赛芬；④ 尉

---

① 我在北京会议上做报告的题目是《试谈理雅各翻译与解释中国古典的具体诠释限制》。这次会议于 2015 年 4 月 10—12 日在北京外国语大学举办的。

② 比丘林用古俄语翻译了"四书"，包括朱熹的注。但这些翻译自从 1815 年完成之后就一直处于抄本的状态（现在至少有三个不完整的抄本），从未在俄国或其他地方出版过。那么，理雅各自然没有机会接触，甚至不知道这一非凡的译本。

③ 晁德莅用古拉丁语翻译了"四书"和《三字经》，然后他又选译了《诗经》和《易经》的卦爻辞，以及部分《礼记》，也是用古雅的拉丁文。理雅各在《中国圣书》第三、四卷的评注中参考过晁德莅翻译的不到十卷的《礼记》译文（《礼记》总共有四十六卷）。

④ 与其他几位汉学巨擘不同，理雅各翻译过的儒经，顾赛芬大部分都翻译过，而且是用两种语言翻译的：现代法语和现代教会拉丁语。他唯一没有翻译的是《易经》，但翻译了《仪礼》。另外，他也没有翻译过道家经典《道德经》和《庄子》。

（卫）礼贤①；还有葡萄牙耶稣会士戈振东（Joaquim Guerra，1908—1993）。②除了这些人之外，还有一些不是传教士的著名汉学家也至少翻译了理雅各翻译过的四种书，包括克罗地亚汉学家玛亚（Maja Milčinski，1956—　）③和德国汉学家顾彬（Wolfgang Kubin，1945—　）。④径直地讲了这些之后，我指出有两项颇具批判性的研究严肃地质疑了理雅各某些译本的性质：韦利（Arthur Waley）1949年发表文章批评理雅各的《孟子》译本，⑤王辉2008年出版著作批评理雅各的两个《中庸》译本。⑥此后，我表示我要指出理雅各译著的各种诠释局限；那是针对我那时阅读理雅各的译著所做出的总结，但现在，7年之后，我要修改和增加一些要点。我的目的只是辨识其中的一些"具体的诠释限制"，但我会时不时地添加一些简短的解释或说明，以突出要点。2015年，我把那些局限分成了"当时已知的"（accessible）和"未能预见的"（inaccessible）两类，意思是前者是

---

① 这两个姓（发音都是 Wèi）是他在不同时期使用的。前者是他在青岛时用的一个姓，后者是他 1924 年出版《易经》译本时自己有意选择的一个姓。卫礼贤是一个多产的翻译家和作家，他用德语翻译了《论语》《道德经》《孟子》，还有《庄子》和《礼记》的大部分篇幅，以及一个不同寻常的《易经》译本。另外，他还选译了《尚书》和《诗经》，但没有出版。

② 理雅各翻译过的儒经，戈振东都用葡萄牙语翻译过，但《诗经》是用英语翻译的。而且，他还用葡萄牙语翻译了《道德经》。

③ 据我所知，玛亚用克罗地亚语翻译了《道德经》和《庄子》，还翻译了"四书"和《易经》。

④ 顾彬是非常著名且多产的汉学翻译家和作家。虽然他翻译过多数理雅各翻译过的儒家和道家作品，但只是主题性的编译。他不仅将之翻译为当代德语，还附有大量评注。也就是说，他没有把那些标准的中文著作做成德语译本（除了《大学》《中庸》《孝经》），而是根据某些主题选了某些特定的篇章。除此之外，他有《论语》《孟子》《老子》（根据郭店竹简译出）、《庄子》译本。另外，他还编译了许多其他中国古代的作品，常常与中国哲学有关。

⑤ 参见 Arthur Waley, Notes on Mencius, *Asia Major* n.s. Vol. 1, No. 1 (1949), pp. 99-108。这篇文章被收录进了现在出版的某些版本的《中国经典》中。

⑥ 参见 Wang Hui, *Translating Chinese Classics in a Colonial Context: James Legge and His Two Versions of the Zhongyong*, Bern, Switzerland: Peter Lang, 2008。

理雅各在其有生之年可以改变的局限，后者是他所不知道的局限，是他在有生之年不可能知道的。

针对理雅各《中国经典》和《中国圣书》当时已知的诠释局限，我要指出以下问题：

（1）理雅各没有遵照朱熹厘定的"四书"顺序，而是把《论语》排在第一位。这显然没有遵照清代御纂的"四书"版本。理雅各这样做的主要原因是，他要批评孔子其人和其教导。这是有问题的。我在《中国圣书》的这些导读文章中已经非常详细地说明了理雅各对孔子的评价发生了巨大的转变，从"嘲讽"转向了真正的"欣赏"，这一转变是从1873年开始的。他在1877年的一篇文章中表达了那一转变的态度，然后是在1880年《中国宗教》的第二章，最后是在1893年在牛津出版的《中国经典》第一卷导论中对孔子评价的修订。

（2）尽管理雅各意识到了清儒焦循《孟子正义》的重要性，但他没有根据焦循的注疏修改他的翻译或评注。他完全可以在1895年出版的《中国经典》第二卷修订本中这样做，但他没有，可能是因为那牵扯到大量额外的工作。

（3）理雅各《中国经典》一个"比较怪异"的方面是他在1871年首次以非诗歌体翻译《诗经》。理雅各的目的是描述《诗经》的思想内容，但出版后遭到了一位英国诗人的严厉批评，这位诗人说他不能接受这样的一个散文体译本，认为那不能充分再现中国古代诗歌。在这种情况下，如我上文所述，理雅各最终在他人的帮助下，出版了一个《诗经》韵律体译本，然后更大胆地用不同的韵律体诗形式翻译了儒家和道家经典中的其他诗体篇章，见于四卷《中国圣书》之中。这次他又面临一个自我决定的诠释局限，并做出了改变，最终克服了这一局限，做出了诗体译文。事实上，这些译文相当巧妙、富有洞察力，有些还很吸引人。

（4）理雅各在《中国经典》中没有非常重视"孝"在文化和人伦方面的重要性。（理雅各把"孝"翻译为"filial piety"〈子女对父母的虔敬〉，也许用"respect for elders"〈尊老〉更为合适。）但这一缺陷在《中国圣书》中得到了弥补，他在《中国圣书》第一卷翻译了《孝经》。他不仅翻译了《孝经》，而且还把《孝经》的主张融入了他对中国古代儒教一神论"神圣性"的理解中。在理雅各看来，儒家"神圣"这一概念有非常强烈的"孝"的维度，"孝"被融入了对"上帝"的祭祀仪式中，也被融入了对祖先的祭祀仪式中。

（5）尽管理雅各知晓许多注解儒经的次级传统，但他从来没有区别过理学和心学这两个后期儒家发展史上的次级传统。其他传教士-学者曾经论述过这个问题，包括花之安（Ernst Faber，1839—1899）、卫礼贤、丁韪良（W. A. P. Martin，1827—1916）、戴遂良（Léon Wieger，1856—1933）、戈振东。

（6）理雅各在《中国经典》中没有利用《说文解字》这部中国古代的字典，然而它对批评宋儒的语文学主张非常重要。但是，在《中国圣书》后几卷中（尤其是第三、四、五卷），他在每卷都引用了一次。

（7）理雅各在《中国经典》和《中国圣书》中都有依据粤语发音把汉字拼音写错的情形。事实上，理雅各最初学的是福建话，后来用了大半生时间学习和说广东话，只是在后期才学标准的北京音，大概始于1865年。结果，他拼错了某些词语的发音，误导了那些不懂粤语发音的读者。例如，在《中国圣书》中，理雅各一直把"周代"和"周公"的"周"字拼写作"*Kâu*"（类似于粤语发音 *jao*，而非 *zhōu*）。在我为《中国圣书》制作的某些"索引"中，我已经指出了他根据粤语发音误拼的专名或词语（尤其是在《诗经》和《易经》

中，但不限于这两部书）。

（8）因为理雅各不接受占卜实践及其主张的价值，他在《易传》（《中国圣书》第二卷）中表达的态度有时是负面的、批评性的，对于那些想了解这些篇章深层意义的读者来说没有什么帮助。这完全是一个诠释前见的问题。

（9）同样，理雅各对待后期道教文本（《中国圣书》第六卷附录）的态度有时候是严厉批评，在原则上拒不接受。这说明他认为这些作品与他重视的《道德经》《庄子》这样的道家经典比较起来，价值不大，也没有什么文学性。对于它们成仙的主张，他依然持一贯的否定态度。显然，理雅各至少有机会查阅晚明的道藏目录，但他不了解构成这一庞大著作集的大部分文本的性质（这一点我将在稍后的评论中再次论及）。

（10）虽然理雅各对待《庄子》的态度有时也非常负面，常给予批评，但支持他观点的是他参考的两位清儒对《庄子》同样的负面评价和批评。他们是林云铭和陆树芝（详见上文）。这一诠释局限不是由于诠释前见，而是因为理雅各认同清儒对《庄子》的批评；所以理雅各的《庄子》评注常常揭示了清儒知识圈对《庄子》的看法。

至于未能预见的诠释局限，可考虑以下几点：

（1）如上所述，理雅各不太了解道藏的性质和复杂性，但这只有到了 1920 年代完整的道藏进入公众的视野时才能被深入研究。所以，从可利用资料的角度看，理雅各在有生之年没有机会接触到广博的道藏研究。[1]

---

[1] 我在《中国圣书》第五卷的"导读"中参考了 2004 年施舟人（Kristopher Schipper）和傅飞岚（Franciscus Verellen）编纂出版的三卷本《道藏通考》（*The Taoist Canon: A Historical Companion to the Daozang*）。

（2）同样，理雅各也没有机会接触到考古发现，包括书写在甲骨、竹简、绢帛上的重要文献。这些是 20 世纪晚期和 21 世纪初才进行的研究。这限制了他对儒家和道家经典文本中某些主题的研究和评注。①

（3）理雅各基本上不知道日语、朝鲜语和越南语中大量的儒学文献。这在很大程度上是因为他不懂这些语言，所以在其著作中几乎没有提到过这些文献。我只记得他在《诗经》中提到过一部研究名物的日本作品，② 还有一部高丽本《礼记》。③

在我报告完这些关于理雅各汉学翻译的当时已知的和未能预见的诠释局限之后，下一位发言者是来自北京师范大学的著名历史学家刘家和教授。由于他之前的一个学生邵东方是我在夏威夷大学的博士同学，所以我有幸在 1990 年代中期结识了刘教授，并且与他和邵东方一起研究《书经》和《春秋左传》。在过去的二十年间，刘教授用中文撰写和发表了许多关于理雅各的文章。在这次会议上，刘教授对我的发言做了深刻的回应。他说的意思大概是这样的：

> 纵观理雅各翻译的中国经典，还有他对那么多评注传统的总结和评价！"四书""五经"，还有道家的经典——真是不可思议的创举。在当今中国，别说把这么多的经典翻译成外语了，

---

① 关于其中的一些问题，可参考 Shirley Chan, ed., *Reading Through Recovered Ancient Chinese Manuscripts*, Sydney: The Oriental Society of Australia, Inc., 2020。中国也有许多处理这些问题的著作，但我想许多中国学者不知道这部书，所以就只提了这部书。
② 参见《中国经典》第四卷导论，第 180 页。这部作品是冈元凤的《毛诗品物图考》，天明四年（1785）刊刻。
③ 参见《中国圣书》第三卷，第 138 页注释 1。

谁有能力把它们翻译成现代汉语？那是一项艰巨的工作，而理雅各完成了。是的，我们的确都有我们自己的诠释局限，理雅各也是像我们一样的人。然而，无论他存在什么样的局限和错误，他的汉学成就是非常了不起的。

2015 年 4 月，我为刘教授的话而深受感动，我所能够做的就是感激他深刻的评论。现在，我更加认真地通读和研究了六卷《中国圣书》，我更加确信，刘教授关于这位非凡的苏格兰传教士-学者和汉学家的评论是极富洞见的。

（丁大刚　田世宇　译

潘琳　校）

附录

《中国经典》和《中国圣书》中的相同文本

在下表中，我分别用 CC 和 SBC 表示《中国经典》和《中国圣书》这两套由理雅各翻译的丛书；两套丛书中的相同文本在《中国经典》栏用新罗马体表示，在《中国圣书》栏用黑体表示。正文引用或"索引"（《中国经典》的"索引"为湛约翰制作，《中国圣书》的"索引"为理雅各制作）中提及的相同文本，以及我的注释和细节情况见我为《中国圣书》各卷制作的索引。"相同文本"栏提到的文本若加中括号，表示理雅各引用的重要古籍，但不在理雅各翻译的《中国经典》或《中国圣书》中。

出版时间	书名	英文译名	丛书/卷/册	相同文本
1861	《论语》	The Confucian Analects, Analects, or *Lun Yu*	CC1/ 1	《尚书》《诗经》《易经》[《周礼》]
1861	《大学》	The Great Learning or *Ta Hsüeh*	CC1/ 1	《论语》《尚书》《诗经》
1861	《中庸》	The Doctrine of the Mean or *Chung Yung*	CC1/ 1	《论语》《诗经》[《周礼》]
1861	《孟子》	The Works of Mencius	CC2/ 2	《中庸》《尚书》《诗经》《礼记》《春秋》
1865	《书经》或《尚书》	The Shoo King or *The Book of Historical Documents*	CC3/ 3 & 4	《论语》《大学》《孟子》《易经》《易传》《诗经》《周礼》《春秋》《左传》
1871	《诗经》	The She King or *The Book of Poetry*	CC4/ 5 & 6	《论语》《中庸》《孟子》《易经》《尚书》《礼记》《周礼》《春秋》《左传》[《仪礼》《国语》《尔雅》《说文解字》《列子》《史记》《康熙字典》《佩文韵府》]
1872	《春秋》和《左传》	The Ch'un Ts'ew & *The Tso Chuen*	CC5/ 7 & 8	《论语》《孟子》《易经》《书经》《诗经》《礼记》《竹书纪年》[《公羊传》《穀梁转》《周礼》《周官》《国语》《家语》《史记》《三字经》《列国志》《说文解字》]

出版时间	书名	英文译名	丛书/卷/册	相同文本
1879	《书经》或《尚书》	*The Shû King* or *Book of Historical Documents*	SBC1	《论语》《中庸》《孟子》《易经》《诗经》《春秋》《左传》《孝经》《竹书纪年》[《史记》《周官》《国语》《荀子》《康熙字典》《康熙补品词库》]
	《诗经》（选）	*The Shih King* or *Book of Poetry* (Selections "illustrating the Religious Views and Practices of the Writers and Their Times)	SBC1	《论语》《大学》《中庸》《孟子》《易经》《书经》《诗经》《礼记》《春秋》《左传》《孝经》[《史记》《周礼》《周官》《仪礼》《国语》《荀子》]
	《孝经》	*The Hsiâo King*① or *Classic of Filial Piety*	SBC1	《论语》《中庸》《孟子》《易经》《易传》《书经》《诗经》《礼记》《春秋》《左传》《公羊传》《縠梁传》《道德经》[《周礼》《仪礼》《说文解字》《史记》《尔雅》《小学》《四库全书提要》]

① 根据威妥玛拼音系统，理雅各这里应该用斜体的 "K"，所以这个字应该拼为 "*King*"。

续表

出版时间	书名	英文译名	丛书/卷/册	相同文本
1882	《易经》	*The Yî King*① or *Book of Changes*	SBC2 （经与传）	《论语》《大学》《中庸》《孟子》《书经》《诗经》《春秋》《左传》
1885	《礼记》	*The Lî Kî or Collection of Treatises on the Rules of Propriety or Ceremonial Usages*	SBC3 SBC4 *(Kung Yung or The State of Equilibrium and Harmony, Tâ Hsio or The Great Learning)*	《论语》《中庸》《孟子》《易经》《易传》《书经》《诗经》《春秋》《左传》《孝经》[《大戴礼记》《周官》《周礼》《仪礼》《公羊传》《尔雅》]《道德经》[《列子》《吕氏春秋》]
1891	《道德经》	*The Tâo Teh King*	SBC5	《论语》《中庸》《孟子》《易经》《易传》《书经》《诗经》《春秋》《左传》《礼记》[《周官》]《庄子》《太上感应篇》《阴符经》[《列子》]
1891	《庄子》	*The Writings of Kwang-ʒze*	SBC5 SBC6	《论语》《中庸》《孟子》《易经》《易传》《诗经》《春秋》《左传》《礼记》[《仪礼》《三字经》]《道德经》[《列子》]

---

① 根据威妥玛拼音系统，理雅各这里应该用斜体的 "K"，所以这个字应该拼为 "*King*"。

出版时间	书名	英文译名	丛书 / 卷 / 册	相同文本
1891	《太上感应篇》	The Thâi-Shang Tractate of Actions and Their Retributions	SBC6	《易传》《礼记》《左传》《道德经》[《康熙字典》]
1891	《清净经》	Khing Kăng King or The Classic of Purity	SBC6	《道德经》《庄子》[《三字经》《佩文韵府》]
1891	《阴符经》	Yin Fû King or Classic of the Harmony of the Seen and the Unseen	SBC6	《易经》《易传》《道德经》《庄子》[《佩文韵府》《史记》]
1891	《玉枢经》	Yü Shû King or The Clasic of the Pivot of Jade	SBC6	《庄子》
1891	《日用经》	Zăh Yung King or Classic of the Directory for a Day	SBC6	《中庸》《诗经》《道德经》《庄子》[《佩文韵府》]
1891	《老子庙碑》	Stone Tablet in Temple of Lâo-ʒze	SBC6	《易经》《礼记》《道德经》《庄子》[《佩文韵府》《史记》]
1891	《庄子祠堂记》	Record for the Sacrificial Hall of Kwang-ʒze	SBE6	《道德经》《庄子》[《史记》《竹书纪年》]

本卷导读

费乐仁

一、引言

　　《中国圣书》第一卷是理雅各为《东方圣书》贡献的第一卷书。[①]《东方圣书》是理雅各著名的同事麦克斯·缪勒主编的一套丛书，总计50卷，理雅各为之贡献了6卷。理雅各1876年在牛津大学基督圣体学院开始了中国语言文学教授的生涯，在他任职仅仅三年后便有了这卷书的出版。此前，理雅各在香港从事传教事业，于1867年从伦敦会退休，结束了他长达20多年的传教士生涯，[②]后来又于1870—1873年在香港佑宁堂（Union Church）担任全职牧师。[③]尽管如此，传教期间的理雅各在很大意义上仍然堪称一位汉学家。[④]与英国国内许多普通基督徒一样，理雅各是支持各个活跃在大清帝国的差会的。因此，我们有必要特别关注理雅各如何把他对中国"圣

[①]　被列为《东方圣书》第三卷。

[②]　事实上，1840年初理雅各就在马六甲的英华书院为伦敦会服务了。1843年，第一次鸦片战争结束后，清政府割让香港岛和其他一些附属土地给英国，香港沦为英国的殖民地，于是理雅各来到了香港。

[③]　1873年初，理雅各辞去了他的牧师工作，然后到华北旅行。理雅各参观了许多地方，尤其对曲阜有特别的兴趣，因为这里有孔府和孔庙。理雅各还游览了北京的许多地方，主要目的是参观天坛。

[④]　我这样写是为纠正熊文华关于理雅各是"后传教时期的英国汉学"代表的说法。参见熊文华《英国汉学史》，学苑出版社2007年版，第52—70页。我在《中国圣书》总论中有更多关于这一问题的讨论。

书"的讨论导向基督徒读者。

作为教授，理雅各不仅要教授学院的课程，还要为整个牛津大学开设讲座。[①] 一般一年要开设两次大学讲座，这些讲座大部分都被认真地记录了下来，所以我们知道在 1879 年这卷书出版之前，理雅各没有讲过其中的任何一部儒经。只是在数年后的 1883 和 1884 年，理雅各才讲了"中国年表"（Chinese Chronology）和中国历史上的不同朝代，这就会提到《尚书》（理雅各喜欢称之为《书经》）里的事件。[②] 后来他有一场"中国诗歌"的讲座，应该会提到《诗经》。[③] 理雅各没有开设过关于《孝经》性质或《孝经》注疏史的讲座。

另外，在 1879 年理雅各教授就在他的正常课程中讲授"中国历史"，[④] 而且在 19 世纪八九十年代继续与学生一起学习不同的史书，尤其是《史记》。[⑤] 从 1886 年开始他才为部分课程讲授了部分《诗经》，但《孝经》本身从未成为任何课程的指定读物。

理雅各贡献的这一卷《中国圣书》是不同寻常的，因为它包含了理雅各曾在《中国经典》系列翻译过的两部儒经，[⑥] 包括《书经》（《中国经典》第三卷，1865 年）和部分《诗经》（《中国经典》第

[①] 这一要求的明确表述可参考后来牛津大学另一个学院的著名英国文学教授的生平。参见 George Sayer, *Jack: C. S. Lewis and His Times*, San Francisco: Harper and Row, 1988, pp. 115–116。

[②] 详见吉瑞德《维多利亚时代翻译中国》附录二"理雅各在牛津大学的讲座与课程（1876—1897）"。需要指出的是，这不是理雅各在牛津大学开设讲座的完整记录，因为缺少 1886、1887 及 1890—1892 年的记录。

[③] 1895 年 10 月 28 日讲座，参见吉瑞德《维多利亚时代翻译中国》，第 540 页。

[④] 同上书，第 541 页。

[⑤] 同上书，第 541—545 页。

[⑥] 非常可惜的是，熊文华在介绍理雅各的汉学贡献时没有充分认识到《中国经典》（1861—1872）与《中国圣书》（1879—1891）的差异，也没有意识到两者有重叠，所以他甚至没有提到这一事实。参见熊文华《英国汉学史》，第 57、63、64、69、70 页。这些段落中的一些日期和其他细节，要么不正确，要么描述不准确。

四卷，1871 年）。后几卷《中国圣书》都没有包含之前出版过的经书。[①] 那么，问题就来了，理雅各是否只是重印了之前他已经翻译和阐释过的《书经》和《诗经》？这样的问题显然有些意外。理雅各作为专注于儒家经典和道家经典的译者和阐释者，这样的问题将揭示他学术生涯的许多面相，将表明他是如何认真地重新思考那些翻译的。我们将看到改译的地方并不多，但这些改变揭示了理雅各在智识上长期浸淫于中国古典文本，这不仅是他在牛津大学的学术模式，更是在他到牛津大学之前就养成了。另外，它也表明理雅各的翻译和阐释并非"完美"，也不是没有错误，但这些翻译和阐释是他在学术上孜孜不倦追求的结果。这其中的许多细节都可在本导读所附的两份表格中看出。

　　如表所示，1879 年前理雅各不仅出版了《书经》的完整译本，而且还有两个完整的《诗经》译本（一个为散文体，一个为英文韵律体）。但他之前从未出版过《孝经》的译本。他为《东方圣书》准备的所有这些译本与《中国经典》最大的不同是，它们仅以英文呈现，而《中国经典》则以中英文对照的形式呈现。鉴此，我们应该认识到《中国经典》针对的不仅是英文读者，也包括中文读者，而且在翻译《中国经典》时理雅各还得到了中国学者的帮助；但《中国圣书》针对的仅仅是英文读者，是理雅各独立完成的。

　　我们还应论及本卷书产生的背景，即理雅各其他方面的经历和活动，但读者可在《中国圣书》总论中发现有这些方面的详细论述。其中包括理雅各对中国经书理解的加深，1873 年他最后一次离开香

---

① 但需要指出的是，理雅各在《中国圣书》第四卷中重新翻译了《中庸》和《大学》，不过用的是《礼记》中的"古本"。也就是说，它们不是《中国经典》第一卷（1861年初版，1893 年修订版）中已经翻译过的朱熹改定的"今本"，而是进行了重译。关于这些问题，我们将在《中国圣书》第四卷"导读"中再详细论述。

港之后到华北旅行的人生经历，及至 1876 年他担任牛津大学基督圣
体学院的教授。

二、关键性的阐释问题

本卷书的读者应该思考几个关键性的阐释问题。第一，为什么
理雅各要选择这三部儒家"圣书"？这三部儒经的英语译文与本卷
书的多种副文本（包括序言、导论、篇章导读、脚注）之间有什么
关系？理雅各创制这么复杂的一个文本，有没有什么文化的和阐释
的洞见？

第二，就这三部儒经的翻译和呈现方式来看，有没有不同于之
前译本的新东西？换句话说，前两部儒经是否只是简单地重复了早
期的译本？理雅各自己对这些翻译的性质有何话可说？除了理雅各
说的之外，我们对于这些翻译还能知道些什么？

第三，理雅各在翻译和阐释这三部"神圣"儒经时，是以怎样
的标准把"宗教内容"融汇其中的？那一阐释的支点如何影响着理
雅各的翻译和阐释？这一"宗教内容"与他之前作为传教士-学者的
职业生涯之间有没有明显的联系？

这些问题将指引我接下来对本卷《中国圣书》的探究、评价
和解释。对于 21 世纪阅读本卷三部经书的中国读者而言，我认为
还有一些重要的挑战要面对。首先，要面对这卷书内部多文本的互
动。其次，中国读者要认识到理雅各的诠释原则明显源自朱熹的诠
释原则和新教圣经诠释原则（有时很明显，但多数情况下是融入
他的诠释案语中的，如他在导论中的评论和译文注释所揭示的那
样）。最后，在理解理雅各在本卷的三个文本中所标识的"宗教主
题"的性质方面，会有一些令人意想不到的东西。我将从中指出一

些洞见，这些洞见有助于解开一些疑问，这些问题关乎理雅各之前作为传教士-学者的事业以及他作为牛津大学教授完成的翻译—阐释工作。

三、《中国圣书》第一卷的普遍特征和独有特征

《中国圣书》第一卷中的一些普遍特征在其他五卷中也能找到。这包括每卷书都有一个"序言"，每部经典都有一篇主要的导论文章。《中国圣书》第一卷的"序言"简要地介绍了它所包含的三部儒经，但也包含了一些独特的论述（详见下文）。此外，这卷书包含有三部儒经，这一点不同于其他几卷"儒教文本"（Texts of Confucianism）只有一部经书。[①] 除了这些主要的普遍特征之外，还有一些也许不被注意或未被研究的特征，但它们也是每卷《中国圣书》都具备的特征。这包括每个章节的"导言"，以及大多数译文页面之下涉及各种问题的脚注。在这第一卷中，"导言"出现在正文中的每个章节前；在之后的几卷中，"导言"则被置于"导论"中（如《礼记》和《庄子》）。[②] 脚注几乎总是出现在页面底部，并以较小字号印刷。[③] 也有一个例外，《道德经》的注释是融入正文之中的。这些注释紧跟在一章的译文之后，而且字号与译文一样大。[④]

---

① "儒教文本"是六卷本《中国圣书》中的前四卷。《中国圣书》第二卷（《东方圣书》第 16 卷）是《易经》及《易传》，理雅各认为它们是两个独立的文本，但他承认在清代儒家精英文化中它们常常被作为一个整体连在一起。《中国圣书》第三卷和第四卷（《东方圣书》第 27 和 28 卷）是《礼记》。

② 《中国圣书》第三卷第 15—60 页中有对《礼记》四十六篇的总结。《中国圣书》第五卷第 127—163 页有对《庄子》三十三篇的总结。

③ 多数脚注都不长，但是《中国圣书》第一卷中关于《书经》和《诗经》的一些脚注，还有《中国圣书》第二卷《易经》中关于卦义的脚注，相当长。有些关于《易经》卦义的脚注比那一页的正文还长。

④ 参见《中国圣书》第五卷，第 47—124 页。

这些副文本与正文有着怎样的互文关系？理雅各显然是为那些不懂中国儒家和道家文本的英文读者而写这些副文本的，但他把解释标准定在了一个相对较高的水平，因此在这些领域有所涉猎或造诣的读者也能从中获取新知。理雅各的具体做法取决于他所翻译和阐释的是哪一部中国经典。我将在为每卷《中国圣书》写的"导读"中解释那些新知，并说明副文本与译文之间的关系是何其重要与精妙。

尤其是考虑到《中国圣书》的英文读者时，理雅各将各种材料纳入到副文本的动机是什么？多数时候理雅各的附加评注摘自中国的评注者，有时候也来自欧洲和美国传教士——学者和汉学家的翻译和阐释。他所摘选的内容都表达着强烈且一以贯之的教育目的。事实上，那些教育的主题具有非常明显的多样性，尤其是要揭示古代中国的宗教内容和精神活动时。有时，在本卷中，他们涉及的民族群体对中国古代族群提出挑战、与之交战，在某些情况下最终融入其文化圈。尽管如此，理雅各仍聚焦于那些被看作代表中国古代文化的人，因此他并没有经常或长时间地深入探讨与这些人偶尔有接触的外来文化的性质。另外，教育主题也会根据文本的不同而发生变化。所以，我将在每卷《中国圣书》的"导读"中重点讨论这些教育主题和与之相关的动机。

毫无疑问，理雅各意识到他的许多英文读者都受到维多利亚时代基督教团体及其亚文化的影响，而且对于那些像他自己一样在苏格兰环境中长大的人，他确实偶尔会提到《圣经》、英格兰和苏格兰的相关文献。这些文献在六卷《中国圣书》中只有零零散散的数条。其中最突出的还是《圣经》的经文，但也很少出现。在这些论述中，理雅各始终试图在他翻译和阐释的中国古代文本中揭示一些重要的真理，从而为他的英文读者提供文化和宗教的洞见。

　　以上所述是《中国圣书》第一卷的普遍特征，但这卷书中还有三个独有的特征需要说明。第一个独有特征是序言开篇部分以简介的方式论述了中国的三大宗教传统（释、儒、道）及其"圣书"的性质。① 理雅各在这个序言中还关注了一些其他问题，其中包括对本卷书第二个独有特征的简要描述。理雅各决定在这卷书中再次呈现整部《书经》，但是他在正文添加了 235 个星号（*）以突出他所认为的那些重要的宗教习俗、仪式、态度、观念等。第三个独有特征是理雅各不打算呈现整部《诗经》，因为此前他已经以另外两种形式完整地翻译过《诗经》（1871、1876）。② 他只在这卷书中收录了那些他认为中国古代文化语境中重要的宗教习俗、仪式和观念。这三个独有特征都值得进一步说明。

　　理雅各在谈论《中国圣书》所包含的全部内容时非常迅速地表明他自己只谈论"儒教"（Confucianism）和"道教"（Taoism），而中国的佛经"不属于我的职责范围"，③ 意即有其他人负责。④ 事实上，理雅各仅仅用了一页的篇幅介绍中国的佛教，⑤ 用了两页介绍道教，⑥ 而介

---

① 参见《中国圣书》第一卷，第 xiii—xxii 页。这部分结尾处在页面中间有一条横线把它与下一节分开了。在这个序言中共有四条这样的分隔线（有一条在第 xxii 页，有两条在第 xxix 页，最后一条在第 xxx 页）。这几节所讨论问题的更详尽论述见下文。

② 第一个《诗经》译本为《中国经典》第四卷，于 1871 年出版。第二个译本是个韵律体译本，《诗经》中的三百首诗全部用英语韵文翻译，于 1876 年在伦敦出版。关于理雅各这三个《诗经》译本的详细比较，读者可参考本文结尾所附的表格。有兴趣了解更多细节的读者可参考我的文章 "James Legge's Metrical Book of Poetry"，*Bulletin of the School of Oriental and African Studies* Vol. 60, No. 1 (February 1997), pp. 64–85。

③ 《中国圣书》第一卷，第 xiii 页。

④ 毕尔（Samuel Beal，1825—1889）用英文翻译了中文《佛所行赞经》，作为《东方圣书》第 19 卷，于 1883 年出版。《佛所行赞经》本来是马鸣（Aśvaghoṣa，80—150）用梵文写成的一部讲述佛陀生平事迹的书。

⑤ 参见《中国圣书》第一卷，第 xiii 页。

⑥ 同上书，第 xxi—xxii 页。

绍儒教"圣书"的影响和性质时则用了 7 页。① 这一对儒教的重视明显地反映了理雅各的学术兴趣，但他也说明了用如此长的篇幅介绍儒经的理由，因为他把儒教当作"中国的正统宗教"②，即中国最优秀的宗教传统。理雅各 1879 年提出这一主张也许会让一些读者感到惊讶，但《中国圣书》第一卷的内容说明了他的主张为什么应该被严肃对待。③

理雅各认为儒教是中国最具代表性和典范性的宗教传统，他通过《中国圣书》第一卷的第二个独有特征来证明这一主张。他在序言结尾简要地描述了这个特征："为了引起读者对《书经》中或显或隐的宗教思想的关注，相关内容之后会用星号（＊）标出。"④ 事实上，理雅各总共为《书经》的这个译本标记了 235 个星号，这说明他确实发现了大量宗教相关问题，这些问题不仅包括对宗教思想的讨论，而且还包括一些篇章谈及宗教礼仪、祭祀仪式、宗庙，以及天、帝或上帝、神等在君主、大臣和普通民众生活中的作用。有趣的是，理雅各没有在这卷书的任何地方给其所谓的"宗教"或"或明或暗的宗教思想"下个定义，因此我们需要在下文对他描述"宗教"的方式做系统、详尽、深入的分析。

关于什么算作"宗教性的"，这与本卷书的第三个独有特征（即选择性地呈现《诗经》）有着直接的关联。理雅各选择性地呈现了《诗经》中的宗教性元素——他收录了诗三百中的一百零五篇，有的是完整的，有的是部分诗节，这仅仅是《诗经》的三分之一——不同寻常的是他重新排列了文本的顺序。理雅各为什么要这么做？我

---

① 参见《中国圣书》第一卷，第 xiv—xx 页。
② 同上书，第 xiv 页。
③ 我在《中国圣书》总论中有对这节序言内容的详细说明和评价。
④ 《中国圣书》第一卷，第 xxx 页。

在 25 年前探讨了这一问题，其中的一些见解我今天仍然认为是正确的，因此我要引用于此：

> 理雅各重新编辑了他 1871 年翻译出版的散文体、学术风格的《诗经》(《中国经典》第四卷)，他重新编排了所有诗篇的顺序。……理雅各根据宗教体验的不同，为之分了层级。在《颂》诗部分，理雅各把原来全译本排在最后一部分的《商颂》排在了首位，然后是全译本排在第一部分的《周颂》，随后是原来排在第二部分的《鲁颂》，但只是选取了其中的几篇。然后理雅各的排列顺序是《小雅》《大雅》《国风》，但只选取了那些有宗教性质的诗篇，而且有些诗篇只选取了其中的某几章。
>
> 关于理雅各构建他"宗教体验等级观"(hierarchical vision of religious experiences)的标准，他清楚地表明《商颂》是这部经典中最古老的诗，也许是最具有一神论性质的诗。因此，理雅各虽然从未全面也从未明确地表述过他的层级概念，但它的基础看起来是建立在对各种宗教体验的价值的复杂理解之上的。这种理解首要的是把那些或隐或显地暗示一神论上帝概念的文本提升到第一个层级。第二个层级是那些指向相信神灵存在的诗篇所描绘的宗教传统，包括祭祀祖先，以及崇拜山川、土地、月亮、星辰之神等。尽管在理雅各自己的理解中，人格神与非人格神有重大区别，但他没有根据这个标准对文本进行重组。第三个层级关乎辨识精神价值的方法（例如卜筮、巫教）以及对祭礼的描述。理雅各之所以把《小雅》和《大雅》放在《国风》之前，是因为这些诗篇被包含在了周王的宗教仪式和祭礼之中，其层级要高于诸侯所行的类似礼仪。①

---

① 参见 Pfister, "James Legge's Metrical Book of Poetry," pp. 66–67。

这两段话总结了理雅各如何重组经文，继而高度选择性地呈现《诗经》中大约三分之一带有宗教主题的诗篇。这一总结虽然提供了不少信息，但它有点过于简单化了，它没有考虑更复杂的文本间的比较情形，即《诗经》处于《书经》之后和《孝经》之前这样的一个情形之中。例如，它没有提到孝的精神影响和宗教意义。它既没有谈到祭祀各种神灵与政治稳定之间的相互关系，也没有谈到天命和社会伦常（如家庭、政府等）之间的关系，也没有谈到战争之后在构想新的社会形态时宗教的意义。这些问题将在下文专门谈论理雅各解释《书经》《诗经》《孝经》中的"宗教"元素时进行处理。

四、探究《中国圣书》第一卷复杂的多元文本特征

吉瑞德认为，理雅各在《中国圣书》中的工作被嘲弄的方式之一，是被 19 世纪的东方学家认为他"仅仅只是一个译者"。[①] 吉瑞德的方法论和评价有一个更大的问题：他的方法是建立在阅读理雅各的"序言"和"导论"的基础上，而非理雅各的译文本身；[②] 他的评价是基于 20、21 世纪的批判性比较宗教理论，相对于儒教和基督教，他更看重道教。[③] 仔细阅读这三部儒经的译文，我们就会发现它事实

[①] 参见 Girardot, *The Victorian Translation of China*, p. 250。

[②] 吉瑞德在其著作的第四章"阐释者理雅各"中频频用到这一方法。参见 Girardot, *The Victorian Translation of China*, 尤其是第 266—285 页。吉瑞德认为理雅各在《中国圣书》第一卷中关于其翻译的断言是完全正确的，而事实上理雅各的谦卑和自我贬低需要在他的三部儒经译文的关照下进行评估。

[③] 例如，吉瑞德根据《圣经》多种翻译引起的"混乱"而反对《圣经》的意义具有单一性。我在总论中讨论了他的反对意见，以及他根据批判性的比较宗教研究而提出的一些其他与"进步"有关的假设。他看重道教文本表现在他对理雅各《道德经》译文的某些方面简短但相对认真的解读中，尤其是在 20 世纪晚期欧洲道教学者评论的关照下对之进行解读（Girardot, *The Victorian Translation of China*, p. 438）。但吉瑞德没有把这种学术的礼貌——仔细阅读翻译本身——贯穿在这三部儒经的译本中。

上不仅仅是"单纯的翻译"（mere translation）。伴随译文一同出现的还有许多副文本，包括理雅各为每个部分撰写的"导论"，以及大量的注释。可以看出，理雅各没有"隐身"于翻译，而是不断地发表他的批判性洞见，对译文中所提出的不同主题进行阐释和评价。这包括丰富的文本内互文和文本间互文，表明理雅各对这些儒家文本有着深刻、透彻的理解。

我首先将以定量的方式来探讨这些问题，然后以定性的方式做更深入的探究。这三部儒经译本的多文本特征——主译文与导读文字和注释之间丰富的互文性——各自又有很大的不同。这使我认为我们应该特别注意理雅各如何运用那些副文本来说明、批评和阐释在译文中发现的各种主题。

在整部《书经》译本中——正文包括241页（每页34行，字体较大），有51篇导读文字置于该古代历史记录的各个篇章之前，还有284条脚注，这足以让那些只注意其译文的人感到惊讶。[①]另外，这些导读文字和脚注的字体较小，所以每页可达42行，每行大约还有10个空格，[②]这说明理雅各是有意用这一方式把这些儒家圣书文本的译文与他的阐释性副文本进行区分。[③]但这并不是说这些副文本不重要。相反，某些长篇的导读文字[④]和注释[⑤]表明理雅各非常专注于

---

① 先不论其内容如何（下文有论），仅从表面来看，理雅各的导读文字平均为每页0.21篇（或曰每页五分之一篇），脚注为每页1.18条。这表明每页都有理雅各的阐释，但事实上并非如此，所以对于这一文本状况需要更深入的统计说明。

② 根据行长和每页行数，导读文字和注释比大字体的译文每页多48%的量。换句话说，从数量上看，理雅各参与阐释的活跃度是很高的。

③ 用这一方法来突出经文不仅在儒家注疏传统中有先例，而且在理雅各那个时代及21世纪的今天出版的《圣经》评注中也是显而易见的。下文我将从《圣经》学的视角解释这些问题。

④ 读者可在《中国圣书》第一卷，第137—139、171—173页发现这些小字体的导读文字长达两页的篇幅，差不多就是《书经》这两部分内容的小型学术文章了。其他如《中国圣书》第一卷，第63—64、124—125、151—152、164—165、181—182、254—255页、265—266页的导读文字也有差不多一整页的篇幅。

⑤ 此这卷中最长的一个注释有50行，超过一页的篇幅（第257—258页）。其他注释

对他要介绍给英语读者的"神圣文本"（sacred texts）进行批判性评价和阐释。若再加上理雅各用于标示《书经》中有关宗教体验、观念、态度和习俗的 235 个星号，这是一组非常不寻常和复杂的副文本，① 因此我们需要重新思考理雅各的阐释工作，② 他把《书经》作为儒家传统的一个神圣的历史文本呈现在读者面前。

理雅各对中国古代历史文本的翻译和阐释非常不同于他对诗歌文本的翻译和阐释。③ 理雅各为《诗经》的每篇诗写的导读文字一般较短，但也因此较为均衡地分布于整个文本。在《诗经》部分，理雅各选取了 105 篇他认为有宗教措辞的诗进行翻译，而且重新为它们排了序。这部分正文只有 147 页，比《书经》少了差不多 100 页。虽然如此，伴随这些古诗散文体译文的却有 113 篇导读文字和 314 条注释，比《书经》译文中的导读文字的篇数和注释条数都多。④ 从另一个角度来看，《书经》译文有 70 页没有注释，但《诗经》译文只有 22 页没有注释。⑤ 另外，在这个《诗经》译本中，有 70 页既有导读文字又有注释，而《书经》中类似的页数只有 33 页。再者，《诗经》译本中最长的导读文字长达 5 页，堪称一篇名副其实的学术论

（接上页）如第 145 页有 31 行，第 140—141 页有 27 行，第 236—237 页有 24 行，第 147 页有 21 行。

① 例如，在《书经》中，有 35 页只有导读文字而没有注释，还有 33 页既有导读文字又有注释。另外，有 45 页译文既无导读文字也无注释，但这其中有 22 页标有星号说明其文本有宗教元素（几乎占 50% 之多）。

② 因此，如果我们除去那些没有任何注释的页面，只计算有注释页面的注释数量，那么平均每页的注释则上升至 1.66 条。

③ 虽然我说的是"诗歌"，但需要注意的是理雅各在这个译本中用的是散文体译文，虽然他在 1876 年出过一部韵律版《诗经》译文。

④ 《诗经》中导读文字的篇数和注释条数密度都很高。若不考虑长度的话，《诗经》平均每页有 0.77 篇导读文字（几乎是《书经》的四倍），2.14 条注释（几乎是《书经》的两倍）。

⑤ 如果我们除去这没有注释的 22 页，平均每页有 2.51 条注释，是《书经》的两倍之多。

文。① 就注释的数量而言，在《诗经》译本中，一页中的注释多达 7 条，这在《书经》译本中是不曾有的。② 就注释的长度而言，《诗经》译本中的注释不如《书经》的长，但有两个注释长达 23 行，③ 还有几个注释也比较长。④ 这表明理雅各在《中国圣书》第一卷的这一部分又在批判性阐释的副文本中付出了巨大的努力，而且副文本的密度更高。

最后，我们需要再次指出《中国圣书》第一卷中的第三部经书是之前理雅各从未翻译出版过的，因此他作为译者对这个文本的阐释需要另一个层次的努力。前两部儒家经典显然要比《孝经》长多，因此理雅各的《孝经》译文仅有 23 页。不同寻常的是，他没有为《孝经》中的 18 个篇章写导读文字；但在译文结尾加了一篇历史性阐释文字。⑤ 比较引人注意的是他为这部相对较短的经书写了 48 条注释，⑥ 而且许多条注释都比较长，其中两条长达 50 多行。⑦

然而，最重要的是定性地看这些副文本所揭示的丰富信息。这表明，为了阐明这些经书的性质和内容，理雅各以批判性阐释者的身份以多样的方式与译文互动，从而为英文读者提供了大量的信息。因此，统计数字只能揭示这些多层次的副文本与译文

---

① 参见《中国圣书》第一卷，第 299—303 页。
② 同上书，第 343 页。第 387 页有 6 条注释。
③ 同上书，第 405、445 页。
④ 例如《中国圣书》第一卷，第 423—424 页有条注释长达 20 行，第 406 页有条注释长达 17 行。
⑤ 同上书，第 488 页。
⑥ 即使如此，《孝经》平均每页的注释数（2.09 条）也比《诗经》少。
⑦ 参见《中国圣书》第一卷，第 453—454 页的注释（54 行）和第 477—478 页的注释（50 行）。其他比较长的注释如第 472—473 页（32 行），第 484—485 页（21 行），第 476 页（20 行），第 471 页（18 行），第 465—466 页（17 行），第 468—469 页（16 行），第 479 页（15 行）。对于这么短的译文来说，这么多长篇注释是非常值得注意的。

之间相互交织的情形，而这些交互文本的动态性质只能通过定性分析才能凸显理雅各在导读文字和注释中表达的多重主题和各种关怀。

　　对于中国读者而言，理雅各在对这三部儒家经典进行复杂阐释的时候，一个不为人知的影响是他在圣经学和基督教解经学方面所接受的诠释学训练在此的应用。例如，1560 年出版的英文版《日内瓦圣经》是第一部"研读本《圣经》"，每卷经文都有简短的导读文字，每章还有简短的总结，有时候译文的侧面空白处还注有相当长的解释及当代的用法。① 自此之后，有许多类似的研读本《圣经》出版，但我要提及两部较新的基督教新教《圣经》。虽然这两部《圣经》都是在 21 世纪出版的，但它们非常有助于我们理解理雅各的基督教新教释经倾向在儒家和道家经文中的应用，以及一些相关的阐释原则。这两部研读本《圣经》是威尔斯比主编的《威尔斯比研读本圣经》，② 以及 2015 年出版的史普罗（Robert Charles Sproul, 1939—2017）主编的第三版《宗教改革研读本圣经》。威尔斯比是美国中西部地区非常著名的一位牧师，他运用广播和出版物的形式把他对《圣经》的领悟应用到当代美国的生活。史普罗则是一位著名的改革宗神学家；他是一位美国人，在欧洲拿到博士学位后，在宾夕法尼亚建立了一个利戈尼尔研究中心（Ligonier Study Center），以更加理性的方式研读《圣经》经文及其神学原则。与《威尔斯比研读本圣经》不同的是，史普罗主编的《圣经》有 50 多位著名的神

---

① 这个版本的《圣经》现在有重印本。参见 *The Bible Geneva Edition, 1ˢᵗ Edition: 1560*, Litchfield Park, Arizona: The Bible Museum, 2006。

② 参见 Warren W. Wiersbe, ed., *The Wiersbe Study Bible, New King James Version*, Nashville, Tennessee: Thomas Nelson Publishers, 2009。第二版出版于 2018 年。虽然书上写着威尔斯比 "主编"，但我们不清楚其他参与这部研读本《圣经》的编纂人员。他也许是这部著作的唯一作者。

学家参与撰写，其中大部分神学家都有博士学位。^①尽管这两部研
读本《圣经》在解经倾向和对读者的帮助方面有着明显的不同——
威尔斯比本更适合牧师，更限制于《圣经》经文；史普罗本更具有
神学性、历史性和理性，除了《圣经》经文之外还包含了一些改革
宗的文献，以及一些论述 21 世纪基督教信仰的文章——但它们有
一些共同的特征。这些特征在《威尔斯比研读本圣经》中有详细描
述，包括导论、全书提纲、全书概览，灵修注释，^②编者撰写的用
作概括主旨的注释（名曰 "catalyst notes"），"研读注释""交叉引
用"（cross-references）（在讨论某处经文时参考其他经文进行阐释
说明或确认所讨论的话题），关键词索引（包括词语在《圣经》中
出现的位置），"布道提纲索引"（突出威尔斯比本为牧师所用的特
征），"地图"（《圣经》经文中提到的地方和时代）。除了"布道提
纲"之外，史普罗研读本《圣经》也具备其他一切特征，只是多了
一些神学、历史和比较宗教的文章。^③

　我提及威尔斯比和史普罗编纂的这两部研读本《圣经》，是因
为它们可与理雅各的《中国圣书》作比较，尤其是包含《书经》《诗
经》《孝经》的第一卷。在所有这些独有的特征背后是"以经解经"
的新教诠释原则，香港牧师和神学家陈终道从 21 个不同的视角解读

---

① 这些人员的名字和头衔及隶属机构都在"参编人员"（Contributors）部分可找到。参
　见 R. C. Sproul, ed., *The Reformation Study Bible, English Standard Version*, Sanford,
　Florida: Reformation Trust, 2015, pp. xii–xvi。另外一处说整个出版团队多达 100 人
　（同上书，第 xx 页）。根据我在写这篇文章时从利戈尼尔学习中心了解到的情况，第
　三版已经销售了 25 万套。早期两个版本的销售情况没有类似的统计数字，《威尔斯
　比研读本圣经》的销售情况也没有统计数字。
② 书中用语是"被转化"（Be Transformed），参见 *Wiersbe Study Bible*, p. xi。
③ 这一点对于阅读"导言"的读者而言不是非常明显，因为它的"特征说明"（Explanation
　of Features）部分只谈了关于交叉引用的体例和注释的细节（参见 *The Reformation
　Study Bible*, pp. xxi–xxii）。尽管如此，浏览一下目录（同上书，第 v–x 页）就可明
　白《威尔斯比研读本圣经》所具备的特征，《宗教改革研读本圣经》也都具备。

了这一原则。^①这一新教诠释原则应用的一个例子可见于《宗教改革研读本圣经》，尤其是当这部书谈论到交叉引用的目的及其各种脚注的性质时。有时候这些交叉引用^②指在另一处《圣经》上下文中使用了同样的词语；另外一些交叉引用指向"相同的主题"，但用词可能不同；还有一些交叉引用有主题的关联，但也可能有一些在原文中未被发现的洞见。还有一种交叉引用表明一段文字引自先前的《圣经》文本，好像所解释的段落是一个引文似的。同样，这部研读本《圣经》还有四种脚注：^③提供"另一种译文"的脚注；解释文中使用的"希腊文和希伯来文术语"的脚注；各种各样的解释性脚注；对于那些难于理解和翻译的篇章提供"技术性翻译注释"的脚注。

在译文之外的副文本方面，包括各种交叉引用和注释，理雅各的《中国圣书》第一卷与这两部研读本《圣经》之间的相似性也很容易看出。理雅各的导读文字和脚注中有对那部儒经中篇章的交叉引用（因而称"文本内"），也有对其他儒经及注疏文献等的引用。文本内的交叉引用较多，这说明理雅各希望通过一部儒经的文内互注来启发读者。《书经》的导读文字中有 21 处文内交叉引用，^④注释中有 57 处文内交叉引用。^⑤《诗经》的导读文字中有 36 处文内交叉引用，注释中有 41 处文内交叉引用。^⑥《孝经》的章节没有导读文

---

① 参见陈终道《以经解经》第二版，香港金灯台出版社于 1997 年出版，第一版出版于 1995 年。关于这本书的更多主张及其与理雅各"圣书"诠释倾向之间关联性的论述，请参阅《中国圣书》"总论"。

② 前三处交叉引用出现在《宗教改革研读本圣经》第 xxi 页；第四处在接下来的一页。

③ 所有这四类，以及前三类脚注下属类别的脚注在《宗教改革研读本圣经》第 xxii 页都可找到。

④ 在一篇导读文字中有两处交叉引用（《中国圣书》第一卷，第 92 页），还有六处提醒读者参考他写的导论文章。

⑤ 其中只有 12 条注释有交叉引用的细节，这说明大多数交叉引用的注释都出现在了其他与《书经》相关的更复杂的论述中。

⑥ 其中只有 9 条注释有交叉引用的细节。

字，而且其注释中只有两处交叉引用。① 我们知道，至 1879 年，理雅各对每部儒经及其注疏传统已经有了非常深厚的了解，因此，他能对他已经以各种形式翻译出版过的那些儒经自由地交叉引用，我们对此一点也不感到奇怪。这些儒经包括《孟子》②《左传》③，两者都被引用了 9 次；④《中庸》⑤ 被引用了 10 次，⑥《大学》⑦ 被引用了 1 次；⑧《论语》⑨

---

① 其中一处指向他的"导论"，另一处指向前面的篇章。分别参见《中国圣书》第一卷，第 465 页注释 1、475 页注释 1。

② 1861 年作为《中国经典》的第二卷在香港英华书院初版。1867 年在伦敦出版现代版。1895 年在牛津出版修订版。理雅各去世之后，1895 年修订版又以多种形式再版。2010 年华东师范大学出版社重印了全套《中国经典》，并附有中文引言。

③ 1872 年作为《中国经典》第五卷出版，1895 年再版但没有修订。

④ 《孟子》在《书经》的导读文字中被引用 4 次，在《诗经》导读文字中被引用 1 次，在注释中被引用 3 次，在《孝经》注释中被引用 1 次。相较之下，《左传》在《孝经》注释中被引用 5 次，但在《诗经》注释中只被引用了 1 次，在《诗经》导读文字中被引用了 3 次。

⑤ 1861 年《中庸》标题被理雅各翻译为 The Doctrine of the Mean，1885 年理雅各在翻译古本《中庸》时把它改为了 The State of Equilibrium and Harmony。理雅各显然喜欢后一个标题。但是，不知什么原因，在 1893 年牛津出版的修订本中理雅各没有改这一标题，也许是出版社不同意改。结果他在 1893 年的修订版中为这个标题增加了一条评注（参见 1893 年版《中国经典》第一卷，第 383 页），说："我在《东方圣书》版中用的标题译文是 The State of Equilibrium and Harmony。"很不幸，The Doctrine of the Mean 成了理雅各《中庸》译本的标准标题。但所幸的是，21 世纪出版的《中庸》英译本质疑了这个不准确的古老翻译。

⑥ 《中庸》在《诗经》导读文字中被引用 3 次，在《诗经》注释中被引用 1 次；在《孝经》注释中被引用 5 次；在《书经》注释中被引用 1 次。

⑦ 《大学》和《中庸》都在 1861 年香港英华书院出版的《中国经典》第一卷中，后来又于 1867 年在伦敦出版了现代版（没有中文）。这些是根据朱熹重订的"新本"翻译的。理雅各后来又在 1885 年翻译《礼记》时翻译了这两部书的"古本"，都在《中国圣书》第四卷中，我们将在第四卷的导读文章中对之详细介绍。后来在 1893 年出版的《中国经典》第一卷修订版中，理雅各重出了这个"新本"译文。

⑧ 这一次引用在《诗经》的一个注释中。参见《中国圣书》第一卷，第 445 页注释 2。

⑨ 《论语》标题的译文 Analects 是理雅各发明的，后来成了《论语》这部书的标准译名。然而理雅各的全译是 Confucian Analects，但这一全译名常常被参考这部书的人忽略。像"四书"中的其他几部书一样，《论语》也是 1861 年首版，1867 年出版现代版，1893 年出版修订版。《中国经典》本《论语》已广为世人认可，现在仍然以各种形式被重印再版，甚至在 21 世纪的这第三个十年还有重印。

12 次，①《春秋》②2 次。③

此外，理雅各还参考引用了一些他未翻译的经书。这包括《礼记》④，被引用多达8次；⑤《易经》⑥，被引用2次；⑦《诗经》中的一篇导读文字⑧ 频频引用《孝经》。除此之外，理雅各还参考引用了许多他未曾翻译出版的著作：《周官》6 次；⑨《国语》3 次；⑩《说文解字》3 次⑪。这并不是说《中国圣书》第一卷中每部圣书的注释就不交叉引用其他两部圣书的篇章。事实上，这卷书中被引用最多的经书是《书经》，被《诗经》中的 11 处注释和 9 处导读文字所引用，被《孝经》中的 11 处注释所引用。同样，该书中被引用次数第二多的经书是《诗经》，被《书经》的副本文引用 3 次，被《孝经》注释引用 14 次。

所有这些细节都表明理雅各作为儒经文本阐释者所达到的精确水平，然而在他为英文读者所书写的导读文字和注释中还有更多的

---

① 在《书经》导读文字中引用 1 次，注释中引用 5 次；在《诗经》注释中引用 3 次，导读文字中引用 1 次；在《孝经》注释中引用 2 次。

② 1872 年作为《中国经典》第五卷出版，附有《左传》译文（有时为解释）。1895 年重印，但没有修订。理雅各 1897 年去世之后很少再版，但若仔细寻找的话，也可发现数个单独的《春秋》译本是他的译文。

③ 参见《中国圣书》第一卷，第 311 页注释 3、346 页注释 1。

④ 这部儒经译本以两卷本的形式于 1885 年出版（《东方圣书》第 27 卷和第 28 卷）。

⑤ 这些不包括对《大学》和《中庸》的引用。对《礼记》其他篇的引用在《书经》导读文字中引用 1 次，在《诗经》注释中引用 1 次，及其导读文字 2 次，在《孝经》注释中引用 2 次。

⑥ 这一卜筮文本及其《大传》（十翼）由理雅各 1882 年翻译出版。（《中国圣书》第二卷，《东方圣书》第 16 卷）。

⑦ 参见《中国圣书》第一卷，第 138 页（在《书经》的一篇导读文字中）、412 页注释 2（《诗经》）。

⑧ 同上书，第 299—300 页。

⑨ 都在《诗经》中，参见《中国圣书》第一卷，第 323 页注释 1、350 页注释 1、384 页注释 1、419 页注释 2、420 页注释 1、445 页注释 2。

⑩ 在《诗经》的三篇导读文字中，参见《中国圣书》第一卷，第 303、317—318、413 页。

⑪ 在《孝经》导读文字中出现 2 次，注释中引用 1 次。参见《中国圣书》第一卷，第 449、453、471 页注释 2。第 471 页注释 2 中的第一个"十"字应为"士"字。

东西值得探讨。其中一个方面就是引用中国的注疏文献来讨论和佐证他的翻译选择，这涉及为数不太多的大儒及其著作。① 理雅各最常引用的大儒是朱熹（*Kû Hsî*，1130—1200）。统计数字表明朱熹在《中国圣书》第一卷副文本（subtexts）中的主导地位：这卷书引用朱熹共计56次；被引用次数第二多的学者是孔安国（Khung An-Kwo，约公元前154—前74），共计引用32次，多在《孝经》中。② 孔安国之后被引用最多的是《史记》的作者司马迁（Sze-mâ *Kh*ien，前139—前86），共被引用26次。③ 西汉《诗经》学者毛苌（Mâo *K*ang，大约活跃于公元前145年左右）被引9次，但与之相关的《诗序》被引21次。④ 东汉大儒郑玄（*K*ăng Hsüän，127—200，有时理雅各称其字郑康成，*K*ăng Khang-*Kh*ăng）被引13次，其中5次在注释中。⑤ 唐代大儒孔颖达（Khung Ying-tâ，574—648）被引5次。⑥ 理雅各引用如此多汉儒的著作有其道理，因为他们对先秦文字的训诂阐释，是批评后来朱熹某些阐释主张的语文学理据。理雅各也明白御纂编者的阐释视角，⑦

① 我说"为数不太多"是将《中国圣书》本《书经》《诗经》相对简短的导读文字和注释与《中国经典》本《书经》《诗经》相对较长的导读文字和注释相比较而言的。

② 只在《书经》中被引用1次，其余都在《孝经》中。

③ 在《书经》导读文字中引用5次（参见《中国圣书》第一卷，第37、53、100、234、245页），脚注中引用3次（同上书，第91页注释1、95页注释1、119页注释1）。另外，在《诗经》导读文字（同上书，第37和443页）和注释（同上书，第307页注释1和392页注释1）各引用《史记》2次。在《孝经》中仅引用了1次（同上书，第450页）。

④ 这些引用都在《诗经》各篇的导读文字中。参见《中国圣书》第一卷，第305、314—316、319—321、323、327—331、333—335、360、368、404、413、419页。

⑤ 都在《诗经》注释中，参见《中国圣书》第一卷，第307页注释1、308页注释2、322页注释2、367页注释4、397页注释2。

⑥ 在《书经》注释引用2次（见《中国圣书》第一卷，第139页注释2、241页注释2，后一个引用与祭礼有关），在《诗经》注释中引用3次（参见《中国圣书》第一卷，第405页注释1、421页注释4和438页注释4）。

⑦ 理雅各在《书经》中提到1次"《书》的最新御纂编者"（参见《中国圣书》第一卷，第147页注释2，即《钦定书经传说汇纂》的编者），然后又在《诗经》中提到3次"御纂编者"（参见《中国圣书》第一卷，第307页注释1、323、331页，即《钦定诗经传说汇纂》的编者）。他还提到过2次"雍正编者"（参见《中国圣书》第一卷，第219—220、333页，即《钦定书经传说汇纂》的编者）。

而且对好辨的反理学（反朱熹）大儒毛奇龄的作品多有兴趣，[1] 这其中的部分原因是毛奇龄的批评与清代朴学学者的学术批评立场相似。清代朴学也是理雅各所欣赏的。

面对宋儒朱熹的解释及其对《孝经》大胆的删削，理雅各的评价是相当复杂的。理雅各对朱熹解释的回应可分四种。理雅各共引朱熹 36 次，其中他明显接受朱熹解释的仅有 10 次；[2] 部分接受朱熹主张的有 5 次；[3] 反对朱熹解释的有 12 次，而常常偏向于"早期学者"（通常为汉儒）的解释和主张；[4] 引用朱熹主张而无评论的有 9 次，我们可称之为"中立引用"，常常是要表明"典型的儒家评注者"如何解释经文中的一个问题，虽然理雅各自己不一定同意朱熹的意见。[5] 虽然理雅各对朱熹的引用可分这四种情况，但是有一点非常重要，那就是理雅各认同朱熹的《诗经》阐释原则，[6] 而且接受大多数宋儒

---

[1] 参见《中国圣书》第一卷，第 461 页，引自毛奇龄《孝经问》。

[2] 《书经》只有一个注释肯定朱熹的解释（参见《中国圣书》第一卷，第 236 页注释 1），《诗经》中有 6 处同意朱熹之注（参见《中国圣书》第一卷，第 319 和 320 页导读文字、319 页注释 1、374 页注释 1、405 页注释 1、436 页注释 2），《孝经》中有 3 处注释接受朱熹的阐释主张和文本批评（参见《中国圣书》第一卷，第 476 页注释 1、472 页注释 1、注释 3）。

[3] 这 4 次都在《诗经》的导读文字中。参见《中国圣书》第一卷，第 336—337 页、399—400、439 页。

[4] 所有这些反对意见都在《诗经》中。参见《中国圣书》第一卷，第 307、315、323、331、334、368、308 页注释 4、354 页注释 1、392 页注释 3、415 页注释 2、435 页注释 3、438 页注释 3。

[5] 《书经》3 次（《中国圣书》第一卷，第 45 页注释 2、145 页注释 1、174 页注释 2）。《诗经》5 次（《中国圣书》第一卷，第 305、431 页、378 页注释 1、407 页注释 1、435 页注释 3）。《孝经》1 次（《中国圣书》第一卷，第 466 页注释 1）。

[6] 理雅各在本卷《诗经》"导论"结尾（《中国圣书》第一卷，第 298 页）详细引用了朱熹的阐释原则。在《中国经典》第四卷"导论"，第 29 页中也有这一引用。理雅各如此描述这一原则："我们必须在诗歌本身中发现诗歌的意义，而不是接受我们所不认识的那些人的阐释，循着这样的阐释只会把许多诗化为荒谬的谜。"

对《孝经》的文本批评。① 这一切都表明理雅各是中国古代经文的积极阐释者和批判性译者，他始终根据中国注疏和其他相关文献为自己的翻译选择提供理据，而且还从支持其观点的那些中国注疏者的著作中寻找阐释原则。

"其他相关文献"指在欧洲出版的传教士或汉学家的著作。因此，从这个方面来讲，理雅各还希望回应那些可能读过这三部儒经的其他欧洲语言译本或文章的英文读者。理雅各经常引用的是法国天主教传教士宋君荣（P. Gaubil，1689—1759）和韩国英（P. Cibot，1727—1780），他们分别翻译过《书经》和《孝经》。② 理雅各常以他们的翻译与自己的翻译做比较。③ 其他法语文献虽然理雅各参考不多，但仍值得注意，其中包括法国汉学家毕瓯（Édouard Biot，1803—1850）的作品，④ 以及另一位法国耶稣会士孙璋（P. Lacharme，1695—1767）的拉丁文版《诗经》。⑤ 理雅各还引用了

---

① 如上文所言理雅各肯定了朱熹对《孝经》的评注。一般而言，理雅各同意朱熹所说，《孝经》所引用的《诗经》文字是后来添加进去的，而且也同意朱熹所说，《孝经》前六章是孔子之言，应视之为"经"。这是一个有趣的肯定，因为理雅各 1861 年曾拒绝接受朱熹在今本《大学》《中庸》中表达的类似主张。从诠释学的角度来看，理雅各知道宋儒重新编订和解释了《大学》《中庸》，他们的编订和解释非常不同于《礼记》中的"古本"《大学》和《中庸》，但《孝经》没有一个明显不同的早期文本可挑战朱熹的主张。

② 《书经》8 次提到宋君荣，参见《中国圣书》第一卷，第 140 页注释 1、141 页注释 2、142 页注释 1、145 页注释 1、147 页注释 1、227 页注释 1、255 页注释 1、269 页注释 1。《孝经》提到韩国英 9 次，参见第 465—466 页注释 3（2 次）、467 页注释 2、471 页注释 2、473 页注释 3、475 页注释 2、476 页注释 2、479 页注释 1（引文为法语）、482 页注释 2。大约一半的情况下，理雅各反对这些法语译文。

③ 理雅各在《孝经》"导论"结尾为韩国英的翻译做了一个总评："我相信我的这个英语译本要比韩国英的法语译本更加准确和贴切。"（参见《中国圣书》第一卷，第 463 页）

④ 有关天文学方面的知识，理雅各在《书经》即《中国圣书》第一卷，第 82 页注释 3 中引用了毕瓯；在《诗经》即《中国圣书》第一卷，第 419 页注释 2 引用毕瓯。

⑤ 参见《中国圣书》第一卷，第 436 页注释 2。

英语世界的传教士学者和汉学家，包括美国传教士，而后成为耶鲁大学中文教授的卫三畏（Samuel Wells Williams，1812—1884），①前英国驻华领事和伦敦国王学院汉学教授道格拉斯（R. K. Douglas，1838—1913），②以及伦敦会传教士学者艾约瑟（Rev. Dr. Edkins，1823—1905）③和麦都思（Walter Henry Medhurst，1796—1857）④，还有英国圣经公会传教士学者、苏格兰人伟烈亚力（Alexander Wylie，1815—1887）⑤。

以上所举理雅各交叉参考的作品以及中外评注者远远不够全面，此外理雅各还参考了许多其他作品和人物，有时候只参考了一次。我的目的首先是表明理雅各不仅仅是一个"单纯的译者"，其次是说明他把自己从《圣经》中学到的阐释原则应用于解读这些古代儒家传统的"圣书"。根据以上所述，可以引申出来的另一个问题是：理雅各引用的文献有多少是新作，即哪些是在他之前的《书经》《诗经》译本所未引用过的著作？这是我们接下来要谈的一个主要问题。

虽然这些交叉引用的特点足以说明理雅各把这些儒经当作"圣书"的严肃态度，也足以揭示他作为"尽心的译者"在为英语读者阐释这些文本方面所付出的努力；但为了让英语读者对那些古代的儒家文本有更多的理解，理雅各在阐释和分析那些经文及其注疏传统方面还运用了一些其他方法。有些问题是理雅各在呈现这些儒经

---

① 对卫三畏作品的引用在《书经》即《中国圣书》第一卷，第 173、179 页导读文字，在《诗经》即《中国圣书》第一卷，第 331 页注释 1。
② 只在《孝经》"导论"提到道格拉斯 1 次（参见《中国圣书》第一卷，第 454 页注释 1）。
③ 提及艾约瑟的作品在《书经》的一篇导读文字（《中国圣书》第一卷，第 172—173 页）和《诗经》的一个注释（《中国圣书》第一卷，第 405 页注释 1）。
④ 因为麦都思翻译出版过《书经》，理雅各在《中国圣书》第一卷，第 141 页注释 2、142 页注释 1 中提到过他的翻译。
⑤ 理雅各在《孝经》中提到过伟烈亚力（参见《中国圣书》第一卷，第 454 页注释 1）。

时特别关注的。例如,《书经》①《诗经》②中都有不同的文体,理雅各
在其导读文字和注释中都进行了一一说明。选译《诗经》中有宗教
倾向的诗歌时,理雅各额外讨论了这些诗歌的创作年代或与确立创
作年代有关的问题。③同样,对于《孝经》文本史上"窜入"或"伪
造"问题的讨论,④也揭示了理雅各为确立自己在这些问题上的立场
而表现出的严谨认真的学术态度。理雅各经常解释人名⑤和称谓⑥,详
细解释译文中出现的大量古代汉语。为了便于读者理解,理雅各还
给出了这些儒经中古代地名的现代地理位置,⑦还解释了中国古代社

---

① 在《书经》的第一篇导读文字中,理雅各就说其中有"六类文献"(参见《中国圣
书》第一卷,第31页)。然后他在之后的导读文字中讨论了典、誓、诰、贡、训、
命这六种文体。有时候就一个文本的归类问题会有争议。参见《中国圣书》第一卷,
第 31、46、57、64、76、86、95、103、112、120、121、133、137、149、151、
164、196、200、220、226 页。

② 有趣的是,理雅各这里为《诗经》诗歌体裁分类用的不是《中国经典》第四卷中提
到的古典儒家分类("赋"〈narrative〉,"比"〈metaphorical〉,"兴"〈allusive〉),
而是描述《圣经·诗篇》的文体用语。参见《中国圣书》第一卷,第336—337页
(比较"祭祀诗"〈sacrificial odes〉与"赞美诗"〈praise odes〉),第341页("游
吟歌谣"〈bardic effusions〉,更像是古代苏格兰的赞歌),第349页("祝贺歌"〈ode
of congratulation〉),第354、355、358页("哀歌"〈lamentation〉),第369页
("皇室颂歌"〈royal ode〉)。

③ 参见《中国圣书》第一卷,第303、314、316、328、336、349、351、355、358、
361、377、407、408、417、419、431、434、439—444 页。

④ 尤其参见《中国圣书》第一卷,第472—473 页注释3。

⑤ 解释人名意义之处参见《中国圣书》第一卷,第32页注释1、80页注释1(尧)、
38页注释1(舜)、46页注释1(禹)、202页注释1(高宗)、256页注释1(黄帝)、
318页(周公及其他人名)、319—320、396页(后稷)、404页(召公或奭)、465
页注释1(仲尼和子思)、465页注释2、473页(曾子)。

⑥ 如《中国圣书》第一卷,第39页注释3(shepherds of men)、第95页注释1和118
页注释1(Buttress and Director)、122页注释1(Grand Master 和 Junior Master)、
78页注释1、119页、161页注释1、250页注释1,都与祭祀中的"尸"(spirit
personators)有关;第228页注释4(又见第44页 Minister of Religion)、257—258
页注释1(Minister of Astronomy and the Calendar)。

⑦ 这样的情况特别多,以《书经》中最多,有时候也会提及《诗经》中的地名。参见
《中国圣书》第一卷,第31、33页注释1和2、35页注释2、36页注释1、37、39
页注释4、41页注释2、52页注释1、60页注释2、63、64页注释1、66页注释1、

会中与宗教仪式不相关的许多细节问题。[①]（下文将会讨论理雅各为许多宗教观念、行为和习俗而做的详细注解。）就理雅各利用的所有这些阐释方法而言，需要注意的是只有少数几处有跨文化阐释。一次他比较"好思辨的"（speculative）希腊人与"务实的"（practical）中国人，但这样比较的目的只是要挑战 18 世纪耶稣会译者宋君荣所做的中国-希腊比较。[②]一次在介绍《小雅》中的一首诗时，理雅各说中国人对天的理解与摩尼教对天的理解很相像，因此把它比作"塞比教徒的观念"（Sabian views）。[③]在整卷书中理雅各只有两次参考《圣经》经文：一处提到把丰收的一部分留给孤儿寡妇，[④]另一处理雅各主张中国古代的一神论类似于《圣经》中的神。[⑤]此外，理雅

（接上页）67 页注释 1、69 页注释 1、70 页注释 1、71 页注释 1，第 76、84、86页注释 1，第 88 页注释 1、93 页注释 1、97 页注释 1、104 页注释 1，第 120、124、125 页注释 1，第 131 页注释 1、133 页注释 1，第 134 页注释 1、4，第 136 页注释 2、3，第 162、163 页注释 1，第 164、174 页注释 1、181—182、199 页注释 1，第 211页注释 1、3，第 235 页注释 2、237 页注释 2。以及第 254、265、268、270、303、316、337、417、426、430、437、439、440、442、444 页等。

① 这些问题有很多，这里谈到的只是一些代表性的主题。这里强调的是一些特殊的主题，但在本卷书的大量注释中还有与特定文本相关的许多历史说明和解释。在《书经》中他特别解释了历法和皇历（《中国圣书》第一卷，第 125 页注释 1、127 页注释 1、152 页注释 1、195 页注释 4、255 页注释 1），详细探讨了各种刑罚（《中国圣书》第一卷，第 40 页注释 4、41 页注释 1、168 页注释 1、255 页注释 2、261 页注释 1 和 2、262 页注释 1），还有一些涉及古代射、御详细情形的短小的注释（分别参见《中国圣书》第一卷，第 59 页注释 1 和 77 页注释 2），五等爵位（《中国圣书》第一卷，第 136 页注释 4、137 页注释 1），中国古代语境中的饮酒及祭祀中的饮酒问题（详见《中国圣书》第一卷，第 171—173 页）。

② 参见《中国圣书》第一卷，第 138 页。

③ 同上书，第 362 页。塞比教徒在《古兰经》中被提到过三次，是同犹太教徒和基督徒一样被早期的穆斯林所容忍的宗教徒。

④ 理雅各提醒读者参考《申命记》24: 19—22。参见《中国圣书》第一卷，第 373 页注释 2。

⑤ 在《孝经》的一处讨论中，理雅各引用康熙帝御定的《孝经衍义》的文字，然后补充说："天接近于绝对神之名——耶和华，就像《出埃及记》15: 14 中所解释的那样；而帝就是 God，是'我们在天上的父'。"参见《中国圣书》第一卷，第 478 页。理雅各所指的应该不是《出埃及记》15: 14，应该是《出埃及记》3: 15。

各还拿"天"与"Providence"比较。①这个术语常常与法国神学家加尔文（Jean Calvin，1509—1564）的主张相关联，虽然理雅各在这些地方不曾提到加尔文的名字。理雅各在这些方面显然是在抑制他的阐释冲动；他关注的是帮助英文读者理解中国的文本，而非用各种中国文本为他的个人偏好提供理据。

五、新旧译本比较

比较《中国经典》和《中国圣书》正文的体例，读者会发现《中国圣书》中有许多新的方面需要考虑。首先，《中国经典》几乎每页正文的上方都有中文原文，这在《中国圣书》完全没有。这背后的原因可能与理雅各的偏好无关，很有可能是麦克斯·缪勒和牛津大学出版社编辑的决定。即使如此，这一明显的不同还是会引发我们的一些疑问。例如，理雅各是否只是照搬了《中国经典》中《书经》和《诗经》的英文翻译？还有，理雅各在《中国圣书》本《书经》《诗经》的副文本中提到的一些难解的中文名称、字词，是否仅仅是选自《中国经典》？有没有具体的例子表明理雅各对《书经》《诗经》的译文和副文本做出了一些改变和新的阐释？

理雅各在《中国圣书》第一卷的"序言"中提到了这一重译本中一个"新"的方面。理雅各说他放弃了《中国经典》的"音译系统"（transliteration system）②——主要依靠马礼逊（Robert Morrison，1782—

① 有一处理雅各认为"天步"相当于"course of Providence"，另一处理雅各把"天"等同于19世纪晚期惯常意义上的"Providence"（与加尔文神学没有严格的意义关联）。参见《中国圣书》第一卷，第376页注释3、434页注释1。

② 我的法国同行贺旦思（Dimitri Drettas）博士说得很正确，他说"音译系统"是用符号来表示在另一书面语言中发现的语音，但由于汉字在不同方言中的发音非常不同（例如粤语、闽南语、沪语、北京话），用于描述其语音的标准方法被称为"转写"或"转写系统"（transcription system），因为一个汉字没有一个特定的语音。

1834）字典的拼音体系，而改用威妥玛（Sir Thomas Wade, 1818—1895）更为现代和准确的拼音体系。理雅各在他的六卷本《中国圣书》中把这一拼音体系应用到了中文专有名词上，包括中国古代的人名、评注者的名字及其著作的标题、地名等。这些专有名词几乎每页都有，因此这一拼音体系的转变对于理雅各而言是一项不小的修订工作。根据本导读文章所附表格，总的来说理雅各是比较顺利地转向了威妥玛的拼音体系，但《诗经》中某些标题和专名有拼写错误，因为理雅各有时给出的是粤语发音，[①] 有些与理雅各纠正早期译本的拼写有关，[②] 有些错误理雅各在《中国圣书》第一卷中还没有纠正过来。[③]

　　若将《中国经典》中《书经》《诗经》的译文与《中国圣书》中《书经》《诗经》（摘选）的译文进行比较，我们发现两者基本上是一样的。我只发现了少数几处《书经》译文两者有很大差别，而这主要是因为理雅各忽略了其中的某些字句或章节。[④] 理雅各说他在《中国圣书》第一卷中重译了这两部书，我们可信以为真。然而，事实是两个译文基本上是相同的（尽管人名、地名音译不同）。理雅各自己也在序言中说，除了年代和新的拼音系统之外，译文没有太大的

---

① 理雅各有三处用了粤语拼音（参见本文结尾的《诗经》三译本比较表的注释，即第123 页注释 3、129 页注释 3、131 页注释 3，原文在《中国经典》第四卷 65、575 页，及 1876 年《诗经》韵律体译本第 89 和 307 页。）

② 有些在 1876 年《诗经》韵律体译本中已经纠正过来了（参见本文结尾所附的《诗经》三译本比较表注释，即第124 页注释 3、126 页注释 5 和 6），有些在《中国圣书》第一卷中纠正了过来（参见《诗经》三译本比较表注释，即第 123 页注释 5、130 页注释 2 和 3、131 页注释 1 和 4、132 页注释 1）。

③ 参见《诗经》三译本比较表注释，即第 124 页注释 1 和 7、128 页注释 4、129 页注释 4—6、131 页注释 5。

④ 我们可以对照中文原文来识别这些具体的章节。参见《中国圣书》第一卷，第 109 页和《中国经典》第三卷，第 237 页，《中国圣书》第一卷，第 111 页和《中国经典》第三卷，第 239 页，《中国圣书》第一卷，第 159 页和《中国经典》第三卷，第 369 页，《中国圣书》第一卷，第 167 页和《中国经典》第三卷，第 387 页，《中国圣书》第一卷，第 177 页和《中国经典》第三卷，第 408 页。

变化。① 虽然如此，这只是对这些译文性质的总体评价，我发现有一章文字是理雅各真的重译了。为了对比两者的差异，我选择把 1865 年版与 1879 年版并置于此。

<table>
<tr><td>1865 年版 ②</td><td>1879 年版 ③</td></tr>
</table>

[vii.] "Seventh, of the examination of doubts. — Having chosen and appointed officers for divining by the tortoise and by the milfoil, they are to be charged *on occasion* to perform their duties. *In doing this*, they will find *the appearances* of rain, clearing up, cloudiness want of connection, and crossing; and *the symbols*, solidity, and repentance. In all *the indications* are seven: — five given by the tortoise, and two by the milfoil, by which the errors *of affairs* may be traced out. These officers having been appointed, when the operations with the tortoise and the milfoil are proceeded with, three men are

vii. 'Seventh, of the (means for the) examination of doubts. — Officers having been chosen and appointed for divining by the tortoise-shell and the stalks of the Achillea, they are to be charged (on occasion) to execute their duties. (In doing this,) they will find (the appearances of) rain, of clea-ring up, of cloudiness, of want of connection, and of crossing; and the inner and outer diagrams. In all (the indications) are seven: — five given by the shell, and two by the stalks; and (by means) of these any errors (in the mind) may be traced out. These officers having been appointed, when the

---

① 参见他在《中国圣书》第一卷，第 xxix—xxx 页关于这件事的完整叙述。他在前一页说"没有必要提那些无足轻重的译文的变化"。这说明这些新译文中没有什么重要的变化，但下面的例子将说明这一表述是不完全正确的。

② 引自《中国经典》第三卷，第 334—335 页。

③ 引自《中国圣书》第一卷，第 145—146 页。

to obtain and interpret the in-dications and symbols, and the *consenting* words of two of them are to be followed.

divination is proceeded with, three men are to interpret the indications, and the (consenting) words of two of them are to be followed.

除了格式或排版风格问题之外，对比这两个译文，我们可以看出理雅各在 1879 年对中国古代卜筮的性质和操作方法有了更深的理解。1879 年时理雅各显然确信中国古代的卜筮之官是用那些依据《易经》卦画而来的符号进行占卜的。1879 年的译文不仅在某些特定术语的翻译方面有变化，英语表达也更流畅，而且从中我们也可看出理雅各对某些关键内容的阐释发生了改变。虽然理雅各觉得这些变化"不足道"，但这些变化确实反映了他的成长，也增加了《洪范》这一篇的意义，并使之更加容易理解了。

另外需要强调的是，理雅各显然是有意选择再现 1871 年的《诗经》散文体译本，而非 1876 年更富创造性、更优美的韵律体译本。这主要是为了尽可能准确地呈现《诗经》中的宗教元素。

我们已经说过，理雅各之前没有翻译出版过《孝经》，因此我们没有一个可比较的早期译本。

《中国经典》与《中国圣书》第一卷之间还有一个非常明显的不同，那就是前者的长篇导论在后者中被大大缩减了。认真比较分析这两个学术性导论，我们可以看出在这个修订版中理雅各所做出的创造性工作。简便起见，我只选取《诗经》的"导论"来说明。①

哪怕是粗略地比较一下《诗经》1871 年散文体译本中的"导论"、1876 年韵律体译本中的"导论"和这个 1879 年的译本中的"导论"，

---

① 这样做我意在表明《书经》"导论"也有同样的情形。再次说明，《孝经》"导论"是全新的。

我们就会立即看出 1876 年本"导论"与 1879 年本"导论"更接近。那么，通过详细比较 1876 年本和 1879 年本导论，我们便能揭示理雅各在修订和重写 1879 年"导论"时所做的创造性工作。简而言之，1879 年本"导论"的第一章是全新的，^① 第二和第三章比较依赖 1876 年本，但仍然有一定程度的变化，^② 第四章的变化最大。^③

除了这些重要的改动之外，我们还可看出理雅各补充了一些最新出版的著作，一些不曾在其《书经》^④《诗经》^⑤ 早期译本中所看到的参考书。若比较《诗经》1871 年译本的注释和 1879 年译本的注释，我们会看到理雅各在 1879 年本中引用的一些中文文献是 1871 年本中所没有的，这一定是理雅各最新研究的结果。^⑥ 因此，理雅各不仅重译了《书经》《诗经》中的许多篇章，而且还认真书写了各种副文本（前言、导论、篇章导读、注释），这些副文本极大地增加了《中国圣书》第一卷的学术价值，也使经文变得更容易理解。然而，还

---

① 参见《中国圣书》第一卷，第 275—279 页。

② 尤其是第三章结尾的语气更为强烈。参见《中国圣书》第一卷，第 289 页。

③ 如果比较 1871 年本"导论"（《中国经典》第四卷，第 23—33 页）和 1879 年本"导论"（《中国圣书》第一卷，第 290—298 页），这一点可以看得更明显。

④ 包括参考艾约瑟于 1879 年 4 月 24 日在北京皇家亚洲学会北中国支会所发表的演讲（参见《中国圣书》第一卷，第 172 页），以及引用卫三畏 1874 年出版的《汉英韵府》（*A Syllabic Dictionary of the Chinese Language*）中关于"酒"的概念（参见《中国圣书》第一卷，第 173 页）。

⑤ 《书经》导论末附有牛津大学萨维利安天文学教授（Savilian Professor of Astronomy）普里查德牧师（Rev. C. Pritchard）制作的天文表（参见《中国圣书》第一卷，第 29 页），替换了 1865 年本中湛约翰（John Chalmers）制作的表（参见《中国经典》第三卷，第 90—104 页）。另外，理雅各还就"串"（串夷）的发音问题引用了金斯密（T. W. Kingsmill）在 1872 年 4 月发表的一篇文章中的说法（参见《中国圣书》第一卷，第 389 页注释 2）。还参考了艾约瑟 1872 年初版、1878 年再版的《中国的宗教》（*Religion in China*）（参见《中国圣书》第一卷，第 405 页注释 1）。

⑥ 这些新添加的中文注疏文献可参见《中国圣书》第一卷，第 407 页注释 1（*Kû Kung-khien* 朱公迁），第 414 页注释 1（引自韩婴《韩诗外传》），第 421 页注释 4（参考了一部不常见的书《神异经》，转引自孔颖达疏《毛诗注疏》），第 424 页注释 1（纠正了 1871 年误拼的一个注疏者的名字）。

有一个问题需要解决，那就是理雅各在阐释这三部儒经的过程中所揭示的中国古代宗教生活及宗教观念的性质。

六、《中国圣书》第一卷的宗教内容

具有讽刺意味的是，理雅各从未给六卷本《中国圣书》中的宗教内容给出明确的界定。吉瑞德提出了这一问题，他说读者也许一开始会期待理雅各"在评价中国古人'对上帝的认识'方面会更加开放。"[①] 因此，他非常敏锐地指出，1877 年理雅各坚决主张中国古代的某些表达对等于"God"这一概念，并因此引起了激烈的争论，此后在《中国圣书》第一卷中理雅各便选择"让文献本身说话"。[②] 随后，吉瑞德发现理雅各在《中国圣书》第一卷序言中详细讨论了中国古代儒家的"上帝观"，并且认为帝尧和帝舜在后来被"神圣化"了，就像古希腊传统中的"历史人物神圣化的过程"（process of euhemerization）一样。[③] 理雅各首先用了 8 页的篇幅详细讨论了这个问题，[④] 然后说他一直坚信他 1865 年作为传教士—译者在《中国经典》第三卷中首次表达的信念，并且在 15 年之后表达得更清晰了。这些问题是吉瑞德所未谈到，也未曾重视的。[⑤] 吉瑞德说理雅各

---

① Girardot, *The Victorian Translation of China*, p. 271. 在这句话的注释（《中国圣书》第一卷，第 653 页注释 121）中，吉瑞德让我们参考 1865 年本《书经》"导论"结尾 6 页与"宗教和迷信"有关的内容（《中国经典》第三卷"导论"，第 192—197页）。事实上，其中只有 1 页半与"上帝观"有关（《中国经典》第三卷"导论"，第 193—194 页）。这与《中国圣书》第一卷"序言"中对"上帝观"的讨论形成了鲜明的对比。（详见下文论述）

② Girardot, *The Victorian Translation of China*, p. 271.

③ Ibid., p. 275.

④ 参见《中国圣书》第一卷，第 xxii—xxix 页。

⑤ 需要注意的是，吉瑞德对于理雅各一贯主张的质疑不是基于理雅各自己的文字，而是一篇书评中提出的问题（参见 Girardot, *The Victorian Translation of China*, pp. 653—

是一个"学术型的评注者—译者—阐释者"，而不是一个"给自己的作品涂上一层传教士'色彩'"的人。① 这表明，吉瑞德认为理雅各不可能一贯地或理性地把他早期的信念和后期的主张统一起来。一位牛津大学的基督徒教授能真正重申他在十几年前在香港作为传教士-学者的理解吗？理雅各说他确实是这样做的，而且他的这一信念在这些年中与日俱增。② 吉瑞德论述的关键是他认为理雅各"在评价中国宗教的性质和意义方面有一些极其微妙的变化"，尤其是他认为理雅各提及的中国宗教语境中的"迷信"是有问题的，但他没有注意到理雅各一直持这样的主张，1865 年理雅各就根据"现代中国学者"的评论做出了对那些迷信的理解。③ 理雅各对这些宗教现象"同情但不中立"的阐释，不仅没有掩盖他对儒教和道教宗教主张的评价，而且促使他在《中国圣书》六卷本中以敏锐的学术头脑诚实地表达他对儒教和道教宗教性质的理解和信念。首先，他为《书经》中有宗教意义的章节标示出了 235 个星号，从而以间接的方式宣称

（接上页）654, footnote 123）。吉瑞德说这位书评者对理雅各的主张"不甚信服"。这在文化意义和历史意义上都很重要，但显然不是理雅各自己的见解。对这些问题更公正的评价应该依据理雅各一年之后出版的《中国宗教》一书（*The Religions of China: Confucianism and Tâoism Described and Compared with Christianity*, London: Hodder and Staughton, 1880.）

① Girardot, *The Victorian Translation of China*, p. 276.

② 通过阅读理雅各的《中国宗教》，我们可确证他的这些主张。《中国宗教》揭示了理雅各以"同情但不中立"的立场评价中国古代儒家传统中的宗教观念和习俗，以及清代的儒教和道教。

③ 参见《中国经典》第三卷导论，第 196 页："现代（中国）学者"说"商朝的人非常迷信"。这些中国的知识分子显然属于那时"最进步的"知识分子，就像 1879 年牛津大学的麦克斯·缪勒一样。吉瑞德好像希望理雅各跟随 20 世纪宗教研究的思潮（"最进步的西方标准"，参见 Girardot, *The Victorian Translation of China*, p. 269），但理雅各是不可能知道这些的。他回应的是他那个时代最优秀的中国知识分子和欧美的汉学家和传教士—学者的著作。根据理雅各用星号认真标示出的那些《书经》中相关章节的宗教观念，我们可看出他在阐释学意义上是对此有所回应的，也在思想上参与了其中。

了他的宗教主张。① 其次，我们可以查阅前四卷《中国圣书》"儒教文本"的主题索引和人名索引，② 但这将使我们超越《中国圣书》第一卷的范围。另外，如果我们看理雅各所选《诗经》后三部分的副标题，可以看出理雅各在寻找那些表示"作者及其时代的宗教观念和宗教实践"（the religious views and practices of the writers and their times）③ 的诗歌，这可以暗示理雅各关注的是什么。事实上，除了他用星号标示的之外，《书经》中还有更多与宗教有关的内容。

理雅各最初关注的重点主要是《书经》中记录的祭祀、祭品，以及举办祭祀活动的场所。（在此需要说明的是，像许多古代历史文本一样，《书经》主要记录中国古代社会王公贵族的宗教仪式和习俗，很少提及普通人的宗教生活。普通人的宗教观念、道德和习俗主要记载在《诗经》和《孝经》这两部书中，但理雅各没有为这两部书中的宗教内容标注星号。）祭祀的对象有上帝④、天⑤、六宗⑥、山川⑦，还有群神⑧，包括崇拜祖先之神以示"孝道"或对长辈的尊敬。⑨祭祀场所有文祖⑩、艺祖⑪、宗庙⑫，还有与之相随的祭坛。⑬ 有好多处

---

① 虽然吉瑞德说理雅各通过添加星号提供了这些暗示，但是他没有统计有多少个星号，也没有基于详细的研究而对这些星号所示的内容做出评价。他只是说了他对理雅各这番努力的总体印象（参见 Girardot, *The Victorian Translation of China*, p. 272）。下文我将提供一些吉瑞德评价中所没有说到的细节。

② 参见《中国圣书》第四卷，第 471—485 页。

③ 参见《中国圣书》第一卷，第 347、377 和 430 页上出现的这同一个副标题。

④ 在《中国圣书》第一卷第 39 页首次提及。

⑤ 同上。

⑥ 同上。

⑦ 同上书，第 39 页中提到过 2 次，然后在第 70—71 页和第 74 页提到了具体的山和泛称的山。

⑧ 也在《中国圣书》第一卷第 39 页提到过。

⑨ 同上书，第 99 页提到过。

⑩ 参见《中国圣书》第一卷，第 38、41 页。

⑪ 同上书，第 40 页。

⑫ 在许多地方都提到过，同上书，第 96、102、195 页。

⑬ 《中国圣书》第一卷，第 40 页提到在 12 个州建了 12 座祭坛。

都强调疏于祭祖是不道德的，而且会灾难临头。① 然后，祭品也要符
合规制，理雅各在注释中对此有详细的解释。有时用特（牡牛），有
时用玄牡。② 祭祀文王、武王只能用骍牛（红牛），因为周天子以红
色为正色。③ 许多祭祀场合都用酒，一次特别准确地说用秬鬯。④ 一
次武王生病很严重，周公在祖庙中祈求代武王去死，理雅各认为周
公这一非凡而又崇高的行为很可敬。⑤

　　这里顺便说一下《中国圣书》第一卷引起的关于"帝"与"God"
对等问题的争论。理雅各在书中主张某些古代儒家语境中的"帝"对
等于"God"，这引起了一些人的愤怒，并影响到了缪勒对理雅各的支
持。然而，1880 年末发生在牛津大学的一件事坚定了缪勒对理雅各主
张的理解和支持。一位日本明治时期的外交官森有礼（1847—1889）
拜访了牛津大学的理雅各和缪勒，他们谈论了这个问题，随后理雅各
还给了他一篇文章，在文章中理雅各重申了自己翻译的正确性。读了
这篇文章之后，森有礼写信给缪勒，说"理雅各博士是正确的。"这
打消了缪勒的疑虑，使他对理雅各主张的支持不再动摇了。⑥

　　君主与神灵之间存在着紧密的宗教关系。这个关系在出现"天
命"（Heavenly Mandate, the appointment of Heaven）一词的上下文中
得到了清晰的阐释；有时候是在出现"天道"（Way of Heaven）的上
下文中进行描述的，但很少出现在《书经》中。⑦ 处于中国古代文化
背景之中的君主和贵族的一般宗教观念和宗教期待可在描述儒家精

---

① 《中国圣书》第一卷，例如第 132、214 页。
② 参见《中国圣书》第一卷，第 40、90 页。
③ 详见《中国圣书》第一卷，第 195 页。
④ 参见《中国圣书》第一卷，第 174、194、242 页。引文"秬鬯"见《中国圣书》第
　　一卷，第 194 页。
⑤ 参见《中国圣书》第一卷，第 153 页理雅各的翻译和注释。
⑥ 引文和详情见 Girarot, *The Victorian Translation of China*, p. 208。
⑦ 理雅各为"天命"标了 10 次星号，但只给"天道"标了 2 次。

神价值的许多句子中得以概括。例如，"至诚感神"[①] "天寿平格"[②] "满招损，谦受益，是乃天道"[③] "皇天无亲，惟德是辅"[④]。

对于那些无德、无义、残暴的君主和贵族而言，所期望的就不是上天的恩宠了，而是其反面。无论是上天和其他神灵的恩宠还是惩罚，都被经常提到，理雅各用星号为《书经》标出了多达上百处这样的内容。[⑤] 另外，卜筮[⑥] 是用于辨识"天意"的一个重要方法，例如决定是否要征伐，[⑦] 营建新的居住地并建宗庙和祭坛，[⑧] 分辨君主及其大臣是否值得上天保佑。[⑨] 如此，人们方能理解为什么君主及其大臣应该"严天威"[⑩] 及"天罚"[⑪]。通过卜筮，通常要寻找的是让各个方面的迹象都与天意吻合，包括君主与卿士的期望，以及根据自然现象而解读出的任何相关的征兆。[⑫] 有时也包括君主做的梦。[⑬] 如果不能完全吻合，那么就对各种变数进行演算，这些变数通常情况下要让步于卜筮。[⑭]

---

① 引自《中国圣书》第一卷，第 52 页。

② 同上书，第 207 页。

③ 同上书，第 52 页，但第 89—90 页也表达了相同的观点。

④ 同上书，第 212 页，但第 99、101 页也表达了相同的观点。

⑤ 占总星号数（235 个）的 43%。

⑥ 卜筮对于著名的《洪范》篇所描述的九条治国大法（九畴）之第七条是非常重要的。参见《中国圣书》第一卷，第 145—147 页。

⑦ 如《中国圣书》第一卷，第 77、83、85、86、90、128、120—122、126、127、129 页所示，都是秉承"天意"要去消灭罪恶之君。

⑧ 参见《中国圣书》第一卷，第 183、190 页。

⑨ 参见《中国圣书》第一卷，第 207 页。

⑩ 引自《中国圣书》第一卷，第 262 页。

⑪ 同上书，第 264 页。

⑫ 详见《中国圣书》第一卷，第 145—147 页《洪范》第七条的描述。第八条也有自然现象（参见《中国圣书》第一卷，第 147—149 页），被看作是上天对君主之统治的肯定。

⑬ 这是在确证未来征讨能成功的背景下提及的。参见《中国圣书》第一卷，第 128 页。

⑭ 理雅各因此认为这些卜筮的规则不合理，是人为操纵的。它只是要强化己意，而非要知天意。所以，理雅各认为这些行为都是迷信（参见《中国经典》第三卷，第 196、197 页）。

需要注意的是,《书经》的这些宗教特征大部分都在《中国经典》第三卷"导论"的最后一节详细探讨过了。但是,这些特征在本卷书中被给予了新的强调,而且理雅各没有为之提供解释,因为1865 年译本中已经有了说明。[1]

有时候,在君主、卿相及庶人的生活中,灾难在所难免。面临灾难之时,中国古代社会各个阶层的人都会祈求上天。[2] 这种情况非常多,以至于《诗经》中有一类"哀诗"(lamentations),用于抒发这种悲伤之情,[3]《孝经》专门有一章《谏净》用于劝说刚愎的长辈和上位者回归天道。[4] 就是在这样的背景下,对各种堕落的精神抵制表明了一种宗教承诺(lèligious commitment),虽然这样的承诺最终能使走上歧途的人回归正道,但它常常引起强烈的个人痛苦。根据《中国圣书》第一卷所反映的宗教价值观,可以说理雅各及其同时代人所说的"孝"(filial piety)——尊敬活着的或逝去的长者,包括那些死后配天的圣君[5] 和贤臣——应该被看作是中国古代文化和宗教意愿的精神支柱。

结　论

我在文章伊始为自己确立了三个关键的阐释问题,意欲借此对

---

[1]　详见《中国经典》第三卷,第 192—197 页。
[2]　舜就每日呼唤上天(参见《中国圣书》第一卷,第 52 页),庶人遇到暴政时也呼唤上天(参见《中国圣书》第一卷,第 127—256 页)。
[3]　《中国圣书》第一卷,第 351—358 页有五首这样的诗。
[4]　参见《中国圣书》第一卷,第 483—484 页《孝经》第十五章。这里把人伦从最高位的君主至最低位的家庭,使谏净成了古代儒家文化背景下最普遍的道德观念。
[5]　舜死后被赋予了这样的地位,所有好的统治者和大臣也都应如此。参见《中国圣书》第一卷,第 45、207 页。奇怪的是,理雅各没有把这一非常重要的宗教概念包括在《中国圣书》第四卷的主题索引中(参见《中国圣书》第四卷,第 472 页)。

理雅各 1879 年出版的《中国圣书》第一卷的性质和价值做出一些决定性的评判。第一个问题与这卷书的多重文本的性质有关，不仅包括三部儒经的英语译文，而且还有大量的副文本。第二个问题是要评价理雅各是否只是一个"单纯的译者"，甚至说得更刻薄一点，他在《中国圣书》第一卷的译文和副文本中是否做了一些重大的改变。第三个问题显然是一个核心问题，不仅影响这卷书的特质，也为判断六卷本《中国圣书》所涉及的中国古代文化中的宗教生活、价值观、态度和习俗设立一个标准。现在，经过十分详尽的论述，我揭示了之前中外学者不曾探讨的关于这卷书的许多方面，并得出了如下结论。

第一，理雅各不仅翻译而且制作了多重副文本，因为他是要把这些中国古书视作"圣书"。这意味着他应该"以经解经"，这是他从自己的新教神学训练以及解读《圣经》经文而得出的阐释原则。因此，理雅各创制的副文本不仅为受过教育的英文读者提供了教育的洞见和学术阐释的工具，也展现了中国古代生活和历史方方面面的细节信息，从而有助于读者对这三部儒经获得新的理解视角。

第二，理雅各不仅是一个有着自主意识的译者——认真评估和修改他之前已经翻译过的《书经》《诗经》，而且还是一个训练有素的伟大阐释者——把自己最优秀的中国学术成果展现给英语读者。他不仅评估和修改之前的译文和阐释性注释，而且还添加了许多新的细节，这些都是从他反复阅读的大量中文和西文参考文献中提取的，包括他那个时代学术圈内流行的最新资料。我已设法从许多不同的方面说明，理雅各无论是作为中国经书的译者还是学者，都是在不断成长的，所以他提供了许多新的阐释、新的文献，而且以新的精神面貌和参考文献突出了他对这三部儒经抱持的信念。

第三，理雅各所谓的"宗教内容"概念是相当宽泛和复杂的，

包括中国古代文化语境中的宗教生活、价值观、态度、习俗；它
所揭示的精神关怀与理雅各所属福音派新教团体的关怀有很多不
同。需要注意的是，理雅各主要关注的是儒家经典文本中最古老的
那些，而在后来中国历史的发展过程中，一些宗教态度和精神性
实践都与这些早期文本中所体现的有不同程度的差异。[①] 我所论述
的理雅各对"宗教内容"的解释都有理雅各翻译的这些古代文本为
证。这使得理雅各有可能成为中国古代儒经和其他经典著作"同情
但不中立"的基督徒阐释者。他还通过一些共同的价值观念、共同
的关怀及生活方式把这三部儒经联系在了一起。这些方面随着时代
的发展虽然会有变化，但某些做法仍然可以揭示儒家的精神倾向。
在这些价值观念中，"孝"无论是在中国古代社会的世俗世界还是
精神世界，都成了支撑祭祀仪式、尊敬长上的主要理由，也是和
平和战争时期维持家庭和集体生计的主要支撑力。理雅各将在接下
来的几卷《中国圣书》的翻译和阐释中继续使用这一"宗教内容"
标准。

（丁大刚　译　潘琳　校）

---

① 例如，《左传》所揭示的春秋后期的宗教态度，就与更古老的《书经》和《诗经》最
　古老部分所揭示的宗教概念、价值观、习俗有很大不同。参见陈来《古代思想文化
　的世界：春秋时代的宗教、伦理与社会思想》（台北市允晨文化，2006 年版）。

附录一

理雅各《尚书》^① 两译本比较表

书名与篇名	1865 年版英译名	1879 年版英译名	页码（1865）	页码（1879）
唐书	**Part I. The Book of T'ang**	**Part I. The Book of Thang**	**15—27**	**31—36**
尧典	The Canon of Yaou	The Canon of Yâo	15—27	31—36
虞书	**Part II. The Books of Yu**	**Part II. The Books of Yü**	**29—90**	**37—62**
舜典	Book I. The Canon of Shun	Book I. The Canon of Shun	29—51	37—45
大禹谟	Book II. The Counsels of the Great Yu	Book II. The Counsels of the Great Yü	52—67	46—52
皋陶谟	Book III. The Counsels of Kaou-Yaou	Book III. The Counsels of Kâo-Yâo	68—75	53—56
益稷	Book IV. Yih and Tseih	Book IV. The Yî and Kî	76—90	56—62
夏书	**Part III. The Books of Hea**	**Part III. The Books of Hsiâ**	**91—171**	**63—83**
禹贡上	Book I. The Tribute of Yu Part I	Book I. The Tribute of Yü [Section 1]^②	92—127	63—72
禹贡下	Book II.^③ The Tribute of Yu Part II	[Section 2]	128—151	72—76
甘誓	Book II. The Speech at Kan	Book II. The Speech at Kan	152—155	76—77
五子之歌	Book III. The Songs of the Five Sons	Book III. The Songs of the Five Sons	156—161	78—80
胤征	Book IV. The Punitive Expedition of Yin	Book IV. The Punitive Expedition of Yin	162—171	81—83
商书	**Part IV. The Books of Shang**	**Part IV. The Books of Shang**	**173—279**	**84—123**

① 理雅各 1865 年译本使用过《尚书》这个书名，但他一直用《书经》来指代这部儒经，无论是 1865 年译本还是 1879 年译本都是如此。

② 我用方括号表示这篇书没有被分成两个不同部分，而是在一本"书"中包含了两个"部分"，这是理雅各在 1879 年译本中的一项创新，1865 年译本中没有，下同。

③ 此处疑似理雅各的一个编次错误，应为"Book I"。

续表

书名与篇名	1865 年版英译名	1879 年版英译名	页码（1865）	页码（1879）
汤誓	Book I. The Speech of T'ang	Book I. The Speech of Thang	173—176	84—86
仲虺之诰	Book II. The Announcement of Chung-Hwuy	Book II. The Announcement of *K*ung-Hui	177—183	86—89
汤诰	Book III. The Announcement of T'ang	Book III. The Announcement of Thang	184—190	89—91
伊训	Book IV. The Instructions of E	Book IV. The Instructions of Î	191—198	92—95
太甲上	Book V. T'ae Kea. Part I	Book V. The Thâi *K*iâ [Section 1]	199—204	95—97
太甲中	Book V. T'ae Kea. Part II	[Section 2]	205—208	97—99
太甲下	Book V. T'ae Kea. Part III	[Section 3]	209—212	99—100
咸有一德	Book VI. Both Possessed Pure Virtue	Book VI. The Common Possession of Pure Virtue	213—219	100—103
盤庚上	Book VII. Pwan-Kang. Part I	Book VII. The Pan-Kăng [Section 1]	220—232	103—107
盤庚中	Book VII. Pwan-Kang. Part II	[Section 2]	233—242	108—110
盤庚下	Book VII. Pwan-Kang. Part III	[Section 3]	243—247	111—112
说命上	Book VIII. The Charge to Yue. Part I	Book VIII. The Charge to Yüeh [Section 1]	248—253	112—115
说命中	Book VIII. The Charge to Yue. Part II	[Section 2]	254—258	115—116
说命下	Book VIII. The Charge to Yue. Part III	[Section 3]	259—263	116—118
高宗肜日	Book IX. The Day of the Supplementary Sacrifice of Kaou-Tsung	Book IX. The Day of the Supplementary Sacrifice to Kâo ʒung	264—267	118—119
西伯戡黎	Book X. The Chief of the West's Conquest of Le	Book X. The Chief of the West's Conquest of Lî	268—272	120—121
微子	Book XI. The Viscount of Wei	Book XI. The Count of Wei	273—279	121—123
周书	**Part V. The Books of Chow**	**Part V. The Books of *K*âu**	**281—630**	**124—272**

书名与篇名	1865 年版英译名	1879 年版英译名	页码（1865）	页码（1879）
泰誓上	Book I. The Great Declaration. Part I	Book I. The Great Declaration [Section 1]	281—288	124—127
泰誓中	Book I. The Great Declaration. Part II	[Section 2]	289—293	127—129
泰誓下	Book I. The Great Declaration. Part III	[Section 3]	294—299①	129—130
牧誓	Book II. The Speech at Muh	Book II. The Speech at Mû	300—305	131—132
武成	Book III. The Successful Completion of the War	Book III. The Successful Completion of the War	306—319	133—137
洪范	Book IV. The Great Plan	Book IV. The Great Plan	320—344	137—149
旅獒	Book V. The Hounds of Leu	Book V. The Hounds of Lü	345—350	149—151
金縢	Book VI. The Metal-bound *Coffer*	Book VI. The Metal-bound Coffer	351—361②	151—156
大诰	Book VII. The Great Announcement	Book VII. The Great Announcement	362—375	156—161
微子之命	Book VIII. The Charge to the Viscount of Wei	Book VIII. The Charge to the Count of Wei	376—380③	161—163
康诰	Book IX. The Announcement to *the Prince of* K'ang④	Book IX. The Announcement to the Prince of Khang	381—398	164—171

① 理雅各在 1865 年《中国经典》第三卷，第 297—299 页附加了清儒江声重构的这篇书的经文。理雅各的目的是批评这一重构，质疑它对儒家传统的价值，但同时也表明某些中国学者认为这篇经文有文本问题。对于《尚书》中某些篇的真伪，理雅各在《周书》的某些篇末常常予以指出，见下文注释。

② 在这篇书末，理雅各附加了宋儒王柏（王鲁斋）对这篇书的质疑文字（只有中文，没有英译文，表明理雅各关于此篇真伪问题持保留意见），见《中国经典》第三卷，第 361 页。这段文字源自王柏的著作《王鲁斋书疑》，它质疑了《尚书》中若干篇的真伪问题，这是理雅各在翻译《周书》时开始认真考虑的问题。理雅各在接下来数篇书的末尾常常参考此书。

③ 理雅各在这篇书末再次引用了王柏对这篇书真伪的质疑文字，见《中国经典》第三卷，第 380 页。

④ 斜体字是中文篇名中没有的，理雅各的这一翻译样式借自钦定本《圣经》。

续表

书名与篇名	1865 年版英译名	1879 年版英译名	页码（1865）	页码（1879）
酒诰	Book X. The Announcement about Drunke-nness	Book X. The Announcement about Drunkenness	399—412	171—179
梓材	Book XI. The Timber of the Tsze Tree	Book XI. The Timber of the Rottlera	413—419	179—181
召诰	Book XII. The Announcement of *the Duke of* Shao	Book XII. The Announcement of the Duke of Shâo	420—433①	181—188
洛诰	Book XIII. The Announcement Concerning Lo	Book XIII. The Announcement Concerning Lo	434—452	188—195
多士	Book XIV. The Numerous Officers	Book XIV. The Numerous Officers	453—463	196—200
无逸	Book XV. Against Luxurious Ease	Book XV. Against Luxurious Ease	464—473	200—205
君奭	Book XVI. Prince Shih	Book XVI. The Prince Shih	474—486	205—210
蔡仲之命	Book XVII. The Charge to Chung of Ts'ae	Book XVII. The Charge to *K*ung of ʒhâi	487—491	211—213
多方	Book XVIII. Numerous Regions	Book XVIII. The Numerous Regions	492—507	213—219
立政	Book XIX. The Establishment of Government	Book XIX. The Establishment of Government	508—522	219—225
周官	Book XX. The Officers of Chow	Book XX. The Officers of *K*âu	523—534	226—231
君陈	Book XXI. Keun-Ch'in	Book XXI. The *K*ün-*K*hăn	535—543	231—234
顾命	Book XXII. The Testamentary Charge	Book XXII. The Testamentary Charge	544—561②	234—242
康王之诰	Book XXIII. The Announcement of King K'ang	Book XXIII. The Announcement of King Khang	562—568	243—245

① 理雅各第三次引用王柏对这篇书真伪的质疑文字，见《中国经典》第三卷，第 433 页。不同的是，它还评论了下一篇《洛诰》的经文。
② 理雅各第四次引用王柏对这篇书真伪的质疑文字，见《中国经典》第三卷，第 561 页。

书名与 篇名	1865 年版英译名	1879 年版英译名	页码 （1865）	页码 （1879）
毕命	Book XXIV. The Charge to *the Duke of* Peih	Book XXIV. The Charge to the Duke of Pî	569—577	245—249
君牙	Book XXV. Keun-Ya	Book XXV. The *Kün*-yâ	578—582	250—251
冏命	Book XXVI. The Charge to Keung	Book XXVI. The Charge to *Kh*iung	583—587	252—253
吕刑	Book XXVII. *The Prince of* Leu upon Punishments	Book XXVII. The Marquis of Lü on Punishments	588—612[1]	254—264
文侯之命	Book XXVIII. The Charge to Prince Wan	Book XXVIII. The Charge to the Marquis Wăn	613—620	265—267
费誓	Book XXIX. The Speech at Pe	Book XXIX. The Speech at Pî	621—625	267—270
秦誓	Book XXX. The Speech of *the Duke of* Ts'in	Book XXX. The Speech of (the Marquis of) *Kh*in[2]	626—630	270—272

---

[1] 理雅各第五次引用王柏对这篇书真伪的质疑文字，见《中国经典》第三卷，第 612 页。由于这篇经文在多个方面都有争议，这是理雅各引用的关于质疑一篇书真伪篇幅最长的文字。

[2] 这里标题中加括号似乎与理雅各的体例不一致。

附录二

理雅各《诗经》三译本比较表 ①

中文名称②	1871/1876 年版译名	1879 年版译名	页码（1871）	页码（1876）	页码（1879）
颂 ③	**Part IV. Odes of the Temple and the Altar**	**Part IV. Odes of the Temple and the Altar**	**569—647**	**350—391**	**299—346**
商颂 ④	Book III. The Sacrificial Odes of Shang	I. The Sacrificial Odes of Shang	631—647	384—391	303—313
那 ⑤	Na ⑥	The Nâ ⑦	631—633	384—385	304—305
烈祖	Lëeh tsoo	The Lieh ʒû	634—635	385—386	305—306
玄鸟	Heuen nëaou	The Hsûan Niâo	636—638	386—387	307—308
长发	Ch'ang fah	The *Khang* Fâ	638—643	387—389	308—311

① 1871 年散文体分诗节译本（*The She-King*, 1871）；1876 年韵律体分诗节译本（*The She King* or *The Book of Ancient Poetry*, 1876）；1879 年散文体分段选译（*The Shih King*, 1879）

② 这里的编次不是理雅各 1871、1876 年译本所用的《诗经》标准编次，而是他 1879 年译本的编次。在 1879 年译本中，理雅各把最后一部分放置在最前，然后只选择了那些有"宗教意义"的诗篇。因此，那些了解标准本《诗经》的读者会意识到，理雅各在这个译本对这部儒经做了非同寻常的改变。

③ 《诗经》主要有四个部分，理雅各称之为"Part I""Part II"等。这些部分的汉字和译文及其在译本中的相应页码，用黑体显示。

④ 理雅各《诗经》译本的每个部分中都有许多卷（Books）。为使这些卷的标题区别于每个部分的标题，所有信息都用粗宋体，字号大小正常。

⑤ 每篇诗的标题及其相关信息不以任何方式加亮或强调。但是，有些诗合称"……之什"（因为其中通常包含 10 首诗，有时候多于 10 首）。标题"……之什"用粗楷体。

⑥ 通常情况下，1871 年译本每篇诗的篇名与 1876 年相同，但 1876 年译本中加有定冠词"The"，在两个译本中都用斜体。若这两个译本每篇诗的译名有任何其他的差异，都会用附注来说明其变化。

⑦ 这里若只写诗的篇名，就说明理雅各是翻译了整个诗篇。但理雅各 1879 年《诗经》译本的一个显著特征是，他有时只翻译一篇诗的某些章。若出现这样的情况，我将明确他选译了哪些章。

续表

中文名称	1871/1876 年版译名	1879 年版译名	页码（1871）	页码（1876）	页码（1879）
殷武	Yin woo	The Yin Wû	643—647	390—391	311—313
周颂	Book I. Sacrificial Odes of Chow	II. The Sacrificial Odes of Kâu	569—610	350—372	313—336
清庙之什	**The Decade of Ts'ing mëaou**①	**The First Decade, or that of *Kh*ing Miào**	569—581	350—356	313—320
清庙	Ts'ing mëaou	The *Kh*ing Miâo	569	350—351	313—314
维天之命	Wei Tëen che ming②	The Wei Thien *K*ih Ming	570—571	351	314—315
维清	Wei ts'ing	The Wei *Kh*ing	571	352	315
烈文	Lëeh wăn	The Lieh Wăn	572—573	352—353	315—316
天作	Tëen tsoh	The Thien ꝛo	574	353	316
昊天有成命	Haou T'ëen yëw shing ming③	The Hâo Thien yû *Kh*ăng Ming	575	353	316—317
我将	Wo tsëang	The Wo *K*iang	575—576	354	317
时迈	She mae	The Shih Mài	577—578	354—355	317—318
执竞	Chih king	The *K*ih *K*ing	578—579	355—356	319
思文	Sze wăn	The Sze Wăn	580—581	356	319—320
臣工之什	**[ii.] The Decade of Shin Kung**④	**The Second Decade, or that of *Kh*ăn Kung**	582—595	357—363	320—328

① 1876 年译本写的是 "Section I. Decade of Ts'ing Meaou"。
② 1876 年译本包括一个英语译文和一个拉丁语译文，后者由孖沙（W. T. Mercer）翻译。
③ 这里 "成" 字的拼写是 "成" 的粤语发音，而非现在所谓的普通话发音。
④ 1876 年译本写的是 "Section II. The Decade of Shin Kung"。

续表

中文名称	1871/1876 年版译名	1879 年版译名	页码（1871）	页码（1876）	页码（1879）
臣工	Shin-kung①	The *Kh*ăn Kung	582—583	357	320—321
噫嘻	E he	The Î Hsî	584	357—358	321—322
振鹭	Chin loo	The *K*âu Lû②	585	358	322
丰年	Fung nëen	The Făng Nien	586	358—359	323
有瞽	Yëw koo	The Yû Kû	587	359	323—324
潜③	Ts'een④	The *Kh*ien	588	359—360	324—325
雝	Yung	The Yung	589—590	360—361	325—326
载见	Tae hëen⑤	The ӡâi Hsien	591—592	361	326—327
有客	Yëw k'ih	The Yû Kho	592—593	361—362	327
武	Woo	The Wû	594—595	362—363	328
闵予小子之什	[iii.] The Decade of Min Yu Seaou-Tsze⑥	**The Third Decade, or that of Min Yü Hsiâo ӡze**	596—610	364—372	328—336

① 1871 年译本在两个汉字的拼写之间是不常加连字符的，所以 1876 年译本中就没有这个连字符。注意这里拼写从"Shin"变为"*Kh*ăn"。理雅各一定是意识到了他过去的拼写或发音错误。

② 把"振"拼写为"Kâu"是不正确的。《诗经》中也没有其他可以如此拼写的一篇诗，似乎也不可能是誊写错误，不知为什么 1879 年译本中会有这样一个不当的拼写。

③ 1871 年译本中这篇诗的篇名以及正文第五个字印刷错误（《中国经典》第四卷，第 588 页），但在注释中这个字印刷正确（《中国经典》第四卷，第 589 页）。

④ 这个篇名中第一个"e"应该拼写为"ë"，1876 年译本拼写正确。

⑤ 这个篇名有一个明显的印刷错误："Tae"应该为"Tsae"。

⑥ 篇名最后两个单词之间的连字符在 1876 年译本中无。另外，"seaou"应该写成"sëaou"，但是 1871、1876 年译本中都没有这样写，但目录中第一篇诗篇名写的是"sëaou"（《中国经典》第四卷，第 x 页），1876 年译本第一篇诗篇名也是这样写的。

中文名称	1871/1876 年版译名	1879 年版译名	页码（1871）	页码（1876）	页码（1879）
闵予小子	Min yu①	The Min Yü	596	364	328—329
访落	Fang loh	The Fang Lo	597—598	364—365	329
敬之	King che	The *King Kih*	598—599	365—366	329—330
小毖	Sëaou pe	The Hsiâo Pî	599—600	366—367	330—331
载芟	Tsai shoo	The ʒâi Shû②	600—603	367—368	331—333
良耜	Lëang sze	The Liang Sze	603—605	369	332—333
丝衣	Sze e	The Sze Î	605—606	370	333—334
酌	Choh	The Ko	606—607	370—371	334—335
桓	Hwan	The Hwan	607—608	371	335
赉	Lae	The Lâi	608	371	335—336
般	Pan or Pwan③	The Pan	609—610	372	336
鲁颂	Book II. Praise-Odes of Loo	III. The Praise Odes of Lû	611—630	373—383	336—346

① 虽然这篇诗的中文名有四个汉字，但理雅各 1871 和 1879 年译本中只拼写了前两个汉字，而 1876 年译本中则全部拼写了出来。
② 我查阅的相关词典中这个字都写作"芟"，发音为 shān。但理雅各在三个译本中给出的是另一种读音。
③ 1876 年译本是"The Pan"，没有标明 1871 年译本的另一个读音。

续表

中文名称	1871/1876 年版译名	1879 年版译名	页码（1871）	页码（1876）	页码（1879）
泮水①	Pwan-shwuy②	The Phan Shui	616—620	376—378	337—340
閟宫	Peih kung	The Pî Kung	620—630	378—383	341—346
小雅	**Part II. Minor Odes of the Kingdom**	**The Minor Odes of the Kingdom③**	**245—425**	**189—283**	**347—376**
鹿鸣之什	**Book I. Decade of Luh Ming④**	**The First Decade, or that of Lû-ming**	245—267	189—202	347—349
伐木⑤	Fah muh	Ode 5, Stanza 1. The Fâ Mû	253—254⑥	194—195⑦	347
天保	T'ëen paou	Ode 6. The Thien Pâo	255—258	196—197	347—349
杕杜	Te too	Ode 9, Stanza 4. The Tî tû⑧	366	201⑨	349
祈父之什	**Book IV. Decade of K'e Foo⑩**	**The Fourth Decade, or that of Khi fû**	298—329	219—231	349—358
斯干	Sze kan	Ode 5, Stanzas 5 to 9. The Sze Kan	305—307	223	349—351

① 《泮水》是《鲁颂》的第三篇。理雅各略去前两篇，是因为他认为前两篇没有宗教元素。
② 这里的连字符 1876 年译本中没有。
③ 理雅各在 1879 年译本中为这一部分加了一个副标题："阐明作者及其时代宗教观念和宗教实践的诗节和诗篇"（Pieces and Stanzas illustrating the Religious Views and Practices of the Writers and their Times.）
④ 注意 1871 年译本自此之下理雅各省略了"Book"。
⑤ 理雅各的选择性现在变得更激进了。每部分所选诗篇的数量和所选的章只在 1879 年译本下标明。
⑥ 这里标明的页码只有第一章。下同。
⑦ 这里标明的页码只有第一章。下同。
⑧ 不知第二个"t"理雅各为什么不大写。这似乎与他 1879 年译本的体例不一致。
⑨ 这篇诗有两个译本，第二个是拉丁译本，由孖沙翻译。
⑩ 1876 年译本中这两个汉字的拼写之间有连字符。

续表

中文名称	1871/1876 年版译名	1879 年版译名	页码（1871）	页码（1876）	页码（1879）
无羊	Woo yang	Ode 6, Stanza 4. The Wû Yang	309	224	351
节南山	Tsëeh nan shan	Ode 7. The *Kieh* Nan Shan	309—314	224—226	351—353
正月	Ching yueh	Ode 8, Stanzas 4, 5, and 7. The *Kâng* yüeh①	316—318	227	354—355
十月之交	Shih yueh che këaou	Ode 9. The Shih yüeh *kih Kiâo*	320—325	229—230	355—357
雨无正	Yu woo ching	Ode 10, Stanzas 1 and 3. The Yü wû *Kâng*	325—327	230—231	257—258
小旻之什	**Book V. Decade of Seaou Min②**	**The Fifth Decade, or that of Hsiâo Min**	330—359	232—246	358—364
小旻	Sëaou min	Ode 1, Stanzas 1, 2, and 3. The Hsiâo Min	330—331	232	358—359
小宛	Sëaou yuen③	Ode 2, Stanzas 1, 2 and 5.④ The Hsiâo Yüan	333—335	233—234	359
小弁	Sëaou pwan⑤	Ode 3, Stanzas 1 and 3. The Hsiâo Pan	336—337	234—235	360
巧言	Keaou yen⑥	Ode 4, Stanza 1. The *Khi*âo Yen	340	236—237	361
巷伯	Hëang pih	Ode 6, Stanzas 5 and 6. The Hsiang Po	348	240	361
大东	Ta fung⑦	Ode 9. The Tâ Tung	353—356	243—244	362—364

① 这里第二个汉字的拼写用的是小写，因为这两个汉字是一个词组，指阴历的第一个月。
② 这个篇名中的"e"应该是"ë"，但理雅各经常丢掉其中的变音符。
③ "宛"在现代汉语中读 wǎn，但古代读 yuān，指楚国的一个地方。
④ 这个篇名只指前两章，但第五章也被收录到了理雅各 1879 年译本。因此，1871 和 1876 年译本的参考页码包含了第五章。
⑤ 现代汉语中"弁"读 biàn，但在这篇诗中读 pán。
⑥ 这个篇名中的"e"应该写成"ë"，理雅各在 1876 年译本中纠正了这个错误。
⑦ "fung"所对应的汉字应读 dōng；理雅各在 1876 年译本中纠正了这个错误，写作"Ta tung"。

续表

中文名称	1871/1876 年版译名	1879 年版译名	页码（1871）	页码（1876）	页码（1879）
北山之什	**Book VI. The Decade of Pih Shan**	**The Sixth Decade, or that of Pei Shan**	360—385	347—260	364—373
小明	Sëaou ming	Ode 3, Stanzas 1, 4 and 5. The Hsiâo Ming	363—366	249—250	364—365
楚茨	Ts'oo ts'ze	Ode 5. The Khû ʒhze	368—373	252—255	365—368
信南山	Sin nan shan	Ode 6. The Hsin Nan Shan	373—376	255—256	368—370
甫田	P'oo t'ëen	Ode 7. The Phû Thien①	376—379	257—258	370—372
大田	Ta t'ëen	Ode 8. The Tâ Thien	380—382	258—259	372—373
桑扈之什	**Book VII. Decade of Sang Hoo**	**The Seventh Decade, or that of Sang Hû**	386—408	261—273	373—376
桑扈	Sang-hoo	Ode 1, Stanza 1. The Sang Hû	386	261	373—374
宾之初筵	Pin che tsoo yen	Ode 6, Stanzas 1 and 2. The Pin Kih Khû Yen	395—397	265—267	374—375
都人士之什	**Book VIII. The Decade of Too Jin Sze**	**The Eighth Decade, or that of Po Hwâ②**	409—425	274—283	376
白华	Pih hwa	Ode 5, Stanzas 1 and 2. The Po Hwâ	416	278	376
大雅	**Part III. Greater Odes of the Kingdom**	**The Major Odes of the Kingdom③**	**427—567**	**284—349**	**377—429**

---

① 1879 年译本中，理雅各把这个篇名变成了与 Fǔtián 对应的读音，但《上海辞书出版社》（1980 年版，第 56 页）保留了这篇诗的读音 Pǔtián。

② 理雅各这里误将"都人士之什"这部分的名称写成了其中一篇诗的名称了。

③ 理雅各为这部分加了一个副标题："Pieces and Stanzas illustrating the Religious Views and Practices of the Writers and their Times"（阐明作者及其时代宗教观念和宗教实践的诗节和诗篇）。

中文名称	1871/1876 年版译名	1879 年版译名	页码（1871）	页码（1876）	页码（1879）
文王之什	**Book I. Decade of King Wan**①	**The First Decade, or that of Wăn Wang**	427—464	284—301	377—396
文王	Wăn wang	Ode 1. The Wăn Wang	427—431	284—286	377—380
大明	Ta ming	Ode 2. The Tâ Ming	432—436	286—289	380—382
绵	Mëen	Ode 3. The Mien	437—441	289—291	382—385
棫朴	Yih p'oh	Ode 4, Stanzas 1 or 2. The Yî Pho②	442—443	291—292	386
旱麓	Han luh	Ode 5. The Han Lû	444—446	292—293	386—387
思齐	Sze chae③	Ode 6. The Sze *Kâi*	446—448	293—294	387—388
皇矣	Hwang e	Ode 7. The Hwang Î	448—455	294—297	389—393
下武	Hëa Woo④	Ode 9. The Hsiâ Wû	458—460	298—299	393—394
文王有声	Wăn wang yëw shing	Ode 10. The Wăn Wang yû Shăng	460—464	299—301	394—396
生民之什	**Book II. Decade of Shang Min**	**The Second Decade, or that of Shăng Min**	465—504	302—320	396—410
生民	Shăng min⑤	Ode 1. The Shăng Min	464—472	302—307⑥	396—399

① 1876 年译本理雅各用的拼写是 "Wăn"。

② 1879 年译本这个篇名两个汉字的拼写显然不正确。第一个汉字应该读作 "yù" 或 "yû"，第二个汉字应该读作 "pǔ" 或 "puh"。

③ 篇名中第二个汉字用的是旧式的拼写，理雅各明白这一点。1876 年译本中，理雅各在两个汉字的拼写之间加了连字符。

④ 1876 年译本中，字母 "W" 没有大写。

⑤ 1876 年译本中，字母 "a" 上没有变音符。

⑥ 1876 年译本中，这篇诗有理雅各两个侄子的两个韵律体译文。

续表

中文名称	1871/1876 年版译名	1879 年版译名	页码（1871）	页码（1876）	页码（1879）
行苇	Hing wei①	Ode 2. The Hsin Wei②	472—475	307—308	399—401
既醉	Ke tsuy	Ode 3. The *Kî* ʒui	475—478	308—309	401—402
凫鹥	Hoo e	Ode 4. The Hû Î	479—481	309—310	402—403
假乐	Këa loh	Ode 5, Stanza 1. The *Kiâ* Lo	481	311	404
卷阿	K'euen o	Ode 8. The *Khüan* Â③	491—495	315—317	404—407
民劳	Min laou	Ode 9, Stanza 1. The Min Lâo	495	317	407
板	Pan	Ode 10. The Pan	499—504	319—320	408—410
荡之什	**Book III. Decade of Tang**	**The Third Deace, or that of Tang**	505—567	321—349	411—429
荡	Tang	Ode 1. The Tang	505—510	321—323	410—412
抑	Yih	Ode 2. The Yî	510—518	323—327	413—417
桑柔	Sang yëw④	Ode 3, Stanzas 1, 2, 3, 4, and 7. The Sang Zâu⑤	519—521 and 523	327—328	417—419

---

① 1876 年译本中，第一个汉字的拼写变成了"Hăng"，可能是"行"在这个位置正常的粤语发音。

② 理雅各这里有误：第一个汉字应该拼写为"Hsing"。

③ 第一个汉字的拼写应该是"Küan"，而非"*Khüan*"，因为在拼音体系中它有一个正常的"j"音，而不是卷舌的"zh"音。

④ 第二个汉字的拼音应该相当于"*róu*"，但在三个译本中都拼错了。

⑤ 理雅各认识到他错拼了第二个汉字的发音，但 1879 年译本中应该拼为"Zou"，而非"Zâu"。

续表

中文名称	1871/1876 年版译名	1879 年版译名	页码（1871）	页码（1876）	页码（1879）
云汉	Yun han①	Ode 4. The Yun Han	528—534	330—334	419—423
崧高	Sung kaou	Ode 5, Stanzas 1, 2, and 4. The Sung Kâo	535—536 and 538	334—335	423—424
烝民	Ching min②	Ode 6, Stanzas 1 and 7. The Kăng Min	541 and 544—545	336 and 338	425—426
韩奕	Han yih	Ode 7, Stanzas 1 and part of 3. The Han Yî	546 and 548	339—341	426
江汉	Këang Han	Ode 8, Stanzas 4 and 5. The *K*iang Han	554	343—344	427—428
瞻卬	Chen jang③	Ode 10, Stanzas 1, 5, 6, and 7. The *K*an Zang④	559—560 and 562—564	346—348	428—429
召旻	Shaou min	Ode 11, Stanzas 1 and 2. The Shâo Min	564—565	348—349	429
国风	**Part I. Lessons from the States**	**Lessons from the States⑤**	**1—243**	**58—188**	**430—446**
召南	Book II. The Odes of Shao and the South⑥	Book II. The Odes of Shâo and the South	20—37	67—75	430—432

---

① 理雅各在 1876 年译本中把篇名中的"H"大写了。
② 1871 和 1876 译本中，第一个汉字都被拼写错了。
③ 1871 年和 1876 年译本中这里有两个拼写错误。第一个汉字拼写中的元音应该是"a"，第二个汉字的拼写开头不应该有辅音，应该是"ang"。
④ 在 1879 年译本中理雅各纠正了第一个错误，但第二个错误仍然保留了下来。
⑤ 1879 年译本中附加了一个副标题："Odes and Stanzas illustrating the Religious Views and Practices of the Writers and their Times"。
⑥ 这一部分里"Book"的角色就像"Decade"，因此被当作"Decade"对待。但事实上，《国风》中有许多部分都超过 10 篇以上。

续表

中文名称	1871/1876 年版译名	1879 年版译名	页码（1871）	页码（1876）	页码（1879）
采蘩	Ts'ae fan	Ode 2. The *Zhâi* Fan	22	68	431—432
采苹	Ts'ae pin①	Ode 4. The *Zhâi* Pin	25	69	432
邶风	Book III. The Odes of P'ei	Book III. The Odes of Phei	38—72	76—92	433—434
日月	Jeh yueh	Ode 4. The *Zǎh* Yüeh	44—46	80	433—434
北门②	Pih mun③	Ode 15, Stanza 1. The Pei Măn	65	89	434
鄘	Book IV. The Odes of Yung	Book IV. The Odes of Yung	73—90	93—101	434—437
柏舟	Peh chow	Ode 1. The Pai *Kâu*	73—74	93—94	434—435
君子偕老	Keun-tsz' këae laou④	Ode 3, Stanza 2. The *Kün-ʒze Kieh Lâo*	76—77	95	435—436
定之方中	Ting che fang chung	Ode 6, Stanzas 1 and 2. The *Ting kih fang Kung*	81—82	96—97	436—437
卫	Book V. The Odes of Wei	Book V. The Odes of Wei	91—109	102—110	437—438
氓	Măng	Ode 4, Stanzas 1 and 2. The Măng	97—98	105	437—438
王	Book VI. The Odes of the Royal Domain	Book VI. The Odes of the Royal Domain	110—123	111—118	438—440

---

① 这里 1871 和 1876 年译本中，第二个汉字应该拼为 "p'in"，但理雅各略去了撇号。1879 年译本中是否需要这个撇号，我们不清楚，因为有其他的办法来标示送气音。

② 1871 年译本中这里的 "北" 字左边有 "土" 字旁，这不正常。

③ 第二个汉字被拼写为 "mun"（而不是 "*mén*"），事实上是 "门" 的粤语发音。理雅各在开始学习官话之前，学习和使用了许多年的粤语。需要指出的是，他在 1879 年译本中纠正了这一拼写。

④ 1876 年译本中，第二个汉字的拼写是 "tsze"，也许说明 1871 年译本中的拼写是一个排印错误。

中文名称	1871/1876 年版译名	1879 年版译名	页码（1871）	页码（1876）	页码（1879）
黍离	Shoo li①	Ode 1, Stanza 1. The Shû Lî	110	111	439
大车	Ta keu	Ode 9, Stanzas 1 and 3. The Tâ *Kü*②	121	117—118	440
唐	Book X. The Odes of T'ang	Book X. The Odes of Thang	174—189	147—156	440—442
鸨羽	Paou yu	Ode 8, Stanza 1. The Pâo Yü	183	151—152	440—441
葛生	Koh sang	Ode 11. The Ko Shǎng	186—187	154—155	441—442
秦	Book XI. The Odes of Ts'in	Book XI. The Odes of *Kh*in	190—204	157—166	442—444
黄鸟	Hwang nëaou③	Ode 6, Stanza 1. The Hwang Niâo	198—199	162—163	443—444
豳	Book XV. The Odes of Pin	Book XV. The Odes of Pin	226—243	180—188	444—446
七月	Ts'ih yueh	Ode 1, Stanza 8. The *Kh*î Yüeh	232—233	183	444—446

---

① 1876 年译本中理雅各把第二个汉字误拼成了 "le"。

② 1879 年译本中，第二个汉字最后一个元音似乎不正确，应该是类似 "-eh" 的拼写。

③ 1876 年译本中，这篇诗有两个韵律体译文，第二个译文的译者是孖沙。

中国圣书（一）

序　言 xiii

在为本卷书中的《书经》译本书写序之前，我认为最好简要介绍一下所谓中国宗教的圣书。中国的三大宗教是儒教、道教和佛教。

一

我先就佛教说几句。翻译佛经不属于我的职责范围，我也没必要多说。据说佛教是在公元前 3 世纪传入中国的；但直到公元 50—75 年才在中国获得权威认可。[①] 随着佛经陆续从印度传入中国，佛经也被逐渐翻译成中文。不久之后，中国就拥有了一整套完备的汉文大藏经。[②] 由梵文翻译来的中译本构成了中国佛教典籍的主要部分，尽管其中也包括许多中国人的原创作品。

二

儒教是中国的正统宗教，其得名于一位圣人，即生活在公元前 xiv

---

① 我不确定佛教引入中国的时间是否在公元前，《隋书·经籍志》中有关于中国佛教史的一篇文章，其编者说，汉朝（始于公元前 202 年）之前，中国未闻佛教。编者还提到了一些相反的说法（"或云"），并且说明了对方主张的原因。（"推寻典籍，自汉已上，中国未传。或云久以流布，遭秦之世，所以湮灭。"——译者注）现在各方一致认为佛教书籍是在公元 60—70 年引入中国的。

② 毕尔《汉文佛典纪要》（ *Catena of Buddhist Scriptures from the Chinese* ）第 1—2 页："中国第一部完整的汉文大藏经可追溯至 7 世纪；第二部更大的大藏经称《南藏》，1410 年刊刻而成；第三部大藏经称《北藏》，1590 年刻成，1723 年重修、增订。"

5 世纪到 6 世纪的孔子。事实上，孔子既不是儒教的创立者，也不是传授儒教教理、规定儒教崇拜形式的第一人。孔子说他是"述而不作，信而好古"；故《中庸》（据说为孔子孙子所作）第三十章说："仲尼祖述尧舜，宪章文武"。

　　孔子在完成他自认为的使命时，并没有根据自己对古人观点的理解著书立说。他只是与弟子畅谈古人的观点，从其弟子那里我们知道了许多孔子说的话。他对古代观点和实践的描述可能不自觉地会带上了其个人的思想色彩。但他最喜欢的教学方法是将弟子的注意力引到中国古代文献上去。他既不会肯定也不会引用一些无法得到权威公认的文献。他自己曾说（《论语·八佾第三》第九章）能言夏代和殷代之礼，但他没有这么做，因为周代这两个朝代的封国（杞国和宋国）没有足够的文献记载和学者，不足以证实他的话。甚至认为他根据那个时代尚存的各种文献编纂了《书》《诗》以及其他典籍也是错误的。那时有一些最古老的文献已经消亡。他对那些留下来的文献进行研究，并劝告他的弟子也要研究它们，这均有助于典籍的保存。他对那些文献意义的书写或解说，我们应该以崇敬的态度接受；要是这些经孔子之手的典籍能完好无损地流传下来，我们外国人也有可能像孔子那样学习中国古代的宗教。我们现在用的本子将与孔子当时用的本子一样。不幸的是，在孔子去世之后，大部分古籍都散佚损毁了。然而，我们至今还拥有这么多的古籍，我们有理由心怀感激。因为没有任何一个国家的古籍能以如此完好的状态流传下来。

　　但是读者必须记住，中国的古籍并不自称受到了启发，也不包含我们所说的启示（revelation）。历史学家、诗人等撰写这些作品，只是有感而发。一篇古诗里也许偶尔会包含上帝说的话，但是我们只能理解这些话是为了使读者注意其前面的内容。*我们还读到天（Heaven）扶植古代伟大的君主和老师，并且以各种方式帮助他们完成自己的事业；**但是所有这一切和现在任何国家的有宗教信仰的人从上天那里接收到的给自己以及他人的引导、帮助与指导并无二样。然而，尽管中国古代的书籍并没有宣称包含任何神启，但涉及宗教观点和实践的内容却很多；读者正可根据这些内容，自己勾勒出早期中国宗教的轮廓。现在我要说明这些古籍是什么。

第一部，也是最重要的一部，是《书》（*The Book of Historical Documents*），自汉朝（始于前 202）以来，开始改称《书经》。《书》记载的内容上至尧在位时期（前 24 世纪），下至周襄王时期（前 651—前 619）。《书》中最早几篇与其描述的事件并非在同时代产生，但其他篇从公元前 22 世纪开始就是了。读者将读到这部书完整无删节的译本。

第二部，几乎与《书》同等重要，是《诗》（*The Book of Poetry*）。《诗》一共有三百零五篇，其中五篇属于商朝（也称为殷，前 1766— xvi 前 1123）。其余诸篇属于周朝，从周文王（生于前 1231）到周定王在位时期（前 606—前 586）。《诗经》分为四部分，最后一部分是《颂》。其他部分中的许多篇也具有宗教性质，但更多的是描述了当时的礼仪、习俗和事件，因此没有包含进本卷书中。本卷书中的所有诗歌，阐明了作者的宗教观点，记叙了同时期的宗教活动。

第三部是《易》（*The Book of Changes*）。孔子非常重视《易》，认为学《易》能够让人纠正自己的品行，使其品格完美。（《论语·述而第七》第十七章）《易》常被外国人称为中国最古老的书。但事实并非如此。无论是孔子时期的《易》，还是现存的《易》，文

---

* 参见《诗经·大雅·皇矣》："帝谓文王……" ——译者
** 参见《尚书·泰誓上》："天佑下民，作之君，作之师，惟其克相上帝，宠绥四方。" ——译者

本中均没有涉及早于文王时期的记载。确实，书中的八卦为伏羲所创。伏羲一般被认为是中华民族的创立者，他在历史年表中的位置大致被归在公元前 34 世纪。八卦继而增加为六十四卦。完整的线条（——）和断开的线条（— —）是形成这些图形的两个基本符号。这两个线条自相叠加，再相互叠加，就形成四个图形；在此基础上，用两个基本线条再以同样的过程叠加，就形成八个图形，即著名的八卦。把这一过程重复三次，便会相继得到十六、三十二和六十四个图形。图形中的线条以等差级数增加，公差为 1；图形的数量以几何级数增加，公比为 2。但是，伏羲为他的基本线条（一条完整的线条和一条断开的线条）赋予了什么思想；他为他的八卦赋予了什么含义；赋予了六十四卦什么含义——如果他自己真的创造了这么多图形；还有，为什么这些图形的数量止于六十四；——这些问题从他那里我们是无从知晓答案的。有理由认为夏商时期这六十四卦之后就有文辞，但这些文辞无一保存下来。可能是文王和他的儿子周公，采用了当时仍存世的文辞，并融合了他们自己对这些图形的解释。但是，只有文王与周公被认为是《易》之文辞的作者。据说，文王在商朝末年被商纣王囚禁，他手持六十四卦，为每卦附加了简短的文字，解释其意义，而这意义是他根据构成那一卦的两个八卦图形在他头脑中演绎出来的；在某些卦中，他还会附上在实际事务中应该怎么做的文辞，那些事务是这一卦的意义所针对的。周公为构成每卦的每条线附加了简短的文字，解释其意义。据说在大约 600 年后孔子开始参与解释《易》。人们认为孔子为《易》作了几篇传，旨在尝试解释伏羲八卦的起源，还有文王和周公的卦爻辞。卦画、文王和周公的卦爻辞、孔子的传，共同构成了《易》。

根据《书》，我们知道《易》从一开始就与占卜密切相关，这在中国古代的宗教活动占据了重要地位。这很好地解释了其晦涩、神

xvii

秘的特征；尽管语焉不详，但是书中有如此多形而上、形而下、道德和宗教话语，逐渐让学者着迷。而且，由于其在占卜上的使用，使得迷信残暴的秦始皇在公元前213年下诏烧毁一切儒学书籍时，它能得以幸免。《易》就这样完好无损地保留了下来，我会给出一个完整的译本。

此外，《易》还是宋朝哲学家汲取他们"无神论政治"（atheo- political）体系的源泉。我将在我的《易经》译本附录中概括说明这一体系，并尝试检验这些作者对《易经》的阐释是否正确。

第四部伟大的经典是《礼记》（*The Record of Rites*），但这只是古代中国（尤其是周朝）典章制度和仪式书籍的一种。它们被统称为"三礼"。一是《周礼》，又名《周官》，后一名称更加准确。《周礼》是一本记载周朝官制的书，一般认为是周公所作。如果不是周公所作，那毫无疑问的一点是，里面的内容来自当王朝由商更替到周时，周公为政府制定的制度规范。这些制度规范从周文王起一直延续到周武王时期。他根据周朝的国情设置了众部门，列举了每个部门的主要以及下属官员，并描述了其各自的职责。秦焚书后，这部书在公元前一世纪就几乎完全复原。毕瓯1851年在法国巴黎出版这部书的完整译本，译得很好。

"三礼"中的第二部书是《仪礼》，曾被翻译为"the Decorum Ritual"和"the Rules of Demeanour"。其复原的时间早于《周礼》，篇幅与《周礼》同等宏大。其内容是士在社会和政府各种场合应该遵循的行为规范。据我所知，现在它还没有被翻译成任何一门欧洲语言。

"三礼"中的第三部是《礼记》，比前两部篇幅更繁浩，也是成书于汉代。在公元前1世纪的时候，其篇目多达二百一十四篇，分为五个部分。当时的学者戴德将二百一十四篇缩减为八十五篇。戴德的侄子戴胜又将八十五篇缩减为四十六篇。在汉末又增添了三篇形成了四十九篇，长期被官方定为"五经"之一，这也就是我们如今见到的《礼记》。嘉略利（J. M. Callery）于 1853 年在都灵出版了一个删减版，译名为 "Lî Kî, ou Memorial des Rites, traduit pour la première fois du Chinois, et accompagné de notes, de commentaires, et du texte original"（《礼记》，首次由中文译成法文，并附有注释、评注和原文）。但是嘉略利的译本只翻译了四十九篇中的三十六篇，并且许多都是原文的缩减版。是否可能在《东方圣书》中完整翻译《礼记》？如果不能做到完整翻译，那么在选择部分内容时该遵循什么准则？这些问题有待进一步商议后决定。孔子对中国祭祀的思考及其背后蕴藏的思想在此书中多有体现，远超其他书。

但是不要忘了，这些礼仪书籍，并没能如更早的《书经》和《诗经》一般更多地揭示中国古代的宗教。这些书籍的内容属于周代，作为当时的记录不会追溯到周代以前，或是更远的尧舜时期。此外，这些书中记载的孔子的观点并不是第一手的，而是距离孔子死后五六百年的汉代学者汇编而成，我们也不能确定这些人有没有将自己的观点借孔子之口说出来，并对那些被认为——无论是或不是——孔子直系弟子的著作进行补充。

最后一部经为孔子所作。孔子称其为《春秋》（*The Spring and Autumn*），是孔子根据鲁国史记编撰的一部非常简略的编年史，记录了鲁国从公元前 722 年到公元前 481 年共 242 年的历史。但是对于"圣书"而言，其中没有多少信息可搜集；若是大费周章地检阅《春秋》三传（《左传》《公羊传》《穀梁传》），又得不偿失。其中《左传》最为重要，我 1872 年在香港出版的《春秋》译本中有其完整的翻译。

还有一部小书也被归在孔子名下，即《孝经》（*Classic of Filial*

Piety）。虽然无法与上面提到的五部经书齐名，但《孝经》是第一部孔子亲自以"经"命名的书——如果我们的信息来源可靠的话。这部作品并不像《春秋》那样直接出自孔子之手，而是以孔子和其弟子曾子之间的对话形式出现，可能是由曾子的弟子记录在册。多个朝代的皇帝都曾关注并且费尽心思为《孝经》做注，这是其他古代文献不曾有的。在我看来，《孝经》试图以孝德为本构建起一个宗教体系，而且在许多方面都容易招致批评。本卷也给出了《孝经》的译文。

　　这些经典书籍常常被称为"五经"和"四书"。"五经"上文已经分别谈到了。"四书"是四子书的缩写。第一本书是《论语》（*Discourses and Conversations*），主要是记录孔子及其与弟子间的对话。第二本书是《孟子》。孟子也许是孔子之后儒家最伟大的思想家和作者。我希望我能将这两本书的译文在《东方圣书》中呈现给大家。第三本书是《大学》（*Great Learning*），与《孝经》一样，它被认为是曾子所作。第四本书是《中庸》（*Doctrine of the Mean*），系孔子之孙，子思所作。然而，《大学》和《中庸》都取自《礼记》。我已于 1861 年完整地翻译出版了"四书"。

三

　　中国的第三个宗教是道教。与儒教一样是本土宗教，公认的创始 xxi
人是李耳，字伯阳，谥号聃。通常被称为老子，有人将其译为"the Old Philosopher"（老哲学家），有人将其译为"the Old Boy"（老男孩）。这个名字的得来源于一个传说。据说，老子的母亲怀胎 72 年才生下老子，所以老子一出生就满头白发。老子生于公元前 604 年，因此他比孔子大 50 到 60 岁左右。关于这两人之间会面和谈话的记述几乎都不可靠。

老子的体系常被英国作者称为理性主义（Rationalism）。但是，若真用理性主义之名，那么这一名称得以一种十分奇怪的意义去理解。老子的教义是"道"，但是"道"这个汉字的意义很难在英文中找到对等的表达。我们唯一可以了解老子思想的著作是《道德经》（*Classic of Tâo and Virtue*），这部著作篇幅不长。《道德经》法译版于 1842 年在巴黎出版，由已故的儒莲翻译，标题为 *Le Livre de la Voie et de la Vertu*。儒莲还对庄子以及其他道家学者十分感兴趣，他说："道无行、无思、无断、无智"，还说，"似乎不可能把道当作创造并主宰这个世界的原初理性（the Primordial Reason）、最高的智性（the Sublime Intelligence）。"

1868 年，广州的湛约翰博士出版了《道德经》的英译本，标题为《老子关于形而上学、政治和道德的思辨》（*The Speculations in Metaphysics, Polity, and Morality, of "The Old Philosopher"*）。湛约翰在他的英文译本中保留了"道"这个词，他说："我认为最好不要翻译'道'这个词，一则'道'一词直接延伸出了这一宗派之名——道家，二则没有一个英语词与'道'完全等同。有三个可能等同的词汇：the Way（道路）、Reason（理性）、the Word（言说）；但是这三个词都可能遭到反对。以词源学来看，'the Way'最接近道最原始的含义，在某一两章中道的含义似乎就是'道路'；但是这个词太唯物，无法达到翻译的目的。'Reason'似乎更像是有意识的存在（Being）具有的品质或属性，而'道'不是。我想用'逻各斯'（Logos）意义上的'the Word'来翻译'道'，但这是一个有争议的问题：中文里的这个'道'是最接近《新约》里'Logos'的一个词，但'Logos'与道之间究竟有多相似？"

《道德经》的另两个译本均为德文：一是史陶斯（Victor von

Strauss）的 "Lao-tsze's Tao Teh King, aus dem Chinesischen ins Deutsche übersetzt, eingeleitet, und commentirt"（莱比锡，1870），二是普郎克纳（Reinhold von Plänckner）的 "Lao-tse，Tao-Te-King，'Der Weg zur Tugend'"，也是在莱比锡出版。史陶斯紧趋儒莲，普郎克纳在处理原作时比较自由。尽管《道德经》已经有了这四个译本，分别用三种不同的欧洲语言阐释老子的意义，但是仍有出版一个新译本的空间，我将在合适的时候为读者提交这个新译本。只有对原文做深入和持久的研究，我们才能对"道"的意义达成一致意见。我不仅要翻译《道德经》，还要翻译《庄子》，庄子是道家早期最杰出的代表人物。

不管老子创立的道意蕴为何，道教随着历史的发展不断借鉴儒教和佛教的思想。在某些方面，它灌输一种高层次的道德，并发展成服务于迷信的一套怪诞的信仰和实践体系，意在养生和延年益寿。《太上感应篇》这部道教最流行的著作展现了这些实用的教导，此外也许在道教的其他一些著作中也有这样的教导。

本卷书中的《书经》译本与我 1865 年出版的《中国经典》第三 xxiii 卷中的《书经》译本基本相同。然而，我还是重新翻译了全文，尽管在这之前不仅有我自己的译本，以及更早的宋君荣（P. Gaubil）法语译本和麦都思博士（Dr. Medhurst）的英译本。相比之前，本卷书我引用了更多中国本土的注疏。经过十二年孜孜不倦潜心钻研中国经典，现在重新翻阅之前的译文，我几乎没有发现任何需要纠正的错误。只是改动了几处用词，以便使意义表达更加清晰。只有一种改动会让熟悉前一译本的读者感到震惊。在《书经》头几篇中多次出现用于尧舜的汉字"帝"，以及在第五部分第二十七篇中出现过一次的汉字"帝"，在我的前一个译本中被翻译为"emperor"；但在本卷中未翻译，而是直接用拼音转写。

　　在做这一改变之前，我考虑过我是否应该将《书》（以及《诗》）中全部的"帝"及其强化形式"上帝"翻译成"God"。宋君荣将大部分的"帝"都翻译成"le Seigneur"，把"上帝"翻译成"le Souverain Maître"，有时在其译文后用括号加上"Tî"或"Shang Tî"。麦都思将"帝"翻译为"the Supreme"或"the Supreme Ruler"，将"上帝"译为"the Supreme Ruler"。早在 25 年前我就认为中文的"帝"等同于我们的"God"，"上帝"也等同于我们的"God"，"上帝"中的"上"等同于英文中的"Supreme"。关于这一点，我一直以来都坚定不移，并且我在至今为止翻译出版的《中国经典》所有卷册中都将两者翻译为"God"。

xxiv　　在本卷书中我没有这样做，因为我认为《东方圣书》的目标是译者应该首先在不掺杂个人观念的情况下翻译这些文本。我自己认为"帝"的意义是"God"，我的这一观点是不是在"译名之争"（关于用合适的汉字翻译"God"和"Spirit"的争论）中形成的？处处都会碰到"God"一词的读者也许会更加重视中国的原始宗教。我是应该不译"帝"和"上帝"？还是说，我应该将其翻译为"Ruler"和"Supreme Ruler"，而不是"God"？我不明白应该选择走哪条路。

　　"天"在《中国经典》中随处可见，表示"至高无上的权力"（the Supreme Power），以全知全能的仁和义统治和管理着人类的一切事务。这一意义模糊的用语常常在同一个段落，甚至在同一句话中，与具有人格意义的"帝"和"上帝"互换。"天"和"帝"的写法完全不同。两者都在最古老的文字之列，并在后来作为声旁与其他汉字组合，构成新的汉字，虽然这些汉字的数量并不是很多。根据中国最古老的字典《说文解字》（成书于公元 100 年）的解释，"天"是由"一"和"大"两个汉字构成的会意字，意为"大无有二"。13世纪的戴侗在其编撰的一部非凡的字典《六书故》中，说"天"上面的一横表示"上"，因此"天"的意思是"在上而大者"。在这两部字典中，"帝"都源于"上"，而且他们说"帝"是形声字，这点我难以苟同。[①]但是戴侗对"帝"的含义给出了以下解释："主宰之 xxv 尊称，故'天'曰'上帝'。五气曰五帝，天子[②]曰帝。"这里"天"隐隐约约地表达了"上帝"的概念；当中国人想以人格之名来称呼"天"时，则用"帝"和"上帝"。我相信，我们的先祖开始使用"God"这个词的时候也是这样的。"帝"这一名称在中国被用来表达这个概念已经足足有 5000 年了。因此，《中国经典》里凡出现"帝"字的地方，都可自然而然地用"God"来翻译，但要除去我在上文讨论的有关帝尧、帝舜的情形。中国人的"帝"从未像希腊人的宙斯（Zeus）一样成为一个专有名称。除了用"God"翻译"帝"和"上帝"，我想不出还有任何其他词可用；就像除了用"man"来翻译"人"一样，没有其他词可用。

以上简短说明了我为什么决定在本卷书中继续用"God"来翻译"帝"和"上帝"，除了引出这些言辞的那些情形外[*]。但是在解释"帝"时，戴侗说："天子曰帝"；而我的大部分读者都知道"皇帝"是中国君主的称号。这一称呼是怎么产生的？是否从一开始"帝"就是统治者或帝王的称号，然后当"天"所传达的模糊概念无法满

---

① 《说文解字》说"帝"的声旁是"朿"（cì）。但是两者之间从形和声来看均没有任何相似之处。也许文本有讹误。湛约翰在《中国人的起源》（*The Origin of the Chinese*）一书中（第 12 页）试图从"帝"字的构形来分析："汉语书面语言的特性很好地说明了对帝的原始信仰。'帝'是'大'在上面'丨'（统治）'冖'（天）和'囗'（地）。"这个解析虽然很新颖，但不能完全令人满意。后三个构成部分确实如此，但把上面的部分说成是"大"，无法令人信服。

② "天子"是中国古代对君主的普遍称呼。这里的"子"最初是一个动词，"天子"等同于"天子之"，即天视之为子，像儿子一样对待。参见《中国圣书》第一卷，第318 页第二行诗。

* 即上文所言《书经》头几篇用于帝尧、帝舜的"帝"字和《吕刑》中的"帝"字用拼音转写。——译者

足某位思想家或宗教崇拜者，并且他希望能表达自己认为有一位人
xxvi 格神，他是自己全能的主宰时，这一称号就被用来指称"至高无上
的权力"（Supreme Power）？如果上述设想能得到肯定的回答，"帝"
被用来称呼至高无上神（Supreme Being），就像我们从父子关系出发
称其为父（Father）一样。又或是帝就像我们的"God"一样，本来
是至高无上的主和统治者的称号，后来才被用于称呼世俗的统治者，
目的是神化他，就像罗马的皇帝被称为"Divus"（神）一样？我认
为是通过后一种方式，"帝"被用于称呼中国的君主；因此再次出版
《书》的译本时，我决定其中凡是"帝"用于称呼尧舜的地方，而且
仅有在这种情况下，我要用音译保留这个中文名称，而不是像之前
那样用"emperor"去翻译。

下面是我经过权衡之后做出这个决定的原因：

第一，在中国历史上第一位真正使用皇帝称号的帝王是秦始皇；
他公元前221年采用了这个称号，也就是在那一年他打败了所有周
王朝分封的诸侯国，建立了一个延续至今的封建专制帝国。

周朝从公元前1122年至前256年，持续了867年，其统治者被
称为王。

周朝之前是商或殷朝，从公元前1766至前1123年，持续了644
年，其统治者也被称为王。

商朝之前是夏朝，从公元前2205年至前1767年，持续了439
年，其统治者被称为王或后。

因此，从公元前2205年大禹开始至前221年接近2000年的时
间，中国并没有帝。在这期间人口数量一直在增加，国土也在不断
扩大。如果之前就存在帝，那么这一高级的称号是怎么被一个低级
的称号取代的呢？

xxvii 夏朝之前，除开尧舜时期，我们所拥有的中国历史记载就只剩

下神话和传说了。可以称得上最古老的历史文献只有《书》里面关于尧、舜的几篇，即使这几篇也不是在尧舜时代记录下来的。更早记载的人物是盘古，据说在他那个时代"天地初分"。盘古之后紧接着是三皇时代，包括十二天皇、十一地皇和九人皇，统治时间总计约5万年。此后又经过众多不同的世系，直到五帝。五帝之首一般认为是伏羲；有时为了使尧、舜位列五帝，就将伏羲和另两位列为三皇。

　　我讨论这些细节，是因为关于秦始皇采用皇帝这个称号我们有这样的记载："王初并天下，自以为德兼三皇，功过五帝，乃更号曰'皇帝'。"三皇纯属虚构，五帝也是神话传说。说在夏朝之前中国就有皇或帝统治，是不被承认的。

　　第二，如上所述，以及《书》"导论"第13—19页（即本书边码）所示，《书》中夏朝前的几篇所述事件并非当时所记的文献，从这个意义上讲它们不是历史文献。他们也承认那些是他们根据更古老的文献编纂而成。当他们称尧舜为帝时，帝是放在名字之前，而非之后；如果"帝"是皇帝的意思，那么根据中国人的惯用法，"帝"应该放在名字之后。"尧皇帝"应该称"尧帝"；但我们看到的是"帝尧"，"帝"在此是一个形容词。周朝的开创者周文王，始终被称为 xxviii "文王"。如果称其为"王文"的话，每一位中国学者都会立即觉得难以容忍；将"帝尧"称为"尧帝"也会引起相同的反应。五年前，我第一次意识到我违背了中文词语的使用规则，错将"帝尧"和"帝舜"翻译成"the emperor Yâo"和"the emperor Shun"。确实，在《书》的头几篇中，有"帝"单独使用的情况，没有附加在尧和舜前，但指的是这两个人物。在这种情况下，它确实是一个名词，但它的意义取决于它在"帝尧""帝舜"中用作形容词的意义。如果能够确定在"帝尧""帝舜"中"帝"的意义是"神化的"（the Deified）；那么单独用作名词时，它的意义就是"神"（Divus 或 the Divine One）。

第三，如上所述，夏商周三代君主均被称为王而不是帝。孔子在《论语》中多次提及尧舜，但从未称他们为帝。孟子在引用《书》中关于尧舜的记载时，却是两者称呼均用。这说明《书》的头几篇流行于周朝中期，与我们今天所见相差无几。现在的问题是，我们能否证明这几篇中的"帝"是如何用于称呼尧舜的。我们能。

《礼记》第四篇为《月令》（ *the Monthly Record of the Proceedings of Government* ），即按月记录政府的事务。祭祀五帝的事务分布在四季。五帝分别为伏羲、神农、有熊或轩辕、金天、高阳，号大皞、炎帝、黄帝、少皞和颛顼。在祭典上，每位帝都配有一位地位低其一级的神。除了名字和月份外，描述每场祭典的语言都一样。因此《月令》开篇第一条为："孟春之月…… 其帝大皞，其神句芒。"句芒是少皞之子，比大皞晚几百年；因此在这一祭典中将此二人联系在一起，只能是在之后的时代才出现的。

无论我们如何解读描写如此简略的祭典；无论我们从中看到的是日益盛行的自然崇拜，还是对古代英雄和圣贤的崇拜；其中"帝"的意义显然就是"God"。这五例中都有一个"帝"和一个"神"，其意思不是皇帝（Emperor）和普通的神灵（Spirit），而是"上帝"（God）和"圣灵"（Spirit）——"圣灵"与"上帝"的关系恰如臣与君的关系。因此，经过一个神化的过程，"帝"开始在周王朝时期用于称呼古代神话和传说中的伟大人物；它也因此被用于称呼尧舜这样的英雄人物。中国人用"皇帝"称呼当今及古代的皇帝，这一称号可能除了让他想到人君之外，并不会引起他的其他想法；但是，因为我认为"帝"的真正含义就是"God"，而且经过一个神化的过程这一称号被用于尧舜，我很满意于这样的解释；所以《书》中凡用"帝"称呼尧舜之时，我不再将之译为"Emperor"，而是在本卷书中将之做不译处理。

———————

译文中其他不重要的改动，就没必要指出了。导论和注释中表示公元前的年份均比之前出版的译本多一年，从而使其与宋君荣译本中的年份以及已故梅辉立非常有用的《中国历史年表》(*Chinese Chronological Tables*) 中的年份一致。

———————

中文专名的拼写变化相当大。对于现在居住在北京的外国人来说，似乎应该采用威妥玛《寻津录》和《语言自迩集》里的拼音 xxx 体系。但是，为了尽可能确保《东方圣书》所有卷册的统一性，我使用的字母是遵照了麦克斯·缪勒教授制定的东方字母表拼音方案 (Scheme for the Transliteration of Oriental Alphabets)。一开始这样做并不容易；因为中国人没有字母表，也不愿意新造一个让人感觉他们好像有似的。但是，我还是不得不用字母表，这使我最终接受了现在用的这种方法。汉语双元音很多，因此不可能把所有的双元音都收录进这个字母表。读者需要知道，在元音或双元音前的 i 近似于 y 的发音，因此整个音还是单音节。r 和 ze 两个音要想被听明白，必须要发出声，音量要大。

———————

为了引起读者对《书经》中或显或隐的宗教思想的关注，相关内容之后会用星号（*）标出。

理雅各

牛津

1879 年 4 月 18 日

（丁大刚　马芙蓉　译

潘琳　校）

《书经》（英译本）导论

一、《书》之性质与历史

1. 释《书经》之名

《书》是中国最古老的典籍，包含从公元前 2357 年至前 627 年间的各种历史文献。"书"字的构成（聿曰）表示"笔说"，*故常指用来表征语言的书面文字。这确实是书最原始的含义，此后"书"字便转义为著述或书籍。"书"被孔子及其他人用于专指古代遗存的历史性著作，而与《诗》《礼》或其他早期文献有别，这并非说没有其他著作称之为"书"，但"书"字用来特指《书》，则历史悠久，且沿用至今。

《书》传到我们之时，已经残缺不全，即使有人声称孔子时代《书》就已经存在，但从来没有说过它包含的就是中国历史，更遑论里面包含历史编年。它仅仅是一部历史记录集，历史跨度约为 1700 年，但篇章之间缺乏联系，甚至相去甚远。

《书》在汉代以前（始于前 202 年）从未被称为"经"。若说孔子把"经"字用于什么典籍的话，也只有《孝经》（见后文《孝经》"导论"）。但是，汉代的学者在收集整理国家古代文献时，为了便

---

* 根据《说文解字》，"書"字"从聿者聲"，可知"書"是形声字。理雅各解之为"笔说"，是错将它当作了会意字。——译者

于区分那些孔子认为最有价值的文献，就将之以"经"命名，意为
正典，具有不容挑战的权威。

2.《书》是在孔子之前就已经存世的一部文献集

　　《论语》中孔子和弟子引用《书》时以"《书》云"开头。《大
学》提到了《书》中的四篇篇名，与我们现在看到的篇名一致。《孟
子》有时用类似孔子的句式说"《书》曰"，有时则直接用具体篇名。
我们可能会很自然地猜想孔子所提之《书》，就是那部名为《书》的
文献集。

　　《孟子》中有一章似乎可以确证当时存在《书》这一文献集。孟
子说："尽信《书》，不如无《书》"，此后他直接提到了《书》中的
一个篇名，说："吾于《武成》，取二三策而已矣。"① 墨子、荀子及周
朝最后两百年的其他作者，都以同样的方式引用《书》，而且经常明
确提及其不同部分，如《虞书》《夏书》《商书》《周书》。最后，《左
传》也多次以同样的方式引用《书》，即使它叙述的是孔子之前很久
的人和事。② 以上论证说明，《书》是在孔子之前就已经存世的一部 3
历史文献集。

3. 孔子没有编纂《书》；孔子时期《书》的篇数；被认为是孔子所作
　　的《书序》

　　根据上一段，我们可以推论说孔子没有编纂《书》这部文献集。
最早断言《书》的编纂者为孔子的是公元前2世纪的孔安国，他是
孔子的十一世孙。孔安国在《尚书序》中叙述了其先祖所作的工作，
他说："［他］讨论坟、典，断自唐虞以下，讫于周。芟夷烦乱，翦

---

① 《孟子·尽心下》第三章。
② 《左传》第一次引用《书》是在隐公六年（前717）。

截浮辞，举其宏纲，撮其机要，足以垂世立教，典、谟、训、诰、誓、命之文，凡百篇。"*司马迁在《史记》（约成书于公元前100年）中也有相同的说法，但是司马迁的信息来源于孔安国。这样的编纂与孔子自称"述而不作，信而好古"①的特点相吻合，也与其孙在《中庸》中说他"祖述尧、舜，宪章文、武"②相吻合。

　　然而，我们知道《书》在孔子时代以及之前就已经存在了。那么它真的就如孔安国所言有100篇吗？他这么说的权威来自《书序》，而《书序》是与《书》的古简在孔安国时代被一同发现的，孔安国对这些简进行了解读。关于这些简的发现我会在下文详谈。但是，孔安国并没有明确说此序为孔子所作，尽管司马迁认为出自孔子之手。《书序》中保存有一百篇中八十一篇文献的篇名。现在中国学者普遍认为，《书序》并非由孔子所作。我完全赞同朱熹弟子蔡沈的观点。蔡沈的《书集传》出版于1210年，现在是《尚书》的正统解释。他说《书序》"识见浅陋，无所发明，其间至有与经相戾者，于已亡之篇，则依阿简略，尤无所补，其非孔子所作明甚。"**

　　《书序》中所提到的八十一篇，或更多，可能在孔子时代的《书》中是存在的。然而，我认为其中有几篇一定是在后来，且在秦始皇之前，就丢失了。是秦始皇把整部《书》都烧掉了。孟子抱怨说在他那个时代诸侯毁坏了许多古籍，这样他们就可以篡位和改制了。***其他的说法也证实了我的这一结论，这里我就不展开了。

---

* 理雅各引文综合了"芟夷烦乱，翦截浮辞，举其宏纲，撮其机要，足以垂世立教"一句，与《尚书序》稍有出入。——译者
① 《论语·述而第七》第一章。
② 《中庸》第三十章，第一节。
** 蔡沈：《书集传》，中华书局2018年版，第302页；亦见《书序》，《钦定书经传说汇纂》，四库全书本，第1页。——译者
*** 《孟子·万章下》第二章。（理雅各的说法与《孟子》原文"诸侯恶其害己也，而皆去其籍"有出入。——译者

4.《书》的文献来源

这里有必要专门用一段来说明《书》的文献来源。我们是否有充分的证据证明《书》中的文献是在古代社会产生、保存，并且被选为历史正典呢？

答案是肯定的。在周朝，上至王室下至诸侯，都有史官，其英语翻译有"Recorders""Annalists""Historiographers"和简单的"Clerks"。"史"分为大史、小史、内史、外史、御史。内史之责为"凡命诸侯及孤、卿、大夫，*则策命之""凡四方之事书，内史读 5
之""内史掌书王命，遂贰之"。外史之责为"掌书外令""掌四方之志""掌三皇五帝之书""掌达书名于四方"。①

这些文字清楚表明，自公元前11世纪周代建国，已经有明文规定编纂和保存帝国政令、记录政府日常运作和各诸侯国历史，以及保存和解释上古文献。孔子说在他早年，史官对于没有充足证据的事会空着不记。②孟子也提及了三本书：晋国的《乘》、楚国的《梼杌》、鲁国的《春秋》，这三本书毋庸置疑来自其各自国家的史官。

上溯至商朝和夏朝是否存在类似的史官，我们现有证据不足。《书经》第五部分第十篇第二章（《周书·酒诰》），似乎说到了商朝的史官（太史友、内史友）。商朝的第十二位君主武丁（前1324—前1264）曾把他做的一个梦告知了大臣，被记录了下来。③还有早于武丁400年，师保伊尹劝谏年轻浮躁的君主太甲，也被记录了下来。④再往前追溯至夏代，仲康朝（前2159—前2145）胤侯号令军

---

*　理雅各此处引文与原文稍有出入，他把"孤、卿、大夫"综合在一起称"其他显贵"（any other dignitary）。——译者
①　以上引文见《周礼》或《周官》卷三十一，第35—42节。
②　《论语·卫灵公第十五》第二十五章。（"吾犹及史之阙文也。"）
③　《商书·说命上》。
④　《商书·太甲上》。

队时引用了《政典》，这使我们认为他参考了某一广为人知的文献。①
还有，夏朝的创立者大禹之孙（前2205—前2196）在《五子之歌》
中提到了大禹的"训"，其语言"训有之"能使我们想起孟子之时在
6 参考公认的权威文献时所常用的"于传有之"这种表述方式。②

　　百科全书编纂家马端临在首次刊刻于1321年的《文献通考》中
说："史官笔自黄帝有之"。《隋书》的编者说："《书》之所兴，盖与
文字俱起。"我认为文字的发明早于黄帝。当文字被发明后，就被用
于记录历史。据称《书》中许多文献的时间较早，在没有进一步查
验的情况下我们没有正当的理由否定它们。更让我们惊讶的或许是
《书》在编纂之时总篇数竟不过一百篇。

5. 秦始皇焚书

　　周朝于公元前256年灭亡，又经过了35年的混乱动荡后，秦王
统一了天下，并自称皇帝。直到此时，《书》没有像其他人类作品那
样随着时间的流逝而遭损毁；但现在它差点全部被毁。公元前213
年，暴君秦始皇下了一道诏书，下令除了那些属于为宫廷服务的博
士官的书和《易》之外，其他古代典籍一律焚毁。秦始皇尤为憎恶
《书》和《诗》。诏书发布30天后，凡是在一起谈论这些作品的儒
生，一经发现即刻处死，凡是拥有这些作品的儒生，一经查出即处
以黥刑，并发配去修建长城4年。

7 　　我们在此不对焚书这一疯狂行为加以解释。除了《易》之外，
当时中国所有的古典文献都付之一炬。诏令被无情地执行，数百名
抗旨的儒生被活埋。《书》几乎从地球上消亡了。

---

① 《夏书·胤征》。
② 《夏书·五子之歌》。

6.《书》的恢复

　　然而，距离焚书令发布不到 4 年时间，即公元前 210 年，秦始皇就去世了。他建立的王朝也在公元前 206 年灭亡。公元前 201 年汉朝建立，公元前 190 年挟书令被正式废止。这些古书遭禁的时间不足四分之一个世纪。如果不是因为公元前 206 年项羽火烧咸阳，恢复这些书可能并不困难。据说，大火把宫殿和公共建筑烧了三个月，这对宫中藏书的破坏不亚于秦始皇诏令对民间藏书的破坏。

　　然而，在秦博士中有一位姓伏的博士。在焚书令颁布后，他将自己的《书》简藏在墙壁中。汉朝建立后，他去找寻那些书简，发现许多已亡佚。他只恢复其中的 29 份文献，根据传统的划分，总共 35 篇。其中一篇恢复难度极大，此处我就不详细讨论了。他以这些篇目教授生徒，各地的学者都来到他门下求学。汉文帝（前 179—前 155）听说了伏生，于是派掌故晁错前来见伏生，并将伏生所恢复之简，也有可能是复制品带回皇宫。竹简采用的是当时流行的文字，与之前几个世纪使用的文字不同，因此被称为"今文尚书"。刘歆受汉哀帝（前 6—前 1）之命编纂的《七略》中包含了一个条目——"《书》二十九卷"，毫无疑问是受自伏生。伏生也为他的《书》做了注。此《书》被刻在汉灵帝（168—189）下令篆刻的石碑上。[*] 汉代有很多学者研究这个文本，将其传授给自己的弟子，并公开发表其成果。然而，在西晋怀帝在位期间（307—312）中国动乱之后，他们的著作没有一本完整保留下来。

　　汉武帝在位期间（前 140—前 85），在孔子故宅的墙壁中发现了《书》《春秋》《孝经》和《论语》的简策。它们在那里藏了多久，我们不得而知。一般的说法是它们被孔家的某个后人藏了起来，使它

---

[*]　即熹平石经。——译者

们得以幸免于秦火。但是简策上面所书的是一种已经废弃不用的文字，几乎没有人能够破解，而且一定是在公元前 5 世纪初留存下来的。简策被交给孔安国保管，他是博士，也是孔氏家族的族长。在伏生今文和其他文献的帮助下，他辨认出了所有保存完好的《书》简，除了伏生的二十九篇外，还有其他一些篇目。他还发现，有三处伏生都将两份不同的文献合并到了一个篇名之下，并没有注意到这是三篇。现在总共有四十六卷"古文尚书"重见天日。它们在刘歆《七略》中的条目是"《尚书》古文经，四十六卷"。

　　公元前 97 年，孔安国将释读出的《尚书》转写为当时通行的文字，上呈皇帝，自己留了一个副本，并受命为之作传。他完成了工作，但在即将上呈皇帝之际，朝廷发生祸乱，一时无暇顾及文事。由于这些原因孔安国《尚书》传注被忽视了一段时间。孔安国公元前 136 年就被立为五经博士，但他的《古文尚书》却"未立于学官"。

　　然而，孔安国的传注并没有丢失；在谈论它之前，我必须提及在公元 1 世纪初第三次关于《书》的大部分内容的恢复。王莽（9—22）篡位期间，有一位名为杜林的学者，他是一位逃亡者，在他身上曾经发生过多次令人惊叹的逃脱。杜林流亡期间，得漆书古文《尚书》一卷，可能是以漆书写在竹简上，或者是书写在上过漆的布帛之上。杜林视其为珍宝，常宝爱不离身。待东汉光武帝平定天下之后，他拿出漆书与其他学者一起交流。卫宏为其做注，此外贾逵、马融和康成（郑玄）都为之做过注解，这些人均为中国经学史上的大人物。杜林的漆书与孔安国的篇数相同，但是其中十三篇中有五篇与安国的不同，还有九篇是安国有而漆书无。郑玄的注解在隋代之前仍存于世，之后便亡佚了。

　　我现在再来谈论孔安国本及其传注的历史。其传承线索可清楚地追溯到西汉末年。虽不甚清晰，但可以肯定的是，我们有证据证明，在东晋初豫章内史梅赜得到了一份抄本，并将其献给元帝（317—322）。其中缺少《舜典》，便依据杜林的文本用马融的注做了补充。从这时起，孔安国的《古文尚书》和传注在太学拥有了自己的位置。《隋书·经籍志》列有《古文尚书》及孔安国"传"。唐朝的第二位皇帝太宗敕令孔颖达在当时多位官员的辅助下编撰《尚 10 书正义》。他们采用了孔安国的"传"，并添加了许多疏解。公元 654 年，他们的著作被下令刊印，并且幸运地一直被保存至今。《尚书正义》的本文即是孔安国恢复的《古文尚书》，后来得到进一步的保护，与其他诸经一起被刻在了唐石碑上。这些碑于公元 837 年刻成，至今仍保存在陕西的长安。

我们没有必要进一步追溯《书》的历史了。从唐朝至今，有 500多部作品涉及《书》或《书》中的部分内容，我们随意就可说出其中几部作品的名称。事实上，在宋代就开始出现了质疑性的批评。这种批评的外部证据相对较少，主要是根据文本的风格来决定其真实性。结果是，这种批评总是根据作者的知识和主观判断而有所不同。许多人认为，所谓孔安国的传并不是真的出自孔安国，而是出自梅赜之手，并假借这位伟大的汉朝学者的名义向世人展示。即使果真如此，这部作品也存在了近 1600 年了。我们对马融、康成和其他汉代早期学者观点的大部分了解，都要归功于唐代学者对它的注疏。无论它的作者是真孔还是伪孔，其价值之大再怎么评价都不为过。但我不相信它是伪造的。所有人都承认孔安国确实曾为他的《古文尚书》做过传。它又亡佚于何时？没有证据可以证明。相反，它的存在恰好证明，它不时出现在中华帝国的经学史中，每个间隔都不算久远，直到如孔颖达所证实的，梅赜从一位名叫张昭的学者那里得到了它。

关于《书》，人们对第一次伏生恢复的文本没有争议；但孔安国 11

后发现的文本很容易理解，所以有人指控孔安国的文本不真实，我对此并不惊讶。在经受这两个文本中共有的一些晦涩难懂之处的折磨后，当我们再去看任意一个文本，我们发现他们只是看起来简单，实则不然。此外，不同篇章的文体因其主题不同而不同。"诰"是所有篇中最难理解的。"命""誓""训"结构则比较简单；孔安国发现的篇目主要是这三种。首先，在破解这些古老的文字时，他利用了伏生《书》。我们认为他的文本没有一味地遵循伏生传下来的文本，两者有差别的章节正是那些批评家们辛勤收集起来的。然而，当他发现伏生《书》中没有的新篇目时，他不得不尽最大的努力破解这些竹简，因为此时他没有了最得力的援手。我们可以想象，当他竭力读完一段的大部分内容后，仍有一些顽固的文字令他百思不得其解，他就根据自己对意义的理解，用他自己的文字将这些地方补全。根据周朝作品对其特定篇目中许多章节的引用，我们发现他的文本总体上是忠实、成功的。这一事实足以引起人们足够的重视与思考。我认为他文本中的每一句重要陈述都有这样的证据做保证。其书的特点使其真实性遭到怀疑，但这并不足以推翻它是在孔宅墙壁中发现的竹简的真实抄本这一主张。

在本章结尾，我得出的结论是，没有什么可以动摇我们对现有《书》各部分内容真实性的信心，它与孔子之前和之后周朝的《书》大体上是相同的。

12　二、《书》中记载内容的可信性

1.《书》中记载内容是否可信

接受上章我得出的结论之后，现在我来探讨《书》中文献是否

是对其所载之事真实可靠的叙述。也许可以立即回答的是，就大部分而言，毫无理由质疑其可信性。当然，我们必须考虑到一个王朝的缔造者在列举被推翻王朝的罪状时会有与事实不符的情况，而受人喜爱的英雄即使失败也有可能被人加以粉饰。但是《书》中的文献要比现在《京报》（*Peking Gazette*）上刊登的事件记录要可信。

　　当然，越近的文献可信度越高。我们已经知道，周朝的制度规定，要保存以前各个朝代的历史记录。但是，我们要知道，其中许多记录会随着时间的流逝而消亡，还有一些会有残缺和讹误。我们发现，事实就是如此。《书》曾经包含的八十一篇中，只有一篇属于尧时期；七篇属于舜时期；四篇属于夏朝，其中较多篇幅叙述了尧时期的事情；三十一篇属于商朝；三十八篇属于周王朝的前五百年。这一切似乎从表面上证明了我的说法。

2.《周书》《商书》《夏书》

　　《周书》与其所记事件在同一时间，其成书不久便公布于众，其真实性毋庸置疑。

　　《商书》也毋庸置疑。藉着《商书》里的文献我们可以自信地上溯到商朝的缔造者成汤。成汤的统治时间在历史年表中始于公元前1766年。　　13

　　关于更早的夏朝，我们只有四篇文献，我们没有证据证明在周朝《书》成之时，其中是否含有更多的文献。这四篇中，第一篇最长，它虽然讲述的是夏朝开创者禹（前2205—前2196）的伟大成就，但实际上属于尧统治时期，不应收录在《夏书》中。其余三篇只能让我们追溯到仲康朝（前2159—前2145），我看不出有什么理由质疑其真实性。其中最后一篇提到了一个天体现象，一直被理解为在秋季最后一个月的第一天在房宿发生了日食。房宿是从天蝎座 π

星到 σ 星约 5½° 的空间。宋君荣通过计算认为这一日食确实发生在仲康五年（前 2155）。然而，正如下一章所示，人们对他计算的准确性产生了怀疑，因此我在此不利用它来确认这篇文献的真实性。

3.《唐书》和《虞书》

我们来看更早的尧舜时期的记录。必须将《夏书》的第一篇《禹贡》与之归为一类。或许得说，没有同样的证据表明这些记录原本如此。

（1）这些文献显然是后来编纂而成的

《尧典》及虞时期的三篇文献，均以"曰若稽古"开篇，因此其自身表明是后来编纂的。编纂者将自己与他所叙述事件发生的时间分开，并声称其文献来源是上古的记录，但以现代为出发点书写。舜时期的最后一篇文献《益稷》在伏生《书》中与前一篇合为一篇，故而也以"曰若稽古"开篇。我将在下文单独讨论《禹贡》。

（2）这些文献是传说

《尧典》和《舜典》以及其他文献中的许多内容有更多传说的色彩而非真实的历史。尧在位七十年之时，他提出让位给他的首席大臣四岳。这位贤人说他不胜此位，尧于是要他推荐堪当此任之人，无论是贵族还是贫民，只要是最贤能的人即可。于是舜就登上了历史舞台。朝廷之上所有的大臣都推荐虞舜[①]——一个地位卑下的单身汉。舜的父亲目盲且顽劣；母亲（或继母）奸诈；弟弟傲慢；但舜以其孝道而能与他们和睦相处，而且使他们在很大程度上能够克己自制，不再作恶。尧很高兴。他之前也曾听说过舜。他决定先考验

---

① "虞"是舜朝之名号，要把它与舜的继任者"禹"区别开来。禹是夏朝的创立者。本生（Bunsen）把这两个称号混在了一起。参见 *Egypt's Place in Universal History*, Vol. III., p. 399。

一下舜。这是一个很奇怪的考验。他把两个女儿嫁给了舜，看他拥有两个妻子的表现，从而决定他是否适合帝位。

舜无疑经受住了考验，尧于是任命其为"百揆"，为时三年。三年后尧让位与舜。舜拒绝继位，但他一直执掌政事，直到公元前2257年尧去世后，舜才在公元前2255年登上帝位。孟子和司马迁对 15 《书》中这些以及其他一些关于尧舜的怪异之事有更详细的叙述，但他们的叙述也同样匪夷所思。我必须认为，《书》中这些最古老的文献并没有给我们讲述尧舜的历史，而是关于他们的传奇故事。

（3）它们的编纂者有古老的文献作为依据

但是，我们必须说，这些篇的编纂者手中有一些尧时代的文献。在我看来，有三件事可以证明这一说法。第一，尧舜大臣的称号与后来相应大臣的称号不同。居于首位的大臣是"四岳"，次之是"百揆"，掌管祭祀的是"秩宗"。这些特别的称谓表明编纂者很可能接受的是古老文献中的说法，而非其个人发明。第二，《唐书》《虞书》的风格在一些细节上与《夏书》《商书》《周书》的风格有所不同。就拿感叹词"吁""咨""都"来说，我们在其他地方没有发现这样的用法。第三，尧命星官根据星星在某个季节的黄昏时刻到达中天位置而确定春分、秋分和夏至、冬至，这不可能是后世的发明。在下一章中我们将发现这些语句曾被用于确定帝尧的年代。关于二分点岁差的知识中国是在公元4世纪中叶才有的，当时没有这样的知识，因此没有编纂者能够捏造尧的命令以符合年表上给他记载的时间。

《唐书》和《虞书》具体什么时候成为今天我们所见到的形式，我们不得而知。很可能是在西周时期，但我怀疑在周代和汉代之间 16 短暂存在的秦王朝时期其文辞曾发生了一些改变，以及在汉朝恢复它们的过程中也有一些字词变化。

4.《禹贡》

现在我们来看《禹贡》。按照现在的编排它属于《夏书》的第一篇，但如前所述，其事件发生在尧时期，或至少在尧舜共同执政时期。因此，它出现的地方与其历史时期不符，并且也像《唐书》《虞书》中的文献一样具有总体的不确定性。

我们不知道尧是哪一年登上帝位的，但他好像突然遭遇了洪灾。洪水滔天，淹没了丘陵。四方百姓，遍地哀号。有没有一个能人可堪治理洪水的重任？所有的大臣都建议尧委派鲧去治理洪水，但这不是尧所想要的人选。鲧经过九年的努力，仍然没有完成任务。他的儿子禹接替了父亲的工作。他从今天中国内地的西陲出发，循着大江大河流经之地，焚烧林木，劈开岩石，凿穿阻挡河流的大山，深挖河道，使大水平缓地向东注入大海。他开挖湖泊，加高坚固的堤岸，直到最终"四隩既宅，九山刊旅，九川涤源，九泽既陂，四海会同。六府孔修，庶土交正，砥慎财赋，咸则三壤，成赋中邦。"禹对工作的热忱，在《益稷》中可见一斑。他在《益稷》中自述道：17 "予乘四载，"——即陆地上的马车、水上的船、冰天雪地里的雪橇、上山时穿的带钉子的鞋子——"随山刊木，暨益奏庶鲜食，"——即捕鱼、鸟、兽——"予决九川，距四海，浚畎浍距川；暨稷播，奏庶艰食鲜食。懋迁有无，化居。烝民乃粒，万邦作义。"还有"在涂山结婚时，仅和妻子在一起四天（娶于涂山，辛壬癸甲）。"孟子说他在治水的时候，三过家门而不入。他自己的话是："启呱呱而泣，予弗子，惟荒度土功。"

除了治理水患外，禹还开展了其他与早期文明相适应的重要工作。我们从《书》中得知，他没有花费很长时间就完成了他的丰功伟业，事实上在尧去世前，这项工程就顺利完成了。这一切都令人难以置信。毕瓯在 1842 年发表在《亚洲杂志》（*Journal Asiatique*）

上的一篇关于《禹贡》的文章中说："如果我们要相信评注者的注疏，禹就成了超自然的存在，他治理中国的大江大河就像治理缓缓流淌的小溪一般容易。"没有理由说"如果我们要相信评注者的注疏"；我们只有理由说"如果我们要相信《书》"，我们也只能据《书》评判禹。

关于《禹贡》，毕瓯得出的总体结论值得我们注意，在他看来，我们在其中发现的仅仅是一个殖民地的大幅扩张。禹是中国这片领土的第一位开拓者。他在中国这片大地的各个区域设立了殖民者或种植园主的据点。他要人们砍伐那些据点周围的树木，开垦出耕地。大禹之后，治理河流，砍伐森林的工作仍然持续了一段时间，而这一切都被归功于禹。毫无疑问，这位法国汉学家的观点道出了一点事实的真相，但是我们最好抛弃禹是中国殖民地领袖的观点。我们认为中国人的发源地是在今山西南部，西边和南边是黄河。禹之子曾在今陕西西安府的一个地方与有扈氏交战。禹的孙子太康曾被囚禁在河南的一个地方，位于黄河南部。大禹及其部族不断向东南西北四个方位扩展，随着人口数量的增加，征服了所行之处的土地。

尧时期的洪水很可能是黄河泛滥，此后黄河多次泛滥，因此有了"中国之殇"（China's Sorrow）之称。禹的卓越之处在于疏通了黄河的水道，缓和了水势，将之引入大海。中国的疆域在夏朝和商朝时期逐渐确立，其各个部分也被数量不断增加的中国人所逐渐占据，并按相应的比例向中央进贡。有资料记载了大禹付出的辛劳，以及他把领土分配给最显贵的追随者。有历史学家认为这个国家的秩序是禹奠定的，于是就把这伟大的成就归功于禹，以此来赞美禹。大约与此同时，流传着关于禹克己的故事，这些故事就被记录在了《益稷》中，然后迅速激发了《禹贡》的构想，而且被人顺利地接受。于是大禹就顺利地与尧舜关联了起来，形成了中国君主政治初始阶段的三人组合。大禹集聚了尧舜的智慧和仁心，还对自己的岗位尽职尽责。他是所有帝王的楷模，将永远鞭策着那些帝王不敢偷懒和放纵自己，激励着他们勤勤恳恳地履行自己的职责。

在第五部分第十九篇（《周书·立政》），周公建议年轻的成王（前1115—前1077）让军队严阵以待，"以陟禹之迹"，巡行天下，令四海臣服。周公提到"禹之迹"，不是为了证明禹确实如《禹贡》所记载的那样到访过那些地方并在那耕耘，而是为了说明这是周朝开创之时的信条，同时它让我们有了一个推测，即当时周王朝的档案中有《禹贡》这篇文献。《禹贡》可能是在夏朝灭亡之前编纂而成，也可能是在商朝时期编纂的。它从商朝传到了周朝，被周朝外史保存了下来，后来被非常恰当地编入了《书》这部历史文献集中。

5. 尧、舜、禹均是历史人物

虽然我们不能认为《书》中最早的六篇文献是在其所载事件发生时所写，但这并不意味着可以质疑尧、舜、禹是历史人物。更何况禹是夏朝的第一任君主，是中国世袭君主制的奠基人，是"传递姓氏和封地"的封建君主。《禹贡》之后的文献，从《甘誓》（前2197年禹之子和继位者启所作）开始，均可被奉为名副其实的古文献。

20

三、中国年表及《书》中的主要年代

1. 根据《书》制定不出详细的年表

我在这里不会详细论述中国年表的问题，只是表明《书》中文献具有上古的性质不存在纪年的困难。关于这些古代文献的性质，我已经在上文详细谈过了。

《书》本身并没有提供任何纪年的方法，以记录它涵盖得那么长

一段历史时期。我们从中得知周朝之前是商（又名殷）朝，商朝之前是夏朝，在夏朝的创立者禹之前是舜和尧的统治时期。正如宋君荣所说，"如果我们只有《书经》，那么我们对其各个部分的时间只会有一个混乱的概念。"这没有什么值得惊讶的。一个民族的纪年，只有在他们感到有必要按照时间顺序有规律地排列其历史事件时，才会发展成一门科学。

2. 系统尝试制作年表始于汉代

直到汉代人们才首次尝试为中国历史做一个年表。学者们为此利用了著名的 60 年一个周期的甲子纪年法。我现在正处在第 76 个周期的第 15 年。据说这个纪年法最初是由公元前黄帝的一位大臣大桡在公元前 2637 年所做，这一年即为第一个周期的第一年。但是中国所有的学者，不管他们是否质疑这个周期的起源，现在都一致认为甲子纪年不是古代的方法，并且不会早于王莽篡位时期（9—22）。

《书》只用甲子纪日。年代的确立是根据君主在位的年数。然 21
而，在《书》中这样确认的年代极其少见。

汉代之前，中国人无疑只能通过帝王世系表和一些帝王在位的时长来推算其民族的历史时期。如果有完整可靠的帝王表和每位帝王统治的年数，这一方法仍是非常令人满意的。但是我们没有这样完整可靠的帝王表和每位帝王统治的年数。甚至在西汉时期，司马迁的父亲和司马迁自己，在其撰写的《史记》（成书于前 100）中仅仅只能按顺序给出商朝和夏朝大多数君主的名字。另外，公元 279 年，魏襄王（卒于前 295）的坟墓被发掘时，里面发现了许多竹简，用古文篆书写成，其中最有价值的是一部编年史，始于黄帝，终于末位周王十六年（前 299）。这部书仍以《竹书纪年》之名流传至今。其中的年表比通用年表少了 200 多年。

如果周朝有哪本书载有从一个确定的时代到作者那个时代中华民族的历史时期，那将是非常有价值的记录。或者，如果准确确定了粗略提及的商朝和夏朝君主统治的时长，那么我们自己就能够大致地计算了。但是在这些书中只有仅存的两段话对我这一设想有用。一是《左传·周宣王三年》里的一段话，说商朝统治时长达 600 年。另一段在《孟子》的最后一章"由尧舜至于汤，五百有余岁。由汤至于文王，五百有余岁。由文王至于孔子，五百有余岁。"我们现在知道孔子出生于公元前 551 年。根据孟子给定的年数，551 加上 1500 余年，就是尧舜时代，大约在公元前 2100 年。通用年表认为禹作为舜的继承人即位于公元前 2205 年。尽管孟子的语言很模糊，但在我经过艰辛的研究之后，除了基于天文考虑的结论外，我认为可以确定中国历史的长度没有比这更为准确的了。

3. 周朝时期

《周书·文侯之命》被认为是周朝的第十三位君主周平王所作。他在历史上的位置是非常确定的。孔子的《春秋》始于公元前 721 年。其中提到的 36 次日食中，第一次发生在三年之后的公元前 719 年的 2 月 14 日；而在此后一个月平王崩。因此这是一个毫无争议的时间点。周朝一个更早的日期也可以得到同样的肯定。《诗经》提到了发生在公元前 776 年 8 月 29 日的日食，即周幽王六年。周幽王在位 11 年，他的前任周宣王在位 46 年，因此其统治始于公元前 826 年。这是中国编年学家都同意的日期。周宣王之前有 10 位统治者，通用年表为其分配的是 295 年，从而使周朝始于公元前 1122 年，与事实相距不远。

4. 商朝时期

对于商朝时期，我们不能通过天文学数据确定任何一个王的统

治年代。通用年表当中记载了 28 代王，持续 644 年，因此商朝始于
公元前 1766 年。《竹书纪年》中记载了 30 代王，统治时长总计只有　23
508 年。孟子曾说从商汤到武丁的 20 位君主中："贤圣之君，六七
作。"由此我们得出结论 28 位君主之数确实属实。《周书·无逸》提
到了三个君主的名字，也提到了他们统治的时长，目的是表明上天
很有可能以统治的时间长短来表彰仁君：太戊统治了 75 年，武丁统
治了 59 年，祖甲统治了 33 年。司马光的年表和《竹书纪年》的年
表在这三位商王的统治时长问题上是一致的，还有另外五位商王的
统治时长也一致。根据《左传》的说法，我之前在上文也提及过，
商朝持续时间为 600 年，以及孟子的说法"商朝五百有余岁"，我们
可以认为比起《竹书纪年》的 508 年，通用年表中的 644 年更为准确。

5. 夏朝时期

　　根据通用年表，夏朝持续的时间是 439 年；根据《竹书纪年》，
它持续的时间是 431 年，这两个年表的差别不大。据前者估计，夏
朝开始于公元前 2205 年，即禹元年。

　　我在上文提及过《夏书·胤征》记载了一次日食，发生于仲康
（禹之孙）朝，并指出宋君荣通过计算确证，这份文献中所述的那月
那天在那个天空区域确实有日食发生，即在仲康五年（前 2156），在
其都城于早晨 6 点 49 分确实可以看见这一现象。1840 年，毕瓯将
宋君荣的计算副本提交给同为法兰西学院的研究员小拉尔热托（the
younger Largeteau），小拉尔热托对照浏览了达莫瓦索月食表（the
lunar tables of Damoiseau）和德朗布尔日食表（the solar tables of
Delambre），结果发现那天确实发生过日食，不过是在当时中国首都　24
太阳升起之前。[①] 我的朋友，广州的湛约翰牧师，在不知道拉尔热托

---

① *Etudes sur l'Astronomie indicnne et sur l'Astronomie Chinoise*, pp. 376–382.

对比结果的情况下，1861 年着手验证这次日食，发现虽然宋君荣给出的年、月、日都正确，但是日食发生在夜间，中国天文学家根本无法看到。因此，《书》中这篇文献提到的这次日食，目前尚不能用来证明中国的通用年表；但我又不愿意完全放弃。毕瓯说："尽管拉尔热托验证这次日食的尝试失败了，但在公元前 22 世纪某个年代找到它的希望并没有完全丧失。我们应该等到月食表的进一步完善，从而让我们有新的发现，据此我们才能形成更为可靠的判断。"

6. 尧舜时期

现在我们来谈《书》中粗略记述的中国历史的最早期——尧舜时期。《书》中说舜与尧共同执政 30 年，又 50 年后舜去世。我们也从中得知，尧在位的第七十年才开始找继承人减轻他为政的辛劳。因此，两者所涵盖的时间是 150 年。两个年表都接受这一说法。加上从舜死到禹即位之间两年的丧期，我们得出公元前 2357 年为尧元年。

据《尧典》记载，帝尧告诉其星官如何确立二分点和二至点的时候，他说春分点可以通过观察鸟星确定，夏至可以通过观察火星确定，秋分可以观察虚星，冬至可以观察昴星。中国学者一向认为尧说"春分之星在鸟"，他的意思是在那个季节的黄昏时观察点上的鸟星达到中天位置。其他同理。现今一位中国天文学家的说法与此一致。

此外，最常见的，也是中国最早的黄道划分，是二十八星宿，形成现在我们所谓的中国黄道带（Chinese zodiac）。这些星宿被分成四宫，每宫七个，占天的四分之一。① 在尧指定的天空，鸟是南四分

① 公元前 12 世纪的著作《周官》卷二十六第二十五章详述了那个时代星官的职责。其中提到了确定"二十有八星位"，意思是"二十八宿之主星"。书中未提及这些星和宿的名称；但充分说明那时的人们是知道这些星和宿的。参见 Biot, *Etudes sur l'Astronomie indienne et sur l'Astronomie Chinoise*, pp. 112-113。

之一天七宿的总名；火是现在称为房的旧名，是东四分之一天的中心宿；虚和昴分别是北和南四分之一天的中心宿。因此，尧的意思是，他的星官可以通过他为这些季节指定的星宿的中天位置来确定二至点和二分点的时间。我们假设，他把春分之星指向了南天鸟星的中央星宿——"星"。现在，在我们的恒星命名法中，中国古时的"星"对应长蛇座 α 星，以及它附近的小星；"火"对应天蝎座 β 星和 δ 星；"虚"对应于水瓶座 β 星；"昴"对应昴宿星。当我们想把尧的指令用于年代查询时，出现的问题是：在中国，上述所说之星在春分、秋分和夏至、冬至黄昏时出现在中天是什么时间？

本生（Bunsen）说，伊德勒（Ideler）把这些星座的位置向后推算，确定尧登上帝位的时间为公元前 2163 年；弗莱雷（Freret）认为这些观察有 3 度的不确定性，相差 210 年。[①] 但是毕瓯从尧的这些指令中确证了通用年表中尧的即位时间——公元前 2357 年。[②] 本导论之后附有牛津大学萨维尔天文学教授查尔斯·普里查德（Charles Pritchard）专门为我制作的公元前 2300 年在中国可以看到的星表。根据他的说明查阅这张表，我们将发现，尧向他的星官指出的现象在那时是确实存在的。这一事实有力地确证了年表的大致正确性，即把尧置于公元前 24 世纪。我在前面说过，2500 多年后，中国人才有了二分点岁差的知识。因此，在周朝时期，也即《书》存在的时期，对于遥远的尧时期分点与至点星在中天的时间是不可能科学推算出来的。《尧典》中无论是尧给出指令的形式，还是其他事情，确实有传说的成分，我也并没有说现存《尧典》就是与尧同期的文献。但我已经说过，《尧典》的编纂者手头上有古代文献，其中一份一定包含了四仲中星的事实，这是我现在努力阐述清楚的事。

26

---

① *Egypt's Place in Universal History*, III, pp. 400, 401.
② *Etudes sur l'Astronomie indienne et sur l'Astronomie Chinoise*, pp. 361–366.

关于四仲中星的记载似乎可以确定尧在年表中的位置是公元前24世纪，并表明在那个遥远的时代，对星象进行观测和记录是一种习俗。鉴于此，我认为《甘誓》（大约在尧之后200年发表）之后那些文献都是在事件发生时同步记载下来的，这绝非虚妄之词。

7. 蚩尤之时

27　　《周书》第二十七篇《吕刑》提到的一件事把历史向尧前推了四个世纪，其文曰："若古有训，蚩尤惟始作乱。"然而，它没有说蚩尤是何时扰乱了先前的幸福安宁；也就是这句话把上古的下限定在了舜时。但是年表将蚩尤置于黄帝时，即公元前27世纪末。有作者描述了蚩尤与黄帝之间的战争，其中龙、雾和指南针的发明在战争中发挥了显著的作用。蚩尤是《书》中唯一提到的比尧更古老的名字，虽然只是粗粗一提；但正是由于《书》我们才知道了这一点，同时也证明了《书》自身是真正的历史文献记载。

――――――――

星表使用说明

这张表旨在大致表示大约公元前2300年，在中国中部任何地方的地平线上方，在任何一天的任何时间，能看到的黄道主星的方位。

为了方便实际应用，建议读者剪出一张纸（最好是硬纸板），使其上边缘与曲线ＡＢＯＣＤ完全吻合，并在靠近纸的底部绘制一条线，与表上的"小时线"（Hour Line）重合。

这样做了之后，如果被问及春分日落时天体的方位，读者要沿着表的水平"小时线"移动纸板底部的线，直到太阳在黄道中的位置在春分点Ｏ刚好接触到纸的弯曲顶部；那么在日落时，所有未被

覆盖的星星都在地平线之上，其中包括毕宿五（Aldebaran）、天狼星
（Sirius）、角宿一（Spica）等；昴宿星团（Pleiades）刚刚落下，轩
辕十四（Regulus）和长蛇座 α 星（α Hydrae）非常接近子午线，半
人马座 β 星（β Centauri）处于上升点，而天蛇座 α 星（α Serpentis）
则远高于地平线。这完全符合尧（据中国历史记载生活在公元前
2300 年左右）向他的星官（羲、和）指明的天体方位，即他会在春
分日落时发现"星"［据说对应长蛇座 α 星（α Hydrae）］到达中天 28
的位置。①

　　第二，如果被要求找到夏至日落时哪个星座到达中天，必须像
之前一样将纸板向右手方向移动，直到太阳的位置在夏至点 G 刚好
接触到水平曲线，这时可以看到巨蛇座 α 星（α Serpentis）和心宿二
（Antares）正处于中天位置，轩辕十四和半人马座 β 星正在落下，而
天鹰座（Aquila）和水瓶座（Aquarius）正在上升；织女星（Vega）
在东方地平线上方清晰可见。这再次吻合了尧对其星官的指示，即
他们发现天蝎座（Scorpio）在当时达到中天。

　　第三，要找出冬至日落时哪个星座达到中天，像之前一样移动
纸板上的水平线，直到太阳的位置在冬至点 F 刚好接触到水平线上，
这时将可以看到白羊座（Aries）和金牛座（Taurus）以及昴宿星团
靠近中天的位置。这也吻合尧的指示。

　　最后，秋分日落时，将纸板上的水平线向左移动，直至点 A 落
在水平线上，在此位置可以看见宝瓶座（Aquarius）的星星达到中
天。这些星星在一年中的四次位置几乎不可能与其他任何时代一致，
除了大约在公元前 2300 年或之前、之后的极少数世纪。

---

① 参见已故的英国皇家天文学会（Royal Astronomical Society）副秘书威廉斯先生
（Mr. Willi-ams）关于中国彗星的优秀研究论文，可于伦敦伯林顿府（Burlington
House）皇家天文学会取阅。

　　读者还可以自己发展出此表的其他许多有趣的应用。通过观察昴宿星团在三个不同时期（公元前2300年，公元1年及公元1878年）的三个位置（在表中用字母 K、L、M 标记），可以立即发现岁差对恒星位置的影响。并且由于岁差的近似作用导致所有星平行于黄道以相同的弧线移动，如果读者想象每颗星分别经由对等于 K L、L M 的空间平行于黄道移动，他会得到公元 1 年和 1878 年天体的位置。

　　下表计算了公元前 2300 年、公元前 1500 年、公元 1 年和公元 1000 年这几年几个主星的位置。除了一个例外，此表确证了毕瓯对公元前 2300 年主星位置的类似计算。

（丁大刚、马芙蓉　译

潘琳　校）

星名	公元前2300年 赤经	公元前2300年 北极距	公元前1500年 赤经	公元前1500年 北极距	公元1年 赤经	公元1年 北极距	公元1000年 赤经	公元1000年 北极距	公元1878年 赤经	公元1878年 北极距
	时 分 秒	° ′	时 分 秒	° ′	时 分 秒	° ″	时 分 秒	° ′	时 分 秒	° ′
仙女座α星	20 33 18	82 1.7	21 13 18	79 1.3	22 27 33	71 49.4	23 18 4	66 28.4	0 2 5	61 35.0
飞马座γ星	20 28 50	96 1.1	21 12 0	92 58.9	22 30 26	85 45.9	23 22 23	80 23.8	0 6 57	75 29.7
鲸鱼座β星	20 40 23	129 55.3	21 32 5	126 40.1	22 59 27	119 2.8	23 53 7	113 33.4	0 37 28	108 39.4
白羊座α星	22 18 8	89 27.4	22 59 59	85 16.6	0 18 20	76 57.2	1 12 25	71 36.3	2 0 18	67 6.9
金牛座η星	23 49 0	86 8.3	0 31 15	81 42.1	1 52 20	73 52.4	2 49 17	69 31.6	3 40 14	66 16.4
毕宿五	0 40 10	90 54.6	1 22 25	86 38.2	2 43 20	79 37.0	3 39 17	76 7.5	4 28 55	73 44.3
五车二	0 43 7	60 13.1	1 22 14	55 56.4	2 55 15	49 3.0	4 4 9	45 54.0	5 7 41	44 7.7
参宿七	1 47 31	111 43.8	2 26 12	107 58.3	3 38 7	102 21.2	4 26 41	99 52.2	5 8 40	98 20.7
猎户座α星	2 5 7	93 37.4	2 46 56	90 4.8	4 6 40	85 9.1	5 1 10	83 22.1	5 48 34	82 37.1
天狼星	3 16 27	112 9.0	4 2 2	108 57.4	5 14 27	106 24.3	6 0 31	106 6.5	6 39 46	106 33.0
北河二	2 54 18	62 4.9	3 44 10	59 14.8	5 22 33	56 27.0	6 29 36	56 35.9	7 26 49	57 50.7
南河三	3 44 27	85 4.8	4 28 20	83 50.0	5 50 36	82 18.3	6 45 52	82 59.1	7 32 55	84 27.8
长蛇座α星	5 45 32	88 32.7	6 28 6	88 43.5	7 46 41	91 25.9	8 38 14	94 39.4	9 21 35	98 7.8
轩辕十四	5 55 10	65 40.6	6 45 15	66 6.8	8 16 11	69 36.6	9 14 2	74 25.8	10 1 52	77 26.2
狮子座β星	7 39 12	55 54.2	8 31 25	58 6.5	10 1 9	64 43.8	10 56 54	69 54.5	11 42 50	74 44.8
角宿一	9 37 49	78 15.6	10 37 29	82 7.8	11 40 35	90 15.5	12 33 13	95 45.2	13 18 46	100 31.4
半人马座β星	10 16 8	127 25.1	10 46 42	131 31.7	12 1 16	139 48.1	12 59 23	145 11.8	13 55 14	149 47.0
大角星	10 36 18	47 58.2	11 22 12	52 16.1	12 39 47	60 40.3	13 28 52	65 48.7	14 10 6	70 10.9
巨蛇座α星	12 10 58	63 47.2	12 51 58	68 11.0	14 6 6	75 46.5	14 55 30	79 58.8	15 38 16	83 11.4
心宿二	12 24 0	98 16.5	13 6 50	102 37.4	14 30 11	109 53.9	15 29 8	113 36.6	16 21 56	116 9.6
天琴座α星	16 8 29	48 3.6	16 36 28	49 51.2	17 28 24	51 38.0	18 3 18	51 43.1	18 32 48	51 19.7
天鹰座α星	16 17 0	82 12.2	16 57 6	83 44.0	18 12 14	84 21.1	19 2 19	83 12.7	19 44 50	81 27.2
宝瓶座α星	18 19 16	103 8.6	18 55 26	102 28.3	20 19 41	98 45.1	21 2 2	94 53.9	21 59 31	90 54.7
北落师门	18 16 30	134 54.0	19 15 43	133 57.8	20 58 57	129 17.4	22 1 5	124 46.9	22 50 54	120 16.1
飞马座α星	19 24 1	92 34.4	20 6 35	90 33.5	21 24 14	84 49.4	22 15 19	80 2.6	22 58 41	75 27.0

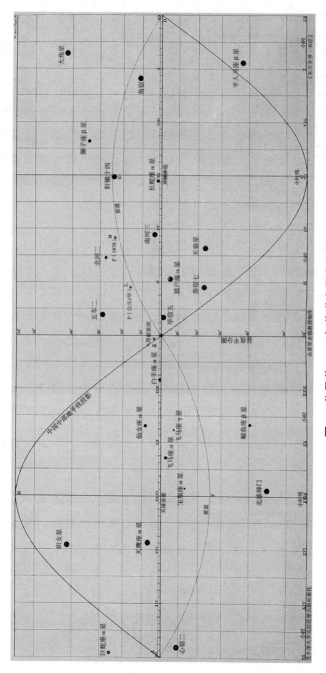

图 1　公元前 2300 年黄道主星方位图

《诗经》（英译本）导论

一、《诗》之名与内容

1."诗"字的含义

在中国经书里，就古老性而言，《书》之后便是《诗》。

汉字"書"由两部分构成："聿"（表示"笔"）和"曰"（表示"说"）。从结构可以看出这个字的主要意义，并为它的各种用法提供了线索。然而，"诗"字的构造原则不同，它是一个形声字——绝大部分汉字都属于这一类。其表意的形旁为"言"，表示大致读音的声旁为"寺"。"诗"字用法不同，意义也有所不同。最常见的意思是诗歌、诗、诗集。《诗》或《诗经》用的是最后一个意思，即诗歌总集。

中国关于诗歌这一主题的论述最早见于《书》，其中舜对他的乐官说："诗言志，歌永言。"《诗大序》也有类似的表述。《诗大序》有人说是孔子所作，不过其创作年代肯定在公元前。其中说："诗者志之所之也，在心为志，发言为诗。情动于中，而形于言，言之不足，故嗟叹之，嗟叹之不足，故永歌之，永歌之不足，不知手之舞之足之蹈之也。……故正得失，动天地，感鬼神，莫近于诗。"

这里需要补充的一点是，韵律是中国诗歌中不可或缺的一部分，《诗》中仅有少数几篇没有韵律。

2.《诗》的内容

《诗经》有三百零五篇，还有六篇仅存篇名。其中时代最近的诗被认为是周定王时期（前 606—前 586）的作品，最古老的五篇被认为是商朝（前 1766—前 1123）的作品。这五篇中，时代最近的一篇应该在公元前 12 世纪，最古老的一篇可能要再向前推 5 个世纪。《诗》中其余诸篇分布于周定王与周文王之间。然而每个时期的分布不均等也不连续，有的时期甚至一篇都没有。

整部《诗经》分为《国风》《大雅》《小雅》《颂》四个部分。

十五《国风》包含一百六十篇，篇幅全都十分短小，记述了周朝几个诸侯国的风俗和事件。有人把"国风"这个标题翻译为"The Manners of the Different States""Les Mœurs des Royaumes"，我倾向于把它翻译为"Lessons from the States"（列国之教训）。

277　　《小雅》，共八卷，包含七十四篇及仅存篇名的六篇，在诸侯宴饮及其朝见天子时演唱。这些诗创作于王畿，描写的是周王室的风俗习惯和治理国家的方式。很难找到一个恰当的英文单词表征这里的"雅"字。孙璋（P. Lacharme）把《小雅》译为"是正确的，但次序较低""Quod rectum est, sed inferiore ordine"，并加注解：《小雅》可以译作 Parvum Rectum，因为这部分描述的风俗习惯总体是正确的，但也有一些偏离了正统"Siâo Yâ, latine Parvum Rectum, quia in hac Parte mores describuntur, recti illi quidem, qui tamen nonnihil a recto deflectunt"。但实际情形是，相较于前面的《国风》或后面的《大雅》，《小雅》所描写的习俗的正确性或不正确性并不亚于他们。我更愿意称这部分为"Minor Odes of the Kingdom"（周王国之小诗），而没有试图翻译"雅"这个字。

《大雅》，共三卷，包含三十一篇，在朝廷的重要场合以及天子在场时演唱。孙璋称其为"Magnum Rectum（Quod rectum est superiore ordine)"。但他使用"正确"(rectum)一词,问题与"小雅"的翻译一样,也会遇到同样的反对意见。我用"Major Odes of the Kingdom"(周王国之大诗)。这一部分诗篇的长度和庄重的程度都使它称得上"Major"(大),以区别于前一部分的"Minor"(小)。

《颂》,共三卷,包含四十篇,其中《周颂》三十一篇,《鲁颂》四篇,《商颂》五篇。孙璋称之为"Parentales Cantus"(父母之歌),很正确。在上文我提到的《诗大序》说:"颂者,美盛德之形容,以其成功告于神明者也。"朱熹说"颂"是"宗庙之乐歌";本朝江永说"颂"是"祭祀之乐歌"。我结合这两个解释,称之为"Odes of the Temple and the Altar"(宗庙和祭坛之诗)。《鲁颂》与其他两颂有 278 别,我将在翻译《鲁颂》时再谈这个问题。

只有第四部分的诗篇具有宗教性质

从以上所述《诗》的内容可以看出,只有第四部分的诗篇具有宗教性质。然而,其他部分的许多诗篇,尤其是第二和第三部分的诗篇,也描写了宗教仪式,表现了作者的宗教思想。

3. 根据体裁和表现手法对诗分类

《诗》中的诗篇有的是民谣(ballads),有的是歌曲(songs),有的是赞美诗(hymns),还有一些难以用英语表达的类型。它们通常被统称为颂歌(odes),即可配乐的抒情诗。

我之所以触及这一点,是因为我们在中国文献中发现了对《诗》(已经结集或正在结集的过程中)最早的记载。《周官》(一般认为是前 12 或前 11 世纪的作品)谈到大师的职责时说:"教六诗,曰风,曰赋,曰比,曰兴,曰雅,曰颂。"《周官》那么早时期结集的《诗》不可能与我们现在看到的《诗》相同;但我们在所谓孔子所作的《诗大序》中也看到了同样的表述。风、雅(包括小雅和大雅)、颂是《诗》的四个部分，我在上节已经谈过了。但什么是赋、比、兴呢？我们也许会认为它们是《诗》的其他部分或卷。但事实并非如此。在《诗》的四个部分中都有赋诗、比诗和兴诗，但在第一部分中尤其多。

"赋"是叙事（narrative）诗，其中诗人把内心所想用简单直接的方式，毫不隐讳地表达出来。诗人在创作中也会自由地使用比喻和其他修辞，这与任何其他语言中的叙事诗并无二致。

"比"是比喻（metaphor）诗，其中诗人想表达的意思与字面上的意思不同，这种隐含的意思与字面上的意思没有任何联系。这种手法可以比作伊索寓言，但是寓言的目的是灌输道德和谨慎的德性，《诗》中的比类诗必须为其寻找一个历史性解释（historical interpretation）。此外，寓言的道德寓意一般是人为附加上去的，这在这些比类诗是不存在的。

"兴"是暗示（allusive）诗。兴类诗非常引人注目，数量上远远多于比类。这些诗开篇几句会在所有诗节中不断被重复，不做任何变化或稍作韵律的变化。有些诗中，不同诗节有自己特定的起兴句。这些起兴句大多是描述动物或植物世界里的某个对象或情形，此后诗人开始进入主题。一般来说，起兴句的意思与接下来诗句的意思相一致；在这种情况下，英国诗人会以 Like 或 As 开篇。它们确实具有比喻的性质，但兴类诗与比类诗的区别在于：前者诗人继续书写她头脑里想好的主题，但后者没有这样的暗示。有时，虽说不上不可能，但很难在起兴句中发现比喻的想法，那么我们只能将之视为叠句。

在结束这个话题之前，还需明确的一点是，有时同一篇诗中会同时出现兴、比、赋三种手法。

二、孔子之前的《诗》及孔子所做的工作

1. 各家观点

司马迁在《孔子世家》中说："古者，诗三千余篇，及至孔子，去其重，取可施于礼义，上采契、后稷，中述殷、周之盛，至幽、厉之缺，……三百〇五篇，孔子皆弦歌之，以求合韶、武、雅、颂之音。"

《隋书·经籍志》说："王泽竭而诗亡，鲁太师挚，次而录之；孔子删诗，上采桑，下取鲁，凡三百篇。"

朱熹的《诗集传》刊印于 1178 年，他没有特别明确地探讨孔子删诗这一问题，但用下面的话总结了孔子为这些诗歌所做的工作："王迹熄而诗亡，其存者缪乱失次，孔子自卫反鲁，复得之他国以归，定著为三百篇。"

我没能找到支持这些说法的证据。我的观点是，孔子生前与身后，《诗》的面貌基本相同；虽然孔子在某种程度上改变了诗歌的编排顺序，但他所做的工作不是编纂（compilation），而是学习和传授。

2. 司马迁的说法无根据

如果我们把司马迁书写《孔子世家》的时间定在公元前 100 年，那么它距离孔子去世已有差不多四百年，也就是说，关于孔子删诗或编纂我们目前的三百多篇诗的说法，距离孔子去世也有差不多四百年；期间没有任何作者曾说到或暗示孔子删诗的事。另外，《隋书》中关于鲁太师的记载也没有任何早期的证据证明这一事件。但是，如果不考虑这些因素的话，有充分的证据证明：第一，孔子之世的诗绝对没有司马迁所说的那么多；第二，这三百篇左右的诗集，其

确立的分类与今天的《诗》相同，在孔子之前就有了。

3. 古诗并没有那么多

说公元前 6 世纪在中国人当中有三千多篇诗流行，并不奇怪。奇怪的是，事实并非如此。但在周朝一部相传为左丘明所著的作品《国语》中，引用的诗有三十一首，全部为孔子之前的王公大夫等所赋；而在这些诗中，不为当今《诗经》所收录的不超过两首，而且这两首中的一首只是用了另外一个名称引用。再者，在左丘明著的《左传》中，引诗至少二百一十九首，其中仅有十三首不在今本《诗经》中。因此，在所谓的孔子编纂《诗经》之前中国已有二百五十首诗流行，其中二百三十六首都在《诗经》中，只有十四首不在其中。用本朝学者赵翼的话说："若使古诗有三千余，则所引逸诗宜多于删存之诗十倍，岂有古诗则十倍于删存诗，而所引逸诗反不及删存诗二三十分之一？以此而推，知古诗三千之说不足凭也。"

282

至于孔子之前就存在的《诗经》被分成四个部分，大体与现在的编排次序相同，可以提出以下四种证据：

第一，上一章最后一节引用和讨论了《周官》中的一段话，其中清楚地提到了《诗》，比孔子早许多世纪，但编排和分类方式与现存《诗》相同。毫无疑问，当时我们的《诗》正在形成过程中。

第二，《诗经》第二部分卷六第四首诗被归在周幽王（前 780—前 770）时代，其中有这样的话：

> 以雅以南，
> 以龠不偕。

因此，早在公元前 8 世纪就有一部诗集了，其中有一些诗被称为"南"，有充足的证据证明就是现在《诗经》第一部分的前两卷

《周南》和《召南》；另外一些是诗被称为"雅"，很有可能就是现在《诗经》的第二和第三部分。

第三，襄公二十九年（前544），孔子仅有八九岁，《左传》载吴公子出使鲁国。吴公子（季札）是当时著名的政治家，很有学问。《左传》说他想听周乐，因为在歌唱方面鲁国比其他任何诸侯国都好，于是就为他歌《周南》《召南》，还有《邶》《墉》《卫》《王》《郑》《齐》《豳》《秦》《魏》《唐》《陈》《郐》《曹》。还为他歌《小雅》《大雅》；最后歌《颂》。因此，在孔子还处于童年，我们就有了现在所谓的《诗经》，包含风、雅、颂。唯一的差别也十分细微——《风》诗各卷的顺序不同。

第四，我们也可诉诸孔子自己的话。《论语》中他两次提及作为一部诗集的诗三百篇。①因为《论语》并非按照任何时间顺序编纂，所以我们不能确定那些话是孔子哪一时期所说；但评注者一致认为他说这些话的时间是在他对《诗》所做工作之前，即司马迁和朱熹所说他删诗、编诗的那个时间之前。

我认为这些证据是确凿的。我们现在所看到的《诗经》在孔子之前很久就在中国流行了。政治家和学者常常在节庆、宴饮等场合引用这些诗。没有包含在其中的诗无疑是少数。孔子也许制作了一个抄本，供自己和弟子使用；但他似乎没有删除之前已被接受的诗，也没有添加之前这个诗集中没有的诗。

4. 孔子为《诗》所做的工作

现在的问题是，孔子究竟为《诗》做了什么，如果他确实做了什么的话。关于这个问题，我们只能根据孔子的话大胆地提一点微

---

① 说"诗三百"，孔子很可能取的是整数。我在前一章说过《诗》总共三百零五篇（这是司马迁给出的数字），还有六篇有目无诗。朱熹等学者认为这些题目只是曲名。更有可能的观点是，这六篇诗的文辞是在孔子去世后亡佚的。

不足道的意见。《论语》第九篇第十四章，孔子说："吾自卫反鲁，然
284 后乐正，雅、颂各得其所。"孔子自卫国返回鲁国时距离其去世仅有
5 年。自此他不再参与政事，通过音乐、读经、书写《春秋》、教授
弟子来安抚自己。他正乐——为诗配乐使其可歌；但至于正在何处，
我们不得而知。他给《雅》《颂》之诗定了正确位置。我们知道，今
本《诗经》中《风》诗各卷的顺序与孔子童年时稍有不同，也可能
这是他所编定的。其余的我们就不得而知了。

　　虽然我们不能找到孔子对《诗》所做的具体工作，虽然我们现
在的《诗经》与孔子之时的《诗》基本相同（见下章），但《诗》的
传承要归功于孔子对《诗》的赞美，以及他对《诗》的热情，并以
之激励弟子。诗是孔子乐于同弟子谈论的话题之一。[1] 孔子说诗可以
让心志得到最好的激励。[2] 在孔子看来，人若不读诗，他就会像面墙
而站，视野受限，无法前行。[3] 孔子特别命令儿子学习的两件事中，
第一件就是学诗。[4] 孔子很可能就是这样传承了《诗经》：首先是保
存刻有诗的简策，继而通过那些敬重其权威及视其为老师的人的记
忆，进行《诗》的传承。

285 ## 三、从孔子时代到现在被公认的《诗经》版本

1. 从孔子到秦代

　　自孔子去世到秦朝兴起这段时间内关于《诗》的研究，我们可
从子思、孟子和荀子的著作中获得充分的证据。孟子被公认的一个

---

① 《论语》第七篇，第十七章。
② 《论语》第八篇，第八章；第十七篇，第九章。
③ 《论语》第十七篇，第十章。
④ 《论语》第十六篇，第十三章。

特点就是精通这些诗，他引用诗的数量特别多。荀子的生命不仅持续到了周朝灭亡，而且到了秦朝。

2. 秦火之后《诗》全部恢复了

秦始皇下令焚书后，除《易》之外，其他经书都被焚毁了，《诗》也在其中。但我已经在《书经》"导论"第 7 页指出，该法令生效不到 25 年秦就灭亡了。几乎全部的诗都恢复了；[①]其中的原因是，这些诗的保存有赖于学者的记忆，而不是刻写在简帛上。

3. 三家《诗》

汉代出现了三种不同的《诗经》本子，即《齐诗》《鲁诗》《韩诗》；也就是从不同地方恢复的《诗经》本子。刘歆《七略》（前 6—1）开篇说《诗经》有三家二十八卷。

（1）《鲁诗》

286

《七略》此后又提到两部《鲁诗》的传注："《鲁故》二十五卷；《鲁说》二十八卷。"《鲁故》的作者是申培，《汉书·儒林传》有其传记。申培是鲁人，从齐地学者浮丘伯学《诗》。浮丘伯有许多弟子跟随他学《诗》，但他只教他们诵诗。汉高祖经过鲁时，申培跟随浮丘伯到鲁南宫与之相见。汉武帝即位初（前 139），召迎申培入宫，其时他已八十多岁的高龄；他好像还活了很多年。他的弟子当中，我们知道名字的有 10 位，都是非常显赫的人物，其中就有孔安国。其后，治《鲁诗》最著名的人物是韦贤，曾官至丞相，作《鲁诗章句》。《汉书》和《魏书》处处可见引诗，它们一定是取自《鲁诗》的这些传授者。但无论是《鲁诗》的经文还是评注性作品都没

[①] 事实上，除了第二部分有目无诗的六篇，其他诗都恢复了。朱熹等学者认为这六篇的文辞在孔子之前就亡佚了。但也有可能是在孔子去世之后亡佚的。参见本卷第 283 页注释 1。

有流传多久。据说它们是在晋朝（265—419）亡佚的。《隋书·经籍志》书写时，这些文本都不存在了。

（2）《齐诗》

《汉书·艺文志》提到了五部《齐诗》著作："《齐后氏故》二十卷，《齐孙氏故》二十七卷，《齐后氏传》三十九卷，《齐孙氏传》二十八卷，《齐杂记》十八卷。"《齐诗》的作者是齐人辕固，《汉书·儒林传》也有他的传记。我们从中得知他是汉景帝朝（前156—前141）的一位著名学者，深受景帝宠爱，尤以治《诗》和主张儒家正统学说而著名。他在武帝时去世，卒年90多岁；据说当时齐地治《诗》显贵者都是他的弟子。其中最著名的是夏侯始昌，夏侯始昌传287《诗》给后苍。后苍是今山东人，《汉书·艺文志》载有他的两部著作。后苍有三位著名弟子，《齐诗》自他们而传授他人，《汉书》很多地方都引用了他们的著作和名字。然而，《齐诗》无论是经文还是评注，其命运都没有比《鲁诗》好到哪里去。《隋书·经籍志》也没有提到它们。据说它们甚至在晋朝之前就灭亡了。

（3）《韩婴诗》

《韩诗》比较幸运。刘歆《七略》载有韩婴的四部著作："《韩故》三十六卷，《韩内传》四卷，《韩外传》六卷，《韩说》四十一卷。"韩婴的姓就这样永久地存在了出自他手的《诗》里。韩婴是燕人，孝文帝时（前179—前155）为"博士"，直到景帝和武帝。《汉书·儒林传》说他"推诗人之意，而作内外传数万言，其语颇与齐、鲁间殊，然归一也。"当然，韩婴创立了一个学派；尽管他的门徒的著作几乎很快就亡佚了，但刚才提到的《韩内传》《韩外传》这两部著作历经多个朝代传到了宋代。《隋书·经籍志》载"《韩诗》二十二卷，《韩诗翼要》十卷，《韩诗外传》十卷。"《旧唐书·经籍志》载"《韩诗》二十卷，《韩诗外传》十卷。"但是，元代刊印的

《宋史·艺文志》只载"《韩诗外传》十卷"；欧阳修（1017—1072）说在他那个时代《韩诗》就只有这些了。《韩诗》就这样全部或几乎全部保存到了今天。

4.《毛诗》

　　鲁、齐、韩三家《诗》除《韩诗》一部分保留下来之外，其他都亡佚了。它们不幸的命运不只是因为中华帝国时常的动荡，从而造成大量典籍被毁，就像我们今天在中国看到的那样，更多是因为 288 第四家《诗》的出现替代了它们，因为这第四家《诗》更为正确，而且受到更多的拥护和评注。这就是所谓的《毛诗》。它比其他三家《诗》晚出；但《汉书·艺文志》载"《毛诗》二十九卷，《毛诗故训传》三十九卷。"郑玄说《毛诗故训传》的作者是鲁人毛亨即大毛公；陆德明说毛亨是荀卿的弟子。这部著作亡佚了。然而，毛亨把他治《诗》的学问传授给了毛苌即小毛公。毛苌是河间献王府的"博士"。这位献王在恢复古书方面最为勤勉，大概是在公元前129年他把《毛诗》和《毛诗故训传》献给了自己的父亲。毛苌有《毛氏诗传》二十九卷遗世；但直到平帝（1—9）时《毛诗》才被立于学官，具有与鲁、齐、韩三家《诗》同等的地位。

　　中国的评论家细致地列出了直到平帝时传授《毛诗》及其传的学者谱系。众学者之名及其著作均已列出。直至公元25年，最著名的学者都致力于《毛诗》。著名的贾逵（30—101）作《毛诗杂义难》，此前汉明帝（58—75）曾令其编撰三家《诗》与《毛诗》异同。著名学者马融（79—165）继之而作《毛诗注》，然后是郑玄或郑康成（127—200）作《毛诗笺》和《诗谱》。《毛诗笺》全部和《诗谱》部分存世。郑玄之后，其他三家《诗》就很少听说了，而那 289 些治《毛诗》的学者之名则迅速为众人所知。《毛诗》甚至被收录在汉灵帝（168—189）的石经中。毛苌墓在今河间府河间县尊福乡。

5. 不同的文本保证了恢复之《诗》的真实性

现在我们重新回到我在第二条谈的秦火之后《诗经》的全部恢复问题。应该说，汉代兴起之后出现的三个不同又相互独立的文本为《诗经》的恢复提供了最令人满意的证据，就如它是继孔子之后而持续存在一般。不幸的是这三家《诗》只有部分文本保留了下来；但是在三家诗仍存于世时，能力出众的学者孜孜不倦地拿它们相互比较，并与《毛诗》比较，最终《毛诗》独存。就目前所知，现行《诗经》包含许多异读现象；我认为它们之间的差异以及与《毛诗》的差异源于这些诗的保存是因讽诵而传。诗歌的韵律有助于记忆。虽然木简、竹帛都毁于秦火，但当暴政过去之后，学者们就渴望背诵他们记忆中的诗了。在中国这样的情况尤其不可避免，因为中国没有字母表，相同的发音由不同的人书写，难免会被写成不同的汉字。

总体来说，以上的证据足以证明《诗经》的恢复问题，我们也没有理由怀疑《诗经》的现行文本，因为它很接近孔子时代流行的文本。

290　　**四、《诗经》的形成；《诗经》为何变得如此简短而不完整；《诗经》的评注及作者；孔子序**

1. 上文第二章已经说明，《诗经》在孔子之前就已经作为诗集存在了。[①] 为了完成这一导论，有必要对本章标题中所指出的问题加以

---

① 就像《书》一样，孔子一般也只用《诗》，从不用《诗经》。然而在《论语》第九篇第十四章，他还提到了"雅"和"颂"；在第十七篇第十章，他说到了《国风》里的前两卷《周南》和《召南》。孟子也同样只用《诗》，在《滕文公上》第四章他提到了《鲁颂》；在《告子下》第三章他发表了对《小弁》和《凯风》两篇诗的看法。

说明。

首先，这些诗是如何收集的？萨尔托恩的安德鲁·弗莱彻爵士（Sir Andrew Fletcher of Saltoun）在他的《关于"一个为了人类普遍利益的正确统治规划"的谈话记录》（*An Account of a Conversation concerning "a Right Regulation of Governments for the Common Good of Mankind"*, Edinburgh, 1704）第 10 页，引用"一个非常聪明的人"的观点，说："如果一个人有机会编纂一个民族的所有民谣，他无需在意谁应该为这个民族立法。"《观察家》（*The Spectator*）第 502 期上一位作者指出在英国早于弗莱彻时代就有类似的观点。他说："我听说伊丽莎白女王统治时期，国务大臣会让人把所有形式的书籍和民谣拿到他面前，不管它是什么种类的书籍和民谣，以便从中考察民情，从而确定使民的最佳方式。"①

中国学者的观点与上述观点一致，他们认为古代帝王有责任了　291 解各诸侯国流传的所有诗歌，并根据这些诗歌来判断诸侯国的统治，以此对诸侯国进行相应的陟罚臧否。

此理论的雏形可以在《尚书·舜典》中找到，但是支持这一理论的一个经典篇章是《礼记·王制》的一段文字："天子五年一巡守……命大师陈诗以观民风。"不幸的是，《王制》这卷书的编纂时间是在汉文帝（前 179—前 155）时。我们可以认为，受命编纂此书的学者一定充分使用了他们手头上的资料。显然他们用到了《孟子》和《仪礼》。那时《周礼》或《周官》还没有恢复。但《孟子》和《仪礼》中都没有提到刚才那句话。《书》提到舜每五年一巡守，但当时没有诗可供他查看；舜及其大臣皋陶被认为是最早尝试诗歌艺术的人。至于夏、殷两代君主们的巡守情况，我们不得而知。我们

---

① 德庇时爵士在其《中国人的诗歌》（*The Poetry of the Chinese*, p.35）中引用了《观察家》上这位作者的话。

知道，周天子是每十二年一巡守。因此，《王制》中的这句话很有可能只是依据传统。

尽管《礼记》这一段读起来困难重重，但是我并不打算完全放弃这一说法。它在一定程度上从我在第278页引用《周官》的一段文字得到了确证，那段文字说明周代已有一部《诗集》，且有风、雅、颂之划分，而由大师负责教授乐师和太学的孩子们。因此可以说，周公在为王朝立法时，下令在天子巡守之时采集各个诸侯国产生的诗，并将之归入周王室大司乐档案中。我们更有理由认为，王畿产生的诗也要在适当的时间采集。

但诸侯是效法周天子的。他们也有自己的大师、乐师和史官。天子巡守并非每个诸侯国都去，这样的话大师便有机会自己采诗。天子在固定的时候会在王国的不同地方去见这些侯、伯、子等，裁定他们的功勋，向他们发布诏令。我们认为诸侯国的乐师会陪同这些诸侯到会见的地方，把他们采集的诗歌呈给天子的乐师。根据以上安排，我们能够明白整个王国的诗是如何集聚到王都而被存档。是否有规定一国之诗在其他诸侯国传播？有充足的证据表明这样的传播在某种程度上是有的。根据《国语》和《左传》的记载，各诸侯国的大夫不仅熟悉他们自己的诗，也熟悉其他诸侯国的诗。他们好像也非常熟悉我们今天《诗经》的各个部分；我们前面已经看到吴国的季札在孔子幼时出访鲁国，《诗经》里的全部诗都被唱给他听了。周王室很可能会定期向各个诸侯国传达那些被认为值得传唱的诗歌。没有地方明确这样说；但可以根据我在《书经》"导论"第4、5页给出的关于王室史官的职责来推论。

2. 但是，如果各个诸侯国的诗都是这样采进王都，然后再传播到整个王国，那么我们也许会推断说这些诗应该要比我们现在看到的更多、更完整。数量少可解释为自武王始几代君主之后王国的混乱和动荡导致。周王朝衰败之后，天子不再巡守，然后诗也就不再采集了。① 春秋时期不见有天子巡守的记载。但在此之前，成王与懿王之间有长达 143 年的间隔，历经康王、昭王、穆王、共王，如果除去《周颂》中两首可疑的诗的话，这些王都没有纪念他们的诗歌。懿王之后的孝王之世同样也没有纪念的诗歌。最晚的诗作于定王之世，距离春秋时期结束还有 100 年。我只能说，成王之后的 143 年间创作和采集了许多诗歌，但它们很有可能在懿王、孝王、夷王和厉王的衰落和动荡之世亡佚了。懿王之世只有五首诗，但朱熹认为其世不详。至于孝王之世，我们上面说过没有诗作。夷王之世只有一首，而且朱熹有充分的理由说它是相当后期的诗作。然后还有四首不详其世，以及归在厉王之世的十一首——其中有的明显有错。继承厉王的是统治时间长久和治理颇为有力的宣王（前 827—前 782），我们可以认为此时恢复了古代的采诗习俗。宣王之世后，周王朝进入大衰败和大动荡时期。也许就是在宣王之世的后期，孔子的先祖正考父（正考甫）从周王室大师那里得到前朝颂诗十二篇，带回到了宋国，宋国是商王朝后裔的封地。这些诗被用于祭祀商朝的先王，也有可能在孔家后来逃难到鲁国时被带到了鲁国。但在这十二首诗中有七首在孔子之世就已经亡佚了。*

　　我们从中得出的总的结论是，现存《诗经》是周代早期几个王统治时期根据《礼记》中记载的制度采集的不同诗集的片段，这些诗集后来有所添加，尤其是在王朝兴盛之时。那么为什么第一部分《国风》包含的诗不足 12 个诸侯国的，而且这些诗只跨越了那些诸侯国历史的很短一段时间：对于这样的问题，我们只能回答说是因

①　参见《孟子》第四篇下，第二十一章。
*　理雅各此段主要资料来源为《钦定诗经传说汇纂》卷首上"作诗时世图"，以及《诗小序》。——译者

294

为时世的破坏和社会动荡的结果。我们只能接受现存的《诗经》本子，而且为此心存感激。至于在孔子之前的什么时间采诗活动停止，我们不得而知。

3. 以上我得出的关于《诗经》如何形成的结论，对于解释其中的许多诗有重要的意义。司马迁等人说孔子从三千篇诗中"取可施于礼义"三百零五篇，是错误的。孔子只是学习和传授了现成的诗，那些诗本来就有说明政教之善恶和道德之美丑的。解诗的最大羁绊莫过于接受朱熹关于《郑风》淫的阐释。但天子巡守之时要求诸侯国采诗和献诗的原因是"观民风"，从而确定其政教得失。作为这些诗的学习者和翻译者，只能让这些诗歌为其自身代言，没有必要纠结于其语言的美与丑。孔子"诗三百，一言以蔽之，思无邪"①这句难解的话，一定得按照我在《论语》中的翻译来理解其意思。*根据我在此提出的所有观点，可以说采集和保存这些诗的目的是促进政治清明和民风向善。这些诗的功用是，它们向我们清晰地展现了这个国家的政治状况，以及人民社会风尚、宗教习惯的好坏。

《诗经》中的诗当然是由那些拥有作诗天赋或自认为有作诗天赋的个人所作。至于说他们都是谁，我们只能依靠诗歌本身的权威性，或与这些诗歌差不多同时期的信史的记载来判断。中国评注者认为这些诗歌大多数由周公所作，这不值得我们质疑，虽然我们承认《书》的第五部分大部分内容为周公所作。不过只有《国风·豳风·鸱鸮》一篇我们有独立的证据可以证明为周公所作。②《国风》中的其他一些诗歌，虽然也是用第一人称写作，而且对这些诗也有非常确定的历史性解释；但是这个第一人称也许是作者虚构的，并

---

① 参见《论语》第二篇，第二章。
* 理雅各把"思无邪"翻译为"Thought without depravity"（思想没有邪念）。——译者
② 参见《书》第五部分，第六章第二节。

非真的是作者自己。

《小雅》中的《节南山》被认为是一位名为家父的周朝贵所作，但我们对他一无所知；《巷伯》的作者被认为是一个叫孟子的寺人；《宾之初筵》，根据所发生之事的外部证据，应该是卫武公（前812—前758）所作。

《大雅》中的《抑》也被认为是卫武公作；《桑柔》被认为是王畿内的芮伯所作；《云汉》被认为是宣王的一个大臣所作，表达王国 296 遭受旱灾危害之时宣王的心情；《崧高》《烝民》被认为是宣王大臣尹吉甫作。

4.《小雅·祈父之什·十月之交》中的一个日期使我们能够非常满意地确定它的创作年份，并证明中国通用年表直到那个日期都是正确的。这首诗是一组诗中的一首，其内容使我们联系到周宣王的儿子周幽王的统治时期，即前781年至前771年。当我们研究他所处时期的年表时，据说他在位的第六年（前776年），发生了一次日食。这首诗开篇写道：

> 十月之交，朔日辛卯，日有食之。

经计算，这次日食发生在公元前776年的8月29日，也就是诗中所写的月和日。

5.《毛诗序》给出了许多诗歌的场景和作者；但我不太看重它的证据。现在它被分为《大序》和《小序》；但是毛氏本人并没有做过这样的划分。关于这个问题，我觉得撮述朱熹的观点就足够了：

> 诗序之作，说者不同，或以为孔子，或以为子夏，或以为国史，皆无明文可考。唯《后汉书·儒林传》以为卫宏作《毛

297 诗序》，① 今传于世，则《序》乃宏作明矣。然郑氏又以为诸序本
自合为一编，毛公始分以诸篇之首，则是毛公之前，其传已久，
宏特增广而润色之耳。故近世诸儒，多以《序》之首句为毛公
所分，而其下推说云云者，为后人所益，理或有之。但今考其
首句，则已有不得诗人之本意，而肆为妄说者矣，况沿袭云云
之误哉。然计其初，犹必自谓出于臆度之私，非经本文，故且
自为一编，别附经后。又以尚有齐、鲁、韩氏之说，并传于世，
故读者亦有以知其出于后人之手，不尽信也。及至毛公引以入
经，乃不缀篇后，而超冠篇端，不为注文，而直作经字，不为
疑辞而遂为决辞，其后三家之传又绝，而毛说孤行，则其抵牾
之迹无复可见。故此《序》者，遂为诗人先所命题，而诗文反
为因《序》以作，于是读者转相尊信，无敢拟议。至于有所不
通，则必为之委曲迁就，穿凿而附合之，宁使经之本文缭戾破
碎不成文理，而终不忍明以《小序》为出于汉儒也。

我想，西方的汉学家几乎没有人会不同意我所认同的朱熹的解
诗原则，即我们必须在诗歌本身中发现诗歌的意义，而不是接受我
们所不认识的那些人的阐释，循着这样的阐释只会把许多诗化为荒
谬的谜。

（丁大刚　马芙蓉　译
　　潘琳　校）

---

① 《后汉书·儒林传》载："谢曼卿善《毛诗》，乃为其训，宏从受学，因作《毛诗序》，
善得风、雅之旨，于今传于世。"

《孝经》(英译本)导论

一、《孝经》之名;《孝经》成书早于汉代;
《孝经》的内容及作者

1. 释"孝"

汉字"孝"可翻译为"Filial Piety",但"孝"也可作形容词,译为"filial",也可作动词,译为"to be filial",也可作副词,译为"filially"。"孝"是一个会意字,其组成部分暗示了其含义。"孝"由两部分组成:上面是表示"老人"或"老"的部分,下面是表示"儿子"的部分。中国最古老的字典《说文》(公元100年成书)说:"孝,子承老也。"从视觉而言,"孝"字呈现的就是一个孩子扶持老人之状。由"孝"作声旁构成的汉字至少有20个,因此"孝"字在很早之前就有了。"经"字已经在《书经》"导论"(第2页)里解释过,因此"孝经"可以翻译为"the Classic of Filial Piety"。

2.《孝经》是由孔子命名的吗?

中国许多评注者认为,《孝经》这部简短的著作是由孔子命名的,它在其他更古老、更重要的经典之前就被称为"经"了。现存 450 《孝经》版本应当归功于唐玄宗(713—755)。玄宗在其《孝经》注本序中说:"子曰:'吾志在《春秋》,行在《孝经》。'"玄宗引用此句,仿佛大家普遍认为这句话出自孔子之口。关于此句话更早的记载见于何休（129—182）的《春秋公羊传解诂·序》中。勤勉的学者将其追溯到更早年代的《孝经钩命决》，此书大约成书于公元1世纪，或公元前1世纪。它是一种纬书，内容充斥着神秘而无用的谶纬之说，从未被广泛认可。很多纬书很快就消失了，但是这部纬书一直保存到了隋朝（581—618），因为当时秘阁里有一份抄本。它现在已经丢失了，但是汉代作者的引文中保留有原作的一些段落。其中有云："孔子云：'欲观我褒贬诸侯之志，在《春秋》；崇人伦之行，在《孝经》。'"因此被认为出自孔子之口的"孝经"二字便先经过何休，后经过玄宗皇帝，最终传给了我们。无论"孝经"二字是否真的出自孔子之口，早在我们的基督纪元之初它就被认为是出自孔子，而且当时人们认为是孔子给了这部经典"经"这一尊贵的名称。

3.《孝经》成书早于汉代

但是《孝经》的成书可以追溯到汉朝前几百年，即孔子死后不到100年的时间。司马迁在《魏世家》说，魏文侯在公元前407年从卜子夏处获得经书，此外还提到孔子另两个弟子，此两人都是文侯的好朋友。文侯为《孝经》作的传注在蔡邕（133—192）时期仍在流传，蔡邕在一部著作中撮述其要。

4.《孝经》的内容及作者

《孝经》在秦火之后的恢复我们将会在下节谈及。这里我们假设《孝经》已近恢复了。翻看此书，我们发现其中尽是孔子与弟子曾子之间的对话，以及众多对话的摘录。然而，曾子仅仅是一个聆听者，孔子将孝置于各种人伦之中，向曾子讲述了他对孝的看法。《孝经》有两个本子：一个本子十八章，一个本子二十二章。十八章的本子，每一章都有一个非常简短的标题。我在译文中给出了这些标题，但这些标题只能追溯到唐玄宗的注本。

何休等人将"吾志在《春秋》，行在《孝经》"之言归于孔子，似乎表明了是孔子自己创作了《孝经》，但是读者很快就意识到《孝经》不可能出自孔子。许多人认为这部著作是在孔子的指导下由曾子写成的；但它的风格和写作方法否定了这一观点。然而，我们没有理由不接受一种更普遍的说法——《孝经》出自曾子学派。用 12 世纪上半叶胡寅的话来说："《孝经》非曾子所自为也。曾子问孝于仲尼，退而与门弟子言之，门弟子类而成书。"

二、汉代《孝经》的恢复及唐玄宗《孝经》注本

452

（一）

1.《孝经》的恢复

《孝经》像其他所有的除《易经》之外的儒学著作一样遭遇了秦火。其后来的恢复与《书》的恢复（第 7—8 页）十分相似。像《书》一样，《孝经》也有一个篇幅较短的今文本和一个篇幅较长的古文本。

据刘歆《七略》记载，有两个版本的《孝经》：一个版本是《孝经古孔氏》，《汉书》作者班固说它有二十二章；另一个版本据班固注有十八章，后来被称为"今文"。在这两个条书目之后，我们发现有《长孙氏说》《江氏说》《后氏说》《翼氏说》。班固说这四家所解说的皆为十八章《孝经》。

2. 今文《孝经》

因此，我们必须认为十八章的副本是首先被恢复的。但这其中

究竟经历了什么，我们不得而知，直到《隋书》中才有记载。《隋书》说秦下令销毁书籍时，《孝经》副本被一位名叫颜芝的学者藏起来，他无疑是孔子最喜欢的弟子颜回所属的颜氏家族的成员。几年后焚书令废止时，颜芝的儿子颜贞将副本从藏匿处取出。这一定是在公元前2世纪，这个副本很可能是由颜贞以当时使用的字体誊写下来的。在文景之世（前179—前141），此副本交由被任命保存古籍的博士保管。

453

3. 古文《孝经》

汉武帝时期（前140—前87），古文《孝经》的木简在孔子故宅壁中被发现。与《书》简一样，一般认为这些简也是被孔安国解读出来的。安国为此《孝经》作传，但它并未出现在刘歆的《七略》里，就像里面也没有提到安国为《书》作传一样。但是，我们在《隋书》里发现了下面的记载："安国之本，亡于梁乱……至隋……于京师访得孔传，送至河间刘炫。"刘炫于是将其公布于众，不久之后被朝廷立为国学，但许多学者认为是刘炫假托安国之名自作。无论此本系刘炫所作与否，古文《孝经》的发现以及孔安国为之作传都是毋庸置疑之事。

4. 古文《孝经》有另一个副本吗？

不过，有人可能会说，公元前1世纪发现了古文《孝经》的另一个副本。公元121年许慎的儿子许冲向安帝进献《说文解字》，在上皇帝书中，他说他父亲使用的《孝经》是"鲁国一老者"献给昭帝（前86—前74）的副本。[1] 以王应麟（字伯厚，1223—1296）为

---

[1] 许冲的上书是这么说的："古文《孝经》者，孝昭帝时，鲁国三老所献。"其中的"三老"很容易让人联想到"三个老人"，但按照中国成语的意思，这两个字也可表示"三等老人"或"三等老人中的一人"。《礼记·文王世子》解释了这个词语的意思，

代表的中国评论家指出，这种说法与孔安国发现古文《孝经》的说 454
法不一致。很难调和这两种说法，参见下面的注释；①但是如果我们 455
知道更多这一发现的细节，以及后来这些竹简是怎么处理的，这个
困难就不存在了。

5. 我们能够完全信赖刘歆收录的副本吗？

当然，公元前 1 世纪，汉朝秘府确实有两个《孝经》副本。如
果刘歆收录进《七略》的这两个副本，确实是颜贞进献的本子，以

（接上页）说文王在太学设宴招待"三老、五更"（即三等老人和五等人），三等老人
分别指 80、90、100 岁三等。昭帝是从其中一等的一个人那里获得了古文《孝经》。
（理雅各对"三老"的理解遵从的是《钦定礼记义疏》杜预注和编者案语。——中译
者）这个人应该是孔子惠（参见下一条注释）；《隋书》说这个人是孔氏家族的一个
人，是他在秦始皇发布焚书令时把《孝经》竹简藏了起来。

① 《四库全书总目》述及《孝经》各副本时首先介绍了从日本获得的《古文孝经孔氏
传》；但《总目》的编者罗列了充分的理由质疑其真实性。大英博物馆中文部藏有
这部著作的一个副本，是 1732 年刊印的一个版本。我在道格拉斯教授和伟烈亚力
先生的帮助下仔细研究过这个版本。它不仅包含了孔安国的传，而且有孔安国的原
序。其中说，在孔子讲堂壁中"石函"内发现古文《孝经》，载于竹牒，字为"科斗
文"，由鲁国"三老"孔子惠献给皇帝。此序还说，皇帝命"学士与博士群儒"用当
时流行的字体抄写了两份，一份给子惠，另一份赐给了皇帝所宠幸的侍中霍光。霍
光很珍视这个抄本，藏之于秘府，小心呵护。
　　这一说明让"鲁国三老"的意思变得非常清楚；但是，我们很难相信这是出自
孔安国。序中没有提到他；然而根据现在的说法，科斗文写成的竹牒是由他首先破
译的。序中也没有提到孔子惠进献的皇帝的名字；然而，毫无疑问，这位皇帝即是
汉昭帝，霍光是他的宠臣。如果序是真实的，那么在子惠将竹牒进献皇帝之时，安
国仍在世。这些竹牒发现于天汉年间（前 100—前 97），而汉昭帝在位时间为公元
前 86 年到公元前 74 年。安国死时年六十岁，至于是哪一年，我们无从得知。他曾
从申公学《诗》，申公卒年不可能晚于公元前 135 年。如果安国出生在公元前 150 年，
若他卒于昭帝即位时，他卒时应该不止 60 岁。因此，我认为从日本获得的《孝经》
的序不是孔安国所作；如果我们否认此序，我们也必须否认它之后的传。
　　这个《孝经》文本几乎与司马光的《孝经》文本（参见原书第 458 页即本书边
码）一模一样；但每章都加了标题（司马光并没有采用这些标题），这些标题添加的
时间早不过唐朝。这也许能说得过去，但传没有为经文带来新意。《四库全书总目》
的编者说其传文"浅陋冗漫，不类汉儒释经之体。"我必须认同他们的观点，即所谓
日本所保存的孔安国的传是伪造的。

及从孔子讲堂壁中发现的古文《孝经》并用汉隶誊写的抄本；那么我们就可以说，秦火之后恢复的《孝经》与周朝时的《孝经》是一样的，关于其恢复的证据正如我们所期望的那样是令人满意的。但是，这其中还有一些问题需要考虑。

据《隋书》，古文《孝经》献于朝廷后，有人注意到它与早期恢复的文本之间有差异，于是刘歆的父亲刘向（前80—前9），奉汉成帝（前32—前7）的旨意对这两个本子进行校对。校对结果是："除其繁惑，以十八章为定。"以前似乎没有将颜贞的副本划分章节。刘向对古文《孝经》做了什么，我们不得而知。唐代颜师古注刘歆目录"孝经古孔氏"条引刘向言曰："庶人章分为二也，曾子敢问章分为三，又多一章。"据了解，古文《孝经》多出来的这一章开头是"闺门之内"。我翻译所据的底本是玄宗注本，但我把来自古文《孝经》的这一章附在了我的译文之后。但《隋书》说这一章在早期今文《孝经》四大评注者之一的长孙氏《孝经》中。

刘歆《七略》中收录的副本来自他父亲典校的两个本子。现存
456 《孝经》的风格和写法不似流传下来的刘向的原作。由于缺乏证据，很难说他对交给他的文本有多大的修改自由。我们现在看到的这两个文本之间的差异是微不足道的。我认为刘向的修改并不重要；但正是由于他的修改，我们才有了二手的《孝经》，这就为朱熹等人对它的处理提供了理据（我将在下一章谈及这个问题）。

（二）

1. 从孔安国到唐玄宗

我在上文已经说过（第450页），对于我们现在所拥有的今文

《孝经》，我们要感谢唐玄宗的注。朱彝尊《经义考》列举了从孔安国到唐玄宗时期共 86 部《孝经》传注作品。其中没有一部幸存下来；但这表明，在其间的几个世纪里，最杰出的学者都为《孝经》做了注，并在保存文本方面做到了相互监督。此外，一些作品横跨整个唐朝，并一直保留到宋朝。《隋书·经籍志》共收录《孝经》著作 19 种。

2. 唐玄宗的注

唐玄宗在序中说他在注解《孝经》时参考了早期的六家注。此六家为：公元 2 世纪和 3 世纪的韦昭、王肃、虞翻、刘邵；公元 6 世纪的刘炫，刘炫所治者为孔安国的传，如前所述，孔安国的传是在他的那个时代被发现并呈现给了他；陆澄（比刘炫更早）批判了郑康成的注。玄宗说："在理或当，何必求人？今故特举六家之异同，会五经之旨趣；约文敷畅，义则昭然。" 457

玄宗本人没有提到古文和今文文本之间的差异，尽管我们知道，这个问题在当朝学者中引起了激烈的争论。他注解的文本共 18 章，其中不包括我在第 455 页（本书边码）提到的一章，即公元前 1 世纪长孙氏《孝经》中的那章。据权威的说法，由于受学者和大臣司马贞的影响，这一章被排除在外。玄宗在《孝经》每章前都加上了一个简短的标题，我在译文中保留了这些内容。这些标题，很可能是他从当朝学者提出的各种各样的标题中挑选出来的。

这篇御注所采用的《孝经》文本现在可以被认为是相当可靠的。不到一个世纪后，这个《孝经》文本被刻在唐石碑上。唐石碑公元 837 年刻成，被立在唐都西安。直到今天，这些石碑仍然保存在那里，几乎没有受到破坏。[①] 不仅如此。皇帝对自己的注非常满意，公

---

① 　一般认为这些石碑所刻为"十三经"经文；但实际上只有 12 部著作，包括《易》《书》《诗》《周礼》《仪礼》《礼记》《春秋左传》《春秋公羊传》《春秋穀梁传》"九

元 745 年，他下令将此《孝经》文本及其注全部刻在四个大石碑上。今天仍然可以在西安的孔庙前看到这些石碑。

458 3. 邢昺的疏

关于《孝经》的保存，在此无需赘述。公元 996 年，宋朝第二位皇帝敕令注解《孝经》。在邢昺（932—1010）的监管下对《孝经》文本及玄宗注给予大量批判性注释以及长篇的疏解，书成于 1001 年。自此，这一著作在中国一直沿用至今。

三、唐代之后的《孝经》批评

1. 司马光和范祖禹评注的古文《孝经》

尽管我在第 455 页已经指出有一章存在问题，但玄宗的文本一般被认为是公元前 2 世纪恢复的代表性今文《孝经》。但是，仍不乏有人继续支持"古文"。宋朝大臣和大学者司马光（1009—1086）1054 年把自己作的《古文孝经指解》上呈朝廷，他在序及各种表文中多次为公元 6 世纪刘炫恢复的古文辩护，力证其真。范祖禹（1041—1098）与司马光为同一世纪的学者，也是司马光的同僚，晚年著《古文孝经说》。他在序中说："二者虽大同而小异，然得其真

（接上页）经"和《论语》《孝经》《尔雅》。顾炎武（1613—1682）说这些石碑上共有 650252 个汉字。戴维斯（T. W. Rhys Davids）估计我们的英文《圣经》有 80 万—95 万个单词（*Buddhism*, p.19）。译文典雅、精炼的"委办本"《诗篇》第一篇有 100 个汉字，而我们的英文则有 130 个单词。唐石碑所刻经典若翻译为英文（如果译者精通这两门语言的话），其部头不会有我们的《圣经》那么大。

者，古文也。臣之说也不无用也。*"①

2. 质疑之声

（1）朱熹的观点

但是，到了宋朝《孝经》仍遭受了严厉的质疑。最具代表的就是朱熹的《孝经刊误》，刊印于1186年。朱熹说他最初看到胡宏［高宗朝（1127—1162）大臣］说《孝经》引《诗》多出后人附会，感到非常震惊。然而经过长时间的考察，朱熹觉得胡宏之言很有道理，而且他认为《孝经》的其他部分也有可疑之处。此外，他还发现孝宗朝（1163—1189）还有一位学者汪应辰指出《孝经》大多内容被汉代学者篡改过。因此，他就有理由表达自己的观点，而不必担心被指责是第一个质疑通行文本的人。

事实上，正如《四库全书总目》编者指出的那样，朱熹一直都坚持他在《孝经刊误》中表明的观点，引用胡、王两人之说只是为了掩盖自己的大胆举动。朱熹将《孝经》分为"经"一章，"传"十四章。但是两部分都被大量删减。他的"经"包含我译文中的前六章，朱子认为这部分是孔子说的一段连续的话。剩余部分不该归于孔子。其中大部分内容出自曾子及其弟子，然而汉代学者篡改了大量的内容。朱熹取古文《孝经》，删去223字。

我们应该注意他删去的那些文句，以及他提出的理由，这些理 460

---

* 最后一句引文为理雅各撮述原序之意，原序为："臣今窃以古为据，而申之以训说，虽不足以明先王之道，庶几有万一之补焉。"——译者

① 现在中国刊行的《孝经》，要么单独刊印，要么与朱熹的《小学》一起刊印。我们发现它用的是古文，没有分章。但是，玄宗的注、司马光的指解和范祖禹的说相继列在每个章句之后。有些部分与我译文所遵从的玄宗和邢昺的章句次序不一致。如前文所说，古文本和唐玄宗的今文本之间的差异很小，甚至还没有我们《新约》中福音书和其他卷各校勘本之间的差异大。

由大体上令人满意。显然，他在很大程度上受到了他所称"程子"即程颐（1033—1107）处理古文《大学》方式的影响，但他更大胆，改得更大刀阔斧，不仅改变了章句的次序，补充了明显的缺陷，还质疑了原文大部分内容的真实性，并毫无顾忌地删除了这些内容。

（2）吴澄的观点

元代大学者吴澄（1249—1333）跟随朱熹的质疑，但有独到之处。朱熹从古文《孝经》，吴澄更喜今文《孝经》，这一版本在我看来也是更为正确的；吴澄认为公元6世纪刘炫恢复的孔安国之经和传是伪作。因此，吴澄以玄宗今文为底本改定《孝经》，撰《孝经章句》（ *the Hsiâo King, in paragraphs and sentences* ）[1]。吴澄从朱熹之例，将《孝经》分为"经"和"传"。经一章与朱熹一致，传只有十二章。当然，他删除了古文特有的一章，我们在前文多次提及这一章，而且将玄宗的十一章和另一章合并，还更改了朱熹其他章的次序。此改定本比古文《孝经》少246字。

3. 后来的《孝经》著作

朱彝尊列举了吴澄之后至明朝之间出现的《孝经》著作近一百二十种。本朝学者对《孝经》的研究并不比前朝少。毛奇龄（1623—1713）著作集中有一本《孝经问》，他以自身的学问加上他一贯的尖刻为通行本《孝经》辩护。他坚称古文与今文无大差别，在这一点上他是对的；但他进一步指出从未有过古文与今文之别，此言没有证据支撑。他讥笑朱熹与吴澄；但是，我认为他在辩护《孝经》为真方面不如辩护孔安国之《书》来得成功。

中国历代帝王都对《孝经》十分重视。在玄宗注之前，东晋

---

① 此书在《四库全书总目》中作《孝经定本》（ *Settlement of the Text of the Hsiâo King* ）。

（317—419）元帝和孝武帝，梁（502—556）武帝和简文帝，以及北魏（386—534）孝明帝均注过《孝经》。本朝满族统治者在《孝经》注疏上也颇有成就。1656 年第一位皇帝作《御注孝经》（*Imperial Commentary on the Hsiâo King*）一卷，1728 年第三位皇帝颁布《孝经集注》（*Collection of Comments*）。在他们之间是著名的康熙朝（1662—1722），清朝最为著名的第二位皇帝康熙帝御定了《孝经衍义》（*Extensive Explanation of the Hsiâo King*）一百卷。其中惟一完整给出的一部分经文是朱熹的经一章；但朱熹传十四章的大部分主题也得到了阐发；整部书都值得认真研究。

4. 关于《孝经》之真实性与完整性的结论

我们看到，肆意删改《孝经》的朱熹和吴澄这两位大学者，认为《孝经》中有孔子之言，整部《孝经》超过五分之一的内容可以准确无误地归在孔子名下，包含大约四百个字，尽管这其中还有朱熹删改的内容。在这一点上我同意他们的意见。其余内容，无论被归在谁的名下，从孔子的直系弟子曾子到刘向（前 80—前 9），公元前 1 世纪就形成了我们现在的样子。读者可能看不出章与章之间的紧密联系，会认为其作者试图扩大"孝"的内涵，使它超过其本有的含义。然而，《孝经》是一部重要的古代经典，展示了中国的道德家和统治者从最古老的时代起就乐于颂扬的美德，认为它是仁之本，是社会幸福的伟大源泉，是国家富强和稳定的纽带。

462

翻译说明

在翻译《孝经》的过程中，我经常参阅之前的四个译本。

其中两个是我自己的译本：一个是 30 年前我为了提高中文水平而做的翻译练习；另一个是 4 年前，我为了全面了解儒家关于"孝"的教导而做的翻译，但当时没有参考我之前的翻译。

第三个是 1835 年《中国丛报》（*The Chinese Repository*）第 4 卷第 345—353 页刊登的译文，其准确性不够，注释也寥寥无几。第四个在《中国杂纂》（*Mémoires concernant les Chinois*, Paris, 1779）第 4 卷，是由韩国英（P. Cibot）撰写的长篇巨著《中国古今孝道》的一部分。韩国英在《孝经》译序中说："卫方济以前把《孝经》翻译成拉丁文。我们的翻译必然与他的不同。他依从古文，我们则依从今文。今文《孝经》是国子监学者们采用的本子。不仅如此，卫方济做的是释义型翻译。我们要做一个忠实的法译本。"我在做这个译本的时候，没有能够参考到卫方济的翻译；但我在做最早的一个译本时，参考了他的翻译。古文和今文之间的差异非常细微，不足以影响它们翻译的性质，但卫方济的译本显然太过冗长。他的著作的标题是《中国六经拉丁译本：大学、中庸、论语、孟子、孝经、小学》（*SINENSIS IMPERII LIBRI CLASSICI SEX, nimirum Adultorum Schola, Immutabile Medium, Liber sententiarum, Mencius, Filialis Observantia, Parvulorum Schola, e Sinico idiomate in Latinum* traducti à P. Fr. Noël, S.J., Prague, 1711）。我认为，与韩国英的法语译本相比，我现在的英文译本更准确、更忠实，就像用中文写成一样。

（丁大刚　马芙蓉　译
潘琳　校）

THE SHÛ KING（书经）

THE SHIH KING（诗经）

THE HSIÂO KING（孝经）

THE

SACRED BOOKS OF CHINA

THE TEXTS OF CONFUCIANISM

TRANSLATED BY

JAMES LEGGE

PART I

THE SHÛ KING

THE RELIGIOUS PORTIONS OF THE SHIH KING

THE HSIÂO KING

Oxford

AT THE CLARENDON PRESS

1879

CONTENTS.

ix

THE SHIH.

INTRODUCTION.

CHAP.

I. THE NAME AND CONTENTS OF THE SHIH . . . 275

The meaning of the character Shih. The contents. Only the pieces of the fourth Part have professedly a religious character. Classification of the pieces from their form and style.

II. THE SHIH BEFORE CONFUCIUS, AND WHAT, IF ANY, WERE HIS LABOURS UPON IT 280

Statement of Sze-mâ *Kh*ien; in the Records of the Sui Dynasty; of *K*û Hsî. View of the author. Groundlessness of *Kh*ien's statement. What Confucius did for the Shih.

THE HSIÂO.

INTRODUCTION.

CHAP.

I. THE NAME OF THE CLASSIC; ITS EXISTENCE BEFORE THE
HAN DYNASTY; ITS CONTENTS, AND BY WHOM IT WAS
WRITTEN 449

Meaning of the character Hsiâo. Was the treatise called
the Hsiâo King by Confucius? It existed before the Han
dynasty during the time of the *K*âu. It came, probably, from
the school of ȝăng-ȝze.

II. THE RECOVERY OF THE HSIÂO UNDER THE HAN
DYNASTY, AND ITS PRESERVATION DOWN TO THE
PUBLICATION OF THE COMMENTARY OF THE THANG
EMPEROR HSÜAN ȝUNG 452

Recovery of the Hsiâo. The shorter or modern text. The
old or longer text. Was another copy in the old text discovered? Can we fully rely on the copies catalogued by Liû
Hin? From Khung An-kwo to the emperor Hsüan ȝung.
The emperor's work. Hsing Ping's work.

III. CRITICISM OF THE HSIÂO SINCE THE THANG DYNASTY 458

Works on the old text by Sze-mâ Kwang and Fan ȝû-yü.
Sceptical criticism ;—views of *K*û Hsî and Wû *Kh*ăng. Con-
clusion regarding the genuineness and integrity of the Hsiâo.
Note on the translation.

PREFACE.

WHILE submitting here some prefatory observations on
the version of the Shû King presented in this volume,
I think it well to prefix also a brief account of what are
regarded as the Sacred Books of the Religions of China.
Those religions are three:—Confucianism, Tâoism, and
Buddhism.

I. I begin with a few words about the last. To translate
any of its books does not belong to my province, and more
than a few words from me are unnecessary. It has been
said that Buddhism was introduced into China in the third
century B.C.; but it certainly did not obtain an authorita-
tive recognition in the empire till the third quarter of our
first century[1]. Its Texts were translated into Chinese, one
portion after another, as they were gradually obtained from
India; but it was not till very long afterwards that the
Chinese possessed, in their own language, a complete copy
of the Buddhist canon[2]. Translations from the Sanskrit
constitute the principal part of the Buddhistic literature
of China, though there are also many original works in
Chinese belonging to it.

---

[1] I put the introduction of Buddhism into China before our Christian era thus
uncertainly, because of what is said in the article on the history of Buddhism in
China, in the Records of the Sui Dynasty (A.D. 589–618), the compilers of which
say that before the Han dynasty (began B.C. 202) Buddhism was not heard of
in China. They refer to contrary statements as what 'some say,' and proceed
to relate circumstances inconsistent with them. It is acknowledged on all sides
that Buddhist books were first brought to China between A.D. 60 and 70.

[2] Mr. Beal (Catena of Buddhist Scriptures from the Chinese, pp. 1, 2) says
that 'the first complete edition of the Buddhist Canon in China dates from the
seventh century; that a second and much enlarged edition of it, called the
Southern Collection, was prepared in A.D. 1410; that a third edition, called the
Northern Collection, appeared about A.D. 1590; which again was renewed and
enlarged in the year 1723.'

II. Confucianism is the religion of China par excellence, and is named from the great sage who lived in the
fifth and sixth centuries B. C. Confucius indeed did not
originate the system, nor was he the first to inculcate its
principles or enjoin its forms of worship. He said of himself (Analects, VII, i) that he was a transmitter and not
a maker, one who believed in and loved the ancients ; and
hence it is said in the thirtieth chapter of the Doctrine of
the Mean, ascribed to his grandson, that 'he handed down
the doctrines of Yâo and Shun, as if they had been his
ancestors, and elegantly displayed the regulations of Wăn
and Wû, taking them as his models.'

In fulfilling what he considered to be his mission, Confucius did little towards committing to writing the views of
antiquity according to his own conception of them. He
discoursed about them freely with the disciples of his
school, from whom we have received a good deal of what
he said; and it is possible that his accounts of the ancient
views and practices took, unconsciously to himself, some
colour from the peculiar character of his mind. But his
favourite method was to direct the attention of his disciples
to the ancient literature of the nation. He would neither
affirm nor relate anything for which he could not adduce
some document of acknowledged authority. He said on
one occasion (Analects, III, ix) that he could describe the
ceremonies of the dynasties of Hsiâ (B. C. 2205-1767) and
Yin (B. C. 1766-1123), but did not do so, because the
records and scholars in the two states of *K*âu, that had
been assigned to the descendants of their sovereigns, could
not sufficiently attest his words. It is an error even to
suppose that he compiled the historical documents, poems,
and other ancient books from various works existing in his
time. Portions of the oldest works had already perished.
His study of those that remained, and his exhortations to
his disciples also to study them, contributed to their preservation. What he wrote or said about their meaning should
be received by us with reverence; but if all the works
which he handled had come down to us entire, we should
have been, so far as it is possible for foreigners to be, in

the same position as he was for learning the ancient religion of his country. Our text-books would be the same
as his. Unfortunately most of the ancient books suffered
loss and injury after Confucius had passed from the stage
of life. We have reason, however, to be thankful that we
possess so many and so much of them. No other literature, comparable to them for antiquity, has come down to
us in such a state of preservation.

But the reader must bear in mind that the ancient books
of China do not profess to have been inspired, or to contain what we should call a Revelation. Historians, poets,
and others wrote them as they were moved in their own
minds. An old poem may occasionally contain what it
says was spoken by God, but we can only understand that
language as calling attention emphatically to the statements to which it is prefixed. We also read of Heaven's
raising up the great ancient sovereigns and teachers, and
variously assisting them to accomplish their undertakings;
but all this need not be more than what a religious man of
any country might affirm at the present day of direction,
help, and guidance given to himself and others from above.
But while the old Chinese books do not profess to contain
any divine revelation, the references in them to religious
views and practices are numerous; and it is from these
that the student has to fashion for himself an outline of
the early religion of the people. I will now state what the
books are.

First, and of greatest importance, there is the Book of
Historical Documents, called the Shû and, since the
period of the Han dynasty (began B.C. 202), the Shû
King. Its documents commence with the reign of Yâo in
the twenty-fourth century B.C., and come down to that of
king Hsiang of the *K*âu dynasty, B.C. 651–619. The earliest
chapters were not contemporaneous with the events which
they describe, but the others begin to be so in the twenty-
second century B.C. The reader will find a translation of
the whole of this work without abridgment.

Second, and nearly as important as the Shû, there is
the Shih, or the Book of Poetry. It contains in all 305

pieces, five of which are of the time of the Shang dynasty (called also the Yin), B.C. 1766–1123. The others belong to the dynasty of Kâu, from the time of its founder, king Wăn, born B.C. 1231, to the reign of king Ting, B.C. 606–586. The whole is divided into four Parts, the last of which is occupied with 'Odes of the Temple and the Altar.' Many pieces in the other Parts also partake of a religious character, but the greater number are simply descriptive of the manners, customs, and events of the times to which they belong, and have no claim to be included in the roll of Sacred Texts. In this volume will be found all the pieces that illustrate the religious views of their authors, and the religious practices of their times.

The third work is the Yî, commonly called the Book of Changes. Confucius himself set a high value on it, as being fitted to correct and perfect the character of the learner (Analects, VII, xvi); and it is often spoken of by foreigners as the most ancient of all the Chinese classics. But it is not so. As it existed in the time of the sage, and as it exists now, no portion of the text is older than the time of king Wăn, mentioned above. There were and are, indeed, in it eight trigrams ascribed to Fû-hsî, who is generally considered as the founder of the Chinese nation, and whose place in chronology should, probably, be assigned in the thirty-fourth century B.C. The eight trigrams are again increased to sixty-four hexagrams. To form these figures, two lines, one of them whole (——) and the other divided (— —), are assumed as bases. Those lines are then placed, each over itself, and each over the other; and four binograms are formed. From these, by the same process with the base lines, are obtained eight figures,—the famous trigrams. Three other repetitions of the same process give us successively sixteen, thirty-two, and sixty-four figures. The lines in the figures thus increase in an arithmetical progression, whose common difference is one, and the number of the figures increases in a geometrical progression, whose common ratio is two. But what ideas Fû-hsî attached to his primary lines,—the whole and the divided; what significance he gave to his trigrams; what to the

sixty-four hexagrams,—if indeed he himself formed so
many figures; and why the multiplication of the figures
was stayed at sixty-four:—of none of these points have we
any knowledge from him.　There is some reason to believe
that there were texts to the hexagrams under the dynasties
of Hsiâ and Shang, but none of them have been preserved.
It may be that king Wăn and his equally famous son, the
duke of *K*âu, adopted much of what they found already
existing, and incorporated it with their own interpretations
of the figures; but they, and they alone, are accepted as
the authors of the text of the Yî.　King Wăn, we are told,
at a time when he was imprisoned by the tyrannical sovereign with whom the dynasty of Shang or Yin ended, took
in hand the ever-changing hexagrams, and appended to
each a brief explanation of the meaning which the trigrams
composing it suggested by their union to his mind; and in
some cases the practical course in affairs to which that
meaning should direct.　His son did for the separate lines
of each hexagram what Wăn had done for the whole figure.
Confucius is said to have entered into their labours about
600 years afterwards.　Several appendixes are ascribed to
him, in which there is an attempt to explain the origin
of the Fû-hsî figures, and many of the interpretations of
Wăn and his son.　The early linear figures; the notes
of Wăn and the duke of *K*âu; and the Confucian appendixes:—these constitute the Yî.
　　The work was from the first intimately connected with
the practice of divination, which, we know from the Shû,
entered largely into the religion of the ancient Chinese.
This goes far to account for its obscure and enigmatical
character; but at the same time there occur in it, though
in a fragmentary manner, so many metaphysical, physical,
moral, and religious utterances, that the student of it is
gradually brought under a powerful fascination.　In consequence, moreover, of its use in divination, it was exempted
by the superstitious tyrant of *K*hin from the flames to
which he condemned all the other Confucian literature in
B.C. 213.　It has thus come down to us entire, and a translation of the whole of it will be given.

An additional interest belongs to the Yî as the fountain-head from which the comparatively modern philosophers of the Sung dynasty (began A. D. 960) professed to draw what has been called their 'atheo-political' system. As an appendix to the translation of the Yî, there will be given an outline of that system, and an attempt will be made to test the correctness of the interpretation of this classic by its authors.

The fourth of the great classics is the Lî *Kî*, or the Record of Rites; but it is only one of a class that we may denominate the Constitutional and Ritual Books of ancient China, especially under the *K*âu dynasty. They are often mentioned together as 'the Three Rituals.' The first of them is called *K*âu Lî, the Rites of *K*âu, and also *K*âu Kwan, the Officers of *K*âu, which latter is the better name for it. It is the official book of the *K*âu dynasty. The prevailing opinion is that it was the production of the duke of *K*âu; and if it were not composed in its present form by him, it contains, no doubt, the substance of the regulations which he made for the administration of the government, after the dynasty of Shang had passed, through the achieve-ments of his father and brother, into that of *K*âu. Under the various departments in which that administration was arranged, it enumerates the principal and subordinate officers belonging to each, and describes their duties. After the fires of *K*hin, the work was recovered nearly complete in the first century B. C. A good translation of the whole work was published in 1851, at Paris, by M. Edouard Biot.

The second Ritual Collection bears the name of Î Lî, which has been translated 'the Decorum Ritual,' and 'the Rules of Demeanour.' It was recovered earlier than the former, and is as voluminous. It consists of the rules by which a scholar or officer should regulate his behaviour on social and state occasions. It has not yet, so far as I know, been translated into any European language.

The third Collection, more voluminous than either of the others, was made also under the Han dynasty. In the first century B. C., it was an immense compilation of 214 books arranged in five divisions. The 214 were reduced

to eighty-five by Tâi Teh, a scholar of the time, and his   xix
eighty-five again to forty-six by a cousin, called Tâi *Kh*ăng.
Three other books were added to these towards the end of
the Han period, forming forty-nine in all, which have come
down to us under the title of Lî *K*î, or 'the Record of
Rites,' and have long constituted by imperial authority one
of the five Ki ng. An abridgment of this work was translated by M. J. M. Callery, at Turin, in 1853, with the
title,—'Lî *K*î, ou Memorial des Rites, traduit pour la
première fois du Chinois, et accompagné de notes, de
commentaires, et du texte original.' Callery's work, however, contains only thirty-six of the forty-nine books of
the Lî *K*î, and most of those thirty-six in a condensed
form. Whether it will be possible to give in these Sacred
Books of the East translations of the whole of these Rituals ;
and if that be not possible, by what principles to be guided
in the selection of portions of them :—these are questions
to be determined after further deliberation. Many passages
contain more of the mind of Confucius himself on the
sacrificial worship of his country, and the ideas underlying
it, than we find elsewhere.

But it must not be forgotten that these ritual books do
not throw so valuable a light on the ancient religion of
China as the older Shû and Shih. They belong to the
period of the *K*âu dynasty, and do not go back as contemporaneous records to the dynasties beyond it and the still
remoter age of Yâo and Shun. The views of Confucius,
moreover, as given in them, do not come to us at first hand.
They were gathered up by the Han scholars five and six
centuries after his death, nor can we be sure that these
did not sometimes put ideas of their own into the mouth of
the sage, and make additions to the writings which were
supposed, correctly or incorrectly, to have come from his
immediate disciples.

We owe the fifth and last of the Ki ngs of China to
Confucius himself. It is what he called *Kh*un *Kh*iû, or
'the Spring and Autumn,' a very brief chronicle compiled
by him of the annals of his native state of Lû for 242
years, from B. C. 722 to 481. But there is not much to be

b 2

xx gleaned from it for the Sacred Texts; and if we were to
launch out into the three supplements to it of Zo *K* hiû--
ming, Kung-yang, and Kû-liang, the result would not repay
the labour. A translation of the whole of Zo's supplement,
much the most important, is given in my work on the
*K*hun *K*hiû, published at Hong Kong in 1872.

There is another short treatise attributed to Confucius,—
the Hsiâo King, or 'Classic of Filial Piety.' Though not
like one of the five great works that have been described,
it was the first to receive the denomination of a King,—
and that from the lips of the sage himself,—if the account
which we have received of the matter is to be relied on.
This little work does not come to us, like the *K*hun *K*hiû,
as directly from the pencil of Confucius, but in the shape of
conversations between him and his disciple Zäng-ʒze, put
on record in the first place, probably, by some members of
Zäng's school. No portion of the ancient literature has
more exercised the minds and engaged the attention of
many of the emperors of successive dynasties. The Hsiâo
seems to me an attempt to construct a religion on the
basis of the cardinal virtue of Filial Piety, and is open
to criticism in many respects. A translation of it is given
in the present volume.

The classical books are often spoken of as being 'the
five King' and 'the four Shû.' The King have all been
separately referred to above; the four Shû is an abbrevia-
tion for the Shû or Books of the four Philosophers. The
first is the Lun Yü, or 'Discourses and Conversations,'
occupied chiefly with sayings of Confucius and conversations
between him and many of his disciples. The second is the
Works of Mencius, perhaps the greatest thinker and writer
of the Confucian school after the Master. I hope to be
able to give both these works. The third of the Shû is
the Tâ Hsio, or 'Great Learning,' ascribed, like the Hsiâo,
to Zäng-ʒze. The fourth is the *K*ung Yung, or 'Doctrine
of the Mean,' the production of Zze-sze, the sage's grandson.
Both of these treatises, however, are taken from the Lî *K*î.
The whole of the Four Books were translated and published
by me in 1861.

III. The third Religion in China is what is called Tâoism.
It was, like Confucianism, of native origin, and its acknowledged founder was Lî *R*, called also Lî Po-yang, and, after
his death, Lî Tan.   More commonly he is designated Lâo-
ʒze, translated by some 'the Old Philosopher,' and by
others 'the Old Boy' from a fabulous story that his mother
carried him in her womb for seventy-two years, so that
when he was at length cut out of it, his hair was already
white.   His birth is referred to the year 604 B.C., so that
he was between fifty and sixty years older than Confucius.   There are accounts, hardly reliable, of interviews and
discussions between the two men.

Lâo-ʒze's system often goes with English writers by the
name of Rationalism; but if that name be retained, the
term must be taken in quite a peculiar sense.   His doctrine was that of the Tâo, but it is not easy to determine
what English term will best express the meaning of the
Chinese character.   The only record which we have of
Lâo-ʒze's views is the Tâo-teh King, or 'Classic of Tâo
and Virtue,' a treatise of no great length.   It was published
at Paris in 1842, with a translation in French, by the late
Stanislas Julien, under the title of 'Le Livre de la Voie
et de la Vertu.'   Appealing to the views of *K*wang-ʒze and
other writers of the Tâoist school, M. Julien says that 'Le
Tâo est dépourvu d'action, de pensée, de jugement, d'intelligence,' and adds that 'it appears impossible therefore to
take it for the primordial reason, the Sublime Intelligence, which created and rules the world.'

A translation in English was published, in 1868, by
the Rev. Dr. Chalmers of Canton, under the title of 'the
Speculations in Metaphysics, Polity, and Morality, of "the
Old Philosopher."'   Dr. Chalmers retains the term Tâo
in his English Text, and says, 'I have thought it better
to leave the word Tâo untranslated, both because it has
given the name to the sect,—the Tâoists,—and because no
English word is its exact equivalent.   Three terms suggest
themselves,—the Way, Reason, and the Word; but they
are all liable to objection.   Were we guided by etymology,
"the Way" would come nearest to the original, and in one

or two passages the idea of a Way seems to be in the term ; but this is too materialistic to serve the purpose of a translation. Reason again seems to be more like a quality or attribute of some conscious Being than Tâo is. I would translate it by the Word in the sense of the Logos, but this would be like settling the question which I wish to leave open, viz. what amount of resemblance there is between the Logos of the New Testament and this Tâo, which is its nearest representative in Chinese.'

Two other translations of the Tâo-teh King have appeared, both in German :—'Lao-tsze's Tao Te King, aus dem Chinesischen ins Deutsche übersetzt, eingeleitet, und commentirt, von Victor von Strauss (Leipzig, 1870),' and 'Lao-tse, Tao-te-king, "Der Weg zur Tugend," aus dem Chinesischen übersetzt und erklärt von Reinhold von Plänckner,' also published at Leipzig. Strauss closely follows Julien, while Plänckner allows himself great freedom in dealing with his original. Notwithstanding these four attempts to give the meaning of 'the Old Philosopher' in three European languages, there is room for a new version, which will be submitted to the reader in due course. It is only by an intense and long-continued study of the original that we can come to an agreement as to the meaning of the Tâo. I propose not only to give a translation of the Tâo-teh King, but also of the works of Kwang-ȝze, the most remarkable of the early writers of the Tâoist school.

Whatever Lâo-ȝze intended by the Tâo, Tâoism has, in the course of time, borrowed largely, both from Confucianism and Buddhism. It inculcates a morality of a high order in some respects, and has developed a system of grotesque beliefs and practices, ministering to superstition, and intended to refine and preserve the breath of life. Its practical teachings will be exhibited in the most popular of all the Tâoist writings,—the treatise on 'Actions and their Recompenses,' and perhaps in one or more, besides, of the characteristic productions of the system.

———

The version of the Shû that appears in this volume is substantially the same as that in the third volume of my large edition of the Chinese Classics, and which was published in 1865. I wrote out the whole afresh, however, having before me not only my own version, but the earlier translations of P. Gaubil in French and Dr. Medhurst in English. Frequent reference was made likewise to a larger apparatus of native commentaries than I had formerly used. Going to the text anew, after more than twelve years devoted mainly to the continuous study of the Chinese classics, I yet hardly discovered any errors which it was necessary to correct. A few verbal alterations were made to make the meaning clearer. Only in one case will a reader, familiar with the former version, be struck with any alteration in this. The Chinese character 帝 (Tî), applied repeatedly to the ancient Yâo and Shun in the commencing books of the classic, and once in the 27th Book of the fifth Part, was there translated by 'emperor,' while it is left untranslated in the present volume, and its name transferred to the English text.

Before adopting this change, I had considered whether I ought to translate Tî in all other instances of its occurrence in the Shû (and invariably in the Shih), and its intensified form Shang Tî (上 帝), by our term 'God.' Gaubil rendered Tî for the most part by 'le Seigneur,' and Shang Tî by 'le Souverain Maître,' adding sometimes to these names Tî and Shang Tî in brackets. Medhurst translated Tî by 'the Supreme,' and 'the Supreme Ruler,' and Shang Tî by 'the Supreme Ruler.' More than twenty-five years ago I came to the conclusion that Tî was the term corresponding in Chinese to our 'God,' and that Shang Tî was the same, with the addition of Shang, equal to 'Supreme.' In this view I have never wavered, and I have rendered both the names by 'God' in all the volumes of the Chinese Classics thus far translated and published.

What made me pause before doing so in the present volume, was the consideration that the object of 'the Sacred Texts of the Religions of the East,' as I understand it, is to give translations of those texts without any colouring in the first place from the views of the translators. Could it be that my own view of Tî, as meaning God, had grown up in the heat of our controversies in China as to the proper characters to be used for the words God and Spirit, in translating the Sacred Scriptures? A reader, confronted everywhere by the word God, might be led to think more highly of the primitive religion of China than he ought to think. Should I leave the names Tî and Shang Tî untranslated? Or should I give for them, instead of God, the terms Ruler and Supreme Ruler? I could not see my way to adopt either of these courses.

The term Heaven (天, pronounced Thien) is used everywhere in the Chinese Classics for the Supreme Power, ruling and governing all the affairs of men with an omnipotent and omniscient righteousness and goodness; and this vague term is constantly interchanged in the same paragraph, not to say the same sentence, with the personal names Tî and Shang Tî. Thien and Tî in their written forms are perfectly distinct. Both of them were among the earliest characters, and enter, though not largely, as the phonetical element into other characters of later formation. According to the oldest Chinese dictionary, the Shwo Wăn (A. D. 100), Thien is formed, 'by association of ideas,' from yî (一), 'one,' and tâ (大), 'great,' meaning— what is one and undivided, and great. Tâi Thung, of our thirteenth century, in his remarkable dictionary, the Liû Shû Kû, explains the top line of it as indicating 'what is above,' so that the significance of the character is 'what is above and great.' In both these dictionaries Tî (帝) is derived from 丄 or ⊥ (shang), 'above,' or 'what is above:' and they say that the whole character is of phonetical formation, in which I am not able to follow them[1];

---

[1] It is said in the Shwo Wăn that the phonetical element in Tî is 朿; but this is pronounced βhze. Neither in form nor sound is there any similitude between it and Tî. An error, probably, has crept into the text. Dr. Chalmers, in his treatise on 'the Origin of the Chinese,' attempts (p. 12) to analyse the character into its constituent parts in the following way :—' The peculiar nature of the Chinese written language has done good service in stereotyping the primi-

but Tâi Thung gives the following account of its meaning:—'Tî is the honourable designation of lordship and rule,' adding, 'Therefore Heaven is called Shang Tî; the five Elementary Powers are called the five Tî; and the Son of Heaven [1]—that is, the Sovereign—is called Tî.' Here then is the name Heaven, by which the idea of Supreme Power in the absolute is vaguely expressed; and when the Chinese would speak of it by a personal name, they use the terms Tî and Shang Tî;—saying, I believe, what our early fathers did, when they began to use the word God. Tî is the name which has been employed in China for this concept for fully 5000 years. Our word God fits naturally into every passage where the character occurs in the old Chinese Classics, save those to which I referred above on p. xxiii. It never became with the people a proper name like the Zeus of the Greeks. I can no more translate Tî or Shang Tî by any other word but God than I can translate *ză*n (人) by anything else but man.

The preceding is a brief abstract of the reasoning by which I was determined to retain the term God for Tî and Shang Tî in this volume, excepting in the cases that have called for these observations. But in the account of Tî which I have adduced from Tâi Thung, it is said that 'the sovereign is also called Tî;' and most of my readers know that Hwang Tî (皇 帝) is the title of the emperor of China. How did this application of the name arise? Was it in the first place a designation of the ruler or emperor; and was it then given to the Supreme Power, when the vague Heaven failed to satisfy the thinker and worshipper,

---

tive belief in one Supreme Tî (帝), who is 大 "great," over, and ｜ '
" ruling," heaven (⌒ = ⌒) and earth (冂).' This is ingenious, but not entirely satisfactory. The three last steps are so; but the finding 大 (great) in the top part of 帝 does not in the same way carry conviction to the mind.

[1] Thien βze, 'the Son of Heaven,' is a common designation of the sovereign of China. Originally βze performed in the expression the part of a verb, and Thien βze was equivalent to ' he whom Heaven sons,' that is, considers and treats as its son. See the second line of the ode, p. 318.

and he wished to express his recognition of a personal Being who was to himself his almighty ruler? If these questions be answered in the affirmative, Tî would be a name applied to the Supreme Being, just as we rise from the paternal relation among ourselves and call him Father. Or, on the other hand, was Tî the designation of the Supreme Lord and Ruler, corresponding to our God, and was it subsequently applied to the earthly ruler, thereby deifying him, just as the title Divus was given to a Roman emperor? I believe that it was in this latter way that Tî came to be used of the sovereigns of China ; and therefore in again publishing a translation of the Shû, I resolved, that where the appellation is given in it to Yâo and Shun, and it is only to them that it is given, I would retain the Chinese term instead of rendering it, as formerly, by ' emperor.'

The following are the reasons which weighed with me in coming to this resolution :

First, the first really historical sovereign of China who used the title of Hwang Tî was the founder of the Khin dynasty ; and he assumed it in B.C. 221, when he had sub-jugated all the sovereignties into which the feudal kingdom of Kâu had become divided, and was instituting the despotic empire that has since subsisted.

The Kâu dynasty had continued for 867 years, from B.C. 1122 to 256, and its rulers had been styled Wang or kings.

Kâu superseded the dynasty of Shang or Yin, that had endured for 644 years, from B.C. 1766 to 1123 ; and its rulers had similarly been styled Wang or kings.

Shang superseded the dynasty of Hsiâ, which had lasted for 439 years, from B.C. 2205 to 1767, and its rulers had been styled Wang, or kings, and Hâu, or sovereigns.

Thus, from the great Yü, B.C. 2205 to B.C. 221, that is, for nearly 2000 years, there was no Tî or emperor in China. During all that time the people had on the whole been increasing in numbers, and the nation growing in territory ;—how did it come to pass, that the higher title, if it had previously existed, gave place to an inferior one?

Prior to the dynasty of Hsiâ, with the exception of the period of Yâo and Shun, the accounts which we have of the history of China have been, and ought to be, pronounced 'fabulous' and 'legendary.' The oldest documents that purport to be historical are the books in the Shû about Yâo and Shun, and even they do not profess to be contemporaneous with those personages. The earlier accounts open with a Phan-kû, in whose time 'heaven and earth were first separated.' To him succeeded the period of the San Hwang, or Three August Lines, consisting of twelve Celestial, eleven Terrestrial, and nine Human Sovereigns, who ruled together about 50,000 years. After them come a host of different Lines, till we arrive at the Wû Tî, or Five Emperors. The first of these is commonly said to be Fû-hsî, while he and two others are sometimes put down as the San Hwang, in order to bring in Yâo and Shun as the last two of the Tîs.

I have entered into these details because of the account which we have of the king of *Kh*in's assuming the title of Hwang Tî. We are told:—'As soon as the king had brought the whole country into subjection, thinking that he united in himself the virtues of the three Hwangs, and that his merits exceeded those of the five Tîs, he changed his title into Hwang Tî.' The three Hwangs are entirely fabulous, and the five Tîs are, to say the least, legendary. That there were either Hwangs or Tîs ruling in China before the age of the Hsiâ dynasty cannot be admitted.

Second, it has been stated above, and is shown in the Introduction to the Shû, pp. 13–19, that the books in the Shû, previous to the Hsiâ dynasty, are not historical in the sense of their being contemporaneous documents of the times about which they speak. They profess to be compilations merely from older documents; and when they speak of Yâo and Shun as Tîs, the title Tî precedes the name or designation, instead of following it, as it ought to do, according to Chinese usage, if Tî is to be taken in the sense of emperor. Yâo Tî would be 'the emperor Yâo,' but we have Tî Yâo, where Tî performs the part of an adjective. King Wăn, the founder of the *K*âu dynasty, is invariably mentioned as Wăn Wang, 'Wăn the king.' To say Wang Wăn would be felt at once by every Chinese scholar to be inadmissible; and not less so is Tî Yâo for 'the emperor Yâo.' It was the perception of this violation of usage in Chinese composition, five years ago, that first showed me the error of translating Tî Yâo and Tî Shun by 'the emperor Yâo' and 'the emperor Shun.' It is true that in the early books of the Shû, we have Tî used alone, without the adjunct of Yâo or Shun, and referring to those personages. In those cases it does perform the part of a substantive, but its meaning depends on that which belonged to it as an adjective in the phrases Tî Yâo and Tî Shun. If it be ascertained that in these it means 'the Deified,' then when used singly as a noun, it will mean Divus, or the Divine One.

Third, the sovereigns of the Hsiâ, the Shang, and the *K*âu dynasties, it has been seen, were styled Wang and not Tî. Confucius speaks repeatedly in the Analects of Yâo and Shun, but he never calls either of them by the title of Tî. Mencius, however, uses it both of the one and the other, when he is quoting in substance from the accounts of them in the Shû. This confirms the view that the early books of the Shû were current after the middle of the *K*âu dynasty, very much in the form in which we now have them; and the question arises whether we can show how the application of the title Tî as given in them to Yâo and Shun arose. We can.

The fourth Book of the Lî *K*î is called Yüeh Ling, 'the Monthly Record of the Proceedings of Government.' In it certain sacrificial observances paid to the five Tîs are distributed through the four seasons. The Tîs are Fû-hsî, Shăn-năng, Yû-hsiung or Hsien-yüan, *K*in-thien, and Kâo-yang, who are styled Thâi Hâo (the Greatly Resplendent), Yen Tî (the Blazing Tî), Hwang Tî (the Yellow Tî), Shâo Hâo (the Less Resplendent), and *K*wan Hsü (the Solely Correct); with each Tî there is associated in the ceremony a personage of inferior rank, who is styled Shăn (神 = a Spirit). The language descriptive of the ceremony is the same in all the cases, with the exception of the names and months. Thus the first entry is :—'In the first month of spring, on such and such days, the Tî is Thâi Hâo, and the Shân is Kâu-mang.' Now this Kâu-mang was a son of Shâo Hâo, several hundreds of years later than Thâi Hâo, so that the associating them together in this ceremony could only have arisen in later times.

However we explain the ceremony thus curtly described; whether we see in it the growing prevalence of nature-worship, or an illustration of the practice of worshipping ancient heroes and worthies :—Tî appears in the account of it plainly used in the sense of God. In each of the five instances, we have a Tî and a Shăn, not an emperor and a spirit, but a God and a Spirit,—a Spirit standing in the same relation to the God, that *K h* ăn (⿴⿱一口 =a subject or minister) stands in to a ruler. Thus it was that, by a process of deification, the title of Tî came to be given, in the time of the *K*âu dynasty, to the great names, fabulous and legendary, of antiquity; and thus it was that it was applied to the heroes Yâo and Shun. It may well be that the title Hwang Tî, used by a Chinese of the present emperor or of any emperor of the past, does not call up to his mind any other idea than that of a human sovereign ; but being satisfied as to the proper signification of Tî as God, and as to the process by which the title came to be applied to the ancient Yâo and Shun, I could no longer render it, when used of them in the Shû, by emperor, and elected to leave it untranslated in the present volume.

To any unimportant changes of translation it is unnecessary to refer. The dates B. C. in the introductions and notes are all one year more than in the translations formerly published. They are thus brought into accordance with those of P. Gaubil and the useful Chinese Chronological Tables of the late Mr. Mayers.

The changes in the transliteration of Chinese names are very considerable. As foreigners are now resident in Peking, it seemed proper to adopt the pronunciation of the capital as given by Sir T. F. Wade in his H sin Ching Lu and Tzŭ Erh Chî. At the same time, in order to secure as near an approach as possible to uniformity in all the volumes of the Sacred Books of the East, the letters employed were made to conform to those in Professor Max Müller's Scheme for the Transliteration of Oriental Alphabets. It was not easy at first to do this, for Chinese, having no alphabet, reluctated against being made to appear as if it had; but use has more than reconciled me to the method now employed. It was not possible to introduce into the table all the diphthongs in which Chinese speech is rich. The reader has to be informed that i before another vowel or a diphthong approximates to the sound of y, so that the whole utterance is still monosyllabic. The powers of *r* and ze must be heard before they can be appreciated.

To call the attention of the reader to passages in the Shû, embodying, more or less distinctly, religious ideas, an asterisk (*) will be found appended to them.

J. L.

Oxford,
18th April, 1879.

THE SHÛ KING

OR

BOOK OF HISTORICAL DOCUMENTS.

THE SHÛ KING

OR

BOOK OF HISTORICAL DOCUMENTS.

INTRODUCTION.

CHAPTER I.

THE NATURE AND HISTORY OF THE SHÛ.

1. The Shû is the most ancient of the Chinese classical books, and contains historical documents of various kinds, relating to the period from about B.C. 2357–627. The

Meaning of the name Shû King. character Shû shows us by its composition that it denotes 'the pencil speaking,' and hence it is often used as a designation of the written characters of the language. This, indeed, was the earliest meaning of it, but from this the transition was easy to its employment in the sense of writings or books, applicable to any consecutive compositions; and we find it further specially employed by Confucius and others to designate the historical remains of antiquity, in distinction from the poems, the accounts of rites, and other monuments of former times. Not that those other monuments might not also be called by the general name of Shû. The peculiar significancy of the term, however, was well established, and is retained to the present day.

The book has come down to us in a mutilated condition; but even as it is said to have existed in the time of Confucius, it did not profess to contain a history of China, and much less, to give the annals of that history. It was simply a collection of historical memorials, extending over a space of about 1700 years, but on no connected method, and with frequent and great gaps between them.

2   The name King (now in Pekinese *K*ing) was not added
to Shû till the time of the Han dynasty (began B. C. 202).
If Confucius applied it to any of the classical works, it was
to the classic of Filial.Piety, as will be seen in the Introduction to the translation of that work.   The Han scholars,
however, when engaged in collecting and digesting the
ancient literary monuments of their country, found it convenient to distinguish the most valuable of them, that had
been acknowledged by Confucius, as King, meaning what
was canonical and of unchallengeable authority.

2. In the Confucian Analects, the sage and one of his
disciples quote from the Shû by the simple formula—

The Shû was
an existing
collection of
documents
before
Confucius.

'The Shû says.'   In the Great Learning, four
different books or chapters of the classic,
all in it as we have it now, are mentioned,
each by its proper name.   Mencius sometimes
uses the same formula as Confucius, and at
other times designates particular books.   It is most natural
for us to suppose that Confucius, when he spoke of the
Shû, had in his mind's eye a collection of documents bearing
that title.

One passage in Mencius seems to put it beyond a doubt
that the Shû existed as such a collection in his time.
Having said that 'it would be better to be without the
Shû than to give entire credit to it,' he makes immediate
reference to one of the books of our classic by name,
and adds, 'In the Completion of the War I select two or
three passages only, and believe them[1].'   In Mo-ʒze, Hsün-
ʒze, and other writers of the last two centuries of the *K*âu
dynasty, the Shû is quoted in the same way, and also frequently with the specification of its parts or larger divisions,—
'The Books of Yü,' ' of Hsiâ,' ' of Shang,' ' of *K*âu.'   And,
in fine, in many of the narratives of ʒo *Kh*iû-ming's commentary on the Spring and Autumn, the Shû is quoted in
the same way, even when the narratives are about men
and events long anterior to the sage[2].   All these consi-

---

[1] Mencius, VII, ii, ch. 3.

[2] The first quotation of the Shû in ʒo is under the sixth year of duke Yin,
B.C. 717.

derations establish the thesis of this paragraph, that the   3
Shû was an existing collection of historical documents
before Confucius.

3. From the above paragraph it follows that Confucius
did not compile the collection of documents that form the

Confucius did
not compile
the Shû. The
number of
documents in
it in his time.
The Preface
ascribed to
him.

Shû. The earliest assertion that he did so we
have from Khung An-kwo, his descendant in
the eleventh generation, in the second century,
B. C. Recounting the labours of his ancestor,
An-kwo says, in the Preface to his edition of
the Shû, that ' he examined and arranged the
old literary monuments and records, deciding
to commence with Yâo and Shun, and to come down to
the times of *K*âu. Of those deserving to be handed down
to other ages and to supply permanent lessons, he made
in all one hundred books, consisting of canons, counsels,
instructions, announcements, speeches, and charges.' The
same thing is stated by Sze-mâ *K*ien in his Historical Records, completed about B. C. 100, but *K*ien's
information was derived from An-kwo. Such a compilation would have been in harmony with the character which
Confucius gave of himself, as 'a transmitter and not a
maker, believing and loving the ancients[1],' and with what
his grandson says of him in the Doctrine of the Mean,
that ' he handed down (the lessons of) Yâo and Shun, as if
they had been his ancestors, and elegantly displayed those
of Wăn and Wû, whom he took for his model[2].'

We have seen, however, that the collection existed in
his time and before it. Did it then, as An-kwo says,
consist of a hundred books? His authority for saying so
was a Preface, which was found along with the old tablets
of the Shû that were discovered in his time and deciphered
by him, as will be related farther on. He does not say, however, that it was the work of Confucius, though *K*ien does.
It still exists,—a list of eighty-one documents in a hundred books. The prevailing opinion of scholars in China
is now, that it was not written by the sage. I entirely

---

[1] Analects, VII, i.   [2] The Doctrine of the Mean, XXX, 1.

B 2

4   agree myself with the judgment of 3*h*âi *K*h*ă*n, the disciple
of *K*û Hsî, whose Collected Comments, first published
A. D. 1210, are now the standard of orthodoxy in the interpretation of the Shû.   He says of the document: 'It
sheds light on nothing, and there are things in it at vari-
ance with the text of the classic.   On the books that are
lost it is specially servile and brief, affording us not the
slightest help.   That it is not the work of Confucius is
exceedingly plain.'

The eighty-one documents mentioned in it, and more,
may have been in the Shû of the time of Confucius.
I think, however, that several of them must have been
lost subsequently, before the rise of the tyrant of *K*h*in,
who doomed the whole collection to the flames.   Mencius
complains that in his days the feudal princes destroyed
many of the records of antiquity that they might the better
perpetrate their own usurpations and innovations[1].   Other
considerations, on the exhibition of which I need not enter,
confirm me in this conclusion.

4. It will be well here to devote a paragraph to the
The sources sources of the Shû. Have we sufficient proofs
of the Shû.   of the composition in ancient times of such
documents as it contains, and of their preservation, so that
they could be collected in a sort of historical canon?

We have.   Under the dynasty of *K*âu (B. C. 1122–256),
at the royal court, and at the courts of the feudal princes
on a smaller scale, there were officers styled Sze, which has
been translated 'Recorders,' 'Annalists,' 'Historiographers,'
and simply 'Clerks.'   There were the Grand Recorder, the
Assistant Recorder, the Recorder of the Interior, the Recorder of the Exterior, and the Recorder in Attendance on
the Sovereign.   Among the duties of the Recorder of the
Interior were the following :—'In case of any charge given
by the king to the prince of a state, or to any other dignitary, he writes it on tablets;' 'In case of any memorials
on business coming in from the different quarters of the
kingdom, he reads them (to the king);' 'It is his business

---

[1] Mencius, V, ii, ch. 2.

to write all charges of the king, and to do so in duplicate.' 5
Of the duties of the Recorder of the Exterior it is said :—
' He has charge of the histories of the states in all parts of
the kingdom ; ' ' He has charge of the most ancient books ; '
' It is his business to publish in all parts of the kingdom
the books and the characters in them[1].'

These entries show that under the *K*âu dynasty there
was provision made for the recording and preservation of
royal charges and ordinances, of the operations of the
general government, and of the histories of the different
states ; and, moreover, for the preservation and interpretation of documents come down from more ancient times.
Confucius himself tells us that in his early days a recorder
would leave a blank in his text, rather than enter anything
of which he had not sufficient evidence[2]. Mencius also
mentions three works, the Shăng of *K*in, the Thâo-wû of
*K*hû, and the *Kh*un *Kh*iû of Lû, which must have come
from the recorders of those states.

Of the existence of a similar class of officers under the
previous dynasties of Shang or Yin (B.C. 1766–1123) and
Hsiâ (B.C. 2205–1765), we have not such abundant evidence. Chapter 2 in the 10th Book of the 5th Part of our
classic, however, seems to speak of them in the time of the
former. Wû-ting (B.C. 1324–1264), the twentieth sovereign of
it, is described as communicating, in writing, a dream which
he had had, to his ministers[3]; and fully four hundred years
earlier, Î Yin, the chief minister, remonstrates, in writing,
with his young and careless sovereign Thâi *K*iâ[4]. Going
back to the dynasty of Hsiâ, we find the prince of Yin,
during the reign of *K*ung Khang (B.C. 2159–2145), in addressing his troops, quotes the Statutes of Government in
a manner which makes us conceive of him as referring to
a well-known written compilation[5]. The grandsons of the
great Yü, its founder (B.C. 2205–2196), likewise, make
mention, in the Songs of the Five Sons, of his Lessons, in
a style that suggests to us the formula that Mencius was

---

[1] See for all these statements the Ritual or Official Book of *K*âu, XXXI, 35–42.
[2] Analects, XV, xxv. [3] Part IV, viii, section 1.
[4] Part IV, v, section 1. [5] Part III, iv.

6   wont to employ when referring to the documents acknowledged to be of authority in his day [1].

Mâ Twan-lin, the encyclopedist, in his General Examination of Records and Scholars, first published A. D. 1321,
says that 'the pencil of the recorders was busy from the
time of Hwang Tî (B. C. 2697).' The compilers of the
records of the Sui dynasty (A. D. 589–617) say that
'historical documents began immediately with the invention of written characters.' That invention I must place
myself at an earlier date than the time assigned to Hwang
Tî. When once the characters were invented, they would
come in time to be employed in the writing of history.
The early dates alleged for many of the documents in the
Shû are no valid reason for rejecting them without further
examination. We may rather be surprised that, when the
compilation was made, it did not contain many more than
a hundred documents.

5. The dynasty of *K*âu came to an end in B. C. 256, and
after an anarchic interval of thirty-five years, the king of
*Kh*in succeeded in uniting all the feudal states under his
own sway, and proclaimed himself emperor.
Up to this time the Shû had sustained no
other damage than all human works are
liable to in the course of time ; but now it
narrowly escaped an entire destruction. An edict went forth
from the tyrant in B. C. 213, commanding that all the old
classical books should be consigned to the flames, excepting
those belonging to the great scholars in the service of the
court, and the Yî. His rage was hottest against the Shû
and the Shih (the Book of Poetry). Death was the doom
of scholars who should be known to meet together and
speak of these works, and all who should be discovered
having copies of them in their possession, when thirty days
had elapsed after the publication of the edict, were to be
branded, and sent to labour for four years on the Great
Wall, which was then building.

This is not the place to explain the reasons that led to

Destruction of the classical literature by the emperor of *Kh*in.

---
[1] Part III, iii.

this insane attempt to extinguish, with the exception of one   7
work, the ancient literary monuments of China. · The edict
was ruthlessly enforced, and hundreds of scholars who refused obedience to the imperial command were buried alive.
The Shû had nearly perished from off the earth.

6. The tyrant, however, died in B. C. 210, within four years
from the issuing of his edict. The dynasty which he had
sought to establish passed away in B. C. 206. That of Han
dates from the year B. C. 202, and in 191 the edict against
the ancient books was formally repealed. They had been
Recovery of under the ban for less than a quarter of a
the Shû. century. There would probably have been
no difficulty in recovering copies of them, but for the sack
of the capital in B. C. 206 by the most formidable opponent
of the founder of the House of Han. Then the fires blazed,
we are told, for three months among the palaces and public
buildings, and proved as destructive to the copies that might
have been preserved about the court as the edict of *Kh*in
had been to those among the people.

Among the scholars of *Kh*in, however, there had been
one, of the surname Fû, who, when the edict was issued,
hid his tablets of the Shû in a wall. Returning for them,
after the rule of Han was established, he found that many
were perished or gone. He recovered only twenty-nine
of the documents, containing, according to the division of
them that has long been followed, thirty-five books in all.·
About one of them there is some difficulty, on the discussion
of which I need not enter. Fû commenced teaching them,
and from all parts scholars resorted to him, and sat at his
feet. The emperor Wăn (B. C. 179–155) heard of him, and
sent one of the recorders of the court to visit him, and
bring the recovered tablets themselves, or a copy of them,
to the capital. They were in the form of the character
that was prevalent at that time, different from that which
had been used in previous centuries, and are known as
'the Shû of the modern text.' The Catalogue of the
Imperial Library, prepared by Liû Hin for the emperor
Âi (B. C. 6–1), contains an entry of 'the text of the Shû
in twenty-nine portions,'—the same, no doubt, which was

8   received from Fû. Fû himself commented on his Shû. The text was engraved on the stone tablets of the emperor Ling (A. D. 168-189). Very many scholars of the Han times laboured on this text, taught it to their disciples, and published their views on it. Not one of their writings, however, survived, in a complete form, the troubles which desolated the empire during the reign of the emperor Hwâi (A. D. 307-312) of the western dynasty of *K*in.

In the reign of the Han emperor Wû (B. C. 140-85) a discovery was made in the wall of the house of the Khung or Confucian family of the tablets of the Shû, the Spring and Autumn, the classic of Filial Piety, and the Lun-yü or Confucian Analects. How long they had lain there we do not know. It is commonly said that they had been hidden by some one of the Khung family to save them from the fires of *Kh*in. But they were in a form of the character that had long gone into disuse, and which hardly any one could decipher, and must have been deposited towards the beginning of the fifth century B. C. They were committed to the care of Khung An-kwo, who was then one of the 'great scholars' of the empire, and the chief of the Khung family. By means of the current text of Fû and other resources he made out all the tablets of the Shû that were in good preservation, and in addition to Fû's twenty-nine documents several others. He found also that Fû had in three cases incorporated two different documents under one name, and taken no note of the division of one other into three books or sections. Altogether there were now forty-six documents or different portions of the old Shû brought anew to light. They appear in Liû Hin's Catalogue as 'the text of the Shû in old characters in forty-six portions.'

When An-kwo had made out the tablets, he presented them to the emperor in B. C. 97, with a transcript of them in the current characters of the time, keeping a second transcript of them for himself; and he received an order to make a commentary on the whole. He did so, but when he was about to lay the result of his labours before the court, troubles had arisen which prevented for several years the paying attention to literary matters. It was

owing to these that his commentary was neglected for a　9
time, and the enlarged text which he had deciphered was
not officially put in charge of the Board of 'Great Scholars,'
to which the care of the five King, so far as they had been
recovered, had been committed in B. C. 136.

An-kwo's commentary, however, was not lost; but
before speaking of it, I must refer to a third recovery of
a large portion of the Shû early in our first century.
A scholar and officer, named Tû Lin, had been a fugitive,
having many wonderful escapes, during the usurpation of
Mang (A. D. 9–22). During his wanderings he discovered
a portion of the Shû on 'lacquered' tablets, or perhaps on
lacquered cloth, which he thenceforth guarded as his richest
treasure, and kept near his person. When the empire was
again settled by the first emperor of the eastern Han, he
communicated his text to other scholars. Wei Hung published a commentary on it, and subsequently *K*iâ Khwei, Mâ
Yung, and *K*ăng Khang-*kh*ăng (all, great names in Chinese
literature) did the same. Tû Lin's 'lacquered' books were
the same in number as An-kwo's, but they contained five
documents in thirteen books, which were not in the text
of the other, and wanted nine documents, also in thirteen
books, which An-kwo's text had. The commentary of
*K*ăng Khang-*kh*ăng continued till the Sui dynasty, after
which we lose sight of it.

I return to the commentary of An-kwo, which, of course,
contained his text. Its transmission from hand to hand
down to the close of the western Han dynasty is clearly
traced. Less distinctly, but surely, we can discover evidence of its preservation, till we come to the commencement
of the eastern dynasty of *K*in, when Mei 3eh, a recorder
of the Interior, having come into possession of a copy, presented it to the emperor Yüan (A. D. 317–322). The
Canon of Shun was wanting in it, and was supplied from
the commentary of Mâ Yung, based on the text of Tû Lin.
From this time the text and commentary of An-kwo had
their place assigned them in the Imperial College. They
are mentioned in the Catalogue of the Imperial Library of
Sui. The second emperor of the Thang dynasty gave orders

10　　for a grand edition of the Shû, under the superintendence
of Khung Ying-tâ, assisted by others. They adopted the
commentary of An-kwo, and enriched it with profuse anno-
tations. In A. D. 654 their work was ordered to be printed,
and happily remains to the present day. The text of the
Shû, that is, of all of it that had been recovered by An-
kwo, was still further secured, being engraved with that of
all the other classics on the Thang tablets of stone which
were completed in the year 837, and are still preserved at
Khang-an, in Shen-hsî.

It is not necessary to trace the history of the Shû further
on. The titles of more than 500 works, on the whole of it
or on portions, from the dynasty of Thang to the present day,
could easily be adduced. Under the Sung dynasty, indeed,
there began the sceptical criticism, which, setting comparatively little store on external evidence, decides on the
genuineness of documents principally from their style.
The results of such criticism always vary according to the
knowledge and the subjective character of the mind of its
author. Many maintain that the commentary said to be
that of An-kwo was not really from him, but was made by
Mei 3eh, and palmed on the world under the name of the
great Han scholar. Even if it were so, the work would
remain, produced nearly 1600 years ago. And to the anno-
tations of the Thang scholars upon it we are indebted for
most of what we know of the earlier views of Mâ Yung,
Kǎng Khang-khǎng, and other writers of the Han period.
Whether its author were the true Khung or a false Khung, its
value cannot be over-estimated. But I do not believe that it
was a forgery. That An-kwo did write a commentary on his
'Shû in the ancient characters' is admitted by all. When
did it perish? There is no evidence that it ever did so.
On the contrary, its existence rises as a fact, here and there,
at no great intervals of time, on the surface of the literary
history of the empire, till we arrive at Mei 3eh, who
received it, as Khung Ying-tâ proves, from a scholar named
3ang 3hâo.

Then as to the text of the Shû, there is no controversy
about the documents which were recovered in the first

place by Fû; but the additional ones found by Khung An-
kwo are so much more easily understood, that I do not
wonder that the charge of not being genuine has been
raised against them. But even they are not easy. They
only appear to be so, when we come to one of them, after
toiling through some of the more contorted portions common to both texts. And, moreover, the style of the different books differs according to their subjects. The
'Announcements' are the hardest to understand of all.
The 'Charges,' 'Speeches,' and 'Instructions' are much
simpler in their construction; and the portions which we
owe to An-kwo consist principally of 'these. In making
out his obsolete characters he had, in the first place, to
make use of the Books of Fû. That he did not servilely
follow his text we conclude from the readings of Fû's
followers, different from his in many passages which the
industry of critics has gathered up. When he came, however, to new books, which were not in Fû's copy, he had to
make out his tablets as he best could. His most valuable
aid had ceased. We can conceive that, when he had
managed to read the greater portion of a paragraph, and
yet there were some stubborn characters that defied him,
he completed it according to his understanding of the
sense with characters of his own. That he was faithful
and successful in the main we find by the many passages
of his peculiar books that are found quoted in writings of
the *K*âu dynasty. This is a fact worthy of the most
attentive consideration. I do not think there is an important statement in his chapters that is not thus vouched
for. The characteristics of his books which have exposed
them to suspicion are not sufficient to overthrow their claims
to be regarded as genuine transcripts of the tablets discovered in the wall of the house of the Khung family.

The conclusion to which I come, at the close of this
chapter, is, that there is nothing seriously to shake our
confidence in the portions of the Shû that we now possess,
as being substantially the same as those which were in
the collection of the *K*âu dynasty both before and after
Confucius.

11

12

CHAPTER II.

THE CREDIBILITY OF THE RECORDS IN THE SHÛ.

1. Accepting the conclusion which I have stated immediately above, I now go on to enquire whether the documents in the Shû can be relied on as genuine narratives of the transactions which they profess to relate. And it may be said at once, in reference to the greater number of them, that there is no reasonable ground to call their credibility in question. Allowance must be made, indeed, for the colouring with which the founders of one dynasty set forth the misdeeds of the closing reigns of that which they were superseding, and for the way in which the failures of a favourite hero may be glossed over. But the documents of the Shû are quite as much entitled to credit as the memorials and edicts which are published at the present day in the Peking Gazette.

Whether the records in the Shû are reliable or not.

The more recent the documents are, the more, of course, are they to be relied on. And provision was made, we have seen, by the statutes of *K*âu, for the preservation of the records of previous dynasties. But it was not to be expected that many of those should not perish in the lapse of time, and others suffer mutilations and corruptions. And this, we find, was the case. Of the eighty-one documents that the Shû at one time contained, only one belonged to the period of Yâo; seven to the period of Shun; four to the dynasty of Hsiâ, much the larger one of which narrates what was done in the time of Yâo; thirty-one to the dynasty of Shang; and thirty-eight to the first 500 years of that of *K*âu. All this seems to bear on the surface of it the stamp of verisimilitude.

2. The Books of *K*âu were contemporaneous with the events which they describe, and became public property not long after their composition. They are to be received without hesitation.

*The Books of K*âu.

Nor are those of the previous dynasty of Shang open   13
The Books to suspicion. We ascend by means of them
of Shang. to Thang the Successful, its founder, with a
confident step. The beginning of his rule is placed chrono-
logically in B. C. 1766.

Of the still earlier dynasty of Hsiâ, there are only four
The Books documents, and we have no evidence that
of Hsiâ. there were any more when the collection of
the Shû was made in the times of *K*âu. The first and
longest of the four, though occupied with the great achievement of Yü, the founder of Hsiâ, whose chronological
place is B. C. 2205–2196, really belongs to the reign of
Yâo, and is out of place among the records of Hsiâ. The
other three documents bring us down only to the reign of
*K*ung Khang (B. C; 2159–2145), and I see no grounds for
doubting their genuineness. In the last of them a celestial
phenomenon is mentioned, which has always been understood to have been an eclipse of the sun in Fang, a space of
about $5\frac{1}{2}°$ from π to σ of Scorpio, on the first day of the
last month of autumn. P. Gaubil thought he had deter-
mined by calculation that such an eclipse really took
place in the fifth year of *K*ung Khang, B. C. 2155. Doubts,
however, have been cast, as will be seen in the next chapter,
on the accuracy of his calculation, and therefore I do not
avail myself of it here as a confirmation of the truth of
the document.

3. We come to the earlier records,—those of the reigns
The Books of Yâo and Shun, with which must be classed
of Thang the Tribute of Yü, the first of the documents
and Yü. of Hsiâ ; and it must be admitted that there
is not the same evidence that they existed originally in
their present form.

i. The Canon of Yâo and three of the four still existing books of the time of Yü, all commence
They are with the words, 'Examining into antiquity,
professedly we find.' They are therefore, on their own
later compi-
lations. showing, the compilations of a later age. The
writer separates himself from the date of the events which
he narrates, and while professing to draw from the records

14   of 'antiquity,' yet writes himself from a modern standpoint. The Yî and *K*î, the last of the documents of the Shun period, formed one book with the preceding in the Shû of Fû, and came under the opening words of that, as being a result 'of 'the examination of antiquity.' I will draw separate attention farther on to the Tribute of Yü.

ii. Much of what is related in the Canons of Yâo and Shun, as well as in the other documents, has more the air of legend than of history. When Yâo has been on the throne for seventy years, he proposes to resign in favour of his principal minister, who is styled the Four Mountains. That worthy declares himself unequal to the office. Yâo then asks him whom he can recommend for it; be the worthiest individual a noble or a poor man, he will appoint him to the dignity. This brings Shun upon the stage. All the officers about the court can recommend him,—Shun of Yü [1], an unmarried man among the lower people. His father, a blind man, was obstinately unprincipled; his mother, or stepmother, was insincere; his brother was arrogant; and yet Shun had been able by his filial piety to live harmoniously with them, and to bring them to a considerable measure of self-government and good conduct. Yâo is delighted. He had himself heard something of Shun. He resolved to give him a preliminary trial. And a strange trial it was. He gave him his own two daughters in marriage, and declared that he would test his fitness for the throne by seeing his behaviour with his two wives.

They are legendary.

    Shun must have stood the test. Yâo continued to employ him as General Regulator for three years, and then called him to ascend the throne. Shun refused to do so, but discharged the royal duties till the death of Yâo in 2257, becoming himself sole ruler in B. C. 2255. These

---

[1] 虞舜.—Yü is the dynastic designation of Shun. It is to be distinguished from Yü (禹), the name of Shun's successor, the founder of the dynasty of Hsiâ. Bunsen confounded the two appellations (Egypt's Place in Universal History, III, p. 399).

and other marvellous notices of Yâo and Shun are 15
largely added to by Mencius and Sze-mâ *Kh*ien, but
their accounts are of the same extraordinary character.
I must believe that the oldest portions of the Shû do not
give us the history of Yâo and Shun, but legendary tales
about them.

At the same time it must be allowed that the compiler
of these books in their present form had in
his possession some documents as old as the
time of Yâo. To my mind three things render this admission necessary. First, the titles
of the high officers of Yâo and Shun are different from those of the corresponding dignitaries at a later
age. The principal personage was called the Four Mountains; next to him was the General Regulator; and the
Minister of Religion was the Arranger of the Ancestral
Temple. It is more probable that the compiler received
these and other peculiar designations from old documents
than that he invented them himself. Second, the style of
these early books is distinguished in several particulars from
the style of those of Hsiâ, Shang, and *K*âu. I need only
specify the exclamations, 'Alas!' 'Ah!' and 'Oh!' which are
expressed by characters that we do not elsewhere find used
in the same way. Third, the directions of Yâo to his astronomers, telling them how to determine the equinoxes and
solstices, by means of the stars culminating at dusk in those
seasons, could not be the inventions of a later age. The
reader will find this subject discussed in the next chapter,
where it is shown how those culminating stars may be
employed to ascertain the era of Yâo. No compiler,
ignorant of the precession of the equinoxes, which was
not known in China till about the middle of our fourth
century, could have framed Yâo's directions with such an
adjustment to the time assigned to him in chronology.

When the Books of Thang and Yü received their present
form, we cannot tell. Probably it was in the early period of
the *K*âu dynasty, though I am not without a suspicion
that some verbal changes were made in them under the
short-lived dynasty of *Kh*in, which intervened between

Their compiler had ancient documents on which to base his representations.

16   the dynasties of *K*âu and Han, and possibly some also
when they were recovered under the latter.

4. It remains for us to consider the case of the Tribute
The Tribute   of Yü, the first, as the books are now arranged,
of Yü.   of those of Hsiâ, but belonging, as has been
already said, to the period of Yâo, or at least to the period
when Yâo and Shun were together on the throne. It thus
appears out of its chronological order, and must share in the
general uncertainty which attaches to the documents of
the first two parts of our classic.

·Yâo, in what year of his reign we are not told, appears
suddenly startled by the ravages of a terrible inundation.
The waters were overtopping the hills, and threatening the
heavens in their surging fury. The people everywhere were
groaning and murmuring Was there a capable man to
whom he could assign the correction of the calamity? All
the nobles recommend one Khwăn, to whom Yâo, against
his own better judgment, delegates the difficult task, on
which Khwăn labours without success for nine years. His
son Yü then entered on the work. From beyond the
western bounds of the present China proper he is represented as tracking the great rivers, here burning the woods,
hewing the rocks, and cutting through the mountains that
obstructed their progress, and there deepening their channels until their waters flow peacefully into the eastern sea.
He forms lakes, and raises mighty embankments, till at
length 'the grounds along the rivers were everywhere made
habitable; the hills cleared of their superfluous wood; and
access to the capital was secured for all within the four
seas. A great order was effected in the six magazines (of
material wealth); the different parts of the country were
subjected to an exact comparison, so that contribution of
revenue could be carefully adjusted according to their
resources. The fields were all classified according to the
three characters of the soil, and the revenues of the Middle
Kingdom were established.' Of the devotion with which
Yü pursued his work, he says himself in the Yî and
*K*î:—'I mounted my four conveyances,'—carriages on
the land, boats on the water, sledges in icy places, and

shoes with spikes in them in ascending the hills,—'and all
along the hills hewed down the woods, at the same time,
along with Yî, showing the people how to get flesh to
eat,'—that is, by capturing fish and birds and beasts. 'I
opened passages for the streams throughout the nine provinces, and conducted them to the sea. I deepened the
channels and canals, and conducted them to the streams,
at the same time, along with *Kî*, sowing grain, and showing
the people how to procure the food of toil in addition to
flesh meat. I urged them to exchange what they had for
what they had not, and to dispose of their accumulated
stores. In this way all the people got grain to eat, and
the myriad regions began to come under good rule.' And
again :—'When I married in Tû-shan, I remained with my
wife only four days.' Mencius says that while engaged on
his task, he thrice passed the door of his house, but did not
enter it. His own words are :—'When *Khî* (my son) was
wailing and weeping, I did not regard him, but kept planning with all my might my labour on the land.'

Along with his operations to assuage the wide-spread
inundation, Yü thus carried on other most important labours
proper to an incipient civilization. We gather from the Shû
that it did not take him many years to accomplish his
mighty undertaking. It was successfully finished before
the death of Yâo. All this is incredible. The younger
Biot, in an article on the Tribute of Yü, published in the
Journal Asiatique, in 1842, says :—'If we are to believe
the commentators, Yü will become a supernatural being,
who could lead the immense rivers of China as if he had
been engaged in regulating the course of feeble stream-
lets.' There is no occasion to say, 'If we are to believe
the commentators ;'—if we are to believe the Shû, this is
the judgment that we must form about Yü.

The general conclusion to which Biot came about the
document under our notice was that we are to find in it
only the progress of a great colony. Yü was the first
explorer of the Chinese world. He established posts of
colonists or planters in different parts of the territory.
He caused the wood around those posts to be cut down,

17

18 and commenced the cultivation of the soil. After Yü, the labours of draining the country and clearing the forests continued during some ages, and the result of all was attributed by Chinese tradition to the first chief. I have no doubt there is an inkling of the truth in this view of the French sinologue, but the idea of Yü's being the leader of a Chinese colony had better be abandoned. We recognise the primitive seat of the Chinese people, in the southern parts of the present Shan-hsî, with the Ho on the west and south of it. His son fought a battle with the Chief of Hû at a place in the present department of Hsî-an, in Shen-hsî, across the Ho, and his grandson was kept a sort of prisoner at large in the present province of Ho-nan, south of the river. The people or tribe extended itself westward, eastward, and southward, and still later northward, as it increased in numbers, and was able to subdue the earth.

The flood of Yâo was probably an inundation of the Ho, similar to many in subsequent times which have procured for that river the name of 'China's Sorrow,' and Yü distinguished himself in the assuaging of it, and the regulation of its course to the sea. The extent of the country came to be ascertained under the dynasties of Hsiâ and Shang, and its different parts were gradually occupied by the increasing numbers of the people, and contributed their various proportions of revenue to the central government. There were memorials of the toils which Yü had undergone, and of allotments of territory which he had made to the most distinguished among his followers. It occurred to some historiographer to form a theory as to the way in which the whole country might have been brought to order by the founder of the Hsiâ dynasty, and he proceeded to glorify Yü by ascribing so grand an achievement to him. About the same time, probably, the popular stories of Yü's self-denial had found their expression in the Yî and Kî, prompting at once the conception of the Tribute of Yü, and obtaining for it a favourable reception. Yü entered well into association with Yâo and Shun, and formed a triad with them

at the beginning of the Chinese monarchy. Their wisdom   19
and benevolence appeared in him, combined with a practical devotion to the duties of his position, in which all
sovereigns would have a model, to win them from indolence
and self-indulgence, and stimulate them to a painstaking
discharge of their responsibilities.

In the nineteenth of the Books of Part V, the duke of
*K*âu counsels his young sovereign, king *Kh*ăng (B. C. 1115–
1077), to have his armies in a good state of preparation,
so that he might go forth 'beyond the footsteps of Yü,' and
travel over all beneath the sky, everywhere meeting with
submission. The duke's reference to 'the footsteps of Yü'
does not prove that Yü really travelled and toiled as the
Tribute of Yü· reports, but only that such was the current
belief at the commencement of the *K*âu dynasty, while it
affords at the same time a presumption that our document
was then among the archives of the kingdom. It may have
been compiled before the end of the Hsiâ dynasty, or under
that of Shang. From Shang it passed to *K*âu, and came
under the care of the recorders of the Exterior. Then
subsequently it was very properly incorporated in the
collection of the Shû.

5. While we are thus unable to receive the six earliest
documents in our classic as contemporaneous in their present form with the events which they relate, it is not meant

Yâo, Shun,
and Yü are
all historical
personages.

to throw doubt on the existence of Yâo,
Shun, and Yü as historical personages. More
especially does Yü stand forth as the first
sovereign of the dynasty of Hsiâ, the man
who laid the foundation of the hereditary monarchy in
China, its feudal sovereign who 'conferred surnames and
lands.' The documents which follow the Tribute of Yü,
commencing with the Speech at Kan, delivered in B.C. 2197
by Yü's son and successor, may all be received as veritable
monuments of antiquity.

20

CHAPTER III.

ON THE CHRONOLOGY OF CHINA, AND THE PRINCIPAL
ERAS IN THE SHÛ.

1. I do not enter here on the subject of the chronology of China further than is necessary to show that there is no chronological difficulty in the way of our accepting the documents of the Shû, which I have just specified, as being possessed of the antiquity ascribed to them.

The Shû itself does not supply the means of laying down
No detailed any scheme of chronology for the long period
chronological of time which it covers. We learn from it that
system can
be made out the dynasty of *K*âu succeeded to that of
from the Shû. Shang (another name for which was Yin), and
the dynasty of Shang to that of Hsiâ, and that prior to Yü, the founder of the Hsiâ, there were the reigns of Shun and Yâo. As P. Gaubil has observed, 'If we had only the Shû King, we should have but confused ideas of the time comprised in the different parts of the book.' There is nothing in this to awaken our surprise. The chronology of a nation comes to be cultivated as a science only when a necessity is felt to arrange the events of its history in regular series on the course of time.

2. It was under the Han dynasty that it was first
Attempts at attempted to construct a chronological
systematic scheme of the history of the nation. For
chronology
began in this purpose its scholars employed the well-
the Han known cycle of sixty years, in the fifteenth
period. year of the seventy-sixth revolution of which
I am now writing. It was assumed that this cycle was first devised by Tâ-nâo, an officer of Hwang Tî, in B.C. 2637, which is the first year of the first cycle. But all scholars in China, whether they call in question this origin of the cycle or not, now agree in saying that the use of the cyclic characters to chronicle years was not the ancient method, and did not begin earlier than the time of the usurper Mang (A.D. 9–22).

In the Shû itself the current cycle is used to chronicle

days, and days only. Years are specified according to their order in the reign of the sovereign to whom they are re-ferred. Such specification of years in it, however, is rare. 21

Before the Han dynasty a list of sovereigns, and of the length of their several reigns, was the only method which the Chinese had of determining the duration of their national history. And it would still be a satisfactory method, if we had a list of sovereigns, and of the years that each reigned, that was complete and reliable. But we do not have this. Even in the early part of the Han dynasty, Sze-mâ *K͟h*ien's father and himself, in their Historical Records, completed about B.C. 100, were obliged to content themselves with giving simply the names and order of most of the rulers of Shang and Hsiâ. It is right to state also that in A.D. 279, when the grave of king Hsiang of Wei (died in B.C. 295) was opened, there were found a number of bamboo tablets in it, written in the ancient seal characters, among which the most valuable portion was a book of annals, beginning with the reign of Hwang Tî, and coming down to the sixteenth year of the last king of *K*âu, B.C. 299. This work is still current under the name of the Annals of the Bamboo Books. The chronology derived from it is shorter than the received system by rather more than 200 years.

Ancient method of determining the length of Chinese history.

If in any of the classical books of the *K*âu dynasty we had a statement of the length of the national history from any given era to the time of the writer, the notice would be exceedingly valuable ; or, if the length of the reigns of the sovereigns of Shang and Hsiâ, cursorily mentioned in it, were correctly given, we should be in a position to make an approximate computation for ourselves. But there are only two passages in all those books which are helpful to us in this point. The former of them is in a narrative in *K͟h*iû-ming's supplement to the Spring and Autumn, under the third year of duke Hsüan, where it is said that the dynasty of Shang possessed the throne for 600 years. The other passage is the last chapter of the works of Men-cius, where that philosopher says that 'from Yâo and Shun to Thang'—a period including all the dynasty of Hsiâ—

22   'there were 500 years and more; from Thang to king Wăn'—the period of the Shang dynasty—'500 years and more; and from king Wăn to Confucius, 500 years and more.' We know that Confucius was born in B. C. 551. Adding 551 to the 1500 years 'and more,' given by Mencius, we have the era of Yâo and Shun at 2100 years 'and more' before our Christian era. And the received chronology places Yü's accession to the throne, as the successor of Shun, in B. C. 2205. Vague as the language of Mencius is, I do not think that with the most painstaking research, apart from conclusions based on astronomical considerations, we can determine anything more precise and definite concerning the length of Chinese history than it conveys.

3. The Charge to the Marquis Wăn, which now forms

The period of the *Kâu* dynasty.

the 28th Book of the 5th Part of the Shû, is understood to have been delivered by king Phing, the thirteenth of his line. His place in historical time is well ascertained. Confucius' chronicle of the Spring and Autumn commences in B. C. 722. The first of the thirty-six solar eclipses mentioned in it took place three years after, on the 14th February (N. S.) 719, and it is recorded that in the month after king Phing died. Here therefore is a point of time about which there can be no dispute. An earlier date in the *K*âu dynasty is known with the same certainty. The Book of Poetry mentions an eclipse of the sun which took place on the 29th August, B. C. 776, in the sixth year of king Yû, who preceded Phing. Yû reigned 'eleven years, and his predecessor, Hsüan, forty-six, whose reign consequently commenced B. C. 827. Up to this date Chinese chronologers agree. To the ten reigns before king Hsüan, the received chronology assigns 295 years, making the dynasty begin in B. C. 1122, which cannot be far from the truth.

4. In the period of the Shang dynasty we cannot fix a

The period of the Shang dynasty.

single reign by means of astronomical facts. The received chronology assigns to it twenty-eight reigns, extending over 644 years, so that its commencement was in B. C. 1766. The scheme derived from the bamboo books makes the sovereigns to 23 be thirty, but the aggregate of their reigns is only 508. Mencius says that between Thang, the founder of the dynasty, and Wû-ting, the twentieth sovereign (in the common scheme), 'there had been six or seven worthy and sage rulers[1],'—leading to the conclusion that the number of twenty-eight sovereigns in all is not beyond the truth. In the fifteenth of the Books of *K*âu the names of three of the Shang rulers are given, and the duration of their reigns,—to show how Heaven is likely to crown a good king with length of sway. They are Thâi Mâu, who reigned seventy-five years; Wû-ting, who reigned fifty-nine; and Зû-*k*iâ, who reigned thirty-three. The two schemes agree in the length of those reigns and of five others. From the statement in the Зo-*k*wan, to which I have referred above, that the Shang dynasty possessed the throne for 600 years, and Mencius' language that it lasted 'for 500 years and more,' we may believe that the 644 years of the common scheme are more likely to be correct than the 508 of the shorter.

5. The dynasty of Hsiâ lasted, according to the received chronology, 439 years, and according to the bamboo books, The period 431; so that the difference here between the of Hsiâ. two schemes is small. The former estimate carries us up to B.C. 2205, as the first year of Yü's reign.

I referred on page 13 to an eclipse of the sun, mentioned in the fourth of the Books of Hsiâ, as having occurred in the reign of·*K*ung Khang, a grandson of Yü, and stated that P. Gaubil had found by calculation that on the day and month stated in the document, and in the quarter of the heavens given, an eclipse did occur in the fifth year of *K*ung Khang, that is, in B.C. 2156, and was visible at his capital at 6^h 49′, A.M. In 1840, J. B. Biot submitted a copy of Gaubil's calculations to the younger Largeteau, a member, like himself, of the Institute of France, who went over them with the lunar tables of Damoiseau and the solar tables of Delambre, and brought out the result that

---

[1] Mencius, II, i, ch. 1.

24   there was indeed an eclipse on the day stated, but before
the rising of the sun at the then capital of China[1]. My
friend, the Rev. Dr. Chalmers of Canton, not knowing anything of the examination made by Largeteau, undertook
to verify the eclipse in 1861, and found that while the year,
the month, and the day, as given by Gaubil, were correct,
the eclipse had taken place during the night, and could not
have been seen by the Chinese astronomers. The eclipse
mentioned in the document of the Shû cannot therefore
be used at present to confirm the received chronology of
China ; but I am unwilling to give it up entirely. M. Biot
says that, 'Notwithstanding the failure of the attempt of
Largeteau to verify the eclipse, the hope of yet finding it
in some one of the years of the twenty-second century
before our era is not entirely lost. We ought to wait till
the further perfecting of the lunar tables brings us new
lights, by means of which we can form a surer judgment.'

6. We come to the earliest period of Chinese history of
which the Shû makes more than a cursory mention,—that

The period   of Yâo and Shun. It says that Shun was
of Yâo   thirty years on the throne with Yâo, and that,
and Shun.   fifty years after, he died and went on high.
We learn from it also that it was in the seventieth year of
his reign that Yâo sought for another to relieve him of the
toils of government. The period covered by the two therefore is 150 years, which both the schemes of chronology
accept. Adding two years of mourning between Shun's
death and Yü's accession to the throne, we have B. C. 2357
as the first year of Yâo.

In the Canon of Yâo, when that personage is giving
directions to his astronomers how to determine the equinoxes and solstices, he tells them that at the vernal equinox
they would find the star in Niâo, and at the autumnal in
Hsü ; at the summer solstice, the star in Hwo, and at the
winter in Mâo. It has always been assumed by Chinese
scholars that when Yâo said, 'The star of mid-spring is in

---

[1] Etudes sur l'Astronomie Indienne et sur l'Astronomie Chinoise, pp. 376–
382.

Niâo,' he meant the star culminating at dusk at that season, at the point of observation. And so of the other stars and seasons. A Chinese astronomer at the present day would similarly express himself.

Further, the most common, and what was the earliest division of the ecliptic in China, is that of the twenty-eight lunar mansions, forming what we may call the Chinese zodiac. These mansions are grouped together in four classes of seven each, assigned to the four quarters of the heavens[1]. Of the celestial spaces which Yâo specified, Niâo is the general name for the seven mansions or constellations belonging to the southern quarter; Hwo is an old name of what is now called Fang, the central constellation of the eastern quarter; Hsü and Mâo are the central constellations of the northern and southern quarters respectively. What Yâo meant therefore was, that his astronomers could determine the solstices and the autumnal equinox by the culmination of the stars in the mansions which he specified for those seasons. And we may assume that he directed them, for the star of the vernal equinox, to Hsing, the central mansion in the southern space Niâo. Now, Hsing corresponds to *a* (Alphard) Hydræ, and small stars near it, in our stellar nomenclature; Hwo, to β, δ in Scorpio; Hsü, to β Aquarii; and Mâo, to Pleiades. When we wish to make the directions of Yâo available for the purpose of chronological enquiry, the question that arises is this :— When did the above-named stars culminate at dusk in China at the equinoctial and solstitial seasons?

Bunsen tells us that Ideler, computing the places of the constellations backwards, fixed the accession of Yâo at B.C. 2163, and that Freret was of opinion that the observations left an uncertainty of 3°, leaving a margin of 210

---

[1] In the Official Book of *K*âu, a work of the twelfth century before our era, Book XXVI, par. 25, in the enumeration of the duties of the astronomer royal of that day, there is mentioned the determination of 'the places of the twenty-eight stars,' meaning 'the principal stars in the twenty-eight lunar mansions.' The names of the stars and their mansions are not mentioned ;—surely a sufficient indication that they were even then well known. See Biot's Etudes sur l'Astronomie Indienne, &c., pp. 112, 113.

26 years [1]. On the other hand, J. B. Biot found in the directions a sufficient confirmation of the received date for Yâo's accession,—B.C. 2357 [2]. Appended to this Introduction is a chart of the stars as they were visible in China in B. C. 2300, which the Rev. C. Pritchard, Savilian Professor of Astronomy in the University of Oxford, kindly prepared for me. An inspection of it, in the manner directed by him, will show that the phenomena indicated by Yâo to his astronomers were all apparent at that date. This fact must be accepted as a strong proof of the approximate correctness of the chronology, which places Yâo in the twenty-fourth century B. C. The precession of the equinoxes, it has already been observed, was not known in China till more than 2500 years after the time assigned to Yâo, so that the culminating stars at the equinoxes and solstices of his remote period could not have been computed back scientifically in the time of the *K*âu dynasty, during which the collection of the Shû existed. The form in which the directions are given, and other things in the Canon, savour, indeed, of legend, and I have not claimed for it that in its present form it be received as a document contemporaneous with the reign of Yâo. I have argued, however, that the compiler of it had before him ancient documents, and one of them must have contained the facts about the culminating of the stars, which I have now endeavoured to set in a clear light.

The mention of these culminating stars does seem to fix Yâo's place in chronology in the twenty-fourth century B. C., and to show that at that remote era it was the custom to make and to record astronomical observations of the heavenly bodies. Having respect to these things, my claim to have the documents of the Shû from the Speech at Kan, nearly two centuries later than Yâo, downwards, regarded as contemporaneous with the events which they describe, cannot be considered extravagant.

7. In the 27th Book of the 5th Part, the Marquis of

---

[1] Egypt's Place in Universal History, III, pp. 400, 401.
[2] Etudes sur l'Astronomie Indienne, &c., pp. 361-366.

Lü on Punishments, there is a historical reference which   27
would carry us back four centuries beyond the time of
Yâo. It is said that, 'According to the teachings of antiquity, *Kh*ih Yû was the first to create disorder.' There
is no intimation, however, of the time when this rebel
disturbed the happy order and innocence which had previously prevailed ; and the very same sentence brings the
review of antiquity down to the time of Shun. But the
chronologers place him in the reign of Hwang Tî, towards
the end of the twenty-seventh century B.C. Other writers
describe the struggle between him and Hwang Tî, in which
dragons, mists, and the invention of the compass play conspicuous parts. It is to the credit of the Shû, and an
evidence of its being a genuine collection of historical memorials, that this cursory reference to *Kh*ih Yû is the only
mention in it of any name older than that of Yâo.

The Use of the Chart.

This chart is intended to represent approximately the aspect of
the principal zodiacal stars as seen above the horizon of any
place in central China, at any hour of any day, about the year
B. C. 2300.

In order to apply the chart to a practical purpose, the reader is
advised to cut out a sheet of paper (cardboard is preferable) with
its upper edge exactly fitting the curved line A B O C D, and to
draw, near to the bottom of the paper, a line coinciding with 'the
hour-line' on the chart.

This being done, if it be asked what will be the aspect of the
heavens when the Sun sets at the Vernal Equinox, the reader is to
move the line at the bottom of the cardboard along the horizontal
'hour-line' of the chart until the place of the Sun in the Ecliptic at
the Vernal Equinox O just touches the curved top of the paper ;
then all the stars not covered over are above the horizon at the time
of that sunset, viz. in this case Aldebaran, Sirius, Spica, &c. ; the
Pleiades are just setting, Regulus and α Hydræ are very near the
meridian, β Centauri is on the point of rising, and α Serpentis is
well up above the horizon. This exactly corresponds with that
state of the heavens which Yâo, (alleged in the Chinese records to
have flourished about B.C. 2300,) indicated to his astronomers (Hsî
and Ho) would be the case, viz. that he would find the star (or the

28   stellar division) Shun Hwo (corresponding, it is said, to *a* Hydræ)
          culminating at the time of sunset at the Vernal Equinox[1].

          Again, if it be required to find what constellation is culminating
at the time of sunset at the Summer Solstice, the cardboard must
be moved, as before, towards the right hand until the position of
the Sun at the Summer Solstice, viz. G, just touches the horizon
curve, when it will be seen that *a* Serpentis and Antares are then
culminating, Regulus and *β* Centauri are just setting, while the
constellations of Aquila and Aquarius are rising; Vega is a conspicuous object above the eastern horizon. This again corresponds
to the indications given by Yâo to his astronomers, viz. that they
would find the constellation Scorpio culminating at the time.

          Thirdly, to find what constellation is culminating at sunset at the
Winter Solstice, the cardboard horizon is to be moved, as before,
until the Sun at F falls upon it, when the constellations Aries and
Taurus with the Pleiades will be seen near to their culmination.
This is a third correspondence with the indications of the astro-
nomical sovereign.

          Lastly, at sunset of the Autumnal Equinox the movable horizon
is to be shifted to the left until the point A falls upon it, where it
will be seen in this position that the stars in Aquarius are culminating at the time. It is scarcely possible that all these indications of the positions of the stars at these several times of the year
could be simultaneously correct at any other epoch than somewhere about B.C. 2300 or a very small number of centuries before
or after.

          The reader may easily make for himself many other interesting
applications of the chart. A general notion of the effects of
precession on the positions of the stars may be seen at once by
observing the three positions of the Pleiades, at the three epochs
B.C. 2300, A.D. 1, and A.D. 1878, marked in the chart by the letters
K, L, M; and as the approximate effect of precession is to cause
all stars to move parallel to the Ecliptic and through the same arc,
if the reader will imagine every star to be shifted parallel to the
Ecliptic through spaces equal respectively to K L, L M, he will get
the aspect of the heavens at the epochs A.D. 1 and A.D. 1878.

          The following table has been calculated for the apparent posi-
tions of the principal stars in the years B.C. 2300, B.C. 1500, A.D. 1,
and A.D. 1000; except in one instance it will be found to confirm
a similar calculation made by Biot for the earliest of these dates.

----

[1] See an excellent memoir by Mr. Williams, the late Assistant Secretary of
the Royal Astronomical Society, on Chinese Comets, procurable at the apartments of the Royal Astronomical Society, Burlington House, London.

Name of Star.	For the year B.C. 2300. R.A. (h. m. s.)	For the year B.C. 2300. N.P.D. (° ')	For the year B.C. 1500. R.A. (h. m. s.)	For the year B.C. 1500. N.P.D. (° ')	For the year A.D. 1. R.A. (h. m. s.)	For the year A.D. 1. N.P.D. (° ')	For the year A.D. 1000. R.A. (h. m. s.)	For the year A.D. 1000. N.P.D. (° ')	For the year A.D. 1878. R.A. (h. m. s.)	For the year A.D. 1878. N.P.D. (° ')
α Andromedæ	20 33 18	82 1.7	21 13 18	79 1.3	22 27 33	71 49.4	23 18 4	66 28.4	0 2 5	61 35.0
γ Pegasi	20 28 50	96 1.1	21 12 0	92 58.9	22 30 26	85 45.9	23 22 23	80 23.8	0 6 57	75 29.7
β Ceti	20 40 23	129 55.3	21 32 0	126 40.1	22 59 27	119 23.8	23 53 17	113 33.4	0 37 28	108 39.4
α Arietis	22 18 8	89 27.4	22 59 59	85 16.6	0 18 20	76 57.2	1 12 25	71 36.3	2 0 18	67 6.9
η Tauri	23 49 0	86 8.3	0 31 15	81 42.1	1 52 20	73 52.4	2 49 17	69 31.6	3 40 14	66 16.4
Aldebaran	0 40 10	90 54.6	1 22 25	86 38.2	2 43 20	79 37.0	3 39 17	76 7.5	4 28 55	73 44.3
Capella	0 43 7	60 13.1	1 22 14	55 56.4	2 55 15	49 3.0	4 4 9	45 54.0	5 7 41	44 7.7
Rigel	1 47 31	111 43.8	2 26 12	107 58.3	3 38 7	102 21.2	4 26 41	99 52.2	5 8 40	98 20.7
α Orionis	2 5 7	93 37.4	2 46 56	90 4.8	4 6 40	85 9.1	5 0 31	83 26.1	5 48 34	82 37.1
Sirius	3 16 27	112 9.0	4 2 2	108 57.4	5 14 27	106 24.3	6 29 36	106 6.5	6 39 46	106 33.0
Castor	2 54 18	62 4.9	3 44 10	59 14.8	5 22 33	56 27.0	6 45 52	56 35.9	7 26 49	57 50.7
Procyon	3 44 27	85 4.8	4 28 20	83 50.0	5 50 36	82 18.3	7 14 14	82 59.1	7 32 55	84 27.8
α Hydræ	5 45 33	88 32.7	6 28 6	88 43.5	7 46 41	91 25.9	9 14 2	94 39.4	9 21 35	57 7.8
Regulus	5 55 10	65 40.6	6 45 15	66 6.8	8 16 10	69 35.6	9 56 54	74 25.8	10 1 52	77 26.2
β Leonis	7 39 12	55 54.2	8 31 25	58 6.5	10 1 9	64 43.8	11 42 50	69 54.5	11 42 50	74 44.8
Spica	9 37 49	78 15.6	10 37 29	82 7.8	11 40 35	90 15.5	13 33 13	95 45.2	13 18 46	100 31.4
β Centauri	10 16 8	127 25.1	10 46 43	131 31.7	11 1 16	139 48.1	12 59 23	145 11.8	13 48 46	149 47.0
Arcturus	10 36 18	47 58.2	11 22 12	52 16.1	12 39 47	60 40.3	14 28 52	65 48.7	14 10 14	70 10.9
α Serpentis	12 10 58	63 47.2	12 51 58	68 11.0	14 6 6	75 46.5	15 55 30	79 58.8	15 38 16	83 11.4
Antares	12 24 0	98 16.5	13 6 50	102 37.4	14 30 11	109 53.9	16 29 8	113 36.6	16 21 56	116 9.6
α Lyræ	16 8 29	48 3.6	16 36 28	49 51.2	17 28 24	51 43.1	18 3 18	51 43.1	18 32 14	38 43.1
α Aquilæ	16 17 0	82 12.2	16 57 0	83 38.0	17 12 14	84 38.0	19 1 18	83 12.7	19 44 50	81 27.2
α Aquarii	18 19 16	103 8.6	18 12 14	83 44.0	20 19 41	98 45.1	21 44 2	94 53.9	21 59 31	90 54.7
Fomalhaut	18 16 30	134 54.0	18 55 26	102 28.3	20 58 57	129 17.4	22 50 ...	124 46.9	22 50 54	120 16.1
α Pegasi	19 24 1	92 34.4	20 6 35	90 33.5	21 24 14	84 49.4	23 ... 19	80 2.6	23 58 41	75 27.0

THE SHÛ KING.

PART I. THE BOOK OF THANG.

THE CANON OF YÂO.

SHÛ KING, the name of the whole work, has been sufficiently
explained in the Introduction. The name of this Part, the
first of the five into which the whole is divided, is the
Book of Thang, Thang being taken as the dynastic designation of Yâo, who before his elevation to the throne had been
marquis of the small state of Thang, the name of which is
supposed to be still retained in Thang, one of the districts of
the department Pâo-ting, in Kih-lî. It is said that after his
elevation he established his capital in Phing-yang, lat. 36° 06′,
long. 111° 33′, in Shan-hsî. But all this is very uncertain. See
on Part III, Book iii, ch. 2. The one Book, forming this Part,
is called the Canon of Yâo. The character which we translate 'Canon' means a document of the most exalted nature,
the contents of which are entitled to the greatest regard. The
name is given expressly only to one other Book in the
Shû. The Canons are the first of the six classes of documents
which the Shû contains.

Yâo is the subject of the Book:—In ch. 1, in his personal character
and the general results of his government; in ch. 2, in his
special care for the regulation of the calendar and the labours
of agriculture; in ch. 3, in his anxiety to find one who could
cope with the ravages of a terrible inundation, and take his
place on the throne. The third chapter introduces to our
notice Shun, the successor of Yâo.

1. Examining into antiquity, (we find that) the Tî Yâo[1] was styled Fang-hsün[2]. He was reverential, intelligent, accomplished, and thoughtful,—naturally and without effort. He was sincerely courteous, and capable of (all) complaisance. The bright (influence of these qualities) was felt through the four quarters (of the land), and reached to (heaven) above and (earth) beneath.

He made the able and virtuous distinguished, and thence proceeded to the love of (all in) the nine classes of his kindred, who (thus) became harmonious. He (also) regulated and polished the people (of his domain), who all became brightly intelligent. (Finally), he united and harmonized the myriad states; and so the black-haired people were transformed. The result was (universal) concord.

2. He commanded the Hsîs and Hos[3], in reverent accordance with (their observation of) the wide heavens, to calculate and delineate (the movements and appearances of) the sun, the moon, the stars, and the zodiacal spaces, and so to deliver respectfully the seasons to be observed by the people.

---

[1] Yâo is to us now the name of the ancient ruler so denominated. The character means 'high,' 'lofty and grand.' It may originally have been an epithet, 'the Exalted One.' On the meaning of Tî in Tî Yâo, see what has been said in the Preface.

[2] The Han scholars held that Fang-hsün was the name of Yâo. Those of Sung, taking the characters as an epithet, make them signify 'the Highly Meritorious.'

[3] The Hsîs and Hos seem to have been brothers of two families, on whom devolved the care of the calendar, principally with a view to regulate the seasons of agriculture. See Parts III, iv, and V, xxvii. On Yâo's directions to them, see the Introduction, pp. 24-28.

He separately commanded the second brother
Hsî to reside at Yü-î¹, in what was called the
Bright Valley, and (there) respectfully to receive
as a guest the rising sun, and to adjust and arrange
the labours of the spring. 'The day,' (said he), 'is
of the medium length, and the star is in Niâo;—you
may thus exactly determine mid-spring. The people
are dispersed (in the fields), and birds and beasts
breed and copulate.'

He further commanded the third brother Hsî to
reside at Nan-*k*iâo², (in what was called the Brilliant Capital), to adjust and arrange the transforma-
tions of the summer, and respectfully to observe the
exact limit (of the shadow). 'The day,' (said he),
' is at its longest, and the star is in Hwo;—you may
thus exactly determine mid-summer. The people
are more dispersed; and birds and beasts have their
feathers and hair thin, and change their coats.'

He separately commanded the second brother
Ho to reside at the west, in what was called the
Dark Valley, and (there) respectfully to convoy the
setting sun, and to adjust and arrange the completing
labours of the autumn. 'The night,' (said he), 'is
of the medium length, and the star is in Hsü;—you
may thus exactly determine mid-autumn. The people
feel at ease, and birds and beasts have their coats in
good condition.'

He further commanded the third brother Ho to

¹ Yü-î is by some identified with Tăng-*k*âu, in Shan-tung,
lat. 37° 48′, long. 121° 4′; by others, it is sought in Corea.

² Nan-*k*iâo was south, it is said, on the border of An-nan
or Cochin-China. The characters for 'in what was called the
Brilliant Capital' are supposed to have dropt out of the text.

34　reside in the northern region, in what was called the Sombre Capital, and (there) to adjust and examine the changes of the winter. 'The day,' (said he), 'is at its shortest, and the star is in Mâo;—you may thus exactly determine mid-winter. The people keep in their houses, and the coats of birds and beasts are downy and thick.'

The Tî said, 'Ah! you, Hsîs and Hos, a round year consists of three hundred, sixty, and six days. Do you, by means of the intercalary month, fix the four seasons, and complete (the period of) the year. (Thereafter), the various officers being regulated in accordance with this, all the works (of the year) will be fully performed.'

3. The Tî said, 'Who will search out (for me) a man according to the times, whom I can raise and employ?' Fang-khî said, '(Your) heir-son Kû[1] is highly intelligent.' The Tî said, 'Alas! he is insincere and quarrelsome :—can he do ?'

The Tî said, 'Who will search out (for me) a man equal to the exigency of my affairs ?' Hwan-tâu[2] said, 'Oh! the merits of the Minister of Works have just been displayed on a wide scale.' The Tî said, 'Alas! when all is quiet, he talks ; but when employed, his actions turn out differently. He is respectful (only) in appearance. See! the floods assail the heavens!'

The Tî said, 'Ho! (President of) the Four

---

[1] In Part II, iv, 2, Yü speaks of this son of Yâo as 'the haughty Kû of Tan,' Tan probably being the name of a state, over which, according to tradition, he had been appointed.

[2] Hwan-tâu and the Minister of Works, whom he recommends, appear in the next Book as great criminals.

Mountains[1], destructive in their overflow are the   35
waters of the inundation.   In their vast extent they
embrace the hills and overtop the great heights,
threatening the heavens with their floods, so that the
lower people groan and murmur! Is there a capable
man to whom I can assign the correction (of this
calamity)?'   All (in the court) said, 'Ah! is there
not Khwăn[2]?'   The Tî said, 'Alas! how perverse is
he! He is disobedient to orders, and tries to injure
his peers.'   (The President of) the Mountains said,
'Well but—.   Try if he can (accomplish the work).'
(Khwăn) was employed accordingly. The Tî said (to
him), 'Go; and be reverent!'   For nine years he
laboured, but the work was unaccomplished.

   The Tî said, 'Ho! (President of) the Four Mountains, I have been on the throne seventy years. You
can carry out my commands ;—I will resign my place
to you.'   The Chief said, 'I have not the virtue ;—
I should disgrace your place.'   (The Tî) said, 'Show
me some one among the illustrious, or set forth
one from among the poor and mean.'   All (then)
said to the Tî, 'There is an unmarried man among
the lower people, called Shun of Yü[3].'   The Tî

---

   [1] (President of) the Four Mountains, or simply Four Mountains, appears to have been the title of the chief minister of Yâo.
The four mountains were—mount Thâi in the east; Hwâ in the
west, in Shan-hsî; Hăng in the south, in Hû-nan; and Hăng in
the north, in _K_ih-lî.   These, probably, were the limits of the
country, so far as known, and all within these points were the care
of the chief minister.
   [2] Khwăn is believed to have been the father of Yü, who afterwards coped successfully with the inundation. We are told that
he was earl of _K_hung, corresponding to the present district of Hû,
in Shen-hsî.
   [3] See on the title of next Book.

D 2

36　said, 'Yes, I have heard of him. What have you to say about him ?' The Chief said, ' He is the son of a blind man. His father was obstinately unprincipled; his (step-)mother was insincere; his (half-)brother Hsiang was arrogant. He has been able, (however), by his filial piety to live in harmony with them, and to lead them gradually to self-government, so that they (no longer) proceed to great wickedness.' The Tî said, ' I will try him ; I will wive him, and thereby see his behaviour with my two daughters.' (Accordingly) he arranged and sent down his two daughters to the north of the Kwei [1], to be wives in (the family of) Yü. The Tî said to them, ' Be reverent !'

---

[1] The Kwei is a small stream in Shan-hsî, which flows into the Ho.

Book I. The Canon of Shun.

THE Books of Yŭ is the name of this Part of the Shû, Yŭ being the dynastic designation of Shun, as Thang was that of Yâo. It does not appear so clearly, however, how it came to be so. Yŭ must be the name of a state, and is commonly identified with the present district of An-yî, in *K*ieh *K*âu, Shan-hsî. Some think that Yâo, after marrying his two daughters to Shun, appointed him lord of this state; but in the first mention of him to Yâo in the last Book, he is called Shun of Yŭ. It is generally said that Shun's ancestors had been lords of the principality of Yŭ up to the time of his father, who lost his patrimony and was reduced to the rank of a private man. But after what has been said, in the Introduction, on the Books in the first two Parts of the Shû, it will not be thought surprising that much in the accounts about Yâo and Shun should be open to suspicion. According to Mencius, IV, Part ii, ch. 1, Shun was from the country of the wild tribes on the east. Sze-mâ *K*hien makes him to have been descended from Hwang-Tî, in which case he and his wives, the daughters of Yâo, would have had the same ancestor. Nothing more injurious to the fame of Yâo and Shun, according to Chinese notions of propriety, could be alleged against them.

Shun is the subject of this Canon, as Yâo was of the former. As it now stands, we may divide it into six chapters:—the first, describing Shun's virtues and gradual advancement; the second, Yâo's satisfaction with his administration of affairs, and associating of Shun with himself on the throne; the third, the acts of Shun in that position; the fourth, the demise of Yâo, and Shun's accession as sole monarch; the fifth, his choice of ministers and complete organization of his government; and the sixth, his death.

38　　　1. Examining into antiquity, (we find that) the Tî Shun[1] was styled *Khung-hwâ*[2]. His character was entirely conformed to (that of) the (former) Tî; he was profound, wise, accomplished, and intelligent. He was mild and courteous, and truly sincere. The report of his mysterious virtue was heard on high, and he was appointed to office.

2. (Shun) carefully set forth the beauty of the five cardinal duties, and they came to be (universally) observed. Being appointed to be General Regulator, the affairs of every (official) department were arranged in their proper seasons. (Being charged) to receive (the princes) from the four quarters of the land, they were all docilely submissive. Being sent to the great plains at the foot of the mountains, notwithstanding the tempests of wind, thunder, and rain, he did not go astray.

The Tî said, 'Come, you Shun. I have consulted you on (all) affairs, and examined your words, and found that they can be carried into practice;—(now) for three years. Do you ascend the seat of the Tî.' Shun wished to decline in favour of some one more virtuous, and not to consent to be (Yâo's) successor. On the first day of the first month, (however), he received (Yâo's) retirement (from his duties) in the temple of the Accomplished Ancestor[3].*

3. He examined the pearl-adorned turning sphere,

---

[1] If Shun be taken as an epithet, it will mean 'the Benevolent and Sage.'

[2] *Khung-hwâ*, the name of Shun according to the Han scholars, may mean 'the Glorious (Yâo) repeated.'

[3] The Accomplished Ancestor would be, probably, the individual in some distant time to whom Yâo traced his possession of the throne.

39

with its transverse tube of jade, and reduced to a harmonious system (the movements of) the Seven Directors [1].

Thereafter, he sacrificed specially, but with the ordinary forms, to God; sacrificed with reverent purity to the Six Honoured Ones; offered their appropriate sacrifices to the hills and rivers; and extended his worship to the host of spirits [2].*

He called in (all) the five jade-symbols of rank; and when the month was over, he gave daily audience to (the President of) the Four Mountains, and all the Pastors [3], (finally) returning their symbols to the various princes.

In the second month of the year he made a tour of inspection eastwards, as far as Thâi-ȝung [4], where he presented a burnt-offering to Heaven, and sacrificed in order to the hills and rivers.* Thereafter he gave audience to the princes of the east. He set in accord their seasons and months, and regulated the days; he made uniform the standard-tubes, with the measures of length and of capacity, and the steelyards; he regulated the five (classes of) ceremonies, with (the various) articles of introduction,—the five

---

[1] Probably the seven stars of the Great Bear.

[2] Who the Six Honoured Ones were cannot be determined with certainty. An-kwo thought they were, 'the seasons, cold and heat, the sun, the moon, the stars, and drought,' that is, certain spirits, supposed to rule over these phenomena and things, and residing probably in different stars. The whole paragraph describes Shun's exercise of the prerogative of the sovereign, so far as religious worship was concerned.

[3] The princes of the various states, whose official chief was the President of the Four Mountains, all 'shepherds of men.'

[4] Thâi-ȝung is mount Thâi, in Shan-tung. See note on the President of the Four Mountains, p. 35.

40 symbols of jade, the three kinds of silk, the two living (animals) and the one dead one. As to the five instruments of rank, when all was over, he returned them. In the fifth month he made a similar tour southwards, as far as the mountain of the south[1], where he observed the same ceremonies as at Thâi. In the eighth month he made a tour westwards, as far as the mountain of the west[1], where he did as before. In the eleventh month he made a tour northwards, as far as the mountain of the north[1], where he observed the same ceremonies as in the west. He (then) returned (to the capital), went to (the temple of) the Cultivated Ancestor[2], and sacrificed a single bull.*

In five years there was one tour of inspection, and there were four appearances of the princes at court. They gave a report (of their government) in words, which was clearly tested by their works. They received chariots and robes according to their merits.

He instituted the division (of the land) into twelve provinces[3], raising altars upon twelve hills in them.* He (also) deepened the rivers.

He exhibited (to the people) the statutory punishments, enacting banishment as a mitigation of the five (great) inflictions[4]; with the whip to be employed in the magistrates' courts, the stick to be

---

[1] See note on the President of the Four Mountains, p. 35.

[2] Probably the same as the Accomplished Ancestor on p. 38.

[3] As Yü, according to Part III, i, divided the land into nine provinces, this division of it into twelve must have been subsequent to the completion of Yü's work. See on the Tribute of Yü.

[4] Those five great inflictions were—branding on the forehead; cutting off the nose; cutting off the feet; castration; and death, inflicted in various ways.

employed ·in schools[1], and money to be received
for redeemable offences.   Inadvertent offences and
those which could be ascribed to misfortune were
to be pardoned, but those who transgressed presumptuously and repeatedly were to be punished
with death. ' Let me be reverent! Let me be
reverent!' (he said to himself.)   ' Let compassion
rule in punishment!'

He banished the Minister of Works to Yû island;
confined Hwan-tâu on mount *Kh*ung; drove (the
chief of) San-miâo (and his people) into San-wei,
and kept them there; and held Khwăn a prisoner
·till death on mount Yü.   These four criminals being
thus dealt with, all under heaven acknowledged the
justice (of Shun's administration)[2].

4. After twenty-eight years the Tî deceased,
when the people mourned for him as for a parent
for three years.   Within the four seas all the eight
kinds of instruments of music were stopped and
hushed.   On the first day of the first month (of the)
next year, Shun went to (the temple of) the Accomplished Ancestor.*

41

---

[1] This punishment was for officers in training; not for boys at
school.

[2] The Minister of Works, Hwan-tâu, and Khwăn are mentioned
in the former Canon.   Yû island, or Yû *K*âu, was in the extreme
north of the present district of Mî-yun, department Shun-thien,
*K*ih-lî.

Mount *Kh*ung was in the district of Yung-ting, Lî *K*âu, Hû-nan.
San-miâo was the name of a territory, embracing the present
departments of Wû-*kh*ang in Hû-pei, Yo-*k*âu in Hû-nan, and
*K*iû-*k*iang in *K*iang-hsî.   San-wei was a tract of country round
a mountain of the same name in the present department of An-
hsî, Kan-sû.   Mount Yü was in the present district of Than-*kh*ǎng,
Shan-tung.

42

5. He deliberated with (the President of) the Four Mountains how to throw open the doors (of communication between himself and the) four (quarters of the land), and how he could see with the eyes, and hear with the ears of all.

He consulted with the twelve Pastors[1], and said to them, ' The food !—it depends on observing the seasons. Be kind to the distant, and cultivate the ability of the near. Give honour to the virtuous, and your confidence to the good, while you discountenance the artful ;—so shall the barbarous tribes lead on one another to make their submission.'

Shun said, ' Ho ! (President of) the Four Mountains, is there any one who can with vigorous service attend to all the affairs of the Tî, whom I may appoint to be General Regulator, to assist me in (all) affairs, managing each department according to its nature ? ' All (in the court) replied, ' There is Po-yü[2], the Minister of Works.' The Tî said, ' Yes. Ho ! Yü, you have regulated the water and the land. In this (new office) exert yourself.' Yü did obeisance with his head to the ground, and wished to decline in favour of the Minister of Agriculture, or Hsieh, or Kâo-yâo. The Tî said, ' Yes, but do you go (and undertake the duties).'

The Tî said, '*Khî*[3], the black-haired people are (still) suffering from famine. Do you, O prince, as

---

[1] These were the twelve princes holding the chief sway and superintendence in his twelve provinces.

[2] Po-yü is the great Yü, the founder of the Hsiâ dynasty. Po denotes, probably, his order as the eldest among his brothers.

[3] *Khî* was the name of the Minister of Agriculture, better known in the Shih and other books as Hâu-*kî*, the progenitor of the kings of *K*âu. See the legend about him in the Shih, Part III, ii, Ode 1.

Minister of Agriculture, (continue to) sow (for them) the various kinds of grain.'

The Tî said, ' Hsieh[1], the people are (still) wanting in affection for one another, and do not docilely observe the five orders of relationship. It is yours, as the Minister of Instruction, reverently to set forth the lessons of duty belonging to those five orders. Do so with gentleness.'

The Tî said, ' Kâo-yâo[2], the barbarous tribes trouble our great land. There are (also) robbers, murderers, insurgents, and traitors. It is yours, as the Minister of Crime, to use the five punishments to deal with their offences. For the infliction of these there are the three appointed places. There are the five cases in which banishment in the appropriate places is to be resorted ·to, to which places, though five, three localities are assigned. Perform your duties with intelligence, and you will secure a sincere (submission).'

The Tî said, 'Who can superintend my works, as they severally require?' All (in the court) replied, 'Is there not *Z*ui[3]?' The Tî said, 'Yes. Ho! *Z*ui, you must be Minister of Works.' ·*Z*ui did obeisance with his head to the ground, and wished. to decline in favour of Shû, *Kh*iang, or Po-yü. The

---

[1] Hsieh was honoured by the kings of the Shang dynasty as their progenitor. See the Shih, Part IV, iii, Odes 3 and 4. ·

[2] See the preliminary note to Book iii.

[3] *Z*ui was not claimed by any great family as its progenitor, but he was handed down by tradition as a great artificer. See a reference to him in Part V, xxii, 2. Shû and *Kh*iang must have been named from their skill in making halberds and axes. The Yü (quite different from the name of the great Yü) in Po-yü gives us no indication of the skill of that individual.

44   Tî said, 'Yes, but do you go (and undertake the duties). Effect a harmony (in all the departments).'

The Tî said, 'Who can superintend, as the nature of the charge requires, the grass and trees, with the birds and beasts on my hills and in my marshes?' All (in the court) replied, 'Is there not Yî[1]?' The Tî said, 'Yes. Ho! Yî, do you be my Forester.' Yî did obeisance with his head to the ground, and wished to decline in favour of *K*û, Hû, Hsiung, or Pî[1]. The Tî said, 'Yes, but do you go (and undertake the duties). You must manage them harmoniously.'

The Tî said, 'Ho! (President of the) Four Mountains, is there any one able to direct my three (religious) ceremonies[2]?' All (in the court) answered, 'Is there not Po-î[3]?' The Tî said, 'Yes. Ho! Po, you must be the Arranger in the Ancestral Temple. Morning and night be reverent. Be upright, be pure.' Po did obeisance with his head to the ground, and wished to decline in favour of Khwei or Lung. The Tî said, 'Yes, but do you go (and undertake the duties). Be reverential!'*

The Tî said, 'Khwei[4], I appoint you to be Director of Music, and to teach our sons, so that the straightforward shall yet be mild; the gentle, dignified; the strong, not tyrannical; and the impetuous,

---

[1] For Yî, see the preliminary note to Book iv. He wishes here to decline his appointment in favour of *K*û ('The Cedar'), Hû ('The Tiger'), Hsiung ('The Bear'), or Pî ('The Grisly Bear').

[2] The three ceremonies were the observances in the worship of the Spirits of Heaven, the Spirits of Earth, and the Spirits of Men.

[3] Po-î was the progenitor of the great family of *K*iang, members of which ruled in *K*hî and other states.

[4] Of Khwei we know nothing more than what is here told us. The character denotes a monstrous animal, 'a dragon with one leg.'

not arrogant. Poetry is the expression of earnest   45
thought; singing is the prolonged utterance of that
expression; the notes accompany that utterance, and
they are harmonized themselves by the standard-
tubes. (In this way) the eight different kinds of
musical instruments can be adjusted so that one
shall not take from or interfere with another; and
spirits and men are brought into harmony.' Khwei
said,'I smite the (sounding-) stone, I gently strike it, and
the various animals lead on one another to dance.'

The Tî said, ' Lung ¹, I abominate slanderous
speakers and destroyers of the (right) ways, who
agitate and alarm my people. I appoint you to
be the Minister of Communication. Early and late
give forth my orders and report to me, seeing that
everything is true.'

The Tî said, ' Ho! you, twenty and two men, be
reverent; so shall you be helpful to the business
(entrusted to me by) Heaven.' *

Every three years there was an examination of
merits, and after three examinations the undeserving
were degraded, and the deserving advanced. (By
this arrangement) the duties of all the departments
were fully discharged; the (people of) San-miâo
(also) were discriminated and separated.

6. In the thirtieth year of his age, Shun was
called to employment. Thirty years he was on the
throne (with Yâo). Fifty years afterwards he went
on high and died ².*

---

¹ We are in ignorance of Lung, as we are of Khwei. The
character denotes ' the dragon.'

² The Chinese text is here difficult to construe. *Kû Hsî* says
that the term ' went on high' is appropriate to the death of the Son
of Heaven; and that the meaning is that Shun went to heaven.

BOOK II. THE COUNSELS OF THE GREAT YÜ.

OF the six classes of documents in the Shû, 'Counsels' are the second, containing the wise remarks and suggestions of high officers on the subject of government.

This Book may be divided into three chapters :—the first, containing counsels of Yü and Yî on principles and methods of government; the second, occupied with Shun's resignation of the administration to Yü, and containing also many sage observations and maxims; and the third, describing Yü's operations against the people of Miâo, and counsels addressed to him by Yî. The style differs from that of the Canons; being more sententious, and falling occasionally into rhyme.

1. Examining into antiquity, (we find that) the Great Yü[1] was styled Wăn-ming[2]. Having arranged and divided (the land), all to the four seas, in reverent response to the Tî, he said, 'If the sovereign can realize the difficulty of his sovereignship, and the minister the difficulty of his ministry, the government will be well ordered, and the black-haired people will sedulously seek to be virtuous.'

The Tî said, 'Yes; let this really be the case, and good words will nowhere lie hidden; no men of virtue and talents will be left neglected, away from court, and the myriad states will all enjoy repose. (But) to obtain the views of all; to give up one's opinion and follow that of others; to keep from oppressing the helpless, and not to neglect the

---

[1] The name Yü, taken as an epithet, would mean 'the Unconstrained.' As an epithet after death, it has the meaning of 'Receiving the Resignation and Perfecting the Merit;' but this is evidently based on the commonly received history of Yü.

[2] Wăn-ming may be translated, 'the Accomplished and the Issuer of Commands.'

straitened and poor;—it was only the (former) Tî   47
who could attain to this.'

Yî said, 'Oh! your virtue, O Tî, is vast and in-
cessant. It is sagely, spirit-like, awe-inspiring, and
adorned with all accomplishments. Great Heaven
regarded you with its favour, and bestowed on you its
appointment. Suddenly you possessed all within the
four seas, and became ruler of all under heaven.'*

.Yü said, 'Accordance with the right leads to good
fortune; following what is opposed to it, to bad ;—
the shadow and the echo.' Yî said, 'Alas! be
cautious! Admonish yourself to caution, when there
seems to be no occasion for anxiety. Do not fail to
observe the laws and ordinances. Do not find your
enjoyment in idleness. Do not go to excess in
pleasure. In your employment of men of worth, let
none come between you and them. Put away evil
without hesitation. Do not carry out plans, of (the
wisdom of) which you have doubts. Study that all
your purposes may be with the light of reason. Do
not go against what is right, to get the praise of the
people. Do not oppose the people's (wishes), to follow
your own desires. (Attend to these things) without
idleness or omission, and the barbarous tribes all
around will come and acknowledge your sovereignty.'

Yü said, 'Oh! think (of these things), O Tî. The
virtue (of the ruler) is seen in (his) good government, and that government in the nourishing of
the people. There are water, fire, metal, wood,
the earth, and grain,—these must be duly regulated; there are the rectification of (the people's)
virtue, (the tools and other things) that supply the
conveniences of life, and the securing abundant
means of sustentation,—these must be harmoniously

48 attended to. When the nine services (thus indicated) have been orderly accomplished, that accomplishment will be hailed by (the people's) songs. Caution them with gentle (words), correct them with the majesty (of law), stimulate them with the songs on those nine subjects,—in order that (your success) may not suffer diminution.' The Tî said, 'The earth has been reduced to order, and the (influences of) heaven produce their complete effect; those six magazines and three departments of (governmental) action are all truly regulated, and may be depended on for a myriad generations :—this is your merit.'

2. The Tî said, 'Come, you Yü. I have occupied my place for thirty and three years. I am between ninety and a hundred years old, and the laborious duties weary me. Do you, eschewing all indolence, take the leading of my people.' Yü replied, 'My virtue is not equal (to the position), and the people will not repose in me. (But there is) Kâo-yâo with vigorous activity sowing abroad his virtue, which has descended on the black-haired people, till they cherish him in their hearts. O Tî, think of him! When I think of him, (my mind) rests on him (as the man fit for this place); when I would put him out of my thoughts, (my mind still) rests on him; when I name and speak of him, (my mind) rests on him (for this); the sincere outgoing of my thoughts about him is that he is the man. O Tî, think of his merits.'

The Tî said, 'Kâo-yâo, that of these my ministers and all (my people) hardly one is found to offend against the regulations of the government is owing to your being Minister of Crime, and intelligent in the use of the five punishments, thereby

assisting (the inculcation of) the five cardinal duties, 49
with a view to the perfection of my government,
and that through punishment there may come to
be no punishments, but the people accord with (the
path of) the Mean. (Continue to) be strenuous.'
Kâo-yâo replied, 'Your virtue, O Tî, is faultless.
You condescend to your ministers with a kindly
ease ; you preside over the multitudes with a generous forbearance. Punishments do not extend to
(the criminal's) heirs, while rewards reach to (succeeding) generations. You pardon inadvertent
faults, however great, and punish purposed crimes,
however small. In cases of doubtful crimes, you
deal with them lightly; in cases of doubtful merit,
you prefer the high estimation. Rather than put an
innocent person to death, you will run the risk of
irregularity and error. This life-loving virtue has
penetrated the minds of the people, and this is why
they do not render themselves liable to be punished
by your officers.' The Tî said, 'That I am able
to follow and obtain what I desire in my government, the people responding everywhere as if moved
by the wind,—this is your excellence.'

The Tî said, 'Come Yü. The inundating waters
filled me with dread, when you accomplished truly
(all that you had represented), and completed your
service ;—thus showing your superiority to other
men. Full of toilsome earnestness in the service of
the country, and sparing in your expenditure on
your family, and this without being full of yourself
and elated,—you (again) show your superiority to
other men. You are without any prideful assumption, but no one under heaven can contest with you
the palm of ability; you make no boasting, but no

[1]   E

50   one under heaven can contest with you the palm of merit. I see how great is your virtue, how admirable your vast achievements. The determinate appointment of Heaven rests on your person; you must eventually ascend (the throne) of the great sovereign.* The mind of man is restless, prone (to err); its affinity to what is right is small. Be discriminating, be uniform (in the pursuit of what is right), that you may sincerely hold fast the Mean. Do not listen to unsubstantiated words; do not follow plans about which you have not sought counsel. Of all who are to be loved, is not the ruler the chief? Of all who are to be feared, are not the people the chief? If the multitude were without their sovereign Head, whom should they sustain aloft? If the sovereign had not the multitude, there would be none to guard the country for him. Be reverential! Carefully maintain the throne which you are to occupy, cultivating (the virtues) that are to be desired in you. If within the four seas there be distress and poverty, your Heaven-conferred revenues will come to a perpetual end. It is the mouth which sends forth what is good, and raises up war. I will not alter my words.'

    Yü said, 'Submit the meritorious ministers one by one to the trial of divination[1], and let the favouring indication be followed.' The Tî replied, '(According to the rules for) the regulation of divination, one should first make up his mind, and afterwards refer (his judgment) to the great tortoise-shell. My mind (in this matter) was determined in the first place; I consulted and deliberated with all (my

---

[1] On Divination, see Part V, iv.

51

ministers and people), and they were of one accord with me. The spirits signified their assent, and the tortoise-shell and divining stalks concurred. Divination, when fortunate, should not be repeated.'* Yü did obeisance with his head to the ground, and firmly declined (the place). The Tî said, 'You must not do so. It is you who can suitably (occupy my place).' On the first morning of the first month, (Yü) received the appointment in the temple (dedicated by Shun) to the spirits of his ancestors[1], and took the leading of all the officers, as had been done by the Tî at the commencement (of his government).*

3. The Tî said, 'Alas! O Yü, there is only the lord of Miâo[2] who refuses obedience; do you go and correct him.' Yü on this assembled all the princes, and made a speech to the host, saying, 'Ye multitudes here arrayed, listen all of you to my orders. Stupid is this lord of Miâo, ignorant, erring, and disrespectful. Despiteful and insolent to others, he thinks that all ability and virtue are with himself. A rebel to the right, he destroys (all the obligations of) virtue. Superior men are kept by him in obscurity, and mean men fill (all) the offices. The people reject him and will not protect him. Heaven

---

[1] Many contend that this was the ancestral temple of Yâo. But we learn from Confucius, in the seventeenth chapter of the Doctrine of the Mean, that Shun had established such a temple for his own ancestors, which must be that intended here.

[2] The lord of Miâo against whom Yü proceeded would not be the one whom Shun banished to San-wei, as related in the former Book, but some chieftain of the whole or a portion of the people, who had been left in their native seat. That Yâo, Shun, and Yü were all obliged to take active measures against the people of Miâo, shows the difficulty with which the Chinese sway was established over the country.

E 2

52 is sending down calamities upon him.* I therefore, along with you, my multitude of gallant men, bear the instructions (of the Tî) to punish his crimes. Do you proceed with united heart and strength, so shall our enterprize be crowned with success.'

At the end of three decades, the people of Miâo continued rebellious against the commands (issued to them), when Yî came to the help of Yü, saying, 'It is virtue that moves Heaven; there is no distance to which it does not reach. Pride brings loss, and humility receives increase;—this is the way of Heaven.* In the early time of the Tî, when he was living by mount Lî[1], he went into the fields, and daily cried with tears to compassionate Heaven, and to his parents, taking to himself all guilt, and charging himself with (their) wickedness.* (At the same time) with respectful service he appeared before Kû-sâu, looking grave and awe-struck, till Kû also became transformed by his example. Entire sincerity moves spiritual beings,—how much more will it move this lord of Miâo!'* Yü did homage to the excellent words, and said, 'Yes.' (Thereupon) he led back his army, having drawn off the troops. The Tî set about diffusing on a grand scale the virtuous influences of peace;—with shields and feathers they danced between the two staircases (in his courtyard). In seventy days, the lord of Miâo came (and made his submission).

---

[1] Mount Lî is found in a hill near Phû Kâu, department of Phing-yang, Shan-hsî. It is difficult to reconcile what Yî says here of Shun 'in his early life' and his father Kû-sâu with the account of it as happening when Shun was fifty years old; see Mencius V, Part i, ch. 5. The whole is legendary, and there were, no doubt, more forms of the legend than one.

BOOK III. THE COUNSELS OF KÂO-YÂO.　53

Kâo-yâo was Minister of Crime to Shun, and is still celebrated in China as the model for all administrators of justice. There are few or no reliable details of his history. Sze-mâ *Kh*ien says that Yü, on his accession to the throne, made Kâo-yâo his chief minister, with the view of his ultimately succeeding him, but that the design was frustrated by Kâo-yâo's death. But if there had been such a tradition in the time of Mencius, he would probably have mentioned it, when defending Yü from the charge of being inferior to Yâo and Shun, who resigned the throne to the worthiest, whereas he transmitted it to his son. Kâo-yâo's surname was Yen, but an end was made of his representatives, when the principality belonging to them was extinguished in the dynasty of *K*âu by the ambitious state of *Kh*û. There is still a family in China with the surname Kâo, claiming to be descended from this ancient worthy ; but Kâo and Yâo are to be taken together in the Shû as his name.

The 'Counsels' in the Book do not appear as addressed directly to Shun, but are found in a conversation between Yü and Kâo-yâo, the latter being the chief speaker. The whole may be divided into four chapters : — the first, enunciating the principle that in government the great thing is for the ruler to pursue the course of his virtue, which will be seen in his knowledge and choice of men for office, thereby securing the repose of the people; the second, illustrating how men may be known; the third, treating of the repose of the people; in the fourth, the speaker asserts the reasonableness of his sentiments, and humbly expresses his own desire to be helpful to the sovereign.

1. Examining into antiquity, (we find that) Kâo-yâo said, 'If (the sovereign) sincerely pursues the course of his virtue, the counsels (offered to him) will be intelligent, and the aids (of admonition that he receives) will be harmonious.' Yü said, 'Yes, but explain yourself.' Kâo-yâo said, 'Oh! let him be careful about his personal cultivation, with thoughts that are far-reaching, and thus he will

54 produce a generous kindness and nice observance
of distinctions among the nine branches of his
kindred. All the intelligent (also) will exert themselves in his service; and in this way from what
is near he will reach to what is distant.' Yü did
homage to the excellent words, and said, ' Yes.'
Kâo-yâo continued, ' Oh! it lies in knowing men,
and giving repose to the people.' Yü said, ' Alas!
to attain to both these things might well be a difficulty even to the Tî. When (the sovereign) knows
men, he is wise, and can put every one into the
office for which he is fit. When he gives repose
to the people, his kindness is felt, and the black-
haired race cherish him in their hearts. When he
can be (thus) wise and kind, what occasion will he
have for anxiety about a Hwan-tâu? what to be
removing a lord of Miâo? what to fear any one
of fair words, insinuating appearance, and great
artfulness?'

2. Kâo-yâo said, ' Oh! there are in all nine
virtues to be discovered in conduct, and when we
say that a man possesses (any) virtue, that is as
much as to say he does such and such things.'
Yü asked, ' What (are the nine virtues)?' Kâo-
yâo replied, ' Affability combined with dignity;
mildness combined with firmness; bluntness combined with respectfulness; aptness for government
combined with reverent caution; docility combined
with boldness; straightforwardness combined with
gentleness; an easy negligence combined with discrimination; boldness combined with sincerity; and
valour combined with righteousness. (When these
qualities are) displayed, and that continuously, have
we not the good (officer)? When there is a daily

display of three (of these) virtues, their possessor 55
could early and late regulate and brighten the clan
(of which he was made chief). When there is a
daily severe and reverent cultivation of six of them,
their possessor could brilliantly conduct the affairs
of the state (with which he was invested). When
(such men) are all received and advanced, the possessors of those nine virtues will be employed in
(the public) service. The men of a thousand and
men of a hundred will be in their offices; the
various ministers will emulate one another; all the
officers will accomplish their duties at the proper
times, observant of the five seasons (as the several
elements predominate in them),—and thus their
various duties will be fully accomplished. Let not
(the Son of Heaven) set to the holders of states
the example of indolence or dissoluteness. Let him
be wary and fearful, (remembering that) in one day
or two days there may occur ten thousand springs
of things. Let him not have his various officers
cumberers of their places. The work is Heaven's;
men must act for it!'*

3. 'From Heaven are the (social) relationships
with their several duties; we are charged with (the
enforcement of) those five duties;—and lo! we have
the five courses of honourable conduct[1]. From
Heaven are the (social) distinctions with their
several ceremonies; from us come the observances
of those five ceremonies;—and lo! they appear in

---

[1] The five duties are those belonging to the five relationships,
which are the constituents of society;—those between husband
and wife, father and son, ruler and subject, elder brother and
younger, friend and friend.

56 regular practice[1]. When (sovereign and ministers show) a common reverence and united respect for these, lo! the moral nature (of the people) is made harmonious. Heaven graciously distinguishes the virtuous ;—are there not the five habiliments, five decorations of them[2]? . Heaven punishes the guilty ;—are there not the five punishments, to be severally used for that purpose ? The business of government !—ought we not to be earnest in it ? ought we not to be earnest in it ? *

'Heaven hears and sees as our people hear and see ; Heaven brightly approves and displays its terrors as our people brightly approve and would awe ;—such connexion is there between the upper and lower (worlds). How reverent ought the masters of territories to be !' *

4. Kâo-yâo said, ' My words are in accordance with reason, and may be put in practice.' Yü said, ' Yes, your words may be put in practice, and crowned with success.' Kâo-yâo added, ' (As to that) I do not know, but I wish daily to be helpful. May (the government) be perfected !'

BOOK IV. THE YÎ AND KÎ.

Yî and *Kî*, the names of Shun's Forester and Minister of Agriculture, both of whom receive their appointments in Book i, occur near the commencement of this Book, and occasion is thence taken to give its title to the whole. But without good reason; for these worthies do not appear at all as interlocutors

---

[1] The five ceremonies are here those belonging to the distinctions of rank in connexion with the five constituent relations of society.
[2] See in next Book, ch. 1.

in it. Yü is the principal speaker; the Book belongs to the 57
class of ' Counsels.'

To Yî there is, of course, assigned an ancient and illustrious
descent; what is of more importance, is that the lords of *Kh*in,
who finally superseded the kings of *K*âu, traced their lineage to
him. *Kh*î was the name of *K*î, the character for the latter term
meaning ' Millet,' and *Kh*î was so styled from his labours in
teaching the people to sow and reap, so that *K*î became equivalent to ' Minister of Agriculture.'

The contents of the Book have been divided into three chapters.
The first gives a conversation between Shun and Yü. Yü
relates his own diligence and achievements as a model to Shun,
and gives him various admonitions, while Shun insists on what
his ministers should be, and wherein he wished them to help
him. In the second chapter, Khwei, the Minister of Music,
makes his appearance; it has no apparent connexion with the
former. In the third, Shun and Kâo-yâo sing to each other
on the mutual relation of the sovereign and his ministers.

1. The Tî said, ' Come Yü, you also must have
excellent words (to bring before me).' Yü did
obeisance, and said, ' Oh! what can I say, O Tî,
(after Kâo-yâo) ? I can (only) think of maintaining
a daily assiduity.' Kâo-yâo said, ' Alas! will you
describe it ?' Yü replied, ' The inundating waters
seemed to assail the heavens, and in their vast
extent embraced the hills and overtopped the great
mounds, so that the people were bewildered and
overwhelmed. I mounted my four conveyances [1],
and all along the hills hewed down the trees, at the
same time, along with Yî, showing the multitudes
how to get flesh to eat. I (also) opened passages for
the streams (throughout the) nine (provinces), and
conducted them to the four seas. I deepened (moreover) the channels and canals, and conducted them
to the streams, sowing (grain), at the same time,

---

[1] See the Introduction, pp. 16, 17.

58 along with *Kî*, and showing the multitudes how to procure the food of toil, (in addition to) the flesh meat. I urged them (further) to exchange what they had for what they had not, and to dispose of their accumulated stores. (In this way) all the people got grain to eat, and the myriad regions began to come under good rule.' Kâo-yâo said, 'Yes, we ought to model ourselves after your excellent words.'

Yü said, 'Oh! carefully maintain, O Tî, the throne which you occupy.' The Tî replied, 'Yes;' and Yü went on, 'Find your repose in your (proper) resting-point. Attend to the springs of things; study stability; and let your assistants be the upright :— then shall your movements be grandly responded to, (as if the people only) waited for your will. Thus you will brightly receive (the favour of) God;— will not Heaven renew its appointment of you, and give you blessing ?' *

The Tî said, 'Alas! what are ministers ?—are they not (my) associates? What are associates ?— are they not (my) ministers?' Yü replied, 'Yes;' and the Tî went on, 'My ministers constitute my legs and arms, my ears and eyes. I wish to help and support my people ;—you give effect to my wishes. I wish to spread the influence (of my government) through the four quarters ;—you act as my agents. I wish to see the emblematic figures of the ancients,—the sun, the moon, the stars, the mountain, the dragons, and the flowery fowl (= the pheasant), which are depicted (on the upper garment); the temple cups, the pondweed, the flames, the grains of rice, the hatchet, and the symbol of distinction, which are embroidered (on the lower garment),—(I wish to see all these) fully displayed in the five colours, so as to form the (ceremonial) robes ;—it is yours to see them clearly (for me). I wish to hear the six pitch-tubes, the five notes (determined by them), and the eight kinds of musical instruments (regulated again by these), examining thereby the virtues and defects of government, according as (the odes that) go forth (from the court, set to music), and come in (from the people), are ordered by those five notes ;—it is yours to hear them (for me). When I am doing wrong, it is yours to correct me ;—do not follow me to my face, and, when you have retired, have other remarks to make. Be reverent, ye associates, who are before and behind and on each side of me ! As to all the obstinately stupid and calumniating talkers, who are found not to be doing what is right, are there not—the target to exhibit (their true character)[1], the scourge to make them recollect, and the book of remembrance[2] ? Do we not wish them to live along with us ? There are also the masters (of music) to receive their compositions, (set them to music), and continually publish them (as corrected by themselves). If they become reformed they are to be received and employed; if they do not, let the terrors (of punishment) overtake them.'

59

---

[1] Archery was anciently made much of in China, and supposed to be a test of character. Unworthy men would not be found hitting frequently, and observing the various rules of the exercise. Confucius more than once spoke of archery as a discipline of virtue; see Analects, III, xvi.

[2] In the Official Book of Kâu, the heads of districts are required to keep a register of the characters of the people. Shun's Book of Remembrance would be a record on wood or cloth. The reference implies the use of writing.

60   Yü said, 'So far good! But let your light shine, O Tî, all under heaven, even to every grassy corner of the sea-shore, and throughout the myriad regions the most worthy of the people will all (wish) to be your ministers. Then, O Tî, you may advance them to office. They will set forth, and you will receive, their reports; you will make proof of them according to their merits; you will confer chariots and robes according to their services. Who will then dare not to cultivate a humble virtue? who will dare not to respond to you with reverence? If you, O Tî, do not act thus, all (your ministers) together will daily proceed to a meritless character.'

'Be not haughty like *Kû* of Tan[1], who found his pleasure only in indolence and dissipation, and pursued a proud oppressive course. Day and night without ceasing he was thus. He would make boats go where there was no water. He introduced licentious associates into his family. The consequence was that he brought the prosperity of his house to an end. I took warning from his course. When I married in Thû-shan[2], (I remained with my wife only the days) hsin, *zăn*, kwei, and *kiâ*. When (my son) *Khî* was wailing and weeping, I did not regard him, but kept planning with all my might my labour on the land. (Then) I assisted in completing the five Tenures[3], extending over 5000 lî[4]; (in appointing) in the provinces twelve Tutors, and in establishing

---

[1] This was the son of Yâo. He must have been made lord of some principality, called Tan.

[2] Yü married the daughter of the lord of Thû-shan, a principality in the present department of Făng-yung, An-hui.

[3] See in the Tribute of Yü, Part II.

[4] The lî is what is called the Chinese mile, generally reckoned to be 360 paces.

in the regions beyond, reaching to the four seas, 61
five Presidents. These all pursue the right path,
and are meritorious ; but there are still (the people
of) Miâo, who obstinately refuse to render their
service. Think of this, O Tî.' The Tî said,
' That my virtue is followed is the result of your
meritorious services so orderly displayed. And now
Kâo-yâo, entering respectfully into your arrangements, is on every hand displaying the (various) punishments, as represented, with entire intelligence.'

2. Khwei said, 'When the sounding-stone is tapped
or struck with force, and the lutes are strongly swept
or gently touched, to accompany the singing, the
progenitors (of the Tî) come (to the service),* the
guest of Yü[1] is in his place, and all the princes
show their virtue in giving place to one another.
(In the court) below (the hall) there are the flutes
and hand-drums, which join in at the sound of the
rattle, and cease at that of the stopper, when the
organ and bells take their place. (This makes)
birds and beasts fall moving. When the nine parts
of the service, as arranged by the Tî, have all been
performed, the male and female phœnix come with
their measured gambolings (into the court).'

Khwei said, 'Oh! when I smite the (sounding-)
stone, or gently strike it, the various animals lead
on one another to dance[2], and all the chiefs of the
official departments become truly harmonious.'

---

[1] *Kû* of Tan.

[2] These last words of Khwei have already appeared in Book i,
ch. 5. They are more in place here, though this second chapter
has no apparent connexion with what precedes. ' The stone '
is the sonorous stone formed, often in the shape of a carpenter's
square, into a musical instrument, still seen everywhere in China.

3. The Tî on this made a song, saying, 'We must deal cautiously with the favouring appointment of Heaven, at every moment and in the smallest particular.'* He then sang,

> ' When the members (work) joyfully,
> The head rises (grandly);
> And the duties of all the offices are fully discharged!'

Kâo-yâo did obeisance with his head to his hands and then to the ground, and with a loud and rapid voice said, ' Think (O Tî). It is yours to lead on and originate things. Pay careful attention to your laws (in doing so). Be reverential! and often examine what has been accomplished (by your officers). Be reverential!' With this he continued the song,

> ' When the head is intelligent,
> The members are good;
> And all affairs will be happily performed!'

Again he continued the song,

> ' When the head is vexatious,
> The members are idle;
> And all affairs will go to ruin!'

The Tî said, ' Yes, go and be reverently (attentive to your duties).'

PART III. THE BOOKS OF HSIÂ.

Book I. The Tribute of Yü.

Hsiâ is the dynastic designation under which Yü and his descendants held the throne for 439 years (B. C. 2205–1767). On the conclusion of his labours, according to what was the universally accepted tradition in the Kâu period, Yü was appointed by Yâo to be earl of Hsiâ, a small principality in Ho-nan, identified with the present Yü-kâu, department Khâi-fäng, which thus still retains the name of Yü.

It has been repeatedly said in the Introduction that the Tribute of Yü describes what was done before the death of Yâo. The reason why it got its place as the first of the Books of Hsiâ was, no doubt, because the merit set forth in it was the ground of Yü's advancement to the throne.

Altogether the Books of Hsiâ are properly no more than three;— a fact which shows that in so early a period the duty of the recorder was little exercised, or that the destruction of its monuments in the course of time was nearly complete. We may assume that it was in consequence of both of these things that, when the collection of the Shû was made, only three documents of Hsiâ were found, to go into it.

The word 'Tribute' in the name of this first Book is not to be understood only in the sense of a contribution paid by one nation to another in acknowledgment of subjection, but also as the contribution of revenue paid by subjects to their proper ruler. The term, moreover, gives a very inadequate idea of the contents, which describe generally the labours of Yü in remedying the disasters occasioned by the inundation with which he had to cope, and how he then defined the boundaries of the different provinces, made other important territorial divisions, and determined the quality of the soil in each province, and the proportion of revenue it should pay, with other particulars. The Book, if we could fully credit it, would be a sort of domesday book of China in the twenty-third century

64   B.C., in the compass of a few pages. In the classification of
the Books of the Shû, according to their subject-matter, this is
rightly considered as a Canon. The first section of it is divided
into one short introductory chapter, and nine others, each containing the account of one province.

Section 1.

1. Yü divided the land. Following the course of
the hills, he cut down the trees. He determined
the highest hills and largest rivers (in the several
regions).

2. With respect to *K*î *K*âu[1], he did his work
at Hû-khâu, and took effective measures at (the
mountains) Liang and *K*hî. Having repaired the
works on Thâi-yüan, he proceeded on to the south
of (mount) Yo. He was successful with his labours
on Tan-hwâi, and went on to the cross-flowing stream
of *K*ang.

The soil of this province was whitish and mellow.
Its contribution of revenue was the highest of the
highest class, with some proportion of the second.
Its fields were the average of the middle class.

---

[1] *K*î *K*âu embraced the present provinces of Shan-hsî, *K*ih-lî,
the three most northern departments of Ho-nan, and the western
portion of Liâo-tung. It had the Ho—what we call the Yellow
river—on three sides of it. On the west was all that part of the
Ho which forms the dividing line between Shen-hsî and Shan-hsî.
At the south-western corner of Shan-hsî, the Ho turns to the
east: and in Yü's time it flowed eastwards to about the place
where *K*ih-lî, Shan-tung, and Ho-nan all touch, forming the
southern boundary of *K*î *K*âu. Thence it ran north and east,
till its waters entered the present gulph of *K*ih-lî, forming, so
far, the eastern boundary of the province. The northern boundary
must be left undefined.

It would be foreign to the object of the present publication of
the Shû, and take too much space, to give notes on the details
of Yü's operations in *K*î *K*âu and the other provinces.

The (waters of the) Hăng and Wei were brought 65
to their proper channels, and Tâ-lü was made capable
of cultivation.

The wild people of the islands (brought) dresses
of skins (i. e. fur dresses); keeping close on the right
to the rocks of *K*ieh, they entered the Ho.

3. Between the *K*î and the Ho was Yen *K*âu[1].

The nine branches of the Ho were made to keep
their proper channels. Lêi-hsiâ was made a marsh,
in which (the waters of) the Yung and the 3ü were
united. The mulberry grounds were made fit for
silkworms, and then (the people) came down from
the heights, and occupied the grounds (below).

The soil of this province was blackish and rich ;
the grass in it was luxuriant, and the trees grew
high. Its fields were the lowest of the middle class.
Its contribution of revenue was fixed at what would
just be deemed the correct amount ; but it was not
required from it, as from the other provinces, till
after it had been cultivated for thirteen years. Its
articles of tribute were varnish and silk, and, in
baskets, woven ornamental fabrics.

They floated along the *K*î and Thâ, and so
reached the Ho.

4. The sea and (mount) Tâi were the boundaries
of *Kh*ing *K*âu[2].

---

[1] Yen *K*âu was a small province, having the Ho on the north,
the *K*î on the south, the gulph of *K*ih-lî on the east, and Yü
*K*âu, Yü's seventh province, on the west. It embraced the
department of Tâ-ming, with portions of those of Ho-*k*ien and
Thien-*k*ing, in *K*ih-lî, and the department of Tung-*kh*ang, with
portions of those of *K*î-nan and Yen-*k*âu, in Shan-tung.

[2] *Kh*ing *K*âu, having mount Tâi and Hsü *K*âu (the next
province) on the west and south, Yen *K*âu and the sea on the
north-west and the north, and the sea on the east and south,

[1]   F

66

(The territory of) Yü-î was defined; and the Wei-
and 3ze were made to keep their (old) channels.

Its soil was whitish and rich. Along the shore
of the sea were wide tracts of salt land. Its fields
were the lowest of the first class, and its contribution of revenue the highest of the second. Its
articles of tribute were salt, fine cloth of dolichos
fibre, productions of the sea of various kinds; with
silk, hemp, lead, pine trees, and strange stones, from
the valleys of Tâi. The wild people of Lâi were
taught tillage and pasturage, and brought in their
baskets the silk from the mountain mulberry tree.

They floated along the Wăn, and so reached
the *K*î.

5. The sea, mount Tâi, and the Hwâi were (the
boundaries of) Hsü *K*âu[1].

The Hwâi and the Î (rivers) were regulated. The
(hills) Măng and Yü were made fit for cultivation.
(The waters of) Tâ-yeh were confined (so as to form

---

would be still smaller than Yen *K*âu, and contain the three
departments of *K*hing-*k*âu, Lâi-*k*âu, and Têng-*k*âu, with the
western portion of that of *K*î-nan, in Shan-tung. From the text
we should never suppose that it passed across the sea which
washes the north and east of Shan-tung, and extended indefinitely
into Liâo-tung and Corla. This, however, is the view of many
Chinese geographers.

[1] The western boundary of Hsü *K*âu, which is not given in
the text, was Yü *K*âu, and part of *K*hing *K*âu. It embraced
the present department of Hsü-*k*âu, the six districts—Thâo-yüan,
*K*hing-ho, An-tung, Hsü-*k*hien, Sui-ning, and Kan-yü, department
of Hwâi-an, with Phei *K*âu and Hâi *K*âu,—all in *K*iang-sû; the
whole of Yen-*k*âu department, Tung-phing *K*âu and the south
of Phing-yin district in the department of Thâi-an, the department
of Î-*k*âu, and portions of those of *K*î-nan and *K*hing-*k*âu,—all
in Shan-tung; with the four districts Hwâi-yüan, Wû-ho, Hung,
and Ling-pî, department of Făng-yang, with Sze *K*âu and Hsü
*K*âu,—all in An-hui.

a marsh); and (the tract of) Tung-yüan was success-fully brought under management. 67

The soil of this province was red, clayey, and rich. Its grass and trees grew more and more bushy. Its fields were the second of the highest class; its con-tribution of revenue was the average of the second. Its articles of tribute were—earth of five different colours, variegated pheasants from the valleys of mount Yü, the solitary dryandra from the south of mount Yî, and the sounding-stones that (seemed to) float on the (banks of the) Sze. The wild tribes about the Hwâi brought oyster-pearls and fish, and their baskets full of deep azure and other silken fabrics, chequered and pure white.

They floated along the Hwâi and the Sze, and so reached the· Ho.

6. The Hwâi and the sea formed (the boundaries of) Yang *K*âu[1].

The (lake of) Phăng-lî was confined to its proper limits, and the sun-birds (= the wild geese) had places

---

[1] The Hwâi was the boundary of Yang *K*âu on the north, and we naturally suppose that the other boundary mentioned, the sea, should be referred to the south of the province. If it were really so, Yang *K*âu must have extended along the coast as far as Cochin-China, and not a few Chinese scholars argue that it did so. But that no southern boundary of the province is mentioned may rather be taken as proving that when this Book was compiled, the country south of the *K*iang—the present Yang-ʒze—was unknown.

Along the greater part of its course, the province was con-terminous on the west with *K*ing *K*âu, and in the north-west with Yü *K*âu. We may safely assign to it the greater portion of An-hui, and a part of the department of Hwang-*k*âu, in Hû-pei. All this would be the northern portion of the province. How far it extended southwards into *K*ê-*k*iang and *K*iang-hsî, it is impos-sible to say.

68 to settle on.   The three *K*iang were led to enter
the sea, and it became possible to still the marsh of
*K*ǎn.   The bamboos, small and large, then spread
about; the grass grew thin and long, and the trees
rose high ; the soil was miry.

The fields of this province were the lowest of the
lowest class ; its contribution of revenue was the
highest of the lowest class, with a proportion of the
class above.   Its articles of tribute were gold, silver,
and copper; yâo and khwǎn stones ; bamboos, small
and large; (elephants') teeth, hides, feathers, hair,
and timber.   The wild people of the islands brought
garments of grass, with silks woven in shell-patterns
in their baskets.   Their bundles contained small
oranges and pummeloes,—rendered when specially
required.

They followed the course of the *K*iang and the
sea, and so reached the Hwâi and the Sze.

7. (Mount) *K*ing and the south of (mount) Hǎng
formed (the boundaries of) *K*ing *K*âu [1].

The *K*iang and the Han pursued their (common)
course to the sea, as if they were hastening to court.
The nine *K*iang were brought into complete order.
The Tho and *Kh*ien (streams) were conducted by

---

[1] Mount *K*ing, which bounded *K*ing *K*âu on the north, is
in the department of Hsiang-yang, Hû-pei, and is called the
southern *K*ing, to distinguish it from another mountain of the
same name farther north in Yung *K*âu.   Mount Hǎng, its southern
boundary, is 'the southern mountain' of the Canon of Shun
in Hǎng-*k*âu department, Hû-nan.   Yang *K*âu was on the east,
and the country on the west was almost unknown.   *K*ing *K*âu
contained the greater portion of the present provinces of Hû-pei
and Hû-nan, and parts also of Kwei-*k*âu and Sze-*kh*üaṇ.   Some
geographers also extend it on the south into Kwang-tung and
Kwang-hsî, which is very unlikely.

their proper channels. The land in (the marsh of)   69
Yün (became visible), and (the marsh of) Măng was
made capable of cultivation.

The soil of this province was miry. Its fields
were the average of the middle class ; and its contribution of revenue was the lowest of the highest
class. Its articles of tribute were feathers, hair,
(elephants') teeth, and hides ; gold, silver, and
copper ; *kh*un trees, wood for bows, cedars, and
cypresses ; grindstones, whetstones, flint stones to
make arrow-heads, and cinnabar ; and the *kh*ün
and lû bamboos, with the hû tree, (all good for
making arrows)—of which the Three Regions were
able to contribute the best specimens. The three-
ribbed rush was sent in bundles, put into cases.
The baskets were filled with silken fabrics, azure
and deep purple, and with strings of pearls that
were not quite round. From the (country of the)
nine *K*iang, the great tortoise was presented when
specially required (and found).

They floated down the *K*iang, the Tho, the *Kh*ien,
and the Han, and crossed (the country) to the Lo,
whence they reached the most southern part of
the Ho.

8. The *K*ing (mountain) and the Ho were (the
boundaries of) Yü *K*âu [1].

The Î, the Lo, the *Kh*an, and the *K*ien were
conducted to the Ho. The (marsh of) Yung-po was

---

[1] Yü *K*âu was the central one of Yü's nine divisions of the
country, and was conterminous, for a greater or less distance, with
all of them, excepting *Kh*ing *K*âu, which lay off in the east by
itself. It embraced most of the present Ho-nan, stretching also
into the east and south, so as to comprehend parts of Shan-tung
and Hû-pei.

70 confined within its proper limits. The (waters of that of) Ko were led to (the marsh of) Măng-*k*û.

The soil of this province was mellow ; in the lower parts it was (in some places) rich, and (in others) dark and thin. Its fields were the highest of the middle class; and its contribution of revenue was the average of the highest class, with a proportion of the very highest. Its articles of tribute were varnish, hemp, fine cloth of dolichos fibre, and the bœhmerea. The baskets were full of chequered silks, and of fine floss silk. Stones for polishing sounding-stones were rendered when required.

They floated along the Lo, and so reached the Ho.

9. The south of (mount) Hwâ and the Black-water were (the boundaries of) Liang *K*âu [1].

The (hills) Min and Po were made capable of cultivation. The Tho and *Kh*ien streams were conducted by their proper channels. Sacrifices were offered to (the hills) ȝhâi and Mâng on the regula-tion (of the country about them).* (The country of) the wild tribes about the Ho was successfully operated on.

---

[1] Liang *K*âu was an extensive province, and it is a remarkable fact that neither the dominions of the Shang nor the *K*âu dynasty, which followed Hsiâ, included it. Portions of it were embraced in the Yü and Yung provinces of *K*âu, but the greater part was considered as wild, savage territory, beyond the limits of the Middle Kingdom. It is difficult to believe that the great Yü operated upon it, as this chapter would seem to indicate. The Hwâ at its north-eastern corner is the western mountain of Shun. The Black-water, or 'the *K*iang of the Golden Sands,' is identified with the present Lû. The province extended over most of the present Sze-*kh*üan, with parts of Shen-hsî and Kan-sû. I can hardly believe, as many do, that it extended far into Yün-nan and Kwei-*k*âu.

The soil of this province was greenish and light. 71
Its fields were the highest of the lowest class; and
its contribution of revenue was the average of the
lowest class, with proportions of the rates immediately above and below. Its articles of tribute were
—the best gold, iron, silver, steel, flint stones to
make arrow-heads, and sounding-stones; with the
skins of bears, foxes, and jackals, and (nets) woven
of their hair.

From (the hill of) Hsî-*kh*ing they came by the
course of the Hwan; floated along the *Kh*ien, and
then crossed (the country) to the Mien; passed to
the Wei, and (finally) ferried across the Ho.

10. The Black-water and western Ho were (the
boundaries of) Yung *K*âu [1].

The Weak-water was conducted westwards. The
*K*ing was led to mingle its waters with those of the
Wei. The *Kh*î and the *Kh*ü were next led in a
similar way (to the Wei), and the waters of the Fêng
found the same receptacle.

(The mountains) *K*ing and *Kh*î were sacrificed to.*
(Those of) *K*ung-nan and *Kh*un-wû (were also regulated), and (all the way) on to Niâo-shû. Successful
measures could now be taken with the plains and
swamps, even to (the marsh of) *K*û-yeh. (The
country of) San-wei was made habitable, and the
(affairs of the) people of San-miâo were greatly
arranged.

---

[1] The Black-water, which was the western boundary of Yung *K*âu,
was a different river from that which, with the same name, ran along
the south of Liang *K*âu. Yung *K*âu was probably the largest of
Yü's provinces, embracing nearly all the present provinces of
Shen-hsî and Kan-sû, and extending indefinitely northwards to the
Desert.

72   The soil of the province was yellow and mellow.
Its fields were the highest of the highest class, and
its contribution of revenue the lowest of the second.
Its articles of tribute were the *kh*iû jade and the
lin, and (the stones called) lang-kan.

Past *Kî*-shih they floated on to Lung-măn on the
western Ho. They then met on the north of the
Wei (with the tribute-bearers from other quarters).

Hair-cloth and skins (were brought from) Khwăn-
lun, Hsî-*k*ih, and *Kh*ü-sâu ;—the wild tribes of the
west (all) coming to (submit to Yü's) arrangements.

Section 2.

The division of the Book into two sections is a convenient arrangement, but modern, and not always followed. The former section
gives a view of Yü's labours in each particular province. This
gives a general view of the mountain ranges of the country, and
of the principal streams; going on to other labours, subsequently, as was seen in the Introduction, ascribed to Yü,—his
conferring lands and surnames, and dividing the whole territory
into five domains. The contents are divided into five chapters:
—the first, describing the mountains; the second, describing
the rivers; the third, containing a summary of all the labours of
Yü thus far mentioned; the fourth, relating his other labours;
and the fifth, celebrating Yü's fame, and the completion of his
work.

1. (Yü) surveyed and described (the hills), begin-
ning with *Kh*ien and *Kh*î and proceeding to mount
*K*ing; then, crossing the Ho, Hû-khâu, and Lêi-
shâu, going on to Thâi-yo. (After these came)
Tî-*k*û and Hsî-*kh*ăng, from which he went on to
Wang-wû; (then there were) Thâi-hang and mount
Hăng, from which he proceeded to the rocks of
*K*ieh, where he reached the sea.

(South of the Ho, he surveyed) Hsî-*kh*ing, *K*û-yü,

and Niâo-shû, going on to Thâi-hwâ; (then) Hsiung-*r*,   73
Wâi-fang, and Thung-pâi, from which he proceeded to
Pei-wei.

He surveyed and described Po-*kh*ung, going on to
(the other) mount *K*ing; and Nêi-fang, from which
he went on to Tâ-pieh.

(He did the same with) the south of mount Min,
and went on to mount Hăng. Then crossing the nine
*K*iang, he proceeded to the plain of Fû-*kh*ien.

2. He traced the Weak-water as far as the Ho-lî
(mountains), from which its superfluous waters went
away among the moving sands.

He traced the Black-water as far as San-wei, from
which it (went away to) enter the southern sea.

He traced the Ho from *K*î-shih as far as Lung-
măn; and thence, southwards, to the north of (mount)
Hwâ; eastward then to Tî-*kh*û; eastward (again)
to the ford of Măng; eastward (still) to the junction
of the Lo; and then on to Tâ-pei. (From this the
course was) northwards, past the *K*iang-water, on to
Tâ-lü; north from which the river was divided, and
became the nine Ho, which united again, and formed
the Meeting Ho, when they entered the sea.

From Po-*kh*ung he traced the Yang, which, flowing
eastwards, became the Han. Farther east it became
the water of 3hang-lang; and after passing the three
Dykes, it went on to Tâ-pieh, southwards from which
it entered the *K*iang. Eastward still, and whirling
on, it formed the marsh of Phăng-lî; and from that
its eastern flow was the northern *K*iang, as which it
entered the sea.

From mount Min he traced the *K*iang, which,
branching off to the east, formed the Tho; eastward
again, it reached the Lî, passed the nine *K*iang, and

74   went on to Tung-ling; then flowing east, and winding
to the north, it joined (the Han) with its eddying
movements. From that its eastern flow was the
middle *K*iang, as which it entered the sea.

He traced the Yen water, which, flowing eastward,
became the *K*î, and entered the Ho. (Thereafter)
it flowed out, and became the Yung (marsh). Eastward, it issued forth on the north of Thâo-*kh*iû, and
flowed farther east to (the marsh of) Ko; then it
went north-east, and united with the Wăn; thence it
went north, and (finally) entered the sea on the
east.

He traced the Hwâi from the hill of Thung-pâi.
Flowing east, it united with the Sze and the Î, and
(still) with an eastward course entered the sea.

He traced the Wei from (the hill) Niâo-shû-thung-
hsüeh. Flowing eastward, it united with the Fêng,
and eastwards again with the *K*ing. Farther east
still, it passed the *Kh*î and the *Kh*ü, and entered
the Ho.

He traced the Lo from (the hill) Hsiung-*r*.
Flowing to the north-east, it united with the *K*ien
and the *Kh*an, and eastwards still with the Î. Then
on the north-east it entered the Ho.

3. (Thus), throughout the nine provinces a
similar order was effected:—the grounds along the
waters were everywhere made habitable; the hills
were cleared of their superfluous wood and sacrificed to;* the sources of the rivers were cleared; the
marshes were well banked; and access to the capital
was secured for all within the four seas.

The six magazines (of material wealth) were fully
attended to; the different parts of the country were
subjected to an exact comparison, so that con-

tribution of revenue could be carefully adjusted
according to their resources. (The fields) were all
classified with reference to the three characters of
the soil; and the revenues for the Middle Region
were established.

4. He conferred lands and surnames. (He
said), ' Let me set the example of a reverent attention to my virtue, and none will act contrary to my
conduct.'

Five hundred lî formed the Domain of the
Sovereign. From the first hundred they brought
as revenue the whole plant of the grain; from the
second, the ears, with a portion of the stalk; from
the third, the straw, but the people had to perform
various services; from the fourth, the grain in the
husk; and from the fifth, the grain cleaned.

Five hundred lî (beyond) constituted the Domain
of the Nobles. The first hundred lî was occupied
by the cities and lands of the (sovereign's) high
ministers and great officers; the second, by the
principalities of the barons; and the (other) three
hundred, by the various other princes.

Five hundred lî (still beyond) formed the Peace-
securing Domain. In the first three hundred, they
cultivated the lessons of learning and moral duties;
in the other two, they showed the energies of war
and defence.

Five hundred lî (remoter still) formed the Domain of Restraint. The (first) three hundred were
occupied by the tribes of the Î; the (other) two
hundred, by criminals undergoing the lesser banishment.

Five hundred lî (the most remote) constituted
the Wild Domain. The (first) three hundred were

76 occupied by the tribes of the Man; the (other) two hundred, by criminals undergoing the greater banishment.

5. On the east, reaching to the sea; on the west, extending to the moving sands; to the utmost limits of the north and south :—his fame and influence filled up (all within) the four seas. Yü presented the dark-coloured symbol of his rank, and announced the completion of his work.

Book II. The Speech at Kan.

With this Book there commence the documents of the Shû that may be regarded, as I have said in the Introduction, as contemporaneous with the events which they describe. It is the first of the 'Speeches,' which form one class of the documents of the classic.

The text does not say who the king mentioned in it was, but the prevalent tradition has always been that he was *Khî*, the son and successor of Yü. Its place between the Tribute of Yü and the next Book belonging to the reign of Thâi Khang, *Khî's* son, corroborates this view.

Kan is taken as the name of a place in the southern border of the principality of Hû, with the lord of which *Khî* fought. The name of Hû itself still remains in the district so called of the department Hsî-an, in Shen-hsî.

The king, about to engage in battle with a rebellious vassal, assembles his generals and troops, and addresses them. He declares obscurely the grounds of the expedition which he had undertaken, and concludes by stimulating the soldiers to the display of courage and observance of order by promises of reward and threats of punishment.

There was a great battle at Kan. (Previous to it), the king called together the six nobles, (the leaders of his six hosts), and said, 'Ah! all ye who

are engaged in my six hosts, I have a solemn   77
announcement to make to you.

'The lord of Hû wildly wastes and despises the
five elements (that regulate the seasons), and has
idly abandoned the three acknowledged commence-
ments of the year[1].   On this account Heaven is
about to destroy him, and bring to an end his
appointment (to Hû); and I am now reverently
executing the punishment appointed by Heaven.*

'If you, (the archers) on the left[2], do not do your
work on the left, it will be a disregard of my orders.
If you, (the spearmen) on the right[2], do not do your
work on the right, it will be a disregard of my
orders.   If you, charioteers[2], do not observe the
rules for the management of your horses, it will be
a disregard of my orders.   You who obey my orders,
shall be rewarded before (the spirits of) my ancestors; and you who disobey my orders, shall be put
to death before the altar of the spirits of the land,
and I will also put to death your children.'*

---

[1] The crimes of the lord of Hû are here very obscurely stated.
With regard to the second of them, we know that Hsiâ commenced
its year with the first month of spring, Shang a month earlier,
and Ⓚâu about mid-winter.   It was understood that every dynasty
should fix a new month for the beginning of the year, and the
dynasty of Ⓚẖin actually carried its first month back into our
November.   If the lord of Hû claimed to begin the year with
another month than that which Yü had fixed, he was refusing
submission to the new dynasty.   No doubt, the object of the
expedition was to put down a dangerous rival.

[2] The chariots were the principal part of an ancient Chinese
army; it is long before we read of cavalry.   A war-chariot generally carried three.   The driver was in the centre; on his left was
an archer, and a spearman occupied the place on his right.   They
all wore mail.

Book III. The Songs of the Five Sons.

This Book ranks in that class of the documents of the Shû which
goes by the name of 'Instructions.' Though the form of it be
poetical, the subject-matter is derived from the Lessons left by
Yü for the guidance of his posterity.

Thâi Khang succeeded to his father in B.C. 2188, and his reign continues in chronology to 2160. His character is given here in the
introductory chapter. *Kh*iung, the principality of Î who took the
field against him, is identified with the sub-department of Tê-
*K*âu, department *K*î-nan, Shan-tung. There is a tradition that
Î, at an early period of his life, was lord of a state in the present
Ho-nan. This would make his movement against Thâi Khang,
'south of the Ho,' more easy for him. The name of Thâi Khang
remains in the district so called of the department *Kh*ăn-*k*âu,
Ho-nan. There, it is said, he died, having never been able to
recross the Ho.

In his song the king's first brother deplores how he had lost
the affections of the people; the second speaks of his dissolute
extravagance; the third mourns his loss of the throne; the
fourth deplores his departure from the principles of Yü, and its
disastrous consequences; and the fifth is a wail over the miserable condition of them all.

1. Thâi Khang occupied the throne like a personator of the dead[1]. By idleness and dissipation he
extinguished his virtue, till the black-haired people
all wavered in their allegiance. He, however,
pursued his pleasure and wanderings without any

---

[1] The character that here as a verb governs the character signifying 'throne' means properly 'a corpse,' and is often used for the
personator of the dead, in the sacrificial services to the dead which
formed a large part of the religious ceremonies of the ancient
Chinese. A common definition of it is 'the semblance of the
spirit,' = the image into which the spirit entered. Thâi Khang
was but a personator on the throne, no better than a sham
sovereign.

self-restraint.   He went out to hunt beyond the Lo,
and a hundred days elapsed without his returning.
(On this) Î, the prince of *Kh*iung, taking advantage
of the discontent of the people, resisted (his return)
on (the south of) the Ho.   The (king's) five brothers
had attended their mother in following him, and were
waiting for him on the north of the Lo; and (when
they heard of Î's movement), all full of dissatisfaction, they related the Cautions of the great Yü in
the form of songs.

2. The first said,
'It was the lesson of our great ancestor :—
The people should be cherished,
And not looked down upon.
The people are the root of a country;
The root firm, the country is tranquil.
When I look at all under heaven,
Of the simple men and simple women,
Any one may surpass me.
If the One man err repeatedly[1],
Should dissatisfaction be waited for till it appears?
Before it is seen, it should be guarded against.
In my dealing with the millions of the people,
I should feel as much anxiety as if I were driving
    six horses with rotten reins.
The ruler of men—
How should he be but reverent (of his duties)?'
    The second said,
'It is in the Lessons :—
When the palace is a wild of lust,
And the country is a wild for hunting;

---

[1] Any king, in the person of Yü, may be understood to be the
speaker.

80   When spirits are liked, and music is the delight;
      When there are lofty roofs and carved walls;—
      The existence of any one of these things
      Has never been but the prelude to ruin.'
          The third said,
      'There was the lord of Thâo and Thang [1],
      Who possessed this region of *K*î.
      Now we have fallen from his ways,
      And thrown into confusion his rules and laws;—
      The consequence is extinction and ruin.'
          The fourth said,
      Brightly intelligent was our ancestor,
      Sovereign of the myriad regions.
      He had canons, he had patterns,
      Which he transmitted to his posterity.
      The standard stone and the equalizing quarter
      Were in the royal treasury.
      Wildly have we dropt the clue he gave us,
      Overturning our temple, and extinguishing our
          sacrifices.' *
          The fifth said,
      'Oh! whither shall we turn?
      The thoughts in my breast make me sad.
      All the people are hostile to us;
      On whom can we rely?
      Anxieties crowd together in our hearts;
      Thick as are our faces, they are covered with blushes.
      We have not been careful of our virtue;
      And though we repent, we cannot overtake the
          past.'

---

[1] The lord of Thâo and Thang is Yâo, who was lord of the principalities of Thâo and Thang, but of which first and which last is uncertain, before his accession to the throne. *K*î is the *K*î *K*âu of the Tribute of Yü.

Book IV. The Punitive Expedition of Yin.

This Book is another of the 'Speeches' of the Shû, belonging to the reign of *K*ung Khang, a brother of Thâi Khang, the fourth of the kings of Shang (B. C. 2159–2147).

Hsî and Ho, the principal ministers of the Board of Astronomy, descended from those of the same name in the time of Yâo, had given themselves over to licentious indulgence in their private cities, and grossly neglected their duties. Especially had they been unobservant of an eclipse of the sun in autumn. The king considered them worthy of death, and commissioned the marquis of Yin to execute on them the sentence of his justice. Where Yin was is not now known.

The principal part of the Book consists of the speech made by the marquis to his troops.

1. When *K*ung Khang commenced his reign over all within the four seas, the marquis of Yin was commissioned to take charge of the (king's) six hosts. (At this time) the Hsî and Ho had neglected the duties of their office, and were abandoned to drink in their (private) cities; and the marquis of Yin received the king's charge to go and punish them.

2. He made an announcement to his hosts, saying, 'Ah! ye, all my men, there are the well-counselled instructions of the sage (founder of our dynasty), clearly verified in their power to give stability and security :—" The former kings were carefully attentive to the warnings of Heaven[1],* and their ministers observed the regular laws (of their offices). All the officers (moreover) watchfully did their duty to

---

[1] That is, here, such warnings as were supposed to be conveyed by eclipses and other unusual celestial phenomena.

[1]   G

82 assist (the government), and their sovereign became
entirely intelligent." Every year, in the first month
of spring, the herald, with his wooden-tongued bell,
goes along the roads[1], (proclaiming), "Ye officers
able to instruct, be prepared with your admonitions.
Ye workmen engaged in mechanical affairs, remonstrate on the subjects of your employments. If any
of you do not attend with respect (to this requirement), the country has regular punishments for
you."

'Now here are the Hsî and Ho. They have
allowed their virtue to be subverted, and are besotted by drink. They have violated the duties of
their office, and left their posts. They have been the
first to let the regulating of the heavenly (bodies) get
into disorder, putting far from them their proper business. On the first day of the last month of autumn,
the sun and moon did not meet harmoniously in
Fang[2]. The blind musicians beat their drums; the
inferior officers galloped, and the common people
(employed about the public offices) ran about[3]. The
Hsî and the Ho, however, as if they were (mere)
personators of the dead in their offices, heard nothing
and knew nothing;—so stupidly went they astray
(from their duties) in the matter of the heavenly
appearances, and rendered themselves liable to the
death appointed by the former kings. The statutes
of government say, "When they anticipate the time,
let them be put to death without mercy; when (their

[1] A similar practice existed in the *K*âu dynasty.
[2] See the Introduction, p. 13.
[3] Similar observances are still practised on occasion of an
eclipse of the sun. See Biot's Etudes sur l'Astronomie Indienne
et Chinoise, pp. 357–360.

reckoning) is behind the time, let them be put to death without mercy."

'Now I, with you all, am entrusted with the execution of the punishment appointed by Heaven.* Unite your strength, all of you warriors, for the royal House. Give me your help, I pray you, reverently to carry out the dread charge of the Son of Heaven.

'When the fire blazes over the ridge of Khwăn[1], gems and stones are burned together; but if a minister of Heaven exceed in doing his duty, the consequences will be fiercer than blazing fire. While I destroy, (therefore), the chief criminals, I will not punish those who have been forced to follow them; and those who have long been stained by their filthy manners will be allowed to renovate themselves.

'Oh! when sternness overcomes compassion, things are surely conducted to a successful issue. When compassion overcomes sternness, no merit can be achieved. All ye, my warriors, exert yourselves, and take warning, (and obey my orders)!'

---

[1] Khwăn is perhaps a part of the Khwăn-lun mountain in the west of the Ko-ko-nor, where the Ho has its sources. The speaker evidently thought of it as volcanic.

PART IV. THE BOOKS OF SHANG.

Book I. The Speech of Thang.

Shang was the name under which the dynasty that superseded Hsiâ (b.c. 1766) held the kingdom for fully 300 years. Yin then began to be used as well as Shang, and the dynasty was called indifferently Shang or Yin, and sometimes Yin-Shang by a combination of the two names. The ruling House traced its origin into the remote times of antiquity, through Hsieh, whose appointment by Shun to be Minister of Instruction is related in the Canon of Shun. For his services Hsieh was invested with the principality of Shang, corresponding to the present small department of the same name in Shen-hsî. From Hsieh to Thang, the founder of the dynasty, there are reckoned fourteen generations, and we find Thang, when he first becomes prominent in history, a long way from the ancestral fief, in 'the southern Po,' corresponding to the present district of Shang-*khiû*, department Kwei-teh, Ho-nan. The title of the dynasty, however, was derived from the original Shang.

There were in the Shû, when the collection was formed, thirty-one documents of Shang in forty Books, of which only eleven remain in seventeen Books, two of them containing each three parts or sections. The Speech of Thang, that is now the first Book in the Part, was originally only the sixth. Thang was the designation of the hero, whose surname, dating from Hsieh, was 3ze, and name Lî. Thang may be translated, 'the Glorious One.' His common style in history is as *Kh*ăng Thang, 'Thang the Completer,' or 'Thang the Successful.'

He had summoned his people to take the field with him against *K*ieh, the cruel and doomed sovereign of Hsiâ, and finding them backward to the enterprise, he sets forth in this Book his reasons for attacking the tyrant, argues against their reluctance, using in the end both promises and threats to induce them to obey his orders.

The king said, 'Come, ye multitudes of the
people, listen all to my words. It is not I, the
little child[1], who dare to undertake a rebellious
enterprise; but for the many crimes of the sovereign
of Hsiâ, Heaven has given the charge to destroy
him.*

· 'Now, ye multitudes, you are saying, "Our prince
does not compassionate us, but (is calling us) away
from our husbandry to attack and punish Hsiâ."
I have indeed heard (these) words of you all; (but)
the sovereign of Hsiâ is guilty, and, as I fear God,
I dare not but punish him.*

'Now you are saying, "What are the crimes of
Hsiâ to us?" The king of Hsiâ in every way
exhausts the strength of his people, and exercises
oppression in the cities of Hsiâ. His multitudes
are become entirely indifferent (to his service), and
feel no bond of union (to him). They are saying,
"When wilt thou, O sun, expire? We will all
perish with thee[2]." Such is the course of (the
sovereign) of Hsiâ, and now I must go (and punish
him).

'Assist, I pray you, me, the One man, to carry
out the punishment appointed by Heaven. I will
greatly reward you. On no account disbelieve me;—
I will not eat my words. If you do not obey the
words which I have thus spoken to you, I will put

85

---

[1] 'The little child' is a designation used humbly of themselves
by the kings of Shang and *K*âu. It is given also to them and
others by such great ministers as Î Yin and the duke of *K*âu.

[2] *K*ieh, it is said, had on one occasion, when told of the danger
he was incurring by his cruelties, pointed to the sun, and said that
as surely as the sun was in the heavens, so firm was he on the
throne.

86   your children to death with you;—you shall find no forgiveness.'

Book II. The Announcement of *K*ung-hui.

This Book is the first of the ' Announcements,' which form a large class of the documents in the Shû. They are distinguished from the Speeches, as being made in a general assembly, or published, for the information of all, whereas the Speeches were made to an army.

*K*ung-hui, of an old family, whose surname was *Z*ăn, with its seat in the territory of Hsieh, corresponding to the present district of Thang, department Yen-*k*âu, Shan-tung, was a minister of Thang. Thang has been successful against *K*ieh, and dethroned him, but is haunted by some feeling of remorse, and afraid that what he has done may be appealed to in future ages as an apology for rebellion. This gives occasion to the Announcement, in which *K*ung-hui vindicates the proceeding of the king, showing, first, that he had only obeyed the guidance of Heaven, and, then, that men consented with Heaven in the matter. He concludes with various counsels addressed to the king.

1. When Thang the Successful was keeping *K*ieh in banishment in Nan-*kh*âo[1], he had a feeling of shame on account of his conduct, and said, ' I am afraid that in future ages men will fill their mouths with me, (as an apology for their rebellious proceedings.) '

2. On this *K*ung-hui made the following announcement: ' Oh! Heaven gives birth to the people with (such) desires, that without a ruler they must fall into all disorders; and Heaven again gives birth

---

[1] Nan-*kh*âo is identified with the present district of *Kh*âo, department Lû-*k*âu, An-hui.

to the man of intelligence to regulate them.* The 87
sovereign of Hsiâ had his virtue all-obscured, and
the people were (as if they had fallen) amid mire
and (burning) charcoal. Heaven hereupon gifted
(our) king with valour and prudence, to serve as
a sign and director to the myriad regions, and
to continue the old ways of Yü. You are now
(only) following the proper course, honouring and
obeying the appointment of Heaven. The king
of Hsiâ was an offender, falsely and calumniously
alleging the sanction of supreme Heaven, to spread
abroad his commands among the people. On this
account God viewed him with disapprobation,
caused our Shang to receive his appointment, and
employed (you) to enlighten the multitudes (of the
people).' *

3. 'Contemners of the worthy and parasites of
the powerful,—many such followers he had indeed ;
(but) from the first our country was to the sovereign
of Hsiâ like weeds among the springing corn, and
blasted grains among the good. (Our people), great
and small, were in constant apprehension, fearful
though they were guilty of no crime. How much
more was this the case, when our (prince's) virtues
became a theme (eagerly) listened to! Our king
did not approach to (dissolute) music and women ;
he did not seek to accumulate property and wealth.
To great virtue he gave great offices, and to great
merit great rewards. He employed others as if
(their excellences) were his own ; he was not slow
to change his errors. Rightly indulgent and rightly
benevolent, from the display (of such virtue), confidence was reposed in him by the millions of the
people.

88　　'When the earl of Ko¹ showed his enmity to the provision-carriers, the work of punishment began with Ko. When it went on in the east, the wild tribes of the west murmured; when it went on in the south, those of the north murmured :—they said, " Why does he make us alone the last ? " To whatever people he went, they congratulated one another in their families, saying, "We have waited for our prince; our prince is come, and we revive." The people's honouring our Shang is a thing of long existence.'

4. ' Show favour to the able and right-principled (among the princes), and aid the virtuous; distinguish the loyal, and let the good have free course. Absorb the weak, and punish the wilfully blind; take their states from the disorderly, and deal summarily with those going to ruin. When you (thus) accelerate the end of what is (of itself) ready to perish, and strengthen what is itself strong to live, how will the states all flourish! When (a sovereign's) virtue is daily being renewed, he is cherished throughout the myriad regions; when his mind is full (only) of himself, he is abandoned by the nine branches of his kindred. Exert yourself, O king, to make your virtue (still more) illustrious, and set up (the standard of) the Mean before the people. Order your affairs

---

¹ Ko was a principality corresponding to the present district of Ning-ling, department of Kwei-teh, Ho-nan. It was thus near the southern Po, which belonged to Thang. Mencius tells us (III, ii, ch. 3) that Thang sent a multitude of his people to assist the farmers of Ko, about the poor produce of which their chief had lamented to him. That chief, however, instead of showing any gratitude, surprised and robbed those who were carrying provisions from Po to the labourers in the field, and committed various atrocities upon them. This aroused Thang's indignation, and he made him the first object of his punitive justice.

by righteousness; order your heart by propriety;—
so shall you transmit a grand example to posterity.
I have heard the saying, " He who finds instructors
for himself, comes to the supreme dominion; he
who says that others are not equal to himself,
comes to ruin. He who likes to put questions,
becomes enlarged; he who uses only his own
views, becomes smaller (than he was)." Oh! he
who would take care for the end must be attentive
to the beginning. There is establishment for the
observers of propriety, and overthrow for the blinded
and wantonly indifferent. To revere and honour
the path prescribed by Heaven is the way ever to
preserve the favouring appointment of Heaven.' *

BOOK III. THE ANNOUNCEMENT OF THANG.

THANG had made an end of the dynasty of Hsiâ, and returned to
Po, when he issued this Announcement, which may be considered as a solemn inauguration of the new dynasty. He
shows how he had taken possession of the throne in reverent
submission to the will of Heaven, what appreciation he had of
the duties devolving on him, and the spirit in which he would
discharge them. In the end he calls on the princes and the
people to sympathize and co-operate with him.

1. When the king returned from vanquishing
Hsiâ and came to Po, he made a grand announcement to the myriad regions.

2. The king said, 'Ah! ye multitudes of the
myriad regions, listen clearly to the announcement
of me, the One man¹. The great God has conferred

---

¹ 'The One man' has occurred before, in the Songs of the
Five Sons, as a designation of the sovereign. It continues to be
so to the present day.

90 (even) on the inferior people a moral sense, compliance with which would show their nature invariably right.* To make them tranquilly pursue the course which it would indicate is the work of the sovereign.

'The king of Hsiâ extinguished his virtue, and played the tyrant, extending his oppression over you, the people of the myriad regions. Suffering from his cruel injuries, and unable to endure the wormwood and poison, you protested with one accord your innocence to the spirits of heaven and earth.* The way of Heaven is to bless the good, and make the bad miserable. It sent down calamities on (the House of) Hsiâ, to make manifest its guilt. Therefore I, the little child, charged with the decree of Heaven and its bright terrors, did not dare to forgive (the criminal). I presumed to use a dark-coloured victim-bull, and, making clear announcement to the Spiritual Sovereign in the high heavens [1], requested leave to deal with the ruler of Hsiâ as a criminal.* Then I sought for the great Sage [2], with whom I might unite my strength, to request the favour (of Heaven) for you, my multitudes. High Heaven truly showed its favour to the inferior people, and the criminal has been degraded and subjected. What Heaven appoints is without error;—brilliantly (now), like the blossoming of plants and trees, the millions of the people show a true reviving.' *

3. 'It is given to me, the One man, to secure the

---

[1] For 'the Spiritual Sovereign in the high heavens,' we have in the Confucian Analects, XX, 1, professing to quote this passage, 'the most great and Sovereign God.'

[2] 'The great Sage' must be Î Yin, Thang's chief adviser and minister, who appears prominently in the next Book.

harmony and tranquillity of your states and clans ;
and now I know not whether I may not offend
against (the Powers) above and below.* I am fearful
and trembling, as if I were in danger of falling into
a deep abyss. Throughout all the regions that
enter on a new life under me, do not, (ye princes),
follow lawless ways ; make no approach to insolence
and dissoluteness; let every one be careful to keep
his statutes;—that so we may receive the favour
of Heaven.* The good in you I will not dare
to keep concealed; and for the evil in me I will
not dare to forgive myself. I will examine these
things in harmony with the mind of God.* When
guilt is found anywhere in you who occupy the
myriad regions, let it rest on me, the One man [1].
When guilt is found in me, the One man, it shall
not attach to you who occupy the myriad regions.

'Oh ! let us attain to be sincere in these things,
and so we shall likewise have a (happy) consummation.'

---

[1] There was a tradition in the *K*âu dynasty, given with variations by Hsün-ʒze, Sze-mâ *K*hien, and others, which may be quoted
to illustrate these noble sentiments of Thang. For seven years
after his accession to the throne, B. C. 1766–1760, there was a great
drought and famine. It was suggested at last that some human
being should be offered in sacrifice to Heaven, and prayer made for
rain. Thang said, 'If a man must be the victim, I will be he.' He
fasted, cut off his hair and nails, and in a plain carriage, drawn by
white horses, clad in rushes, in the guise of a sacrificial victim, he
proceeded to a forest of mulberry trees, and there prayed, asking
to what error or crime of his the calamity was owing. He had not
done speaking when a copious rain fell.

BOOK IV. THE INSTRUCTIONS OF Î.

THANG died in B.C. 1754 or 1753, and was succeeded, so far as the evidence of the Shû goes, by his grandson, known as Thâi Kiâ. The chief minister of Thang had been Î Yin, who delivers these Instructions to his young sovereign soon after his accession. Î was a great and wise man, 'a great sage,' as Thang calls him in the last Book, and is classed by Mencius among other celebrated ministers as 'the one most inclined to take office.' He reasons thus :—'Heaven's plan with mankind is that they who are first informed should instruct those who are later in being informed, and they who first apprehend principles should instruct those who are later in doing so.' He thought he was one of the former class, and a fire burned within him, impelling him to seek for office with a view to benefit the ignorant and erring. There were many legends about him in the times of Kâu. He was surnamed Î, from having been born near the river of that name, an affluent of the Ho. His name is said to have been Kih, and also Â-hăng (see the beginning of next Book). Yin was his designation. Thang had, probably, entrusted to him the guardianship of his grandson, and so he now went over the history of the kingdom from Yü, till it was transferred from the line of Hsiâ to that of Shang, celebrated the virtues of Thang and his government, and warned the young king of the fate that he must incur, if he neglected the instructions given to him.

1. In the twelfth month of the first year, on (the day) Yî-khâu, Î Yin sacrificed to the former king, and presented the heir-king reverently before (the shrine of) his grandfather.* All the princes from the domain of the nobles and the royal domain were present; all the officers (also), each continuing to discharge his particular duties, were there to receive the orders of the chief minister. Î Yin then clearly described the complete virtue of the Meritorious Ancestor for the instruction of the (young) king.

2. He said, 'Oh! of old the former kings of Hsiâ   93
cultivated earnestly their virtue, and then there
were no calamities from Heaven. The spirits of
the hills and rivers likewise were all in tranquillity;
and the birds and beasts, the fishes and tortoises, all
enjoyed their existence according to their nature.*
But their descendant did not follow (their example),
and great Heaven sent down calamities, employing
the agency of our (ruler) who was in possession of
its favouring appointment.* The attack (on Hsiâ)
may be traced to (the orgies in) Ming-thiâo[1], but our
(rise) began in Po. Our king of Shang brilliantly
displayed his sagely prowess ; for oppression he sub-
stituted his generous gentleness; and the millions
of the people gave him their hearts. Now your
Majesty is entering on the inheritance of his
virtue ;—all depends on (how) you commence your
reign. To set up love, it is for you to love (your
relations) ; to set up respect, it is for you to respect
(your elders). The commencement is in the family
and the state; the consummation is in (all within)
the four seas.'

3. 'Oh! the former king began with careful
attention to the bonds that hold men together.
He listened to expostulation, and did not seek to
resist it; he conformed to (the wisdom of) the
ancients ; occupying the highest position, he displayed intelligence ; occupying an inferior position,
he displayed his loyalty ; he allowed (the good
qualities of) the men (whom he employed), and did

---

[1] Ming-thiâo was a place not far from the capital of *K*ieh (in the
present district of An-yî, Hâi *K*âu, Shan-hsî). He had a palace
there, where the vilest orgies were celebrated that alienated the
minds of the people from him.

94 not seek that they should have every talent ; in the government of himself, he seemed to think that he could never (sufficiently) attain. It was thus he arrived at the possession of the myriad regions.— How painstaking was he in these things !

' He extensively sought out wise men, who should be helpful to you, his descendant and heir. He laid down the punishments for officers, and warned those who were in authority, saying, " If you dare to have constant dancing in your palaces, and drunken singing in your chambers,—that is called the fashion of sorcerers; if you dare to set your hearts on wealth and women, and abandon your-selves to wandering about or to the chase,—that is called the fashion of extravagance; if you dare to despise sage words, to resist the loyal and up-right, to put far from you the aged and virtuous, and to seek the company of procacious youths,—that is called the fashion of disorder. Now if a high noble or officer be addicted to one of these three fashions with their ten evil ways[1], his family will surely come to ruin; if the prince of a country be so addicted, his state will surely come to ruin. The minister who does not (try to) correct (such vices in the sovereign) shall be punished with branding." These rules were minutely inculcated (also) on the sons of officers and nobles in their lessons.'

4. ' Oh! do you, who now succeed to the throne, revere (these warnings) in your person. Think of

---

[1] The 'ten evil ways' are those mentioned in connexion with the three evil fashions ;—two under the sorcerers' fashion, and four under each of the other two fashions.

them !—sacred counsels of vast importance, admira- 95
ble words forcibly set forth ! (The ways) of God
are not invariable :— on the good-doer he sends
down all blessings, and on the evil-doer he sends
down all miseries.* Do you but be virtuous, be it
in small things (or in large), and the myriad regions
will have cause for rejoicing. If you be not virtuous, be it in large things (or in small), it will bring
the ruin of your ancestral temple.'

Book V. The Thâi *K*iâ.

THIS Book also belongs to the class of 'Lessons or Instructions,' and
is called ' the Thâi *K*iâ,' because the Instructions were addressed
to the young monarch so named. It is divided into three sections or parts. Î Yin finds the young sovereign disobedient to his
counsels, and proceeds to a high-handed measure. He removes
him from his palace and companions, and keeps him in a sort of
easy confinement, near the grave of his grandfather, all the period
of mourning ; and Thâi *K*iâ becomes sincerely penitent and virtuous. This is related in the first section. In the second, Î Yin
brings the king back with honour to Po, to undertake the duties
of the government, and congratulates him on his reformation.
The king responds suitably, and asks the minister to continue to
afford him his counsels, which the other at once proceeds to do.
The third section is all occupied with further and important
counsels.

Section 1.

1. The king, on succeeding to the throne, did not
follow (the advice of) Â-hăng[1]. (Â-hăng or) Î Yin

---

[1] Â-hăng, it is said by Sze-mâ *Kh*ien, was the name of Î. Others
make it the title of the chief minister under the dynasty of Shang, =
'the Support and Steelyard,' 'the Buttress and Director.'

96   then made the following writing[1] :—'The former king kept his eye continually on the bright requirements of Heaven, and so he maintained the worship of the spirits of heaven and earth, of those presiding over the land and the grain, and of those of the ancestral temple;—all with a sincere reverence.* Heaven took notice of his virtue, and caused its great appointment to light on him, that he should soothe and tranquillize the myriad regions.* I, Yin, then gave my assistance to my sovereign in the settlement of the people; and thus it is that you, O heir-king, have received the great inheritance. I have seen it myself in Hsiâ with its western capital[2], that when its rulers went through a prosperous course to the end, their ministers also did the same, and afterwards, when their successors could not attain to such a consummation, neither did their ministers. Take warning, O heir-king. Reverently use your sovereignty. If you do not play the sovereign, as the name requires, you will disgrace your grandfather.'

    2. The king would not think (of these words), nor listen to them. On this Î Yin said, 'The former king, before it was light, sought to have large and clear views, and then sat waiting for the dawn (to carry them into practice). He (also) sought on every side for men of ability and virtue, to instruct and guide his posterity. Do not frustrate his charge (to me), and bring on yourself your own overthrow. Be careful to strive after the virtue

---

    [1] This is the first direct statement in the Shû of a communication made in writing.

    [2] An-yî, the capital of Hsiâ, might be described as 'western,' from the standpoint of Po.

of self-restraint, and cherish far-reaching plans. Be like the forester, who, when he has adjusted the spring, goes to examine the end of the arrow, whether it be placed according to rule, and then lets go; reverently determine your aim, and follow the ways of your grandfather. Thus I shall be delighted, and be able to show to all ages that I have discharged my trust.'

3. The king was not yet able to change (his course). Î Yin said (to himself), 'This is (real) unrighteousness, and is becoming by practice (a second) nature. I cannot bear to be near (so) disobedient (a person). I will build (a place) in the palace at Thung[1], where he can be in silence near (the grave of) the former king. This will be a lesson which will keep him from going astray all his life.' The king went (accordingly) to the palace at Thung, and dwelt during the period of mourning. In the end he became sincerely virtuous.

Section 2.

1. On the first day of the twelfth month of his third year, Î Yin escorted the young king in the royal cap and robes back to Po. (At the same time) he made the following writing :—

'Without the sovereign, the people cannot have that guidance which is necessary to (the comfort of) their lives ; without the people, the sovereign would have no sway over the four quarters (of the kingdom).

---

[1] Thung was the place where Thang's tomb was ; probably in the present district of Yung-ho, department of Phû-kâu, Shan-hsî. The site or supposed site of the grave there was washed away in an overflow of the Fân river under the Yüan dynasty, and a stone coffin was removed to another position, near which a royal tomb has been built.

98 Great Heaven has graciously favoured the House of Shang, and granted to you, O young king, at last to become virtuous.* This is indeed a blessing that will extend without limit to ten thousand generations.'

2. The king did obeisance with his face to his hands and his head to the ground, saying, ' I, the little child, was without understanding of what was virtuous, and was making myself one of the unworthy. By my desires I was setting at nought all rules of conduct, and violating by my self-indulgence all rules of propriety, and the result must have been speedy ruin to my person. Calamities sent by Heaven may be avoided, but from calamities brought on by one's self there is no escape.* Heretofore I turned my back on the instructions of you, my tutor and guardian ;—my beginning has been marked by incompetency. Let me still rely on your correcting and preserving virtue, keeping this in view that my end may be good !'

3. Î Yin did obeisance with his face to his hands and his head on the ground, and said, ' To cultivate his person, and by being sincerely virtuous, bring (all) below to harmonious concord with him ;—this is the work of the intelligent sovereign. The former king was kind to the distressed and suffering, as if they were his children, and the people submitted to his commands,—all with sincere delight. Even in the states of the neighbouring princes, (the people) said, " We are waiting for our sovereign ; when our sovereign comes, we shall not suffer the punishments (that we now do)."

' O king, zealously cultivate your virtue. Regard (the example of) your meritorious grandfather. At no time allow yourself in pleasure and idleness. In worshipping your ancestors, think how you can prove your filial piety ;* in receiving your ministers, think how you can show yourself respectful ; in looking to what is distant, try to get clear views; have your ears ever open to lessons of virtue;—then shall I acknowledge (and respond to) the excellence of your majesty with an untiring (devotion to your service).

99

Section 3.

1. Î Yin again made an announcement to the king, saying, ' Oh! Heaven has no (partial) affection;—only to those who are reverent does it show affection.* The people are not constant to those whom they cherish ;—they cherish (only) him who is benevolent. The spirits do not always accept the sacrifices that are offered to them ;—they accept only the sacrifices of the sincere.* A place of difficulty is the Heaven-(conferred) seat. When there are (those) virtues, good government is realized; when they are not, disorder comes. To maintain the same principles as those who secured good government will surely lead to prosperity ; to pursue the courses of disorder will surely lead to ruin. He who at last, as at first, is careful as to whom and what he follows is a truly intelligent sovereign. The former king was always zealous in the reverent cultivation of his virtue, so that he was the fellow of God[1].* Now, O king, you have entered on the inheritance of his excellent line ;—fix your inspection on him.'

2. '(Your course must be) as when in ascending

---

[1] This phrase is used, as here, with reference to the virtue of a sovereign, making him as it were the mate of God, ruling on earth as He rules above ; and with reference to the honours paid to a departed sovereign, when he is associated with God in the great sacrificial services.

H 2

100 high you begin from where it is low, and when in travelling far you begin from where it is near. Do not slight the occupations of the people;—think of their difficulties. Do not yield to a feeling of repose on your throne;—think of its perils. Be careful for the end at the beginning. When you hear words that are distasteful to your mind, you must enquire whether they be not right; when you hear words that accord with your own views, you must enquire whether they be not contrary to what is right. Oh! what attainment can be made without anxious thought? what achievement can be made without earnest effort? Let the One man be greatly good, and the myriad regions will be rectified by him.'

3. 'When the sovereign does not with disputatious words throw the old rules of government into confusion, and the minister does not, for favour and gain, continue in an office whose work is done,—then the country will lastingly and surely enjoy happiness.'

BOOK VI.
THE COMMON POSSESSION OF PURE VIRTUE.

THIS is the last of the 'Instructions' of Î Yin;—addressed, like those of the last two Books, to Thâi *Ki*â, but at a later period when the great minister wished to retire from the toils of administration. He now disappears from the stage of history, though according to Sze-mâ *Kh*ien, and a notice in the Preface to the Shû, he lived on to B.C. 1713, the eighth year of Thâi *Ki*â's son and successor.

In this Book, his subject is 'Pure or Single-eyed Virtue,' and the importance of it to the ruler of the kingdom. He dwells on the fall of *Ki*eh through his want of this virtue, and the elevation of Thang through his possession of it; treats generally on its nature and results; and urges the cultivation of it on Thâi *Ki*â.

1. Î Yin, having returned the government into

the hands of his sovereign, and being about to announce his retirement, set forth admonitions on the subject of virtue.

101

2. He said, 'Oh! it is difficult to rely on Heaven;—its appointments are not constant.* (But if the sovereign see to it that) his virtue be constant, he will preserve his throne; if his virtue be not con-stant, the nine provinces will be lost by him. The king of Hsiâ could not maintain the virtue (of his ancestors) unchanged, but contemned the spirits and oppressed the people. Great Heaven no (longer) extended its protection to him. It looked out among the myriad regions to give its guidance to one who should receive its favouring appointment, fondly seeking (a possessor of) pure virtue, whom it might make lord of all the spirits.* Then there were I, Yin, and Thang, both possessed of pure virtue, and able to satisfy the mind of Heaven. He received (in consequence) the bright favour of Heaven, so as to become possessor of the multitudes of the nine provinces, and proceeded to change Hsiâ's com-mencement of the year. It was not that Heaven had any private partiality for the lord of Shang;—it simply gave its favour to pure virtue.* It was not that Shang sought (the allegiance of) the lower people;—the people simply turned to pure virtue. Where (the sovereign's) virtue is pure, his enter-prizes are all fortunate; where his virtue is wavering and uncertain, his enterprizes are all unfortunate. Good and evil do not wrongly befal men, but Heaven sends down misery or happiness according to their conduct.' *

3. 'Now, O young king, you are newly entering on your (great) appointment,—you should be seeking to

102 make new your virtue. At last, as at first, have this as your one object, so shall you make a daily renovation. Let the officers whom you employ be men of virtue and ability, and let the ministers about you be the right men. The minister, in relation to (his sovereign) above him, has to promote his virtue, and, in relation to the (people) beneath him, has to seek their good. How hard must it be (to find the proper man)! what careful attention must be required! (Thereafter) there must be harmony (cultivated with him), and a oneness (of confidence placed in him).

'There is no invariable model of virtue ;—a supreme regard to what is good gives the model of it. There is no invariable characteristic of what is good that is to be supremely regarded ;—it is found where there is a conformity to the uniform consciousness (in regard to what is good). (Such virtue) will make the people with their myriad surnames all say, "How great are the words of the king!" and also, "How single and pure is the king's heart!" It will avail to maintain in tranquillity the rich possession of the former king, and to secure for ever the (happy) life of the multitudes of the people.'

4. 'Oh! (to retain a place) in the seven-shrined temple [1] of ancestors is a sufficient witness of virtue.* To be acknowledged as chief by the myriad heads of families is a sufficient evidence of one's government.

---

[1] It is beyond a doubt that the ancestral temple of the kings of *K*âu contained seven shrines or seven small temples, for the occupancy of which, by the spirit-tablets of such and such kings, there were definite rules, as the line of sovereigns increased. It would appear from the text that a similar practice prevailed in the time of the Shang dynasty.

The sovereign without the people has none whom 103
he can employ ; and the people without the sovereign
have none whom they can serve. Do not think yourself so large as to deem others small. If ordinary
men and women do not find the opportunity to give
full development to their ability, the people's lord
will be without the proper aids to complete his
merit.'

BOOK VII. THE PAN-KĂNG.

PAN-KĂNG was the seventeenth sovereign in the line of Thang. From
Thâi *K*iâ to him, therefore, there was a space of 321 years, which
are a gap in the history of the Shang dynasty, so far as the existing
documents of the Shû are concerned. When the collection was
complete, there were seven other documents between 'the Common Possession of Pure Virtue' and ' the Pan-kăng,' but the latest
of them belonged to the reign of Ẑû-yî, B.C. 1525-1507.

The reign of Pan-kăng extended from B. C. 1401 to 1374, and is
remarkable as that in which the dynasty began to be called Yin,
instead of Shang. The Book belongs to the class of 'Announcements,' and is divided into three sections.

The contents centre round the removal of the capital from the
north of the Ho to Yin on the south of it. The king saw that
the removal was necessary, but had to contend with the unwill-
ingness' of the people to adopt such a step, and the opposition of
the great families. The first section relates how he endeavoured
to vindicate the measure, and contains two addresses, to the
people and to those in high places, respectively, designed to
secure their cordial co-operation. The second section brings before
us the removal in progress, but there continue to be dissatisfactions, which the king endeavours to remove by a long and
earnest defence of his course. The third section opens with the
removal accomplished. The new city has been founded, and
the plan of it laid out. The king makes a fresh appeal to the
people and chiefs, to forget all their heart-burnings, and join
with him in building up in the new capital a great destiny for
the dynasty.

Section 1.

1. Pan-kăng wished to remove (the capital) to Yin[1], but the people would not go to dwell there. He therefore appealed to all the discontented, and made the following protestations. 'Our king, (3û-yî), came, and fixed on this (Kăng for his capital). He did so from a deep concern for our people, and not because he would have them all die, where they cannot (now) help one another to preserve their lives. I have consulted the tortoise-shell, and obtained the reply—" This is no place for us." When the former kings had any (important) business, they gave reverent heed to the commands of Heaven.* In a case like this especially they did not indulge (the wish for) constant repose,—they did not abide ever in the same city. Up to this time (the capital has been) in five regions[2]. If we do not follow (the example) of these old times, we shall be refusing to acknowledge that Heaven is making an end of our dynasty (here);—how little can it be said of us that we are following the meritorious course of the former kings! As from the stump of a felled tree there are sprouts and shoots, Heaven will perpetuate its decree in our favour in this new city;—the great inheritance of the former kings will be continued and renewed, and tranquillity will be secured to the four quarters (of the kingdom).' *

---

[1] The removal was probably necessitated by an inundation of the Ho. Kăng had been fixed on by 3û-yî for his capital. The Yin to which Pan-kăng removed was in the present district of Yen-sze, department Ho-nan, Ho-nan.

[2] This fact—the frequent change of capital—does not give us a great idea of the stability and resources of the Shang dynasty.

2. Pan-kăng, in making the people aware of his
views, began with those who were in (high) places,
and took the constantly-recurring circumstances of
former times to lay down the right law and measure
(for the present emergency), saying, 'Let none of
you dare to suppress the remonstrances of the poor
people.' The king commanded all to come to him
in the courtyard (of his palace).

. The king spoke to this effect :—'Come, all of
you; I will announce to you my instructions. Take
counsel how to put away your (selfish) thoughts.
Do not with haughty (disregard of me) follow after
your own ease. Of old, our former kings planned
like me how to employ the men of old families to
share in (the labours of) government. When they
wished to proclaim and announce what was to be
attended to, these did not conceal the royal views;
and on this account the kings greatly respected them.
They did not exceed the truth (in their communica-
tions with the people), and on this account the people
became greatly changed (in their views). Now,(however), you keep clamouring, and get the confidence
(of the people) by alarming and shallow speeches ;—
I do not know what you are wrangling about. (In
this movement) I am not myself abandoning my
proper virtue, but you conceal the goodness of my
intentions, and do not stand in awe of me, the One
man. I see you as clearly as one sees a·fire ; but I,
likewise, by my undecided plans, have produced your
error.

'When the net has its line, there is order and not
confusion ; and when the husbandman labours upon
his fields, and reaps with all his might, there is the
(abundant) harvest. If you can put away your

106 (selfish) thoughts, and bestow real good upon the people, reaching (also) to your own relatives and friends, you may boldly venture to make your words great, and say that you have accumulated merit. But you do not fear the great evils which (through our not removing) are extending far and near; (you are like) idle husbandmen, who yield themselves to ease, and are not strong to toil and labour on their acres, so that they cannot get their crop of millets. You do not speak in a spirit of harmony and goodness to the people, and are only giving birth to bitter evils for yourselves. You play the part of destroyers and authors of calamity, of villains and traitors, to bring down misery on your own persons. You set the example of evil, and must feel its smart;—what will it avail you (then) to repent? Look at the poor people;—they are still able to look to one another and give expression to their remonstrances, but when they begin to speak, you are ready with your extravagant talk;—how much more ought you to have me before your eyes, with whom it is to make your lives long or short! Why do you not report (their words) to me, but go about to excite one another by empty speeches, frightening and involving the multitudes in misery? When a fire is blazing in the flames so that it cannot be approached, can it still be beaten out? So, it will not be I who will be to blame, that you all cause dispeace in this way, (and must suffer the consequences.)

'*Kh*ih *Z*ăn [1] has said, "In men we seek those of old families; in vessels, we do not seek old ones,

---

[1] Who *Kh*ih *Z*ăn was is not known. The general opinion is, that he was an ancient historiographer. A *K*'âu *Z*ăn is introduced in a similar way in the Confucian Analects, XVI, i.

but new." Of old, the kings, my predecessors, and   107
your forefathers and fathers shared together the
ease and labours (of the government) ;—how should
I dare to lay undeserved afflictions on you ?   For
generations the toils of your (fathers) have been
approved, and I will not conceal your goodness.
Now when I offer the great sacrifices to my predecessors, your forefathers are present to share in
them.*   (They all observe) the happiness I confer
and the sufferings I inflict, and I cannot dare to
reward virtue that does not exist.

  ' I have announced to you the difficulties (of the
intended movement), being bent on it, like an archer
(whose only thought is to hit).   Do not you despise
the old and experienced, and do not make little of
the helpless and young.   Seek every one long continuance in this (new city), which is to be your abode ;
exert yourselves and put out your strength (in fur-
thering the removal), and listen to the plans of me,
the One man.   I will make no distinction between
men as being more distantly or more nearly related
to me ;—the criminal (in this matter) shall die the
death, and the good-doer shall have his virtue distinguished.   The prosperity of the country (ought
to) come from you all.   If it fail of prosperity, that
must arise from me, the One man, erring in the
application of punishment.   Be sure, all of you, to
make known this announcement.   From this time
forward, attend respectfully to your business; have
(the duties of) your offices regularly adjusted; bring
your tongues under the rule of law :—lest punishment come upon you, when repentance will be of no
avail.'

Section 2.

1. Pan-kăng arose, and (was about to) cross the Ho with the people, moving (to the new capital). Accordingly, he addressed himself to those of them who were (still) dissatisfied, and made a full announcement to their multitudes, to induce a sincere acquiescence (in the measure). They all attended, and (being charged) to take no liberties in the royal courtyard, he called them near, and said, ' Listen clearly to my words, and do not disregard my commands.

' Oh ! of old time my royal predecessors cherished, every one and above every other thing, a respectful care of the people, who (again) upheld their sovereign with a mutual sympathy. Seldom was it that they were not superior to any (calamitous) time sent by Heaven. When great calamities came down on Yin, the former kings did not fondly remain in their place. What they did was with a view to the people's advantage, and therefore they moved (their capitals). Why do you not reflect that I, according to what I have heard of the ancient sovereigns, in my care of you and actings towards you, am only wishing to rejoice with you in a common repose ? It is not that any guilt attaches to you, so that (this movement) should be like a punishment. If I call upon you to cherish this new city, it is simply on your account, and as an act of great accordance with your wishes. My present undertaking to remove with you, is to give repose and stability to the country. You, (however), have no sympathy with the anxieties of my mind; but you all keep a great reserve in declaring your minds, (when you might) respectfully think by your sincerity to move me, the One man. You only exhaust and distress yourselves. The case is like that of sailing in a boat ;—if you do not cross the stream (at the proper time), you will destroy all the cargo. Your sincerity does not respond to mine, and we are in danger of going together to destruction. You, notwithstanding, will not examine the matter ;—though you anger yourselves, what cure will that bring ?

' You do not consult for a distant day, nor think of the calamity that must befal you (from not removing). You greatly encourage one another in what must prove to your sorrow. Now you have the present, but you will not have the future ;—what prolongation of life can you look for from above ? My measures are forecast to prolong your (lease of) life from Heaven ;—do I force you by the terrors of my power ? My object is to support and nourish you all. I think of my ancestors, (who are now) the spiritual sovereigns;* when they made your forefathers toil (on similar occasions it was only for their good), and I would be enabled in the same way greatly to nourish you and cherish you.'

2. ' Were I to err in my government, and remain long here, my high sovereign, (the founder of our dynasty), would send down on me great punishment for my crime, and say, " Why do you oppress my people ?"* If you, the myriads of the people, do not attend to the perpetuation of your lives, and cherish one mind with me, the One man, in my plans, the former kings will send down on you great punishment for your crime, and say, " Why do you not agree with our young grandson, but go on to forfeit

110

your virtue ?" When they punish you from above, you will have no way of escape.* Of old, my royal predecessors made your ancestors and fathers toil (only for their good). You are equally the people whom I (wish to) cherish. But your conduct is injurious ;—it is cherished in your hearts. Whereas my royal predecessors made your ancestors and fathers happy, they, your ancestors and fathers, will (now) cut you off and abandon you, and not save you from death.* Here are those ministers of my government, who share with me in the offices (of the kingdom) ;—and yet they (only think of hoarding up) cowries and gems. Their ancestors and fathers earnestly represent (their course) to my high sovereign, saying, "Execute great punishments on our descendants." So do they advise my high sovereign to send down great calamities (on those men).' *

3. 'Oh! I have now told you my unchangeable purpose ;—do you perpetually respect (my) great anxiety; let us not get alienated and removed from one another; share in my plans and thoughts, and think (only) of following me; let every one of you set up the true rule of conduct in his heart. If there be bad and unprincipled men, precipitously or carelessly disrespectful (to my orders), and taking advantage of this brief season to play the part of villains or traitors, I will cut off their noses, or utterly exterminate them. I will leave none of their children. I will not let them perpetuate their seed in this new city.

'Go! preserve and continue your lives. I will now transfer you (to the new capital), and (there) establish your families for ever.'

Section 3.

1. Pan-kăng having completed the removal, and settled the places of residence, proceeded to adjust the several positions (of all classes at an assembly); and then he soothed and comforted the multitudes, saying to them, ' Do not play nor be idle, but exert yourselves to build (here) a great destiny (for us).

' Now I have disclosed my heart and belly, my reins and bowels, and fully declared to you, my people, all my mind. I will not treat any of you as offenders; and do not you (any more) help one another to be angry, and form parties to defame me, the One man.

' Of old, my royal predecessor, (Thang), that his merit might exceed that of those who were before him, proceeded to the hill-site [1]. Thereby he removed our evils, and accomplished admirable good for our country. Now you, my people, were by (your position) dissipated and separated, so that you had no abiding place. (And yet) you asked why I was troubling your myriads and requiring you to remove. But God, being about to renew the virtuous service of my high ancestor, and secure the good order of our kingdom, I, with the sincere and respectful (of my ministers), felt a reverent care for the lives of the people, and have made a lasting settlement in (this) new city.*

' I, a youth, did not neglect your counsels;— I (only) used the best of them. Nor did any of

---

[1] It is supposed that this 'hill-site' of Thang was the same as that which Pan-kăng had fixed on, but this does not clearly appear in the text.

112   you presumptuously oppose the decision of the
tortoise-shell; — so we are here to enlarge our
great inheritance.'*

2. 'Oh! ye chiefs of regions, ye heads of departments, all ye, the hundreds of officers, would that
ye had a sympathy (with my people)! I will exert
myself in the choice and guiding of you;—do ye
think reverently of my multitudes. I will not employ those who are fond of enriching themselves;
but will use and revere those who are vigorously,
yet reverently, labouring for the lives and increase
of the people, nourishing them and planning for
their enduring settlement.

'I have now brought forward and announced to
you my mind, whom I approve and whom I dis-
allow;—let none of you but reverence (my will).
Do not seek to accumulate wealth and precious
things, but in fostering the life of the people, seek
to find your merit. Reverently display your virtue
in behalf of the people. For ever maintain this
one purpose in your hearts.'

BOOK VIII. THE CHARGE TO YÜEH.

AFTER Pan-kăng came the reigns of Hsiâo-hsin and Hsiâo-yî, of
which we have no accounts in the Shû. Hsiâo-yî was followed by
Wû-ting (B. c. 1324–1264), to the commencement of whose reign
this Book, in three sections, belongs. His name is not in it,
but that he is the king intended appears from the prefatory
notice, and the Confucian Analects, XIV, xliii. The Book is the
first of the 'Charges' of the Shû. They relate the designation
by the king of some officer to a particular charge or to some fief,
with the address delivered by him on the occasion. Here the
charge is to Yüeh, in the first section, on his appointment to be

chief minister. In the other two sections Yüeh is the principal 113
speaker, and not the king. They partake more of the nature of
the 'Counsels.' Yüeh had been a recluse, living in obscurity.
The king's attention was drawn to him in the manner related
in the Book, and he was discovered in Fû-yen, or amidst 'the
Crags of Fû,' from which he was afterwards called Fû Yüeh, as
if Fû had been his surname.

The first section tells us how the king met with Yüeh, and appointed
him to be his chief minister, and how Yüeh responded to the
charge that he received. In the second section, Yüeh counsels the
king on a variety of points, and the king responds admiringly.
In the third, the king introduces himself as a pupil at the feet of
Yüeh, and is lectured on the subject of enlarging his knowledge.
In the end the king says that he looks to Yüeh as another Î Yin,
to make him another Thang.

Section 1.

1. The king passed the season of sorrow in
the mourning shed for three years[1], and when the
period of mourning was over, he (still) did not
speak (to give any commands). All the ministers
remonstrated with him, saying, 'Oh! him who is
(the first) to apprehend we pronounce intelligent,
and the intelligent man is the model for others.
The Son of Heaven rules over the myriad regions,
and all the officers look up to and reverence him.
They are the king's words which form the commands (for them). If he do not speak, the ministers have no way to receive their orders.' On this
the king made a writing, for their information, to
the following effect :—'As it is mine to serve as the

---

[1] A young king, mourning for his father, had to 'afflict' himself
in various ways for twenty-five months, nominally for three years.
Among other privations, he had to exchange the comforts of a
palace for a rough shed in one of the courtyards. During the time
of mourning, the direction of affairs was left to the chief minister.

114 director for the four quarters (of the kingdom), I have been afraid that my virtue is not equal to (that of my predecessors), and therefore have not spoken. (But) while I was reverently and silently thinking of the (right) way, I dreamt that God gave me a good assistant who should speak for me.'* He then minutely recalled the appearance (of the person whom he had seen), and caused search to be made for him everywhere by means of a picture. Yüeh, a builder in the wild country of Fû-yen, was found like to it.

2. On this the king raised and made (Yüeh) his prime minister, keeping him (also) at his side.

He charged him, saying, 'Morning and evening present your instructions to aid my virtue. Suppose me a weapon of steel;—I will use you for a whetstone. Suppose me crossing a great stream;—I will use you for a boat with its oars. Suppose me in a year of great drought;—I will use you as a copious rain. Open your mind, and enrich my mind. (Be you) like medicine, which must distress the patient, in order to cure his sickness. (Think of me) as one walking barefoot, whose feet are sure to be wounded, if he do not see the ground.

'Do you and your companions all cherish the same mind to assist your sovereign, that I may follow my royal predecessors, and tread in the steps of my high ancestor, to give repose to the millions of the people. Oh! respect this charge of mine;— so shall you bring your work to a (good) end.'

3. Yüeh replied to the king, saying, 'Wood by the use of the line is made straight, and the sovereign who follows reproof is made sage. When the sovereign can (thus) make himself sage, his ministers,

without being specially commanded, anticipate his
orders;—who would dare not to act in respectful
compliance with this excellent charge of your
Majesty?'

115

Section 2.

1. Yüeh having received his charge, and taken
the presidency of all the officers, he presented himself before the king, and said, ' Oh! intelligent kings
act in reverent accordance with the ways of Heaven.
The founding of states and the setting up of capitals,
the appointing of sovereign kings, of dukes and other
nobles, with their great officers and heads of departments, were not designed to minister to the idleness
and pleasures (of one), but for the good government
of the people.　It is Heaven which is all-intelligent
and observing;—let the sage (king) take it as his
pattern.*　Then his ministers will reverently accord
with him, and the people consequently will be well
governed.

'It is the mouth that gives occasion for shame;
they are the coat of mail and helmet that give occasion to war.　The upper robes and lower garments
(for reward should not be lightly taken from) their
chests; before spear and shield are used, one should
examine himself.　If your Majesty will be cautious
in regard to these things, and, believing this about
them, attain to the intelligent use of them, (your
government) will in everything be excellent.　Good
government and bad depend on the various officers.
Offices should not be given to men because they are
favourites, but only to men of ability.　Dignities
should not be conferred on men of evil practices, but
only on men of worth.

I 2

116 'Anxious thought about what will be best should precede your movements, which also should be taken at the time proper for them. Indulging the consciousness of being good is the way to lose that goodness; being vain of one's ability is the way to lose the merit it might produce.

'For all affairs let there be adequate preparation;— with preparation there will be no calamitous issue. Do not open the door for favourites, from whom you will receive contempt. Do not be ashamed of mistakes, and (go on to) make them crimes. Let your mind rest in its proper objects, and the affairs of your government will be pure. Officiousness in sacrificing is called irreverence;* and multiplying ceremonies leads to disorder. To serve the spirits acceptably (in this way) is difficult.' *

2. The king said, 'Excellent! your words, O Yüeh, should indeed be put in practice (by me). If you were not so good in counsel, I should not have heard these rules for my conduct.' Yüeh did obeisance with his head to the ground, and said, 'It is not the knowing that is difficult, but the doing. (But) since your Majesty truly knows this, there will not be the difficulty, and you will become really equal in complete virtue to our first king. Wherein I, Yüeh, refrain from speaking (what I ought to speak), the blame will rest with me.'

Section 3.

1. The king said, 'Come, O Yüeh. I, the little one, first learned with Kan Pan[1]. Afterwards I lived

---

[1] From Part V, xvi, 2, we learn that Kan Pan was a great minister of Wû-ting. It is supposed that he had been minister to Wû-ting's father, and died during the king's period of mourning.

concealed among the rude countrymen, and then I   117
went to (the country) inside the Ho, and lived there [1].
From the Ho I went to Po ;—and the result has
been that I am unenlightened. Do you teach me
what should be my aims. Be to me as the yeast
and the malt in making sweet spirits, as the salt and
the prunes in making agreeable soup. Use various
methods to cultivate me ; do not cast me away ;—so
shall I attain to practise your instructions.'

Yüeh said, ' O king, a ruler should seek to learn
much (from his ministers), with a view to establish
his affairs ; but to learn the lessons of the ancients
is the way to attain this. That the affairs of one,
not making the ancients his masters, can be perpetuated for generations, is what I have not heard.

' In learning there should be a humble mind and
the maintenance of a constant earnestness ;—in such
a case (the learner's) improvement will surely come.
He who sincerely cherishes these things will find all
truth accumulating in his person. Teaching is the
half of learning ; when a man's thoughts from first
to last are constantly fixed on learning, his virtuous
cultivation comes unperceived.

' Survey the perfect pattern of our first king ;—so
shall you for ever be preserved from error. Then
shall I be able reverently to meet your views, and
on every side to look out for men of eminence to
place in the various offices.'

2. The king said, ' Oh! Yüeh, that all within the four

---

[1] We do not know the events of Wû-ting's early life sufficiently to
explain his language here. His living concealed among the rude
people of the country, and then crossing to the north of the Ho,
was owing probably to troubles in the kingdom.

118   seas look up to my virtue is owing to you. As his
legs and arms form the man, so does a good minister
form the sage (king). Formerly, there was the first
premier of our dynasty, Pâo-hăng[1], who raised up
and formed its royal founder. He said, "If I cannot
make my sovereign like Yâo or Shun, I shall feel
ashamed in my heart, as if I were beaten in the
market-place." If any common man did not get
(all he should desire), he said, "It is my fault."
(Thus) he assisted my meritorious ancestor, so that
he became equal to great Heaven.* Do you give
your intelligent and preserving aid to me, and let
not Â-hăng engross all the good service to the
House of Shang.

'The sovereign should share his government with
none but worthy officers. The worthy officer should
accept his support from none but the proper sovereign. May you now succeed in making your sovereign a (true) successor of the founder of his line, and
in securing the lasting happiness of the people!'

Yüeh did obeisance with his head to the ground,
and said, 'I will venture to respond to, and display
abroad, your Majesty's excellent charge.'

Book IX. The Day of the Supplementary Sacrifice to Kâo ƺung.

Kâo ƺung was the title given to Wû-ting, after his death, in the
ancestral temple. A supplementary sacrifice was offered on the
day following the regular and more solemn service. What
special idea was connected with it, it would be difficult to say;

---

[1] Styled Â-hăng in the beginning of 'the Thâi-kiâ.' Pâo-hăng =
'the Protector and Steelyard.'

but at the close of it, the representatives or personators of the
dead in the sacrifice of the preceding day were all feasted.
The title of this short Book leaves it uncertain whether the sacrifice
was offered to Wû-ting or by him. The prefatory notice proceeds
on the former view. Many critics of great intelligence decide
. for the latter, which a renewed consideration of the text has
induced me to adopt. The king then is Зû-kăng, Wû-ting's son.
Something irregular or excessive in his sacrificing to his father
was the thing which his monitor Зû *Kî* wished to censure,
taking occasion to do so from the incident mentioned in the first
sentence.

On the day of the supplementary sacrifice of
Kâo Зung, there appeared a crowing pheasant [1].
Зû *Kî* said, 'To rectify this affair, the king must
first be corrected.' He delivered accordingly a
lesson to the king, saying, 'In its inspection of men
below, Heaven's first consideration is of their righteousness, and it bestows on them (accordingly) length
of years or the contrary.* It is not Heaven that
cuts short men's lives; they bring them to an end
themselves. Some men who have not complied with
virtue will yet not acknowledge their offences, and
when Heaven has by evident tokens charged them
to correct their conduct, they still say, "What are
these things to us?"

'Oh! your Majesty's business is to care reverently for the people. And all (your ancestors) were
the heirs of (the kingdom by the gift of) Heaven;—
in attending to the sacrifices (to them), be not so
excessive in those to your father.'*

---

[1] Sze-mâ *Kh*ien, after the prefatory notice, says that the pheasant
sat on the ear—one of the handles—of a tripod.

120

BOOK X.

THE CHIEF OF THE WEST'S CONQUEST OF Lî.

THE reigns of seven more kings of Yin or Shang have passed, and
this Book brings us to the time of *K*âu-hsin or Shâu, its last sovereign, B.C. 1154–1123. The House of *K*âu begins to come to the
front, for 'the Chief of the West' was one of the acknowledged
founders of the *K*âu dynasty;—whether *Kh*ang, known as king
Wăn, or his son Fâ, known as king Wû, is uncertain. *Kh*ang's
father, the duke of *K*âu in the present department of Făng-hsiang,
Shen-hsî, had been appointed Chief of the West, that is, of all the
western portion of the kingdom, embracing Yü's provinces of
Yung, Liang, and *K*ing. The same jurisdiction descended to his
son and grandson. The state of Lî, the conquest of which is
mentioned, was in the present department of Lû-an, Shan-hsî,
within the royal domain, so that the Chief of the West was no
longer confining himself to the west, but threatening the king
himself.

Zû Î, a loyal officer, hears of the conquest of Lî, and hurries away
to inform the king and warn him of the danger threatening the
dynasty through his evil conduct. The king gives no heed to
his remonstrances, and Zû Î retires, sighing over the ruin, which
he sees is not to be averted.

The Book is classed, it would be hard to tell why, among the
'Announcements.'

The Chief of the West having subdued Lî, Zû Î
was afraid, and hastened to report it to the king.

He said, 'Son of Heaven, Heaven is bringing to
an end the dynasty of Yin;* the wisest men and the
shell of the great tortoise do not presume to know
anything fortunate for it.* It is not that the former
kings do not aid us, the men of this later time;*
but by your dissoluteness and sport you are bringing on the end yourself. On this account Heaven
has cast us off, and there are no good harvests to
supply us with food.* Men have no regard to their

heavenly nature, and pay no obedience to the sta- 121
tutes (of the kingdom). (Yea), our people now all
wish (the dynasty) to perish, saying, "Why does not
Heaven send down its indignation? Why does not
(some one with) its great appointment make his
appearance? What has the present king to do
with us?"'

The king said, 'Oh! was not my birth in
accordance with the appointment of Heaven (in
favour of my House)?' (On this) Ȝû Î returned
(to his own city), and said, 'Your crimes, which are
many, are registered above, and can you still appeal
to the appointment of Heaven in your favour?*
Yin will perish very shortly. As to all your deeds,
can they but bring ruin on your country?'

Book XI. The Count of Wei.

THE conversation recorded here—called, like the last Book, and
with as little reason, an 'Announcement'—is referred to B. C.
1123, the year in which the dynasty of Shang perished.
Wei was a principality in the royal domain, corresponding to the
present district of Lû-khăng, department Lû-an, Shan-hsî, the lords
of which were counts. The count who appears here was, most
probably, an elder brother of the king, and by the same mother,
who was, however, only a concubine when the count was born,
but raised to be queen before the birth of Kâu-hsin. Saddened
with the thought of the impending ruin of the dynasty, the count
seeks the counsel of two other high nobles, and asks them to
tell him what was to be done. One of them replies to him in
still stronger language about the condition and prospects of the
kingdom, and concludes by advising the count to make his
escape, and declaring that he himself would remain at his post,
and share in the unavoidable ruin.

122

1. The Count of Wei spoke to the following effect:—'Grand-Master and Junior-Master[1], (the House of) Yin, we may conclude, can no longer exercise rule over the four quarters (of the kingdom). The great deeds of our founder were displayed in former ages, but by our maddened indulgence in spirits, we have destroyed (the effects of) his virtue in these after-times. (The people of) Yin, small and great, are given to highway robberies, villainies, and treachery. The nobles and officers imitate one another in violating the laws, and there is no certainty that criminals will be apprehended. The smaller people (consequently) rise up, and commit violent outrages on one another. Yin is now sinking in ruin;—its condition is like that of one crossing a stream, who can find neither ford nor bank. That Yin should be hurrying to ruin at the present pace!'

He added, 'Grand-Master and Junior-Master, we are manifesting insanity. The most venerable members of our families are withdrawn to the wilds; and you indicate no course (to be taken), but (only) tell me of the impending ruin;—what is to be done?'

2. The Grand-Master made about the following reply:—'O son of our (former) king, Heaven in anger is sending down calamities, and wasting the country of Yin.* Hence has arisen that mad indulgence in spirits. (The king) has no reverence

---

[1] For high ministers with these titles under the *K*âu dynasty, see next Part, Book xx. The individuals whom the count of Wei consulted were probably the count of *K*î and Pî-kan, who are classed with him in the Confucian Analects, XVIII, 1.

for things which he ought to reverence, but does 123
despite to the venerable aged, the men who have
long been in .office. The people of Yin will now
steal even the pure and perfect victims devoted to
the spirits of heaven and earth ; * and their conduct
is connived at, and though they proceed to eat the
victims, they suffer no punishment. (On the other
hand), when I look down and survey the people of
Yin, the methods by which they are governed are
hateful exactions, which call forth outrages and
hatred ;—and this without ceasing. Such crimes
equally belong to all in authority, and multitudes
are starving with none to whom to appeal. Now
is the time of Shang's calamity ;—I will arise and
share in its ruin. When ruin overtakes Shang,
I will not be the servant (of another House).
(But) I tell you, O king's son, to go away, as being
the course (for you). Formerly I injured you by
what I said ; if you do not (now) go away, our
(sacrifices) will entirely perish. Let us rest quietly
(in our several parts), and each present himself to
the former kings [1] (as having done so).* I do not
think of making my escape.'

---

[1] It is understood that the former king, the father of both *Khî*
and *K*âu-hsin, had wished to leave the throne to *Khî*, and that the
Grand-Master had advocated such a measure ;—thereby injuring
Khî when it did not take effect, through making *K*âu-hsin jealous
of him.

PART V. THE BOOKS OF *K*ÂU.

Book I. The Great Declaration.

*K*ÂU is the dynastic designation under which king Wû and his descendants possessed the throne from B. C. 1122 to 256, a period of 867 years. They traced their lineage up to *K*hî, who was Minister of Agriculture under Shun. He was invested with the principality of Thâi, the present district of Fû-făng, department of Făng-hsiang, Shen-hsî. Long afterwards Than-fû, claiming to be one of his descendants, appears in B.C. 1326, founding the state of *K*âu, near mount *K*hî, in the same department of Făng-hsiang. This Than-fû was the great-grandfather of king Wû. The family surname was *K*î.

When the collection of the Shû was complete, it contained thirty-eight different documents of the *K*âu dynasty, of which twenty-eight remain, twenty of them being of undisputed genuineness.

This first Book, 'the Great Declaration,' is one of the contested portions; and there is another form of it, that takes the place of this in some editions. It has appeared in the Introduction that the received text of the Shû was formed with care, and that everything of importance in the challenged Books is to be found in quotations from them, while the collection was complete, that have been gathered up by the industry of scholars.

King Wû, having at last taken the field against *K*âu-hsin, the tyrant of Shang, made three speeches to his officers and men, setting forth the reasons for his enterprise, and urging them to exert themselves with him in the cause of humanity and Heaven. They are brought together, and constitute 'the Great Declaration.'

'In the first Part,' says a Chinese critic, 'king Wû addresses himself to the princes and nobles of inferior rank; in the second, to their hosts; and in the third, to his officers. The ruling idea in the first is the duty of the sovereign,—what he ought to be

and to do; with this it begins and ends. There is not the same
continuity of thought in the second, but the will and purpose of
Heaven is the principal thing insisted on. The last Part shows
the difference between the good sovereign and the bad, and
touches on the consent that there is between Heaven and men.
There is throughout an unsparing exhibition of the wickedness
of *K*âu-hsin.

Section 1.

In the spring of the thirteenth year[1] there was
a great assembly at Mâng-*k*ing[2]. The king said,
'Ah! ye hereditary rulers of my friendly states, and
all ye my officers, managers of my affairs, hearken
clearly to my declaration.

'Heaven and earth is the parent of all creatures;
and of all creatures man is the most highly endowed.*
The sincerely intelligent (among men) becomes the
great sovereign; and the great sovereign is the
parent of the people. But now, Shâu, the king of
Shang, does not reverence Heaven above, and inflicts
calamities on the people below.* Abandoned to
drunkenness and reckless in lust, he has dared to
exercise cruel oppression. He has extended the
punishment of offenders to all their relatives. He
has put men into offices on the hereditary principle.
He has made it his pursuit to have palaces, towers,
pavilions, embankments, ponds, and all other extra-
vagances, to the most painful injury of you, the
myriads of the people. He has burned and roasted
the loyal and good. He has ripped up pregnant

---

[1] The thirteenth year is reckoned from king Wû's succeeding
to his father as 'the Chief of the West.'

[2] Mâng-*k*ing, or 'the Ford of Mâng,' is still the name of a
district in the department of Ho-nan, Ho-nan.

125

126 women. Great Heaven was moved with indignation, and charged my deceased father Wăn to display its terrors; but (he died) before the work was
completed.*

'On this account, I, Fâ, the little child, have by
means of you, the hereditary rulers of my friendly
states, contemplated the government of Shang; but
Shâu has no repentant heart. He sits squatting
on his heels, not serving God nor the spirits of
heaven and earth, neglecting also the temple of his
ancestors, and not sacrificing in it. * The victims
and the vessels of millet all become the prey of
wicked robbers, and still he says, "The people are
mine; the (heavenly) appointment is mine," never
trying to correct his contemptuous mind.*

'Heaven, for the help of the inferior people, made
for them rulers, and made for them instructors, that
they might be able to be aiding to God, and secure
the tranquillity of the four quarters (of the kingdom).
In regard to who are criminals and who are not, how
dare I give any allowance to my own wishes ? *

'"Where the strength is the same, measure the
virtue of the parties; where the virtue is the same,
measure their righteousness." Shâu has hundreds
of thousands and myriads of officers, but they have
hundreds of thousands and myriads of minds; I have
(but) three thousand officers, but they have one mind.
The iniquity of Shang is full. Heaven gives command
to destroy it. If I did not obey Heaven, my iniquity
would be as great.*

'I, the little child, early and late am filled with
apprehensions. I have received the command of
my deceased father Wăn; I have offered special
sacrifice to God; I have performed the due ser-

vices to the great earth; and I lead the multitude   127
of you to execute the punishment appointed by
Heaven. *   Heaven compassionates the people.
What the people desire, Heaven will be found to
give effect to.*   Do you aid me, the One man, to
cleanse for ever (all within) the four seas. Now
is the time!—It should not be lost.'

Section 2.

On (the day) Wû-wû[1], the king halted on the
north of the Ho. When all the princes with their
hosts were assembled, the king reviewed the hosts,
and made the following declaration :—' Oh ! ye multitudes of the west, hearken all to my words.

' I have heard that the good man, doing good,
finds the day insufficient; and that the evil man,
doing evil, also finds the day insufficient. Now
Shâu, the king of Shang, with strength pursues
his lawless way. He has driven away the time-
worn sires, and cultivates intimacies with wicked
men. Dissolute, intemperate, reckless, oppressive,
his ministers have become assimilated to him; and
they form combinations and contract animosities,
and depend on their power to exterminate one
another. The innocent cry to Heaven. The odour
of such a state is felt on high. *

' Heaven loves the people, and the sovereign
should reverently carry out (this mind of) Heaven.
*K*ieh, the sovereign of Hsiâ, would not follow the

---

[1] In Book iii we are told that Wû commenced his march to
attack *K*âu-hsin, on Kwei-*k*î, the 2nd day of the moon. Calcu-
lating on to the day Wû-wû, we find that it was the 28th day of
the same moon.

128 example of Heaven, but sent forth his poisonous injuries through the states of the kingdom:—Heaven therefore gave its aid to Thang the Successful, and charged him to make an end of the appointment of Hsiâ.* But the crimes of Shâu exceed those of *K*ieh. He has degraded from office the greatly good man[1]; he has behaved with cruel tyranny to his reprover and helper[2]. He says that with him is the appointment of Heaven; he says that a reverent care of his conduct is not worth observing; he says that sacrifice is of no use; he says that tyranny is no harm.* The beacon for him to look to was not far off;—it was that king of Hsiâ. It would seem that Heaven is going by means of me to rule the people. My dreams coincide with my divinations; the auspicious omen is double.* My attack on Shang must succeed.

'Shâu has hundreds of thousands and millions of ordinary men, divided in heart and divided in practice;—I have of ministers, able to govern, ten men[3], one in heart and one in practice. Though he has his nearest relatives with him, they are not like my virtuous men. Heaven sees as my people see; Heaven hears as my people hear.* The people are blaming me, the One man, for my delay;—I must now go forward. My military prowess is displayed, and I enter his territories to take the wicked tyrant. My punishment (of evil) will be great, and more glorious than that executed by Thang. Rouse ye,

---

[1] The count of Wei.   [2] Pî-kan.

[3] Confucius tells us, in the Analects, VIII, xx, that one of these ten was a woman; but whether the lady was Wû's wife or mother is disputed.

my heroes! Do not think that he is not to be feared;—better think that he cannot be withstood. (His) people stand in trembling awe of him, as if the horns were falling from their heads. Oh! unite your energies, unite your hearts;—so shall you forthwith surely accomplish the work, to last for all ages!'

Section 3.

The time was on the morrow, when the king went round his six hosts in state, and made a clear declaration to all his officers. He said, 'Oh! my valiant men of the west, from Heaven are the illustrious courses of duty, of which the (several) requirements are quite plain. And now Shâu, the king of Shang, treats with contemptuous slight the five regular (virtues), and abandons himself to wild idleness and irreverence. He has cut himself off from Heaven, and brought enmity between himself and the people.*

' He cut through the leg-bones of those who were wading in the morning[1]; he cut out the heart of the worthy man[2]. By the use of his power, killing and murdering, he has poisoned and sickened all within the four seas. His honours and confidence are given to the villainous and bad. He has driven from him his instructors and guardians. He has thrown to the winds the statutes and penal laws. He has imprisoned and enslaved the upright officer[3]. He neglects the sacrifices to heaven and earth. He

---

[1] This was in winter. Observing some people then wading through a stream, *K*âu-hsin caused their legs to be cut through at the shank-bone, that he might see their marrow.

[2] Pî-kan.

[3] The count of *K*hî; see Book iv.

130 has discontinued the offerings in the ancestral temple. He makes contrivances of wonderful device and extraordinary cunning to please his wife[1].—God will no longer indulge him, but with a curse is sending down on him this ruin.* Do ye with untiring zeal support me, the One man, reverently to execute the punishment appointed by Heaven. The ancients have said, " He who soothes us is our sovereign ; he who oppresses us is our enemy." This solitary fellow Shâu, having exercised great tyranny, is your perpetual enemy. (It is said again), " In planting (a man's) virtue, strive to make it great; in putting away (a man's) wickedness, strive to do it from the roots." Here I, the little child, by the powerful help of you, all my officers, will utterly exterminate your enemy. Do you, all my officers, march forward with determined boldness to sustain your prince. Where there is much merit, there shall be large reward; where you do not so advance, there shall be conspicuous disgrace.

' Oh! (the virtue of) my deceased father Wăn was like the shining of the sun and moon. His brightness extended over the four quarters of the land, and shone signally in the western region. Hence it is that our _K_âu has received (the allegiance of) many states. If I subdue Shâu, it will not be from my prowess, but from the faultless (virtue of) my deceased father Wăn. If Shâu subdue me, it will not be from any fault of my deceased father Wăn, but because I, the little child, am not good.'

---

[1] The notorious Tâ-_k_î, the accounts of whose shameless wickedness and atrocious cruelties almost exceed belief.

Book II. The Speech at Mû.

It is the morning of the day of battle, for which the king has prepared his host by the three speeches of the last Book. Once more he addresses his confederate princes, his officers, and his men. He sets forth more briefly the intolerable wickedness of Shâu, and instructs and warns his troops how they are to behave in the fight.

Mû was in the south of the present district of *Khî*, department Wei-hui, Ho-nan, a tract of open country stretching into the district of *Kî*, and at no great distance from the capital of Shâu.

1. The time was the grey dawn of the day *Kiâ*-ʒze. On that morning the king came to the open country of Mû, in the borders of Shang, and addressed his army. In his left hand he carried a battle-axe, yellow with gold, and in his right he held a white ensign, which he waved, saying, 'Far are ye come, ye men of the western regions!' He added, 'Ah! ye hereditary rulers of my friendly states; ye managers of affairs,—the Ministers of Instruction, of War, and of Works; the great officers subordinate to these, and the many other officers; the master of my body-guards; the captains of thousands and captains of hundreds; and ye, O men of Yung, Shû, *K*iang, Mâo, Wei, Lû, Phang, and Pho[1], lift up your lances, join your shields, raise your spears :— I have a speech to make.'

---

[1] These are the names of eight different tribes or confederations of tribes of the south and west. We are to look for their sites in Sze-*kh*üan, Yün-nan, and Hû-pei. They were, no doubt, an important portion of Wû's army, but only as auxiliaries. It is too much to ascribe, as some have done, the overthrow of Shang to an irruption of barbarous people from the west.

K 2

132

2. The king (then) said, ' The ancients have said, " The hen does not announce the morning. The crowing of a hen in the morning (indicates) the sub-version of the family." Now Shâu, the king of Shang, follows only the words of his wife. In his blindness he has neglected the sacrifices which he ought to offer, and makes no response (for the favours that he has received) ;* he has also cast off his paternal and maternal relations, not treating them properly. They are only the vagabonds from all quarters, loaded with crimes, whom he honours and exalts, whom he employs and trusts, making them great officers and high nobles, so that they can tyrannize over the people, and exercise their vil-lainies in the cities of Shang.

' Now, I, Fâ, am simply executing respectfully the punishment appointed by Heaven.* In to-day's business do not advance more than six or seven steps, and then stop and adjust your ranks ;—my brave men, be energetic! Do not exceed four blows, five blows, six blows, or seven blows, and then stop and adjust your ranks ;—my brave men, be energetic! Display a martial bearing. Be like tigers and panthers, like bears and grisly bears,—(here) in the borders of Shang. Do not rush on those who fly (to us in submission), but receive them to serve our western land ;—my brave men, be energetic! If you be not energetic (in all these matters), you will bring destruction on your-selves.'

· Book III.

133

The Successful Completion of the War.

I have divided this Book into three chapters:—one, consisting of brief historical notes of the commencement and close of Wû's expedition; a second, giving the address (or a part of it) delivered by Wû to his nobles and officers on occasion, we may suppose, of their recognition of him as king, and his confirming some of them in their old states or appointments, and giving new ones to others; the third again historical, and relating several incidents of the battle between Wû and Shâu, and going on to subsequent events and important governmental measures of the new dynasty.

Most Chinese critics hold that portions of the Book are lost, and that the paragraphs of it are, besides, erroneously arranged. In what division of the documents of the Shû it should be classified, it is not easy to say. It is more like a 'Canon' than anything else.

1. In the first month, the day Zăn-khăn immediately followed the end of the moon's waning. The next day was Kwei-kî, when the king, in the morning, marched from Kâu¹ to attack and punish Shang. In the fourth month, at the first appearance of the moon, the king came from Shang to Făng², when he hushed all the movements of war, and proceeded to cultivate the arts of peace. He sent back his horses to the south of mount Hwâ,

---

¹ Kâu is, probably, Wû's capital, called Hâo, about ten miles south of the present district city of Khang-an, and not quite so far from his father's capital of Făng. The river Făng ran between them.

² In Făng there was the ancestral temple of the lords of Kâu, and thither from the capital of Shang, Wû now repaired for the purpose of sacrificing.

134 and let loose his oxen in the open country of Thâo-
lin ¹, showing to all under heaven that he would not
use them (again).

On the day Ting-wei, he sacrificed in the ancestral
temple of *K*âu, when (the princes) of the royal domain,
and of the Tien, Hâu, and Wei domains, all hurried
about, carrying the dishes.* The third day after was
Kăng-hsü, when he presented a burnt-offering to
Heaven, and worshipped towards the hills and
rivers, solemnly announcing the successful completion of the war.*

After the moon began to wane, the hereditary
princes of the various states, and all the officers,
received their appointments from *K*âu ².

2. The king spoke to the following effect :—'Oh !
ye host of princes, the first of our kings ³ founded
his state, and commenced (the enlargement of) its
territory. Kung Liû ⁴ was able to consolidate the
services of his predecessor. But it was the king
Thâi who laid the foundations of the royal inheritance. The king *K*î was diligent for the royal
House ; and my deceased father, king Wăn, completed his merit, and grandly received the appoint-

---

¹ The country about the hill of Mû-niû or Khwâ-fû, in the south-
east of the present department of Thung-*k*âu. Thâo-lin may be
translated 'Peach-forest.'

² The new dynasty of *K*âu was now fully inaugurated.

³ By 'the first of our kings,' we must understand *K*hî, Shun's
Minister of Agriculture ; and his state was that of Thâi.

⁴ Kung Liû, perhaps 'duke Liû,' appears in Pin, the present
Pin *K*âu of Shen-hsî, about the beginning of the eighteenth
century B.C., reviving the fallen fortunes of the House of *K*hî.
History is then silent about the family for more than four centuries,
when we find Than-fû, called here 'king Thâi,' founding the state
of *K*âu.

ment of Heaven, to soothe the regions of our great
land.*   The great states feared his strength ; the
small states thought fondly of his virtue.   In nine
years, however, the whole kingdom was not united
under his rule, and it fell to me, the little child, to
carry out his will.

'Detesting the crimes of Shang, I announced to
great Heaven and the sovereign Earth, to the famous
hill ¹ and the great river ¹ by which I passed, saying,
"I, Fâ, the principled, king of *K*âu by a long
descent, am about to administer a great correction
to Shang.   Shâu, the present king of Shang, is
without principle, cruel and destructive to the creatures of Heaven, injurious and tyrannical to the
multitudes of the people, lord of all the vagabonds
under heaven, who collect about him as fish in the
deep, and beasts in the prairie.   I, the little child,
having obtained (the help of) virtuous men, presume
reverently to comply with (the will of) God, and make
an end of his disorderly ways.*   Our flowery and great
land, and the tribes of the south and north, equally
follow and consent with me.   Reverently obeying
the determinate counsel of Heaven, I pursue my
punitive work to the east, to give tranquillity to its
men and women.   They meet me with their baskets
full of dark-coloured and yellow silks, thereby showing (the virtues) of us, the kings of *K*âu.   Heaven's
favours stir them up, so that they come with their
allegiance to our great state of *K*âu.   And now,
ye spirits, grant me your aid, that I may relieve
the millions of the people, and nothing turn out to
your shame."' *

135

---

¹ Probably mount Hwâ and the Ho.

136

3. On the day Wû-wû, the army crossed the ford of Mâng, and on Kwei-hâi it was drawn up in array in the borders of Shang, waiting for the gracious decision of Heaven. On *K*iâ-ʒze, at early dawn, Shâu led forward his troops, (looking) like a forest, and assembled them in the wild of Mû. But they offered no opposition to our army. Those in the front inverted their spears, and attacked those behind them, till they fled; and the blood flowed till it floated the pestles of the mortars. Thus did (king Wû) once don his armour, and the kingdom was grandly settled. He overturned the (existing) rule of Shang, and made government resume its old course. He delivered the count of *K*hî from prison, and raised a mound over the grave of Pî-kan. He bowed forward to the cross-bar of his carriage at the gate of Shang Yung's village [1]. He dispersed the treasures of the Stag Tower [2], and distributed the grain of *K*ü-*kh*iâo [3], thus conferring great gifts on all within the four seas, so that the people joyfully submitted to him.

He arranged the nobles in five orders [4], assigning the territories to them according to a threefold

---

[1] Shang Yung must have been some worthy in disgrace with Shâu, and living in the retirement of his village.

[2] The Stag Tower was the name of a place in the present department of Wei-hui, Ho-nan, where Shâu had accumulated great treasures. He fled to it after his defeat, and burned himself to death ; but it would appear he had not succeeded in consuming at the same time all his wealth.

[3] *K*ü-*kh*iâo was in the present district of *K*hü-*k*âu, department Kwang-phing, *K*ih-lî, where Shâu had collected great stores of grain.

[4] Dukes, marquises, earls, counts, and barons.

scale [1]. He gave offices only to the worthy, and   137
employments only to the able.   He attached great
importance to the people's being taught the duties
of the five relations of society, and to measures
for ensuring a sufficient supply of food, attention
to the rites of mourning, and to sacrifices.*   He
showed the reality of his truthfulness, and proved
clearly his righteousness.   He honoured virtue,
and rewarded merit.   Then he had only to let
his robes fall down, and fold his hands, and the
kingdom was orderly ruled.

BOOK IV. THE GREAT PLAN.

THE Great Plan, ordinarily classed among the 'Counsels' or
among the 'Instructions' of the Shû, might as well have a
place among the 'Canons.' It is a remarkable production, and
though it appears among the documents of the *K*âu dynasty,
there is claimed for the substance of it a much greater antiquity.
According to the introductory sentences, king Wû, the founder
of *K*âu, obtained it from the count of *K*hî in the same year, the
thirteenth of his dignity as Chief of the West, that he took the
field against the tyrant of Shang. The count of *K*hî, it is
understood, was the Grand-Master at the court of Shang, who
appears in the concluding Book of the last Part. He says there,
that, when ruin overtook the House of Shang, he would not be
the servant of another dynasty. Accordingly, he refused to
acknowledge the sovereignty of king Wû, who had delivered
him from the prison in which he had been confined by *K*âu-
hsin, and fled—or purposed perhaps to flee—to Corea. Wû
respected and admired his fidelity to the fallen dynasty, and
invested him with that territory. He then, it is said, felt con-
strained to appear at the court of *K*âu, when the king consulted

---

[1] Dukes and marquises had the same amount of territory assigned
to them, and counts and barons also.

138　　him on the principles of government; and the result was that
he communicated to him this Great Plan, with its nine divisions.
When we read the Book, we see that it belonged originally to
the time of Hsiâ, and that the larger portion of it should be
ascribed to the Great Yü, and was as old, indeed, as the reign
of Yâo. How it had come into the possession of the count of
Khî we cannot tell. Nor does it appear how far the language
of it should be ascribed to him. That the larger portion of
it had come down from the times of Hsiâ is not improbable.
The use of the number nine and other numbers, and the
naming of the various divisions of the Plan, are in harmony
with Yü's style and practice in his Counsels in the second
Part of our Classic, and in the second Part also of the Tribute
of Yü. We are told in the introductory sentences, that Heaven
or God gave the Plan with its divisions to Yü. To explain
the way in which the gift was made, there is a tradition about
a mysterious tortoise that appeared in the waters of the Lo,
bearing well-defined marks on its back from one to nine, and
that thereupon Yü determined the meaning of those marks and
of their numbers, and completed the nine divisions of the Plan.
Of this legend, however, it is not necessary to speak in connexion with the Shû, which does not mention it; it will come up
in connexion with the translation of the Yî King.

The Great Plan means the great model for the government of the
nation,—the method by which the people may be rendered
happy and tranquil, in harmony with their condition, through
the perfect character of the king, and his perfect administration
of government.

P. Gaubil says that the Book is a treatise at once of physics,
astrology, divination, morals, politics, and religion, and that
it has a sufficiently close resemblance to the work of Ocellus
the Lucanian. There is a shadowy resemblance between the
Great Plan and the curious specimen of Pythagorean doctrine
which we have in the treatise on the Universe; but the dissimi-
larities are still greater and more numerous. More especially
are the differences between the Greek mind, speculative,
and the Chinese mind, practical, apparent in the two works.
Where the Chinese writer loses himself in the sheerest follies of
his imagining, he yet gropes about for a rule to be of use in the
conduct of human affairs.

The whole of the treatise is divided into three chapters. The
first is introductory, and relates how the Great Plan with its

nine divisions was at first made known to Yü, and came at this
time to be communicated to king Wû; the second contains
the names of the nine divisions of the Plan; and in the third
we have a description of the several divisions. 'The whole,'
says a Chinese writer, 'exhibits the great model for the government of the nation.' The fifth or middle division on royal
perfection is the central one of the whole, about which the
Book revolves. The four divisions that precede it show how
this royal perfection is to be accomplished, and the four that
follow show how it is to be maintained.

1. In the thirteenth year [1], the king went to
enquire of the count of *Khî*, and said to him,
'Oh! count of *Khî*, Heaven, (working) unseen, secures the tranquillity of the lower people, aiding
them to be in harmony with their condition [2]. I
do not know how the unvarying principles (of its
method in doing so) should be set forth in due
order.'

The count of *Khî* thereupon replied, 'I have
heard that in old time Khwăn dammed up the
inundating waters, and thereby threw into disorder
the arrangement of the five elements. God was
consequently roused to anger, and did not give
him the Great Plan with its nine divisions, and
thus the unvarying principles (of Heaven's method)
were allowed to go to ruin.* Khwăn was therefore

---

[1] See the commencement of Book i.

[2] Khung Ying-tâ of the Thang dynasty says on this:—'The
people have been produced by supreme Heaven, and both body and
soul are Heaven's gift. Men have thus the material body and the
knowing mind, and Heaven further assists them, helping them to
harmonize their lives. The right and the wrong of their language,
the correctness and errors of their conduct, their enjoyment of
clothing and food, the rightness of their various movements ;—all
these things are to be harmonized by what they are endowed with
by Heaven.'

kept a prisoner till his death, and his son Yü rose up
(and entered on the same undertaking). To him
Heaven gave the Great Plan with its nine divisions, and the unvarying principles (of its method)
were set forth in their due order.' *

2. '(Of those divisions) the first is called " the
five elements ; " the second, " reverent attention to
the five (personal) matters ; " the third, " earnest
devotion to the eight (objects of) government ; "
the fourth, " the harmonious use of the five dividers
of time ; " the fifth, " the establishment and use of
royal perfection ; " the sixth, " the discriminating
use of the three virtues ; " the seventh, " the intelligent use of (the means for) the examination of
doubts ; " the eighth, " the thoughtful use of the
various verifications ; " the ninth, " the hortatory use
of the five (sources of) happiness, and the awing
use of the six (occasions of) suffering." '

3. i. ' First, of the five elements [1].—The first is

---

[1] Gaubil gives here 'les cinq hing,' without translating the
Chinese term. English sinologists have got into the habit of
rendering it by ' elements,' but it hardly seems possible to determine what the Chinese mean by it. We intend by ' elements '
' the first principles or ingredients of which all things are composed.' The Pythagoreans, by their four elements of earth, water,
air, and fire, did not intend so much the nature or essence
of material substances, as the forms under which matter is actually
presented to us. The character hsing, meaning ' to move,' ' to
be in action,' shows that the original conception of the Chinese
is of a different nature ; and it is said in the Khang-hsî Dictionary,
' The five hsing move and revolve between heaven and earth,
without ever ceasing, and hence they are named.' The editors of
the latest imperial edition of the Shû say, ' Distributed through the
four seasons, they make " the five dividers of time ; " exhibited in
prognostications, they give rise to divination by the tortoise-shell
and the reeds ; having lodgment in the human body, they produce
" the five personal matters ; " moved by good fortune and bad, they

water; the second is fire; the third, wood; the fourth, metal; and the fifth, earth. (The nature of) water is to soak and descend; of fire, to blaze and ascend; of wood, to be crooked and straight; of metal, to yield and change; while (that of) earth is seen in seed-sowing and in-gathering. That which soaks and descends becomes salt; that which blazes and ascends becomes bitter; that which is crooked and straight becomes sour; that which yields and changes becomes acrid; and from seed-sowing and in-gathering comes sweetness.'

ii. 'Second, of the five (personal) matters [1].—The first is the bodily demeanour; the second, speech; the third, seeing; the fourth, hearing; the fifth, thinking. (The virtue of) the bodily appearance is respectfulness; of speech, accordance (with reason); of seeing, clearness; of hearing, distinctness; of thinking, perspicaciousness. The respectfulness becomes manifest in gravity; accordance (with reason), in orderliness; the clearness, in wisdom; the distinctness, in deliberation; and the perspicaciousness, in sageness.'

iii. 'Third, of the eight (objects of) government [2].—

---

produce "the various verifications;" communicated to organisms, they produce the different natures, hard and soft, good and evil; working out their results in the changes of those organisms, they necessitate—here benevolence and there meanness, here longevity and there early death:—all these things are from the operation of the five hsing. But if we speak of them in their simplest and most important character, they are what man's life depends on, what the people cannot do without.' After all this, I should still be sorry to be required to say what the five hsing are.

[1] These five 'matters' are represented as being in the human person what the five hsing are in nature. Demeanour is the human correspondency of water, speech that of fire, &c.

[2] Medhurst calls the eight (objects of) government 'the eight

142 The first is food; the second, wealth and articles
of convenience; the third, sacrifices; the fourth, (the
business of) the Minister of Works; the fifth, (that
of) the Minister of Instruction; the sixth, (that of)
the Minister of Crime; the seventh, the observances
to be paid to guests; the eighth, the army.'

iv. 'Fourth, of the five dividers of time[1].—The
first is the year (or the planet Jupiter); the second,
the moon; the third, the sun; the fourth, the stars
and planets, and the zodiacal spaces; and the fifth,
the calendaric calculations.'

v. · 'Fifth, of royal perfection[2].—The sovereign,
having established (in himself) the highest degree
and pattern of excellence, concentrates in his own
person the five (sources of) happiness, and proceeds
to diffuse them, and give them to the multitudes
of the people. Then they, on their part, embodying your perfection, will give it (back) to you, and
secure the preservation of it. Among all the multitudes of the people there will be no unlawful con-
federacies, and among men (in office) there will be
no bad and selfish combinations;—let the sovereign

---

regulators,' and Gaubil calls them 'les huit règles du gouverne-
ment.' The phrase means the eight things to be attended to in
government,—its objects and departments.

[1] 'The five dividers of time' are with Medhurst 'the five
arrangers,' and with Gaubil 'les cinq périodes.' This division of
the Great Plan is substantially the same as Yâo's instructions to his
astronomers.

[2] By 'royal perfection' we are to understand the sovereign
when he is, or has made himself, all that he ought to be. 'Perfection' is 'the utmost point,' the extreme of excellence, realized in
the person of the sovereign, guiding his administrative measures,
and serving as an example and attractive influence to all below,
both ministers and people.

establish in (himself) the highest degree and pattern
of excellence.

143

'Among all the multitudes of the people there
will be those who have ability to plan and to act,
and who keep themselves (from evil):—do you
keep such in mind; and there will be those who,
not coming up to the highest point of excellence,
yet do not involve themselves in evil:—let the
sovereign receive such. And when a placid satisfaction appears in their countenances, and they say,
" Our love is fixed on virtue," do you then confer
favours on them;—those men will in this way advance to the perfection of the sovereign. Do not
let him oppress the friendless and childless, nor let
him fear the high and distinguished. When men
(in office) have ability and administrative power,
let them be made still more to cultivate their conduct; and the prosperity of the country will be promoted. All (such) right men, having a competency,
will go on in goodness. If you cannot cause them
to have what they love in their families, they will
forthwith proceed to be guilty of crime. As to
those who have not the love of virtue, although
you confer favours (and emoluments) on them, they
will (only) involve you in the guilt of employing the
evil.

'Without deflection, without unevenness,
Pursue the royal righteousness.
Without selfish likings,
Pursue the royal way.
Without selfish dislikings,
Pursue the royal path.
Avoid deflection, avoid partiality;—
Broad and long is the royal way.

144

> Avoid partiality, avoid deflection;—
> Level and easy is the royal way.
> Avoid perversity, avoid one-sidedness;—
> Correct and straight is the royal way.
> (Ever) seek for this perfect excellence,
> (Ever) turn to this perfect excellence.'

He went on to say, ' This amplification of the royal perfection contains the unchanging (rule), and is the (great) lesson;—yea, it is the lesson of God.* All the multitudes of the people, instructed in this amplification of the perfect excellence, and carrying it into practice, will thereby approximate to the glory of the Son of Heaven, and say, " The Son of Heaven is the parent of the people, and so becomes the sovereign of all under the sky." '

vi. ' Sixth, of the three virtues [1].—The first is correctness and straightforwardness; the second, strong rule; and the third, mild rule. In peace and tranquillity, correctness and straightforwardness (must sway); in violence and disorder, strong rule; in harmony and order, mild rule. For the reserved and retiring there should be (the stimulus of) the strong rule; for the high(-minded) and distinguished, (the restraint of) the mild rule.

' It belongs only to the sovereign to confer dignities and rewards, to display the terrors of majesty, and to receive the revenues (of the kingdom). There should be no such thing as a minister's conferring dignities or rewards, displaying the terrors of majesty, or receiving the revenues. Such

---

[1] ' The three virtues' are not personal attributes of the sovereign, but characteristics of his rule, the varied manifestations of the perfection described in the preceding division.

a thing is injurious to the clans, and fatal to the
states (of the kingdom); smaller affairs are thereby
managed in a one-sided and perverse manner, and
the people fall into assumptions and excesses.' ·

145

vii. 'Seventh, of the (means for the) examination
of doubts[1].—Officers having been chosen and appointed for divining by the tortoise-shell and the

---

[1] The practice of divination for the satisfaction of doubts was
thus used in China from the earliest times. In the Counsels of
Yü, p. 50, that sage proposes to Shun to submit the question of
who should be his successor on the throne to divination, and Shun
replies that he had already done so. Gaubil says that according to
the Great Plan divination was only used in doubtful cases; but if
such was the practice of the sages, diviners and soothsayers must
have formed, as they do now, a considerable and influential class in
society. The old methods of divination have fallen into disuse,
and we do not know how far other methods are employed and
sanctioned by the government. Those old methods were by
means of the tortoise-shell, and the stalks of the *Khî* plant. 'The
tortoise,' says *Kû* Hsî, 'after great length of years becomes intelligent; and the *Khî* plant will yield, when a hundred years old, a
hundred stalks from one root, and is also a spiritual and intelligent thing. The two divinations were in reality a questioning of
spiritual beings, the plant and the shell being employed, because
of their mysterious intelligence, to indicate their intimations. The
way of divination by the shell was by the application of fire to
scorch it till the indications appeared on it; and that by the stalks
of the plant was to manipulate in a prescribed way forty-nine of
them, eighteen different times, till the diagrams were formed.'
The outer shell of the tortoise was removed, leaving the inner
portion on which were the marks of the lines of the muscles of the
creature. This was smeared with a black pigment, and, fire being
applied beneath, the pigment was examined, and according as it
had been variously dried by the heat, presented the indications
mentioned in the text. The *Khî* plant was probably the Achillea
millefolium. It is cultivated largely on the mound over the grave
of Confucius. I brought from that two bundles of the dried stalks
in 1873.

[I]   L

146   stalks of the Achillea, they are to be charged (on occasion) to execute their duties. (In doing this), they will find (the appearances of) rain, of clearing up, of cloudiness, of want of connexion, and of crossing; and the inner and outer diagrams. In all (the indications) are seven;—five given by the shell, and two by the stalks; and (by means) of these any errors (in the mind) may be traced out. These officers having been appointed, when the divination is proceeded with, three men are to interpret the indications, and the (consenting) words of two of them are to be followed.*

'When you have doubts about any great matter, consult with your own mind; consult with your high ministers and officers; consult with the common people; consult the tortoise-shell and divining stalks. If you, the shell, the stalks, the ministers and officers, and the common people, all agree about a course, this is what is called a great concord, and the result will be the welfare of your person and good fortune to your descendants. If you, the shell, and the stalks agree, while the ministers, and officers, and the common people oppose, the result will be fortunate. If the ministers and officers, with the shell and stalks, agree, while you and the common people oppose, the result will be fortunate. If the common people, the shell, and the stalks agree, while you, with the ministers and officers, oppose, the result will be fortunate. If you and the shell agree, while the stalks, with the ministers and officers, and the common people, oppose, internal operations will be fortunate, and external under-takings unlucky. When the shell and stalks are both opposed to the views of men, there will be

good fortune in being still, and active operations   147
will be unlucky.'*

viii. 'Eighth, of the various verifications[1].—
They are rain, sunshine, heat, cold, wind, and
seasonableness. When the five come, all complete,
and each in its proper order, (even) the various
plants will be richly luxuriant. Should any one of
them be either excessively abundant or excessively
deficient, there will be evil.*

'There are the favourable verifications[2]:—namely,

---

[1] P. Gaubil renders by 'les apparences' the characters which I
have translated 'the various verifications,' observing that he could
not find any word which would cover the whole extent of the
meaning. He says, 'In the present case, the character signifies
meteors, phenomena, appearances, but in such sort that these have
relation to some other things with which they are connected;—
the meteor or phenomenon indicates some good or some evil. It
is a kind of correspondency which is supposed, it appears, to exist
between the ordinary events of the life of men and the constitution
of the air, according to the different seasons;—what is here said
supposes—I know not what physical speculation of those times. It
is needless to bring to bear on the text the interpretation of the
later Chinese, for they are full of false ideas on the subject of
physics. It may be also that the count of *Khî* wanted to play the
physicist on points which he did not know.' There seems to
underlie the words of the count that feeling of the harmony
between the natural and spiritual worlds, which occurs at times to
most men, and strongly affects minds under deep religious thought
or on the wings of poetic rapture, but the way in which he endeavours to give the subject a practical application can only be
characterised as grotesque.

[2] Compare with this what is said above on the second division of
the Plan, 'the five (personal) matters.' It is observed here by *B*hâi
*Kh*än, the disciple of *K*û Hsî, and whose commentary on the Shû
has, of all others, the greatest authority:—'To say that on occasion
of such and such a personal matter being realized, there will be
the favourable verification corresponding to it, or that, on occasion
of the failure of such realization, there will be the corresponding

L 2

148 of gravity, which is emblemed by seasonable rain;
of orderliness, emblemed by seasonable sunshine; of
wisdom, emblemed by seasonable heat; of deliberation, emblemed by seasonable cold; and of sageness,
emblemed by seasonable wind. There are (also)
the unfavourable verifications :—namely, of recklessness, emblemed by constant rain; of assumption,
emblemed by constant sunshine; of indolence, emblemed by constant heat; of hastiness, emblemed
by constant cold; and of stupidity, emblemed by
constant wind.' *

He went on to say, ' The king should examine
the (character of the whole) year; the high ministers
and officers (that of) the month; and the inferior
officers (that of) the day. If, throughout the year,
the month, the day, there be an unchanging seasonableness, all the grains will be matured; the measures
of government will be wise; heroic men will stand
forth distinguished; and in the families (of the
people) there will be peace and prosperity. If,
throughout the year, the month, the day, the seasonableness be interrupted, the various kinds of grain
will not be matured; the measures of government
will be dark and unwise; heroic men will be kept in

---

unfavourable verification, would betray a pertinacious obtuseness,
and show that the speaker was not a man to be talked with on the
mysterious operations of nature. It is not easy to describe the
reciprocal meeting of Heaven and men. The hidden springs
touched by failure and success, and the minute influences that
respond to them:—who can know these but the man that has
apprehended all truth?' This is in effect admitting that the statements in the text can be of no practical use. And the same
thing is admitted by the latest imperial editors of the Shû on the
use which the text goes on to make of the thoughtful use of the
verifications by the king and others.

obscurity; and in the families (of the people) there will be an absence of repose.

149

'By the common people the stars should be examined. Some stars love wind, and some love rain. The courses of the sun and moon give winter and summer. The way in which the moon follows the stars gives wind and rain.'

ix. 'Ninth, of the five (sources of) happiness [1].— The first is long life; the second, riches; the third, soundness of body and serenity of mind; the fourth, the love of virtue; and the fifth, fulfilling to the end the will (of Heaven).* Of the six extreme evils, the first is misfortune shortening the life; the second, sickness; the third, distress of mind; the fourth, poverty; the fifth, wickedness; the sixth, weakness [2].'

Book V. The Hounds of Lü.

Lü was the name of one of the rude tribes of the west, lying beyond the provinces of *K*âu. Its situation cannot be more exactly defined. Its people, in compliment to king Wû, and impressed by a sense of his growing power, sent to him some of their hounds, and he having received them, or intimated that he would do so, the Grand-Guardian remonstrated with him, showing that to receive such animals would be contrary to precedent, dangerous to the virtue of the sovereign, and was not the way to deal with outlying tribes and nations. The Grand-Guardian, it is supposed, was the duke of Shâo, author of the Announcement which forms the twelfth Book of this Part. The Book is one of the 'Instructions' of the Shû.

---

[1] It is hardly possible to see how this division enters into the scheme of the Great Plan.

[2] 'Wickedness' is, probably, boldness in what is evil, and 'weakness,' feebleness of will in what is good.

150 　　1. After the conquest of Shang, the way being open to the nine tribes of the Î[1] and the eight of the Man[1], the western tribe of Lü sent as tribute some of its hounds, on which the Grand-Guardian made 'the Hounds of Lü,' by way of instruction to the king.

2. He said, 'Oh! the intelligent kings paid careful attention to their virtue, and the wild tribes on every side acknowledged subjection to them. The nearer and the more remote all presented the productions of their countries,—in robes, food, and vessels for use. The kings then displayed the things thus drawn forth by their virtue, (distributing them) to the (princes of the) states of different surnames from their own, (to encourage them) not to neglect their duties. The (more) precious things and pieces of jade they distributed among their uncles in charge of states, thereby increasing their attachment (to the throne). The recipients did not despise the things, but saw in them the power of virtue.

'Complete virtue allows no contemptuous familiarity. When (a ruler) treats superior men with such familiarity, he cannot get them to give him all their hearts; when he so treats inferior men, he cannot get them to put forth for him all their strength. Let him keep from being in bondage to his ears and eyes, and strive to be correct in all his measures. By trifling intercourse with men, he ruins his virtue; by finding his amusement in things (of mere pleasure),

---

[1] By 'the nine Î and eight Man' we are to understand generally the barbarous tribes lying round the China of *K*âu. Those tribes are variously enumerated in the ancient books. Generally the Î are assigned to the east, the *Z*ung to the west, the Tî to the north, and the Man to the south.

he ruins his aims. His aims should repose in what   151
is right;· he should listen to words (also) in their
relation to what is right.

'When he does not do what is unprofitable to the
injury of what is profitable, his merit can be completed. When he does not value strange things to
the contemning things that are useful, his people
will be able to supply (all that he needs). (Even)
dogs and horses that are not native to his country
he will not keep. Fine birds and strange animals
he will not nourish in his state. When he does
not look on foreign things as precious, foreigners
will come to him; when it is real worth that is
precious to him, (his own) people near at hand will
be in a state of repose.

'Oh! early and late never be but earnest. If you
do not attend jealously to your small actions, the
result will be to affect your virtue in great matters ;
—in raising a mound of nine fathoms, the work may
be unfinished for want of one basket (of earth). If
you really pursue this course (which I indicate), the
people will preserve their possessions, and the throne
will descend from generation to generation.'

Book VI. The Metal-bound Coffer.

A CERTAIN chest or coffer, that was fastened with bands of metal,
and in which important state documents were deposited, plays
an important part among the incidents of the Book, which is
therefore called 'the Metal-bound Coffer.' To what class
among the documents of the Shû it should be assigned is
doubtful.

King Wû is very ill, and his death seems imminent. His brother,
the duke of *K*âu, apprehensive of the disasters which such an

152 event would occasion to their infant dynasty, conceives the idea
of dying in his stead, and prays to 'the three kings,' their immediate progenitors, that he might be taken and king Wû left.
Having done so, and divined that he was heard, he deposits
the prayer in the metal-bound coffer. The king gets well,
and the duke is also spared; but five years later, Wû does die,
and is succeeded by his son, a boy only thirteen years old.
Rumours are spread abroad that the duke has designs on the
throne, and he withdraws for a time from the court. At length,
in the third year of the young king, Heaven interposes. He has
occasion to open the coffer, and the prayer of the duke is found.
His devotion to his brother and to the interests of their family
is brought to light. The boy-monarch weeps because of the
unjust suspicions he had harboured, and welcomes the duke
back to court, amid unmistakeable demonstrations of the
approval of Heaven.

The whole narrative is a very pleasing episode in the history of
the times. It divides itself naturally into two chapters :—the
first, ending with the placing the prayer in the coffer; and the
second, detailing how it was brought to light, and the consequences of the discovery.

It is in this Book that we first meet in the Shû with the duke of
*K*âu, a name in Chinese history only second to that of Confucius. He was the legislator and consolidator of the dynasty of
*K*âu, equally mighty in words and in deeds,—a man of counsel
and of action. Confucius regarded his memory with reverence,
and spoke of it as a sign of his own failing powers, that the
duke of *K*âu no longer appeared to him in his dreams. He
was the fourth son of king Wăn; his name was Tan, and
he had for his appanage the territory of *K*âu, where Than-fû,
canonized by him as king Thâi, first placed the seat of his
family in B.C. 1327, and hence he is commonly called 'the duke
of *K*âu.'

1. Two years after the conquest of Shang[1], the
king fell ill, and was quite disconsolate. The two
(other great) dukes[2] said, 'Let us reverently consult

---

[1] B.C. 1121.

[2] These were the duke of Shâo, to whom the preceding Book
is ascribed, and Thâi-kung, who became the first of the lords
of *Kh*î.

the tortoise-shell about the king;' but the duke of   153
*K*âu said, 'You must not so distress our former
kings[1].' He then took the business on himself, and
reared three altars of earth on the same cleared
space; and having made another altar on the south
of these, and facing the north, he took there his own
position. Having put a round symbol of jade (on
each of the three altars), and holding in his hands the
lengthened symbol (of his own rank), he addressed
the kings Thâi, *K*î, and Wăn.*

The (grand) historiographer had written on tablets
his prayer, which was to this effect:—'A. B., your
great descendant, is suffering from a severe and
violent disease;—if you three kings have in heaven
the charge of (watching over) him, (Heaven's) great
son, let me Tan be a substitute for his person[2].
I was lovingly obedient to my father; I am possessed
of many abilities and arts, which fit me to serve
spiritual beings. Your great descendant, on the
other hand, has not so many abilities and arts as
I, and is not so capable of serving spiritual beings.
And moreover he was appointed in the hall of God
to extend his aid all over the kingdom, so that he
might establish your descendants in this lower earth.
The people of the four quarters all stand in reverent

---

[1] He negatives their proposal, having determined to take the
whole thing on himself.

[2] Two things are here plain:—first, that the duke of *K*âu offered
himself to die in the room of his brother; and second, that he
thought that his offer might somehow be accepted through the
intervention of the great kings, their progenitors. He proceeds to
give his reasons for making such an offer, which are sufficiently
interesting. It was hardly necessary for Chinese scholars to take
the pains they have done to free the duke from the charge of
boasting in them.

154 awe of him. Oh! do not let that precious Heaven-conferred appointment fall to the ground, and (all the long line of) our former kings will also have one in whom they can ever rest at our sacrifices.* I will now seek for your determination (in this matter) from the great tortoise-shell. If you grant me (my request), I will take these symbols and this mace, and return and wait for your orders. If you do not grant it, I will put them by¹.'*

The duke then divined with the three tortoise-shells, and all were favourable. He opened with a key the place where the (oracular) responses were kept, and looked at them, and they also were favourable. He said, 'According to the form (of the prognostic) the king will take no injury. I, the little child, have got the renewal of his appointment from the three kings, by whom a long futurity has been consulted for. I have now to wait for the issue. They can provide for our One man.'*

When the duke returned, he placed the tablets (of the prayer) in a metal-bound coffer², and next day the king got better.

2. (Afterwards), upon the death of king Wû, (the duke's) elder brother, he of Kwan, and his younger brothers, spread a baseless report through the king-

---

¹ I suppose that the divination took place before the altars, and that a different shell was used to ascertain the mind of each king. The oracular responses would be a few lines, kept apart by themselves, and consulted, on occasion, according to certain rules which have not come down to the present day.

² Many scholars think that it was this coffer which contained the oracles of divination mentioned above. It may have been so ; but I rather suppose it to have been different, and a special chest in which important archives of the dynasty, to be referred to on great emergencies, were kept.

dom, to the effect that the duke would do no good   155
to the (king's) young son.   On this the duke said to
the two (other great) dukes, ' If I do not take the
law (to these men), I shall not be able to make my
report to the former kings¹.' *

He resided (accordingly) in the east for two years²,
when the criminals were taken (and brought to justice).   Afterwards he made a poem to present to
the king, and called it ' the Owl³.'   The king on
his part did not dare to blame the duke.

In the autumn, when the grain was abundant and
ripe, but before it was reaped, Heaven sent a great
storm of thunder and lightning, along with wind, by
which the grain was all broken down, and great trees
torn up.   The people were greatly terrified ; and
the king and great officers, all in their caps of state,
proceeded to open the metal-bound coffer and examine the writings in it, where they found the words
of the duke when he took on himself the business
of being a substitute for king Wû.   The two (great)
dukes and the king asked the historiographer and
all the other officers (acquainted with the transaction) about the thing, and they replied, ' It was
really thus ; but ah ! the duke charged us that we

---

¹ Wû died in B. C. 1116, and was succeeded by his son Sung,
who is known in history as king *Kẖăng*, or ' the Completer.'
He was at the time only thirteen years old, and his uncle, the
duke of *K*âu, acted as regent.   The jealousy of his elder brother
Hsien, ' lord of Kwan,' and two younger brothers, was excited, and
they spread the rumour which is referred to, and entered into a
conspiracy with the son of the tyrant of Shang, to overthrow the
new dynasty.

² These two years were spent in military operations against the
revolters.

³ See the Book of Poetry, Part I, xv, Ode 2.

156 should not presume to speak about it.' The king held the writing in his hand, and wept, saying, 'We need not (now) go on reverently to divine. Formerly the duke was thus earnest for the royal House, but I, being a child, did not know it. Now Heaven has moved its terrors to display his virtue. That I, the little child, (now) go with my new views and feelings to meet him, is what the rules of propriety of our kingdom require.'*

The king then went out to the borders (to meet the duke), when Heaven sent down rain, and, by virtue of a contrary wind, the grain all rose up. The two (great) dukes gave orders to the people to take up the trees that had fallen and replace them. The year then turned out very fruitful.*

BOOK VII. THE GREAT ANNOUNCEMENT.

THIS 'Great Announcement' was called forth by the emergency referred to in the second chapter of the last Book. The prefatory notice says, 'When king Wû had deceased, the three overseers and the wild tribes of the Hwâi rebelled. The duke of *K*âu acted as minister for king *K*hǎng, and having purposed to make an end of the House of Yin (or Shang), he made 'the Great Announcement.' Such was the occasion on which the Book was composed. The young king speaks in it the words and sentiments of the duke of *K*âu; and hence the style in which it commences, 'The king speaks to the following effect.'

The young sovereign speaks of the responsibility lying on him to maintain the kingdom gained by the virtues and prowess of his father, and of the senseless movements of the House of Shang to regain its supremacy. He complains of the reluctance of many of the princes and high officers to second him in putting down revolt, and proclaims with painful reiteration the support and assurances of success which he has received from the divining shell. His traitorous uncles, who were confederate with the son of the tyrant of Shang, are only alluded to.

1. The king speaks to the following effect :—' Ho!   157
I make a great announcement to you, (the princes
of) the many states, and to you, the managers of my
affairs.—We are unpitied, and Heaven sends down
calamities on our House, without the least inter-
mission¹.*   It greatly occupies my thoughts that I,
so very young, have inherited this illimitable patrimony with its destinies and domains. I cannot
display wisdom and lead the people to prosperity;
and how much less should I be able to reach the
knowledge of the decree of Heaven!*   Yes, I who
am but a little child am in the position of one who
has to go through a deep water ;—I must go and seek
where I can cross over. I must diffuse the elegant
institutions of my predecessor and display the
appointment which he received (from Heaven) ;—
so shall I not be forgetful of his great work. Nor
shall I dare to restrain the majesty of Heaven in
sending down its inflictions (on the criminals)².' *

2. ' The Tranquillizing king ³ left to me the great
precious tortoise-shell, to bring into connexion with
me the intelligence of Heaven. I divined by it, and
it told me that there would be great trouble in the
region of the west ⁴, and that the western people
would not be still⁴.*   Accordingly we have these
senseless movements. Small and reduced as Yin

---

¹ With reference, probably, to the early death of his father, and
the revolt that followed quickly upon it.
² The duke had made up his mind that he would deal stern
justice even on his own brothers.
³ King Wû.
⁴ The troubles arose in the east, and not in the west. We
do not know the facts in the state of the kingdom sufficiently to
explain every difficulty in these Books. Perhaps the oracular
response had been purposely ambiguous.

158   now is, (its prince) greatly dares to take in hand its
(broken) line.   Though Heaven sent down its terrors
(on his House), yet knowing of the evils in our
kingdom, and that the people are not tranquil, he
says, "I will recover (my patrimony);" and so (he
wishes to) make our *K*âu a border territory again.

'One day there was a senseless movement, and
the day after, ten men of worth appeared among the
people, to help me to go forward to restore tranquillity and perpetuate the plans (of my father)[1].
The great business I am engaging in will (thus)
have a successful issue.   I have divined (also) by the
tortoise-shell, and always got a favourable response.*
Therefore I tell you, the princes of my friendly states,
and you, the directors of departments, my officers,
and the managers of my affairs,—I have obtained
a favourable reply to my divinations.   I will go forward with you from all the states, and punish those
vagabond and transported ministers of Yin.'

3. '(But) you the princes of the various states,
and you the various officers and managers of my
affairs, all retort on me, saying, "The hardships will
be great, and that the people are not quiet has its
source really in the king's palace and in the mansions
of the princes in that (rebellious) state[2].   We little
ones, and the old and reverend men as well, think
the expedition ill-advised;—why does your Majesty
not go contrary to the divinations?"   I, in my youth,
(also) think continually of these hardships, and say,

---

[1] Who these 'ten men of worth' were, we do not know, nor
the circumstances in which they came forward to help the
government.

[2] Here is an allusion, as plain as the duke could permit himself
to make, to the complicity of his brothers in the existing troubles.

Alas! these senseless movements will deplorably   159
afflict the wifeless men and widows! But I am the
servant of Heaven, which has assigned me this
great task, and laid the hard duty on my person.*
I therefore, the young one, do not pity myself; and
it would be right in you, the many officers, the
directors of departments, and the managers of my
affairs, to comfort me, saying, " Do not be distressed
with sorrow. We shall surely complete the plans of
your Tranquillizing father."

‘Yes, I, the little child, dare not disregard the
charge of God¹.* Heaven, favourable to the Tranquillizing king, gave such prosperity to our small
country of *K*âu. The Tranquillizing king divined
and acted accordingly, and so he calmly received
his (great) appointment. Now when Heaven is
(evidently) aiding the people, how much more should
we follow the indications of the shell! Oh! the
clearly intimated will of Heaven is to be feared :—
it is to help my great inheritance !’ *

4. The king says, ‘You, who are the old ministers,
are fully able to remember the past ; you know how
great was the toil of the Tranquillizing king. Where
Heaven (now) shuts up (our path) and distresses us,
is the place where I must accomplish my work ;—
I dare not but do my utmost to complete the plans
of the Tranquillizing king. It is on this account that
I use such efforts to remove the doubts and carry
forward the inclinations of the princes of my friendly
states. And Heaven assists me with sincere expressions (of sympathy), which I have ascertained among

---

¹ Probably the charge understood to be conveyed by the result
of the divinations spoken of above.

160   the people ;—how dare I but aim at the completion
of the work formerly begun by the Tranquillizer ?
Heaven, moreover, is thus toiling and distressing the
people ;—it is as if they were suffering from disease ;
how dare I allow (the appointment) which my predecessor, the Tranquillizer, received, to be without its
happy fulfilment ?' *

The king says, ' Formerly, at the initiation of this
expedition, I spoke of its difficulties, and thought of
them daily. But when a deceased father, (wishing)
to build a house, had laid out the plan, if his son be
unwilling to raise up the hall, how much less will he
be willing to complete the roof ! Or if the father
had broken up the ground, and his son be unwilling
to sow the seed, how much less will he be willing to
reap the crop ! In such a case could the father, (who
had himself) been so reverently attentive (to his
objects), have been willing to say, " I have a son
who will not abandon his patrimony?"—How dare
I therefore but use all my powers to give a happy
settlement to the great charge entrusted to the
Tranquillizing king ? If among the friends of an elder
brother or a deceased father there be those who
attack his son, will the elders of the people encourage (the attack), and not (come to the) rescue ?'

5. The king says, ' Oh ! take heart, ye princes of
the various states, and ye managers of my affairs.
The enlightening of the country was from the wise,
even from the ten men¹ who obeyed and knew the

---

¹ 'The ten men' here can hardly be the ' ten men of worth'
above in the second chapter. We must find them rather in the
' ten virtuous men, one in heart and one in practice, capable
of good,' mentioned by king Wû, in the second Part of the
Great Declaration.

charge of God,* and the real assistance given by　161
Heaven. ˊAt that time none of you presumed to
change the rules (prescribed by the Tranquillizing
king).　And now when Heaven is sending down
calamity on the country of *K*âu, and the authors of
these great distresses (make it appear on a grand
scale as if) the inmates of a house were mutually
to attack óne another, you are without any knowledge that the decree of Heaven is not to be
changed ! *

' I ever think and say, Heaven in destroying Yin was
doing husbandman's work[1];—how dare I but complete
the work on my fields ?　Heaven will thereby show
its favour to my predecessor, the Tranquillizer.　How
should I be all for the oracle of divination, and presume not to follow (your advice)? *　I am following
the Tranquillizer, whose purpose embraced all within
the limits of the land.　How much more must I
proceed, when the divinations are all favourable !　It
is on these accounts that I make this expedition in
force to the east.　There is no mistake about the
decree of Heaven.　The indications given by the
tortoise-shell are all to the same effect.' *

Book VIII. The Charge to the Count of Wei.

The count of Wei was the principal character in the eleventh
Book of the last Part,- from which it appeared that he was
a brother of the tyrant *K*âu-hsin.　We saw how his friends
advised him to withdraw from the court of Shang, and save

---

[1] That is, thorough work,—clearing the ground of weeds, and
not letting their roots remain.

[I]　　　　　　　　M

162   himself from the destruction that was impending over their House. He had done so, and king Wû had probably continued him in the possession of his appanage of Wei, while Wû-kăng, the son of the tyrant, had been spared, and entrusted with the duty of continuing the sacrifices to the great Thang and the other sovereigns of the House of Shang. Now that Wû-kăng has been punished with death for his rebellion, the duke of *K*âu summons the count of Wei to court, and in the name of king *K*hăng invests him with the dukedom of Sung, corresponding to the present department of Kwei-teh, Ho-nan, there to be the representative of the line of the departed kings of Shang.

The king speaks to the following effect:—'Ho! eldest son of the king of Yin, examining into antiquity, (I find) that the honouring of the virtuous (belongs to their descendants) who resemble them in worth, and (I appoint) you to continue the line of the kings your ancestors, observing their ceremonies and taking care of their various relics. Come (also) as a guest to our royal House[1], and enjoy the prosperity of our kingdom, for ever and ever without end.

'Oh! your ancestor, Thang the Successful, was reverent and sage, (with a virtue) vast and deep. The favour and help of great Heaven lighted upon him, and he grandly received its appointment, to soothe the people by his gentleness, and remove the wicked oppressions from which they were suffering.* His achievements affected his age, and his virtue was transmitted to his posterity. And you are the one who pursue and cultivate his plans;—this praise

---

[1] Under the dynasty of *K*âu, the representatives of the two previous dynasties of Shang and Hsiâ were distinguished above the other princes of the kingdom, and denominated 'guests' of the sovereign, coming to his court and assisting in the services in his ancestral temple, nearly on a footing of equality with him.

has belonged to you for long. Reverently and care-   163
fully have you discharged your filial duties ; gravely
and respectfully you behave to spirits and to men.*
I admire your virtue, and pronounce it great and not
to be forgotten. God will always enjoy your offerings ; the people will be reverently harmonious
(under your sway).* I raise you therefore to the
rank of high duke, to rule this eastern part of our
great land[1].

' Be reverent. Go and diffuse abroad your instructions. Be carefully observant of your robes and
(other accompaniments of) your appointment[2]; follow
and observe the proper statutes ;—so as to prove
a bulwark to the royal House. Enlarge (the fame
of) your meritorious ancestor; be a law to your
people ;—so as for ever to preserve your dignity.
(So also) shall you be a help to me, the One man ;
future ages will enjoy (the benefit of) your virtue ;
all the states will take you for a pattern ;—and thus
you will make our dynasty of *K*âu never weary
of you.

' Oh! go, and be prosperous. Do not disregard
my charge.'

---

[1] Sung lay east from Făng and Hâo, the capitals of Wăn and
Wû, which were in the present department of Hsî-an, Shen-hsî.

[2] Meaning probably that he was to bear in mind that, however
illustrious his descent, he was still a subject of the king of *K*âu.

164

Book IX.

The Announcement to the Prince of Khang.

Of the ten sons of king Wăn, the ninth was called Fâng, and is generally spoken of as Khang Shû, or 'the uncle, (the prince of) Khang.' We must conclude that Khang was the name of Făng's appanage, somewhere in the royal domain. This Book contains the charge given to him on his appointment to be marquis of Wei (the Chinese name is quite different from that of the appanage of the count of Wei), the chief city of which was *K*âo-ko, that had been the capital of *K*âu-hsin. It extended westward from the present Khâi *K*âu, department Tâ-ming, *K*îh-lî, to the borders of the departments of Wei-hui and Hwâi-*kh*ing, Ho-nan.

The Book is called an 'Announcement,' whereas it properly belongs to the class of 'Charges.' Whether the king who speaks in it, and gives the charge be Wû, or his son king *Kh*ăng, is a point on which there is much difference of opinion among Chinese critics. The older view that the appointment of Făng to be marquis of Wei, and ruler of that part of the people who might be expected to cling most tenaciously to the memory of the Shang dynasty, took place after the death of Wû-kăng, the son of the tyrant, and was made by the duke of *K*âu, in the name of king *Kh*ăng, is on the whole attended with the fewer difficulties.

The first paragraph, which appears within brackets, does not really belong to this Book, but to the thirteenth, where it will be found again. How it got removed from its proper place, and prefixed to the charge to the prince of Khang, is a question on which it is not necessary to enter. The key-note of the whole charge is in what is said, at the commencement of the first of the five chapters into which I have divided it, about king Wăn, that 'he was able to illustrate his virtue and be careful in the use of punishments.' The first chapter celebrates the exhibition of these two things given by Wăn, whereby he laid the foundations of the great destiny of his House, and set an example to his descendants. The second inculcates on Făng how he should illustrate his virtue, as the basis of his good government of the people entrusted to him. The third inculcates on him how he should be careful in the use of

punishments, and sets forth the happy effects of his being so. 165
The fourth insists on the influence of virtue, as being superior
in government to that of punishment, and how punishments
should all be regulated by the ruler's virtue. The last chapter
winds the subject up with a reference to the uncertainty of the
appointments of Heaven, and their dependance for permanence
on the discharge of the duties connected with them by those
on whom they have lighted.

[On the third month, when the moon began to
wane, the duke of *K*âu commenced the foundations,
and proceeded to build the new great city of Lo, of
the eastern states. The people from every quarter
assembled in great harmony. From the Hâu, Tien,
Nan, 3hâi, and Wei domains, the various officers
stimulated this harmony of the people, and introduced them to the business there was to be done
for *K*âu. The duke encouraged all to diligence, and
made a great announcement about the performance
(of the works).]

1. The king speaks to this effect :—' Head of the
princes[1], and my younger brother[2], little one[2], Făng,
it was your greatly distinguished father, the king
Wăn, who was able to illustrate his virtue and be careful in the use of punishments. He did not dare to
treat with contempt (even) wifeless men and widows.
He employed the employable, and revered the reverend; he was terrible to those who needed to be
awed :—so getting distinction among the people.
It was thus he laid the foundations of (the sway
of) our small portion of the kingdom[3], and the one

---

[1] Făng had, no doubt, been made chief or leader of all the
feudal lords in one of the *K*âu or provinces of the kingdom.

[2] The duke of *K*âu, though speaking in the name of king
*Kh*ăng, yet addresses Făng from the standpoint of his own
relation to him.

[3] Referring to the original principality of *K*âu.

166 or two (neighbouring) regions were brought under his improving influence, until throughout our western land all placed in him their reliance. The fame of him ascended up to the high God, and God approved. Heaven accordingly gave a grand charge to king Wăn, to exterminate the great (dynasty of) Yin, and grandly receive its appointment, so that the various countries belonging to it and their peoples were brought to an orderly condition.* Then your unworthy elder brother[1] exerted himself; and thus it is that you Făng, the little one, are here in this eastern region.'

2. The king says, 'Oh! Făng, bear these things in mind. Now (your success in the management of) the people will depend on your reverently following your father Wăn ;—do you carry out his virtuous words which you have heard, and clothe yourself with them. (Moreover), where you go, seek out among (the traces of) the former wise kings of Yin what you may use in protecting and regulating their people. (Again), you must in the remote distance study the (ways of) the old accomplished men of Shang, that you may establish your heart, and know how to instruct (the people). (Further still), you must search out besides what is to be learned of the wise kings of antiquity, and employ it in tranquillizing and protecting the people. (Finally), enlarge (your thoughts) to (the comprehension of all) heavenly (principles), and virtue will be richly displayed in your person, so that you will not render nugatory the king's charge.'

---

[1] Is it strange that the duke should thus speak of king Wû? Should we not think the better of him for it?

The king says, 'Oh! Făng, the little one, be respectfully careful, as if you were suffering from a disease. Awful though Heaven be, it yet helps the sincere.* The feelings of the people can for the most part be discerned; but it is difficult to preserve (the attachment of) the lower classes. Where you go, employ all your heart. Do not seek repose, nor be fond of ease and pleasure. I have read the saying,—" Dissatisfaction is caused not so much by great things, or by small things, as by (a ruler's) observance of principle or the reverse, and by his energy of conduct or the reverse." Yes, it is yours, O little one,—it is your business to enlarge the royal (influence), and to protect the people of Yin in harmony with their feelings. Thus also shall you assist the king, consolidating the appointment of Heaven, and renovating the people.'*

3. The king says, 'Oh! Făng, deal reverently and intelligently in your infliction of punishments. When men commit small crimes, which are not mischances, but purposed, they of themselves doing what is contrary to the laws intentionally, though their crimes be but small, you may not but put them to death. But in the case of great crimes, which were not purposed, but from mischance and misfortune, accidental, if the transgressors confess their guilt without reserve, you must not put them to death.'

The king says, 'Oh! Făng, there must be the orderly regulation (of this matter). When you show a great discrimination, subduing (men's hearts), the people will admonish one another, and strive to be obedient. (Deal firmly yet tenderly with evil), as if it were a disease in your own person, and the people

168   will entirely put away their faults. (Deal with them) as if you were protecting your own infants, and the people will be tranquil and orderly. It is not you, O Făng, who (can presume to) inflict a (severe) punishment or death upon a man ;—do not, to please yourself, so punish a man or put him to death.' Moreover, he says, 'It is not you, O Făng, who (can presume to inflict a lighter punishment), cutting off a man's nose or ears ;—do not, to please yourself, cause a man's nose or ears to be cut off.'

The king says, 'In things beyond (your immediate supervision), have laws set forth which the officers may observe, and these should be the penal laws of Yin which were rightly ordered.' He also says, 'In examining the evidence in (criminal) cases, reflect upon it for five or six days, yea, for ten days or three months. You may then boldly come to a decision in such cases[1].'

The king says, 'In setting forth the business of the laws, the punishments will be determined by (what were) the regular laws of Yin. But you must see that those punishments, and (especially) the penalty of death, be righteous. And you must not let them be warped to agree with your own inclinations, O Făng. Then shall they be entirely accordant with right, and you may say, " They are properly ordered ;" yet you must say (at the same time), " Perhaps they are not yet entirely accordant with right." Yes, though you are the little one, who has a heart like you, O Făng ? My heart and my virtue are also known to you.

---

[1] This is supposed to refer to a case where guilt would involve death, so that there could be no remedying a wrong decision.

'All who of themselves commit crimes, robbing, stealing, practising villainy and treachery, and who kill men or violently assault them to take their property, being reckless and fearless of death;— these are abhorred by all.'

The king says, 'O Făng, such great criminals are greatly abhorred, and how much more (detestable) are the unfilial and unbrotherly!—as the son who does not reverently discharge his duty to his father, but greatly wounds his father's heart, and the father who can (no longer) love his son, but hates him; as the younger brother who does not think of the manifest will of Heaven, and refuses to respect his elder brother, and the elder brother who does not think of the toil of their parents in bringing up their children, and is very unfriendly to his junior. If we who are charged with government do not treat parties who proceed to such wickedness as offenders, the laws (of our nature) given by Heaven to our people will be thrown into great disorder and destroyed. You must resolve to deal speedily with such according to the penal laws of king Wăn, punishing them severely and not pardoning.

'Those who are disobedient (to natural principles) are to be thus subjected to the laws;—how much more the officers employed in your state as the instructors of the youth, the heads of the official departments, and the smaller officers charged with their several commissions, when they propagate other lessons, seeking the praise of the people, not thinking (of their duty), nor using (the rules for their offices), but distressing their ruler! These lead on (the people) to wickedness, and are an abomination to me. Shall they be let alone? Do you speedily, according to what is right, put them to death.

'And you will be yourself ruler and president;— if you cannot manage your own household, with your smaller officers, and the heads of departments in the state, but use only terror and violence, you will greatly set aside the royal charge, and be trying to regulate your state contrary to virtue. You must in everything reverence the statutes, and proceed by them to the happy rule of the people. There were the reverence of king Wăn and his caution;—in proceeding by them to the happy rule of the people, say, " If I could only attain to them —." So will you make me, the One man, to rejoice.'

4. The king says, 'O Făng, when I think clearly of the people, I see that they should be led (by example) to happiness and tranquillity. I think of the virtue of the former wise kings of Yin, whereby they tranquillized and regulated the people, and rouse myself to make it my own. Moreover, the people now are sure to follow a leader. If one do not lead them, he cannot be said to exercise a government in their state.'

The king says, 'O Făng, I cannot dispense with the inspection (of the ancients), and I make this declaration to you about virtue in the use of punishments. Now the people are not quiet; they have not yet stilled their minds; notwithstanding my leading of them, they have not come to accord (with my government). I clearly consider that severe as are the inflictions of Heaven on me, I dare not murmur. The crimes (of the people), though they were not great or many, (would all be chargeable on me), and how much more shall this be said

when the report of them goes up so manifestly to   171
heaven !'

The king says, ' Oh! Făng, be reverent! Do not
what will cause murmurings; and do not use bad
counsels and uncommon ways. With the determination of sincerity, give yourself to imitate the active
virtue (of the ancients). Hereby give repose to
your mind, examine your virtue, send far forward
your plans; and thus by your generous forbearance
you will make the people repose in what is good,
and I shall not have to blame you or cast you off.'

5. The king says, ' Oh! you, Făng, the little one,
(Heaven's) appointments are not unchanging.* Think
of this, and do not make me deprive you of your
dignity. Make illustrious the charge which you
have received; exalt (the instructions) which you
have heard, and tranquillize and regulate the people
accordingly.'

The king speaks to this effect: 'Go, Făng. Do
not disregard the statutes you should reverence;
hearken to what I have told you;—so shall you
among the people of Yin enjoy (your dignity), and
hand it down to your posterity.'

Book X.

The Announcement about Drunkenness.

This Announcement was, like the last, made to Făng, the
prince of Khang, about the time when he was invested with
the principality of Wei. Mention has often been made in
previous documents of the Shû of the drunken debauchery of
*K*ieh as the chief cause of the downfal of the dynasty of Hsiâ,
and of the same vice in *K*âu-hsin, the last of the kings of

172 Shang. The people of Shang had followed the example of their sovereign, and drunkenness, with its attendant immoralities, characterised both the highest and lowest classes of society. One of Făng's most difficult tasks in his administration would be, to correct this evil habit, and he is called in this Book to the undertaking. He is instructed in the proper use and the allowable uses of spirits; the disastrous consequences of drunkenness are set forth ; and he is summoned to roll back the flood of its desolation from his officers and people.

I have divided the Book into two chapters :—the one preliminary, showing the original use and the permissible uses of ardent spirits; the other, showing how drunkenness had proved the ruin of the Shang dynasty, and how they of Kâu, and particularly Făng in Wei, should turn the lesson to account.

The title might be translated—' The Announcement about Spirits,' but the cursory reader would most readily suppose that the discourse was about Spiritual Beings. The Chinese term Kiû, that is here employed, is often translated by win e, but it denotes, it seems to me, ardent spirits. As Gaubil says, ' We have here to do with le vin du riz, the art of which was discovered, according to most writers, in the time of Yü, the founder of the first dynasty. The grape was not introduced to China till that of the first Han.'

[Since the above sentences were in manuscript, the Rev. Dr. Edkins of Pekin has stated at a meeting of the North-China branch of the Royal Asiatic Society, and in a letter to myself (April 24th), that he has lately investigated the question whether the Kiû of the ancient Chinese was spirits or not, and found that distillation was first known in China in the Mongol or Yüan dynasty (A. D. 1280–1367), so that the Arabs must have the credit of the invention; that the process in making Kiû was brewing, or nearly so, but, as the term b e e r is inadmissible in a translation of the classics, he would prefer to use the term w in e ; and that Kiû with S h â o ('fired,' 'ardent') before it, means spirits, but without Shâo, it means wine.

If the whole process of Dr. Edkins' investigation were before me, I should be glad to consider it, and not hesitate to alter my own view, if I saw reason to do so. Meanwhile, what he says makes me glad that I adopted ' the Announcement about Drunkenness' as the title of this chapter. It is drunkenness, by whatever liquor occasioned, that the king of Kâu condemns and denounces.

What we commonly understand by w i n e is never intended by 173
· *Kiû* in the Chinese classics, and therefore I cannot use that
term. After searching as extensively as I could do in this
country, since I received Dr. Edkins' letter, I have found nothing
to make me think that the Chinese term is not properly translated by 'spirits.'
Dr. Williams, in his Syllabic Dictionary of the Chinese Language
(Shanghai, 1874), gives this account of *Kiû* :—' Liquor ; it in-
cludes spirits, wine, beer, and other drinks. The Chinese make
no wine, and chiefly distil their liquors, and say that Tû Khang,
a woman of the Tî tribes, first made it.' This account is to a
considerable extent correct. The Chinese distil their liquors.
I never saw beer or porter of native production among them,
though according to Dr. Edkins they had been brewing 'or
nearly so' for more than 3000 years. Among his examples of
the use of *Kiû*, Williams gives the combinations of 'red *Kiû*'
for claret, 'white *Kiû*' for sherry, and 'pî (simply phonetical)
Kiû' for beer, adding that they 'are all terms of foreign origin.'
What he says about the traditional account of the first maker of
Kiû is not correct. It is said certainly that this was Tû Khang,
but who he was, or when he lived, I have never been able to
discover. Some identify him with Î-tî, said by Williams to have
been 'a woman of the Tî tribes.' The attributing of the invention
to Î-tî is probably an independent tradition. We find it in the
'Plans of the Warring States' (ch. xiv, art. 10), a work covering
about four centuries from the death of Confucius:—' Anciently,
the daughter of the Tî ordered Î-tî to make *Kiû*. She admired it,
and presented some to Yü, who drank it, and found it pleasant.
He then discarded Î-tî, and denounced the use of such generous
Kiû, saying, " In future ages there are sure to be those who by
Kiû will lose their states."' According to this tradition intoxi-
cating *Kiû* was known in the time of Yü—in the twenty-third
century B. C. The daughter of the Tî would be Yü's wife, and
Î-tî would probably be their cook. It does not appear as the
name of a woman, or one from the wild Tî tribes.
With regard to the phrase S h â o *Kiû*, said to be the proper term
for ardent spirits, and unknown in China till the Yüan dynasty,
a reference to the Khang-hsî Tonic Thesaurus of the language
will show instances of its use as early at least as the Thang
dynasty (A. D. 618–906).]

1. The king speaks to the following effect :—' Do

174　you clearly make known my great commands in the country of Mei[1].

'When your reverent father, the king Wăn, laid the foundations of our kingdom in the western region, he delivered announcements and cautions to (the princes of) the various regions, and to all his (high) officers, with their assistants, and the managers of affairs, saying, morning and evening, " At sacrifices spirits should be employed."* When Heaven was sending down its favouring decree, and laying the foundations of (the eminence of) our people, (spirits) were used only at the great sacrifices. When Heaven sends down its terrors, and our people are thereby greatly disorganized and lose their virtue, this may be traced invariably to their indulgence in spirits; yea, the ruin of states, small and great, (by these terrors), has been caused invariably by their guilt in the use of spirits [2].

---

[1] There is a place called 'the village of Mei,' in the north of the present district of *Khî*, department Wei-hui, Ho-nan;—a relic of the ancient name of the whole territory. The royal domain of Shang, north from the capital, was all called Mei. Făng's principality of Wei must have embraced most of it.

[2] Kû Hsî says upon the meaning of the expressions 'Heaven was sending down its favouring decree' (its order to make *Kiû*, as he understood the language), and 'when Heaven sends down its terrors,' in this paragraph :—'*Kang* Nan-hsien has brought out the meaning of these two statements much better than any of the critics who went before him, to the following effect:—*Kiû* is a thing intended to be used in offering sacrifices and in entertaining guests;—such employment of it is what Heaven has prescribed. But men by their abuse of *Kiû* come to lose their virtue, and destroy their persons;—such employment of it is what Heaven has annexed its terrors to. The Buddhists, hating the use of things where Heaven sends down its terrors, put away as well the use of them which Heaven has prescribed. It is not so with us of the learned (i. e. the Confucian or orthodox) school;—we only put

'King Wăn admonished and instructed the young 175
nobles, who were charged with office or in any employment, that they should not ordinarily use spirits;
and throughout all the states, he required that such
should drink spirits only on occasion of sacrifices,
and that then virtue should preside so that there
might be no drunkenness[1].'

He said, 'Let my people teach their young men
that they are to love only the productions of the
soil, for so will their hearts be good. Let the young
also hearken wisely to the constant instructions of
their fathers; and let them look at all virtuous
actions, whether great or small, in the same light
(with watchful heed).

'(Ye people of) the land of Mei, if you can employ
your limbs, largely cultivating your millets, and
hastening about in the service of your fathers and
elders; and if, with your carts and oxen, you traffic
diligently to a distance, that you may thereby filially
minister to your parents; then, when your parents
are happy, you may set forth your spirits clear and
strong, and use them[2].

'Hearken constantly to my instructions, all ye my
(high) officers and ye heads of departments, all ye,
my noble chiefs;—when ye have largely done your

---

away the use of things to which Heaven has annexed its terrors,
and the use of them, of which it approves, remains as a matter
of course.'

[1] In sacrificing, the fragrant odour of spirits was supposed to be
acceptable to the Beings worshipped. Here the use of spirits
seems to be permitted in moderation to the worshippers after the
sacrifices. Observe how king Wăn wished to guard the young
from acquiring the habit of drinking spirits.

[2] Here is another permissible use of spirits;—at family feasts,
with a view especially to the comfort of the aged.

176 duty in ministering to your aged, and serving your ruler, ye may eat and drink freely and to satiety. And to speak of greater things:—when you can maintain a constant, watchful examination of yourselves, and your conduct is in accordance with correct virtue, then may you present the offerings of sacrifice,* and at the same time indulge yourselves in festivity. In such case you will indeed be ministers doing right service to your king, and Heaven likewise will approve your great virtue, so that you shall never be forgotten in the royal House.'*

2. The king says, 'O Făng, in our western region, the princes of states, and the young (nobles), sons of the managers of affairs, who in former days assisted king Wăn, were all able to obey his lessons, and abstain from excess in the use of spirits; and so it is that I have now received the appointment which belonged to Yin.'

The king says, 'O Făng, I have heard it said, that formerly the first wise king of Yin manifested a reverential awe of the bright principles of Heaven and of the lower people, acting accordingly, steadfast in his virtue, and holding fast his wisdom.* From him, Thang the Successful, down to Tî-yî[1], all completed their royal virtue and revered their chief ministers, so that their managers of affairs respectfully discharged their helping duties, and dared not to allow themselves in idleness and pleasure;—how much less would they dare to indulge themselves in drinking! Moreover, in the exterior domains, (the princes of) the Hâu, Tien,

---

[1] Tî-yî was the father of Kâu-hsin, the twenty-seventh Shang sovereign. The sovereigns between Thang and him had not all been good, but the duke of Kâu chooses here to say so.

Nan, and Wei (states)[1], with their presiding chiefs; 177
and in the interior domain, all the various officers,
the directors of the several departments, the inferior
officers and employés, the heads of great houses, and
the men of distinguished name living in retirement, all
eschewed indulgence in spirits. Not only did they
not dare to indulge in them, but they had not leisure
to do so, being occupied with helping to complete
the sovereign's virtue and make it more illustrious,
and helping the directors of affairs reverently to
attend to his service.

'I have heard it said likewise, that the last
successor of those kings was addicted to drink, so
that no charges came from him brightly before the
people, and he was (as if) reverently and unchangingly
bent on doing and cherishing what provoked resent-
ment. Greatly abandoned to extraordinary lewdness
and dissipation, for pleasure's sake he sacrificed all
his majesty. The people were all sorely grieved
and wounded in heart; but he gave himself wildly
up to drink, not thinking of restraining himself, but
continuing his excess, till his mind was frenzied, and
he had no fear of death. His crimes (accumulated)
in the capital of Shang; and though the extinction
of the dynasty (was imminent), this gave him no
concern, and he wrought not that any sacrifices of
fragrant virtue might ascend to Heaven. * The
rank odour of the people's resentments, and the
drunkenness of his herd of creatures, went loudly
up on high, so that Heaven sent down ruin on Yin,

---

[1] These were the first, second, third, and fifth domains or territorial divisions of the land under *K*âu, counting back from the
royal domain. It appears here that an arrangement akin to that of
*K*âu had been made in the time of Shang.

178 and showed no love for it,—because of such excesses. There is not any cruel oppression of Heaven; people themselves accelerate their guilt, (and its punishment.)'*

The king says, ' O Făng, I make you this long announcement, not (for the pleasure of doing so); but the ancients have said, " Let not men look into water; let them look into the glass of other people." Now that Yin has lost its appointment, ought we not to look much to it as our glass, (and learn) how to secure the repose of our time ?   I say to you,— Strenuously warn the worthy ministers of Yin, and (the princes) in the Hâu, the Tien, the Nan, and the Wei domains; and still more your friends, the great Recorder and the Recorder of the Interior, and all your worthy ministers, the heads of great Houses; and still more those whom you serve, with whom you calmly discuss matters, and who carry out your measures; and still more those who are, as it were, your mates,—your Minister of War who deals with the rebellious, your Minister of Instruction who is like a protector to the people, and your Minister of Works who settles the boundaries; and above all, do you strictly keep yourself from drink.

' If you are informed that there are companies that drink together, do not fail to apprehend them all, and send them here to Kâu, where I may put them to death.   As to the ministers and officers of Yin who were led to it and became addicted to drink, it is not necessary to put them to death (at once);—let them be taught for a time. If they follow these (lessons of mine), I will give them bright distinction. If they disregard my lessons, then I, the One man, will show them no pity.   As

they cannot change their way, they shall be classed
with those who are to be put to death.'

The king says, ' O Făng, give constant heed to
my admonitions. If you do not rightly manage the
officers, the people will continue lost in drunkenness.'

179

BOOK XI. THE TIMBER OF THE ROTTLERA.

' THE wood of the Ȝze tree '—the Rottlera Japonica, according to
Dr. Williams—is mentioned in the Book, and was adopted as
the name for it. The Ȝze was esteemed a very valuable tree for
making articles of furniture and for the carver's art. The title
perhaps intimates that the administrator of government ought to
go about his duties carefully and skilfully, as the cabinet-maker
· and carver deal with their materials.

The Book is wanting in unity. Divided into two chapters, the
first may be taken as a charge to ' the prince of Khang.' He
is admonished of his duty to promote a good understanding
between the different classes in his state, and between them all
and the sovereign; and that, in order to this, his rule must be
gentle, eschewing the use of punishments. The second chapter
is of a different character, containing not the charges of a
sovereign, but the admonitions or counsels of a minister, loyally
cautioning him, and praying for the prosperity of his reign.
We might suppose them the response of Făng to the previous
charge, but the text does not indicate the introduction of a new
speaker.

1. The king says, ' O Făng, to secure a good
understanding between the multitudes of his people
and his ministers.(on the one hand), and the great
families (on the other); and (again) to secure the
same between all the subjects under his charge, and
the sovereign :—is the part of the ruler of a state.

' If you regularly, in giving out your orders, say,
" My instructors whom I am to follow, my Minister
of Instruction, my Minister of War, and my Minister

N 2

180　　of Works; my heads of departments, and all ye, my officers, I will on no account put any to death oppressively[1]"——. Let the ruler also set the example of respecting and encouraging (the people), and these will (also) proceed to respect and encourage them. Then let him go on, in dealing with villainy and treachery, with murderers and harbourers of criminals, to exercise clemency (where it can be done), and these will likewise do the same with those who have assaulted others and injured their property. When sovereigns appointed overseers (of states), they did so in order to the government of the people, and said to them, " Do not give way to violence or oppression, but go on to show reverent regard for the friendless, and find helping connexions for (destitute) women[2]." Deal with all according to this method, and cherish them. And when sovereigns gave their injunctions to the rulers of states, and their managers of affairs, what was their charge? It was that they should lead (the people) to the enjoyment of plenty and peace. Such was the way of the kings from of old. An overseer is to eschew the use of punishments.'

(The king) says, 'As in the management of a field, when the soil has been all laboriously turned up, they have to proceed by orderly arrangements to make its boundaries and water-courses; as in building a house, after all the toil on its walls, they have to plaster and thatch it; as in working with the wood of the rottlera, when the toil of the coarser and finer operations has been completed, they have

---

[1] The sentence here is incomplete. Many of the critics confess that the text is unintelligible to them.

[2] It is difficult to say what the exact meaning here is.

to apply the paint of red and other colours;—(so do   181
you finish for me the work which I have begun in
the state of Wei.)'

2. Now let your majesty say, ' The former kings
diligently employed their illustrious virtue, and produced such attachment by their cherishing (of the
princes), that from all the states they brought offerings, and came with brotherly affection from all
quarters, and likewise showed their virtue illustrious.
Do you, O sovereign, use, their methods to attach
(the princes), and all the states will largely come
with offerings. Great Heaven having given this
Middle Kingdom with its people and territories to
the former kings, do you, our present sovereign,
display your virtue, effecting a gentle harmony
among the deluded people, leading and urging
them on;—so (also) will you comfort the former
kings, who received the appointment (from
Heaven).*

'Yes, make these things your study. I say so
simply from my wish that (your dynasty) may continue for myriads of years, and your descendants
always be the protectors of the people.'

Book XII.

The Announcement of the Duke of Shâo.

Shâo was the name of a territory within the royal domain, corresponding to the present district of Hwan-*kh*ü, *K*iang *K*âu,
Shan-hsî. It was the appanage of Shih, one of the ablest of the
men who lent their aid to the establishment of the dynasty of
*K*âu. He appears in this Book as the Grand-Guardian at the
court of king *Kh*ăng, and we have met with him before in

182　　the Hounds of Lü and the Metal-bound Coffer. He is introduced here in connexion with one of the most important enterprises of the duke of *K*âu, the building of the city of Lo, not
very far from the present city of Lo-yang, in Ho-nan, as a new
and central capital of the kingdom. King Wû had conceived
the idea of such a city; but it was not carried into effect till the
reign of his son, and is commonly assigned to *Kh*äng's seventh
year, in B.C. 1109.

Shih belonged to the royal House, and of course had the surname *K*î. He is styled the duke of Shâo, as being one of the
'three dukes,' or three highest officers of the court, and also the
chief of Shâo, all the country west of Shen being under him,
as all the east of it was under the duke of *K*âu. He was
invested by Wû with the principality of 'the Northern Yen,'
corresponding to the present department of Shun-thien, *K*îh-lî,
which was held by his descendants fully nine hundred years. It
was in Lo—while the building of it was proceeding—that he
composed this Book, and sent it by the hands of the duke of
*K*âu to their young sovereign.

The whole may be divided into three chapters. The first contains
various information about the arrangements for the building of
Lo, first by the duke of Shâo, and then by the duke of *K*âu;
and about the particular occasion when the former recited the
counsels which he had composed, that they might be made
known to the king. These form the second chapter. First, it
sets forth the uncertainty of the favour of Heaven, and urges the
king to cultivate the ' virtue of reverence,' in order to secure its
permanence, and that he should not neglect his aged and experienced ministers. It speaks next of the importance and
difficulty of the royal duties, and enforces the same virtue of
reverence by reference to the rise and fall of the previous dynasties. Lastly, it sets forth the importance, at this early period
of his reign, of the king's at once setting about the reverence
which was thus described. There is a concluding chapter,
where the duke gives expression to his loyal and personal
feelings for the king, and the purpose to be served by the
offerings, which he was then sending to the court.

The burden of the Announcement is 'the virtue of reverence.'
Let the king only feel how much depended on his attending
reverently to his duties, and all would be well. The people
would love and support the dynasty of *K*âu, and Heaven would
smile upon and sustain it.

1. In the second month, on the day Yî-wei, six   183
days after full moon, the king proceeded in the
morning from *K*âu to Făng[1]. (Thence) the Grand-
Guardian went before the duke of *K*âu to survey
the locality (of the new capital); and in the third
month, on the day Wû-shăn, the third day after the
first appearance of the moon on Ping-wû, he came
in the morning to Lo. He divined by the tortoise-
shell about the (several) localities, and having obtained
favourable indications, he set about laying out the
plan (of the city).* On Kăng-hsü, the third day
after, he led the people of Yin to prepare the various
sites on the north of the Lo; and this work was
completed on *K*iâ-yin, the fifth day after.

On Yî-mâo, the day following, the duke of *K*âu
came in the morning to Lo, and thoroughly inspected
the plan of the new city. On Ting-sze, the third day
after, he offered two bulls as victims in the (northern
and southern) suburbs[2]; and on the morrow, Wû-wû,
at the altar to the spirit of the land in the new city,
he sacrificed a bull, a ram, and a-boar.* After seven
days, on *K*iâ-ʒze, in the morning, from his written
(specifications) 'he gave their several orders to the
people of Yin, and to the presiding chiefs of the
princes from the Hâu, Tien, and Nan domains.
When the people of Yin had thus received their
orders, they arose and entered with vigour on
their work.

(When the work was drawing to a completion),

---

[1] That is, from Wû's capital of Hâo to king Wăn's at Făng.

[2] By the addition to the text here of 'northern and southern,'
I intimate my opinion that the duke of *K*âu offered two sacrifices,
one to Heaven at the altar in the southern suburb, and one to
Earth in the northern suburb.

184

the Grand-Guardian went out with the hereditary princes of the various states to bring their offerings (for the king)[1]; and when he entered again, he gave them to the duke of *K*âu, saying, 'With my hands to my head and my head to the ground, I present these to his Majesty and your Grace[2]. Announcements for the information of the multitudes of Yin must come from you, with whom is the management of affairs.'

2. 'Oh! God (dwelling in) the great heavens has changed his decree respecting his great son and the great dynasty of Yin. Our king has received that decree. Unbounded is the happiness connected with it, and unbounded is the anxiety :—Oh! how can he be other than reverent ?*

'When Heaven rejected and made an end of the decree in favour of the great dynasty of Yin, there were many of its former wise kings in heaven.* The king, however, who had succeeded to them, the last of his race, from the time of his entering into their appointment, proceeded in such a way as at last to keep the wise in obscurity and the vicious in office. The poor people in such a case, carrying their children and leading their wives, made their moan to Heaven. They even fled away, but were apprehended again. Oh! Heaven had compassion on the people of the four quarters; its favouring

---

[1] These 'offerings' were the 'presents of introduction,' which the feudal princes brought with them to court, when they were to have audience of the king. This has led many critics to think that the king was now in Lo, which was not the case.

[2] The original text here is difficult and remarkable ;—intended probably to indicate that the king's majesty was revered in the person of the duke of *K*âu, who was regent.

decree lighted on our earnest (founders). Let the   185
king sedulously cultivate the virtue of reverence. *

'Examining the men of antiquity, there was the
(founder of the) Hsiâ dynasty. Heaven guided (his
mind), allowed his descendants (to succeed him),
and protected them. * He acquainted himself with
Heaven, and was obedient to it. But in process of
time the decree in his favour fell to the ground.*
So also is it now when we examine the case of Yin.
There was the same guiding (of its founder), who
corrected (the errors of Hsiâ), and (whose descendants) enjoyed the protection (of Heaven). He
(also) acquainted himself with Heaven, and was
obedient to it. * But now the decree in favour of
him has fallen to the ground. Our king has now
come to the throne in his youth ;—let him not slight
the aged and experienced, for it may be said of
them that they have studied the virtuous conduct
of the ancients, and have matured their counsels in
the sight of Heaven.

'Oh! although the king is young, yet he is the
great son (of God).* Let him effect a great harmony
with the lower people, and that will be the blessing
of the present time. Let not the king presume to
be remiss in this, but continually regard and stand
in awe of the perilous (uncertainty) of the people's
(attachment).

'Let the king come here as the vice-gerent of
God, and undertake (the duties of government) in
this centre of the land.* Tan [1] said, "Now that this
great city has been built, from henceforth he may

---

[1] Tan was the name of the duke of *Kâu*, and his brother duke
here refers to him by it, in accordance with the rule that 'ministers

186   be the mate of great Heaven, and reverently sacrifice to (the spirits) above and beneath ; from henceforth he may from this central spot administer
successful government." Thus shall the king enjoy
the favouring regard (of Heaven) all-complete, and the
government of the people will now be prosperous.*

'Let the king first subdue to himself those who
were the managers of affairs under Yin, associating
them with the managers of affairs for our *K*âu.
This will regulate their (perverse) natures, and they
will make daily advancement. Let the king make
reverence the resting-place (of his mind) ;—he must
maintain the virtue of reverence.

'We should by all means survey the dynasties of
Hsiâ and Yin. I do not presume to know and say,
" The dynasty of Hsiâ was to enjoy the favouring
decree of Heaven just for (so many) years," nor do
I presume to know and say, " It could not continue
longer." * The fact simply was, that, for want of
the virtue of reverence, the decree in its favour
prematurely fell to the ground. (Similarly), I do
not presume to know and say, " The dynasty of Yin
was to enjoy the favouring decree of Heaven just
for (so many) years," nor do I presume to know
and say, " It could not continue longer." * The fact
simply was, that, for want of the virtue of reverence,
the decree in its favour fell prematurely to the
ground. The king has now inherited the decree,—
the same decree, I consider, which belonged to those
two dynasties. Let him seek to inherit (the virtues

---

should be called by their names in the presence of the sovereign.'
King *K*̌hăng, indeed, was not now really present in Lo, but he
was represented by his uncle, the regent.

of) their meritorious (sovereigns) ;—(let him do this   187
especially) at this commencement of his duties.

'Oh! it is as on the birth of a son, when all
depends on (the training of) his early life, through
which he may secure his wisdom in the future, as if
it were decreed to him.   Now Heaven may have
decreed wisdom (to the king); it may have decreed
good fortune or bad; it may have decreed a (long)
course of years ;—we only know that now is with
him the commencement of his duties.   Dwelling in
this new city, let the king now sedulously cultivate
the virtue of reverence.   When he is all-devoted to
this virtue, he may pray to Heaven for a long-abiding
decree in his favour. *

'In the position of king, let him not, because of
the excesses of the people in violation of the laws,
presume also to rule by the violent infliction of
death ;—when the people are regulated gently, the
merit (of government) is seen.   It is for him who is
in the position of king to overtop all with his virtue.
In this case the people will imitate him throughout the kingdom, and he will become still more
illustrious.

'Let the king and his ministers labour with a
mutual sympathy, saying, "We have received the
decree of Heaven, and it shall be great as the long-
continued years of Hsiâ ;—yea, it shall not fail of
the long-continued years of Yin."   I wish the king,
through (the attachment of) the lower people, to
receive the long-abiding decree of Heaven.'*

3. (The duke of Shâo) then did obeisance with
his hands to his head and his head to the ground,
and said, 'I, a small minister, presume, with the king's
(heretofore) hostile people and all their officers,

188 and with his (loyal) friendly people, to maintain and receive his majesty's dread command and brilliant virtue. That the king should finally obtain the decree all-complete, and that he should become illustrious,—this I do not presume to labour for. I only bring respectfully these offerings to present to his majesty, to be used in his prayers to Heaven for its long-abiding decree.' *

BOOK XIII.   THE ANNOUNCEMENT CONCERNING LO.

THE matters recorded in this Book are all connected, more or less nearly, with Lo, the new capital, the arrangements for the building of which are related at the commencement of the last Book. According to the summary of the contents given by the commentator 3hâi *Kh*ăn, 'The arrangements for the building having been made, the duke of *K*âu sent a messenger to inform the king of the result of his divinations. The historiographer recorded this as the Announcement about Lo, and at the same time related a dialogue between the king and his minister, and how the king charged the duke to remain at Lo, and conduct the government of it.' Passing over the commencing paragraph, which I have repeated here from the ninth Book, 3hâi divides all the rest into seven chapters. Ch. 1 contains the duke's message concerning his divinations; and the next gives the king's reply. Ch. 3 is occupied with instructions to the king about the measures which he should pursue on taking up his residence at Lo. In ch. 4, the king charges the duke to remain at Lo, and undertake its government. In ch. 5, the duke responds, and accepts the charge, dwelling on the duties which the king and himself would have to perform. Ch. 6 relates the action of the duke in reference to a message and gift from the king intended for his special honour. In ch. 7, the historiographer writes of sacrifices offered by the king in Lo, and a proclamation that he issued, and tells how long the duke continued in his government;—showing how the duke began the city and completed it, and how king *Kh*ăng, after offering the sacrifices and inaugurating the government, returned to Hâo, and did not, after all, make his capital at Lo.

Many critics make much to do about the want of historical order in the Book, and suppose that portions have been lost, and other portions transposed; but the Book may be explained without resorting to so violent a supposition.

[In the third month, · when the moon began to wane, the duke of *K*âu commenced the foundations and proceeded to build the new great city of Lo of the eastern states. The people from every quarter assembled in great harmony. From the Hâu, Tien, Nan, 3hâi, and Wei domains, the various officers stimulated this harmony of the ͘ people, and introduced them to the business that was to be done for *K*âu. The duke encouraged all to diligence, and made a great announcement about the performance (of the works)[1].]

1. The duke of *K*âu did obeisance with his hands to his head and his head to the ground[2], saying, 'Herewith I report (the execution of my commission) to my son, my intelligent sovereign. The king appeared as if he would not presume to be present at Heaven's founding here the appointment (of our dynasty), and fixing it, whereupon I followed the (Grand-)Guardian, and made a great survey of this eastern region, hoping to found the place where he should become the intelligent sovereign of the people. On the day Yî-mâo, I came in the morning to this capital of Lo. I (first) divined by the shell concerning (the ground about) the Lî-water on the north of the Ho. I then divined concerning the east of the *K*ien-water, and the west of the *K*ʰan, when the (ground near the) Lo was indicated. Again I

---

[1] See the introductory note to Book ix.

[2] In sending his message to the king, the duke does obeisance as if he were in the presence of his majesty. The king responds with a similar ceremony.

190 divined concerning the east of the *Kh*an-water, when the (ground near the) Lo was also indicated. I (now) send a messenger with a map, and to present the (result of the) divinations.'*

2. The king did obeisance with his hands to his head and his head to the ground, saying, ' The duke did not presume not to acknowledge reverently the favour of Heaven, and has surveyed the locality where our *K*âu may respond to that favour. Having settled the locality, he has sent his messenger to show me the divinations, favourable and always auspicious. We two must together sustain the responsibility. He has made provision for me (and my successors), for myriads and tens of myriads of years, there reverently to acknowledge the favour of Heaven.* With my hands to my head and my head to the ground, (I receive) his instructive words.'

3. The duke of *K*âu said [1], ' Let the king at first employ the ceremonies of Yin, and sacrifice in the new city,* doing everything in an orderly way, but without display. I will marshal all the officers to attend you from *K*âu, merely saying that probably there will be business to be done (in sacrificing). Let the king instantly issue an order to the effect that the most meritorious (ministers) shall have the first place in the sacrifices ; and let him also say in an order, " You, in whose behalf the above order is issued, must give me your assistance with sincere earnestness." Truly display the record of merits, for

---

[1] We must suppose that the duke of *K*âu, after receiving the reply to his message, had himself returned to Hâo, to urge upon the king the importance of his repairing in person to Lo, and solemnly inaugurating the new city as the capital of the kingdom.

it is you who must in everything teach the officers. 191
My young son, can you indulge partiality? Eschew
it, my young son. (If you do not), the consequence
hereafter will be like a fire, which, a spark at first,
blazes up, and by and by cannot be extinguished.
Let your observance of the constant rules of right,
and your soothing measures be like mine. Take
only the officers that are in *K*âu with you to the
new city, and make them there join their (old)
associates, with intelligent vigour establishing
their merit, and with a generous largeness (of
soul) completing (the public manners); — so shall
you obtain an endless fame.'

. The duke said, 'Yes, young as you are, be it
yours to complete (the work of your predecessors).
Cultivate (the spirit of) reverence, and you will know
who among the princes (sincerely) present their
offerings to you, and who do not. In connexion
with those offerings there are many observances. If
the observances are not equal to the articles, it must
be held that there is no offering. When there is no
service of the will in the offerings (of the princes),
all the people will then say, "We need not (be
troubled about) our offerings," and affairs will be
disturbed by errors and usurpations.

'.Do you, my young son, manifest everywhere my
unwearied diligence, and listen to my instructions to
you how to help the people to observe the constant
rules of right. If you do not bestir yourself in these
things, you will not be of long continuance. If you
sincerely and . fully carry out the course of your
Directing father, and follow exactly my example,
there will be no venturing to disregard your orders.
Go, and be .reverent. Henceforth I will study

192 husbandry[1]. There do you generously rule our people, and there is no distance from which they will not come to you.'

4. The king spoke to this effect[2], 'O duke, you are the enlightener and sustainer of my youth. You have set forth the great and illustrious virtues, that I, notwithstanding my youth, may display a brilliant merit like that of Wăn and Wû, reverently responding to the favouring decree of Heaven; and harmonize and long preserve the people of all the regions, settling the multitudes (in Lo); and that I may give due honour to the great ceremony (of recording) the most distinguished (for their merits), regulating the order for the first places at the sacrifices, and doing everything in an orderly manner without display.

'But your virtue, O duke, shines brightly above and beneath, and is displayed actively throughout the four quarters. On every hand appears the deep reverence (of your virtue) in securing the establishment of order, so that you fail in nothing of the earnest lessons of Wăn and Wû. It is for me, the youth, (only) to attend reverently, early and late, to the sacrifices.' *

The king said, 'Great, O duke, has been your merit in helping and guiding me;—let it ever continue so.'

---

[1] By this expression the duke indicates his wish and intention now to retire from public life, and leave the government and especially the affairs of Lo in the king's hands.

[2] From the words of the king in this chapter, we receive the impression that they were spoken in Lo. He must have gone there with the duke from Hâo. He deprecates the duke's intention to retire into private life; intimates his own resolution to return to Hâo; and wishes the duke to remain in Lo, accomplishing all that was still necessary to the establishment of their dynasty.

The king said, 'O duke, let me, the little child, 193
return to my sovereignty in *K*âu, and I charge you,
O duke, to remain behind (here). Order has been
initiated throughout the four quarters of the kingdom,
but the ceremonies to be honoured (by general observance) have not yet been settled, and I cannot look
on your service as completed. Commence on a
great scale what is to be done by your remaining
here, setting an example to my officers and greatly
preserving the people whom Wǎn and Wû received;
—by your good government you will be a help to
the whole kingdom.'

The king said, 'Remain, O duke. I will certainly
go. Your services are devoutly acknowledged and
reverently rejoiced in. Do not, O duke, occasion
me this difficulty. I on my part will not be weary
in seeking the tranquillity (of the people);—do not
let the example which you have afforded me be
intermitted. So shall the kingdom enjoy for generations (the benefit of your virtue).'

5. The duke of *K*âu did obeisance with his hands
to his head and his head to the ground, saying, 'You
have charged me, O king, to come here. I undertake (the charge), and will protect the people whom
your accomplished grandfather, and your glorious
and meritorious father, king Wû, received by the
decree (of . Heaven). I will enlarge the reverence
which I cherish for you. (But), my son, come (frequently), and inspect this settlement. Pay great
honour to (old) statutes, and to the good and wise
men of Yin. Good government (here) will make
you (indeed) the new sovereign of the kingdom, and
an example of (royal) respectfulness to all your
successors of *K*âu.'

[1]   o

(The duke) proceeded to say, 'From this time, by the government administered in this central spot, all the states will be conducted to repose; and this will be the completion of your merit, O king.

'I, Tan, with the numerous officers and managers of affairs, will consolidate the achievements of our predecessors, in response to (the hopes of) the people. I will afford an example of sincerity to (future ministers of) *K*âu, seeking to render complete the pattern intended for the enlightenment of you, my son, and thus to carry fully out the virtue of your accomplished grandfather.'

6. (Afterwards, on the arrival of a message and gifts from the king, the duke said[1]), '(The king) has sent messengers to admonish (the people of) Yin, and with a soothing charge to me, along with two flagons of the black-millet herb-flavoured spirits, saying, "Here is a pure sacrificial gift, which with my hands to my head and my head to the ground I offer for you to enjoy its excellence!"* I dare not keep this by me, but offer it in sacrifice to king Wăn and king Wû.' (In doing so, he prayed), 'May he be obedient to, and observant of your course! Let him not bring on himself any evil or illness! Let him satisfy his descendants for myriads of years with your virtue! Let (the people of) Yin enjoy prolonged (prosperity)!'* (He also said to the messengers), 'The king has sent you to Yin,

---

[1] We must suppose that the king had returned to Hâo, and now sends a message to the duke with an extraordinary gift, doing honour to him as if he were a departed spirit, continuing in heaven the guardianship of the dynasty which he had so long efficiently discharged on earth. This gives occasion for the duke to exhibit anew his humility, piety, and loyalty.

and we have received his well-ordered charges, 195
(sufficient to direct us) for myriads of years, but let
(the people) ever (be able to) observe the virtue
cherished by my son.'

7. On the day Wû-*kh*ăn, the king, being in the
new city [1], performed the annual winter sacrifice,
offering (moreover) one red bull to king Wăn and
another to king Wû.* He then ordered a declaration to be prepared, which was done by Yî [2] in the
form of a prayer, and it simply announced the remaining behind of the duke of *K*âu. The king's
guests [3], on occasion of the killing of the victims
and offering the sacrifice, were all present. The
king entered the grand apartment, and poured out
the libation.* He gave a charge to the duke of
*K*âu to remain, and Yî, the preparer of the document, made the announcement; — in the twelfth
month. (Thus) the duke of *K*âu grandly sustained
the decree which Wăn and Wû had received through
the space of seven years [4].

---

[1] The duke had asked the king to come frequently to the new
city; he is there now accordingly.

[2] Yî was the name of the Recorder who officiated on the
occasion.

[3] All the princes present and assisting at the sacrifices, and
especially the representatives of the previous dynasties.

[4] These seven years are to be calculated from the seventh year
of king *Kh*ăng, after the duke had served as administrator of
the government seven years from the death of king Wû. Many
think, however, that the 'seven years' are only those of the duke's
regency.

196   BOOK XIV.   THE NUMEROUS OFFICERS.

WE have in this Book another 'Announcement,' addressed to the
people of Yin or Shang, and especially to the higher classes
among them,—'the numerous officers,'—to reconcile them to
their lot as subjects of the new dynasty. From the preceding
two Books it appears that many of the people of Yin had been
removed to the country about the Lo, before the dukes of Shâo
and *K*âu commenced the building of the new city.   Now that
the city was completed, another and larger migration of them, we
may suppose, was ordered, and the duke of *K*âu took occasion
to issue the announcement that is here preserved.

I have divided it into four chapters.   The first vindicates the kings
of *K*âu for superseding the line of Shang, not from ambition,
but in obedience to the will of God.   The second unfolds the
causes why the dynasty of Yin or Shang had been set aside.
The third shows how it had been necessary to remove them to
Lo, and with what good intention the new capital had been
built.   The fourth tells how comfort and prosperity were open
to their attainment at Lo, while by perseverance in disaffection
they would only bring misery and ruin upon themselves.

1. In the third month, at the commencement (of
the government) of the duke of *K*âu in the new city
of Lo, he announced (the royal will) to the officers
of the Shang dynasty, saying, 'The king speaks to
this effect:—" Ye numerous officers who remain
from the dynasty of Yin, great ruin came down on
Yin from the cessation of forbearance in compassionate Heaven, and we, the lords of *K*âu, received
its favouring decree.*   We felt charged with its
bright terrors, carried out the punishments which
kings inflict, rightly disposed of the appointment of
Yin, and finished (the work of) God.*   Now, ye numerous officers, it was not our small state that dared
to aim at the appointment belonging to Yin.   But
Heaven was not with (Yin), for indeed it would not

strengthen its misrule. It (therefore) helped us;—
did we dare to seek the throne of ourselves? God
was not for (Yin), as appeared from the mind and
conduct of our inferior people, in which there is the
brilliant dreadfulness of Heaven."' *

2. 'I have heard the saying, "God leads men to
tranquil security," * but the sovereign of Hsiâ would
not move to such security, whereupon God sent
down corrections, indicating his mind to him. (*K*ieh),
however, would not be warned by God, but proceeded to greater dissoluteness and sloth and excuses
for himself. Then Heaven no longer regarded nor
heard him, but disallowed his great appointment, and
inflicted extreme punishment. Then it charged your
founder, Thang the Successful, to set Hsiâ aside,
and by means of able men to rule the kingdom.
From Thang the Successful down to Tî-yî, every
sovereign sought to make his virtue illustrious, and
duly attended to the sacrifices. * And thus it was
that, while Heaven exerted a great establishing
influence, preserving and regulating the House of
Yin, its sovereigns on their part were humbly
careful not to lose (the favour of) God, and strove
to manifest a good-doing corresponding to that of
Heaven. * But in these times, their successor
showed himself greatly ignorant of (the ways of)
Heaven, and much less could it be expected of him
that he would be regardful of the earnest labours of
his fathers for the country. Greatly abandoned to
dissolute idleness, he gave no thought to the bright
principles of Heaven, and the awfulness of the
people. * On this account God no longer protected
him, but sent down the great ruin which we have
witnessed. Heaven was not with him, because he

198 did not make his virtue illustrious.* (Indeed), with regard to the overthrow of all states, great and small, throughout the four quarters of the kingdom, in every case reasons can be given for their punishment.'

'The king speaks to this effect :—" Ye numerous officers of Yin, the case now is this, that the kings of our *K*âu, from their great goodness, were charged with the work of God. There was the charge to them, 'Cut off Yin.' (They proceeded to perform it), and announced the execution of their service to God. In our affairs we have followed no double aims ;—ye of the royal House (of Yin) must (now simply) follow us." ' *

3. ' " May I not say that you have been very lawless ? I did not (want to) remove you. The thing came from your own city[1]. When I consider also how Heaven has drawn near to Yin with so great tribulations, it must be that there was (there) what was not right."

' The king says, " Ho ! I declare to you, ye numerous officers, it is simply on account of these things that I have removed you and settled you here in the west [2] ;—it was not that I, the One man, considered it a part of my virtue to interfere with your tranquillity. The thing was from Heaven ; do not offer resistance ; I shall not presume to have any subsequent (charge concerning you) ; do not murmur against me. Ye know that your fathers of the Yin dynasty had their archives and statutes, (showing

---

[1] That is, your conduct in your own city.

[2] Lo is often called 'the eastern capital,' as being east from Hâo, the capital of king Wû ; but it was west from *K*âo-ko, the capital of Yin.

how) Yin superseded the appointment of Hsiâ. 199
Now, indeed, ye say further, ' (The officers of) Hsiâ
were chosen and employed in the royal court (of
Shang), and had their duties among the mass of
its officers.' (But) I, the One man, listen only to
the virtuous, and employ them; and it was with
this view that I ventured to seek you in your
capital of Shang (once sanctioned by) Heaven, (and
removed you here to Lo.) I thereby follow (the
ancient example), and have pity on you. (Your
present non-employment) is no fault of mine;—it is
by the decree of Heaven."*

' The king says, " Ye numerous officers, formerly,
when I came from Yen¹, I greatly mitigated the
penalty and spared the lives of the people of your
four states². At the same time I made evident
the punishment appointed by Heaven, and removed
you to this distant abode, that you might be near
the ministers who had served in our honoured
(capital)³, and (learn) their much obedience."

' The king says, " I declare to you, ye numerous
officers of Yin, now I have not put you to death,
and therefore I reiterate the declaration of my
charge⁴. I have now built this great city here in

---

¹ Yen was the name of a territory, corresponding to the present
district of *Kh*ü-fâu, in Shan-tung. The wild tribe inhabiting it,
had joined with Wû-kăng and the king's uncles a few years before;
and the crushing of the Yen had been the last act in the sup-
pression of their rebellion.

² The royal domain of Yin, which had been allotted to Wû-kăng
and the king's three uncles.

³ Hâo. There were, no doubt, at this time many ministers and
officers from Hâo in Lo; but the duke had intended that they
should in the mass remove from the old to the new capital.

⁴ The charge which had been delivered on the first removal of
many of them to the neighbourhood of Lo.

200 Lo, considering that there was no (central) place in which to receive my guests from the four quarters, and also that you, ye numerous officers, might here with zealous activity perform the part of ministers to us, with the entire obedience (ye would learn). Ye have still here, I may say, your grounds, and may still rest in your duties and dwellings. If you can reverently obey, Heaven will favour and compassionate you. If you do not reverently obey, you shall not only not have your lands, but I will also carry to the utmost Heaven's inflictions on your persons. Now you may here dwell in your villages, and perpetuate your families; you may pursue your occupations and enjoy your years in this Lo; your children also will prosper;—(all) from your being removed here."

' The king says—[1]; and again he says, "Whatever I may now have spoken is on account of (my anxiety about) your residence here."'

Book XV. Against Luxurious Ease.

The name of this Book is taken from two characters in the first sentence of it, which are the key-note of the whole. It is classified among the 'Instructions' of the Shû, and was addressed to king *Kh*äng by the duke of *K*âu soon after he had resigned the administration of the government into his hands.

There are six pauses in the course of the address, which is resumed always with 'The duke of *K*âu said, "Oh."' This suggests a division into seven chapters.

In the first, the duke suggests to the king to find a rule for himself in the laborious toils that devolve on the husbandman. In the second, he refers to the long reigns of three of the Yin sovereigns,

---

[1] There are probably some sentences lost here.

and the short reigns of others, as illustrating how the blessing of   201
Heaven rests on the diligent monarch. In the third, the example
of their own kings, Thâi, *K*î, and Wăn, is adduced with the
same object. In the fourth, the duke addresses the king directly,
and exhorts him to follow the pattern of king Wăn, and flee from
that of *K*âu-hsin. In the fifth, he stimulates him, by reference to
ancient precedents, to adopt his counsels, and shows the evil
effects that will follow if he refuse to do so. In the sixth, he
shows him, by the cases of the good kings of Yin and of king
Wăn, how he should have regard to the opinions of the common
people, and gird himself to diligence. The seventh chapter is a
single admonition that the king should lay what had been said
to heart.

1. The duke of *K*âu said, ' Oh! the superior man
rests in this,—that he will indulge in no luxurious
ease. He first understands how the painful toil
of sowing and reaping conducts to ease, and thus
he understands how the lower people depend on
this toil (for their support). I have observed among
the lower people, that where the parents have
diligently laboured in sowing and reaping, their sons
(often) do not understand this painful toil, but
abandon themselves to ease, and to village slang,
and become quite disorderly. Or where they do
not do so, they (still) throw contempt on their
parents, saying, " Those old people have heard
nothing and know nothing." '

2. The duke of *K*âu said, ' Oh! I have heard
that aforetime *K*ung ʒung, one of the kings of Yin[1],
was grave, humble, reverential, and timorously
cautious. He measured himself with reference to
the decree of Heaven, and cherished a reverent
apprehension in governing the people, not daring

---

[1] *K*ung ʒung was the sacrificial title of Thâi-wû, the seventh of
the kings of Shang or Yin, who reigned B. C. 1637–1563.

202 to indulge in useless ease.* It was thus that he enjoyed the throne seventy and five years. If we come
to the time of Kâo 3ung¹, he toiled at first away
from the court, and was among the lower people².
When he came to the throne, and occupied the
mourning shed, it may be said that he did not speak
for three years. (Afterwards) he was (still inclined)
not to speak; but when he. did speak, his words
were full of harmonious (wisdom). He did not dare
to indulge in useless ease, but admirably and tranquilly presided over the regions of Yin, till throughout them all, small and great, there was not a single
murmur. It was thus that he enjoyed the throne
fifty and nine years. In the case of 3û-kiâ³, he
refused to be king unrighteously, and was at first
one of the lower people. When he came to the
throne, he knew on what they must depend (for
their support), and was able to exercise a protecting
kindness towards their masses, and did not dare to
treat with contempt the wifeless men and widows.
Thus it was that he enjoyed the throne thirty and
three years. The kings that arose after these,
from their birth enjoyed ease. Enjoying ease from
their birth, they did not know the painful toil of
sowing and reaping, and had not heard of the hard
labours of the lower people. They sought for
nothing but excessive pleasure; and so not one
of them had long life. They (reigned) for ten years,

---

¹ Kâo 3ung was the sacrificial title of Wû-ting, the nineteenth
sovereign of the Yin line, who reigned B.C. 1324–1266. He has
already appeared in the 8th and 9th Books of Part IV.

² Compare Part IV, viii, sect. 3, ch. 1.

³ 3û-kiâ was the twenty-first of the Yin sovereigns, and reigned
B.C. 1258–1226.

for seven or eight, for five or six, or perhaps (only)   203
for three or four.'

3. The duke of *K*âu said, 'Oh! there likewise
were king Thâi and king *K*î of our own *K*âu, who
were humble and reverentially cautious. King Wăn
dressed meanly, and gave himself to the work of
tranquillization and to that of husbandry. Admirably mild and beautifully humble, he cherished and
protected the inferior people, and showed a fostering
kindness to the wifeless men and widows. From
morning to mid-day, and from mid-day to sun-
down, he did not allow himself leisure to eat;—thus
seeking to secure the happy harmony of the myriads
of the people. King Wăn did not dare to go to
excess in his excursions or his hunting, and from
the various states he would receive only the correct amount of contribution. The appointment (of
Heaven) came to him in the middle of his life[1],
and he enjoyed the throne for fifty years.'*

4. The duke of *K*âu said, 'Oh! from this time
forward, do you who have succeeded to the throne
imitate Wăn's avoiding of excess in his sight-seeing,
his indulgence in ease, his excursions, his hunting;
and from the myriads of the people receive only the
correct amount of contribution. Do not allow yourself the leisure to say, "To-day I will indulge in
pleasure." This would not be holding out a lesson
to the people, nor the way to secure the favour
of Heaven. Men will on the contrary be prompt
to imitate you and practise evil. Become not like

---

[1] This can only be understood of Wăn's succeeding to his father
as duke of *K*âu and chief of the West in B.C. 1185. He died
in 1135, leaving it to his son Wû to overthrow the dynasty of
Shang.

204 Shâu the king of Yin, who went quite astray, and became abandoned to drunkenness.'

5. The duke of *K*âu said, 'Oh! I have heard it said that, in the case of the ancients, (their ministers) warned and admonished them, protected and loved them, taught and instructed them; and among the people there was hardly one who would impose on them by extravagant language or deceiving tricks. If you will not listen to this (and profit by it), your ministers will imitate you, and so the correct laws of the former kings, both small and great, will be changed and disordered. The people, blaming you, will disobey and rebel in their hearts;—yea, they will curse you with their mouths.'

6. The duke of *K*âu said, 'Oh! those kings of Yin,—*K*ung 3ung, Kâo 3ung, and 3û-*k*iâ, with king Wăn of our *K*âu,—these four men carried their knowledge into practice. If it was told them, "The lower people murmur against you and revile you," then they paid great and reverent attention to their conduct; and with reference to the faults imputed to them they said, "Our faults are really so," thus not simply shrinking from the cherishing of anger. If you will not listen to this (and profit by it), when men with extravagant language and deceptive tricks say to you, "The lower people are murmuring against you and reviling you," you will believe them. Doing this, you will not be always thinking of your princely duties, and will not cultivate a large and generous heart. You will confusedly punish the guiltless, and put the innocent to death. There will be a general murmuring, which will be concentrated upon your person.'

7. The duke of *K*âu said, ' Oh ! let the king, who　205
has succeeded to the throne, make a study of these
things.'

Book XVI.　The Prince Shih.

The words ' Prince Shih ' occur at the commencement of the
Book, and are taken as its title. Shih was the name of the
duke of Shâo, the author of Book xii. To him the address
or announcement here preserved was delivered, and his name is
not an inappropriate title for it.

The common view of Chinese critics is that the duke of Shâo had
announced his purpose to withdraw from office on account of
his age, when the duke of *K*âu persuaded him to remain at his
post, and that the reasons which he set before him were recorded
in this Book. It may have been so, but the language is far
from clearly indicating it. A few expressions, indeed, may be
taken as intimating a wish that Shih should continue at court,
but some violence has to be put upon them.

I have divided the whole into four chapters, but the two principal
ideas in the address are these :—that the favour of Heaven can
be permanently secured for a dynasty only by the virtue of its
sovereigns; and that that virtue is secured mainly by the counsels
and help of virtuous ministers. The ablest sovereigns of Shang
are mentioned, and the ministers by whose aid it was, in a great
measure, that they became what they were. The cases of Wăn
and Wû of their own dynasty, similarly aided by able men, are
adduced in the same way; and the speaker adverts to the services which they—the two dukes—had already rendered to their
sovereign, and insists that they must go on to the end, and
accomplish still greater things.

1. The duke of *K*âu spoke to the following
effect :—' Prince Shih, Heaven, unpitying, sent
down ruin on Yin. Yin has lost its appointment
(to the throne), which our House of *K*âu has received. I do not dare, however, to say, as if I knew

206 it, "The foundation will ever truly abide in prosperity. If Heaven aid sincerity,"—¹.* Nor do
I dare to say, as if I knew it, "The end will issue in
our misfortunes." Oh! you have said, O prince, "It
depends on ourselves." I also do not dare to rest
in the favour of God, not forecasting at a distance
the terrors of Heaven in the present time, when
there is no murmuring or disobedience among the
people;* — (the issue) is with men. Should our
present successor to his fathers prove greatly unable
to reverence (Heaven) above and (the people) below,
and so bring to an end the glory of his predecessors,
could we in (the retirement of) our families be
ignorant of it? The favour of Heaven is not easily
preserved; Heaven is difficult to be depended on.
Men lose its favouring appointment, because they
cannot pursue and carry out the reverence and
brilliant virtue of their forefathers.* Now I, Tan,
the little child, am not able to make (the king)
correct. I would simply conduct him to the glory of
his fathers, and make him, who is my young charge,
partaker of that.' He also said, 'Heaven is not to
be trusted. Our course is only to seek the prolongation of the virtue of the Tranquillizing king,
that Heaven may not find occasion to remove its
favouring decree which king Wăn received.'*

2. The duke said, 'Prince Shih, I have heard
that aforetime, when Thang the Successful had
received the appointment (to the throne), he had
with him Î Yin, making (his virtue) like that of
great Heaven;* that Thâi _K_iâ had (the same

---

¹ The text is here defective; or perhaps the speaker purposely
left his meaning only half expressed.

Î Yín), the Pâo-hăng¹; that Thâi-wû² had Î   207
*K*ih² and *K*hăn Hû², through whom (his virtue)
was made to affect God,* and Wû Hsien³ who
regulated the royal House; that 3û-yî³ had Wû
Hsien's son; and that Wû-ting had Kan Phan⁴.
(These ministers) carried out (their principles), and
displayed (their merit), preserving and regulating
the dynasty of Yin, so that, while its ceremonies
lasted, (those sovereigns), when deceased, were assessors to Heaven⁵,* and its duration extended over
many years. Heaven thus determinately maintained
its favouring appointment, and Shang was replen-
ished with men. The various heads of great surnames and members of the royal House, holding
employments, all held fast their virtue, and showed
an anxious solicitude (for the kingdom). The smaller
ministers, and the guardian princes in the Hâu and
Tien domains, hurried about on their services. Thus
did they all exert their virtue and aid their sovereign, so that whatever affairs he, the One man,
had in hand, throughout the land, an entire faith
was reposed in their justice as in the indications of
the shell or the divining stalks.'*

The duke said, ' Prince Shih, Heaven gives length
of days to the just and the intelligent; (it was thus

---

¹ See Part IV, v, sect. 1, ch. 1, where Î Yin is called Â-hăng,
nearly = Pâo-hăng.

² Thâi-wû is the *K*ung 3ung of last Book. Î *K*ih would be a
son or grandson of Î Yin. Of *K*hăn Hû we know only what is
stated here.

³ 3û-yî was the eleventh Yin sovereign, reigning B. C. 1525–1507.
We know of Wû Hsien only that he was 3û-yî's minister.

⁴ See Part IV, viii, sect. 3, ch. 1.

⁵ That is, they were associated with Heaven in the sacrifices
to it.

that those ministers) maintained and regulated the dynasty of Yin.* He who came last to the throne granted by Heaven was extinguished by its terrors. Do you think of the distant future, and we shall have the decree (in favour of *K*âu) made sure, and its good government will be brilliantly exhibited in our newly-founded state.'

3. The duke said, 'Prince Shih, aforetime when God was inflicting calamity (on Yin), he encouraged anew the virtue of the Tranquillizing king, till at last the great favouring decree was concentrated in his person. (But) that king Wăn was able to conciliate and unite the portion of the great kingdom which we came to possess, was owing to his having (such ministers) as his brother of Kwo, Hung Yâo, San Î-shăng, Thâi Tien, and Nan-kung Kwo.'

He said further, 'But for the ability of those men to go and come in his affairs, developing his constant lessons, there would have been no benefits descending from king Wăn on the people. And it also was from the determinate favour of Heaven that there were these men of firm virtue, and acting according to their knowledge of the dread majesty of Heaven, to give themselves to enlighten king Wăn, and lead him forward to his high distinction and universal rule, till his fame reached the ears of God, and he received the appointment that had been Yin's.* There were still four of those men who led on king Wû to the possession of the revenues of the kingdom, and afterwards, along with him, in great reverence of the majesty of Heaven, slew all his enemies.* These four men, moreover, made king Wû so illustrious that his glory overspread the kingdom, and (the people) universally and greatly proclaimed his

virtue. Now with me Tan, the little child, it is as 209
if I were floating on a great stream ;—with you,
O Shih, let me from this time endeavour to cross
it. Our young sovereign is (powerless), as if he
had not yet ascended the throne. You must by
no means lay the whole burden on me ; and if you
draw yourself up without an effort to supply my
deficiencies, no good will flow to the people from
our age and experience. We shall not hear the
voices of the phœnixes[1], and how much less can it
be thought that we shall be able to make (the king's
virtue) equal (to Heaven) ! ' *

The duke said, 'Oh! consider well these things,
O prince. We have received the appointment to
which belongs an unlimited amount of blessing, but
having great difficulties attached to it. What I
announce to you are counsels of a generous largeness.—I cannot allow the successor of our kings
to go astray.'

4. The duke said, 'The former king laid bare his
heart, and gave full charge to you, constituting you
one of the guides and patterns for the people, saying,
"Do you with intelligence and energy second and
help the king ; do you with sincerity support and
convey forward the great decree. Think of the
virtue of king Wăn, and enter greatly into his
boundless anxieties." '

The duke said, 'What I tell you, O prince, are
my sincere thoughts. O Shih, the Grand-Protector,
if you can but reverently survey with me the decay
and great disorders of Yin, and thence consider the

---

[1] As a token of the goodness of the government and the general
prosperity. See Part II, iv, ch. 3.

[1]   P

210 dread majesty of Heaven (which warns) us!—Am I not to be believed that I must reiterate my words? I simply say, " The establishment (of our dynasty) rests with us two." Do you agree with me? Then you (also) will say, "It rests with us two." And the favour of Heaven has come to us so largely :— it should be ours to feel as if we could not sufficiently respond to it. If you can but reverently cultivate your virtue (now), and bring to light our men of eminent ability, then when you resign (your position) to some successor in a time of established security, (I will interpose no objection.)

'Oh! it is by the earnest service of us two that we have come to the prosperity of the present day. We must both go on, abjuring all idleness, to complete the work of king Wăn, till it has grandly overspread the kingdom, and from the corners of the sea, and the sunrising, there shall not be one who is disobedient to the rule (of *Kʻâu*).'

The duke said, 'O prince, have I not spoken in accordance with reason in these many declarations? I am only influenced by anxiety about (the appointment of) Heaven, and about the people.'

The duke said, 'Oh! you know, O prince, the ways of the people, how at the beginning they can be (all we could desire); but it is the end (that is to be thought of). Act in careful accordance with this fact. Go and reverently exercise the duties of your office.'

BOOK XVII. THE CHARGE TO *K*UNG OF З̣HÂI. 211

З̣HÂI was the name of the small state or territory, which had been conferred on Tû, the next younger brother of the duke of *K*âu. The name still remains in the district of Shang-з̣hâi, department Zû-ning, Ho-nan. Tû was deprived of his state because of his complicity in the rebellion of Wû-*k*ăng; but it was subsequently restored to his son Hû by this charge. Hû is here called *K*ung, that term simply denoting his place in the roll of his brothers or cousins. King *Kh*ăng and Hû were cousins,—' brothers' according to Chinese usage of terms, and Hû being the younger of the two, was called З̣hâi *K*ung, ' the second or younger brother,—of З̣hâi.'

The Book consists of two chapters. The former is of the nature of a preface, giving the details necessary to explain the appointment of Hû. The second contains the king's charge, delivered in his name by the duke of *K*âu, directing Hû how to conduct himself, so that he might blot out the memory of his father's misdeeds, and win the praise of the king.

1. When the duke of *K*âu was in the place of prime minister and directed all the officers, the (king's) uncles spread abroad an (evil) report, in consequence of which (the duke) put to death the prince of Kwan in Shang[1]; confined the prince of З̣hâi in Kwo-lin[2], with an attendance of seven chariots; and reduced the prince of Hwo[3] to be a private man, causing his name to be erased from the registers for three years. The son of the prince

---

[1] The prince of Kwan—corresponding to the present *Kh*ăng *K*âu, department Khâi-făng, Ho-nan—was the third of the sons of king Wăn, and older than the duke of *K*âu. The Shang where he was put to death was probably what had been the capital of the Shang kings.

[2] We do not know where Kwo-lin was.

[3] The name of Hwo remains in Hwo *K*âu, department Phing-yang, Shan-hsî. The prince of Hwo was the eighth of Wăn's sons.

P 2

212 of 3hâi having displayed a reverent virtue, the duke of *K*âu made him a high minister, and when his father died, requested a decree from the king, investing him with the country of 3hâi.

2. 'The king speaks to this effect :—"My little child, Hû, you follow the virtue (of our ancestors), and have changed from the conduct (of your father); you are able to take heed to your ways;—I therefore appoint you to be a marquis in the east. Go to your fief, and be reverent!

"In order that you may cover the faults of your father, be loyal, be filial[1]. Urge on your steps in your own way, diligent and never idle, and so shall you hand down an example to your descendants. Follow the constant lessons of your grandfather king Wǎn, and be not, like your father, disobedient to the royal orders.

"Great Heaven has no partial affections;—it helps only the virtuous.* The people's hearts have no unchanging attachment;—they cherish only the kind. Acts of goodness are different, but they contribute in common to good order. Acts of evil are different, but they contribute in common to disorder. Be cautious!

"In giving heed to the beginning think of the end;—the end will then be without distress. If you do not think of the end, it will be full of distress, even of the greatest.

"Exert yourself to achieve your proper merit. Seek to be in harmony with all your neighbours.

---

[1] Hû's father had not been filial. When he is told to be filial, there underlies the words the idea of the solidarity of the family. His copying the example of his grandfather would be the best service he could render to his father.

Be a fence to the royal House. Live in amity 　213
with your brethren. Tranquillize and help the
lower people.

" Follow the course of the Mean, and do not by
aiming to be intelligent throw old statutes into
confusion. Watch over what you see and hear, and
do not for one-sided words deviate from the right
rule. Then I, the One man, will praise you."

' The king says, " Oh! my little child, Hû, go,
and do not idly throw away my charge." '

Book XVIII.　The Numerous Regions.

The king has returned to his capital in triumph, having put down
rebellion in the east, and specially extinguished the state or
tribe of Yen. The third chapter of Book xiv contained a
reference to an expedition against Yen. Critics are divided
on the point of whether the expedition mentioned in this Book
was the same as that, or another; and our sources of information
are not sufficient to enable us to pronounce positively in the
case. If we may credit what Mencius says, the Records of
the Shû do not tell us a tithe of the wars carried on by the
duke of *K*âu to establish the new dynasty :—' He smote Yen,
and after three years put its ruler to death. He drove Fei-lien
to a corner by the sea, and slew him. The states which he
extinguished amounted to fifty ' (Mencius, III, ii, ch. 9).
However this point be settled, on the occasion when the announcement in this Book was delivered, a great assembly of princes
and nobles—the old officers of Yin or Shang, and chiefs
from many regions—was met together. They are all supposed
to have been secretly, if not openly, in sympathy with the
rebellion which has been trampled out, and to grudge to yield
submission to the rule of *K*âu. The king, by the duke of *K*âu,
reasons and expostulates with them. He insists on the leniency
with which they had been treated in the ' past ; and whereas
they might be saying that *K*âu's overthrow of the Yin dynasty
was a usurpation, he shows that it was from the will of Heaven.

214   The history of the nation is then reviewed, and it is made to
appear that king Wû had displaced the kings of Yin or Shang,
just as Thang, the founder of the Shang dynasty, had displaced
those of Hsiâ. It was their duty therefore to submit to *K*âu.
If they did not avail themselves of its leniency, they should be
dealt with in another way.

Having thus spoken, the duke turns, in the fourth of the five
chapters into which I have divided the Book, and addresses
the many officers of the states, and especially those of Yin, who
had been removed to Lo, speaking to them, as 'the Numerous
Officers,' after the style of Book xiv. Finally, he admonishes
them all that it is time to begin a new course. If they do well,
it will be well with them; if they continue perverse, they will
have to blame themselves for the consequences.

1. In the fifth month, on the day Ting-hâi, the
king arrived from Yen, and came to (Hâo), the
honoured (capital of) *K*âu. The duke of *K*âu said,
'The king speaks to the following effect: "Ho! I
make an announcement to you of the four states,
and the numerous (other) regions. Ye who were the
officers and people of the prince of Yin, I have dealt
very leniently as regards your lives, as ye all know.
You kept reckoning greatly on (some) decree of
Heaven, and did not keep with perpetual awe
before your thoughts (the preservation of) your
sacrifices[1].*

'"God sent down correction on Hsiâ, but the
sovereign (only) increased his luxury and sloth, and
would not speak kindly to the people. He showed
himself dissolute and dark, and would not yield
for a single day to the leadings of God:—this is
what you have heard.* He kept reckoning on the

---

[1] The extinction of the sacrifices of a state was its utter overthrow. None were left—or if some might be left, none of them
were permitted—to continue the sacrifices to its founder and his
descendants.

decree of God (in his favour), and did not cultivate   215
the means for the people's support.* By great
inflictions of punishment also he increased the disorder of the states of Hsiâ. The first cause (of his
evil course) was the internal misrule [1], which made
him unfit to deal well with the multitudes. Nor did
he endeavour to find and employ men whom he could
respect, and who might display a generous kindness
to the people; but where any of the people of Hsiâ
were covetous and fierce, he daily honoured them,
and they practised cruel tortures in the cities.
Heaven on this sought a (true) lord for the people,
and made its distinguished and favouring decree
light on Thang the Successful, who punished and
destroyed the sovereign of Hsiâ.* Heaven's refusal
of its favour (to Hsiâ) was decided. The righteous
men of your numerous regions were not permitted
to continue long in their posts of enjoyment, and
the many officers whom Hsiâ's (last sovereign)
honoured were unable intelligently to maintain the
people in the enjoyment (of their lives), but, on the
contrary, aided one another in oppressing them, till
of the hundred ways of securing (prosperity) they
could not promote (one).

'" In the case indeed of Thang the Successful, it
was because he was the choice of your numerous
regions that he superseded Hsiâ, and became the
lord of the people. He paid careful attention to the
essential virtue (of a sovereign) [2], in order to stimulate the people, and they on their part imitated him

---

[1] The vile debaucheries of which *K*ieh was guilty through his
connexion with the notorious Mei-hsî.

[2] That is, to benevolence or the love of the people.

216   and were stimulated. From him down to Tî-yî, the sovereigns all made their virtue illustrious, and were cautious in the use of punishments;—thus also exercising a stimulating influence (over the people). When they, having examined the evidence in criminal cases, put to death those chargeable with many crimes, they exercised the same influence; and they did so also when they liberated those who were not purposely guilty. But when the throne came to your (last) sovereign, he could not with (the good will of) your numerous regions continue in the enjoyment of the favouring decree of Heaven." ' *

    2. ' Oh! the king speaks to the following effect :—" I announce and declare to you of the numerous regions, that Heaven had no set purpose to do away with the sovereign of Hsiâ or with the sovereign of Yin. But it was the case that your (last) ruler, being in possession of your numerous regions, abandoned himself to great excess, and reckoned on the favouring decree of Heaven, making trifling excuses for his conduct. And so in the case of the (last) sovereign of Hsiâ; his plans of government were not of a tendency to secure his enjoyment (of the kingdom), and Heaven sent down ruin on him, and the chief of the territory (of Shang) put an end (to the line of Hsiâ). In truth, the last sovereign of your Shang was luxurious to the extreme of luxury, while his plans of government showed neither purity nor progress, and thus Heaven sent down such ruin on him [1].*

---

[1] There must have been something remarkable in the closing period of *K*âu-hsin's history, to which the duke alludes in the subsequent specification of five years. We do not know the events of the times sufficiently to say what it was.

'" The wise, through not thinking, become foolish,　217
and the foolish, by thinking, become wise. Heaven
for five years waited kindly, and forbore with the
descendant (of Thang), to see if he would indeed
prove himself the ruler of the people; but there was
nothing in him deserving to be regarded. Heaven
then sought among your numerous regions, making
a great impression by its terrors to stir up some one
who would look (reverently) to it, but in all your
regions there was not one deserving of its favouring
regard. But there were the kings of our *K*âu, who
treated well the multitudes of the people, and were
able to sustain the burden of virtuous (government).
They could preside over (all services to) spirits and
to Heaven.* Heaven thereupon instructed us, and
increased our excellence, made choice of us, and gave
us the decree of Yin, to rule over your numerous
regions."'*

3. '"Why do I now presume to make (these) many
declarations? I have dealt very leniently as regards
the lives of you, the people of these four states.
Why do you not show a sincere and generous obedience in your numerous regions? Why do you not
aid and co-operate with the kings of our *K*âu, to
secure the enjoyment of Heaven's favouring decree?
You now still dwell in your dwellings, and cultivate
your fields;—why do you not obey our kings, and
consolidate the decree of Heaven? The paths
which you tread are continually those of disquietude;
—have you in your hearts no love for yourselves?
do you refuse so greatly to acquiesce in the ordin-
ance of Heaven? do you triflingly reject that
decree? do you of yourselves pursue unlawful
courses, scheming (by your alleged reasons) for the

218 approval of upright men ? I simply instructed you,
and published my announcement[1]; with trembling
awe I secured and confined (the chief criminals) :—
I have done so twice and for three times. But if
you do not take advantage of the leniency with
which I have spared your lives, I will proceed to
severe punishments, and put you to death. It is
not that we, the sovereigns of *K*âu, hold it virtuous
to make you untranquil, but it is you yourselves
who accelerate your crimes (and sufferings)." '

4. 'The king says, "Oh ! ho ! I tell you, ye many
officers of the various regions, and you, ye many
officers of Yin, now have ye been hurrying about,
doing service to my overseers for five years. There
are among you the inferior assistants, the chiefs, and
the numerous directors, small and great ;—see that ye
all attain to the discharge of your duties. Want of
harmony (in the life) rises from (the want of it in)
one's (inner) self ;—strive to be harmonious. Want
of concord in your families (arises from the want
of it in your conduct) ;—strive to be harmonious.
When intelligence rules in your cities, then will you
be proved to be attentive to your duties. Do not
be afraid, I pray you, of the evil ways (of the
people) ; and moreover, by occupying your offices
with a reverent harmony, you will find it possible to
select from your cities individuals on whose assistance you can calculate. You may thus long continue in this city of Lo[2], cultivating your fields.
Heaven will favour and compassionate you, and we,

---

[1] Referring probably to 'the Great Announcement' in Book vii.

[2] It would almost seem from this that the announcement was
made in Lo; and some critics have argued that Lo was 'the
honoured capital' in the first sentence.

the sovereigns of *K*âu, will greatly help you, and   219
confer rewards, selecting you to stand in our royal
court. Only be attentive to your duties, and you
may rank among our great officers."

'The king says, "Oh! ye numerous officers, if
you cannot exhort one another to pay a sincere
regard to my charges, it will further show that you
are unable to honour your sovereign ; and all the
people will (also) say, 'We will not honour him.'
Thus will ye be proved slothful and perverse,
greatly disobedient to the royal charges. Throughout your numerous regions you will bring on yourselves the terrors of Heaven, and I will then inflict
on you its punishments, removing you far from your
country."'

5. 'The king says, "I do not (wish to) make
these many declarations, but it is in a spirit of awe
that I lay my commands before you." He further
says, "You may now make a (new) beginning. If
you cannot reverently realize the harmony (which I
enjoin), do not (hereafter) murmur against me."'

BOOK XIX. THE ESTABLISHMENT OF GOVERNMENT.

THE phrase, 'the Establishment of Government,' occurs several
times in the course of the Book, and is thence taken to denominate it,—appropriately enough. The subject treated of
throughout, is how good government may be established.

Some Chinese critics maintain that the text as it stands is very
confused, 'head and tail in disorder, and without connexion,'
and various re-arrangements of it have been proposed, for
which, however, there is no manuscript authority. Keeping
to the received text, and dividing it into six chapters, we may
adopt a summary of its contents approved by the editors of
the Shû, which was published in the Yung-*k*ǎng reign of the

220　　present dynasty.—In government there is nothing more important than the employment of proper men; and when such
men are being sought, the first care should be for those to
occupy the three highest positions. When these are properly
filled, all the other offices will get their right men, and royal
government will be established: The appointment of the officers
of business, of pastoral oversight, and of the law, is the great
theme of the whole Book, and the concluding words of chapter 1
are its pulse,—may be felt throbbing everywhere in all the sentiments. Chapters 2 and 3 illustrate the subject from the history
of the dynasties of Hsiâ and Shang; and in chapter 4 it is
shown how kings Wăn and Wû selected their officers, and
initiated the happy state which was still continuing. In chapter 5
there is set forth the duty of the king to put away from him
men of artful tongues; to employ the good, distinguished by
their habits of virtue; to be always well prepared for war; and
to be very careful of his conduct in the matter of litigations.
Chapter 6 seems to have hardly any connexion with the rest
of the Book, and is probably a fragment of one of the lost
Books of the Shû, that has got tacked on to this.

The Book belongs to the class of 'Instructions,' and was made,
I suppose, after the duke of *K*âu had retired from his regency.

1. The duke of *K*âu spoke to the following
effect :—'With our hands to our heads and our
heads to the ground, we make our declarations to
the Son of Heaven, the king who has inherited the
throne.' In such manner accordingly all (the other
ministers) cautioned the king, saying, 'In close
attendance on your majesty there are the regular
presidents[1], the regular ministers[2], and the officers
of justice ;—the keepers of the robes (also), and the
guards.' The duke of *K*âu said, 'Oh! admirable
are these (officers). Few, however, know to be
sufficiently anxious about them.'

---

[1] We must understand by these the chiefs or presidents who·
had a certain jurisdiction over several states and their princes.

[2] The high ministers of Instruction, War, Works, &c.

2. 'Among the ancients who exemplified (this   221
anxiety) there was the founder of the Hsiâ dynasty.
When his House was in its greatest strength, he
sought for able men who should honour God (in the
discharge of their duties).* (His advisers), when
they knew of men thoroughly proved and trust-
worthy in the practice of the nine virtues[1], would
then presume to inform and instruct their sovereign,
saying, "With our hands to our heads and our
heads to the ground, O sovereign, we would say,
Let (such an one) occupy one of your high offices:
Let (such an one) be one of your pastors: Let
(such an one) be one of your officers of justice.
By such appointments you will fulfil your duty as
sovereign. If you judge by the face only, and
therefrom deem men well schooled in virtue, and
appoint them, then those three positions will all
be occupied by unrighteous individuals." The way
of *K*ieh, however, was not to observe this precedent.
Those whom he employed were cruel men;—and he
left no successor.'

3. 'After this there was Thang the Successful,
who, rising to the throne, grandly administered the
bright ordinances of God.* He employed, to fill
the three (high) positions, those who were equal to
them; and those who were called possessors of the
three kinds of ability[2] would display that ability.

---

[1] See chapter 2 of 'the Counsels of Kâo-yâo' in Part II.

[2] Some suppose that men are intended here who possessed
'the three virtues' of 'the Great Plan.' I think rather that men
are intended who had talents and virtue which would make them
eligible to the three highest positions. Thang had his notice fixed
on such men, and was prepared to call them to office at the
proper time.

222   He then studied them severely, and greatly imitated them, making the utmost of them in their three positions and with their three kinds of ability. The people in the cities of Shang[1] were thereby all brought to harmony, and those in the four quarters of the kingdom were brought greatly under the influence of the virtue thus displayed. Oh! when the throne came to Shâu, his character was all violence. He preferred men of severity, and who deemed cruelty a virtue, to share with him in the government of his states; and at the same time, the host of his associates, men who counted idleness a virtue, shared the offices of his court. God then sovereignly punished him, and caused us to possess the great land, enjoy the favouring decree which Shâu had (afore) received, and govern all the people in their myriad realms.' *

4. ' Then subsequently there were king Wăn and king Wû, who knew well the minds of those whom they put in the three positions, and saw clearly the minds of those who had the three grades of ability. Thus they could employ them to serve God with reverence, and appointed them as presidents and chiefs of the people. In establishing their government, the three things which principally concerned them were to find the men for (high) offices, the officers of justice, and the pastors. (They had also) the guards; the keepers of the robes; their equerries; their heads of small departments; their personal attendants; their various overseers; and their treasurers. They had their governors of the larger and smaller cities assigned in the royal domain to the

---

[1] That is, within the royal domain.

nobles; their men of arts[1]; their overseers whose   223
offices were beyond the court; their grand historiographers ; and their heads of departments ;—all good
men of constant virtue.

'(In the external states) there were the Minister
of Instruction, the Minister of War, and the Minister
of Works, with the many officers subordinate to them.
Among the wild tribes, such as the Wei, the Lû,
and the *Kʰăng*[2], in the three Po, and at the dangerous passes, they had wardens.

' King Wăn was able to make the minds of those
in the (three high) positions his own, and so it was
that he established those regular officers and super-
intending pastors, so that they were men of ability
and virtue. He would not appear himself in the
various notifications, in litigations, and in precautionary measures. There were the officers and
pastors (to attend to them), whom he (simply)
taught to be obedient (to his wishes), and not to
be disobedient. (Yea), as to litigations and precautionary measures, he (would seem as if he) did
not presume to know about them. He was followed
by king Wû, who carried out his work of settlement, and did not presume to supersede his righteous and virtuous men, but entered into his plans,
and employed, as before, those men. Thus it was
that they unitedly received this vast inheritance.'

---

[1] All who employed their arts in the service of the government;—
officers of prayer, clerks, archers, charioteers, doctors, diviners, and
the practisers of the various mechanical arts, &c.

[2] Compare what is said in ' the Speech at Mû,' ch. 1. The
Kʰăng are not mentioned there. It would seem to be the
name of a wild tribe. The three Po had all been capitals of the
Shang kings, and their people required the special attention of
the sovereigns of *Kâu*.

224

5. 'Oh! young son, the king, from this time forth be it ours to establish the government, appointing the (high) officers, the officers of the laws, and the pastors;—be it ours clearly to know what courses are natural to these men, and then fully to employ them in the government, that they may aid us in the management of the people whom we have received, and harmoniously conduct all litigations and precautionary measures. And let us never allow others to come between us and them. (Yea), in our every word and speech, let us be thinking of (these) officers of complete virtue, to regulate the people that we have received.

'Oh! I, Tan, have received these excellent words of others[1], and tell them all to you, young son, the king. From this time forth, O accomplished son (of Wû), accomplished grandson (of Wăn), do not err in regard to the litigations and precautionary measures;—let the proper officers manage them. From of old to the founder of Shang, and downwards to king Wăn of our *K*âu, in establishing government, when they appointed (high) officers, pastors, and officers of the laws, they settled them in their positions, and allowed them to unfold their talents;—thus giving the regulation of affairs into their hands. In the kingdom, never has there been the establishment of government by the employment of artful-tongued men; (with such men), unlessoned in virtue, never can a government be distinguished in the world. From this time forth, in establishing government, make no use of artful-tongued men,

---

[1] Probably all the other officers or ministers referred to in ch. 1. They are there prepared to speak their views, when the duke of *K*âu takes all the discoursing on himself.

but (seek for) good officers, and get them to use   225
all their powers in aiding the government of our
country.　Now, O accomplished son (of Wû),
accomplished grandson (of Wăn), young son, the
king, do not err in the matter of litigations;—there
are the officers and pastors (to attend to them).

'Have well arranged (also) your military accoutre-
ments and weapons, so that you may go forth beyond
the steps of Yü, and traverse all under the sky, even
to beyond the seas, everywhere meeting with submission:—so shall you display the bright glory of
king Wăn, and render more illustrious the great
achievements of king Wû[1].

'Oh! from this time forth, may (our) future kings,
in establishing the government, be able to employ
men of constant virtue!'

6. The duke of *K*âu spoke to the following
effect:—'O grand historiographer, the duke of Sû,
the Minister of Crime, dealt reverently with all the
criminal matters that came before him, and thereby
perpetuated the fortunes of our kingdom. Here
was an example of anxious solicitude (for future
ministers), whereby they may rank with him in the
ordering of the appropriate punishments[2].'

---

[1] At the close of his address to prince Shih, Book xvi, the
duke of *K*âu breaks all at once into a warlike mood, as he does
here.

[2] I have said in the introductory note that this chapter does
not seem to have any connexion with the rest of the Book. From
a passage in the 8o *K*wan, under the eleventh year of duke *K*hăng,
we learn that a Sû Făn-shăng, or Făn-shăng of Sû, was Minister
of Crime to king Wû. It is probably to him that the duke here
alludes.

[1]　　　　Q

226

Book XX. The Officers of *K*âu.

'The Officers of *K*âu' contains a general outline of the official system of the *K*âu dynasty, detailing the names and functions of the principal ministers about the court and others, to whom, moreover, various counsels are addressed by the king who speaks in it,—no doubt, king *K*ＡＮＧ. Chinese critics class it with the 'Instructions' of the Shû, but it belongs rather to the 'Announcements.'

There is no mention in it of the duke of *K*âu; and its date must therefore be in some year after he had retired from the regency, and resigned the government into the king's own hands.

The Book has a beginning, middle, and end, more distinctly marked than they are in many of the documents in the Shû. The whole is divided into five chapters. The first is introductory, and describes the condition of the kingdom, when the arrangements of the official system were announced. In the second, the king refers to the arrangements of former dynasties. In the third, he sets forth the principal offices of state, the ministers of which had their residence at court, and goes on to the arrangements for the administration of the provinces. The two other chapters contain many excellent advices to the ministers and officers to discharge their duties so that the fortunes of the dynasty might be consolidated, and no dissatisfaction arise among the myriad states.

1. The king of *K*âu brought the myriad regions (of the kingdom) to tranquillity; he made a tour of inspection through the Hâu and Tien tenures; he punished on all sides the chiefs who had refused to appear at court; thus securing the repose of the millions of the people, and all the (princes in the) six tenures acknowledging his virtue. He then returned to the honoured capital of *K*âu, and strictly regulated the officers of the administration.

2. The king said, 'It was the grand method of former times to regulate the government while there

was no confusion, and to secure the country while   227
there was no danger.' He said, 'Yâo and Shun,
having studied antiquity[1], established a hundred
officers. At court, there were the General Regulator and (the President of) the Four Mountains;
abroad, there were the pastors of the provinces and
the princes of states. Thus the various departments
of government went on harmoniously, and the myriad
states all enjoyed repose. Under the dynasties of
Hsiâ and Shang, the number of officers was doubled,
and they were able still to secure good government.
(Those early) intelligent kings, in establishing their
government, cared not so much about the number
of the offices as about the men (to occupy them).
Now I, the little child, cultivate with reverence my
virtue, concerned day and night about my deficiencies; I look up to (those) former dynasties,
and seek to conform to them, while I instruct and
direct you, my officers.'

3. 'I appoint the Grand - Master, the Grand -
Assistant, and the Grand-Guardian. These are the
three Kung[2]. They discourse about the principles

---

[1] It is the same phrase here, which occurs at the beginning
of the Canons of Yâo and Shun, and of some other Books. It
may be inferred, as P. Gaubil says, that Yâo and Shun had certain
sources of knowledge, that is to say, some history of the times
anterior to their own.

[2] That is, 'the three dukes;' but the term is here a name of
office, more than of nobility, as is evident from the name of the
three Kû, who were next to them. Kû was not used as a term
expressing any order of nobility. It would seem to indicate that,
while the men holding the office were assistant to the Kung, they
yet had a distinct standing of their own. The offices of Grand-
Master &c. had existed under the Shang dynasty; see Book xi,
Part IV.

228

of reason¹ and adjust the states, harmonizing (also) and regulating the operations (in nature) of heaven and earth². These offices need not (always) be filled; there must (first) be the men for them.

'(I appoint) the Junior Master, the Junior Assistant, and the Junior Guardian. These are called the three Kû³. They assist the Kung to diffuse widely the transforming influences, and display brightly with reverence (the powers of) heaven and earth,—assisting me, the One man.

'(I appoint) the Prime Minister, who presides over the ruling of the (various) regions, has the general management of all the other officers, and secures uniformity within the four seas; the Minister of Instruction, who presides over the education in the states, diffuses a knowledge of the duties belonging to the five relations of society, and trains the millions of the people to obedience; the Minister of Religion, who presides over the (sacred) ceremonies of the country, regulates the services rendered to the spirits and manes, and makes a harmony between high and low⁴;* the Minister of War, who presides over the (military) administration of the

---

¹ Meaning, I suppose, the courses or ways, which it was right for the king, according to reason, to pursue.

² That is, probably, securing the material prosperity of the kingdom, in good seasons, &c.

³ See note 2 on the preceding page.

⁴ The name here for ' the Minister of Religion' is the same as that in the Canon of Shun. ' The spirits and manes ' are 'the spirits of heaven, earth, and deceased men.' All festive, funeral, and other ceremonies, as well as those of sacrifices, came under the department of the Minister of Religion, who had therefore to define the order of rank and precedence. This seems to be what is meant by his ' making a harmony between high and low.'

country, commands the six hosts, and secures the 229
tranquillity of all the regions; the Minister of Crime,
who presides over the prohibitions of the country,
searches out the villainous and secretly wicked, and
punishes oppressors and disturbers of the peace;
and the Minister of Works, who presides over the
land of the country, settles the four classes of the
people, and secures at the proper seasons the produce of the ground[1].

' These six ministers with their different duties
lead on their several subordinates, and set an
example to the nine pastors of the provinces, enriching and perfecting the condition of the millions
of the people. In six years (the lords of) the five
tenures appear once at the royal court; and after
a second six years, the king makes a tour of inspection in the four seasons, and examines the (various)
regulations and measures at the four mountains.
The princes appear before him each at the mountain of his quarter; and promotions and degrada-
tions are awarded with great intelligence.'

4. The king said, ' Oh! all ye men of virtue, my
occupiers of office, pay reverent attention to your
charges. Be careful in the commands you issue;
for, once issued, they must be carried into effect,
and cannot be retracted. Extinguish all selfish
aims by your public feeling, and the people will
have confidence in you, and be gladly obedient.
Study antiquity as a preparation for entering on

---

[1] Out of these six ministers and their departments have grown
the Six Boards of the Chinese Government of the present day :—
the Board of Civil Office; the Board of Revenue; the Board of
Rites; the Board of War; the Board of Punishment; and the
Board of Works.

230 your offices. In deliberating on affairs, form your determinations by help (of such study), and your measures will be free from error. Make the regular statutes of (our own) dynasty your rule, and do not with artful speeches introduce disorder into your offices. To accumulate doubts is the way to ruin your plans; to be idle and indifferent is the way to ruin your government. Without study, you stand facing a wall, and your management of affairs will be full of trouble.

'I warn you, my high ministers and officers, that exalted merit depends on the high aim, and a patrimony is enlarged only by diligence; it is by means of bold decision that future difficulties are avoided. Pride comes, along with rank, unperceived, and extravagance in the same way with emolument. Let reverence and economy be (real) virtues with you, unaccompanied with hypocritical display. Practise them as virtues, and your minds will be at ease, and you will daily become more admirable. Practise them in hypocrisy, and your minds will be toiled, and you will daily become more stupid. In the enjoyment of favour think of peril, and never be without a cautious apprehension;—he who is without such apprehension finds himself amidst what is really to be feared. Push forward the worthy, and show deference to the able; and harmony will prevail among all your officers. When they are not harmonious, the government becomes a mass of confusion. If those whom you advance be able for their offices, the ability is yours; if you advance improper men, you are not equal to your position.'

5. The king said, 'Oh! ye (charged) with the

threefold business (of government)[1], and ye great   231
officers, reverently attend to your departments, and
conduct well the affairs under your government, so
as to assist your sovereign, and secure the lasting
happiness of the millions of the people;—so shall
there be no dissatisfaction throughout the myriad
states.'

Book XXI. The *Kün-khăn*.

Kün-khăn was the successor in 'the eastern capital' of the duke
of *Kâu*, who has now passed off the stage of the Shû, which
he occupied so long. Between 'the Officers of *Kâu*' and this
Book, there were, when the Shû was complete, two others,
which are both lost. We must greatly deplore the loss of the
second of them, for it contained an account of the death of
the duke of *Kâu*, and an announcement made by king *Khăng*
by his bier.

Who *Kün-khăn*, the charge to whom on entering on his important
government is here preserved, really was, we are not informed.
Some have supposed that he was a son of the duke of *Kâu*;
but we may be sure, from the analogy of other charges, that
if he had been so, the fact would have been alluded to in the
text. *Kün-khăn* might be translated 'the prince *Khăn*,' like
Kün Shih in the title of Book xvi, but we know nothing of any
territory with which he was invested.

The following summary of the contents is given by a Chinese
critic:—'The whole Book may be divided into three chapters.
The first relates *Kün-khăn*'s appointment to the government
of the eastern capital. The concluding words, "Be reverent,"

---

[1] 'The threefold business of government' is the appointment
of the men of office, the officers of law, and the pastors, 'the three
concerns of those in the three highest positions,' as described in
the last Book, ch. 4. The king, probably, intends the Kung, the
Kû, and the six ministers, whose duties he has spoken of. The
'great officers' will be all the officers inferior to these in their
several departments.

232　are emphatic, and give the key-note to all that follows. The
second chapter enjoins on him to exert himself to illustrate
the lessons of the duke of *K*âu, and thereby transform the
people of Yin. The third requires him to give full development to those lessons, and instances various particulars in
which his doing so would appear;—all illustrative of the command at the commencement, that he should be reverent.'

1. The king spake to the following effect:—
'*K*ün-*kh*ăn, it is you who are possessed of excellent virtue, filial and respectful. Being filial, and
friendly with your brethren, you can display these
qualities in the exercise of goverment. I appoint
you to rule this eastern border. Be reverent.'

2. 'Formerly, the duke of *K*âu acted as teacher
and guardian of the myriads of the people, who
cherish (the remembrance of) his virtue. Go and
with sedulous care enter upon his charge; act in
accordance with his regular ways, and exert yourself to illustrate his lessons;—so shall the people
be regulated. I have heard that he said, " Perfect
government has a piercing fragrance, and influences the spiritual intelligences.* It is not the
millet which has the piercing fragrance; it is bright
virtue." Do you make this lesson of the duke
of *K*âu your rule, being diligent from day to day,
and not presuming to indulge in luxurious ease.
Ordinary men, while they have not yet seen a
sage, (are full of desire) as if they should never
get a sight of him; and after they have seen him,
they are still unable to follow him. Be cautioned
by this! You are the wind; the inferior people
are the grass. In revolving the plans of your
government, never hesitate to acknowledge the
difficulty of the subject. Some things have to be
abolished, and some new things to be enacted;—

going out and coming in, seek the judgment of your people about them, and, when there is a general agreement, exert your own powers of reflection. When you have any good plans or counsels, enter and lay them before your sovereign in the palace. Thereafter, when you are acting abroad in accordance with them, say, " This plan or this view is all due to our sovereign." Oh! if all ministers were to act thus, how excellent would they be, and how distinguished!'

3. The king said, '*Kün-kh*ăn, do you give their full development to the great lessons of the duke of *K*âu. Do not make use of your power to exercise oppression; do not make use of the laws to practise extortion. Be gentle, but with strictness of rule. Promote harmony by the display of an easy forbearance.

'When any of the people of Yin are amenable to punishment, if I say " Punish," do not you therefore punish ; and if I say " Spare," do not you therefore spare. Seek the due middle course. Those who are disobedient to your government, and uninfluenced by your instructions, you will punish, remembering that the end of punishment is to make an end of punishing. Those who are inured to villainy and treachery, those who violate the regular duties of society, and those who introduce disorder into the public manners :—those three classes you will not spare, though their particular offences be but small.

'Do not cherish anger against the obstinate, and dislike them. Seek not every quality in one individual. You must have patience, and you will be successful ; have forbearance, and your virtue will

234 be great. Mark those who discharge their duties well, and also mark those who do not do so, (and distinguish them from one another.) Advance the good, to induce those who may not be so to follow (their example).

'The people are born good, and are changed by (external) things,* so that they resist what their superiors command, and follow what they (themselves) love. Do you but reverently observe the statutes, and they will be found in (the way of) virtue; they will thus all be changed, and truly advance to a great degree of excellence. Then shall I, the One man, receive much happiness, and your excellent services will be famous through long ages!'

Book XXII. The Testamentary Charge.

This Book brings us to the closing act of the life of king *Kh*äng, whose reign, according to the current chronology, lasted thirty-seven years, ending in b.c. 1079. From the appointment of *Kün-khä*n to his death, the king's history is almost a blank. The only events chronicled by Sze-mâ *Kh*ien are a coinage of round money with a square hole in the centre,—the prototype of the present cash; and an enactment about the width and length in which pieces of silk and cloth were to be manufactured.

King *Kh*äng, feeling that his end is near, calls his principal ministers and other officers around his bed, and commits his son *K*âo to their care and guidance. The record of all these things and the dying charge form a chapter that ends with the statement of the king's death. The rest of the Book forms a second chapter, in which we have a detailed account of the ceremonies connected with the publication of the charge, and the accession of *K*âo to the throne. It is an interesting account of the ways of that distant time on such occasions.

1. In the fourth month, when the moon began to wane, the king was indisposed. On the day *K'i*â-

žze, he washed his hands and face; his attendants   235
put on him his cap and robes[1]; (and he sat up),
leaning on a gem-adorned bench[2]. He then called
together the Grand-Guardian Shih, the earls of Zui
and Thung, the duke of Pî, the marquis of Wei, the
duke of Mâo, the master of the warders, the master
of the guards, the heads of the various departments,
and the superintendents of affairs[3].

The king said, 'Oh! my illness has greatly increased, and it will soon be over with me. The
malady comes on daily with more violence, and
maintains its hold. I am afraid I may not find
(another opportunity) to declare my wishes about
my successor, and therefore I (now) lay my charge
upon you with special instructions. The former
rulers, our kings Wăn and Wû, displayed in succession their equal glory, making sure provision for
the support of the people, and setting forth their

---

[1] The king's caps or crowns and robes were many, and for
each there was the appropriate occasion. His attendants, no
doubt, now dressed king Khăng as the rules of court fashions
required.

[2] In those days they sat on the ground upon mats; and for
the old or infirm benches or stools were placed, in front of them,
to lean forward on. The king had five kinds of stools variously
adorned. That with gems was the most honourable.

[3] The Grand-Guardian Shih, or the duke of Shâo, and the other
five dignitaries were, no doubt, the six ministers of the 20th Book.
Zui is referred to the present district of Kâo-yî, department Hsî-an;
and Thung to Hwâ Kâu, department Thung-kâu;—both in Shen-
hsî. The earl of Zui, it is supposed, was Minister of Instruction,
and he of Thung Minister of Religion. Pî corresponded to the
present district of Khang-an, department Hsî-an. The duke of
Pî was Minister of War, called Duke or Kung, as Grand-Master.
It is not known where Mâo was. The lord of it was Minister
of Works, and Grand-Assistant. The marquis of Wei,—see on
Book ix. He was now, it is supposed, Minister of Crime.

236 instructions. (The people) accorded a practical submission, without any opposition, and the influence (of their example and instructions) extended to Yin, and the great appointment (of Heaven) was secured*. After them, I, the stupid one, received with reverence the dread (decree) of Heaven, and continued to keep the great instructions of Wăn and Wû, not daring blindly to transgress them.*

'Now Heaven has laid affliction on me, and it seems as if I should not again rise or be myself. Do you take clear note of these my words, and in accordance with them watch reverently over my eldest son *K*âo, and greatly assist him in the difficulties of his position. Be kind to those who are far off, and help those who are near. Promote the tranquillity of the states, small and great, and encourage them (to well-doing). I think how a man has to govern himself in dignity and with decorum; —do not you allow *K*âo to proceed heedlessly on the impulse of improper motives.' Immediately on receiving this charge, (the ministers and others) withdrew. The tent[1] was then carried out into

---

[1] The tent had been prepared when the king sent for his ministers and officers to give them his last charge, and set up outside his chamber in the hall where he was accustomed to hold 'the audience of government.' He had walked or been carried to it, and then returned to his apartment when he had expressed his last wishes, while the tent—the curtains and canopy—was carried out into the courtyard.

The palace was much more long or deep than wide, consisting of five series of buildings continued one after another, so that, if all the gates were thrown open, one could walk in a direct line from the first gate to the last. The different parts of it were separated by courts that embraced a large space of ground, and were partly open overhead. The gates leading to the different parts had their particular names, and were all fronting

the court; and on the next day, (being) Yî-*kh*âu,   237
the king died.

2. The Grand-Guardian then ordered Kung
Hwan[1] and Nan-Kung Mâo[1] to instruct Lü *K*î,
the marquis of *Kh*î[2], with two shield-and-spearmen,
and a hundred guards, to meet the prince *K*âo outside the south gate[3], and conduct him to (one of)
the side-apartments (near to that where the king
lay), there to be as chief mourner[4].

On the day Ting-mâo, (two days after the king's
death), he ordered (the charge) to be recorded on

---

the south. Outside the second was held 'the outer levee,' where
the king received the princes and officers generally. Outside the
fifth was held 'the audience of government,' when he met his
ministers to consult with them on the business of the state. Inside
this gate were the buildings which formed the private apartments,
in the hall leading to which was held 'the inner audience,' and
where the sovereign feasted those whom he designed specially
to honour. Such is the general idea of the ancient palace given
by *K*û Hsî. The gateways included a large space, covered by a
roof, supported on pillars.

[1] We know nothing more of these officers but what is here
related.

[2] The marquis of *Kh*î was the son of Thâi-kung, a friend and
minister of king Wǎn, who had been enfeoffed by king Wû with
the state of *Kh*î, embracing the present department of *Kh*ing-*k*âu,
in Shan-tung, and other territory. His place at court was that of
master of the guards.

[3] All the gates might be called ' south gates.' It is not certain
whether that intended here was the outer gate of all, or the last,
immediately in front of the hall, where the king had given his
charge. Whichever it was, the meeting *K*âo in the way described
was a public declaration that he had been appointed successor
to the throne.

[4] ' The mourning shed,' spoken of in Part IV, viii, ch. 1, had
not yet been set up, and the apartment here indicated—on the
east of the hall of audience—was the proper one for the prince
to occupy in the mean time.

238　tablets, and the forms (to be observed in publishing it). Seven days after, on Kwei-yû, as chief (of the west) and premier, he ordered the (proper) officers to prepare the wood (for all the requirements of the funeral) [1].

The salvage men [2] set out the screens [3], ornamented with figures of axes, and the tents. Between the window (and the door), facing the south, they placed the (three)fold mat of fine bamboo splints, with its striped border of white and black silk, and the usual bench adorned with different-coloured gems. In the side-space on the west, which faced the east, they placed the threefold rush mat, with its variegated border, and the usual bench adorned with beautiful shells. In the side-space on the east, which faced the west, they placed the threefold mat of fine grass, with its border of painted silk, and the usual bench carved, and adorned with gems. Before the western side-chamber, and facing the south, they placed the threefold mat of fine bamboo, with its dark mixed border, and the usual lacquered bench [4].

---

[1] On the seventh day after his death the king had been shrouded and put into his coffin. But there were still the shell or outer coffin, &c., to be provided.

[2] These 'salvage men' were, I suppose, natives of the wild Tî tribes, employed to perform the more servile offices about the court. Some of them, we know, were enrolled among the guards.

[3] The screens were ornamented with figures of axe-heads, and placed behind the king, under the canopy that overshadowed him.

[4] All these arrangements seem to have been made in the hall where king *Khäng* had delivered his charge. He had been accustomed to receive his guests at all the places where the tents, screens, and mats were now set. It was presumed he would be present in spirit at the ceremony of proclaiming his son, and

(They set forth) also the five pairs of gems (or 239
jade), and the precious things of display. There
were the red knife, the great lessons, the large
round-and-convex symbol of jade, and the rounded
and pointed maces,—all in the side-space on the
west; the large piece of jade, the pieces contributed
by the wild tribes of the east, the heavenly sounding-
stone, and the river-Plan,—all in the side-space
on the east; the dancing habits of Yin, the large
tortoise-shell, and the large drum,—all in the western
apartment; the spear of Tûi, the bow of Ho, and
the bamboo arrows of *Kh*ui,—all in the eastern
apartment [1].

The grand carriage was by the guests' steps,
facing (the south); the next was by the eastern
(or host's) steps, facing (the south). The front
carriage was placed before the left lobby, and the
one that followed it before the right lobby [2].

---

making known to him his dying charge; and as they could not
tell at what particular spot the spirit would be, they made all the
places ready for it.

[1] The western and eastern apartments were two rooms, east
and west of the hall, forming part of the private apartments,
behind the side rooms, and of large dimensions. The various
articles enumerated were precious relics, and had been favourites
with king *Kh*äng. They were now displayed to keep up the
illusion of the king's still being present in spirit. 'They were set
forth,' it is said, 'at the ancestral sacrifices to show that the king
could preserve them, and at the ceremony of announcing a testamentary charge to show that he could transmit them.' About
the articles themselves it is not necessary to append particular
notes. They perished thousands of years ago, and the accounts
of them by the best scholars are little more than conjectural.

[2] The royal carriages were of five kinds, and four of them at
least were now set forth inside the last gate, that everything might
again be done, as when the king was alive. On the west side
of the hall were the guests' steps (or staircase), by which visitors

240   Two men in brownish leather caps, and holding
three-cornered halberts, stood inside the gate leading
to the private apartments. Four men in caps of
spotted deer-skin, holding spears with blades up-
turned from the base of the point, stood, one on
each side of the steps east and west, and near to
the platform of the hall. One man in a great
officer's cap, and holding an axe, stood in the hall,
(near the steps) at the east (end). One man in a
great officer's cap, and holding an axe of a different
pattern, stood in the hall, (near the steps) at the
west end. One man in a great officer's cap, and
holding a lance, stood at the front and east of
the hall, close by the steps. One man in a great
officer's cap, and holding a lance of a different
pattern, stood in the corresponding place on the
west. One man in a great officer's cap, and holding
a pointed weapon, stood by the steps on the north
side of the hall.

The king, in a linen cap and the variously figured
skirt, ascended by the guests' steps, followed by
the high ministers, (great) officers, and princes of
states, in linen caps and dark-coloured skirts[1].
Arrived in the hall, they all took their (proper)
places. The Grand-Guardian, the Grand-Historio-
grapher, and the Minister of Religion were all in

---

ascended, and on the east were those used by the host himself.
If one of the royal carriages was absent on this occasion, it must
have been that used in war, as not being appropriate at such
a time.

[1] All was now ready for the grand ceremony, and the performers,
in their appropriate mourning and sacrificial array, take their
places in the hall. *Kâo* is here for the first time styled 'king;'
but still he goes up by the guests' steps, not presuming to ascend
by the others, while his father's corpse was in the hall.

linen caps and red skirts. The Grand-Guardian 241
bore the great mace. The Minister of Religion
bore the cup and the mace-cover. These two
ascended by the steps on the east[1]. The Grand-
Historiographer bore the testamentary charge. He
ascended by the guests' steps (on the west), and
advanced to the king with the tablets containing
the charge, and said, ' Our royal sovereign, leaning
on the gem-adorned bench, declared his last charge,
and commanded you to continue (the observance of)
the lessons, and to take the rule of the kingdom of
*K*âu, complying with the great laws, and securing the
harmony of all under the sky, so as to respond to and
display the bright instructions of Wăn and Wû.'

The king twice bowed (low), and then arose, and
replied, ' I am utterly insignificant and but a child,
how should I be able to govern the four quarters
(of the kingdom) with a corresponding reverent
awe of the dread majesty of Heaven!' * He then
received the cup and the mace-cover. Thrice he
slowly and reverently advanced with a cup of spirits
(to the east of the coffin); thrice he sacrificed (to the
spirit of his father);* and thrice he put the cup down.
The Minister of Religion said, ' It is accepted[2].' *

---

[1] The Grand-Guardian and the Minister of Religion ascended
by the eastern steps, because the authority of king *K*ăng was
in their persons, to be conveyed by the present ceremony to his
son. ' The great mace' was one of the emblems of the royal
sovereignty, and ' the cup' also must have been one that only the
king could use. ' The mace-cover' was an instrument by which
the genuineness of the symbols of their rank conferred on the
different princes was tested.

[2] According to Khung Ying-tâ, when the king received the record
of the charge, he was standing at the top of the eastern steps, a
little eastwards, with his face to the north. The Historiographer
stood by king *K*ăng's coffin, on the south-west of it, with his face

[1]   R

242

The Grand-Guardian received the cup, descended the steps, and washed his hands [1]. He then took another cup, (placed it on) a half-mace which he carried, and repeated the sacrifice [2].* He then gave the cup to one of the attendants of the Minister of Religion, and did obeisance. The king returned the obeisance. The Grand-Guardian took a cup again, and poured out the spirits in sacrifice.* He then just tasted the spirits, returned to his place, gave the cup to the attendant, and did obeisance. The king returned the obeisance. The Grand-Guardian descended from the hall, after which the various (sacrificial) articles were removed, and the princes all went out at the temple gate [3] and waited.

---

to the east. There he read the charge, after which the king bowed twice, and the Minister of Religion, on the south-west of the king, presented the cup and mace-cover. The king took them, and, having given the cover in charge to an attendant, advanced with the cup to the place between the pillars where the sacrificial spirits were placed. Having filled a cup, he advanced to the east of the coffin, and stood with his face to the west; then going to the spot where his father's spirit was supposed to be, he sacrificed, pouring out the spirits on the ground, and then he put the cup on the bench appropriated for it. This he repeated three times. At the conclusion the Minister of Religion conveyed to him a message from the spirit of his father, that his offering was accepted.

[1] Preparatory, that is, to his offering a sacrifice.

[2] That is, probably, repeated the sacrifice to the spirit of king Khăng, as if to inform him that his charge had been communicated to his son. The half-mace was used as a handle for the sacrificial cup. This ceremony appears to have been gone through twice. The Grand-Guardian's bowing was to the spirit of king Khăng, and the new king returned the obeisance for his father.

[3] Meaning the fifth or last gate of the palace. The private apartments had for the time, through the presence of the coffin and by the sacrifices, been converted into a sort of ancestral temple.

Book XXIII.

243

The Announcement of King Khang.

KHANG was the honorary sacrificial title conferred on *Kâo*, the son and successor of king *Khäng*. His reign lasted from B.C. 1078 to 1053. Khang, as an honorary title, has various meanings. In the text it probably denotes—'Who caused the people to be tranquil and happy.'
Immediately on his accession to the throne, as described in the last Book, king Khang made the Announcement which is here recorded. Indeed the two Books would almost seem to form only one, and as such they appeared in the Shû of Fû, as related in the Introduction.
The princes, with whose departure from the inner hall of the palace the last Book concludes, are introduced again to the king in the court between the fourth and fifth gates, and do homage to him after their fashion, cautioning also and advising him about the discharge of his high duties. He responds with the declaration which has given name to the Book, referring to his predecessors, and asking the assistance of all his hearers, that his reign may be a not unworthy sequel of theirs. With this the proceedings terminate, and the king resumes his mourning dress which he had put off for the occasion. The whole thus falls into three chapters.

1. The king came forth and stood (in the space) within the fourth gate of the palace, when the Grand-Guardian led in the princes of the western regions by the left (half) of the gate, and the duke of Pî those of the eastern regions by the right (half)[1]. They then all caused their teams of light bay horses, with their manes and tails dyed red, to be exhibited; —and, (as the king's) guests, lifted up their rank-symbols, and (the other) presents (they had brought)[2],

---

[1] See note on these ministers, p. 235.
[2] These presents were in addition to the teams of horses exhibited in the courtyard;—silks and lighter productions of their various territories.

R 2

244　saying, 'We your servants, defenders (of the throne), venture to bring the productions of our territories, and lay them here.' (With these words) they all did obeisance twice, laying their heads on the ground. The king, as the righteous successor to the virtue of those who had gone before him, returned their obeisance.

The Grand-Guardian and the earl of *Z*ui, with all the rest, then advanced and bowed to each other, after which they did obeisance twice, with their heads to the ground, and said, 'O Son of Heaven, we venture respectfully to declare our sentiments. Great Heaven altered its decree which the great House of Yin had received, and Wăn and Wû of our *K*âu grandly received the same, and carried it out, manifesting their kindly government in the western regions. His recently ascended majesty,* rewarding and punishing exactly in accordance with what was right, fully established their achievements, and transmitted this happy state to his successors. Do you, O king, now be reverent. Maintain your armies in great order, and do not allow the rarely equalled appointment of our high ancestors to come to harm.'*

2. The king spoke to the following effect:—'Ye princes of the various states, chiefs of the Hâu, Tien, Nan, and Wei domains, I, *K*âo, the One man, make an announcement in return (for your advice). The former rulers, Wăn and Wû, were greatly just and enriched (the people). They did not occupy them-selves to find out people's crimes. Pushing to the utmost and maintaining an entire impartiality and sincerity, they became gloriously illustrious all under heaven. Then they had officers brave as bears and

grisly bears, and ministers of no double heart, who 245
(helped them) to maintain and regulate the royal
House. Thus (did they receive) the true favouring decree from God, and thus did great Heaven
approve of their ways, and give them the four
quarters (of the land).* Then they appointed and
set up principalities, and established bulwarks (to
the throne), for the sake of us, their successors.
Now do ye, my uncles[1], I pray you, consider with
one another, and carry out the service which the
dukes, your predecessors, rendered to my predecessors. Though your persons be distant, let your
hearts be in the royal House. Enter thus into my
anxieties, and act in accordance with them, so that
I, the little child, may not be put to shame.'

3. The dukes and all the others, having heard
this charge, bowed to one another, and hastily withdrew. The king put off his cap, and assumed again
his mourning dress.

BOOK XXIV. THE CHARGE TO THE DUKE OF PÎ.

THE king who delivers the charge in this Book was Khang, and
the only events of his reign of twenty-six years of which we
have any account in the Shû and in Sze-mâ *Kh*ien are it and
the preceding announcement.

Book xxi relates the appointment of *K*ün-*kh*ăn, by king *Kh*ăng,
to the charge which was now, on his death, entrusted to the
duke of Pî, who is mentioned at the commencement of 'the
Testamentary Charge.' By the labours of the duke of *K*âu
and *K*ün-*kh*ăn a considerable change had been effected in the
character of the people of Yin, who had been transferred to
the new capital and its neighbourhood; and king Khang now

---

[1] Meaning the various princes, and especially those bearing the
same surname as himself.

246　　appoints the duke of Pî to enter into and complete their
work.

After an introductory paragraph, the charge, in three chapters,
occupies all the rest of the Book. The first of them speaks
of what had been accomplished, and the admirable qualities of
the duke which fitted him to accomplish what remained to be
done. The second speaks of the special measures which were
called for by the original character and the altered character of
the people. The third dwells on the importance of the charge,
and stimulates the duke, by various considerations, to address
himself to fulfil it effectually.

1. In the sixth month of his twelfth year, the day
of the new moon's appearance was Kăng-wû, and on
Zăn-shăn, the third day after, the king walked in the
morning from the honoured capital of Kâu to Făng[1],
and there, with reference to the multitudes of Khăng-
kâu[2], gave charge to the duke of Pî[3] to protect and
regulate the eastern border.

2. The king spoke to the following effect :—
'Oh! Grand-Master, it was when Wăn and Wû
had diffused their great virtue all under heaven,
that they therefore received the appointment which
Yin had enjoyed.* The duke of Kâu acted as
assistant to my royal predecessors, and tranquillized
and established their kingdom. Cautiously did he
deal with the refractory people of Yin, and removed
them to the city of Lo, that they might be quietly
near the royal House, and be transformed by its

---

[1] That is, he went from Hâo, founded by king Wû, to Făng
the capital of Wăn. The king wished to give his charge in the
temple of king Wăn, because the duke of Pî had been one of
his ministers.

[2] Khăng-kâu was a name of the new or 'lower' capital of
Lo, perhaps as giving 'completion,' or full establishment to the
dynasty.

[3] The duke of Pî had succeeded the duke of Kâu, in the office
of Grand-Master, under king Khăng.

lessons. Six and thirty years have elapsed[1]; the   247
generation has been changed; and manners have
altered. Through the four quarters of the land
there is no occasion for anxiety, and I, the One
man, enjoy repose.

' The prevailing ways now tend to advancement
and now to degeneracy, and measures of government must be varied according to the manners
(of the time). If you (now) do not manifest your
approval of what is good, the people will not be led
to stimulate themselves in it. But your virtue,
O duke, is strenuous, and you are cautiously attentive to the smallest things. You have been helpful
to and brightened four reigns [2]; with deportment all
correct leading on the inferior officers, so that there
is not one who does not reverently take your words
as a law. Your admirable merits were many (and
great) in the times of my predecessors; I, the little
child, have but to let my robes hang down, and fold
my hands, while I look up for the complete effect
(of your measures).'

3. The king said, ' Oh ! Grand-Master, I now
reverently charge you with the duties of the duke of
*K*âu. Go! Signalize the good, separating the bad
from them; give tokens of your approbation in their
neighbourhoods[3], making it ill for the evil by such
distinction of the good, and thus establishing the
influence and reputation (of their virtue). When
the people will not obey your lessons and statutes,

---

[1] Probably, from the death of the duke of *K*âu.

[2] Those of Wăn, Wû, *K*hăng, and the existing reign of Khang.

[3] Setting up, that is, some conspicuous monument, with an
inscription testifying his approbation. All over China, at the
present day, such testimonials are met with.

248 　mark off the boundaries of their hamlets, making them fear (to do evil), and desire (to do good). Define anew the borders and frontiers, and be careful to strengthen the guard-posts through the territory, in order to secure tranquillity (within) the four seas. In measures of government to be consistent and constant, and in proclamations a combination of completeness and brevity, are valuable. There should not be the love of what is extraordinary. Among the customs of Shang was the flattery of superiors; sharp-tonguedness was the sign of worth. The remains of these manners are not yet obliterated. Do you, O duke, bear this in mind. I have heard the saying, "Families which have for generations enjoyed places of emolument seldom observe the rules of propriety. They become dissolute, and do violence to virtue, setting themselves in positive opposition to the way of Heaven. They ruin the formative principles of good; encourage extravagance and display; and tend to carry all (future ages) on the same stream with them." Now the officers of Yin had long relied on the favour which they enjoyed. In the confidence of their prideful extravagance they extinguished their (sense of) righteousness. They displayed before men the beauty of their robes, proud, licentious, arrogant, and boastful;—the natural issue was that they should end in being thoroughly bad. Although their lost minds have (in a measure) been recovered, it is difficult to keep them under proper restraint. If with their property and wealth they can be brought under the influence of instruction, they may enjoy lengthened years, virtue, and righteousness!— these are the great lessons. If you do not follow

in dealing with them these lessons of antiquity,   249
wherein will you instruct them?'

4. The king said, 'Oh! Grand-Master, the security or the danger of the kingdom depends on those
officers of Yin. If you are not (too) stern with them
nor (too) mild, their virtue will be truly cultivated.
The duke of *K*âu exercised the necessary caution at
the beginning (of the undertaking); *K*ün-*kh*ăn displayed the harmony proper to the middle of it; and
you, O duke, can bring it at last to a successful issue.
You three princes will have been one in aim, and
will have equally pursued the proper way. The
penetrating power of your principles, and the good
character of your measures of government, will exert
an enriching influence on the character of the people,
so that the wild tribes, with their coats buttoning on
the left[1], will all find their proper support in them,
and I, the little child, will long enjoy much happiness. Thus, O duke, there in *Kh*ăng-*k*âu will you
establish for ever the power (of *K*âu), and you will
have an inexhaustible fame. Your descendants will
follow your perfect pattern, governing accordingly.

'Oh! do not say, "I am unequal to this;" but
exert your mind to the utmost. Do not say, "The
people are few;" but attend carefully to your business. Reverently follow the accomplished achievements of the former kings, and complete the excellence of the government of your predecessors.'

---

[1] Confucius once praised Kwan *K*ung, a great minister of *Khî*,
in the seventh century B.C., for his services against the wild tribes
of his time, saying, that but for him they in China would be wearing their hair dishevelled, and buttoning the lappets of their coats
on the left side. See Analects, XIV, xviii. The long robes and
jackets of the Chinese generally stretch over on the right side of
the chest, and are there buttoned.

250

BOOK XXV. THE *K*ÜN-YÂ.

ACCORDING to the note in the Preface to the Shû, the charge delivered in this Book to *K*ün-yâ, or possibly 'the prince Yâ,' was by king Mû; and its dictum is not challenged by any Chinese critic. The reign of king *K*hâo, who succeeded to Khang, is thus passed over in the documents of the Shû. Mû was the son and successor of *K*hâo, and reigned from B.C. 1001 to 947.

*K*ün-yâ's surname is not known. He is here appointed to be Minister of Instruction, and as it is intimated that his father and grandfather had been in the same office, it is conjectured that he was the grandson of the earl of *Z*ui, who was Minister of Instruction at the beginning of the reign of king Khang.

The Book is short, speaking of the duties of the office, and stimulating Yâ to the discharge of them by considerations drawn from the merits of his forefathers, and the services which he would render to the dynasty and his sovereign.

1. The king spoke to the following effect :— 'Oh! *K*ün-yâ, your grandfather and your father, one after the other, with a true loyalty and honesty, laboured in the service of the royal House, accomplishing a merit that was recorded on the grand banner [1]. I, the little child, have become charged by inheritance with the line of government transmitted from Wăn and Wû, from *K*hăng and Khang; I also keep thinking of their ministers who aided them in the good government of the kingdom; the trembling anxiety of my mind makes me feel as if I were treading on a tiger's tail, or walking upon spring ice. I now give you charge to assist me;

---

[1] The grand banner was borne aloft when the king went to sacrifice. There were figures of the sun and moon on it, and dragons lying along its breadth, one over the other, head above tail. The names of meritorious ministers were inscribed on it during their lifetime, preparatory to their sharing in the sacrifices of the ancestral temple after their death.

be as my limbs to me, as my heart and backbone.   251
Continue their old service, and do not disgrace your
grandfather and father.

' Diffuse widely (the knowledge of) the five invariable relations (of society), and reverently seek
to produce a harmonious observance of the duties
belonging to them among the people.   If you are
correct in your own person, none will dare to be
but correct.   The minds of the people cannot
attain to the right mean (of duty) ;—they must be
guided by your attaining to it.   In the heat and
rains of summer, the inferior people may be described as murmuring and sighing.   And so it is
with them in the great cold of winter.   How great
are their hardships!   Think of their hardships in
order to seek to promote their ease ; and the people
will be tranquil.   Oh! how great and splendid were
the plans of king Wăn!   How greatly were they
carried out by the energy of king Wû!   All in
principle correct, and deficient in nothing, they are
for the help and guidance of us their descendants.
Do you with reverence and wisdom carry out your
instructions, enabling me to honour and follow the
example of my (immediate) predecessors, and to
respond to and display the bright decree conferred
on Wăn and Wû ;—so shall you be the mate of your
by-gone fathers.'

2. The king spoke to the following effect :—
' *K*ün-yâ, do you take for your rule the lessons
afforded by the courses of your excellent fathers.
The good or the bad order of the people depends
on this.   You will thus follow the practice of your
grandfather and father, and make the good government of your sovereign illustrious.'

Book XXVI. The Charge to *Kh*iung.

THE charge recorded here, like that in the last Book, is assigned
to king Mû. It was delivered on the appointment of a *Kh*iung
or Po-*kh*iung (that is, the eldest *Kh*iung, the eldest brother
in his family) to be High Chamberlain. Of this *Kh*iung we
know nothing more than we learn from the Shû. He was no
high dignitary of state. That the charge to him found a place
in the Shû, we are told, shows how important it was thought
that men in the lowest positions, yet coming into contact with
the sovereign, should possess correct principles and an earnest
desire for his progress in intelligence and virtue.

King Mû represents himself as conscious of his own incompetencies,
and impressed with a sense of the high duties devolving on
him. His predecessors, much superior to himself, were yet
greatly indebted to the aid of the officers about them;—how
much more must this be the case with him!

He proceeds to appoint *Kh*iung to be the High Chamberlain,
telling him how he should guide correctly all the other servants
about the royal person, so that none but good influences should
be near to act upon the king;—telling him also the manner
of men whom he should employ, and the care he should exercise
in the selection of them.

The king spoke to the following effect:—'Po-
*kh*iung, I come short in virtue, and have succeeded
to the former kings, to occupy the great throne.
I am fearful, and conscious of the peril (of my position). I rise at midnight, and think how I can avoid
falling into errors. Formerly Wăn and Wû were
endowed with all intelligence, august and sage,
while their ministers, small and great, all cherished
loyalty and goodness. Their servants, charioteers,
chamberlains, and followers were all men of correctness; morning and evening waiting on their sovereign's wishes, or supplying his deficiencies. (Those
kings), going out and coming in, rising up and sitting

down, were thus made reverent. Their every warn- 253
ing or command was good. The people yielded a
reverent obedience, and the myriad regions were all
happy. But I, the One man, am destitute of goodness, and really depend on the officers who have
places about me to help my deficiencies, applying
the line to my faults, and exhibiting my errors, thus
correcting my bad heart, and enabling me to be the
successor of my meritorious predecessors.

'Now I appoint you to be High Chamberlain,
to see that all the officers in your department and
my personal attendants are upright and correct, that
they strive to promote the virtue of their sovereign,
and together supply my deficiencies. Be careful in
selecting your officers. Do not employ men of
artful speech and insinuating looks, men whose
likes and dislikes are ruled by mine, one-sided men
and flatterers; but employ good men. When these
household officers are correct, the sovereign will be
correct; when they are flatterers, the sovereign will
consider himself a sage. His virtue or his want of
it equally depends on them. Cultivate no intimacy
with flatterers, nor get them to do duty for me as
my ears and eyes;—they will lead their sovereign
to disregard the statutes of the former kings. If
you choose the men not for their personal goodness,
but for the sake of their bribes, their offices will be
made of no effect, your great want of reverence for
your sovereign will be apparent, and I will hold you
guilty.'

The king said, 'Oh! be reverent! Ever help
your sovereign to follow the regular laws of duty
(which he should exemplify).'

254

Book XXVII.

The Marquis of Lü on Punishments.

The charge or charges recorded in this Book were given in the hundredth year of the king's age. The king, it is again understood, was Mû; and the hundredth year of his age would be b. c. 952. The title of the Book in Chinese is simply 'Lü's Punishments,' and I conclude that Lü, or the marquis of Lü, was a high minister who prepared, by the king's orders, a code of punishments for the regulation of the kingdom, in connexion with the undertaking, or the completion, of which the king delivered to his princes and judges the sentiments that are here preserved.

The common view is that Lü is the name of a principality, the marquis of which was Mû's Minister of Crime. Where it was is not well known, and as the Book is quoted in the Lî Kî several times under the title of 'Fû on Punishments,' it is supposed that Lü and Fû (a small marquisate in the present Ho-nan) were the same.

The whole Book is divided into seven chapters. The first is merely a brief introduction, the historiographer's account of the circumstances in which king Mû delivered his lessons. Each of the other chapters begins with the words, 'The king said.' The first two of them are an historical resumé of the lessons of antiquity on the subject of punishments, and an inculcation on the princes and officers of justice to give heed to them, and learn from them. The next two tell the princes of the diligence and carefulness to be employed in the use of punishments, and how they can make punishments a blessing. The fourth chapter treats principally of the commutation or redemption of punishments, and has been very strongly condemned by critics and moralists. They express their surprise that such a document should be in the Shû, and, holding that the collection was made by Confucius, venture to ask what the sage meant by admitting it. There is, in fact, no evidence that the redemption of punishments on the scale here laid down, existed in China before Mû's time. It has entered, however, into the penal code of every subsequent dynasty. Great official corruption and depravation of the general morality would seem to be inseparable from such a system. The fifth chapter returns again to the

reverence with which punishments should be employed; and the 255
sixth and last is addressed to future generations, and directs
them to the ancient models, in order that punishments may
never be but a blessing to the kingdom.

A Chinese critic says that throughout the Book 'virtue' and 'exact
adaptation' are the terms that carry the weight of the meaning.
Virtue must underlie the use of punishments, of which their
exact adaptation will be the manifestation.

1. In reference to the charge to (the marquis of)
Lü:—When the king had occupied the throne till he
reached the age of a hundred years, he gave great
consideration to the appointment of punishments,
in order to deal with (the people of) the four
quarters.

2. The king said, 'According to the teachings of
ancient times, *Kh*ih Yû was the first to produce disorder, which spread among the quiet, orderly people,
till all became robbers and murderers, owl-like and
yet self-complacent in their conduct, traitors and
villains, snatching and filching, dissemblers and
oppressors[1].

'Among the people of Miâo, they did not use
the power of goodness, but the restraint of punishments. They made the five punishments engines
of oppression[2], calling them the laws. They

---

[1] *Kh*ih Yû, as has been observed in the Introduction, p. 27, is
the most ancient name mentioned in the Shû, and carries us back,
according to the Chinese chronologists, nearly to the beginning of
the twenty-seventh century b. c. P. Gaubil translates the characters
which appear in the English text here as 'According to the
teachings of ancient times' by 'Selon les anciens documents,'
which is more than the Chinese text says.—It is remarkable that
at the commencement of Chinese history, Chinese tradition placed
a period of innocence, a season when order and virtue ruled in
men's affairs.

[2] I do not think it is intended to say here that 'the five punishments' were invented by the chiefs of the Miâo; but only that

256　　slaughtered the innocent, and were the first also to go to excess in cutting off the nose, cutting off the ears, castration, and branding. All who became liable to those punishments were dealt with without distinction, no difference being made in favour of those who could offer some excuse. The people were gradually affected by this state of things, and became dark and disorderly. Their hearts were no more set on good faith, but they violated their oaths and covenants. The multitudes who suffered from the oppressive terrors, and were (in danger of) being murdered, declared their innocence to Heaven. God surveyed the people, and there was no fragrance of virtue arising from them, but the rank odour of their (cruel) punishments.*

'The great Tî[1] compassionated the innocent multitudes that were (in danger of) being murdered, and made the oppressors feel the terrors of his majesty. He restrained and (finally) extinguished the people of Miâo, so that they should not con-

---

these used them excessively and barbarously. From two passages in the Canon of Shun, we conclude that that monarch was acquainted with 'the five great inflictions or punishments,' and gave instructions to his minister Kâo-yâo as to their use.

[1] Here is the name—Hwang Tî—by which the sovereigns of China have been styled from B.C. 221, since the emperor of *Kh*in, on his extinction of the feudal states, enacted that it should be borne by himself and his descendants. I have spoken of the meaning of Tî and of the title Hwang Tî in the note on the translation of the Shû appended to the Preface. There can be no doubt that it was Shun whom king Mû intended by the name. A few sentences further on, the mention of Po-î and Yü leads us to the time subsequent to Yâo, and there does not appear to be any change of subject in the paragraph. We get from this Book a higher idea of the power of the Miâo than from the Books of Part II.

tinue to future generations. Then he commissioned   257
*Kh*ung and Lî[1] to make an end of the communica-
tions between earth and heaven ; and the descents
(of spirits) ceased[1]. From the princes down to the

---

[1] *Kh*ung and Lî are nowhere met with in the previous parts of
the Shû, nor in any other reliable documents of history, as officers
of Shun. Ȝhâi *Kh*än and others would identify them with the
Hsî and Ho of the Canon of Yâo, and hold those to have been
descended from a *Kh*ung and a Lî, supposed to belong to the
time of Shâo Hâo in the twenty-sixth century B.C.

Whoever they were, the duty with which they were charged
was remarkable. In the Narratives of the States (a book of
the *K*âu dynasty), we find a conversation on it, during the lifetime of Confucius, between king *Kh*âo of *Kh*û (B.C. 515–489)
and one of his ministers, called Kwan Yî-fû. ' What is meant,'
asked the king, ' by what is said in one of the Books of *K*âu
about *Kh*ung and Lî, that they really brought it about that there
was no intercourse between heaven and earth? If they had not
done so, would people have been able to ascend to heaven?'
The minister replied that that was not the meaning at all, and
gave his own view of it at great length, to the following effect.—
Anciently, the people attended to the discharge of their duties
to one another, and left the worship of spiritual beings—the
seeking intercourse with them, and invoking and effecting their
descent on earth—to the officers who were appointed for that
purpose. In this way things proceeded with great regularity.
The people minded their own affairs, and the spirits minded
theirs. Tranquillity and prosperity were the consequence. But
in the time of Shâo Hâo, through the lawlessness of *K*iû-lî, a
change took place. The people intruded into the functions of
the regulators of the spirits and their worship. They abandoned
their duties to their fellow men, and tried to bring down spirits
from above. The spirits themselves, no longer kept in check
and subjected to rule, made their appearance irregularly and
disastrously. All was confusion and calamity, when *K*wan Hsü
(B.C. 2510–2433) took the case in hand. He appointed *Kh*ung,
the Minister of the South, to the superintendency of heavenly
things, to prescribe the laws for the spirits, and Lî, the Minister
of Fire, to the superintendency of earthly things, to prescribe the
rules for the people. In this way both spirits and people were

258 inferior officers, all helped with clear intelligence (the spread of) the regular principles of duty, and the solitary and widows were no longer overlooked. The great Tî with an unprejudiced mind carried his enquiries low down among the people, and the solitary and widows laid before him their complaints against the Miâo. He awed the people by the majesty of his virtue, and enlightened them by its brightness. He thereupon charged the three princely (ministers)[1] to labour with compassionate anxiety in the people's behalf. Po-î delivered his statutes to prevent the people from rendering themselves obnoxious to punishment; Yü reduced to order the water and the land, and presided over the naming of the hills and rivers; Kî spread abroad a knowledge of agriculture, and (the people) extensively cultivated the admirable grains. When the three princes had accomplished their work, it was abundantly well with the people. The Minister of Crime[2] exercised among them the restraint of

---

brought back to their former regular courses, and there was no unhallowed interference of the one with the other. This was the work described in the text. But subsequently the chief of San-miâo showed himself a Kiû-lî redivivus, till Yâo called forth the descendants of Khung and Lî, who had not forgotten the virtue and functions of their fathers, and made them take the case in hand again.

According to Yî-fû's statements Khung's functions were those of the Minister of Religion, and Lî's those of the Minister of Instruction ; but Hsî and Ho were simply Ministers of Astronomy and the Calendar, and their descendants continue to appear as such in the Shû to the reign of Kung Khang, long after we know that men of other families were appointed to the important ministries of Khung and Lî.

[1] Those immediately mentioned,—Po-î, Yü, and Kî. See the Canon of Shun and other Books of Part II.

[2] Kâo-yâo.

punishment in exact adaptation to each offence, and taught them to reverence virtue. The greatest gravity and harmony in the sovereign, and the greatest intelligence in those below him, thus shining forth to all quarters (of the land), all were rendered diligent in cultivating their virtue. Hence, (if anything more were wanted), the clear adjudication of punishments effected the regulation of the people, and helped them to observe the regular duties of life. The officers who presided over criminal cases executed the law (fearlessly) against the powerful, and (faithfully) against the wealthy. They were reverent and cautious. They had no occasion to make choice of words to vindicate their conduct. The virtue of Heaven was attained to by them; from them was the determination of so great a matter as the lives (of men). In their low sphere they yet corresponded (to Heaven) and enjoyed (its favour).' *

3. The king said, ' Ah! you who direct the government and preside over criminal cases through all the land, are you not constituted the shepherds of Heaven? * To whom ought you now to look as your pattern? Is it not to Po-î, spreading among the people his lessons to avert punishments? And from whom ought you now to take warning? Is it not from the people of Miâo, who would not examine into the circumstances of criminal cases, and did not make choice of good officers that should see to the right apportioning of the five punishments, but chose the violent and bribe-snatchers, who determined and administered them, so as to oppress the innocent, until God would no longer hold them guiltless, and sent down calamity on

259

260   Miâo, when the people had no plea to allege in
mitigation of their punishment, and their name was
cut off from the world?'*

4. The king said, 'Oh! lay it to heart. My
uncles, and all ye, my brethren and cousins, my sons
and my grandsons[1], listen all of you to my words, in
which, it may be, you will receive a most important
charge. You will only tread the path of satisfaction
by being daily diligent;—do not have occasion to
beware of the want of diligence. Heaven, in its
wish to regulate the people, allows us for a day to
make use of punishments.* Whether crimes have
been premeditated, or are unpremeditated, depends
on the parties concerned;—do you (deal with them
so as to) accord with the mind of Heaven, and thus
serve me, the One man. Though I would put them
to death, do not you therefore put them to death;
though I would spare them, do not you therefore
spare them. Reverently apportion the five punishments, so as fully to exhibit the three virtues[2].
Then shall I, the One man, enjoy felicity; the
people will look to you as their sure dependance;
the repose of such a state will be perpetual.'

5. The king said, 'Ho! come, ye rulers of states
and territories[3], I will tell you how to make punishments a blessing. It is yours now to give repose to
the people;—what should you be most concerned

---

[1] Meaning all the princes of the same surname as himself. As
he was a hundred years old, there might well be among them
those who were really his sons and grandsons.

[2] 'The three virtues' are those of the Great Plan; those of
'correctness and straightforwardness,' of 'strong government,' and
of 'mild government.'

[3] Meaning all the princes;—of the king's own and other surnames.

about the choosing of ?　Should it not be the proper　261
men ?　What should you deal with the most reverently ?　Should it not be punishments ?　What
should you calculate the most carefully ?　Should
it not be to whom these will reach ?

'When both parties are present, (with their documents and witnesses) all complete, let the judges
listen to the fivefold statements that may be made[1].
When they have examined and fully made up their
minds on those, let them adjust the case to one of
the five punishments.　If the five punishments do
not meet it, let them adjust it to one of the five
redemption-fines; and if these, again, are not sufficient for it, let them reckon it among the five cases
of error[2].

'In (settling) the five cases of error there are
evils (to be guarded against);—being warped by
the influence of power, or by private grudge, or by
female solicitation, or by bribes, or by applications.
Any one of these things should be held equal to
the crime (before the judges).　Do you carefully
examine, and prove yourselves equal to (every
difficulty).

'When there are doubts as to the infliction of
any of the five punishments, that infliction should
be forborne.　When there are doubts as to the

---

[1] That is, the statements, with the evidence on both sides,
whether incriminating or exculpating.　They are called fivefold, as
the case might have to be dealt with by one or other of 'the five
punishments.'

[2] That is, the offences of inadvertence.　What should ensue
on the adjudication of any case to be so ranked does not appear.
It would be very leniently dealt with, and perhaps pardoned.　In
'the Counsels of Yü,' Kâo-yâo says to Shun, 'You pardon inadvertent offences however great.'

infliction of any of the five fines, it should be forborne. Do you carefully examine, and prove yourselves equal to overcome (every difficulty). When you have examined and many things are clear, yet form a judgment from studying the appearance of the parties. If you find nothing out on examination, do not listen (to the case any more). In everything stand in awe of the dread majesty of Heaven.*

'When, in a doubtful case, the punishment of branding is forborne, the fine to be laid on instead is 600 ounces (of copper); but you must first have satisfied yourselves as to the crime. When the case would require the cutting off the nose, the fine must be double this;—with the same careful determination of the crime. When the punishment would be the cutting off the feet, the fine must be 3000 ounces;—with the same careful determination of the crime. When the punishment would be castration[1], the fine must be 3600 ounces;—with the same determination. When the punishment would be death, the fine must be 6000 ounces;—with the same determination. Of crimes that may be redeemed by the fine in lieu of branding there are 1000; and the same number of those that would otherwise incur cutting off the nose. The fine in lieu of cutting off the feet extends to 500 cases; that in lieu of castration, to 300; and that in lieu of death, to 200. Altogether, set against the five punishments, there are 3000 crimes. (In the case of others not exactly defined), you must class them with the (next) higher or (next) lower offences, not

---

[1] Or solitary confinement in the case of a female.

admitting assumptive and disorderly pleadings, and 263
not using obsolete laws. Examine and act lawfully,
judging carefully, and proving yourselves equal (to
every difficulty).

'Where the crime should incur one of the higher
punishments, but there are mitigating circumstances,
apply to it the next lower. Where it should incur one
of the lower punishments, but there are aggravating
circumstances, apply to it the next higher. The light
and heavy fines are to be apportioned (in the same
way) by the balance of circumstances. Punishments
and fines should (also) be light in one age, and
heavy in another. To secure uniformity in this
(seeming) irregularity, there are certain relations of
things (to be considered), and the essential principle
(to be observed).

'The chastisement of fines is short of death, yet
it will produce extreme distress. They are not
(therefore) persons of artful tongues who should
determine criminal cases, but really good persons,
whose awards will hit the right mean. Examine
carefully where there are any discrepancies in the
statements ; the view which you were resolved not
to follow, you may see occasion to follow ; with
compassion and reverence settle the cases ; examine carefully the penal code, and deliberate with
all about it, that your decisions may be likely to
hit the proper mean and be correct ;—whether it be
the infliction of a punishment or a fine, examining
carefully and mastering every difficulty. When the
case is thus concluded, all parties will acknowledge
the justice of the sentence ; and when it is reported,
the sovereign will do the same. In sending up
reports of cases, they must be full and complete.

264   If a man have been tried on two counts, his two punishments (must be recorded).'

6. The king said, ' Oh ! let there be a feeling of reverence. Ye judges and princes, of the same surname with me, and of other surnames, (know all) that I speak in much fear. I think with reverence of the subject of punishment, for the end of it is to promote virtue. Now Heaven, wishing to help the people, has made us its representatives here below.* Be intelligent and pure in hearing (each) side of a case. The right ordering of the people depends on the impartial hearing of the pleas on both sides ;—do not seek for private advantage to yourselves by means of those pleas. Gain (so) got by the decision of cases is no precious acquisition ; it is an accumulation of guilt, and will be recompensed with many judgments :—you should ever stand in awe of the punishment of Heaven.* It is not Heaven that does not deal impartially with men, but men ruin themselves. If the punishment of Heaven were not so extreme, nowhere under the sky would the people have good government.'

7. The king said, ' Oh ! ye who shall hereafter inherit (the dignities and offices of) the present time, to whom are ye to look for your models ? Must it not be to those who promoted the virtue belonging to the unbiassed nature of the people ? I pray you give attention to my words. The wise men (of antiquity) by their use of punishments obtained boundless fame. Everything relating to the five punishments exactly hit with them the due mean, and hence came their excellence. Receiving from your sovereigns the good multitudes, behold in the case of those men punishments made felicitous ! '

BOOK XXVIII.

265

THE CHARGE TO THE MARQUIS WĂN.

THE king to whom this charge is ascribed was Phing (B. C. 770–719). Between him and Mû there was thus a period of fully two centuries, of which no documents are, or ever were, in the collection of the Shû. The time was occupied by seven reigns, the last of which was that of Nieh, known as king Yû, a worthless ruler, and besotted in his attachment to a female favourite, called Pâo-sze. For her sake he degraded his queen, and sent their son, Î-*kh*iû, to the court of the lord of Shăn, her father, 'to learn good manners.' The lord of Shăn called in the assistance of some barbarian tribes, by which the capital was sacked, and the king slain; and with him ended the sway of 'the Western *K*âu.' Several of the feudal princes went to the assistance of the royal House, drove away the barbarians, brought back Î-*kh*iû from Shăn, and hailed him as king. He is known as king Phing, 'the Tranquillizer.' His first measure was to transfer the capital from the ruins of Hâo to Lo, thus fulfilling at length, but under disastrous circumstances, the wishes of the duke of *K*âu; and from this time (B. C. 770) dates the history of 'the Eastern *K*âu.'

Among king Phing's early measures was the rewarding the feudal lords to whom he owed his throne. The marquis of *K*in was one of them. His name was *Kh*iû, and that of Î-ho, by which he is called in the text, is taken as his 'style,' or designation assumed by him on his marriage. Wăn, 'the Accomplished,' was his sacrificial title. The lords of *K*in were descended from king Wû's son, Yü, who was appointed marquis of Thang, corresponding to the present department of Thâi-yüan, in Shan-hsî. The name of Thang was afterwards changed into *K*in. The state became in course of time one of the largest and most powerful in the kingdom.

The charge in this Book is understood to be in connexion with Wăn's appointment to be president or chief of several of the other princes. The king begins by celebrating the virtues and happy times of kings Wăn and Wû, and the services rendered by the worthy ministers of subsequent reigns. He contrasts with this the misery and distraction of his own times, deploring his want of wise counsellors and helpers, and praising the

266

marquis for the services which he had rendered. He then concludes with the special charge by which he would reward the prince's merit in the past, and stimulate him to greater exertions in the future.

1. The king spoke to the following effect:— 'Uncle Î-ho, how illustrious were Wăn and Wû! Carefully did they make their virtue brilliant, till it rose brightly on high, and the fame of it was widely diffused here below. Therefore God caused his favouring decree to light upon king Wăn.* There were ministers also (thereafter), who aided and illustriously served their sovereigns, following and carrying out their plans, great and small, so that my fathers sat tranquilly on the throne.

'Oh! an object of pity am I, who am (but as) a little child. Just as I have succeeded to the throne, Heaven has severely chastised me.* Through the interruption of the (royal) bounties that ceased to descend to the inferior people, the invading barbarous tribes of the west have greatly (injured) our kingdom. Moreover, among the managers of my affairs there are none of age and experience and distinguished ability in their offices. I am (thus) unequal (to the difficulties of my position), and say to myself, " My grand-uncles and uncles, you ought to compassionate my case." Oh! if there were those who could establish their merit in behalf of me, the One man, I might long enjoy repose upon the throne.

'Uncle Î-ho, you render still more glorious your illustrious ancestor. You were the first to imitate the example of Wăn and Wû, collecting (the scattered powers), and continuing (the all but broken line of) your sovereign. Your filial piety goes back

to your accomplished ancestor, (and is equal to his.) 267
You have. done much to repair my (losses), and
defend me in my difficulties, and of you, being such,
I am full of admiration.'

2. The king said, 'Uncle Î-ho, return home,
survey your multitudes, and tranquillize your state.
I reward you with a jar of spirits, distilled from the
black millet, and flavoured with odoriferous herbs[1],
with a red bow, and a hundred red arrows[2]; with
a black bow, and a hundred black arrows; and with
four horses. Go, my uncle. Show kindness to
those that are far off, and help those who are
near at hand; cherish and secure the repose of
the inferior people; do not idly seek your ease;
exercise an inspection and (benign) compassion in
your capital (and all your borders);—thus completing your illustrious virtue.'

BOOK XXIX. THE SPEECH AT PÎ.

THE Speech at Pî carries us back from the time of Phing to
that of king *Kh*ăng. In the Preface to the Shû it is attributed
to Po-*kh*in, the son of the duke of *K*âu; and there is a general
acquiescence of tradition and critics in this view. We may
account for its position out of the chronological order from

---

[1] Compare king *Kh*ăng's gift to the duke of *K*âu, in the
Announcement concerning Lo, ch. 6.

[2] The conferring on a prince of a bow and arrows, invested
him with the power of punishing throughout the states within his
jurisdiction all who were disobedient to the royal commands, but
not of taking life without first reporting to the court. The gift
was also a tribute to the merit of the receiver. See the Book of
Poetry, II, iii, ode 1.

268   the Book's being the record not of any royal doings, but of
      the words of the ruler of a state.
      The speech has reference to some military operations against the
      wild tribes on the Hwâi river and in other parts of the pro-
      vince of Hsü; and we have seen that they were in insurrection
      many times during the reign of *Kh*ăng. We thus cannot tell
      exactly the year in which the speech was delivered. Po-*kh*in
      presided over his state of Lû for the long period of fifty-three
      ,years, and died b. c. 1063.
      The name of Pî is retained in the district still so called of the
      .department of Î-*kâ*u. At first it was an independent territory,
      but attached to Lû, and under the jurisdiction of its marquises,
      by one of whom it had been incorporated with Lû before the
      time of Confucius.
      Po-*kh*in appears at the head of his host, approaching the scene
      of active operations. Having commanded silence, he issues his
      orders, first, that the soldiers shall have their weapons in good
      order; next, that the people of the country shall take care of
      the oxen and horses of the army; further, that the troops on no
      account leave their ranks or go astray; and finally, he names
      the day when he will commence operations against the enemy,
      and commands all the requisite preparations to be made.

The duke said, ' Ah! ye men, make no noise, but
listen to my commands.   We are going (to punish)
those wild tribes of the Hwâi and of Hsü, which
have risen up together.

' Have in good repair your buff coats and helmets;
have the laces of your shields well secured;—presume not to have any of them but in perfect order.
Prepare your bows and arrows; temper your lances
and spears; sharpen your pointed and edged weapons;—presume not to have any of them but in
good condition.

' We must now largely let the oxen and horses
loose, and not keep them in enclosures;—(ye
people), do you close your traps and fill up your
pitfalls, and do not presume to injure any of the
animals (so let loose). If any of them be injured,

you shall be dealt with according to the regular   269
punishments.

'When the horses or cattle are seeking one
another, or when your followers, male or female,
abscond, presume not to leave the ranks to pursue
them. But let them be carefully returned. I will
reward you (among the people) who return them
according to their value. But if you leave your
places to pursue them, or if you who find them do
not restore them, you shall be dealt with according
to the regular punishments.

'And let none of you presume to commit any
robbery or detain any creature that comes in your
way, to jump over enclosures and walls to steal
(people's) horses or oxen, or to decoy away their
servants or female attendants. If you do so, you
shall be dealt with according to the regular punishments.

'On the day Kiâ-hsü I will take action against
the hordes of Hsü ;—prepare the roasted grain and
other provisions, and presume not to have any defi-
ciency. If you have, you shall suffer the severest
punishment. Ye men of Lû, from the three environing territories and the three tracts beyond [1],

---

[1] Outside the capital city was an environing territory called the
Kiâo, and beyond the Kiâo was the Sui. The Kiâo of the royal
domain was divided again into six Hsiang, which furnished the six
royal hosts, while the Sui beyond furnished subsidiary hosts. The
Kiâo and Sui of a large state furnished three hosts, and if need
were, subsidiary battalions. The language of the text is equivalent,
I conceive, simply to 'ye men of the army of Lû;' but, as P. Gaubil
observes, it is difficult at the present day to get correct ideas of
what is meant by the designations, and to account for the mention
of three Kiâo and three Sui.

270   be ready with your posts and planks.   On *K*iâ-hsü
I will commence my intrenchments;—dare not but
be provided with a supply of these.   (If you be not
so provided), you shall be subjected to various
punishments, short only of death.   Ye men of Lû,
from the three environing territories and the three
tracts beyond, be ready with the forage, and do not
dare to let it be other than abundant.   (If you do),
you shall suffer the severest punishment.'

Book XXX.

The Speech of (the Marquis of) *K*hin.

The state of *K*hin, at the time to which this speech belongs, was
one of the most powerful in the kingdom, and already giving
promise of what it would grow to.   Ultimately, one of its princes
overthrew the dynasty of *K*âu, and brought feudal China to an
end.   Its earliest capital was in the present district of *K*häng-
shui, *K*hin *K*âu, Kan-sû.

*K*hin and *K*in were   engaged together in в. c. 631 in besieging the
capital of *K*äng, and threatened to extinguish that state.   The
marquis of *K*hin, however, was suddenly induced to withdraw
his troops, leaving three of his officers in friendly relations with
the court of *K*äng, and under engagement to defend the state
from aggression.   These men played the part of spies in the
interest of *K*hin, and in в. c. 629, one of them, called *K*hî-ʒze,
sent word that he was in charge of one of the gates, and if
an army were sent to surprise the capital, *K*äng might be
added to the territories of *K*hin.   The marquis—known in
history as duke Mû—laid the matter before his counsellors.
The most experienced of them—Pâi-lî Hsî and *K*hien-shû—
were against taking advantage of the proposed treachery; but
the marquis listened rather to the promptings of ambition; and
the next year he sent a large force, under his three ablest commanders, hoping to find *K*äng unprepared for any resistance.
The attempt, however, failed; and the army, on its way back to

*K͟h*in, was attacked by the forces of *K*in, and sustained a terrible   271
defeat. It was nearly annihilated, and the three commanders
were taken prisoners.

The marquis of *K*in was intending to put these captives to death,
but finally sent them to *K͟h*in, that duke Mû might himself sacrifice them to his anger for their want of success.   Mû, however,
did no such thing.   He went from his capital to meet the dis-
graced generals, and comforted them, saying that the blame of
their defeat was due to himself, who had refused to listen to the
advice of his wise counsellors.   Then also, it is said, he made
the speech here preserved for the benefit of all his ministers,
describing the good and bad minister, and the different issues of
listening to them, and deploring how he had himself foolishly
rejected the advice of his aged counsellors, and followed that
of new men ;—a thing which he would never do again.

The duke[1] said, 'Ah! my officers, listen to me
without noise.   I solemnly announce to you the
most important of all sayings.   (It is this which)
the ancients have said, " Thus it is with all people,
—they mostly love their ease.   In reproving others
there is no difficulty, but to receive reproof, and
allow it to have free course,—this is difficult."   The
sorrow of my heart is, that the days and months
have passed away, and it is not likely they will
come again, (so that I might pursue a different
course.)

' There were my old counsellors[2].—I said, " They
will not accommodate themselves to me," and I
hated them.   There were my new counsellors, and
I would for the time give my confidence to them[3].
So indeed it was with me; but hereafter I will

---

[1] The prince of *K͟h*in was only a marquis ; but the historiographers or recorders of a state always gave their ruler the higher
title.   This shows that this speech is taken from the chronicles of
*K͟h*in.

[2] Pâi-lî Hsî and *K͟h*ien-shû.

[3] *K͟h*î-ʒze and others.

272   take advice from the men of yellow hair, and then I shall be free from error. That good old officer! —his strength is exhausted, but I would rather have him (as my counsellor). That dashing brave officer!—his shooting and charioteering are faultless, but I would rather not wish to have him. As to men of quibbles, skilful at cunning words, and able to make the good man change his purposes, what have I to do to make much use of them?

'I have deeply thought and concluded.—Let me have but one resolute minister, plain and sincere, without other ability, but having a straightforward mind, and possessed of generosity, regarding the talents of others as if he himself possessed them; and when he finds accomplished and sage men, loving them in his heart more than his mouth expresses, really showing himself able to bear them: —such a minister would be able to preserve my descendants and people, and would indeed be a giver of benefits.

'But if (the minister), when he finds men of ability, be jealous and hates them; if, when he finds accomplished and sage men, he oppose them and does not allow their advancement, showing himself really not able to bear them:—such a man will not be able to protect my descendants and people; and will he not be a dangerous man?

'The decline and fall of a state may arise from one man. The glory and tranquillity of a state may also arise from the goodness of one man.'

THE SHIH KING

OR

BOOK OF POETRY:

ALL THE PIECES AND STANZAS IN IT ILLUSTRATING
THE RELIGIOUS VIEWS AND PRACTICES OF
THE WRITERS AND THEIR TIMES.

THE SHIH KING

OR

·BOOK OF POETRY.

INTRODUCTION.

CHAPTER I.

THE NAME AND CONTENTS OF THE CLASSIC.

1. Among the Chinese classical books next after the Shû in point of antiquity comes the Shih or Book of Poetry.

The character Shû[1], as formed by the combination of

The meaning of the character Shih. two others, one of which signified 'a pencil,' and the other 'to speak,' supplied, we saw, in its structure, an indication of its primary significance, and furnished a clue to its different applications. The character Shih[2] was made on a different principle,— that of phonetical formation, in the peculiar sense of these words when applied to a large class of Chinese terms. The significative portion of it is the character for 'speech,' but the other half is merely phonetical, enabling us to approximate to its pronunciation or name. The meaning of the compound has to be learned from its usage. Its most common significations are 'poetry,' 'a poem, or poems,' and 'a collection of poems.' This last is its meaning when we speak of the Shih or the Shih King.

The earliest Chinese utterance that we have on the subject of poetry is that in the Shû by the ancient Shun, when he said to his Minister of Music, 'Poetry is the expression of earnest thought, and singing is the prolonged

[1]書   [2]詩

T 2

276   utterance of that expression.' To the same effect is the
language of a Preface to the Shih, sometimes ascribed to
Confucius, and certainly older than our Christian era :—
'Poetry is the product of earnest thought. Thought cherished in the mind becomes earnest; then expressed in words,
it becomes poetry. The feelings move inwardly, and are
embodied in words. When words are insufficient for them,
recourse is had to sighs and exclamations. When sighs and
exclamations are insufficient for them, recourse is had to
the prolonged utterance of song. When this again is insufficient, unconsciously the hands begin to move and the
feet to dance. . . . . To set forth correctly the successes
and failures (of government), to affect Heaven and Earth,
and to move spiritual beings, there is no readier instrument
than poetry.'

Rhyme, it may be added here, is a necessary accompaniment of poetry in the estimation of the Chinese. Only
in a very few pieces of the Shih is it neglected.

2. The Shih King contains 305 pieces and the titles of
The contents six others. The most recent of them are
of the Shih. assigned to the reign of king Ting of the
*K*âu dynasty, B. C. 606 to 586, and the oldest, forming a
group of only five, to the period of the Shang dynasty
which preceded that of *K*âu, B. C. 1766 to 1123. Of those
five, the latest piece should be referred to the twelfth century
B. C., and the most ancient may have been composed five
centuries earlier. All the other pieces in the Shih have
to be distributed over the time between Ting and king
Wăn, the founder of the line of *K*âu. The distribution,
however, is not equal nor continuous. There were some
reigns of which we do not have a single poetical fragment.

The whole collection is divided into four parts, called the
Kwo Făng, the Hsiâo Yâ, the Tâ Yâ, and the Sung.

The Kwo Făng, in fifteen Books, contains 160 pieces,
nearly all of them short, and descriptive of manners and
events in several of the feudal states of *K*âu. The title
has been translated by The Manners of the Different
States, 'Les Mœurs des Royaumes,' and, which I prefer,
by Lessons from the States.

The Hsiâo Yâ, or Lesser Yâ, in eight Books, contains 277
seventy-four pieces and the titles of six others, sung at
gatherings of the feudal princes, and their appearances at
the royal court. They were produced in the royal territory,
and are descriptive of the manners and ways of the government in successive reigns. It is difficult to find an English
word that shall fitly represent the Chinese Yâ as here used.
In his Latin translation of the Shih, P. Lacharme translated Hsiâo Yâ by 'Quod rectum est, sed inferiore ordine,'
adding in a note :—'Siâo Yâ, latine Parvum Rectum, quia
in hac Parte mores describuntur, recti illi quidem, qui tamen
nonnihil a recto deflectunt.' But the manners described are
not less correct or incorrect, as the case may be, than those
of the states in the former Part or of the kingdom in the
next. I prefer to call this Part 'Minor Odes of the Kingdom,' without attempting to translate the term Yâ.

The Tâ Yâ or Greater Yâ, in three Books, contains
thirty-one pieces, sung on great occasions at the royal
court and in the presence of the king. P. Lacharme called
it 'Magnum Rectum (Quod rectum est superiore ordine).'
But there is the same objection here to the use of the
word 'correct' as in the case of the pieces of the previous
Part. I use the name 'Major Odes of the Kingdom.'
The greater length and dignity of most of the pieces justify
the distinction of the two Parts into Minor and Major.

The Sung, also in three Books, contains forty pieces,
thirty-one of which belong to the sacrificial services at the
royal court of *K*âu; four, to those of the marquises of Lû;
and five to the corresponding sacrifices of the kings of
Shang. P. Lacharme denominated them correctly 'Parentales Cantus.' In the Preface to the Shih, to which I have
made reference above, it is said, 'The Sung are pieces in
admiration of the embodied manifestation of complete
virtue, announcing to the spiritual Intelligences their
achievement thereof.' *K*û Hsî's account of the Sung was—
'Songs for the Music of the Ancestral Temple;' and that of
*K*iang Yung of the present dynasty—'Songs for the Music
at Sacrifices.' I have united these two definitions, and call
the Part—'Odes of the Temple and the Altar.' There is

278   a difference between the pieces of Lû and the other two collections in this Part, to which I will call attention in giving the translation of them.

From the above account of the contents of the Shih,

Only the pieces of the fourth Part have professedly a religious character. it will be seen that only the pieces in the last of its four Parts are professedly of a religious character. Many of those, however, in the other Parts, especially the second and third, describe religious services, and give expression to religious ideas in the minds of their authors.

3. Some of the pieces in the Shih are ballads, some are songs, some are hymns, and of others the nature can hardly be indicated by any English denomination.

Classification of the pieces from their form and style. They have often been spoken of by the general name of odes, understanding by that term lyric poems that were set to music.

My reason for touching here on this point is the earliest account of the Shih, as a collection either already formed or in the process of formation, that we find in Chinese literature. In the Official Book of *K*âu, generally supposed to be a work of the twelfth or eleventh century B. C., among the duties of the Grand Music-Master there is 'the teaching,' (that is, to the musical performers,) 'the six classes of poems:—the Făng; the Fû; the Pî; the Hsing; the Yâ; and the Sung.' That the collection of the Shih, as it now is, existed so early as the date assigned to the Official Book could not be; but we find the same account of it given in the so-called Confucian Preface. The Făng, the Yâ, and the Sung are the four Parts of the classic described in the preceding paragraph, the Yâ embracing both the Minor and Major Odes of the Kingdom. But what were the Fû, the Pî, and the Hsing? We might suppose that they were the names of three other distinct Parts or Books. But they were not so. Pieces so discriminated are found in all the four Parts, though there are more of them in the first two than in the others.

The Fû may be described as Narrative pieces, in which the writers tell what they have to say in a simple, straightforward manner, without any hidden meaning reserved in

the mind. The metaphor and other figures of speech enter   279
into their composition as freely as in descriptive poems
in any other language.

The Pî are Metaphorical pieces, in which the poet has
under his language a different meaning from what it expresses,—a meaning which there should be nothing in that
language to indicate. Such a piece may be compared
to the Æsopic fable; but, while it is the object of the
fable to inculcate the virtues of morality and prudence,
an historical interpretation has to be sought for the metaphorical pieces of the Shih. Generally, moreover, the
moral of the fable is subjoined to it, which is never done
in the case of these pieces.

The Hsing have been called Allusive pieces. They are
very remarkable, and more numerous than the metaphorical.
They often commence with a couple of lines which are repeated without change, or with slight rhythmical changes, in
all the stanzas. In other pieces different stanzas have allusive
lines peculiar to themselves. Those lines are descriptive,
for the most part, of some object or circumstance in the
animal or vegetable world, and after them the poet proceeds to his proper subject. Generally, the allusive lines
convey a meaning harmonizing with those which follow,
where an English poet would begin the verses with Like or
As. They are really metaphorical, but the difference between an allusive and a metaphorical piece is this,—that
in the former the writer proceeds to state the theme which
his mind is occupied with, while no such intimation is given
in the latter. Occasionally, it is difficult, not to say impossible, to discover the metaphorical idea in the allusive
lines, and then we can only deal with them as a sort of
refrain.

In leaving this subject, it is only necessary to say further
that the allusive, the metaphorical, and the narrative elements sometimes all occur in the same piece.

280

CHAPTER II.

THE SHIH BEFORE CONFUCIUS, AND WHAT, IF ANY, WERE HIS LABOURS UPON IT.

1. Sze-mâ *K͟h*ien, in his memoir of Confucius, says:—
'The old poems amounted to more than 3000. Confucius removed those which were only repetitions of others, and selected those which would be serviceable for the inculca-

Statement of Sze-mâ *K͟h*ien.
tion of propriety and righteousness. Ascending as high as Hsieh and Hâu-*k*î, and descending through the prosperous eras of Yin and *K*âu to the times of decadence under kings Yû and Lî, he selected in all 305 pieces, which he sang over to his lute, to bring them into accordance with the musical style of the Shâo, the Wû, the Yâ, and the Făng.'

In the History of the Classical Books in the Records of the Sui Dynasty (A. D. 589 to 618), it is said :—'When royal

The writer of the Records of the Sui Dynasty.
benign rule ceased, and poems were no more collected, *K*ih, the Grand Music-Master of Lû, arranged in order those that were existing, and made a copy of them. Then Confucius expurgated them; and going up to the Shang dynasty, and coming down to the state of Lû, he compiled altogether 300 pieces.'

*K*û Hsî, whose own standard work on the Shih appeared in A. D. 1178, declined to express himself positively on the expurgation of the odes, but summed up his view of what Confucius did for them in the following words:—

Opinion of *K*û Hsî.
'Royal methods had ceased, and poems were no more collected. Those which were extant were full of errors, and wanting in arrangement. When Confucius returned from Wei to Lû, he brought with him the odes that he had gotten in other states, and digested them, along with those that were to be found in Lû, into a collection of 300 pieces.'

I have not been able to find evidence sustaining these

representations, and must adopt the view that, before the　281
View of the birth of Confucius, the Book of Poetry existed,
author.　substantially the same as it was at his death,
and that while he may have somewhat altered the arrangement of its Books and pieces, the service which he rendered
to it was not that of compilation, but the impulse to study it
which he communicated to his disciples.

2. If we place *Kh*ien's composition of the memoir of
Confucius in B.C. 100, nearly four hundred years will have
Groundlessness elapsed between the death of the sage and
of *Kh*ien's any statement to the effect that he expurgated
statement. previously existing poems, or compiled the
collection that we now have; and no writer in the interval
affirmed or implied any such things. The further statement in the Sui Records aboût the Music-Master of Lû
is also without any earlier confirmation. But independently
of these considerations, there is ample evidence to prove,
first, that the poems current before Confucius were not
by any means so numerous as *Kh*ien says, and, secondly,
that the collection of 300 pieces or thereabouts, digested
under the same divisions as in the present classic, existed
before the sage's time.

3. i. It would not be surprising, if, floating about and
current among the people of China in the sixth century
before our era, there had been more than 3000 pieces of
poetry. The marvel is that such was not the case. But in
the Narratives of the States, a work of the *K*âu dynasty,
and ascribed by many to 3o *Kh*iû-ming, there occur
quotations from thirty-one poems, made by statesmen and
others, all anterior to Confucius; and of those poems there
are not more than two which are not in the present classic.
Even of those two, one is an ode of it quoted under another
name. Further, in the 3o *K*wan, certainly the work of
*Kh*iû-ming, we have quotations from not fewer than 219
poems, of which only thirteen are not found in the classic.
Thus of 250 poems current in China before the supposed
compilation of the Shih, 236 are found in it, and only
fourteen are absent. To use the words of *K*âo Yî, a
scholar of the present dynasty, 'If the poems existing in

282   Confucius' time had been more than 3000, the quotations of poems now lost in these two works should have been ten times as numerous as the quotations from the 305 pieces said to have been preserved by him, whereas they are only between a twenty-first and twenty-second part of the existing pieces. This is sufficient to show that *Kh*ien's statement is not worthy of credit.'

ii. Of the existence of the Book of Poetry before Confucius, digested in four Parts, and much in the same order as at present, there may be advanced the following proofs :—

First. There is the passage in the Official Book of *K*âu, quoted and discussed in the last paragraph of the preceding chapter. We have in it a distinct reference to poems, many centuries before the sage, arranged and classified in the same way as those of the existing Shih. Our Shih, no doubt, was then in the process of formation.

Second. In the ninth piece of the sixth decade of the Shih, Part II, an ode assigned to the time of king Yû, B. C. 781 to 771, we have the words,

     ' They sing the Yâ and the Nan,
     Dancing to their flutes without error.'

So early, therefore, as the eighth century B. C. there was a collection of poems, of which some bore the name of the Nan, which there is much reason to suppose were the *K*âu Nan and the Shâo Nan, forming the first two Books of the first Part of the present Shih ; and of which others bore the name of the Yâ, being, probably, the earlier pieces that now compose a large portion of the second and third Parts.

Third. In the narratives of 3o *Kh*iû-ming, under the twenty-ninth year of duke Hsiang, B. C. 544, when Confucius was only seven or eight years old, we have an account of a visit to the court of Lû by an envoy from Wû, an eminent statesman of the time, and a man of great learning. We are told that as he wished to hear the music of *K*âu, which he could do better in Lû than in any other state, they sang to him the odes of the *K*âu Nan and the Shâo Nan ; thóse of Phei, Yung, and Wei ; of the Royal Domain ; of Kăng ; of *Kh*î ; of Pin ; of *Kh*in ; of Wei ; of

Thang ; of *Kh*ăn ; of Kwei ; and of 3*h*âo. They sang to   283
him also the odes of the Minor Yâ and the Greater Yâ ;
and they sang finally the pieces of the Sung. We have
thus, existing in the boyhood of Confucius, what we may
call the present Book of Poetry, with its Făng, its Yâ, and
its Sung. The only difference discernible is slight,— in the
order in which the Books of the Făng followed one another.

Fourth. We may appeal in this matter to the ̄words of
Confucius himself. Twice in the Analects he speaks of the
Shih as a collection consisting of 300 pieces[1]. That work
not being made on any principle of chronological order,
we cannot positively assign those sayings to any particular
years of Confucius' life ; but it is, I may say, the unanimous
opinion of Chinese critics that they were spoken before the
time to which *Kh*ien and *K*û Hsî refer his special labour
on the Book of Poetry.

To my own mind the evidence that has been adduced
is decisive on the points which I specified. The Shih,
arranged very much as we now have it, was current in
China before the time of Confucius, and its pieces were
in the mouths of statesmen and scholars, constantly quoted
by them on festive and other occasions. Poems not included
in it there doubtless were, but they were comparatively few.
Confucius may have made a copy for the use of himself
and his disciples ; but it does not appear that he rejected
any pieces which had been previously received into the
collection, or admitted any which had not previously found
a place in it.

4. The question now arises of what Confucius did for the
Shih, if, indeed, he did anything at all. The only thing
from which we can hazard an opinion on the
point we have from himself. In the Analects,
IX, xiv, he tells us : —' I returned from Wei
to Lû, and then the music was reformed, and the pieces in

What Confucius
did for the
Shih.

---

[1] In stating that the odes were 300, Confucius probably preferred to use the
round number. There are, as I said in the former chapter, altogether 305
pieces, which is the number given by Sze-mâ *Kh*ien. There are also the titles
of six others. It is contended by *K*û Hsî and many other scholars that these
titles were only the names of tunes. More likely is the view that the text of the
pieces so styled was lost after Confucius' death.

284 the Yâ and the Sung received their proper places.' The
return from Wei to Lû took place only five years before the
sage's death. He ceased from that time to take an active
part in political affairs, and solaced himself with music, the
study of the ancient literature of his nation, the writing
of 'the Spring and Autumn,' and familiar intercourse with
those of his disciples who still kept around him. He
reformed the music,—that to which the pieces of the Shih
were sung; but wherein the reformation consisted we
cannot tell. And he gave to the pieces of the Yâ and
the Sung their proper places. The present order of the
Books in the Fǎng, slightly differing from what was
common in his boyhood, may have now been determined
by him. More than this we cannot say.

While we cannot discover, therefore, any peculiar and
important labours of Confucius on the Shih, and we have
it now, as will be shown in the next chapter, substantially
as he found it already compiled to his hand, the subsequent preservation of it may reasonably be attributed to
the admiration which he expressed for it, and the enthu-
siasm for it with which he sought to inspire his disciples.
It was one of the themes on which he delighted to con-
verse with them[1]. He taught that it is from the poems
that the mind receives its best stimulus[2]. A man ignorant
of them was, in his opinion, like one who stands with his
face towards a wall, limited in his view, and unable to
advance[3]. Of the two things that his son could specify as
enjoined on him by the sage, the first was that he should
learn the odes[4]. In this way Confucius, probably, contributed largely to the subsequent preservation of the Shih,—
the preservation of the tablets on which the odes were
inscribed, and the preservation of it in the memory of all
who venerated his authority, and looked up to him as their
master.

---

[1] Analects, VII, xvii. [2] Analects, VIII, viii, XVII, ix.
[3] Analects, XVII, x. [4] Analects, XVI, xiii.

· CHAPTER III.   285

THE SHIH FROM THE TIME OF CONFUCIUS TILL
THE GENERAL ACKNOWLEDGMENT OF THE
PRESENT TEXT.

1. Of the attention paid to the study of the Shih from
the death of Confucius to the rise of the *Kh*in dynasty, we
From Con-   have abundant evidence in the writings of his
fucius to the   grandson 3ze-sze, of Mencius, and of Hsün
rise of the   *Kh*ing. One of the acknowledged distinctions
Khin dynasty.
of Mencius is his acquaintance with the odes,
his quotations from which are very numerous; and Hsün
*Kh*ing survived the extinction of the *K*âu dynasty, and
lived on into the times of *Kh*in.

2. The Shih shared in the calamity which all the other
classical works, excepting the Yî, suffered, when the tyrant
of *Kh*in issued his edict for their destruction. But I have
shown, in the Introduction to the Shû, p. 7, that that edict
was in force for less than a quarter of a century. The
The Shih was   odes were all, or very nearly all[1], recovered;
all recovered   and the reason assigned for this is, that their
after the fires preservation depended on the memory of
of *Kh*in.
scholars more than on their inscription on
tablets of bamboo and on silk.

3. Three different texts of the Shih made their appearance early in the Han dynasty, known as the Shih of Lû,
Three different of *Kh*î, and of Han; that is, the Book of
texts.   Poetry was recovered from three different
quarters. Liû Hin's Catalogue of the Books in the
Imperial Library of Han (B.C. 6 to 1) commences, on the
Shih King, with a collection of the three texts, in twenty-
eight chapters.

---

[1] All, in fact, unless we except the six pieces of Part II, of which we have
only the titles. It is contended by *K*û Hsî and others that the text of these
had been lost before the time of Confucius. It may have been lost, however,
after the sage's death; see note on p. 283.

286   i. Immediately after the mention of the general collection
in the Catalogue come the titles of two works of commentary on the text of Lû. The former of
The text of Lû. them was by a Shăn Phei of whom we have
some account in the Literary Biographies of Han. He was
a native of Lû, and had received his own knowledge of the
odes from a scholar of *Khî*, called Fâu *Kh*iû-po. He was
resorted to by many disciples, whom he taught to repeat
the odes. When the first emperor of the Han dynasty was
passing through Lû, Shăn followed him to the capital of
that state, and had an interview with him. Subsequently
the emperor Wû (B.C. 140 to 87), in the beginning of his
reign, sent for him to court when he was more than eighty
years old ; and he appears to have survived a considerable
number of years beyond that advanced age. The names
of ten of his disciples are given, all of them men of
eminence, and among them Khung An-kwo. Rather later,
the most noted adherent of the school of Lû was Wei
Hsien, who arrived at the dignity of prime minister (from
B.C. 71 to 67), and published the Shih of Lû in Stanzas and
Lines. Up and down in the Books of Han and Wei are
to be found quotations of the odes, that must have been
taken from the professors of the Lû recension ; but neither
the text nor the writings on it long survived. They are
said to have perished during the *K*in dynasty (A.D. 265 to
419). When the Catalogue of the Sui Library was made,
none of them were existing.

ii. The Han Catalogue mentions five different works on
the Shih of *Khî*. This text was from a Yüan Kû, a native
of *Khî*, about whom we learn, from the same
The text of *Khî*. collection of Literary Biographies, that he was
one of the great scholars of the court in the time of the
emperor *K*ing (B.C. 156 to 141),—a favourite with him, and
specially distinguished for his knowledge of the odes and
his advocacy of orthodox Confucian doctrine. He died in
the succeeding reign of Wû, more than ninety years old ;
and we are told that all the scholars of *Khî* who got a
name in those days for their acquaintance with the Shih
sprang from his school. Among his disciples was the well-

known name of Hsiâ-hâu Shih-*kh*ang, who communicated   287
his acquisitions to Hâu 3*h*ang, a native of the present
Shan-tung province, and author of two of the works in the
Han Catalogue. Hâu had three disciples of note, and by
them the Shih of *Kh*î was transmitted to others, whose
names, with quotations from their writings, are scattered
through the Books of Han. Neither text nor commentaries,
however, had a better fate than the Shih of Lû. There
is no mention of them in the Catalogue of Sui. They are
said to have perished even before the rise of the *K*in
dynasty.

iii. The text of Han was somewhat more fortunate.
Hin's Catalogue contains the names of four works, all by
The text of   Han Ying, whose surname is thus perpetuated
Han Ying.   in the text of the Shih that emanated from
him. He was a native, we are told, of Yen, and a great
scholar in the time of the emperor Wăn (B.C. 179 to 155),
and on into the reigns of *K*ing and Wû. 'He laboured,'
it is said, 'to unfold the meaning of the odes, and published
an Explanation of the Text, and Illustrations of the Poems,
containing several myriads of characters. His text was
somewhat different from the texts of Lû and *Kh*î, but
substantially of the same meaning.' Of course, Han founded
a school; but while almost all the writings of his followers
soon perished, both the works just mentioned continued on
through the various dynasties to the time of Sung. The Sui
Catalogue contains the titles of his Text and two works on
it; the Thang, those of his Text and his Illustrations; but
when we come to the Catalogue of Sung, published under
the Yüan dynasty, we find only the Illustrations, in ten
books or chapters; and Âu-yang Hsiû (A.D. 1017 to
1072) tells us that in his time this was all of Han that
remained. It continues entire, or nearly so, to the present
day.

4. But while those three different recensions of the Shih
all disappeared, with the exception of a single treatise of
Han Ying, their unhappy fate was owing not more to the
convulsions by which the empire was often rent, and the
consequent destruction of literary monuments such as we

288   have witnessed in China in our own day, than to the A fourth text; appearance of a fourth text, which displaced that of Mâo. them by its superior correctness, and the ability with which it was advocated and commented on. This was what is called the Text of Mâo. It came into the field rather later than the others; but the Han Catalogue contains the Shih of Mâo, in twenty-nine chapters, and a Commentary on it in thirty-nine. According to *K*ăng Hsüan, the author of this was a native of Lû, known as Mâo Hăng or 'the Greater Mâo,' who had been a disciple, we are told by Lü Teh-ming, of Hsün *Kh*ing. The work is lost. He had communicated his knowledge of the Shih, however, to another Mâo,—Mâo *K*ang, 'the Lesser Mao,' who was a great scholar, at the court of king Hsien of Ho-*k*ien, a son of the emperor *K*ing. King Hsien was one of the most diligent labourers in the recovery of the ancient books, and presented the text and work of Hăng at the court of his father,—probably in B.C. 129. Mâo *K*ang published Explanations of the Shih, in twenty-nine chapters, —a work which we still possess; but it was not till the reign of Phing (A.D. 1 to 5) that Mâo's recension was received into the Imperial College, and took its place along with those of Lû, *Kh*î, and Han Ying.

The Chinese critics have carefully traced the line of scholars who had charge of Mâo's Text and Explanations down to the reign of Phing. The names of the men and their works are all given. By the end of the first quarter of our first century we find the most famous scholars addicting themselves to Mâo's text. The well-known *K*iâ Khwei (A. D. 30 to 101) published a work on the Meaning and Difficulties of Mâo's Shih, having previously compiled a digest of the differences between its text and those of the other three recensions, at the command of the emperor Ming (A. D. 58 to 75). The equally celebrated Mâ Yung (A. D. 79 to 166) followed with another commentary;—and we arrive at *K*ăng Hsüan or *K*ăng Khang-*kh*ăng (A. D. 127 to 200), who wrote a Supplementary Commentary to the Shih of Mâo, and a Chronological Introduction to the Shih. The former of these two works complete, and

portions of the latter, are still extant.　After the time of
*K*ăng the other three texts were little heard of, while the
name of the commentators on Mâo's text speedily becomes
legion.　It was inscribed, moreover, on the stone tablets of
the emperor Ling (A. D. 168 to 189).　The grave of Mâo
*K*ăng is still shown near the village of Ȝun-fû, in the
departmental district of Ho-*k*ien, *K*ih-lî.

5. Returning now to what I said in the second paragraph,
it will be granted that the appearance of three different and
independent texts, soon after the rise of the
Han dynasty, affords the most satisfactory
evidence of the recovery of the Book of
Poetry as it had continued from the time
of Confucius.　Unfortunately, only fragments
of those texts remain now; but they were, while they were
current, diligently compared with one another, and with
the fourth text of Mâo, which subsequently got the field to
itself.　When a collection is made of their peculiar readings,
so far as it can now be done, it is clear that their variations from one another and from Mâo's text arose from
the alleged fact that the preservation of the odes was
owing to their being transmitted by recitation.　The rhyme
helped the memory to retain them, and while wood,
bamboo, and silk had all been consumed by the flames
of *K*hin, when the time of repression ceased, scholars would
be eager to rehearse their stores.　It was inevitable, and
more so in China than in a country possessing an alphabet,
that the same sounds when taken down by different writers
should be represented by different characters.

The different texts guarantee the genuineness of the recovered Shih.

On the whole, the evidence given above is as full as could
be desired in such a case, and leaves no reason for us to
hesitate in accepting the present received text of the Shih
as a very close approximation to that which was current in
the time of Confucius.

289

[1]　　　U

290 CHAPTER IV.

THE FORMATION OF THE COLLECTION OF THE SHIH;
HOW IT CAME TO BE SO SMALL AND INCOMPLETE;
THE INTERPRETATION AND AUTHORS OF THE PIECES;
ONE POINT OF TIME CERTAINLY INDICATED IN IT;
AND THE CONFUCIAN PREFACE.

1. It has been shown above, in the second chapter, that the Shih existed as a collection of poetical pieces before the time of Confucius[1]. In order to complete this Introduction to it, it is desirable to give some account of the various subjects indicated in the heading of the present chapter.

How were the odes collected in the first place? In his Account of a Conversation concerning 'a Right Regulation of Governments for the Common Good of Mankind' (Edinburgh, 1704), p. 10, Sir Andrew Fletcher, of Saltoun, tells us the opinion of 'a very wise man,' that 'if a man were permitted to make all the ballads of a nation, he need not care who should make its laws.' A writer in the Spectator, no. 502, refers to a similar opinion as having been entertained in England earlier than the time of Fletcher. 'I have heard,' he says, 'that a minister of state in the reign of Elizabeth had all manner of books and ballads brought to him, of what kind soever, and took great notice how they took with the people; upon which he would, and certainly might, very well judge of their present dispositions, and of the most proper way of applying them according to his own purposes[2].'

---

[1] As in the case of the Shû, Confucius generally speaks of 'the Shih,' never using the name of 'the Shih King.' In the Analects, IX, xiv, however, he mentions also the Yâ and the Sung; and in XVII, x, he specifies the Kâu Nan and the Shâo Nan, the first two books of the Kwo Fäng. Mencius similarly speaks of 'the Shih;' and in III, i, ch. 4, he specifies 'the Sung of Lû,' Book ii of Part IV. In VI, ii, ch. 3, he gives his views of the Hsiâo Phan, the third ode of decade 5, Part II, and of the Khâi Fung, the seventh ode of Book iii of Part I.

[2] This passage from the Spectator is adduced by Sir John Davis in his treatise on the Poetry of the Chinese, p. 35.

In harmony with the views thus expressed is the theory   291
of the Chinese scholars, that it was the duty
The theory of
the Chinese of the ancient kings to make themselves
scholars about acquainted with all the poems current in the
a collection of
poems for different states, and to judge from them of
governmental the rule exercised by the several princes, so
purposes.
that they might minister praise or blame,
reward or punishment accordingly.

The rudiments of this theory may be found in the Shû,
in the Canon of Shun ; but the one classical passage which
is appealed to in support of it is in the Record of Rites,
III, ii, parr. 13, 14 :—' Every fifth year, the Son of Heaven
made a progress through the kingdom, when the Grand
Music-Master was commanded to lay before him the poems
of the different states, as an exhibition of the manners and
government of the people.' Unfortunately, this Book of
the Lî *K*î, the Royal Ordinances, was compiled only in the
reign of the emperor Wăn of the Han dynasty (B.C. 179 to
155). The scholars entrusted with the work did their best,
we may suppose, with the materials àt their command.
They made much use, it is evident, of Mencius, and of the
Î Lî. The *K*âu Lî, or the Official Book of *K*âu, had not
then been recovered. But neither in Mencius nor in the
Î Lî do we meet with any authority for the statement
before us. The Shû mentions that Shun every fifth year
made a tour of inspection ; but there were then no odes for
him to examine, for to him and his minister Kâo-yâo is
attributed the first rudimentary attempt at the poetic art.
Of the progresses of the Hsiâ and Yin sovereigns we have
no information ; and those of the kings of *K*âu were made,
we know, only once in twelve years. The statement in the
Royal Ordinances, therefore, was probably based only on
tradition.

Notwithstanding the difficulties that beset this passage
of the Lî *K*î, I am not disposed to reject it altogether. It
derives a certain amount of confirmation from the passage
quoted from the Official Book of *K*âu on p. 278, showing
that in the *K*âu dynasty there was a collection of poems,
under the divisions of the Făng, the Yâ, and the Sung,

292   which it was the business of the Grand Music-Master to
teach the musicians of the court. It may be accepted then,
that the duke of *K*âu, in legislating for his dynasty, enacted
that the poems produced in the different feudal states
should be collected on occasion of the royal progresses,
and lodged thereafter among the archives of the bureau
of music at the royal court. The same thing, we may
presume à fortiori, would be done, at certain other stated
times, with those produced within the royal domain itself.

But the feudal states were modelled after the pattern of
the royal state. They also had their music-masters, their

The music-master of the king would get the odes of each state from its music-master. musicians, and their historiographers. The
kings in their progresses did not visit each
particular state, so that the Grand Music-
Master could have the opportunity to collect
the odes in it for himself. They met, at well-
known points, the marquises, earls, barons, &c., of the
different quarters of the kingdom ; there gave audience to
them ; adjudicated on their merits, and issued to them their
orders. We are obliged to suppose that the princes were
attended to the places of rendezvous by their music-
masters, carrying with them the poetical compositions
gathered in their several regions, to present them to their
superior of the royal court. We can understand how, by
means of the above arrangement, the poems of the whole
kingdom were accumulated and arranged among the
archives of the capital. Was there any provision for dis-

How the collected poems were disseminated throughout the states. seminating thence the poems of one state
among all the others? There is sufficient
evidence that such dissemination was effected
in some way. Throughout the Narratives of
the States, and the details of 3o *K*hiû-ming on the history
of the Spring and Autumn, the officers of the states
generally are presented to us as familiar not only with the
odes of their particular states, but with those of other states
as well. They appear equally well acquainted with all the
Parts and Books of our present Shih; and we saw how the
whole of it was sung over to *K*î *K*â of Wû, when he visited
the court of Lû in the boyhood of Confucius. There was,

probably, a regular communication from the royal court to   293
the courts of the various states of the poetical pieces that
for one reason or another were thought worthy of preservation. This is nowhere expressly stated, but it may be
contended for by analogy from the accounts which I have
given, in the Introduction to the Shû, pp. 4, 5, of the duties
of the royal historiographers or recorders.

2. But if the poems produced in the different states were
thus collected in the capital, and thence again disseminated
throughout the kingdom, we might conclude that the collection would have been far more extensive and complete than
How the Shih we have it now. The smallness of it is to be
is so small and accounted for by the disorder into which the
incomplete. kingdom fell after the lapse of a few reigns
from king Wû. Royal progresses ceased when royal government fell into decay, and then the odes were no more collected[1]. We have no account of any progress of the kings
during the *K͟hun K͟hiû* period. But before that period
there is a long gap of nearly 150 years between kings
K͟hăng and Î, covering the reigns of Khang, *K͟âo*, Mû,
and Kung, if we except two doubtful pieces among the
Sacrificial Odes of *K͟âu*. The reign of Hsiâo, who succeeded
to Î, is similarly uncommemorated; and the latest odes are
of the time of Ting, when 100 years of the *K͟hun K͟hiû*
period had still to run their course. Many odes must have
been made and collected during the 140 and more years
after king *K͟hăng*. The probability is that they perished
during the feeble reigns of Î and the three monarchs who
followed him. Then came the long and vigorous reign of
Hsüan (B. C. 827 to 782), when we may suppose that the
ancient custom of collecting the poems was revived. After
him all was in the main decadence and confusion. It was
probably in the latter part of his reign that *K͟ăng-khâo*,
an ancestor of Confucius, obtained from the Grand Music-
Master at the court of *K͟âu* twelve of the sacrificial odes
of the previous dynasty, as will be related under the Sacrificial Odes of Shang, with which he returned to Sung,

---

[1] See Mencius, IV, ii, ch. 21.

294   which was held by representatives of the line of Shang. They were used there in sacrificing to the old Shang kings; yet seven of the twelve were lost before the time of the sage.

The general conclusion to which we come is, that the existing Shih is the fragment of various collections made during the early reigns of the kings of *K*âu, and added to at intervals, especially on the occurrence of a prosperous rule, in accordance with the regulation that has been preserved in the Lî *K*î. How it is that we have in Part I odes of comparatively few of the states into which the kingdom was divided, and that the odes of those states extend only over a short period of their history :—for these things we cannot account further than by saying that such were the ravages of time and the results of disorder. We can only accept the collection as it is, and be thankful for it. How long before Confucius the collection was closed we cannot tell.

3. The conclusions which I have thus sought to establish concerning the formation of the Shih as a collection have an important bearing on the interpretation of many of the pieces. The remark of Sze-mâ *K*ĥien that 'Confucius

Bearing of these views on the interpretation of particular pieces. selected those pieces which would be serviceable for the inculcation of propriety and righteousness' is as erroneous as the other, that he selected 305 pieces out of more than 3000. The sage merely studied and taught the pieces which he found existing, and the collection necessarily contained odes illustrative of bad government as well as of good, of licentiousness as well as of a pure morality. Nothing has been such a stumbling-block in the way of the reception of *K*û Hsî's interpretation of the pieces as the readiness with which he attributes a licentious meaning to many of those in the seventh Book of Part I. But the reason why the kings had the odes of the different states collected and presented to them was, 'that they might judge from them of the manners of the people,' and so come to a decision regarding the government and morals of their rulers. A student and translator of the odes has simply to allow them to speak for themselves, and has no more reason to be surprised by references to vice in some of them than by the language of virtue in many others. Confucius said, indeed, in his own enigmatical way, that the single sentence, ' Thought without depravity,' covered the whole 300 pieces[1]; and it may very well be allowed that they were collected and preserved for the promotion of good government and virtuous manners. The merit attaching to them is that they give us faithful pictures of what was good and what was bad in the political state of the country, and in the social, moral, and religious habits of the people.

The pieces were of course made by individuals who possessed the gift, or thought that they possessed the gift, The writers of. of poetical composition. Who they were we the odes. could tell only on the authority of the pieces themselves, or of credible historical accounts, contemporaneous with them or nearly so. It is not worth our while to question the opinion of the Chinese critics who attribute very many of them to the duke of *K*âu, to whom we owe so much of the fifth Part of the Shû. There is, however, independent testimony only to his composition of a single ode,—the second of the fifteenth Book in Part I[2]. Some of the other pieces in that Part, of which the historical interpretation may be considered as sufficiently fixed, are written in the first person ; but the author may be personating his subject.

In Part II, the seventh ode of decade 2 was made by a *K*iâ-fû, a noble of the royal court, but we know nothing more about him ; the sixth of decade 6, by a eunuch styled Măng-ʒze ; and the sixth of decade 7, from a concurrence of external testimonies, should be ascribed to duke Wû of Wei, B. C. 812 to 758.

In the third decade of Part III, the second piece was composed by the same duke Wû ; the third by an earl of *Z*ui in the royal domain ; the fourth must have been made by one of king Hsüan's ministers, to express the king's

---

[1] Analects, II, ii.   [2] See the Shû, V, vi, par. 2.

296　feelings under the drought that was exhausting the kingdom ; and the fifth and sixth claim to be the work of Yin *Kî-fû*, one of Hsüan's principal officers.

4. The ninth ode of the fourth Book, Part II, gives us a note of time that enables us to fix the year of its composition in a manner entirely satisfactory, and proves also the correctness, back to that date, of the ordinary Chinese chronology. The piece is one of a group which their contents lead us to refer to the reign of king Yû, the son of Hsüan, B. C. 781 to 771. When we examine the chronology of his period, it is said that in his sixth year, B. C. 776, there was an eclipse of the sun. Now the ode commences :—

'At the conjunction (of the sun and moon) in the tenth month, on the first day of the moon, which was Hsin-mâo, the sun was eclipsed.'

This eclipse is verified by calculation as having taken place in B. C. 776, on August 29th, the very day and month assigned to it in the poem.

5. In the Preface which appeared along with Mâo's text of the Shih, the occasion and authorship of many of the odes are given ; but I do not allow much weight to its The Preface to testimony. It is now divided into the Great the Shih. Preface and the Little Preface ; but Mâo himself made no such distinction between its parts. It will be sufficient for me to give a condensed account of the views of *Kû* Hsî on the subject :—

'Opinions of scholars are much divided as to the authorship of the Preface. Some ascribe it to Confucius ; some to (his disciple) 3ze-hsiâ ; and some to the historiographers of the states. In the absence of clear testimony it is impossible to decide the point, but the notice about Wei Hung (first century) in the Literary Biographies of Han[1] would seem to make it clear that the Preface was

---

[1] The account is this : 'Hung became the disciple of Hsieh Man-*kh*ing, who was famous for his knowledge of Mâo's Shih ; and he afterwards made the Preface to it, remarkable for the accuracy with which it gives the meaning of the pieces in the Făng and the Yâ, and which is now current in the world.'

his work. We must take into account, however, on the   297
other hand, the statement of *K*ǎng Khang - *k*hǎng, that
the Preface existed as a separate document when Mâo
appeared with his text, and that he broke it up, prefixing
to each ode the portion belonging to it. The natural conclusion is, that the Preface had come down from a remote
period, and that Hung merely added to it, and rounded it
off. In accordance with this, scholars generally hold that
the first sentences in the introductory notices formed
the original Preface, which Mâo distributed, and that the
following portions were subsequently added.

' This view may appear reasonable; but when we examine
those first sentences themselves, we find that some of them
do not agree with the obvious meaning of the odes to
which they are prefixed, and give only rash and baseless
expositions. Evidently, from the first, the Preface was
made up of private speculations and conjectures on the
subject-matter of the odes, and constituted a document
by itself, separately appended to the text. Then on its
first appearance there were current the explanations of the
odes that were given in connexion with the texts of Lû,
*K*hî, and Han Ying, so that readers could know that it was
the work of later hands, and not give entire credit to it.
But when Mâo no longer published the Preface as a separate document, but each ode appeared with the introductory
notice as a portion of the text, this seemed to give it the
authority of the text itself. Then after the other texts
disappeared and Mâo's had the field to itself, this means
of testing the accuracy of its prefatory notices no longer
existed. They appeared as if they were the production
of the poets themselves, and the odes seemed to be made
from them as so many themes. Scholars handed down a
faith in them from one to another, and no one ventured to
express a doubt of their authority. The text was twisted
and chiseled to bring it into accordance with them, and no
one would undertake to say plainly that they were the
work of the scholars of the Han dynasty.'

There is no western sinologist, I apprehend, who will

298   not cordially concur with me in the principle of *Kû Hsî*
that we must find the meaning of the poems in the poems
themselves, instead of accepting the interpretation of them
given by we know not whom, and to follow which would
reduce many of them to absurd enigmas.

ODES OF THE TEMPLE AND THE ALTAR.

IT was stated in the Introduction, p. 278, that the poems in the fourth Part of the Shih are the only ones that are professedly religious; and there are some even of them, it will be seen, which have little claim on internal grounds to be so considered. I commence with them my selections from the Shih for the Sacred Books of the Religions of the East. I will give them all, excepting the first two of the Praise Odes of Lû, the reason for omitting which will be found, when I come to that division of the Part.

The Odes of the Temple and the Altar are, most of them, connected with the ancestral worship of the sovereigns of the Shang and *K*âu dynasties, and of the marquises of Lû. Of the ancestral worship of the common people we have almost no information in the Shih. It was binding, however, on all, and two utterances of Confucius may be given in illustration of this. In the eighteenth chapter of the Doctrine of the Mean, telling how the duke of *K*âu, the legislator of the dynasty so called, had 'completed the virtuous course of Wăn and Wû, carrying up the title of king to Wăn's father and grandfather, and sacrificing to the dukes before them with the royal ceremonies,' he adds, 'And this rule he extended to the feudal princes, the great officers, the other officers, and the common people. In the mourning and other duties rendered to a deceased father or mother, he allowed no difference between the noble and the mean.' Again, his summary in the tenth chapter of the Hsiâo King, of the duties

300

of filial piety, is the following:—'A filial son, in serving his parents, in his ordinary intercourse with them, should show the utmost respect; in supplying them with food, the greatest delight; when they are ill, the utmost solicitude; when mourning for their death, the deepest grief; and when sacrificing to them, the profoundest solemnity. When these things are all complete, he is able to serve his parents.'

Of the ceremonies in the royal worship of ancestors, and perhaps on some other occasions, we have much information in the pieces of this Part, and in many others in the second and third Parts.` They were preceded by fasting and various purifications on the part of the king and the parties who were to assist in the performance of them. There was a great concourse of the feudal princes, and much importance was attached to the presence among them of the representatives of former dynasties; but the duties of the occasion devolved mainly on the princes of the same surname as the royal House. Libations of fragrant spirits were made, especially in the *K*âu period, to attract the Spirits, and their presence was invoked by a functionary who took his place inside the principal gate. The principal victim, a red bull in the temple of *K*âu, was killed by the king himself, using for the purpose a knife to the handle of which small bells were attached. With this he laid bare the hair, to show that the animal was of the required colour, inflicted the wound of death, and cut away the fat, which was burned along with southernwood to increase the incense and fragrance. Other victims were numerous, and the fifth ode of the second decade, Part II, describes all engaged in the service as greatly exhausted with what they had to do, flaying the carcases, boiling the flesh, roasting it, broiling it, arranging it on trays and stands, and setting it forth. Ladies from the palace are present to give their assistance; music peals; the cup goes round. The description is that of a feast as much as of a sacrifice; and in fact, those great seasonal occasions were what we might call grand family reunions, where the dead and the living met, eating and drinking together, where the living worshipped the dead, and the dead blessed the living.

This characteristic of these ceremonies appeared most strikingly in the custom which required that the departed ancestors should be represented by living relatives of the same surname, chosen according to certain rules that are not mentioned in the Shih. These took for the time the place of the dead, received the

The royal worship of ancestors.

honours which were due to them, and were supposed to be 301
possessed by their spirits. They ate and drank as those whom
they personated would have done; accepted for them the homage
rendered by their descendants; communicated their will to the
principal in the service, and pronounced on him and on his
line their benediction, being assisted in this point by a mediating
priest, as we may call him for want of a more exact term. On
the next day, after a summary repetition of the ceremonies of
the sacrifice, those personators of the dead were specially feasted,
and, as it is expressed in the second decade of Part III, ode 4,
'their happiness and dignity were made complete.' We have
an allusion to this strange custom in Mencius (VI, i, ch. 5),
showing how a junior member of a family, when chosen to
represent one of his ancestors, was for the time exalted above
his elders, and received the demonstrations of reverence due to
the ancestor.

When the sacrifice to ancestors was finished, the king feasted his
uncles and younger brothers or cousins, that is, all the princes
and nobles of the same surname with himself, in another apartment. The musicians who had discoursed with instrument and
voice during the worship and entertainment of the ancestors,
followed the convivial party 'to give their soothing aid at the
second blessing.' The viands that had been provided, we have
seen, in great abundance, were brought in from the temple,
and set forth anew. The guests ate to the full and drank to
the full, and at the conclusion they all did obeisance, while one
of them declared the satisfaction of the Spirits, and assured the
king of their favour to him and his posterity, so long as they
did not neglect those observances. During the feast the king
showed particular respect to those among his relatives who
were aged, filled their cups again and again, and desired 'that
their old age might be blessed, and their bright happiness ever
increased.'

The above sketch of the seasonal sacrifices to ancestors shows
that they were intimately related to the duty of filial piety, and
were designed mainly to maintain the unity of the family connexion. There was implied in them a belief in the continued
existence of the spirits of the departed; and by means of them
the ancestors of the kings were raised to the position of the
Tutelary spirits of the dynasty; and the ancestors of each family
became its Tutelary spirits. Several of the pieces in Part IV
are appropriate, it will be observed, to sacrifices offered to some

302   one monarch. They would be used on particular occasions connected with his achievements in the past, or when it was supposed that his help would be valuable in contemplated enterprises. With regard to all the ceremonies of the ancestral temple, Confucius gives the following account of the purposes which they were intended to serve, hardly adverting to their religious significance, in the nineteenth chapter of the Doctrine of the Mean :—' By means of them they distinguished the royal kindred according to their order of descent. By arranging those present according to their rank, they distinguished the more noble and the less. By the apportioning of duties at them, they made a distinction of talents and worth. In the ceremony of general pledging, the inferiors presented the cup to their superiors, and thus something was given to the lowest to do. At the (concluding) feast places were given according to the hair, and thus was marked the distinction of years.'

The Shih does not speak of the worship which was paid to God,

The worship paid to God.   unless it be incidentally. There were two grand occasions on which it was rendered by the sovereign,—the summer and winter solstices. These two sacrifices were offered on different altars, that in winter being often described as offered to Heaven, and that in summer to Earth; but we have the testimony of Confucius, in the nineteenth chapter of the Doctrine of the Mean, that the object of them both was to serve Shang-Tî. Of the ceremonies on these two occasions, however, I do not speak here, as there is nothing said about them in the Shih. But there were other sacrifices to God, at stated periods in the course of the year, of at least two of which we have some intimation in the pieces of this fourth Part. The last in the first decade of the Sacrificial Odes of *K*âu is addressed to Hâu *K*î as having proved himself the correlate of Heaven, in teaching men to cultivate the grain which God had appointed for the nourishment of all. This was appropriate to a sacrifice in spring, offered to God to seek His blessing on the agricultural labours of the year, Hâu *K*î, as the ancestor of the House of *K*âu, being associated with Him in it. The seventh piece of the same decade again was appropriate to a sacrifice to God in autumn, in the Hall of Light, at a great audience to the feudal princes, when king Wăn was associated with Him as being the founder of the dynasty of *K*âu.

With these preliminary observations to assist the reader in understanding the pieces in this Part, I proceed to give—

I. The Sacrificial Odes of Shang. 303

THESE odes of Shang constitute the last Book in the ordinary
editions of the Shih. I put them here in the first place, because
they are the oldest pieces in the collection. There are only five
of them.

The sovereigns of the dynasty of Shang occupied the throne from
B.C. 1766 to 1123. They traced their lineage to Hsieh, who
appears in the Shû as Minister of Instruction to Shun. By Yâo
or by Shun, Hsieh was invested with the principality of Shang,
corresponding to the small department which is so named in
Shen-hsî. Fourteenth in descent from him came Thien-yî,
better known as *Kh*ăng Thang, or Thang the Successful, who
dethroned the last descendant of the line of Hsiâ, and became
the founder of a new dynasty. We meet with him first at a
considerable distance from the ancestral fief (which, however,
gave name to the dynasty), having as his capital the southern Po,
which seems correctly referred to the present district of Shang-
*kh*iû, in the department of Kwei-teh, Ho-nan. Among the
twenty-seven sovereigns who followed Thang, there were three
especially distinguished :—Thâi *K*iâ, his grandson and successor
(B.C. 1753 to 1721), who received the title of Thâi 3ung; Thâi
Mâu (B.C. 1637 to 1563), canonized as *K*ung 3ung; and Wû-
ting (B.C. 1324 to 1266), known as Kâo 3ung. The shrines
of these three sovereigns and that of Thang retained their places
in the ancestral temple ever after they were first set up, and if
all the sacrificial odes of the dynasty had been preserved, most
of them would have been in praise of one or other of the four.
But it so happened that at least all the odes of which Thâi 3ung
was the subject were lost; and of the others we have only the
small portion that has been mentioned above.

Of how it is that we have even these, we have the following account
in the Narratives of the States, compiled, probably, by a con-
temporary of Confucius. The count of Wei was made duke
of Sung by king Wû of *K*âu, as related in the Shû, V, viii, there
to continue the sacrifices of the House of Shang; but the government of Sung fell subsequently into disorder, and the memorials of
the dynasty were lost. In the time of duke Tâi (B.C. 799 to 766),
one of his ministers, *K*ăng-khâo, an ancestor of Confucius, received from the Grand Music-Master at the court of *K*âu twelve

of the sacrificial odes of Shang with which he returned to Sung,
where they were used in sacrificing to the old Shang kings. It is
supposed that seven of these were lost subsequently, before the
collection of the Shih was formed.

ODE 1. THE NÂ[1].

APPROPRIATE TO A SACRIFICE TO THANG, THE FOUNDER OF THE
SHANG DYNASTY, DWELLING ESPECIALLY ON THE MUSIC AND THE
REVERENCE WITH WHICH THE SACRIFICE WAS PERFORMED.

We cannot tell by which of the kings of Shang the sacrifice here
referred to was first performed. He is simply spoken of as 'a
descendant of Thang.' The ode seems to have been composed
by some one, probably a member of the royal House, who had
taken part in the service.

How admirable! how complete! Here are set
our hand-drums and drums. The drums resound
harmonious and loud, To delight our meritorious
ancestor [2].

The descendant of Thang invites him with this
music, That he may soothe us with the realization
of our thoughts [3]. Deep is the sound of our hand-

---

[1] The piece is called the Nâ, because a character so named is
an important part of the first line. So generally the pieces in the
Shih receive their names from a character or phrase occurring in
them. This point will not be again touched on.

[2] The 'meritorious ancestor' is Thang. The sacrifices of the
Shang dynasty commenced with music; those of the *K*âu with
libations of fragrant spirits;—in both cases with the same object,
to attract the spirit, or spirits, sacrificed to, and secure their presence
at the service. *K*ǎn Hâo (Ming dynasty) says, 'The departed
spirits hover between heaven and earth, and sound goes forth,
filling the region of the air. Hence in sacrificing, the people of
Yin began with a performance of music.'

[3] The Lî *K*î, XXIV, i, parr. 2, 3, tells us, that the sacrificer, as
preliminary to the service, had to fast for some days, and to think
of the person of his ancestor,—where he had stood and sat, how
he had smiled and spoken, what had been his cherished aims,

drums and drums; Shrilly sound the flutes; All   305
harmonious and blending together, According to
the notes of the sonorous gem. Oh! majestic is the
descendant of Thang; Very admirable is his music.

The large bells and drums fill the ear; The
various dances are grandly performed[1]. We have
the admirable visitors[2], Who are pleased and
delighted.

From of old, before our time, The former men
set us the example;—How to be mild and humble
from morning to night, And to be reverent in
discharging the service.

May he regard our sacrifices of winter and
autumn[3], (Thus) offered by the descendant of
Thang!

ODE 2. THE LIEH 3ô.

PROBABLY LIKE THE LAST ODE, APPROPRIATE TO A SACRIFICE TO
THANG, DWELLING ON THE SPIRITS, THE SOUP, AND THE GRAVITY
OF THE SERVICE, AND ON THE ASSISTING PRINCES.

Neither can we tell by which of the kings of Shang this ode was
first used. *K*û Hsî says that the object of the sacrifice was
Thang. The Preface assigns it to Thâi Mâu, the *K*ung Zung,
or second of the three 'honoured ones.' But there is not a

---

pleasures, and delights; and on the third day he would have a
complete image of him in his mind's eye. Then on the day of
sacrifice, when he entered the temple, he would seem to see him
in his shrine, and to hear him, as he went about in the discharge
of the service. This line seems to indicate the realization of all this.

[1] Dancing thus entered into the service as an accompaniment
of the music. Two terms are employed; one denoting the movements appropriate to a dance of war, the other those appropriate
to a dance of peace.

[2] The visitors would be the representatives of the lines of Hsiâ,
Shun, and Yâo.

[3] Two of the seasonal sacrifices are thus specified, by synec-
doche, for all the four.

[1]   X

306

word in praise of *K*ung ßung, and the 'meritorious ancestor' of the first line is not to be got over. Still more clearly than in the case of the former ode does this appear to have been made by some one who had taken part in the service, for in line 4 he addresses the sacrificing king as 'you.'

Ah! ah! our meritorious ancestor! Permanent are the blessings coming from him, Repeatedly conferred without end ;—They have come to you in this place.

The clear spirits are in our vessels, And there is granted to us the realization of our thoughts. There are also the well-tempered soups, Prepared beforehand, with the ingredients rightly proportioned. By these offerings we invite his presence, without a word, Without (unseemly) contention (among the worshippers). He will bless us with the eyebrows of longevity, With the grey hair and wrinkled face in unlimited degree.

With the naves of their wheels bound with leather, and their ornamented yokes, With the eight bells at their horses' bits all tinkling, (The princes) come to assist at the offerings[1]. We have received the appointment in all its greatness, And from Heaven is our prosperity sent down, Fruitful years of great abundance. (Our ancestor) will come and enjoy (our offerings), And confer on us happiness without limit.

May he regard our sacrifices of winter and autumn, (Thus) offered by the descendant of Thang!

---

[1] These lines are descriptive of the feudal princes, who were present and assisted at the sacrificial service. The chariot of each was drawn by four horses yoked abreast, two insides and two outsides, on each side of the bits of which small bells were attached.

ODE 3. THE HSÜAN NIÂO.

307

APPROPRIATE TO A SACRIFICE IN THE ANCESTRAL TEMPLE OF SHANG ;—
INTENDED SPECIALLY TO DO HONOUR TO THE KING WÛ-TING.

If this ode were not intended to do honour to Wû-ting, the Kâo
Zung of Shang, we cannot account for the repeated mention of
him in it. Kû Hsî, however, in his note on it, says nothing
about Wû-ting, but simply that the piece belonged to the
sacrifices in the ancestral temple, tracing back the line of the
kings of Shang to its origin, and to its attaining the sovereignty of
the kingdom. Not at all unlikely is the view of Kǎng Hsüan,
that the sacrifice was in the third year after the death of Wû-ting,
and offered to him in the temple of Hsieh, the ancestor of the
Shang dynasty.

Heaven commissioned the swallow, To descend
and give birth to (the father of our) Shang[1]. (His
descendants) dwelt in the land of Yin, and became
great. (Then) long ago God appointed the martial
Thang, To regulate the boundaries throughout the
four quarters (of the kingdom).

(In those) quarters he appointed the princes,
And grandly possessed the nine regions[2]. The

---

[1] The father of Shang is Hsieh, who has already been mentioned. The mother of Hsieh was a daughter of the House of the
ancient state of Sung, and a concubine of the ancient ruler Khû
(B. C. 2435). According to Mâo, she accompanied Khû, at the
time of the vernal equinox, when the swallow made its appearance, to sacrifice and pray to the first match-maker, and the
result was the birth of Hsieh. Sze-mâ Khien and Kǎng make
Hsieh's birth more marvellous :—The lady was bathing in some
open place, when a swallow made its appearance, and dropt an
egg, which she took and swallowed; and from this came Hsieh.
The editors of the imperial edition of the Shih, of the present
dynasty, say we need not believe the legends ;—the important
point is to believe that the birth of Hsieh was specially ordered by
Heaven..

[2] 'The nine regions' are the nine provinces into which Yü
divided the kingdom.

X 2

308 first sovereign of Shang[1] Received the appointment without any element of instability in it, And it is (now) held by the descendant of Wû-ting[2].

The descendant of Wû-ting Is a martial sovereign, equal to every emergency. Ten· princes, (who came) with their dragon-emblazoned banners, Bear the large dishes of millet.

The royal domain of a thousand lî Is where the people rest; But the boundaries that reach to the four seas commence there.

From the four seas[3] they come (to our sacrifices); They come in multitudes. King has the Ho for its outer border[4]. That Yin[5] should have received the appointment (of Heaven) was entirely right;—(Its sovereign) sustains all its dignities.

ODE 4. THE KHANG FÂ.

CELEBRATING HSIEH, THE ANCESTOR OF THE HOUSE OF SHANG; HSIANG-THÛ, HIS GRANDSON; THANG, THE FOUNDER OF THE DYNASTY; AND Î-YIN, THANG'S CHIEF MINISTER AND ADVISER.

It does not appear on occasion of what sacrifice this piece was made. The most probable view is that of Mâo, that it was the

---

[1] That is, Thang.

[2] If this ode were used, as Kǎng supposes, in the third year after Wû-ting's death, this 'descendant' would be his son Zû-kǎng, B. C. 1265 to 1259.

[3] This expression, which occurs also in the Shû, indicates that the early Chinese believed that their country extended to the sea, east, west, north, and south.

[4] Kû Hsî says he did not understand this line; but there is ground in the Zo Kwan for our believing that King was the name of a hill in the region where the capital of Shang was.

[5] We saw in the Shû that the name Shang gave place to Yin after the time of Pan-kǎng, B.C. 1401 to 1374. Wû-ting's reign was subsequent to that of Pan-kǎng.

'great Tî sacrifice,' when the principal object of honour would   309
be the ancient Khû, the father of Hsieh, with Hsieh as his
correlate, and all the kings of the dynasty, with the earlier lords
of Shang, and their famous ministers and advisers, would have
their places at the service. I think this is the oldest of the odes
of Shang.

Profoundly wise were (the lords of) Shang, And
long had there appeared the omens (of their dignity).

When the waters of the deluge spread vast
abroad, Yü arranged and divided the regions of
the land, And assigned to the exterior great states
their boundaries, With their borders extending all
over (the kingdom). (Even) then the chief of Sung
was beginning to be great, And God raised up the
son (of his daughter), and founded (the line of)
Shang[1].

The dark king exercised an effective sway[2].
Charged with a small state, he commanded success;
Charged with a large state, he commanded success[3].
He followed his rules of conduct without error;
Wherever he inspected (the people), they responded
(to his instructions)[4]. (Then came) Hsiang-thû all
ardent[5], And all within the four seas, beyond (the
middle regions), acknowledged his restraints.

---

[1] This line refers to the birth of Hsieh, as described in the
previous ode, and his being made lord of Shang.

[2] It would be hard to say why Hsieh is here called 'the dark
king.' There may be an allusion to the legend about the connexion of the swallow,—'the dark bird,'—with his birth. He never
was 'a king;' but his descendants here represented him as such.

[3] All that is meant here is, that the territory of Shang was
enlarged under Hsieh.

[4] There is a reference here to Hsieh's appointment by Shun to
be Minister of Instruction.

[5] Hsiang-thû appears in the genealogical lists as grandson of
Hsieh. We know nothing of him but what is related here.

310 　　The favour of God did not leave (Shang), And in Thang was found the fit object for its display. Thang was not born too late, And his wisdom and reverence daily advanced:—Brilliant was the influence of his character (on Heaven) for long. God he revered, And God appointed him to be the model for the nine regions.

　　He received the rank-tokens of the states, small and large, Which depended on him like the pendants of a banner:—So did he receive the blessing of Heaven. He was neither violent nor remiss, Neither hard nor soft. Gently he spread his instructions abroad, And all dignities and riches were concentrated in him.

　　He received the tribute of the states, small and large, And he supported them as a strong steed (does its burden):—So did he receive the favour of Heaven. He displayed everywhere his valour, Unshaken, unmoved, Unterrified, unscared:—All dignities were united in him.

　　The martial king displayed his banner, And with reverence grasped his axe. It was like (the case of) a blazing fire which no one can repress. The root, with its three shoots, Could make no progress, no growth[1]. The nine regions were effectually secured by Thang. Having smitten (the princes of) Wei and Kû, He dealt with (him of) Kün-wû and with Kieh of Hsiâ.

　　Formerly, in the middle of the period (before

---

[1] By ' the root ' we are to understand Thang's chief opponent, Kieh, the last king of Hsiâ. Kieh's three great helpers were ' the three shoots,'—the princes of Wei, Kû, and Kün-wû ; but the exact sites of their principalities cannot be made out.

Thang), There was a time of shaking and peril[1].　311
But truly did Heaven (then) deal with him as a son,
And sent him down a high minister, Namely,
Â-hăng[2], Who gave his assistance to the king of
Shang.

ODE 5. THE YIN WÛ.

CELEBRATING THE WAR OF WÛ-TING AGAINST *KING-KHÛ*, ITS SUCCESS,
AND THE GENERAL HAPPINESS AND VIRTUE OF HIS REIGN ;—MADE,
PROBABLY, WHEN A SPECIAL AND PERMANENT TEMPLE WAS BUILT
FOR HIM AS THE 'HIGH AND HONOURED' KING OF SHANG.

The concluding lines indicate that the temple was made on the
occasion which I thus assign to it. After Wû-ting's death, his
spirit-tablet would be shrined in the ancestral temple, and he
would have his share in the seasonal sacrifices; but several
reigns would elapse before there was any necessity to make any
other arrangement, so that his tablet should not be removed,
and his share in the sacrifices not be discontinued. Hence the
composition of the piece has been referred to the time of Tî-yî,
the last but one of the kings of Shang.

Rapid was the warlike energy of (our king of)
Yin, And vigorously did he attack *King-Khû*[3].

---

[1] We do not know anything of this time of decadence in the
fortunes of Shang between Hsieh and Thang.

[2] Â-hăng is Î Yin, who plays so remarkable a part in the
Shû, IV, Books iv, v, and vi.

[3] *King*, or *Khû*, or *King-Khû*, as the two names are combined
here, was a large and powerful half-savage state, having its capital
in the present Wû-pei. So far as evidence goes, we should say,
but for this ode, that the name of *Khû* was not in use till long
after the Shang dynasty. The name *King* appears several times
in 'the Spring and Autumn' in the annals of duke *K*wang (B.C. 693
to 662), and then it gives place to the name *Khû* in the first year
of duke Hsî (B.C. 659), and subsequently disappears itself altogether. In consequence of this some critics make this piece out
to have been composed under the *K*âu dynasty. The point cannot
be fully cleared up; but on the whole I accept the words of the
ode as sufficient proof against the silence of other documents.

312   Boldly he entered its dangerous passes, And
brought the multitudes of *K*ing together, Till the
country was reduced under complete restraint:—
Such was the fitting achievement of the descendant
of Thang!

'Ye people,' (he said), 'of *K*ing-*Kh*û, Dwell in
the southern part of my kingdom. Formerly, in
the time of Thang the Successful, Even from the
*K*iang of Tî[1], They dared not but come with their
offerings; (Their chiefs) dared not but come to
seek acknowledgment[2]:—Such is the regular rule
of Shang.'

Heaven had given their appointments (to the
princes), But where their capitals had been assigned within the sphere of the labours of Yü,
For the business of every year they appeared
before our king[3], (Saying), 'Do not punish nor
reprove us; We have not been remiss in our
husbandry.'

When Heaven by its will is inspecting (the kingdom), The lower people are to be feared. (Our
king) showed no partiality (in rewarding), no excess
(in punishing); He dared not to allow himself in
indolence:—So was his appointment (established)

---

[1] The Tî *K*iang, or *K*iang of Tî, still existed in the time of the
Han dynasty, occupying portions of the present Kan-sû.

[2] The chiefs of the wild tribes, lying beyond the nine provinces
of the kingdom, were required to present themselves once in their
lifetime at the royal court. The rule, in normal periods, was for
each chief to appear immediately after he had succeeded to the
headship of his tribe.

[3] The feudal lords had to appear at court every year. They
did so, we may suppose, at the court of Wû-ting, the more so
because of his subjugation of *K*ing-*Kh*û.

over the states, And he made his happiness   313
grandly secure.

The capital of Shang was full of order, . The
model for all parts of the kingdom. Glorious was
(the king's) fame ; Brilliant his energy. Long lived
he and enjoyed tranquillity, And so he preserves
us, his descendants.

We ascended the hill of *K*ing [1], Where the pines
and cypresses grew symmetrical. We cut them
down and conveyed them here ; We reverently
hewed them square. Long are the projecting beams
of pine ; Large are the many pillars. The temple
was completed,—the tranquil abode (of the martial king of Yin).

II. THE SACRIFICIAL ODES OF *K*ÂU.

IN this division we have thirty-one sacrificial odes of *K*âu,
arranged in three decades, the third of which, however, contains
eleven pieces. They belong mostly to the time of king Wăn,
the founder of the *K*âu dynasty, and to the reigns of his son
and grandson, kings Wû and *K*hăng. The decades are named
from the name of the first piece in each.

The First Decade, or that of *K*hing Miâo.

ODE 1. THE *K*HING MIÂO.

CELEBRATING THE REVERENTIAL MANNER IN WHICH A SACRIFICE TO
KING WĂN WAS PERFORMED, AND FURTHER PRAISING HIM.

Chinese critics agree in assigning this piece to the sacrifice mentioned in the Shû, in the end of the thirteenth Book of Part V,
when, the building of Lo being finished, king *K*hăng came to

---

[1] See on the last line but two of ode 3.

314   the new city, and offered a red bull to Wăn, and the same to Wû. It seems to me to have been sung in honour of Wăn, after the service was completed. This determination of the occasion of the piece being accepted, we should refer it to B. C. 1108.

Oh! solemn is the ancestral temple in its pure stillness. Reverent and harmonious were the distinguished assistants[1]; Great was the number of the officers[2]:—(All) assiduous followers of the virtue of (king Wăn). In response to him in heaven, Grandly they hurried about in the temple. Distinguished is he and honoured, And will never be wearied of among men.

ODE 2. THE WEI THIEN *K*IH MING.

CELEBRATING THE VIRTUE OF KING WĂN AS COMPARABLE TO THAT OF HEAVEN, AND LOOKING TO HIM FOR BLESSING IN THE FUTURE.

According to the Preface, there is an announcement here of the realization of complete peace throughout the kingdom, and some of the old critics refer the ode to a sacrifice to king Wăn by the duke of *K*âu, when he had completed the statutes for the new dynasty. But there is nothing to authorize a more definite argument of the contents than I have given.

The ordinances of Heaven,—How deep are they and unintermitting! And oh! how illustrious Was the singleness of the virtue of king Wăn[3]!

How does he (now) show his kindness? We will receive it, Striving to be in accord with him, our

---

[1] These would be the princes who were assembled on the occasion, and assisted the king in the service.

[2] That is, the officers who took part in the libations, prayers, and other parts of the sacrifice.

[3] See what Ʒze-sze says on these four lines in the Doctrine of the Mean, XXVI, par. 10.

king Wăn ;   And may his remotest descendant be   315
abundantly the same!

Ode 3.   The Wei *Khing*.

**APPROPRIATE AT SOME SACRIFICE TO KING WĂN, AND CELEBRATING HIS
STATUTES.**

Nothing more can, with any likelihood of truth, be said of this
short piece, which moreover has the appearance of being a
fragment.

Clear and to be preserved bright,   Are the statutes of king Wăn.   From the first sacrifice (to
him),   Till now when they have issued in our complete state,   They have been the happy omen of
(the fortunes of) *K*âu.

Ode 4.   The Lieh Wăn.

**A SONG IN PRAISE OF THE PRINCES WHO HAVE ASSISTED AT A SACRIFICE,
AND ADMONISHING THEM.**

The Preface says that this piece was made on the occasion of
king *Kh*äng's accession to the government, when he thus addressed the princes who had assisted him in the ancestral
temple. *K*û Hsî considers that it was a piece for general use
in the ancestral temple, to be sung when the king presented
a cup to his assisting guests, after they had thrice presented the
cup to the representatives of the dead. There is really nothing
in it to enable us to decide in favour of either view.

Ye, brilliant and accomplished princes,   Have
conferred on me this happiness.   Your favours to
me are without limit,   And my descendants will
preserve (the fruits of) them.

Be not mercenary nor extravagant in your states,
And the king will honour you.   Thinking of this

316 great service, He will enlarge the dignity of your successors.

What is most powerful is the being the man :— Its influence will be felt throughout your states. What is most distinguished is the being virtuous :— It will secure the imitation of all the princes. Ah! the former kings cannot be forgotten!

Ode 5. The Thien 3o.

APPROPRIATE TO A SACRIFICE TO KING THÂI.

We cannot tell what the sacrifice was; and the Preface, indeed, says that the piece was used in the seasonal sacrifices to all the former kings and dukes of the House of *K*âu. King Thâi was the grandfather of king Wăn, and, before he received that title, was known as ' the ancient duke Than-fû.' In B.C. 1327, he moved with his followers from Pin, an earlier seat of his House, and settled in the plain of *K*hî, about fifty lî to the north-east of the present district city of *K*hî-shan, in Shen-hsî.

Heaven made the lofty hill[1], And king Thâi brought (the country about) it under cultivation. He made the commencement with it, And king Wăn tranquilly (carried on the work), (Till) that rugged (mount) *K*hî Had level roads leading to it. May their descendants ever preserve it!

Ode 6. The Hâo Thien yû *K*hăng Ming.

APPROPRIATE TO A SACRIFICE TO KING *K*HĂNG.

*K*hăng was the honorary title of Sung, the son and successor of king Wû, B.C. 1115 to 1079.

Heaven made its determinate appointment, Which our two sovereigns received[2]. King *K*hăng did not dare to rest idly in it, But night and day enlarged

---

[1] Meaning mount *K*hî.   [2] Wăn and Wû.

its foundations by his deep and silent virtue.　How 317
did he continue and glorify (his heritage),　Exerting
all his heart,　And so securing its tranquillity!

ODE 7.　THE WO *K*IANG.

APPROPRIATE TO A SACRIFICE TO KING WĂN, ASSOCIATED WITH HEAVEN,
IN THE HALL OF AUDIENCE.

There is, happily, an agreement among the critics as to the
occasion to which this piece is referred.　It took place in the
last month of autumn, in the Hall of Audience, called also 'the
Brilliant Hall,' and 'the Hall of Light.'　We must suppose that
the princes are all assembled at court, and that the king receives
them in this hall.　A sacrifice is then presented to God, and
with him is associated king Wăn, the two being the fountain
from which, and the channel through which, the sovereignty had
come to *K*âu.

I have brought my offerings,　A ram and a bull.
May Heaven accept them [1]!

I imitate and follow and observe the statutes of
king Wăn,　Seeking daily to secure the tranquillity
of the kingdom.　King Wăn, the Blesser, has descended on the right, and accepted (the offerings).

Do I not, night and day,　Revere the majesty of
Heaven,　Thus to preserve (its favour)?

ODE 8.　THE SHIH MÂI.

APPROPRIATE TO KING WÛ'S SACRIFICING TO HEAVEN, AND TO THE
SPIRITS OF THE HILLS AND RIVERS, ON A PROGRESS THROUGH THE
KINGDOM, AFTER THE OVERTHROW OF THE SHANG DYNASTY.

Here again there is an agreement among the critics.　We find
from the *ß*o *K*wan and 'the Narratives of the States,' that the

---

[1] This is a prayer.　The worshipper, it is said, in view of the
majesty of Heaven, shrank from assuming that God would certainly accept his sacrifice.　He assumes, below, that king Wăn
does so.

318 piece was, when those compilations were made, considered to be the work of the duke of *K*âu; and, no doubt, it was made by him soon after the accession of Wû to the kingdom, and when he was making a royal progress in assertion of his being appointed by Heaven to succeed to the rulers of Shang. The 'I' in the fourteenth line is, most probably, to be taken of the duke of *K*âu, who may have recited the piece on occasion of the sacrifices, in the hearing of the assembled princes and lords.

Now is he making a progress through his states; May Heaven deal with him as its son!

Truly are the honour and succession come from it to the House of *K*âu. To his movements All respond with tremulous awe. He has attracted and given rest to all spiritual beings [1], Even to (the spirits of) the Ho and the highest hills. Truly is the king our sovereign lord.

Brilliant and illustrious is the House of *K*âu. He has regulated the positions of the princes; He has called in shields and spears; He has returned to their cases bows and arrows [2]. I will cultivate admirable virtue, And display it throughout these great regions. Truly will the king preserve the appointment.

---

[1] .'All spiritual beings' is, literally, 'the hundred spirits,' meaning the spirits presiding, under Heaven, over all nature, and especially the spirits of the rivers and hills throughout the kingdom. Those of the Ho and the lofty mountains are mentioned, because if their spirits were satisfied with Wû, those of all other mountains and hills, no doubt, were so.

[2] Compare with these lines the last chapter of 'the Completion of the War' in the Shû.

ODE 9. THE *K*IH *K*ING.

319

AN ODE APPROPRIATE IN SACRIFICING TO THE KINGS WÛ, *K*HĂNG, AND KHANG.

The Chinese critics differ in the interpretation of this ode, the Preface and older scholars restricting it to a sacrifice to king Wû, while *K*û Hsî and others find reference in it, as to me also seems most natural, to *K*hăng and Khang, who succeeded him.

The arm of king Wû was full of strength ; Irresistible was his ardour. Greatly illustrious were *K*hăng and Khang [1], Kinged by God.

When we consider how *K*hăng and Khang Grandly held all within the four quarters (of the kingdom), How penetrating was their intelligence !

The bells and drums sound in harmony; The sounding-stones and flutes blend their notes ; Abundant blessing is sent down.

Blessing is sent down in large measure. Careful and exact is all our deportment; We have drunk, and we have eaten, to the full; Our happiness and dignity will be prolonged.

ODE 10. THE SZE WĂN.

APPROPRIATE TO ONE OF THE BORDER SACRIFICES, WHEN HÂU-*K*Î WAS WORSHIPPED AS THE CORRELATE OF GOD, AND CELEBRATING HIM.

Hâu-*k*î was the same as *K*hî, who appears in Part II of the Shû, as Minister of Agriculture to Yâo and Shun, and co-operating with

---

[1] If the whole piece be understood only of a sacrifice to Wû, this line will have to be translated—' How illustrious was he, who completed (his great work), and secured its tranquillity.' We must deal similarly with the next line. This construction is very forced; nor is the text clear on the view of *K*û Hsî.

320   Yü in his labours on the flooded land. The name Hâu belongs to
him as lord of Thâi ; that of *K*î, as Minister of Agriculture. However the combination arose, Hâu-*k*î became historically the name
of *Kh*î of the time of Yâo and Shun, the ancestor to whom the
kings of *K*âu traced their lineage. He was to the people the
Father of Husbandry, who first taught men to plough and sow
and reap. Hence, when the kings offered sacrifice and prayer
to God at the commencement of spring for his blessing on
the labours of the year, they associated Hâu-*k*î with him at the
service.

O accomplished Hâu-*k*î, Thou didst prove thy-
self the correlate of Heaven. Thou didst give
grain-food to our multitudes :—The immense gift of
thy goodness. Thou didst confer on us the wheat
and the barley, Which God appointed for the
nourishment of all. And without distinction of
territory or boundary, The rules of social duty
were diffused throughout these great regions.

The Second Decade, or that of *Kh*ăn Kung.

ODE 1. THE *Kh*ăn Kung.

INSTRUCTIONS GIVEN TO THE OFFICERS OF HUSBANDRY.

The place of this piece among the sacrificial odes makes us assign
it to the conclusion of some sacrifice ; but what the sacrifice
was we cannot tell. The Preface says that it was addressed,
at the conclusion of the spring sacrifice to ancestors, to the
princes who had been present and taken part in the service.
*K*û Hsî says nothing but what I have stated in the above
argument of the piece.

Ah ! ah ! ministers and officers, Reverently attend
to your public duties. The king has given you
perfect rules ;—Consult about them, and consider
them.

Ah ! ah ! ye·assistants,· It is now the end of

spring¹; And what have ye to seek for? (Only)   321
how to manage the new fields and those of the third
year. How beautiful are the wheat and the barley!
The bright and glorious God Will in them give us
a good year. Order all our men To be provided
with their spuds and hoes:—Anon we shall see the
sickles at work.

ODE 2. THE Î Hsî.

FURTHER INSTRUCTIONS TO THE OFFICERS OF HUSBANDRY.

Again there is a difficulty in determining to what sacrifice this
piece should be referred. The Preface says it was sung on the
occasions of sacrifice by the king to God, in spring and summer,
for a good year. But the note on the first two lines will show
that this view cannot be accepted without modification.

Oh! yes, king *Kh*ăng² Brightly brought himself near². Lead your husbandmen To sow their
various kinds of grain, Going vigorously to work

---

¹ It is this line which makes it difficult to determine after
what sacrifice we are to suppose these instructions to have been
delivered. The year, during the Hsiâ dynasty, began with the
first month of spring, as it now does in China, in consequence of
Confucius having said that that was the proper time. Under the
Shang dynasty, it commenced a month earlier; and during the
*K*âu period, it ought always to have begun with the new moon
preceding the winter solstice,—between our November 22 and
December 22. But in the writings of the *K*âu period we find
statements of time continually referred to the calendar of Hsiâ,—
as here.

² These first two lines are all but unmanageable. The old
critics held that there was no mention of king *Kh*ăng in them;
but the text is definite on this point. We must suppose that a
special service had been performed at his shrine, asking him to
intimate the day when the sacrifice after which the instructions
were given should be performed; and that a directing oracle had
been received.

[I]   Y

322   on your private fields[1], All over the thirty lî [2].
Attend to your ploughing, With your ten thousand
men all in pairs.

ODE 3. THE *Kâu* Lû.

CELEBRATING THE REPRESENTATIVES OF FORMER DYNASTIES, WHO
HAD COME TO COURT TO ASSIST AT A SACRIFICE IN THE ANCESTRAL
TEMPLE.

This piece may have been used when the king was dismissing his
distinguished guests in the ancestral temple. See the introductory note to this Part, pp. 300, 301.

A flock of egrets is flying, About the marsh
there in the west [3]. My visitors came, With an
(elegant) carriage like those birds.

There, (in their states), not disliked, Here, (in
*K*âu), never tired of; — They are sure, day and
night, To perpetuate their fame.

---

[1] The mention of 'the private fields' implies that there were
also 'the public fields,' cultivated by the husbandmen in common,
in behalf of the government. As the people are elsewhere introduced, wishing that the rain might first fall on 'the public fields,'
to show their loyalty, so the king here mentions only 'the private
fields,' to show his sympathy and consideration for the people.

[2] For the cultivation of the ground, the allotments of single
families were separated by a small ditch; ten allotments, by a
larger; a hundred, by what we may call a brook; a thousand, by
a small stream; and ten thousand, by a river. The space occupied
by 10,000 families formed a square of a little more than thirty-two
lî. We may suppose that this space was intended by the round
number of thirty lî in the text. So at least *K*ang Khang-*kh*ang
explained it.

[3] These two lines make the piece allusive. See the Introduction, p. 279.

ODE 4. THE FĂNG NIEN.

323

AN ODE OF THANKSGIVING FOR A PLENTIFUL YEAR.

The Preface says the piece was used at sacrifices in autumn and winter. *K'û Hsî* calls it an ode of thanksgiving for a good year,—without any specification of time. He supposes, however, that the thanks were given to the ancient Shăn-năng, 'the father of Agriculture,' Hâu-*k'î*, 'the first Husbandman,' and the spirits presiding over the four quarters of the heavens. To this the imperial editors rightly demur, saying that the blessings which the piece speaks of could come only from God.

Abundant is the year with much millet and much rice; And we have our high granaries, With myriads, and hundreds of thousands, and millions (of measures in them); For spirits and sweet spirits, To present to our forefathers, male and female, And to supply all our ceremonies. The blessings sent down on us are of every kind.

ODE 5. THE YÛ KÛ.

THE BLIND MUSICIANS OF THE COURT OF *K'ÂU*; THE INSTRUMENTS OF MUSIC; AND THEIR HARMONY.

The critics agree in holding that this piece was made on occasion of the duke of *K'âu*'s completing his instruments of music for the ancestral temple, and announcing the fact at a grand performance in the temple of king Wăn. It can hardly be regarded as a sacrificial ode.

There are the blind musicians; there are the blind musicians; In the court of (the temple of) *K'âu* [1].

---

[1] The blind musicians at the court of *K'âu* were numerous. The blindness of the eyes was supposed to make the ears more acute in hearing, and to be favourable to the powers of the voice. In the Official Book of *K'âu*, III, i, par. 22, the enumeration of

324　　　There are (the music-frames with their) face-
boards and posts, The high toothed-edge (of the
former), and the feathers stuck (in the latter); With
the drums, large and small, suspended from them ;
And the hand-drums and sounding-stones, the instrument to give the signal for commencing, and the
stopper. These being all complete, the music is
struck up. The pan-pipe and the double flute begin
at the same time [1].

. Harmoniously blend their sounds; In solemn
unison they give forth their notes. Our ancestors
will give ear. Our visitors will be there ;—Long to
witness the complete performance.

ODE 6. THE *KHIEN*.

SUNG IN THE LAST MONTH OF WINTER, AND IN SPRING, WHEN THE
KING PRESENTED A FISH IN THE ANCESTRAL TEMPLE.

Such is the argument of this piece given in the Preface, and in
which the critics generally concur. In the Lî *Kî*, IV, vi, 49, it
is recorded that the king, in the third month of winter, gave
orders to his chief fisher to commence his duties, and went
himself to see his operations. He partook of the fish first
captured, but previously presented some as an offering in the
back apartment of the ancestral temple. In the third month of
spring, again, when the sturgeons began to make their appearance
(Lî *Kî*, IV, i, 25), the king presented one in the same place. On

---

these blind musicians gives 2 directors of the first rank, and 4
of the second; 40 performers of the first grade, 100 of the
second, and 160 of the third; with 300 assistants who were
possessed of vision. But it is difficult not to be somewhat in-
credulous as to this great collection of blind musicians about the
court of *K*âu.

[1] All the instruments here enumerated were performed on in
the open court below the hall. Nothing is said of the stringed
instruments which were used in the hall itself; nor is the enumeration of the instruments in the courtyard complete.

these passages, the prefatory notice was, no doubt, constructed. 325
Choice specimens of the earliest-caught fish were presented by
the sovereign to his ancestors, as an act of duty, and an acknowledgment that it was to their favour that he and the people were
indebted for the supplies of food, which they received from the
waters.

Oh! in the *Khî* and the *Khü*, There are many
fish in the warrens;—Sturgeons, large and snouted,
Thryssas, yellow-jaws, mud-fish, and carp;—For
offerings, for sacrifice, That our bright happiness
may be increased.

Ode 7. The Yung.

APPROPRIATE, PROBABLY, AT A SACRIFICE BY KING WÛ TO HIS FATHER
WĂN.

From a reference in the Analects, III, ii, to an abuse of this ode
in the time of Confucius, we learn that it was sung when the
sacrificial vessels and their contents were being removed.

They come full of harmony; They are here in
all gravity;—The princes assisting, While the Son
of Heaven looks profound.

(He says), 'While I present (this) noble bull,
And they assist me in setting forth the sacrifice,
O great and august Father, Comfort me, your
filial son.

'With penetrating wisdom thou didst play the man,
A sovereign with the gifts both of peace and war,
Giving rest even to great Heaven[1], And ensuring
prosperity to thy descendants.

---

[1] To explain this line one commentator refers to the seventh
stanza of the first piece in the Major Odes of the Kingdom, where
it is said, 'God surveyed the four quarters of the kingdom, seeking
for some one to give settlement and rest to the people;' and adds,
'Thus what Heaven has at heart is the settlement of the people.
When they have rest given to them, then Heaven is at rest.'

326

'Thou comfortest me with the eyebrows of longevity; Thou makest me great with manifold
blessings, I offer this sacrifice to my meritorious
father, And to my accomplished mother¹.'

ODE 8. THE 3ÂI HSIEN.

APPROPRIATE TO AN OCCASION WHEN THE FEUDAL PRINCES HAD BEEN
ASSISTING KING *KHĂNG* AT A SACRIFICE TO HIS FATHER.

They appeared before their sovereign king, To
seek from him the rules (they were to observe).
With their dragon - emblazoned banners, flying
bright, The bells on them and their front-boards
tinkling, And with the rings on the ends of the
reins glittering, Admirable was their majesty and
splendour.

He led them to appear before his father shrined
on the left², Where he discharged his filial duty,
and presented his offerings;—That he might have
granted to him long life, And ever preserve (his
dignity). Great and many are his blessings. They
are the brilliant and accomplished princes, Who
cheer him with his many sources of happiness,

---

¹ At sacrifices to ancestors, the spirit tablets of wives were
placed along with those of their husbands in their shrines, so
that both shared in the honours of the service. So it is now
in the imperial ancestral temple in Peking. The 'accomplished
mother' here would be Thâi Sze, celebrated often in the pieces of
the first Book of Part I, and elsewhere.

² Among the uses of the services of the ancestral temple,
specified by Confucius and quoted on p. 302, was the distinguishing
the order of descent in the royal House. According to the rules
for that purpose, the characters here used enable us to determine
the subject of this line as king Wû, in opposition to his father
Wăn.

Enabling him to perpetuate them in their bright- 327
ness as pure blessing.

ODE 9. THE YÛ KHO.

CELEBRATING THE DUKE OF SUNG ON ONE OF HIS APPEARANCES
AT THE CAPITAL TO ASSIST AT THE SACRIFICE IN THE ANĊESTRAL
TEMPLE OF *K*ÂU;—SHOWING HOW HE WAS ESTEEMED AND CHERISHED
BY THE KING.

The mention of the white horses here in the chariot of the
visitor sufficiently substantiates the account in the Preface that
he was the famous count of Wei, mentioned in the Shu, IV, xi,
and whose subsequent investiture with the duchy of Sung, as
the representative of the line of the Shang kings, is also related
in the Shû, V, viii. With the dynasty of Shang white had been
the esteemed and sacred colour, as red was with *K*âu, and
hence the duke had his carriage drawn by white horses. 'The
language,' says one critic, 'is all in praise of the visitor, but it
was sung in the temple, and is rightly placed therefore among
the Sung.' There is, in the last line, an indication of the
temple in it.

The noble visitor! The noble visitor! Drawn,
like his ancestors, by white horses! The reverent
and dignified, Polished members of his suite!

The noble guest will stay (but) a night or two!
The noble guest will stay (but) two nights or four!
Give him ropes, To bind his horses[1].

I will convoy him (with a parting feast); I will
comfort him in every possible way. Adorned with
such great dignity, It is very natural that he should
be blessed.

---

[1] These four lines simply express the wish of the king to detain
his visitor, from the delight that his presence gave him. Compare
the similar language in the second ode of the fourth decade of
Part II.

328

Ode 10. The Wû.

SUNG IN THE ANCESTRAL TEMPLE TO THE MUSIC REGULATING THE
DANCE IN HONOUR OF THE ACHIEVEMENTS OF KING wû.

This account of the piece, given in the Preface, is variously cor-
roborated, and has not been called in question by any critic.
Perhaps this brief ode was sung as a prelude to the dance, or
it may be that the seven lines are only a fragment. This, indeed,
is most likely, as we have several odes in the next decade, all
said to have been used at the same occasion.

Oh! great wast thou, O king Wû, Displaying
the utmost strength in thy work. Truly accomplished was king Wăn, Opening the path for his
successors. Thou didst receive the inheritance from
him. Thou didst vanquish Yin, and put a stop to
its cruelties ;—Effecting the firm establishment of
thy merit.

The Third Decade, or that of Min Yü Hsiâo 3ze.

Ode 1. The Min Yü.

APPROPRIATE TO THE YOUNG KING *KHĂNG*, DECLARING HIS SENTIMENTS
IN THE TEMPLE OF HIS FATHER.

The speaker in this piece is, by common consent, king *Khăng*.
The only question is as to the date of its composition, whether
it was made for him, in his minority, on his repairing to the
temple when the mourning for his father was completed, or
after the expiration of the regency of the duke of *Kâu*. The
words ' little child,' according to their usage, are expressive of
humility and not of age. They do not enable us to determine
the above point.

Alas for me, who am a little child, On whom has
devolved the unsettled state! Solitary am I and full
of distress. Oh! my great Father, All thy life long,
thou wast filial.

Thou didst think of my great grandfather, (Seeing

him, as it were) ascending and descending in the   329
court, I, the little child, Day and night will be
as reverent.

Oh! ye great kings, As your successor, I will
strive not to forget you.

ODE 2. THE FANG LO.

THE YOUNG KING TELLS OF HIS DIFFICULTIES AND INCOMPETENCIES;
ASKS FOR COUNSEL TO KEEP HIM TO COPY THE EXAMPLE OF HIS
FATHER; STATES HOW HE MEANT TO DO SO; AND CONCLUDES WITH
AN APPEAL OR PRAYER TO HIS FATHER.

This seems to be a sequel to the former ode. We can hardly say
anything about it so definite as the statement in the Preface,
that it relates to a council held by *Khāng* and his ministers in
the ancestral temple.

I take counsel at the beginning of my (rule),
How I can follow (the example of) my shrined
father. Ah! far-reaching (were his plans), And
I am not yet able to carry them out. However
I endeavour to reach to them, My continuation
of them will still be all-deflected. I am a little
child, Unequal to the many difficulties of the
state. Having taken his place, (I will look for him)
to go up and come down in the court, To ascend
and descend in the house. Admirable art thou,
O great Father, (Condescend) to preserve and
enlighten me.

ODE 3. THE KING KIH.

KING KHÄNG SHOWS HIS SENSE OF WHAT WAS REQUIRED OF HIM TO
PRESERVE THE FAVOUR OF HEAVEN, A CONSTANT JUDGE; INTIMATES
HIS GOOD PURPOSES; AND ASKS THE HELP OF HIS MINISTERS TO
BE ENABLED TO PERFORM THEM.

Let me be reverent! Let me be reverent! (The
way of) Heaven is evident, And its appointment

330 　is not easily preserved[1]. Let me not say that it is high aloft above me. It ascends and descends about our doings; It daily inspects us wherever we are.

I am a little child, Without intelligence to be reverently (attentive to my duties); But by daily progress and monthly advance, I will learn to hold fast the gleams (of knowledge), till I arrive at bright intelligence. Assist me to bear the burden (of my position), And show me how to display a virtuous conduct.

Ode 4.　The Hsiâo Pî.

KING *KH*ĂNG ACKNOWLEDGES THAT HE HAD ERRED, AND STATES HIS PURPOSE TO BE CAREFUL IN THE FUTURE; HE WILL GUARD AGAINST THE SLIGHT BEGINNINGS OF EVIL; AND IS PENETRATED WITH A SENSE OF HIS OWN INCOMPETENCIES.

This piece has been considered by some critics as the conclusion of the council in the ancestral temple, with which the previous two also are thought to be connected. The Preface says that the king asks in it for the assistance of his ministers, but no such request is expressed. I seem myself to see in it, with Sû *Kh*eh and others, a reference to the suspicions which *Kh*ăng at one time, we know, entertained of the fidelity of the duke of *K*âu, when he was inclined to believe the rumours spread against him by his other uncles, who joined in rebellion with the son of the last king of Shang.

I condemn myself (for the past), And will be on my guard against future calamity. I will have nothing to do with a wasp, To seek for myself its painful sting. At first indeed it seemed to be

---

[1] The meaning is this: 'The way of Heaven is very clear, to bless the good, namely, and punish the bad. But its favour is thus dependent on men themselves, and hard to preserve.'

(but) a wren[1], But it took wing, and became a large bird. I am unequal to the many difficulties of the kingdom, And am placed in the midst of bitter experiences.

331

ODE 5. THE 3ÂI SHÛ.

THE CULTIVATION OF THE GROUND FROM THE FIRST BREAKING OF IT UP, TILL IT YIELDS ABUNDANT HARVESTS ;—AVAILABLE SPECIALLY FOR SACRIFICES AND FESTIVE OCCASIONS. WHETHER INTENDED TO BE USED ON OCCASIONS OF THANKSGIVING, OR IN SPRING WHEN PRAYING FOR A GOOD YEAR, CANNOT BE DETERMINED.

The Preface says that this ode was used in spring, when the king in person turned up some furrows in the field set apart for that purpose, and prayed at the altars of the spirits of the land and the grain, for an abundant year. *K̂û Hsî* says he does not know on what occasion it was intended to be used; but comparing it with the fourth ode of the second decade, he is inclined to rank it with that as an ode of thanksgiving. There is nothing in the piece itself to determine us in favour of either view. It brings before us a series of pleasing pictures of the husbandry of those early times. The editors of the imperial edition say that its place in the Sung makes it clear that it was an accompaniment of some royal sacrifice. We need not controvert this ; but the poet evidently singled out some large estate, and describes the labour on it, from the first bringing it under cultivation to the state in which it was before his eyes, and concludes by saying that the picture which he gives of it had long been applicable to the whole country.

They clear away the grass and the bushes; And the ground is laid open by their ploughs.

In thousands of pairs they remove the roots, Some in the low wet land, some along the dykes.

---

[1] The Chinese characters here mean, literally, 'peach-tree insect,' or, as Dr. Williams has it, ' peach-bug.' Another name for the bird is ' the clever wife,' from the artistic character of its nest, which would point it out as the small ' tailor bird.' But the name is applied to various small birds.

332   There are the master and his eldest son; His younger sons, and all their children; Their strong helpers, and their hired servants. How the noise of their eating the viands brought to them resounds! (The husbands) think lovingly of their wives; (The wives) keep close to their husbands. (Then) with their sharp ploughshares They set to work on the south-lying acres.

They sow their various kinds of grain, Each seed containing in it a germ of life.

In unbroken lines rises the blade, And, well nourished, the stalks grow long.

Luxuriant looks the young grain, And the weeders go among it in multitudes.

Then come the reapers in crowds, And the grain is piled up in the fields, Myriads, and hundreds of thousands, and millions (of stacks); For spirits and for sweet spirits, To offer to our ancestors, male and female, And to provide for all ceremonies.

Fragrant is their aroma, Enhancing the glory of the state. Like pepper is their smell, To give comfort to the aged.

It is not here only that there is this (abundance); It is not now only that there is such a time:— From of old it has been thus.

ODE 6. THE LIANG SZE.

PRESUMABLY, AN ODE OF THANKSGIVING IN THE AUTUMN TO THE
SPIRITS OF THE LAND AND GRAIN.

Very sharp are the excellent shares, With which they set to work on the south-lying acres.

They sow their various kinds of grain, Each seed containing in it a germ of life.

There are those who come to see them, With   333
their baskets round and square, Containing the
provisions of millet.

With their light splint hats on their heads, They
ply their hoes on the ground, Clearing away the
smartweed on the dry land and wet.

The weeds being decayed, The millets grow
luxuriantly.

They fall rustling before the reapers. The
gathered crop is piled up solidly, High as a wall,
United together like the teeth of a comb; And
the hundred houses are opened (to receive the
grain) [1].

Those hundred houses being full, The wives and
children have a feeling of repose.

(Now) we kill this black-muzzled tawny bull [2],
with his crooked horns, To imitate and hand down,
To hand down (the observances of) our ancestors.

ODE 7. THE SZE Î.

AN ODE APPROPRIATE TO THE PREPARATIONS AND PROGRESS OF A
FEAST AFTER A SACRIFICE.

The Preface and the editors of the Yung-*khăng* Shih say that the
piece has reference to the entertainment given, the day after a

---

[1] 'The hundred houses,' or chambers in a hundred family
residences, are those of the hundred families, cultivating the space
which was bounded by a brook ;—see note on the second ode of
the preceding decade. They formed a society, whose members
helped one another in their field work, so that their harvest might
be said to be carried home at the same time. Then would come
the threshing or treading, and winnowing, after which the grain
would be brought into the houses.

[2] It has been observed that under the *K*âu dynasty, red was the

334　　　sacrifice, in the ancestral temple, to the personators of the dead, described on p. 301. *Kû* Hsî denies this, and holds simply that it belongs to the feast after a sacrifice, without further specifying what sacrifice. The old view is probably the more correct.

In his silken robes, clean and bright, With his cap on his head, looking so respectful, From the hall he goes to the foot of the stairs, And (then) from the sheep to the oxen [1]. (He inspects) the tripods, large and small, And the curved goblet of rhinoceros horn [2]. The good spirits are mild, (But) there is no noise, no insolence :—An auspice (this) of great longevity.

Ode 8.　The *Ko*.

AN ODE IN PRAISE OF KING WÛ, AND RECOGNISING THE DUTY TO FOLLOW HIS COURSE.

This was sung, according to the Preface, at the conclusion of the dance in honour of king Wû;—see on the last piece of the second decade.

Oh! powerful was the king's army, But he nursed it, in obedience to circumstances, while the

---

colour of the sacrificial victims. So it was for the ancestral temple ; but in sacrificing to the spirits of the land and grain, the victim was a ' yellow' bull with black lips.

[1] The subject of these lines must be an ordinary officer, for to such the silk robes and a purple cap were proper, when he was assisting at the sacrifices of the king or of a feudal prince. There were two buildings outside the principal gate leading to the ancestral temple, and two corresponding inside, in which the personators of the departed ancestors were feasted. We must suppose the officer in question descending from the upper hall to the vestibule of the gate, to inspect the dishes, arranged for the feast, and then proceeding to see the animals, and the tripods for boiling the flesh, &c.

[2] The goblet of rhinoceros horn was to be drained, as a penalty, by any one offending at the feast against the rules of propriety ; but here there was no occasion for it.

time was yet dark. When the time was clearly 335
bright, He thereupon donned his grand armour.
We have been favoured to receive What the martial
king accomplished. To deal aright with what we
have inherited, We have to be sincere imitators
of thy course, (O king).

ODE 9. THE HWAN.

CELEBRATING THE MERIT AND SUCCESS OF KING WÛ.

According to a statement in the Ʒo *K*wan, this piece also was
sung in connexion with the dance of Wû. The Preface says
it was used in declarations of war, and in sacrificing to God
and the Father of War. Perhaps it came to be used on such
occasions; but we must refer it in the first place to the reign
of king *Kh*ăng.

There is peace throughout our myriad regions.
There has been a succession of plentiful years :—
Heaven does not weary in its favour. The martial
king Wû Maintained (the confidence of) his officers,
And employed them all over the kingdom, So
securing the establishment of his family. Oh!
glorious was he in the sight of Heaven, Which
kinged him in the room (of Shang).

ODE 10. THE LÂI.

CELEBRATING THE PRAISE OF KING WĂN.

This is the only account of the piece that can be given from itself.
The Ʒo *K*wan, however, refers it to the dance of king Wû;
and the Preface says it contains the words with which Wû
accompanied his grant of fiefs and appanages in the ancestral
temple to his principal followers.

King Wăn laboured earnestly :—Right is it we
should have received (the kingdom). We will diffuse (his virtue), ever cherishing the thought of

336   him; Henceforth we will seek only the settlement (of the kingdom). It was he through whom came the appointment of *K*âu. Oh! let us ever cherish the thought of him.

ODE 11. THE PAN.

CELEBRATING THE GREATNESS OF *K*ÂU, AND ITS FIRM POSSESSION OF THE KINGDOM, AS SEEN IN THE PROGRESSES OF ITS REIGNING SOVE-REIGN.

In the eighth piece of the first decade we have an ode akin to this, relating a tentative progress of king Wû, to test the acceptance of his sovereignty. This is of a later date, and should be referred, probably, to the reign of king *Kh*ăng, when the dynasty was fully acknowledged. Some critics, however, make it, like the three preceding, a portion of what was sung at the Wû dance.

Oh! great now is *K*âu. We ascend the high hills, Both those that are long and narrow, and the lofty mountains. Yes, and (we travel) along the regulated Ho, All under the sky, Assembling those who now respond to me. Thus it is that the appointment belongs to *K*âu.

III. THE PRAISE ODES OF LÛ.

IT is not according to the truth of things to class the Sung of Lû among the sacrificial odes, and I do not call them such. *K*û Hsî says:—'King *Kh*ăng, because of the great services rendered by the duke of *K*âu, granted to Po-*kh*in, (the duke's eldest son, and first marquis of Lû), the privilege of using the royal ceremonies and music, in consequence of which Lû had its Sung, which were sung to the music in its ancestral temple. Afterwards, they made in Lû other odes in praise of their rulers,

which they also called Sung.' In this way it is endeavoured 337
to account for there being such pieces in this part of the Shih
as the four in this division of it. Confucius, it is thought, found
them in Lû, bearing the name of Sung, and so he classed them
with the true sacrificial odes, bearing that designation. If we
were to admit, contrary to the evidence in the case, that the
Shih was compiled by Confucius, this explanation of the place
of the Sung of Lû in this Part would not be complimentary to
his discrimination.

Whether such a privilege as *K*û states was really granted to the
first marquis of Lû, is a point very much controverted. Many
contend that the royal ceremonies were usurped in the state, in
the time of duke Hsî (B.C. 659 to 627). But if this should be
conceded, it would not affect the application to the odes in this
division of the name of Sung. They are totally unlike the Sung
of Shang and of *K*âu. It has often been asked why there are
no Făng of Lû in the first Part of the Shih. The pieces here
are really the Făng of Lû, and may be compared especially with
the Făng of Pin.

Lû was one of the states in the east, having its capital in *Kh*û-
fâu, which is still the name of a district in the department of
Yen-*k*âu, Shan-tung. According to *K*û, king *Kh*ăng invested
the duke of *K*âu's eldest son with the territory. According to
Sze-mâ *Kh*ien, the duke of *K*âu was himself appointed marquis
of Lû ; but being unable to go there in consequence of his
duties at the royal court, he sent his son instead. After the
expiration of his regency, the territory was largely augmented,
but he still remained in *K*âu.

I pass over the first two odes, which have no claim to a place
among 'sacred texts.' And only in one stanza of the third is
there the expression of a religious sentiment. I give it entire,
however.

ODE 3. THE PHAN SHUI.

IN PRAISE OF SOME MARQUIS OF LÛ, CELEBRATING HIS INTEREST IN
THE STATE COLLEGE, WHICH HE HAD, PROBABLY, REPAIRED, TESTI-
FYING HIS VIRTUES, AND AUSPICING FOR HIM A COMPLETE TRIUMPH
OVER THE TRIBES OF THE HWÂI, WHICH WOULD BE CELEBRATED
IN THE COLLEGE.

The marquis here celebrated was, probably, Shăn, or 'duke Hsî,'
mentioned above. The immediate occasion of its composition

[1]   Z

338　　must have been some opening or inauguration service in connexion with the repair of the college.

1. Pleasant is the semicircular water[1], And we gather the cress about it. The marquis of Lû is coming to it, And we see his dragon-figured banner. His banner waves in the wind, And the bells of his horses tinkle harmoniously. Small and great, All follow the prince in his progress to it.

2. Pleasant is the semicircular water, And we gather the pondweed in it. The marquis of Lû has come to it, With his horses so stately. His horses are grand; His fame is brilliant. Blandly he looks and smiles; Without any impatience he delivers his instructions.

3. Pleasant is the semicircular water, And we gather the mallows about it. The marquis of Lû has come to it, And in the college he is drinking. He is drinking the good spirits. May there be

---

[1] It is said in the tenth ode of the first decade of the Major Odes of the Kingdom, that king Wû in his capital of Hâo built 'his hall with its circlet of water.' That was the royal college built in the middle of a circle of water; each state had its grand college with a semicircular pool in front of it, such as may now be seen in front of the temples of Confucius in the metropolitan cities of the provinces. It is not easy to describe all the purposes which the building served. In this piece the marquis of Lû appears feasting in it, delivering instructions, taking counsel with his ministers, and receiving the spoils and prisoners of war. The Lî *Kî*, VIII, ii, 7, refers to sacrifices to Hâu-*kî* in connexion with the college of Lû. There the officers of the state in autumn learned ceremonies; in winter, literary studies; in spring and summer, the use of arms; and in autumn and winter, dancing. There were celebrated trials of archery; there the aged were feasted; there the princes held council with their ministers. The college was in the western suburb of each capital.

given to him such old age as is seldom enjoyed!
May he accord with the grand ways, So subduing
to himself all the people!

4. Very admirable is the marquis of Lû, Reverently displaying his virtue, And reverently watching
over his deportment, The pattern of the people.
With great qualities, both civil and martial, Brilliantly he affects his meritorious ancestors[1]. In
everything entirely filial, He seeks the blessing
that is sure to follow.

5. Very intelligent is the marquis of Lû, Making
his virtue illustrious. He has made this college
with its semicircle of water, And the tribes of the
Hwâi will submit to him[2]. His martial-looking
tiger-leaders Will here present the left ears (of
their foes)[3]. His examiners, wise as Kâo-yâo[4],
Will here present the prisoners.

6. His numerous officers, Men who have enlarged their virtuous minds, With martial energy
conducting their expedition, Will drive far away
those tribes of the east and south. Vigorous and

---

[1] The meaning is that the fine qualities of the marquis 'reached
to' and affected his ancestors in their spirit-state, and would draw
down their protecting favour. Their blessing, seen in his prosperity, was the natural result of his filial piety.

[2] The Hwâi rises in the department of Nan-yang, Ho-nan, and
flows eastward to the sea. South of it, down to the time of this
ode, were many rude and wild tribes that gave frequent occupa-
tion to the kings of *K*âu.

[3] When prisoners refused to submit, their left ears were cut off,
and shown as trophies.

[4] The ancient Shun's Minister of Crime. The 'examiners'
were officers who questioned the prisoners, especially the more
important of them, to elicit information, and decide as to the
amount of their guilt and punishment.

340   grand, Without noise or display, Without appeal to'the judges[1], They will here present (the proofs of) their merit.

7. How they draw their bows adorned with bone! How their arrows whiz forth! Their war chariots are very large! Their footmen and charioteers never weary! They have subdued the tribes of Hwâi, And brought them to an unrebellious submission. Only lay your plans securely, And all the tribes of the Hwâi will be won [2].

8. They come flying on the wing, those owls, And settle on the trees about the college; They eat the fruit of our mulberry trees, And salute us with fine notes [3]. So awakened shall be those tribes of the Hwâi. They will come presenting their precious things, Their large tortoises, and their elephants' teeth, And great contributions of the southern metals [4].

---

[1] The 'judges' decided all questions of dispute in the army, and on the merits of different men who had distinguished themselves.

[2] In this stanza the poet describes a battle with the wild tribes, as if it were going on before his eyes.

[3] An owl is a bird with a disagreeable scream, instead of a beautiful note; but the mulberries grown about the college would make them sing delightfully. And so would the influence of Lû, going forth from the college, transform the nature of the tribes about the Hwâi.

[4] That is, according to 'the Tribute of Yü,' in the Shû, from *K*ing-*k*âu and Yang-*k*âu.

Ode 4. The Pî Kung.

341

IN PRAISE OF DUKE HSÎ, AND AUSPICING FOR HIM A MAGNIFICENT
CAREER OF SUCCESS, WHICH WOULD MAKE LÛ ALL THAT IT HAD
EVER BEEN:—WRITTEN, PROBABLY, ON AN OCCASION WHEN HSÎ HAD
REPAIRED THE TEMPLES OF THE STATE, OF WHICH PIOUS ACT HIS
SUCCESS WOULD BE THE REWARD.

There is no doubt that duke Hsî is the hero of this piece. He is
mentioned in the third stanza as 'the son of duke *K*wang,' and
the Hsî-sze referred to in the last stanza as the architect under
whose superintendence the temples had been repaired was his
brother, whom we meet with elsewhere as 'duke's son, Yü.' The
descriptions of various sacrifices prove that the lords of Lû,
whether permitted to use royal ceremonies or not, did really
do so. The writer was evidently in a poetic rapture as to
what his ruler was, and would do. The piece is a genuine
bardic effusion.

The poet traces the lords of Lû to *K*iang Yüan and her son
Hâu-*k*î. He then comes to the establishment of the *K*âu
dynasty, and under it of the marquisate of Lû; and finally to
duke Hsî, dilating on his sacrificial services, the military power
of Lû, and the achievements which he might be expected to
accomplish in subjugating all the territory lying to the east, and
a long way south, of Lû.

1. How pure and still are the solemn temples,
In their strong solidity and minute completeness!
Highly distinguished was *K*iang Yüan[1], Of virtue
undeflected. God regarded her with favour, And
without injury or hurt, Immediately, when her
months were completed, She gave birth to Hâu-*k*î!
On him were conferred all blessings,—(To know)
how the (ordinary) millet ripened early, and the
sacrificial millet late; How first to sow pulse

---

[1] About *K*iang Yüan and her conception and birth of Hâu-*k*î,
see the first piece in the third decade of the Major Odes of the
Kingdom. There also Hâu-*k*î's teaching of husbandry is more
fully described.

342 and then wheat. Anon he was invested with an
inferior state, And taught the people how to sow
and to reap, The (ordinary) millet and the sacrificial, Rice and the black millet; Ere long over
the whole country :— (Thus) continuing the work
of Yü.

2. Among the descendants of Hâu-*kî*, There
was king Thâi¹, Dwelling on the south of (mount)
Khî, Where the clipping of Shang began. In
process of time Wăn and Wû Continued the work
of king Thâi, And (the purpose of) Heaven was
carried out in its time, In the plain of Mû². 'Have
no doubts, no anxieties,' (it was said), 'God is with
you³.' Wû disposed of the troops of Shang; He
and his men equally shared in the achievement.
(Then) king (*Kh* ăng) said, 'My uncle⁴, I will set
up your eldest son, And make him marquis of Lû.
I will greatly enlarge your territory there, To be
a help and support to the House of *K*âu.'

3. Accordingly he appointed (our first) duke of
Lû, And made him marquis in the east, Giving
him the hills and rivers, The lands and fields, and
the attached states⁵. The (present) descendant of
the duke of *K*âu, The son of duke *K*wang, With
dragon-emblazoned banner, attends the sacrifices,
(Grasping) his six reins soft and pliant. In spring

---

¹ See on the Sacrificial Odes of *K*âu, decade i, ode 5.
² See the Shû, V, iii.
³ Shang-fû, one of Wû's principal leaders, encouraged him at
the battle of Mû with these words.
⁴ That is, the duke of *K*âu.
⁵ That is, small territories, held by chiefs of other surnames, but
acknowledging the jurisdiction of the lords of Lû, and dependent
on them for introduction to the royal court.

and autumn he is not remiss; His offerings are　343
all without error[1]. To the great and sovereign
God, And to his great ancestor Hâu-*kî*, He
offers the victims, red and pure[2]. They enjoy, they
approve, And bestow blessings in large number.
The duke of *K*âu, and (your other) great ancestors,
Also bless you.

4. In autumn comes the sacrifice of the season[3],
But the bulls for it have had their horns capped
in summer[4]; They are the white bull and the red
one[5]. (There are) the bull-figured goblet in its
dignity[6]; Roast pig, minced meat, and soups; The
dishes of bamboo and wood, and the large stands[7],
And the dancers all complete. The filial descendant

---

[1] These lines refer to the seasonal sacrifices in the temple of
ancestors, two seasons being mentioned for all the four, as in
some of the odes of Shang.

[2] From the seasonal sacrifices the poet passes to the sacrifice to
God at the border altar in the spring,—no doubt the same which is
referred to in the last ode of the first decade of the Sacrificial
Odes of *K*âu.

[3] The subject of the seasonal sacrifices is resumed.

[4] A piece of wood was fixed across the horns of the victim-
bulls, to prevent their injuring them by pushing or rubbing
against any hard substance. An animal injured in any way was
not fit to be used in sacrifice.

[5] In sacrificing to the duke of *K*âu, a white bull was used by
way of distinction. His great services to the dynasty had obtained for him the privilege of being sacrificed to with royal
ceremonies. A white bull, such as had been offered to the kings
of Shang, was therefore devoted to him; while for Po-*kh*in, and
the other marquises (or dukes as spoken of by their own subjects), a victim of the orthodox *K*âu colour was employed.

[6] This goblet, fashioned in the shape of a bull, or with a bull
pictured on it, must have been well known in connexion with
these services.

[7] 'The large stand' was of a size to support half the roasted
body of a victim.

344   will be blessed. (Your ancestors) will make you gloriously prosperous, They will make you long-lived and good, To preserve this eastern region, Long possessing the state of Lû, Unwaning, un-fallen, Unshaken, undisturbed! They will make your friendship with your three aged (ministers)[1] Like the hills, like the mountains.

5. Our prince's chariots are a thousand, And (in each) are (the two spears with their) vermilion tassels, and (the two bows with their) green bands. His footmen are thirty thousand, With shells on vermilion strings adorning their helmets[2]. So numerous are his ardent followers, To deal with the tribes of the west and north, And to punish those of *K*ing and Shû[3], So that none of them will dare to withstand us. (The spirits of your ancestors) shall make you grandly prosperous; They

---

[1] Referring, probably, to the three principal ministers of the state.

[2] These lines describe Hsî's resources for war. A thousand chariots was the regular force which a great state could at the utmost bring into the field. Each chariot contained three mailed men;—the charioteer in the middle, a spearman on the right, and an archer on the left. Two spears rose aloft with vermilion tassels, and there were two bows, bound with green bands to frames in their cases. Attached to every chariot were seventy-two foot-soldiers and twenty-five followers, making with the three men in it, 100 in all; so that the whole force would amount to 100,000 men. But in actual service the force of a great state was restricted to three 'armies' or 375 chariots, attended by 37,500 men, of whom 27,500 were foot-soldiers, put down here in round numbers as 30,000.

[3] *K*ing is the *K*ing-*kh*û of the last of the Sacrificial Odes of Shang, and the name Shû was applied to several half-civilized states to the east of it, which it brought, during the *Kh*un *Kh*iû period, one after another under its jurisdiction.

shall make you long-lived and wealthy. The hoary 345
hair and wrinkled back, Marking the aged men,
shall always be in your service. They shall grant
you old age, ever vigorous, For myriads and thousands of years, With the eyebrows of longevity,
and ever unharmed.

6. The mountain of Thâi is lofty, Looked up to
by the state of Lû [1]. We grandly possess also Kwei
and Măng [2]; And we shall extend to the limits
of the east, Even the states along the sea. The
tribes of the Hwâi will seek our alliance; All
will proffer their allegiance:—Such shall be the
achievements of the marquis of Lû.

7. He shall maintain the possession of Hû and
Yî [3], And extend his sway to the regions of
Hsü [4], Even to the states along the sea. The
tribes of the Hwâi, the Man, and the Mo [5], And
those tribes (still more) to the south, All will
proffer their allegiance ;—Not one will dare not to
answer to his call, Thus showing their obedience
to the marquis of Lû.

8. Heaven will give great blessing to our prince,
So that with the eyebrows of longevity he shall

---

[1] Mount Thâi is well known, the eastern of the four great
mountains of China in the time of Shun. It is in the department of Thâi-an, Shan-tung.

[2] These were two smaller hills in Lû.

[3] These were two hills of Lû, in the present district of 3âu.

[4] Hsü was the name of one of Yü's nine provinces, embracing
portions of the present Shan-tung, *K*iang-sû, and An-hui.

[5] Mo was properly the name of certain wild tribes in the
north, as Man was that of the tribes of the south. But we
cannot suppose any tribes to be meant here but such as lay
south of Lû.

346 maintain Lû. He shall possess *K*ang and Hsü [1],
And recover all the territory of the duke of *K*âu.
Then shall the marquis of Lû feast and be glad,
With his admirable wife and aged mother; With
his excellent ministers and all his (other) officers [2].
Our region and state shall he hold, Thus receiving
many blessings, To hoary hair, and with teeth ever
renewed like a child's.

9. The pines of 3û-lâi [3], And the cypresses of
Hsin-fû [3], Were cut down and measured, With
the cubit line and the eight cubits' line. The projecting beams of pine were made very large; The
grand inner apartments rose vast. Splendid look
the new temples, The work of Hsî-sze, Very
wide and large, Answering to the expectations of
all the people.

---

[1] *K*ang was a city with some adjacent territory, in the present
district of Thăng, that had been taken from Lû by *K*hî. Hsü,
called in the Spring and Autumn 'the fields of Hsü,' was west
from Lû, and had been granted to it as a convenient place for its
princes to stop at on their way to the royal court; but it had been
sold or parted with to *K*ăng in the first year of duke Hwan
(B.C. 711). The poet desires that Hsî should recover these and
all other territory which had at any time belonged to Lû.

[2] He would feast with the ladies in the inner apartment of
the palace, suitable for such a purpose; with his ministers in the
outer banqueting-room.

[3] These were two hills, in the present department of Thâi-an.

The First Decade, or that of Lû-ming.

ODE 5, STANZA 1. THE FÂ MÛ.

THE FÂ MÛ IS A FESTAL ODE, WHICH WAS SUNG AT THE ENTERTAIN-
MENT OF FRIENDS;—INTENDED TO CELEBRATE THE DUTY AND VALUE
OF FRIENDSHIP, EVEN TO THE HIGHEST.

On the trees go the blows *kǎng-kǎng*; And
the birds cry out *ying-ying*. One issues from the
dark valley, And removes to the lofty tree. *Ying*
goes its cry, Seeking with its voice its companion.
Look at the bird, Bird as it is, seeking with its
voice its companion; And shall a man Not seek
to have his friends? Spiritual beings will then
hearken to him[1]; He shall have harmony and
peace.

ODE 6. THE THIEN PÂO.

A FESTAL ODE, RESPONSIVE TO ANY OF THE FIVE THAT PRECEDE IT.
THE KING'S OFFICERS AND GUESTS, HAVING BEEN FEASTED BY HIM,
CELEBRATE HIS PRAISES, AND DESIRE FOR HIM THE BLESSING OF
HEAVEN AND HIS ANCESTORS.

Ascribed, like the former, to the duke of *K*âu.

Heaven protects and establishes thee, With the
greatest security; Makes thee entirely virtuous.

---

[1] This line and the following show the power and value of the
cultivation of friendship in affecting spiritual beings. That designation is understood in the widest sense.

348   That thou mayest enjoy every happiness; Grants thee much increase, So that thou hast all in abundance.

Heaven protects and establishes thee. It grants thee all excellence, So that thine every matter is right, And thou receivest every Heavenly favour. It sends down to thee long-during happiness, Which the days are not sufficient to enjoy.

Heaven protects and establishes thee, So that in everything thou dost prosper. Like the high hills and the mountain masses, Like the topmost ridges and the greatest bulks, Like the stream ever coming on, Such is thine increase.

With happy auspices and purifications thou bringest the offerings, And dost filially present them, In spring, summer, autumn, and winter, To the dukes and former kings[1]; And they say, ' We give to thee myriads of years, duration unlimited[2].'

The spirits come[3], And confer on thee many blessings. The people are simple and honest, Daily enjoying their meat and drink. All the black-haired race, in all their surnames, Universally practise thy virtue.

Like the moon advancing to the full, Like the sun ascending the heavens, Like the everlasting southern hills, Never waning, never falling, Like

---

[1] These dukes and former kings are all the ancestors of the royal House of *K*âu, sacrificed to at the four seasons of the year.

[2] Here we have the response of the dukes and kings communicated to the sacrificing king by the individuals chosen to represent them at the service.

[3] The spirits here are, of course, those of the former dukes and kings.

the luxuriance of the fir and the cypress; — May 349
such be thy succeeding line!

ODE 9, STANZA 4. THE TÎ TÛ.

THE TÎ TÛ IS AN ODE OF CONGRATULATION, INTENDED FOR THE MEN
WHO HAVE RETURNED FROM MILITARY DUTY AND SERVICE ON THE
FRONTIERS.

The congratulation is given in a description of the anxiety and
longing of the soldiers' wives for their return. We must suppose
one of the wives to be the speaker throughout. The fourth
stanza shows how she had resorted to divination to allay her
fears about her husband.

They have not packed up, they do not come.
My sorrowing heart is greatly distressed. The
time is past, and he is not here, To the multiplication of my sorrows. Both by the tortoise-shell
and the reeds have I divined, And they unite in
saying he is near. My warrior is at hand.

The Fourth Decade, or that of *Khî* fû.

ODE 5, STANZAS 5 TO 9. THE SZE KAN.

THE SZE KAN WAS PROBABLY MADE FOR A FESTIVAL ON THE COM-
PLETION OF A PALACE; CONTAINING A DESCRIPTION OF IT, AND
PROCEEDING TO GOOD WISHES FOR THE BUILDER AND HIS POSTE-
RITY. THE STANZAS HERE GIVEN SHOW HOW DIVINATION WAS RE-
SORTED TO FOR THE INTERPRETATION OF DREAMS.

The piece is referred to the time of king Hsüan (B.C. 827 to 782).

Level and smooth is the courtyard, And lofty
are the pillars around it. Pleasant is the exposure
of the chamber to the light, And deep and wide
are its recesses. Here will our noble lord repose.

On the rush-mat below and that of fine bamboos
above it, May he repose in slumber! May he sleep

350   and awake, (Saying), 'Divine for me my dreams [1]. What dreams are lucky? They have been of bears and grisly bears; They have been of cobras and (other) snakes.'

The chief diviner will divine them. 'The bears and grisly bears Are the auspicious intimations of sons; The cobras and (other) snakes Are the auspicious intimations of daughters [2].'

Sons shall be born to him :—They will be put to sleep on couches; They will be clothed in robes; They will have sceptres to play with; Their cry will be loud. They will be (hereafter) resplendent with red knee-covers, The (future) king, the princes of the land.

Daughters shall be born to him:—They will be put to sleep on the ground; They will be clothed with wrappers; They will have tiles to play with [3]. It will be theirs neither to do wrong nor to do good [4]. Only about the spirits and the food will

---

[1] In the Official Book of *K*âu, ch. 24, mention is made of the Diviner of Dreams and his duties :—He had to consider the season of the year when a dream occurred, the day of the cycle, and the then predominant influence of the two powers of nature. By the positions of the sun, moon, and planets in the zodiacal spaces he could determine whether any one of the six classes of dreams was lucky or unlucky. Those six classes were ordinary and regular dreams, terrible dreams, dreams of thought, dreams in waking, dreams of joy, and dreams of fear.

[2] The boy would have a sceptre, a symbol of dignity, to play with; the girl, a tile, the symbol of woman's work, as, sitting with a tile on her knee, she twists the threads of hemp.

[3] That is, the red apron of a king and of the prince of a state.

[4] The woman has only to be obedient. That is her whole duty. The line does not mean, as it has been said, that 'she is incapable of good or evil;' but it is not her part to take the initiative even in what is good.

they have to think, And to cause no sorrow to 351
their parents.

ODE 6, STANZA 4. THE WÛ YANG.

THE WÛ YANG IS SUPPOSED TO CELEBRATE THE LARGENESS AND
EXCELLENT CONDITION OF KING HSÜAN'S FLOCKS AND HERDS. THE
CONCLUDING STANZA HAS REFERENCE TO THE DIVINATION OF THE
DREAMS OF HIS HERDSMEN.

Your herdsmen shall dream, Of multitudes and
then of fishes, Of the tortoise-and-serpent, and
then of the falcon, banners[1]. The chief diviner
will divine the dreams ;—How the multitudes, dissolving into fishes, Betoken plentiful years ; How
the tortoise-and-serpent, dissolving into the falcon,
banners, Betoken the increasing population of the
kingdom.

ODE 7. THE *K*IEH NAN SHAN.

A LAMENTATION OVER THE UNSETTLED STATE OF THE KINGDOM ;
DENOUNCING THE INJUSTICE AND NEGLECT OF THE CHIEF MINISTER,
BLAMING ALSO THE CONDUCT OF THE KING, WITH APPEALS TO
HEAVEN, AND SEEMINGLY CHARGING IT WITH CRUELTY AND INJUS-
TICE.

This piece is referred to the time of king Yû (B.C. 781 to 771),
the unworthy son of king Hsüan. The 'Grand-Master' Yin
must have been one of the 'three Kung,' the highest ministers
at the court of *K*âu, and was, probably, the chief of the three,
and administrator of the government under Yû.

Lofty is that southern hill[2], With its masses of
rocks ! Awe-inspiring are you, O (Grand-)Master

---

[1] The tortoise-and-serpent banner marked the presence in a
host of its leader on a military expedition. On its field were the
figures of tortoises, with snakes coiled round them. The falcon
banners belonged to the commanders of the divisions of the host.
They bore the figures of falcons on them.

[2] 'The southern hill' was also called the *K*ung-nan, and rose
right to the south of the western capital of *K*âu.

352   Yin, And the people all look to you! A fire burns in their grieving hearts; They do not dare to speak of you even in jest. The kingdom is verging to extinction;—How is it that you do not consider the state of things?

Lofty is that southern hill, And vigorously grows the vegetation on it! Awe-inspiring are you, O (Grand-)Master Yin, But how is it that you are so unjust? Heaven is continually redoubling its inflictions; Deaths and disorder increase and multiply; No words of satisfaction come from the people; And yet you do not correct nor bemoan yourself.

The Grand-Master Yin Is the foundation of our *K*âu, And the balance of the kingdom is in his hands. He should be keeping its four quarters together; He should be aiding the Son of Heaven, So as to preserve the people from going astray. O unpitying great Heaven, It is not right he should reduce us all to such misery!

He does nothing himself personally, And the people have no confidence in him. Making no enquiry about them, and no trial of their services, He should not deal deceitfully with superior men. If he dismissed them on the requirement of justice, Mean men would not be endangering (the commonweal); And his mean relatives Would not be in offices of importance.

Great Heaven, unjust, Is sending down these exhausting disorders. Great Heaven, unkind, Is sending down these great miseries. Let superior men come (into office), And that would bring rest to the people's hearts. Let superior men execute their justice, And the animosities and angers would 353 disappear[1].

O unpitying great Heaven, There is no end to the disorder! With every month it continues to grow, So that the people have no repose. I am as if intoxicated with the grief of my heart. Who holds the ordering of the kingdom? He attends not himself to the government, And the result is toil and pain to the people.

I yoke my four steeds, My four steeds, long-necked. I look to the four quarters (of the kingdom); Distress is everywhere; there is no place I can drive to.

Now your evil is rampant[2], And I can see your spears. Anon you are pacified and friendly as if you were pledging one another.

From great Heaven is the injustice, And our king has no repose. (Yet) he will not correct his heart, And goes on to resent endeavours to rectify him.

I, *Kiâ-fû*, have made this poem, To lay bare the king's disorders. If you would but change your heart, Then would the myriad regions be nourished.

---

[1] In this stanza, as in the next and the last but one, the writer complains of Heaven, and charges it foolishly. He does so by way of appeal, however, and indicates the true causes of the misery of the kingdom,—the reckless conduct, namely, of the king and his minister.

[2] The parties spoken of here are the followers of the minister, 'mean men,' however high in place and great in power, now friendly, now hostile to one another.

[1]   A a

354　　ODE 8, STANZAS 4, 5, AND 7.　THE *K*ĂNG YÜEH.

THE *K*ĂNG YÜEH IS, LIKE THE PRECEDING ODE, A LAMENTATION OVER
THE MISERIES OF THE KINGDOM, AND THE RUIN COMING ON IT;
WITH A SIMILAR, BUT MORE HOPEFULLY EXPRESSED, APPEAL TO
HEAVEN, 'THE GREAT GOD.'

Look into the middle of the forest;　There are
(only) large faggots and small branches in it [1].　The
people now amidst their perils　Look to Heaven,
all dark;　But let its determination be fixed,　And
there is no one whom it will not overcome.　There
is the great God,—Does he hate any one?

If one say of a hill that it is low,　There are its
ridges and its large masses.　The false calumnies
of the people,—How is it that you do not repress
them [2]?　You call those experienced ancients, You
consult the diviner of dreams.　They all say, 'We
are very wise,　But who can distinguish the male
and female crow [3]?'

Look at the rugged and stony field;—Luxuriantly
rises in it the springing grain.　(But) Heaven moves
and shakes me,　As if it could not overcome me [4].

---

[1] By introducing the word 'only,' I have followed the view of
the older interpreters, who consider the forest, with merely some
faggots and twigs left in it, to be emblematic of the ravages of
oppressive government in the court and kingdom.　*K*û Hsî takes
a different view of them:—'In a forest you can easily distinguish
the large faggots from the small branches, while Heaven appears
unable to distinguish between the good and bad.'

[2] The calumnies that were abroad were as absurd as the assertion in line 1, and yet the king could not, or would not, see through
them and repress them.

[3] This reference to the diviners of dreams is in derision of their
pretensions.

[4] That is, the productive energy of nature manifests itself in the
most unlikely places; how was it that 'the great God, who hates
no one,' was contending so with the writer?

They sought me (at first) to be a pattern (to them), 355
(Eagerly) as if they could not get me; (Now) they
regard me with great animosity, And will not use
my strength.

ODE 9. THE SHIH YÜEH *KIH* *K*ĬÂO.

THE LAMENTATION OF AN OFFICER OVER THE PRODIGIES CELESTIAL
AND TERRESTRIAL, ESPECIALLY AN ECLIPSE OF THE SUN, THAT
WERE BETOKENING THE RUIN OF *K*ÂU. HE SETS FORTH WHAT HE
CONSIDERED TO BE THE TRUE CAUSES OF THE PREVAILING MISERY,
WHICH WAS BY NO MEANS TO BE CHARGED ON HEAVEN.

Attention is called in the Introduction, p. 296, to the date of the
solar eclipse mentioned in this piece.

At the conjunction (of the sun and moon) in the
tenth month, On the first day of the moon, which
was hsin-mâo, The sun was eclipsed, A thing
of very evil omen. Before, the moon became small,
And now the sun became small. Henceforth the
lower people Will be in a very deplorable case.

The sun and moon announce evil, Not keeping
to their proper paths. Throughout the kingdom
there is no (proper) government, Because the good
are not employed. For the moon to be eclipsed
Is but an ordinary matter. Now that the sun has
been eclipsed,—How bad it is!

Grandly flashes the lightning of the thunder.
There is a want of rest, a want of good. The
streams all bubble up and overflow. The crags on
the hill-tops fall down. High banks become valleys;
Deep valleys become hills. Alas for the men of
this time! How does (the king) not stop these
things?

Hwang-fû is the President; Fan is the Minister

A a 2

356 of Instruction; *K*iâ-po is the (chief) Administrator;
*K*ung-yün is the chief Cook; Ʒâu is the Recorder
of the Interior; Khwei is Master of the Horse;
Yü is Captain of the Guards; And the beautiful
wife blazes, now in possession of her place [1].

This Hwang-fû Will not acknowledge that he
is acting out of season. But why does he call us
to move, Without coming and consulting with us?
He has removed our walls and roofs; And our
fields are all either a marsh or a moor. He says,
'I am not injuring you; The laws require that
thus it should be.'

Hwang-fû is very wise; He has built a great
city for himself in Hsiang. He chose three men
as his ministers, All of them possessed of great
wealth. He could not bring himself to leave a
single minister, Who might guard our king. He
(also) selected those who had chariots and horses,
To go and reside in Hsiang [2].

---

[1] We do not know anything from history of the ministers of Yû
mentioned in this stanza. Hwang-fû appears to have been the leading
minister of the government at the time when the ode was written,
and, as appears from the next two stanzas, was very crafty, oppressive, and selfishly ambitious. The mention of 'the chief Cook'
among the high ministers appears strange; but we shall find that
functionary mentioned in another ode; and from history it appears
that 'the Cook,' at the royal and feudal courts, sometimes played
an important part during the times of *K*âu. 'The beautiful
wife,' no doubt, was the well-known Sze of Pâo, raised by king Yû
from her position as one of his concubines to be his queen, and
whose insane folly and ambition led to her husband's death, and
great and disastrous changes in the kingdom.

[2] Hsiang was a district of the royal domain, in the present district of Măng, department of Hwâi-*kh*ing, Ho-nan. It had been
assigned to Hwang-fû, and he was establishing himself there, without any loyal regard to the king. As a noble in the royal domain,

I have exerted myself to discharge my service,　357
And do not dare to make a report of my toils.
Without crime or offence of any kind,　Slanderous
mouths are loud against me.　(But) the calamities
of the lower people　Do not come down from
Heaven.　A multitude of (fair) words, and hatred
behind the back;—The earnest, strong pursuit of
this is from men.

Distant far is my village,　And my dissatisfaction
is great.　In other quarters there is ease,　And
I dwell here, alone and sorrowful.　Everybody is
going into retirement,　And I alone dare not seek
rest.　The ordinances of Heaven are inexplicable,
But I will not dare to follow my friends, and leave
my post.

ODE 10, STANZAS 1 AND 3.　THE YÜ WÛ KĂNG.

THE WRITER OF THIS PIECE MOURNS OVER THE MISERABLE STATE
OF THE KINGDOM, THE INCORRIGIBLE COURSE OF THE KING, AND
OTHER EVILS, APPEALING ALSO TO HEAVEN, AND SURPRISED THAT
IT ALLOWED SUCH THINGS TO BE.

Great and wide Heaven,　How is it you have
contracted your kindness,　Sending down death
and famine,　Destroying all through the kingdom?
Compassionate Heaven, arrayed in terrors,　How
is it you exercise no forethought, no care?　Let
alone the criminals :—They have suffered for their
guilt.　But those who have no crime　Are indis-
criminately involved in ruin.

---

he was entitled only to two ministers, but he had appointed three
as in one of the feudal states, encouraging, moreover, the resort to
himself of the wealthy and powerful, while the court was left weak
and unprotected.

358   How is it, O great Heaven, That the king will not hearken to the justest words? He is like a man going (astray), Who knows not where he will proceed to. All ye officers, Let each of you attend to his duties. How do ye not stand in awe of one another? Ye do not stand in awe of Heaven.

The Fifth Decade, or that of Hsiâo Min.

ODE 1, STANZAS 1, 2, AND 3. THE HSIÂO MIN.

A LAMENTATION OVER THE RECKLESSNESS AND INCAPACITY OF THE KING AND HIS COUNSELLORS. DIVINATION HAS BECOME OF NO AVAIL, AND HEAVEN IS DESPAIRINGLY APPEALED TO.

This is referred, like several of the pieces in the fourth decade, to the time of king Yû.

The angry terrors of compassionate Heaven Extend through this lower world. (The king's) counsels and plans are crooked and bad; When will he stop (in his course)? Counsels that are good he will not follow, And those that are not good he employs. When I look at his counsels and plans, I am greatly pained.

Now they agree, and now they defame one another;—The case is greatly to be deplored. If a counsel be good, They are all found opposing it. If a counsel be bad, They are all found according with it. When I look at such counsels and plans, What will they come to?

Our tortoise-shells are wearied out, And will not tell us anything about the plans. The counsellors are very many, But on that account nothing is accomplished. The speakers fill the court, But

who dares to take any responsibility on himself?　359
We are as if we consulted (about a journey) without
taking a step in advance, And therefore did not
get on on the road.

ODE 2, STANZAS 1 AND 2.　THE HSIÂO YÜAN.

SOME OFFICER IN A TIME OF DISORDER AND MISGOVERNMENT URGES
ON HIS BROTHERS THE DUTY OF MAINTAINING THEIR OWN VIRTUE,
AND OF OBSERVING THE GREATEST CAUTION.

Small is the cooing dove, But it flies aloft to
heaven. My heart is wounded with sorrow, And
I think of our forefathers. When the dawn is
breaking, and I cannot sleep, The thoughts in my
breast are of our parents.

Men who are grave and wise, Though they
drink, are mild and masters of themselves; But
those who are benighted and ignorant Become
devoted to drink, and more so daily. Be careful,
each of you, of your deportment; What Heaven
confers, (when once lost), is not regained[1].

The greenbeaks come and go, Picking up grain
about the stackyard. Alas for the distressed and
the solitary, Deemed fit inmates for the prisons!
With a handful of grain I go out and divine[2], How
I may be able to become good.

---

[1] 'What Heaven confers' is, probably, the good human nature,
which by vice, and especially by drunkenness, may be irretrievably
ruined.

[2] A religious act is here referred to, on which we have not sufficient information to be able to throw much light. It was the
practice to spread some finely ground rice on the ground, in connexion with divination, as an offering to the spirits. The poet
represents himself here as using a handful of grain for the purpose,—probably on account of his poverty.

360   ODE 3, STANZAS 1 AND 3. THE HSIÂO PAN.

THE ELDEST SON AND HEIR-APPARENT OF KING YÛ BEWAILS HIS DEGRA-
DATION, APPEALING TO HEAVEN AS TO HIS INNOCENCE, AND COM-
PLAINING OF ITS CASTING HIS LOT IN SUCH A TIME.

It is allowed that this piece is clearly the composition of a banished
son, and there is no necessity to call in question the tradition
preserved in the Preface which prefers it to Î-khiû, the eldest
son of king Yû. His mother was a princess of the House of
Shän; but when Yû became enamoured of Sze of Pâo, the queen
was degraded, and the son banished to Shän.

With flapping wings the crows   Come back, flying
all in a flock [1].   Other people are happy,   And I
only am full of misery.   What is my offence against
Heaven?   What is my crime?   My heart is sad;—
What is to be done?

Even the mulberry trees and the rottleras   Must
be regarded with reverence [2];   But no one is to be
looked up to like a father,   No one is to be depended on as a mother.   Have I not a connexion
with the hairs (of my father)?   Did I not dwell
in the womb (of my mother)?   O Heaven, who
gave me birth!   How was it at so inauspicious
a time?

----

[1] The sight of the crows, all together, suggests to the prince his
own condition, solitary and driven from court.

[2] The mulberry tree and the rottlera were both planted about
the farmsteadings, and are therefore mentioned here. They carried
the thoughts back to the father or grandfather, or the more remote
ancestor, who first planted them, and so a feeling of reverence
attached to themselves.

ODE 4, STANZA 1. THE *KHIÂO* YEN.

SOME ONE, SUFFERING FROM THE KING THROUGH SLANDER, APPEAL'S TO HEAVEN, AND GOES ON TO DWELL ON THE NATURE AND EVIL OF SLANDER.

This piece has been referred to the time of king Lî, B.C. 878 to 828.

O vast and distant Heaven, Who art called our parent, That, without crime or offence, I should suffer from disorders thus great! The terrors of great Heaven are excessive, But indeed I have committed no crime. (The terrors of) great Heaven are very excessive, But indeed I have committed no offence.

ODE 6, STANZAS 5 AND 6. THE HSIANG PO.

A EUNUCH, HIMSELF THE VICTIM OF SLANDER, COMPLAINS OF HIS FATE, AND WARNS AND DENOUNCES HIS ENEMIES; APPEALING AGAINST THEM, AS HIS LAST RESORT, TO HEAVEN.

The proud are delighted, And the troubled are in sorrow. O azure Heaven! O azure Heaven! Look on those proud men, Pity those who are troubled.

Those slanderers! Who devised their schemes for them? I would take those slanderers, And throw them to wolves and tigers. If these refused to devour them, I would cast them into the north[1]. If the north refused to receive them, I would throw them into the hands of great (Heaven)[2].

---

[1] 'The north,' i.e. the region where there are the rigours of winter and the barrenness of the desert.

[2] 'Great Heaven;' 'Heaven' has to be supplied here, but there

362   ODE 9. THE TÂ TUNG.

AN OFFICER OF ONE OF THE STATES OF THE EAST DEPLORES THE
EXACTIONS MADE FROM THEM BY THE GOVERNMENT, COMPLAINS
OF THE FAVOUR SHOWN TO THE WEST, CONTRASTS THE MISERY OF
THE PRESENT WITH THE HAPPINESS OF THE PAST, AND APPEALS TO
THE STARS OF HEAVEN IDLY BEHOLDING THEIR CONDITION.

I give the whole of this piece, because it is an interesting instance
of Sabian views. The writer, despairing of help from men,
appeals to Heaven ; but he distributes the Power that could help
him among many heavenly bodies, supposing that there are
spiritual beings in them, taking account of human affairs.

Well loaded with millet were the dishes, And
long and curved were the spoons of thorn-wood.
The way to *K*âu was like a whetstone, And
straight as an arrow. (So) the officers trod it,
And the common people looked on it. When I
look back and think of it, My tears run down in
streams.

In the states of the east, large and small, The
looms are empty. Then shoes of dolichos fibre
Are made to serve to walk on the hoar-frost.
Slight and elegant gentlemen[1] Walk along that
road to *K*âu. Their going and coming makes my
heart sad.

Ye cold waters, issuing variously from the spring,
Do not soak the firewood I have cut. Sorrowful
I awake and sigh;—Alas for us toiled people!
The firewood has been cut;—Would that it were

---

is no doubt as to the propriety of doing so ; and, moreover, the
peculiar phraseology of the line shows that the poet did not rest
in the thought of the material heavens.

[1] That is, 'slight-looking,' unfit for toil; and yet they are
obliged to make their journey on foot.

conveyed home! Alas for us the toiled people! 363
Would that we could have rest[1]!

The sons of the east Are summoned only (to
service), without encouragement; While the sons
of the west Shine in splendid dresses. The sons of
boatmen Have furs of the bear and grisly bear.
The sons of the poorest families Form the officers
in public employment.

If we present them with spirits, They regard
them as not fit to be called liquor. If we give
them long girdle pendants with their stones, They
do not think them long enough.

There is the Milky Way in heaven[2], Which looks
down on us in light; And the three stars together
are the Weaving Sisters[3], Passing in a day through
seven stages (of the sky).

Although they go through their seven stages,
They complete no bright work for us. Brilliant
shine the Draught Oxen[4], But they do not serve
to draw our carts. In the east there is Lucifer[5];
In the west there is Hesperus[6]; Long and curved

---

[1] This stanza describes, directly or by symbol, the exactions
from which the people of the east were suffering.

[2] 'The Milky Way' is here called simply the Han,＝in the sky
what the Han river is in China.

[3] 'The Weaving Sisters, or Ladies,' are three stars in Lyra, that
form a triangle. To explain what is said of their passing through
seven spaces, it is said: 'The stars seem to go round the circum-
ference of the heavens, divided into twelve spaces, in a day and
night. They would accomplish six of them in a day; but as their
motion is rather in advance of that of the sun, they have entered
into the seventh space by the time it is up with them again.'

[4] 'The Draught Oxen' is the name of some stars in the neck of
Aquila.

[5] Liû Î (Sung dynasty) says: 'The metal star (Venus) is in the

364　is the Rabbit Net of the sky[1];—But they only occupy their places.

In the south is the Sieve[2], But it is of no use to sift. In the north is the Ladle[3], But it lades out no liquor. In the south is the Sieve, Idly showing its mouth. In the north is the Ladle, Raising its handle in the west.

The Sixth Decade, or that of Pei Shan.

ODE 3, STANZAS 1, 4, AND 5. THE HSIÂO MING.

AN OFFICER, KEPT LONG ABROAD ON DISTANT SERVICE, APPEALS TO HEAVEN, DEPLORING THE HARDSHIPS OF HIS LOT, AND TENDERS GOOD ADVICE TO HIS MORE FORTUNATE FRIENDS AT COURT.

O bright and high Heaven, Who enlightenest and rulest this lower world! I marched on this expedition to the west, As far as this wilderness of *Khiû*. From the first day of the second month, I have passed through the cold and the heat. My heart is sad; The poison (of my lot) is too bitter. I think of those (at court) in their offices, And my tears flow down like rain. Do I not wish to return? But I fear the net for crime.

Ah! ye gentlemen, Do not reckon on your rest

---

east in the morning, thus "opening the brightness of the day;" and it is in the west in the evening, thus "prolonging the day."' The author of the piece, however, evidently took Lucifer and Hesperus to be two stars.

[1] 'The Rabbit Net' is the Hyades.

[2] 'The Sieve' is the name of one of the twenty-eight constellations of the zodiac,—part of Sagittarius.

[3] 'The Ladle' is the constellation next to 'the Sieve,'—also part of Sagittarius.

being permanent. Quietly fulfil the duties of your   365
offices, Associating with the correct and upright;
So shall the spirits hearken to you, And give you
good.

Ah! ye gentlemen, Do not reckon on your
repose being permanent. Quietly fulfil the duties
of your offices, Loving the correct and upright;
So shall the spirits hearken to you, And give you
large measures of bright happiness.

ODE 5. THE *KHÛ* 3HZE.

SACRIFICIAL AND FESTAL SERVICES IN THE ANCESTRAL TEMPLE; AND
THEIR CONNEXION WITH ATTENTION TO HUSBANDRY.

See the remarks on the Services of the Ancestral Temple,
pp. 300, 301.

Thick grew the tribulus (on the ground), But
they cleared away its thorny bushes. Why did they
this of old ? That we might plant our millet and
sacrificial millet; That our millet might be abundant, And our sacrificial millet luxuriant. When
our barns are full, And our stacks can be counted
by tens of myriads, We proceed to make spirits
and prepared grain, For offerings and sacrifice.
We seat the representatives of the dead, and urge
them to eat [1]:—Thus seeking to increase our bright
happiness.

---

[1] The poet hurries on to describe the sacrifices in progress.
The persons selected to personate the departed were necessarily
inferior in rank to the principal sacrificer, yet for the time they
were superior to him. This circumstance, it was supposed, would
make them feel uncomfortable; and therefore, as soon as they
appeared in the temple, the director of the ceremonies instructed
the sacrificer to ask them to be seated, and to place them at ease;
after which they were urged to take some refreshment.

366   With correct and reverent deportment, The bulls and rams all pure, We proceed to the winter and autumnal sacrifices. Some flay (the victims); some cook (their flesh); Some arrange (the meat); some adjust (the pieces of it). The officer of prayer sacrifices inside the temple gate [1], And all the sacrificial service is complete and brilliant. Grandly come our progenitors; Their spirits happily enjoy the offerings; Their filial descendant receives blessing :—They will reward him with great happiness, With myriads of years, life without end.

They attend to the furnaces with reverence; They prepare the trays, which are very large;— Some for the roast meat, some for the broiled. Wives presiding are still and reverent [2], Preparing the numerous (smaller) dishes. The guests and visitors [3] Present the cup all round [4]. Every form is according to rule; Every smile and word are as they should be. The spirits quietly come, And respond

---

   [1] The *Kû*, who is mentioned here, was evidently an officer, 'one who makes or recites prayers.' The sacrifice he is said to offer was, probably, a libation, the pouring out fragrant spirits, as a part of the general service, and likely to attract the hovering spirits of the departed, on their approach to the temple. Hence his act was performed just inside the gate.

   [2] 'Wives presiding,' i. e. the wife of the sacrificer, the principal in the service, and other ladies of the harem. The dishes under their care, the smaller dishes, would be those containing sauces, cakes, condiments, &c.

   [3] 'The guests and visitors' would be nobles and officers of different surnames from the sacrificer, chosen by divination to take part in the sacrificial service.

   [4] 'Present the cup all round' describes the ceremonies of drinking, which took place between the guests and visitors, the representatives of the dead, and the sacrificer.

with great blessings,—Myriads of years as the   367
(fitting) reward.

We are very much exhausted, And have performed every ceremony without error. The able officer of prayer announces (the will of the spirits) [1], And goes to the filial descendant .to convey it [1]:— 'Fragrant has been your filial sacrifice, And the spirits have enjoyed your spirits and viands. They confer on you a hundred blessings ; Each as it is desired, Each as sure as law. You have been exact and expeditious ; You have been correct and careful ; They will ever confer on you the choicest favours, In myriads and tens of myriads.'

The ceremonies having thus been completed, And the bells and drums having given their warning [2], The filial descendant goes to his place [3], And the able officer of prayer makes his announcement, 'The spirits have drunk to the full.' The great representatives of the dead then rise, And the bells and drums escort their withdrawal, (On which) the spirits tranquilly return (to whence they came) [4]. All the servants, and the presiding wives, Remove (the trays and dishes) without delay. The

---

[1] The officer of prayer had in the first place obtained, or professed to have obtained, this answer of the progenitors from their personators.

[2] The music now announced that the sacrificial service in the temple was ended.

[3] The sacrificer, or principal in the service, now left the place which he had occupied, descended from the hall, and took his position at the foot of the steps on the east,—the place appropriate to him in dismissing his guests.

[4] Where did they return to? According to *K*âng Hsüan, ' To heaven.'

368   (sacrificer's) uncles and cousins All repair to the private feast [1].

The musicians all go in to perform, And give their soothing aid at the second blessing [2]. Your [3] viands are set forth ; There is no dissatisfaction, but all feel happy. They drink to the full, and eat to the full ; Great and small, they bow their heads, (saying), 'The spirits enjoyed your spirits and viands, And will cause you to live long. Your sacrifices, all in their seasons, Are completely discharged by you. May your sons and your grandsons Never fail to perpetuate these services !'

ODE 6. THE HSIN NAN SHAN.

HUSBANDRY TRACED TO ITS FIRST AUTHOR ; DETAILS ABOUT IT, GOING ON TO THE SUBJECT OF SACRIFICES TO ANCESTORS.

The Preface refers this piece to the reign of king Yû ; but there is nothing in it to suggest the idea of its having been made in a time of disorder and misgovernment. 'The distant descendant' in the first stanza is evidently the principal in the sacrifice of the last two stanzas :—according to *K*û, a noble or great landholder in the royal domain ; according to others, some one of the kings of *K*âu. I incline myself to this latter view. The three pieces,

---

[1] These uncles and cousins were all present at the sacrifice, and of the same surname as the principal. The feast to them was to show his peculiar affection for his relatives.

[2] The feast was given in the apartment of the temple behind the hall where the sacrifice had been performed, so that the musicians are represented as going in to continue at the feast the music they had discoursed at the sacrifice.

[3] The transition to the second person here is a difficulty. We can hardly make the speech, made by some one of the guests on behalf of all the others, commence here. We must come to the conclusion that the ode was written, in compliment to the sacrificer, by one of the relatives who shared in the feast ; and so here he addresses him directly.

of which this is the middle one, seem all to be royal odes. The 369
mention of ' the southern hill ' strongly confirms this view.

Yes, (all about) that southern hill Was made
manageable by Yü [1]. Its plains and marshes being
opened up, It was made into fields by the distant
descendant. We define their boundaries, We
form their smaller divisions, And make the acres
lie, here to the south, there to the east.

The heavens overhead are one arch of clouds,
Snowing in multitudinous flakes ; There is super-
added the drizzling rain. When (the land) has
received the moistening, Soaking influence abundantly, It produces all our kinds of grain.

The boundaries and smaller divisions are nicely
adjusted, And the millets yield abundant crops,
The harvest of the distant descendant. We proceed to make therewith spirits and food, To
supply our representatives of the departed, and
our guests ;— To obtain long life, extending over
myriads of years.

In the midst of the fields are the huts [2], And

---

[1] There is here a recognition of the work of the great Yü, as
the real founder of the kingdom of China, extending the territory
of former elective chiefs, and opening up the country. ' The
southern hill' bounded the prospect to the south from the capital
of *K*âu, and hence the writer makes mention of it. He does not
mean to confine the work of Yü to that part of the country ; but,
on the other hand, there is nothing in his language to afford a confirmation to the account given in the third Part of the Shû of that
hero's achievements.

[2] In every *K*ing, or space of 900 Chinese acres or mâu, assigned
to eight families, there were in the centre 100 mâu of ' public
fields,' belonging to the government, and cultivated by the husbandmen in common. In this space of 100 mâu, two mâu and
a half were again assigned to each family, and on them were

370   along the bounding divisions are gourds. The fruit is sliced and pickled, To be presented to our great ancestors, That their distant descendant may have long life, And receive the blessing of Heaven [1].

We sacrifice (first) with clear spirits, And then follow with a red bull; Offering them to our ancestors, (Our lord) holds the knife with tinkling bells, To lay open the hair of the victim, And takes the blood and fat [2].

Then we present, then we offer; All round the fragrance is diffused. Complete and brilliant is the sacrificial service; Grandly come our ancestors. They will reward (their descendant) with great blessing, Long life, years without end.

ODE 7. THE PHÙ THIEN.

PICTURES OF HUSBANDRY, AND SACRIFICES CONNECTED WITH IT. HAPPY UNDERSTANDING BETWEEN THE PEOPLE AND THEIR SUPERIORS.

It is difficult to say who the 'I' in the piece is, but evidently he and the 'distant descendant' are different persons. I suppose he may have been an officer, who had charge of the farms, as we may call them, in the royal domain.

Bright are those extensive fields, A tenth of whose produce is annually levied [3]. I take the old

---

erected the huts in which they lived, while they were actively engaged in their agricultural labours.

[1] Here, as in so many other places, the sovereign Power, ruling in the lots of men, is referred to as Heaven.

[2] The fat was taken from the victim, and then burnt along with fragrant herbs, so as to form a cloud of incense. On the taking of the 'blood,' it is only said, that it was done to enable the sacrificer to announce that a proper victim had been slain.

[3] This line, literally, is, 'Yearly are taken ten (and a) thousand;' meaning the produce of ten acres in every hundred, and of a thousand in every ten thousand.

stores, And with them feed the husbandmen. From of old we have had good years ; And now I go to the south-lying acres, Where some are weeding, and some gather the earth about the roots. The millets look luxuriant; And in a spacious resting-place, I collect and encourage the men of greater promise[1].

With my vessels full of bright millet, And my pure victim-rams, We sacrificed at the altar of the spirits of the land, and at (the altars of those of the four) quarters[2]. That my fields are in such good condition Is matter of joy to the husbandmen. With lutes, and with drums beating, We will invoke the Father of Husbandry[3], And pray for sweet rain, To increase the produce of our millets, And to bless my men and their wives.

The distant descendant comes, When their wives and children Are bringing food to those (at work) in the south-lying acres. The surveyor of the fields (also) comes and is glad. He takes (of the food) on the left and the right, And tastes whether

---

[1] The general rule was that the sons of husbandmen should continue husbandmen; but their superior might select those among them in whom he saw promising abilities, and facilitate their advancement to the higher grade of officers.

[2] The sacrifices here mentioned were of thanksgiving at the end of the harvest of the preceding year. The one was to ' sovereign Earth,' supposed to be the supreme Power in correlation with Heaven, or, possibly, to the spirits supposed to preside over the productive energies of the land; the other to the spirits presiding over the four quarters of the sky, and ruling all atmospherical influences.

[3] This was the sacrifice that had been, or was about to be, offered in spring to ' the Father of Husbandry,'—probably the ancient mythical Tî, Shăn Năng.

372

it be good or not. The grain is well cultivated, all
the acres over; Good will it be and abundant. The
distant descendant has no displacency; The husbandmen are encouraged to diligence.

The crops of the distant descendant Look (thick)
as thatch, and (swelling) like a carriage-cover. His
stacks will stand like islands and mounds. He will
seek for thousands of granaries; He will seek for
tens of thousands of carts. The millets, the paddy,
and the maize Will awake the joy of the husbandmen; (And they will say), 'May he be rewarded
with great happiness, With myriads of years, life
without end!'

ODE 8. THE TÂ THIEN.

FURTHER PICTURES OF HUSBANDRY, AND SACRIFICES CONNECTED WITH IT.

Large are the fields, and various is the work to be
done. Having selected the seed, and looked after
the implements, So that all preparations have been
made for our labour, We take our sharp ploughshares, And commence on the south-lying acres.
We sow all the kinds of grain, Which grow up
straight and large, So that the wish of the distant
descendant is satisfied.

It ears and the fruit lies soft in its sheath; It
hardens and is of good quality; There is no wolf's-
tail grass nor darnel. We remove the insects that
eat the heart and the leaf, And those that eat the
roots and the joints, ·So that they shall not hurt
the young plants of our fields. May the spirit, the
Father of Husbandry [1], Lay hold of them, and put
them in the blazing fire!

---

[1] The ancient Shăn Năng, as in the preceding ode.

The clouds form in dense masses,　And the rain 373
comes down slowly.　May it first rain on our public
fields [1],　And then come to our private [1] !　Yonder
shall be young grain unreaped,　And here some
bundles ungathered ;　Yonder shall be handfuls left
on the ground,　And here ears untouched :—For
the benefit of the widow [2].

The distant descendant will come,　When their
wives and children　Are bringing food to those
(at work) on the south-lying acres.　The surveyor
of the fields (also) will come and be glad.　They
will come and offer pure sacrifices to (the spirits
of the four) quarters,　With their victims red and
black [3],　With their preparations of millet :—Thus
offering, thus sacrificing,　Thus increasing our bright
happiness.

The Seventh Decade, or that of Sang Hû.

ODE 1, STANZA 1.　THE SANG HÛ.

THE KING, ENTERTAINING THE CHIEF AMONG THE FEUDAL PRINCES,
EXPRESSES HIS ADMIRATION OF THEM, AND GOOD WISHES FOR THEM.

They flit about, the greenbeaks [4],　With their

---

[1] These are two famous lines, continually quoted as showing the
loyal attachment of the people to their superiors in those ancient
times.

[2] Compare the legislation of Moses, in connexion with the harvest, for the benefit of the poor, in Deuteronomy xxiv. 19–22.

[3] They would not sacrifice to these spirits all at once, or all
in one place, but in the several quarters as they went along on
their progress through the domain.　For each quarter the colour
of the victim was different.　A red victim was offered to the spirit
of the south, and a black to that of the north.

[4] The greenbeaks appeared in the second ode of the fifth
decade.　The bird had many names, and a beautiful plumage,

374   variegated wings. To be rejoiced in are these
princes! May they receive the blessing of Heaven[1]!

ODE 6, STANZAS 1 AND 2. THE PIN KIH KHÛ YEN.

AGAINST DRUNKENNESS. DRINKING ACCORDING TO RULE AT ARCHERY
CONTESTS AND THE SEASONAL SACRIFICES, AND DRINKING TO
EXCESS.

There are good grounds for referring the authorship of this piece
to duke Wû of Wei (B.C. 812 to 758), who played an important
part in the kingdom, during the affairs which terminated in
the death of king Yû, and the removal of the capital from
Hâo to Lo. The piece, we may suppose, is descriptive of
things as they were at the court of king Yû.

When the guests first approach the mats[2], They
take their places on the left and the right in an
orderly manner. The dishes of bamboo and wood
are arranged in rows, With the sauces and kernels
displayed in them. The spirits are mild and good,
And they drink, all equally reverent. The bells and
drums are properly arranged[3], And they raise their
pledge-cups with order and ease[4]. (Then) the great

---

made use of here to compliment the princes on the elegance of
their manners, and perhaps also the splendour of their equipages.
The bird is here called the 'mulberry Hû,' because it appeared
when the mulberry tree was coming into leaf.

[1] This line is to be understood, with Kû Hsî, as a prayer of
the king to Heaven for his lords.

[2] The mats were spread on the floor, and also the viands of the
feast. Chairs and tables were not used in that early time.

[3] The archery took place in the open court, beneath the hall or
raised apartment, where the entertainment was given. Near the
steps leading up to the hall was the regular place for the bells and
drums, but it was necessary now to remove them more on one side,
to leave the ground clear for the archers.

[4] The host first presented a cup to the guest, which the latter
drank, and then he returned a cup to the host. After this pre-

target is set up; The bows and arrows are made 375
ready for the shooting. The archers are arranged
in classes ; 'Show your skill in shooting,' (it is said
by one). ' I shall hit that mark ' (is the response),
' And pray you to drink the cup¹.'

The dancers move with their flutes to the notes
of the organ and drum, While all the instruments
perform in harmony. All this is done to please
the meritorious ancestors, Along with the observance of all ceremonies. When all the ceremonies
have been fully performed, Grandly and fully,
(The personators of the dead say), 'We confer on
you great blessings, And may your descendants
also be happy!' These are happy and delighted,
And each of them exerts his ability. A guest²
draws the spirits ; An attendant enters again with
a cup, And fills it,—the cup of rest². Thus are
performed your seasonal ceremonies ³.

---

liminary ceremony, the company all drank to one another,—'took
up their cups,' as it is here expressed.

¹ Each defeated archer was obliged to drink a large cup of
spirits as a penalty.

² This guest was, it is supposed, the eldest of all the scions of
the royal House present on the occasion. At this point, he presented a cup to the chief among the personators of the ancestors,
and received one in return. He then proceeded to draw more
spirits from one of the vases of supply, and an attendant came in
and filled other cups,—we may suppose for all the other personators. This was called 'the cup of répose or comfort;' and the
sacrifice was thus concluded,—in all sobriety and decency.

³ The three stanzas that follow this, graphically descriptive of the
drunken revel, are said to belong to the feast of the royal relatives
that followed the conclusion of the sacrificial service, and is called
'the second blessing' in the sixth ode of the preceding decade.
This opinion probably is correct; but as the piece does not itself
say so, and because of the absence from the text of religious sentiments, I have not given the stanzas here.

376　　　The Eighth Decade, or that of Po Hwâ.

ODE 5, STANZAS 1 AND 2.　THE PO HWÂ.

THE QUEEN OF KING YÛ COMPLAINS OF BEING DEGRADED AND
FORSAKEN.

The fibres from the white-flowered rush　Are
bound with the white grass[1]. This man's sending
me away makes me dwell solitary.

The light and brilliant clouds　Bedew the rush
and the grass[2]. The way of Heaven is hard and
difficult[3];—This man does not conform (to good
principle).

---

[1] The stalks of the rush were tied with the grass in bundles, in
order to be steeped;—an operation which ladies in those days might
be supposed to be familiar with. The two lines suggest the idea
of the close connexion between the two plants, and the necessa-
riness of the one to the other;—as it should be between husband
and wife.

[2] The clouds bestowed their dewy influence on the plants, while
her husband neglected the speaker.

[3] 'The way of Heaven' is equivalent to our 'The course of
Providence.' The lady's words are, literally, 'The steps of Heaven.'
She makes but a feeble wail; but in Chinese opinion discharges
thereby, all the better, the duty of a wife.

The First Decade, or that of Wăn Wang.

ODE 1. THE WĂN WANG.

CELEBRATING KING WĂN, DEAD AND ALIVE, AS THE FOUNDER OF THE DYNASTY OF *K*âu, SHOWING HOW HIS VIRTUES DREW TO HIM THE FAVOURING REGARD OF HEAVEN OR GOD, AND MADE HIM A BRIGHT PATTERN TO HIS DESCENDANTS AND THEIR MINISTERS.

The composition of this and the other pieces of this decade is attributed to the duke of *K*âu, king Wăn's son, and was intended by him for the benefit of his nephew, the young king *Kh*ăng. Wăn, it must be borne in mind, was never actually king of China. He laid the foundations of the kingly power, which was established by his son king Wû, and consolidated by the duke of *K*âu. The title of king was given to him and to others by the duke, according to the view of filial piety, that has been referred to on p. 299.

King Wăn is on high. Oh! bright is he in heaven. Although *K*âu was an old country, The (favouring) appointment lighted on it recently [1]. Illustrious was the House of *K*âu, And the

---

[1] The family of *K*âu, according to its traditions, was very ancient, but it did not occupy the territory of *K*âu, from which it subsequently took its name, till b.c. 1326; and it was not till the time of Wăn (b.c. 1231 to 1135) that the divine purpose concerning its supremacy in the kingdom was fully manifested.

378 appointment of God came at the proper season. King Wăn ascends and descends On the left and the right of God [1].

Full of earnest activity was king Wăn, And his fame is without end. The gifts (of God) to *K*âu Extend to the descendants of king Wăn, In the direct line and the collateral branches for a hundred generations [2]. All the officers of *K*âu Shall (also) be illustrious from age to age.

They shall be illustrious from age to age, Zealously and reverently pursuing their plans. Admirable are the many officers, Born in this royal kingdom. The royal kingdom is able to produce them, The supporters of (the House of) *K*âu. Numerous is the array of officers, And by them king Wăn enjoys his repose.

Profound was king Wăn; Oh! continuous and bright was his feeling of reverence. Great is the appointment of Heaven! There were the descendants of (the sovereigns of) Shang [3]—The descendants of the sovereigns of Shang Were in number more

---

[1] According to *K*û Hsî, the first and last two lines of this stanza are to be taken of the spirit of Wăn in heaven. Attempts have been made to explain them otherwise, or rather to explain them away. But language could not more expressly intimate the existence of a supreme personal God, and the continued existence of the human spirit.

[2] The text, literally, is, 'The root and the branches:' the root (and stem) denoting the eldest sons, by the recognised queen, succeeding to the throne; and the branches, the other sons by the queen and concubines. The former would grow up directly from the root; and the latter, the chief nobles of the kingdom, would constitute the branches of the great *K*âu tree.

[3] The Shang or Yin dynasty of kings superseded by *K*âu.

than hundreds of thousands. But when God gave 379
the command, They became subject to *K*âu.

They became subject to *K*âu, (For) the appointment of Heaven is not unchangeable. The officers
of Yin, admirable and alert, Assist at the libations in our capital[1]. They assist at those
libations, Always wearing the hatchet-figures on
their lower garments and their peculiar cap[2].
O ye loyal ministers of the king, Ever think
of your ancestor!

Ever think of your ancestor, Cultivating your
virtue, Always seeking to accord with the will
(of Heaven):—So shall you be seeking for much
happiness, Before Yin lost the multitudes, (Its
kings) were the correlates of God[3]. Look to Yin
as a beacon; The great appointment is not easily
preserved.

The appointment is not easily (preserved):—Do
not cause your own extinction. Display and make
bright your righteousness and fame, And look
at (the fate of) Yin in the light of Heaven. The
doings of high Heaven Have neither sound nor

---

[1] These officers of Yin would be the descendants of the Yin
kings and of their principal nobles, scions likewise of the Yin stock.
They would assist, at the court of *K*âu, at the services in the ancestral temple, which began with a libation of fragrant spirits to
bring down the spirits of the departed.

[2] These, differing from the dress worn by the representatives
of the ruling House, were still worn by the officers of Yin or Shang,
by way of honour, and also by way of warning.

[3] There was God in heaven hating none, desiring the good of
all the people; there were the sovereigns on earth, God's vicegerents,
maintained by him so long as they carried out in their government
his purpose of good.

380　smell [1].　Take your pattern from king Wăn,　And the myriad regions will repose confidence in you.

ODE 2. THE TÂ MING.

HOW THE APPOINTMENT OF HEAVEN OR GOD CAME FROM HIS FATHER TO KING WĂN, AND DESCENDED TO HIS SON, KING WÛ, WHO OVER-THREW THE DYNASTY OF SHANG BY HIS VICTORY AT MÛ; CELE-BRATING ALSO THE MOTHER AND WIFE OF KING WĂN.

The illustration of illustrious (virtue) is required below, And the dread majesty is on high [2]. Heaven is not readily to be relied on; It is not easy to be king. Yin's rightful heir to the heavenly seat Was not permitted to possess the kingdom.

Zăn, the second of the princesses of *K*îh [3], From (the domain of) Yin-shang, Came to be married to (the prince of) *K*âu, And became his wife in his

---

[1] These two lines are quoted in the last paragraph of the Doctrine of the Mean, as representing the ideal of perfect virtue. They are indicative of Power, operating silently, and not to be perceived by the senses, but resistless in its operations.

[2] 'The first two lines,' says the commentator Yen *3*ăan, 'contain a general sentiment, expressing the principle that governs the relation between Heaven and men. According to line 1, the good or evil of a ruler cannot be concealed; according to 2, Heaven, in giving its favour or taking it away, acts with strict decision. When below there is the illustrious illustration (of virtue), that reaches up on high. When above there is the awful majesty, that exercises a survey below. The relation between Heaven and men ought to excite our awe.'

[3] The state of *K*îh must have been somewhere in the royal domain of Yin. Its lords had the surname of *Z*ăn, and the second daughter of the House became the wife of *K*î of *K*âu. She is called in the eighth line Thâi-*s*ăn, by which name she is still famous in China. 'She commenced,' it is said, 'the instruction of her child when he was still in her womb, looking on no improper sight, listening to no licentious sound, uttering no word of pride.'

capital. Both she and king *Kî* Were entirely   381
virtuous. (Then) Thâi-*z*ăn became pregnant, And
gave birth to our king Wăn.

This king Wăn, Watchfully and reverently, With
entire intelligence served God, And so secured the
great blessing. His virtue was without deflection;
And in consequence he received (the allegiance of)
the states from all quarters.

Heaven surveyed this lower world; And its
appointment lighted (on king Wăn). In his early
years, It made for him a mate[1];—On the north
of the Hsiâ, On the banks of the Wei. When
king Wăn would marry, There was the lady in
a large state.[2]

In a large state was the lady, Like a fair
denizen of heaven. The ceremonies determined
the auspiciousness (of the union)[3], And in person
he met her on the Wei. Over it he made a
bridge of boats; The glory (of the occasion) was
illustrious.

The favouring appointment was from Heaven,
Giving the throne to our king Wăn, In the capital
of *K*âu. The lady-successor was from Hsin, Its
eldest daughter, who came to marry him. She was
blessed to give birth to king Wû, Who was preserved, and helped, and received (also) the appoint-

---

[1] Heaven is here represented as arranging for the fulfilment of
its purposes beforehand.

[2] The name of the state was Hsin, and it must have been near
the Hsiâ and the Wei, somewhere in the south-east of the present
Shen-hsî.

[3] 'The ceremonies' would be various; first of all, divination by
means of the tortoise-shell.

382 ment, And in accordance with it smote the great Shang.

The troops of Yin-shang Were collected like a forest, And marshalled in the wilderness of Mû. We rose (to the crisis); 'God is with you,' (said Shang-fû to the king), 'Have no doubts in your heart [1].'

The wilderness of Mû spread out extensive; Bright shone the chariots of sandal; The teams of bays, black-maned and white-bellied, galloped along; The Grand-Master Shang-fû Was like an eagle on the wing, Assisting king Wû, Who at one onset smote the great Shang. That morning's encounter was followed by a clear, bright (day).

ODE 3. THE MIEN.

SMALL BEGINNINGS AND SUBSEQUENT GROWTH OF THE HOUSE OF *K*ÂU IN *K*ÂU. ITS REMOVAL FROM PIN UNDER THAN-FÛ, WITH ITS FIRST SETTLEMENT IN *K*ÂU, WITH THE PLACE THEN GIVEN TO THE BUILDING OF THE ANCESTRAL TEMPLE, AND THE ALTAR TO THE SPIRITS OF THE LAND. CONSOLIDATION OF ITS FORTUNES BY KING WĂN.

'The ancient duke Than-fû' was the grandfather of king Wăn, and was canonized by the duke of *K*âu as 'king Thâi.' As mentioned in a note on p. 316, he was the first of his family to settle in *K*âu, removing there from Pin, the site of their earlier settlement, 'the country about the *Kh*ü and the *Kh*î.'

In long trains ever increasing grow the gourds [2]. When (our) people first sprang, From the country about the *Kh*ü and the *Kh*î [3], The ancient duke

---

[1] See the account of the battle of Mû in the third Book of the fifth Part of the Shû. Shang-fû was one of Wû's principal leaders and counsellors, his 'Grand-Master Shang-fû' in the next stanza.

[2] As a gourd grows and extends, with a vast development of its tendrils and leaves, so had the House of *K*âu increased.

[3] These were two rivers in the territory of Pin, which name still

Than-fû Made for them kiln-like huts and caves,
Ere they had yet any houses [1].

The ancient duke Than-fû Came in the morning, galloping his horses, Along the banks of the western rivers, To the foot of mount *Kh*î[2]; And there he and the lady *K*iang[3] Came and together looked out for a site.

The plain of *K*âu looked beautiful and rich, With its violets, and sowthistles (sweet) as dumplings. There he began by consulting (with his followers); There he singed the tortoise-shell, (and divined). The responses were there to stay and then; And they proceeded there to build[4].

He encouraged the people, and settled them; Here on the left, there on the right. He divided the ground, and subdivided it; He dug the ditches; he defined the acres. From the east to the west, There was nothing which he did not take in hand[5].

---

remains in the small department of Pin *K*âu, in Shen-hsî. The *Kh*ü flows into the Lo, and the *Kh*î into the Wei.

[1] According to this ode then, up to the time of Than-fû, the *K*âu people had only had the dwellings here described; but this is not easily reconciled with other accounts, or even with other stanzas of this piece.

[2] See a graphic account of the circumstances in which this migration took place, in the fifteenth chapter of the second Part of the first Book of Mencius, very much to the honour of the ancient duke.

[3] This lady is known as Thâi-*k*iang, the worthy predecessor of Thâi-*s*ăn.

[4] This stanza has reference to the choice—by council and divination—of a site for what should be the chief town of the new settlement.

[5] This stanza describes the general arrangements for the occupancy and cultivation of the plain of *K*âu, and the distribution of the people over it.

384   He called his Superintendent of Works; He called his Minister of Instruction; And charged them with the rearing of the houses. With the line they made everything straight; They bound the frame-boards tight, so that they should rise regularly: Uprose the ancestral temple in its solemn grandeur [1].

Crowds brought the earth in baskets; They threw it with shouts into the frames; They beat it with responsive blows. They pared the walls repeatedly, till they sounded strong. Five thousand cubits of them arose together, So that the roll of the great drums did not overpower (the noise of the builders)[2].

They reared the outer gate (of the palace), Which rose in lofty state. They set up the gate of audience, Which rose severe and exact. They reared the great altar to the spirits of the land, From which all great movements should proceed [3].

---

[1] This stanza describes the preparations and processes for erecting the buildings of the new city. The whole took place under the direction of two officers, in whom we have the germ probably of the Six Heads of the Boards or Departments, whose functions are described in the Shû and the Official Book of *K*âu. The materials of the buildings were earth and lime pounded together in frames, as is still to be seen in many parts of the country. The first great building taken in hand was the ancestral temple. Than-fû would make a home for the spirits of his fathers, before he made one for himself. However imperfectly directed, the religious feeling asserted the supremacy which it ought to possess.

[2] The bustle and order of the building all over the city is here graphically set forth.

[3] Than-fû was now at leisure to build the palace for himself, which appears to have been not a very large building, though the Chinese names of its gates are those belonging to the two which

Thus though he could not prevent the rage   385
of his foes [1], He did not let fall his own fame.
The oaks and the buckthorns were (gradually)
thinned, And roads for travellers were opened.
The hordes of the Khwăn disappeared, Startled
and panting.   .

(The chiefs of) Yü and Zui [2] were brought to an
agreement By king Wăn's stimulating their natural
virtue. Then, I may say, some came to him, previously not knowing him; Some, drawn the last
by the first; Some, drawn by his rapid successes; And some by his defence (of the weak)
from insult.

---

were peculiar to the palaces of the kings of Kâu in the subsequent
times of the dynasty. Outside the palace were the altars appropriate to the spirits of the four quarters of the land, the 'great'
or royal altar being peculiar to the kings, though the one built by
Than-fû is here so named. All great undertakings, and such as
required the co-operation of all the people, were preceded by a
solemn sacrifice at this altar.

   [1] Referring to Than-fû's relations with the wild hordes, described
by Mencius, and which obliged him to leave Pin. As the new
settlement in Kâu grew, they did not dare to trouble it.

   [2] The poet passes on here to the time of king Wăn. The story of
the chiefs of Yü and Zui (two states on the east of the Ho) is this:—
They had a quarrel about a strip of territory, to which each of them
laid claim. Going to lay their dispute before the lord of Kâu, as soon
as they entered his territory, they saw the ploughers readily yielding
the furrow, and travellers yielding the path, while men and women
avoided one another on the road, and old people had no burdens
to carry. At his court, they beheld the officers of each inferior
grade giving place to those above them. They became ashamed
of their own quarrel, agreed to let the disputed ground be an open
territory, and withdrew without presuming to appear before Wăn.
When this affair was noised abroad, more than forty states, it
is said, tendered their submission to Kâu.

[1]   C C

386

ODE 4, STANZAS 1 AND 2. THE YÎ PHO.

IN PRAISE OF KING WĂN, CELEBRATING HIS INFLUENCE, DIGNITY IN THE
TEMPLE SERVICES, ACTIVITY, AND CAPACITY TO RULE.

Abundant is the growth of the buckthorn and
shrubby trees, Supplying firewood; yea, stores of
it [1]. Elegant and dignified was our prince.and king;
On the left and the right they hastened to him.

Elegant and dignified was our prince and king;
On his left and his right they bore their half-
mace (libation-cups) [2] :—They bore them with solemn
gravity, As beseemed such eminent officers.

ODE 5. THE HAN LÛ.

IN PRAISE OF THE VIRTUE OF KING WĂN, BLESSED BY HIS ANCESTORS,
AND RAISED TO THE HIGHEST DIGNITY WITHOUT SEEKING OF HIS
OWN.

Look at the foot of the Han [3], How abundantly
grow the hazel and arrow-thorn [4]. Easy and self-
possessed was our prince, In his pursuit of dignity
(still) easy and self-possessed.

Massive is that libation-cup of jade, With the

---

[1] It is difficult to trace the connexion between these allusive
lines and the rest of the piece.

[2] Here we have the lord of *K*âu in his ancestral temple, assisted
by his ministers or great officers in pouring out the libations to the
spirits of the departed. The libation-cup was fitted with a handle
of jade, that used by the king having a complete kwei, the obelisk-
like symbol of rank, while the cups used by a minister had for a
handle only half a kwei.

[3] Where mount Han was cannot now be determined.

[4] As the foot of the hill was favourable to vegetable growth,
so were king Wăn's natural qualities to his distinction and
advancement.

yellow liquid sparkling in it [1].   Easy and self-pos-   387
sessed was our prince,   The fit recipient of blessing
and dignity.

The hawk flies up to heaven,   The fishes leap
in the deep [2].   Easy and self-possessed was our
prince :—Did he not exert an influence on men ?

His clear spirits were in the vessels ;   His red
bull was ready [3];—To offer, to sacrifice,   To increase
his bright happiness.

Thick grow the oaks and the buckthorn,   Which
the people use for fuel [4].   Easy and self-possessed
was our prince,   Cheered and encouraged by the
spirits [4].

Luxuriant are the dolichos and other creepers,
Clinging to the branches and stems.   Easy and self-
possessed was our prince,   Seeking for happiness
by no crooked ways.

ODE 6.   THE SZE *K*ÂI.

THE VIRTUE OF WĂN, WITH HIS FILIAL PIETY AND CONSTANT REVERENCE,
AND THEIR WONDERFUL EFFECTS.   THE EXCELLENT CHARACTER OF
HIS MOTHER AND WIFE.

Pure and reverent was Thâi *Z*ăn [5],   The mother
of king Wăn.   Loving was she to *K*âu *K*iang [6];—

---

[1] As a cup of such quality was the proper receptacle for the
yellow, herb-flavoured spirits, so was the character of Wăn such
that all blessing must accrue to him.

[2] It is the nature of the hawk to fly and of fishes to swim, and so
there went out an influence from Wăn unconsciously to himself.

[3] Red, we have seen, was the proper colour for victims in the
ancestral temple of *K*âu.

[4] As it was natural for the people to take the wood and use it,
so it was natural for the spirits of his ancestors, and spiritual
beings generally, to bless king Wăn.

[5] Thâi *Z*ăn is celebrated, above, in the second ode.

[6] *K*âu *K*iang is ' the lady *K*iang ' of ode 3, the wife of Than-fû or

CC 2

388

A wife becoming the House of *K*âu. Thâi Sze[1] inherited her excellent fame, And from her came a hundred sons[2].

He conformed to the example of his ancestors, And their spirits had no occasion for complaint. Their spirits had no occasion for dissatisfaction; And his example acted on his wife, Extended to his brethren, And was felt by all the clans and states.

Full of harmony was he in his palace; Full of reverence in the ancestral temple. Unseen (by men), he still felt that he was under inspection[3]: Unweariedly he maintained his virtue.

Though he could not prevent (some) great calamities, His brightness and magnanimity were without stain. Without previous instruction he did what was right; Without admonition he went on (in the path of goodness).

So, grown up men became virtuous (through him), And young men made (constant) attainments. (Our) ancient prince never felt weariness, And from him were the fame and eminence of his officers.

---

king Thâi, who came with him from Pin. She is here called *K*âu, as having married the lord of *K*âu.

[1] Thâi Sze, the wife of Wăn, we are told in ode 2, was from the state of Hsin. The surname Sze shows that its lords must have been descended from the Great Yü.

[2] We are not to suppose that Thâi Sze had herself a hundred sons. She had ten, and her freedom from jealousy so encouraged the fruitfulness of the harem, that all the sons born in it are ascribed to her.

[3] Where there was no human eye to observe him, Wăn still felt that he was open to the observation of spiritual beings.

Ode 7. The Hwang Î.

SHOWING THE RISE OF THE HOUSE OF *K*ÂU TO THE SOVEREIGNTY OF THE
KINGDOM THROUGH THE FAVOUR OF GOD. THE ACHIEVEMENTS OF
KINGS THÂI AND *K*Î, AND ESPECIALLY OF KING WĂN.

Great is God, Beholding this lower world in majesty. He surveyed the four quarters (of the kingdom), Seeking for some one to give establishment to the people. Those two earlier dynasties [1] Had failed to satisfy him with their government; So, throughout the various states, He sought and considered For one on whom he might confer the rule. Hating all the great states, He turned his kind regards on the west, And there gave a settlement (to king Thâi).

(King Thâi) raised up and removed The dead trunks and the fallen trees. He dressed and regulated The bushy clumps and the (tangled) rows. He opened up and cleared The tamarisk trees and the stave trees. He hewed and thinned The mountain mulberry trees. God having brought about the removal thither of this intelligent ruler, The Kwan hordes fled away [2]. Heaven had raised up a helpmeet for him, And the appointment he had received was made sure.

God surveyed the hills, Where the oaks and the buckthorn were thinned, And paths made through the firs and cypresses. God, who had raised the

---

[1] Those of Hsiâ and Shang.

[2] The same as 'the hordes of the Khwăn' in ode 3. Mr. T. W. Kingsmill says that 'Kwan' here should be 'Chun,' and charges the transliteration Kwan with error (Journal of the Royal Asiatic Society for April, 1878). He had not consulted his dictionary for the proper pronunciation of the Chinese character.

390   state, raised up a proper ruler[1] for it,—From the time of Thâi-po and king Kî (this was done)[1]. Now this king Kî In his heart was full of brotherly duty. Full of duty to his elder brother, He gave himself the more to promote the prosperity (of the country), And secured to him the glory (of his act)[2]. He accepted his dignity and did not lose it, And (ere long his family) possessed the whole kingdom.

This king Kî Was gifted by God with the power of judgment, So that the fame of his virtue silently grew. His virtue was highly intelligent,—Highly intelligent, and of rare discrimination; Able to lead, able to rule, To rule over this great country; Rendering a cordial submission, effecting a cordial union[3]. When (the sway) came to king Wăn, His

---

[1] King Wăn is 'the proper ruler' intended here, and the next line intimates that this was determined before there was any likelihood of his becoming the ruler even of the territory of Kâu;—another instance of the foreseeing providence ascribed to God. Thâi-po was the eldest son of king Thâi, and king Kî was, perhaps, only the third. The succession ought to have come to Thâi-po; but he, seeing the sage virtues of Khang (afterwards king Wăn), the son of Kî, and seeing also that king Thâi was anxious that this boy should ultimately become ruler of Kâu, voluntarily withdrew from Kâu altogether, and left the state to Kî and his son. See the remark of Confucius on Thâi-po's conduct, in the Analects, VIII, i.

[2] The lines from six to ten speak of king Kî in his relation to his elder brother. He accepted Thâi-po's act without any failure of his own duty to him, and by his own improvement of it, made his brother more glorious through it. His feeling of brotherly duty was simply the natural instinct of his heart. Having accepted the act, it only made him the more anxious to promote the good of the state, and thus he made his brother more glorious by showing what advantages accrued from his resignation and withdrawal from Kâu.

[3] This line refers to Kî's maintenance of his own loyal duty

virtue left nothing to be dissatisfied with, He re-   391
ceived the blessing of God, And it was extended
to his descendants.

God said to king Wăn[1], 'Be not like those who
reject this and cling to that; Be not like those who
are ruled by their likings and desires;' So he grandly
ascended before others to the height (of virtue). The
people of Mî[2] were disobedient, Daring to oppose
our great country, And invaded Yüan, marching to
Kung[3]. The king rose, majestic in his wrath; He
marshalled his troops, To stop the invading foes;
To consolidate the prosperity of *K*âu; To meet
the expectations of all under heaven.

He remained quietly in the capital, But (his
troops) went on from the borders of Yüan. They
ascended our lofty ridges, And (the enemy) arrayed
no forces on our hills, On our hills, small or large,
Nor drank at our springs, Our springs or our
pools. He then determined the finest of the plains,
And settled on the south of *K*hî[4], On the banks of

---

to the dynasty of Shang, and his making all the states under his
presidency loyal also.

[1] The statement that 'God spake to king Wăn,' repeated in
stanza 7, vexes the Chinese critics, and they find in it simply
an intimation that Wăn's conduct was 'in accordance with the
will of Heaven.' I am not prepared to object to that view of
the meaning; but it is plain that the writer, in giving such a form
to his meaning, must have conceived of God as a personal Being,
knowing men's hearts, and able to influence them.

[2] Mî or Mî-hsü was a state in the present *K*ing-ning *K*âu, of
Phing-liang department, Kan-sû.

[3] Yüan was a state adjacent to Mî,—the present *K*ing *K*âu,
and Kung must have been a place or district in it.

[4] Wăn, it appears, made now a small change in the site of his
capital, but did not move to Făng, where he finally settled.

392   the Wei, The centre of all the states, The resort of the lower people.

God said to king Wăn, ' I am pleased with your intelligent virtue, Not loudly proclaimed nor pourtrayed, Without extravagance or changeableness, Without consciousness of effort on your part, In accordance with the pattern of God.' God said to king Wăn, ' Take measures against the country of your foes. Along with your brethren, Get ready your scaling ladders, And your engines of onfall and assault, To attack the walls of *Kh*ung¹.'

The engines of onfall and assault were (at first) gently plied, Against the walls of *Kh*ung high and and great; Captives for the question were brought in, one after another; The left ears (of the slain) were taken leisurely². He had sacrificed to God and to the Father of War³, Thus seeking to induce

---

¹ *Kh*ung was a state, in the present district of Hû, department Hsî-an, Shen-hsî. His conquest of *Kh*ung was an important event in the history of king Wăn. He moved his capital to it, advancing so much farther towards the east, nearer to the domain of Shang. According to Sze-mâ *Kh*ien the marquis of *Kh*ung had slandered the lord of *K*âu, who was president of the states of the west, to *K*âu-hsin, the king of Shang, and our hero was put in prison. His friends succeeded in effecting his deliverance by means of various gifts to the tyrant, and he was reinstated in the west with more than his former power. Three years afterwards he attacked the marquis of *Kh*ung.

² So far the siege was prosecuted slowly and, so to say, tenderly, Wăn hoping that the enemy would be induced to surrender without great sacrifice of life.

³ The sacrifice to God had been offered in *K*âu, at the commencement of the expedition; that to the Father of War, on the army's arriving at the borders of *Kh*ung. We can hardly tell who is intended by the Father of War. *K*û Hsî and others would require the plural ' Fathers,' saying the sacrifice was to Hwang Tî and *Kh*ih Yû, who are found engaged in hostilities far back in the

submission, And throughout the region none had
dared to insult him. The engines of onfall and
assault were (then) vigorously plied, Against the
walls of *Kh*ung very strong. He attacked it, and
let loose all his forces; He extinguished (its sacrifices)¹, and made an end of its existence; And
throughout the kingdom none dared to oppose him.

ODE 9. THE HSIÂ WÛ.

IN PRAISE OF KING WÛ, WALKING IN THE WAYS OF HIS FOREFATHERS,
AND BY HIS FILIAL PIETY SECURING THE THRONE TO HIMSELF AND
HIS POSTERITY.

Successors tread in the steps (of their predecessors)
in our *K*âu. For generations there had been wise
kings; The three sovereigns were in heaven²;
And king (Wû) was their worthy successor in his
capital³.

King (Wû) was their worthy successor in his
capital, Rousing himself to seek for the hereditary
virtue, Always striving to be in accordance with the

---

mythical period of Chinese history. But *Kh*ih Yû appears as a
rebel, or opposed to the One man in all the country who was then
fit to rule. It is difficult to imagine how they could be associated,
and sacrificed to together.

¹ The extinction of its sacrifices was the final act in the extinction of a state. Any members of its ruling House who might
survive could no longer sacrifice to their ancestors as having been
men of princely dignity. The family was reduced to the ranks
of the people.

² 'The three sovereigns,' or 'wise kings,' are to be understood
of the three celebrated in ode 7,—Thâi, *K*î, and Wăn. We are
thus obliged, with all Chinese scholars, to understand this ode
of king Wû. The statement that 'the three kings were in heaven'
is very express.

³ The capital here is Hâo, to which Wû removed in B.C. 1134,
the year after his father's death. It was on the east of the river
Făng, and only about eight miles from Wăn's capital of Făng.

393

394   will (of Heaven); And thus he secured the confidence due to a king.

He secured the confidence due to a king, And became the pattern of all below him. Ever thinking how to be filial, His filial mind was the model (which he supplied).

Men loved him, the One man, And responded (to his example) with a docile virtue. Ever thinking how to be filial, He brilliantly continued the doings (of his fathers).

Brilliantly! and his posterity, Continuing to walk in the steps of their forefathers, For myriads of years, Will receive the blessing of Heaven.

They will receive the blessing of Heaven, And from the four quarters (of the kingdom) will felicitations come to them. For myriads of years Will there not be their helpers?

ODE 10. THE WĂN WANG YÛ SHĂNG.

THE PRAISE OF KINGS WĂN AND WÛ :—HOW THE FORMER DISPLAYED HIS MILITARY PROWESS ONLY TO SECURE THE TRANQUILLITY OF THE PEOPLE ; AND HOW THE LATTER, IN ACCORDANCE WITH THE RESULTS OF DIVINATION, ENTERED IN HIS NEW CAPITAL OF HÂO, INTO THE SOVEREIGNTY OF THE KINGDOM WITH THE SINCERE GOOD WILL OF ALL THE PEOPLE.

King Wăn is famous; Yea, he is very famous. What he sought was the repose (of the people); What he saw was the completion (of his work). A sovereign true was king Wăn!

King Wăn received the appointment (from Heaven), And achieved his martial success. Having overthrown *Kh*ung[1] He fixed his (capital) city in Făng[2]. A sovereign true was king Wăn!

---

[1] As related in ode 7.
[2] Făng had, probably, been the capital of *Kh*ung, and Wăn

He repaired the walls along the (old) moat. His establishing himself in Fǎng was according to (the pattern of his forefathers), It was not that he was in haste to gratify his wishes ;—It was to show the filial duty that had come down to him. A sovereign true was the royal prince !

His royal merit was brightly displayed By those walls of Fǎng. There were collected (the sympathies of the people of) the four quarters, Who regarded the royal prince as their protector. A sovereign true was the royal prince !

The Fǎng-water flowed on to the east (of the city), Through the meritorious labour of Yü. There were collected (the sympathies of the people of) the four quarters, Who would have the great king as their ruler. A sovereign true was the great king[1] !

In the capital of Hâo he built his hall with its circlet of water[2]. From the west to the east, From the south to the north, There was not a thought but did him homage. A sovereign true was the great king !

He examined and divined, did the king, About settling in the capital of Hâo. The tortoise-shell decided the site[3], And king Wû completed the city. A sovereign true was king Wû !

395

---

removed to it, simply making the necessary repairs and alterations. This explains how we find nothing about the divinations which should have preceded so important a step as the founding of a new capital.

[1] The writer has passed on to Wû, who did actually become king.

[2] See on the third of the Praise Odes of Lû in Part IV.

[3] Hâo was built by Wû, and hence we have the account of his divining about the site and the undertaking.

396   By the Făng-water grows the white millet [1];—
Did not king Wû show wisdom in his employment of officers? He would leave his plans to his
descendants, And secure comfort and support to
his son. A sovereign true was king Wû!

The Second Decade, or that of Shăng Min.

ODE 1. THE SHĂNG MIN.

THE LEGEND OF HÂU-KÎ :—HIS CONCEPTION; HIS BIRTH; THE PERILS
OF HIS INFANCY; HIS BOYISH HABITS OF AGRICULTURE; HIS SUBSE-
QUENT METHODS AND TEACHING OF AGRICULTURE; HIS FOUNDING
OF CERTAIN SACRIFICES; AND THE HONOURS OF SACRIFICE PAID TO
HIM BY THE HOUSE OF KÂU.

Of Hâu-kî there is some notice on the tenth ode of the first
decade of the Sacrificial Odes of Kâu. To him the kings of
Kâu traced their lineage. Of Kiang Yüan, his mother, our
knowledge is very scanty. It is said that she was a daughter
of the House of Thâi, which traced its lineage up to Shăn-nung
in præhistoric times. From the first stanza of this piece it
appears that she was married, and had been so for some time
without having any child. But who her husband was it is
impossible to say with certainty. As the Kâu surname was Kî,
he must have been one of the descendants of Hwang Tî.

The first birth of (our) people [2]   Was from Kiang
Yüan. How did she give birth to (our) people?
She had presented a pure offering and sacrificed [3],

---

[1] 'The white millet,' a valuable species, grown near the Făng,
suggests to the writer the idea of all the men of ability whom Wû
collected around him.

[2] Our 'people' is of course the people of Kâu. The whole
piece is about the individual from whom the House of Kâu sprang,
of which were the kings of the dynasty so called.

[3] To whom Kiang Yüan sacrificed and prayed we are not told,
but I receive the impression that it was to God,—see the next
stanza,—and that she did so all alone with the special object which
is mentioned.

That her childlessness might be taken away. She   397
then trod on a toe-print made by God, and was
moved[1], In the large place where she rested. She
became pregnant; she dwelt retired; She gave
birth to, and nourished (a son), Who was Hâu-*kî*.

When she had fulfilled her months, Her first-
bórn son (came forth) like a lamb. There was no
bursting, nor rending, No injury, no hurt; Showing how wonderful he would be. Did not God give
her the comfort? Had he not accepted her pure
offering and sacrifice, So that thus easily she
brought forth her son?

He was placed in a narrow lane, But the sheep
and oxen protected him with loving care[2]. He was
placed in a wide forest, Where he was met with by
the wood-cutters. He was placed on the cold ice,
And a bird screened and supported him with its
wings. When the bird went away, Hâu-*kî* began
to wail. His cry was long and loud, So that his
voice filled the whole way[2].

---

[1] The 'toe-print made by God' has occasioned much speculation
of the critics. We may simply draw the conclusion that the poet
meant to have his readers believe with him that the conception of
his hero was supernatural. We saw in the third of the Sacrificial
Odes of Shang that there was also a legend assigning a præter-
natural birth to the father of the House of Shang.

[2] It does not appear from the ode who exposed the infant to
these various perils; nor did Chinese tradition ever fashion any
story on the subject. Mâo makes the exposure to have been made
by *K*iang Yüan's husband, dissatisfied with what had taken place;
*K*äng, by the mother herself, to show the more the wonderful
character of her child. Readers will compare the accounts with
the Roman legends about Romulus and Remus, their mother and
her father; but the two legends differ according to the different
characters of the Chinese and Roman peoples.

398
     When he was able to crawl, He looked majestic and intelligent. When he was able to feed himself, He fell to planting beans. The beans grew luxuriantly; His rows of paddy shot up beautifully; His hemp and wheat grew strong and close; His gourds yielded abundantly.

     The husbandry of Hâu-*ki* Proceeded on the plan of helping (the growth). Having cleared away the thick grass, He sowed the ground with the yellow cereals. He managed the living grain, till it was ready to burst; Then he used it as seed, and it sprang up; It grew and came into ear; It became strong and good; It hung down, every grain complete; And thus he was appointed lord of Thâi [1].

     He gave (his people) the beautiful grains ;—The black millet and the double-kernelled, The tall red and the white. They planted extensively the black and the double-kernelled, Which were reaped and stacked on the ground. They planted extensively the tall red and the white, Which were carried on their shoulders and backs, Home for the sacrifices which he founded [2].

     And how as to our sacrifices (continued from him)?

---

   [1] Hâu-*ki*'s mother, we have seen, was a princess of Thâi, in the present district of Wû-kung, *Kh*ien *K*âu, Shen-hsî. This may have led to his appointment to that principality, and the transference of the lordship from *K*iangs to *K*îs. Evidently he was appointed to that dignity for his services in the promotion of agriculture. Still he has not displaced the older Shăn-nung, with whom on his father's side he had a connexion, as 'the Father of Husbandry.'

   [2] This is not to be understood of sacrifice in general, as if there had been no such thing before Hâu-*ki*; but of the sacrifices of the House of *K*âu,—those in the ancestral temple and others,—which began with him as its great ancestor.

Some hull (the grain); some take it from the 399
mortar; Some sift it; some tread it. It is rattling
in the.dishes; It is distilled, and the steam floats
about. We consult[1]; we observe the rites of puri-
fication; We take southernwood and offer it with
the fat; We sacrifice a ram to the spirit of the
path[2]; We offer roast flesh and broiled :—And
thus introduce the coming year[3].

We load the stands with the offerings, The stands
both of wood and of earthenware. As soon as the
fragrance ascends, God, well pleased, smells the
sweet savour. Fragrant it is, and in its due season[4].
Hâu-*kî* founded our sacrifices, And no one, we
presume, has given occasion for blame or regret in
regard to them, Down to the present day.

ODE 2. THE HSIN WEI.

A FESTAL ODE, CELEBRATING SOME ENTERTAINMENT GIVEN BY THE
KING TO HIS RELATIVES; WITH THE TRIAL OF ARCHERY AFTER THE
FEAST; CELEBRATING ESPECIALLY THE HONOUR DONE ON SUCH
OCCASIONS TO THE AGED.

This ode is given here, because it is commonly taken as a prelude
to the next. *Kû* Hsî interprets it of the feast, given by the

---

[1] That is, we divine about the day, and choose the officers to
take part in the service.

[2] A sacrifice was offered to the spirit of the road on commencing
a journey, and we see here that it was offered also in connexion
with the king's going to the ancestral temple or the border altar.

[3] It does not appear clearly what sacrifices the poet had in view
here. I think they must be all those in which the kings of *Kâu*
appeared as the principals or sacrificers. The concluding line is
understood to intimate that the kings were not to forget that a prosperous agriculture was the foundation of their prosperity.

[4] In this stanza we have the peculiar honour paid to Hâu-*kî* by
his descendants at one of the great border sacrifices to God,—the
same to which the last ode in the first decade of the Sacrificial
Odes of *Kâu* belongs.

400   king, at the close of the sacrifice in the ancestral temple, to the princes of his own surname. There are difficulties in the interpretation of the piece on this view, which, however, is to be preferred to any other.

In thick patches are those rushes, Springing by the way-side:—Let not the cattle and sheep trample them. Anon they will grow up; anon they will be completely formed, With their leaves soft and glossy [1]. Closely related are brethren; Let none be absent, let all be near. For some there are mats spread; For some there are given stools [2].

The mats are spread, and a second one above; The stools are given, and there are plenty of servants. (The guests) are pledged, and they pledge (the host) in return; He rinses the cups (and refills them, but the guests) put them down, Sauces and pickles are brought in, With roasted meat and broiled. Excellent provisions there are of tripe and palates; With singing to lutes, and with drums.

The ornamented bows are strong, And the four arrows are all balanced. They discharge the arrows, and all hit, And the guests are arranged according to their skill. The ornamented bows are drawn to the full, And the arrows are grasped in the hand. They go straight to the mark as if planted

---

[1] In the rushes growing up densely from a common root we have an emblem of brothers all sprung from the same ancestor; and in the plants developing so finely, when preserved from injury, an emblem of the happy fellowships of consanguinity, when nothing is allowed to interfere with mutual confidence and good feeling.

[2] In a previous note I have said that chairs and tables had not come into use in those early times. Guests sat and feasts were spread on mats on the floor; for the aged, however, stools were placed on which they could lean forward.

in it,   And the guests are arranged according to
the humble propriety of their behaviour.

The distant descendant presides over the feast;
His sweet spirits are strong.   He fills their cups
from a large vase,   And prays for the hoary old
(among his guests) :— That with hoary age and
wrinkled back,   They may lead on one another (to
virtue), and support one another (in it);   That so
their old age may be blessed,   And their bright
happiness ever increased.

Ode 3.   The *Kî* Βui.

RESPONSIVE TO THE LAST :—THE UNCLES AND BRETHREN OF THE KING
EXPRESS THEIR SENSE OF HIS KINDNESS, AND THEIR WISHES FOR HIS
HAPPINESS, MOSTLY IN THE WORDS IN WHICH THE PERSONATORS OF
THE DEPARTED ANCESTORS HAD CONVEYED THEIR SATISFACTION
WITH THE SACRIFICE OFFERED TO THEM, AND PROMISED TO HIM
THEIR BLESSING.

You have made us drink to the full of your spirits;
You have satiated us with your kindness.   May you
enjoy, O our lord, myriads of years!   May your
bright happiness (ever) be increased!

You have made us drink to the full of your spirits;
Your viands were set out before us.   May you enjoy,
O our lord, myriads of years!   May your bright
intelligence ever be increased!

May your bright intelligence become perfect,
High and brilliant, leading to a good end!   That
good end has (now) its beginning :—The personators
of your ancestors announced it in their blessing.

What was their announcement ?   ' (The offerings)
in your dishes of bamboo and wood are clean and

402   fine. Your friends¹, assisting in the service, Have done their part with reverent demeanour.

'Your reverent demeanour was altogether what the occasion required; And also that of your filial son². For such filial piety, continued without ceasing, There will ever be conferred blessings upon you.'

What will the blessings be? 'That along the passages of your palace, You shall move for ten thousand years, And there will be granted to you for ever dignity and posterity.'

How as to your posterity? 'Heaven invests you with your dignity; Yea, for ten thousand years, The bright appointment is attached (to your line).'

How is it attached? 'There is given you a heroic wife. There is given you a heroic wife, And from her shall come the (line of) descendants.'

ODE 4. THE HÛ Î.

AN ODE APPROPRIATE TO THE FEAST GIVEN TO THE PERSONATORS OF THE DEPARTED, ON THE DAY AFTER THE SACRIFICE IN THE ANCES-TRAL TEMPLE.

This supplementary sacrifice on the day after the principal service in the temple appeared in the ninth Book of the fourth Part of the Shû; and of the feast after it to the personators of the dead I have spoken on p. 301.

The wild-ducks and widgeons are on the *K*ing³;

---

¹ That is, the guests, visitors, and officers of the court.

² Towards the end of the sacrificial service, the eldest son of the king joined in pledging the representatives of their ancestors.

³ The *K*ing is an affluent of the Wei, not far from Wû's capital of Hâo. The birds, feeling at home in its waters, on its sands, &c., serve to introduce the parties feasted, in a situation where they might relax from the gravity of the preceding day, and be happy.

The personators of your ancestors feast and are   403
happy. Your spirits are clear; Your viands are
fragrant. The personators of your ancestors feast
and drink;—Their happiness and dignity are made
complete.

The wild-ducks and widgeons are on the sand;
The personators of the dead enjoy the feast, their
appropriate tribute. Your spirits are abundant;
Your viands are good. The personators of your
ancestors feast and drink;—Happiness and dignity
lend them their aids.

The wild-ducks and widgeons are on the islets;
The personators of your ancestors feast and enjoy
themselves. Your spirits are strained; Your viands
are in slices. The personators of your ancestors
feast and drink;—Happiness and dignity descend
on them.

The wild-ducks and widgeons are where the
waters meet; The personators of your ancestors
feast and are honoured. The feast is spread in the
ancestral temple, The place where happiness and
dignity descend. The personators of your ancestors
feast and drink;—Their happiness and dignity are
at the highest point.

The wild-ducks and widgeons are in the gorge;
The personators of your ancestors rest, full of
complacency. The fine spirits are delicious; Your
meat, roast and broiled, is fragrant. The personators
of your ancestors feast and drink;—No troubles will
be theirs after this.

404

ODE 5, STANZA 1. THE *K*IÂ LO.

IN PRAISE OF SOME KING, WHOSE VIRTUE SECURED TO HIM THE FAVOUR OF HEAVEN.

Perhaps the response of the feasted personators of the ancestors.

Of our admirable, amiable sovereign　Most illustrious is the excellent virtue. He orders rightly
the people, orders rightly the officers, And receives
his dignity from Heaven, Which protects and helps
him, and (confirms) his appointment, By repeated
acts of renewal from heaven.

ODE 8. THE *K*HÜAN Â.

ADDRESSED, PROBABLY, BY THE DUKE OF SHÂO TO KING *K*HĂNG, DESIRING FOR HIM LONG PROSPERITY, AND CONGRATULATING HIM, IN ORDER TO ADMONISH HIM, ON THE HAPPINESS OF HIS PEOPLE, THE NUMBER OF HIS ADMIRABLE OFFICERS, AND THE AUSPICIOUS OMEN ARISING FROM THE APPEARANCE OF THE PHŒNIX.

The duke of Shâo was the famous Shih, who appears in the fifth
and other Books of the fifth Part of the Shû, the colleague of the
duke of *K*âu in the early days of the *K*âu dynasty. This piece
may have been composed by him, but there is no evidence in it
that it was so. The assigning it to him rests entirely on the
authority of the preface. The language, however, is that in
which an old statesman of that time might express his complacency in his young sovereign.

Into the recesses of the large mound　Came the
wind, whirling from the south. There was (our)
happy, courteous sovereign, Rambling and singing;
And I took occasion to give forth my notes.

'Full of spirits you ramble ; Full of satisfaction
you rest. O happy and courteous sovereign, May
you fulfil your years, And end them like your
ancestors !

'Your territory is great and glorious, And per-

fectly secure. O happy and courteous sovereign, 405
May you fulfil your years, As the host of all the
spirits[1]!

'You have received the appointment long acknowledged, With peace around your happiness and
dignity. O happy and courteous sovereign, May
you fulfil your years, With pure happiness your
constant possession!

'You have helpers and supporters, Men of filial
piety and of virtue, To lead you on, and act as
wings to you, (So that), O happy and courteous
sovereign, You are a pattern to the four quarters
(of the kingdom).

'Full of dignity and majesty (are they), Like a

---

[1] 'Host of the hundred—i.e., of all—the spirits' is one of the
titles of the sovereign of China. It was and is his prerogative to
offer the great 'border sacrifices' to Heaven and Earth, or, as Confucius explains them, to God, and to the spirits of his ancestors in
his ancestral temple; and in his progresses (now neglected), among
the states, to the spirits of the hills and rivers throughout the kingdom. Every feudal prince could only sacrifice to the hills and
streams within his own territory. Under the changed conditions of
the government of China, the sacrificial ritual of the emperor still
retains the substance of whatever belonged to the sovereigns in
this respect from the earliest dynasties. On the text here, Khung
Ying-tâ of the Thang dynasty said, 'He who possesses all under the
sky, sacrifices to all the spirits, and thus he is the host of them all.'
Kû Hsî said on it, 'And always be the host of (the spirits of)
Heaven and Earth, of the hills and rivers, and of the departed.'
The term 'host' does not imply any superiority of rank on the
part of the entertainer. In the greatest sacrifices the emperor
acknowledges himself as 'the servant or subject of Heaven.' See
the prayer of the first of the present Manchâu line of emperors, in
announcing that he had ascended the throne, at the altar of Heaven
and Earth, in 1644, as translated by the Rev. Dr. Edkins in the
chapter on Imperial Worship, in the recent edition of his 'Religion
in China.'

jade-mace(in its purity), The subject of praise, the contemplation of hope. O happy and courteous sovereign, (Through them) the four quarters (of the kingdom) are guided by you.

' The male and female phœnix fly about [1], Their wings rustling, While they settle in their proper resting-place. Many are your admirable officers, O king, Ready to be employed by you, Loving you, the Son of Heaven.

' The male and female phœnix fly about, Their wings rustling, As they soar up to heaven. Many are your admirable officers, O king, Waiting for your commands, And loving the multitudes of the people.

' The male and female phœnix give out their notes, On that lofty ridge. The dryandras grow, On those eastern slopes. They grow luxuriantly ; And harmoniously the notes resound.

---

[1] The phœnix (so the creature has been named) is a fabulous bird, 'the chief of the 360 classes of the winged tribes.' It is mentioned in the fourth Book of the second Part of the Shû, as appearing in the courtyard of Shun ; and the appearance of a pair of them has always been understood to denote a sage on the throne and prosperity in the country. Even Confucius (Analects, IX, viii) could not express his hopelessness about his own times more strongly than by saying that 'the phœnix did not make its appearance.' He was himself also called ' a phœnix,' in derision, by one of the recluses of his time (Analects, XVIII, v). The type of the bird was, perhaps, the Argus pheasant, but the descriptions of it are of a monstrous creature, having ' a fowl's head, a swallow's chin, a serpent's neck, a fish's tail,' &c. It only lights on the dryandra cordifolia, of which tree also many marvellous stories are related. The poet is not to be understood as saying that the phœnix actually appeared ; but that the king was sage and his government prosperous, as if it had appeared.

'Your chariots, O sovereign, Are numerous, 407
many. Your horses, O sovereign, Are well trained
and fleet. I have made my few verses, In prolongation of your song.'

ODE 9, STANZA 1. THE MIN LÂO.

IN A TIME OF DISORDER AND SUFFERING, SOME OFFICER OF DISTINC-
TION CALLS ON HIS FELLOWS TO JOIN WITH HIM TO EFFECT A
REFORMATION IN THE CAPITAL, AND PUT AWAY THE PARTIES WHO
WERE THE CAUSE OF THE PREVAILING MISERY.

With the *Kh*üan Â, what are called the 'correct' odes of Part III,
or those belonging to a period of good government, and the
composition of which is ascribed mainly to the duke of *K*âu, come
to an end; and those that follow are the 'changed' Major Odes
of the Kingdom, or those belonging to a degenerate period, commencing with this. Some among them, however, are equal to
any of the former class. The Min Lâo has been assigned to
duke Mû of Shâo, a descendant of duke Khang, the Shih of the
Shû, the reputed author of the *Kh*üan Â, and was directed
against king Lî, B.C. 878 to 828.

The people indeed are heavily burdened, But
perhaps a little relief may be got for them. Let
us cherish this centre of the kingdom, To secure
the repose of the four quarters of it. Let us give
no indulgence to the wily and obsequious, In order
to make the unconscientious careful; And to repress
robbers and oppressors, Who have no fear of the
clear will (of Heaven)[1]. Then let us show kindness
to those who are distant, And help those who are
near,—Thus establishing (the throne of) our king.

---

[1] 'The clear will,' according to *K*û Hsî, is 'the clear appointment
of Heaven;' according to *K*û Kung-*kh*ien, 'correct principle.'
They both mean the law of human duty, as gathered from the
nature of man's moral constitution conferred by Heaven.

ODE 10. THE PAN.

AN OFFICER OF EXPERIENCE MOURNS OVER THE PREVAILING MISERY; COMPLAINS OF THE WANT OF SYMPATHY WITH HIM SHOWN BY OTHER OFFICERS; ADMONISHES THEM, AND SETS FORTH THE DUTY RE-QUIRED OF THEM, ESPECIALLY IN THE ANGRY MOOD IN WHICH IT MIGHT SEEM THAT HEAVEN WAS.

This piece, like the last, is assigned to the time of king Lî.

God has reversed (his usual course of procedure)[1], And the lower people are full of distress. The words which you utter are not right; The plans which you form are not far-reaching. As there are not sages, you think you have no guidance;—You have no real sincerity. (Thus) your plans do not reach far, And I therefore strongly admonish you.

Heaven is now sending down calamities;—Do not be so complacent. Heaven is now producing such movements;—Do not be so indifferent. If your words were harmonious, The people would become united. If your words were gentle and kind, The people would be settled.

Though my duties are different from yours, I am your fellow-servant. I come to advise with you, And you hear me with contemptuous indifference. My words are about the (present urgent) affairs;— Do not think them matter for laughter. The ancients had a saying:—'Consult the gatherers of grass and firewood[2].'

---

[1] The proof of God's having reversed his usual course of procedure was to be found in the universal misery of the people, whose good He was understood to desire, and for the securing of which government by righteous kings was maintained by him.

[2] If ancient worthies thought that persons in such mean employments were to be consulted, surely the advice of the writer deserved to be taken into account by his comrades.

Heaven is now exercising oppression;—Do not in   409
such a way make a mock of things.   An old man,
(I speak) with entire sin'cerity;   But you, my juniors,
are full of pride.   It is not that my words are those
of age,   But you make a joke of what is sad.   But
the troubles will multiply like flames,   Till they
are beyond help or remedy.

Heaven is now displaying its anger;—Do not be
either boastful or flattering,   Utterly departing from
all propriety of demeanour,   Till good men are
reduced to personators of the dead [1].   The people
now sigh and groan,   And we dare not examine
(into the causes of their trouble).   The ruin and
disorder are exhausting all their means of living,
And we show no kindness to our multitudes.

Heaven enlightens the people [2],   As the bamboo
flute responds to the earthen whistle;   As two half-
maces form a whole one;   As you take a thing,
and bring it away in your hand,   Bringing it away,
without any more ado.   The enlightenment of the
people is very easy.   They have (now) many per-
versities;—Do not you set up your perversity
before them.

Good men are a fence;   The multitudes of the
people are a wall;   Great states are screens;   Great
families are buttresses;   The cherishing of virtue

---

[1] During all the time of the sacrifice, the personators of the dead
said not a word, but only ate and drank.   To the semblance of
them good men were now reduced.

[2] The meaning is, that Heaven has so attuned the mind to virtue,
that, if good example were set before the people, they would certainly and readily follow it.   This is illustrated by various instances
of things, in which the one succeeded the other freely and as if
necessarily ; so that government by virtue was really very easy.

410   secures repose;   The circle of (the king's) relatives
is a fortified wall.   We must not let the fortified
wall get destroyed;   We must not let (the king)
be solitary and consumed with terrors.

Revere the anger of Heaven,   And presume not
to make sport or be idle.   Revere the changing
moods of Heaven,   And presume not to drive about
(at your pleasure).   Great Heaven is intelligent,
And is with you in all your goings.   Great Heaven
is clear-seeing,   And is with you in your wanderings
and indulgences.

The Third Decade, or that of Tang.

ODE 1.   THE TANG.

WARNINGS, SUPPOSED TO BE ADDRESSED TO KING LÎ, ON THE ISSUES
OF THE COURSE WHICH HE WAS PURSUING, SHOWING THAT THE
MISERIES OF THE TIME AND THE IMMINENT DANGER OF RUIN WERE
TO BE ATTRIBUTED, NOT TO HEAVEN, BUT TO HIMSELF AND HIS
MINISTERS.

This ode, like the ninth of the second decade, is attributed to duke
Mû of Shâo.   The structure of the piece is peculiar, for, after
the first stanza, we have king Wăn introduced delivering a series
of warnings to *K*âu-hsin, the last king of the Shang dynasty.
They are put into Wăn's mouth, in the hope that Lî, if, indeed,
he was the monarch whom the writer had in view, would
transfer the figure of *K*âu-hsin to himself, and alter his course
so as to avoid a similar ruin.

How vast is God,   The ruler of men below!   How
arrayed in terrors is God,   With many things irregular in his ordinations.   Heaven gave birth to
the multitudes of the people,   But the nature it
confers is not to be depended on.   All are (good)

at first,　But few prove themselves to be so at
the last [1].

King Wăn said, ' Alas!　Alas! you sovereign
of Shang,　That you should have such violently
oppressive ministers,　That you should have such
extortionate exactors,　That you should have them
in offices,　That you should have them in the conduct
of affairs!　"Heaven made them with their insolent
dispositions;"　But it is you who employ them, and
give them strength.'

King Wăn said, ' Alas!　Alas! you (sovereign
of) Yin-shang,　You ought to employ such as are
good,　But (you employ instead) violent oppressors,
who cause many dissatisfactions.　They respond
to you with baseless stories,　And (thus) robbers
and thieves are in your court.　Hence come oaths
and curses,　Without limit, without end.'

King Wăn said, 'Alas!　Alas! you (sovereign of)
Yin-shang,　You show a strong fierce will in the
centre of the kingdom,　And consider the con-
tracting of enmities a proof of virtue.　All-unintelli-
gent are you of your (proper) virtue,　And so you
have no (good) men behind you, nor by your side.
Without any intelligence of your (proper) virtue,
You have no (good) intimate adviser or minister.'

King Wăn said, 'Alas!　Alas! you (sovereign of)
Yin-shang,　It is not Heaven that flushes your face
with spirits,　So that you follow what is evil and
imitate it.　You go wrong in all your conduct;　You
make no distinction between the light and the

---

[1] The meaning seems to be that, whatever miseries might prevail, and be ignorantly ascribed to God, they were in reality owing
to men's neglect of the law of Heaven inscribed on their hearts.

412   darkness; But amid clamour and shouting, You turn the day into night [1].'

King Wăn said, 'Alas! Alas! you (sovereign of) Yin-shang, (All round you) is like the noise of cicadas, Or like the bubbling of boiling soup. Affairs, great and small, are approaching to ruin, And still you (and your creatures) go on in this course. Indignation is rife against you here in the Middle Kingdom, And extends to the demon regions [2].'

King Wăn said, 'Alas! Alas! you (sovereign of) Yin-shang, It is not God that has caused this evil time, But it arises from Yin's not using the old (ways). Although you have not old experienced men, There are still the ancient statutes and laws. But you will not listen to them, And so your great appointment is being overthrown.'

King Wăn said, 'Alas! Alas! you (sovereign of) Shang, People have a saying, "When a tree falls utterly, While its branches and leaves are yet un-injured, It must first have been uprooted." The beacon of Yin is not far distant;—It is in the age of the (last) sovereign of Hsiâ.'

---

[1] We speak of 'turning night into day.' The tyrant of Shang turned day into night. Excesses, generally committed in darkness, were by him done openly.

[2] These 'demon regions' are understood to mean the seat of the Turkic tribes to the north of China, known from the earliest times by various names—'The hill *Z*ung,' 'the northern Lî,' 'the Hsien-yun,' &c. Towards the beginning of our era, they were called Hsiung-nû, from which, perhaps, came the name Huns; and some centuries later, Thû-*k*üeh (Thuh-*k*üeh), from which came Turk. We are told in the Yî, under the diagram *K*î-*k*î, that Kâo *3*ung (B.C. 1324–1266) conducted an expedition against the demon regions, and in three years subdued them.

ODE 2. THE Yî.

CONTAINING VARIOUS COUNSELS WHICH DUKE WÛ OF WEI MADE TO
ADMONISH HIMSELF, WHEN HE WAS OVER HIS NINETIETH YEAR;
ESPECIALLY ON THE DUTY OF A RULER TO BE CAREFUL OF HIS
OUTWARD DEMEANOUR, FEELING THAT HE IS EVER UNDER THE IN-
SPECTION OF SPIRITUAL BEINGS, AND TO RECEIVE WITH DOCILITY
INSTRUCTIONS DELIVERED TO HIM.

The sixth ode in the seventh decade of the Minor Odes of the
Kingdom is attributed to the same duke of Wei as this; and the
two bear traces of having proceeded from the same writer. The
external authorities for assigning this piece to duke Wû are the
statement of the preface and an article in the 'Narratives of the
States,' a work already referred to as belonging to the period of
the *K*âu dynasty. That article·relates how Wû, at the age of
ninety-five, insisted on all his ministers and officers being instant,
in season and out of season, to admonish him on his conduct,
and that 'he made the warnings in the Î to admonish himself.'
The Î is understood to·be only another name for this Yî. Thus
the speaker throughout the piece is Wû, and 'the young son,'
whom he sometimes addresses, is himself also. The conception
of the writer in taking such a method to admonish himself, and
give forth the lessons of his long life, is very remarkable; and
the execution of it is successful.

Outward demeanour, cautious and grave,　Is an
indication of the (inward) virtue.　People have the
saying,　'There is no wise man who is not (also)
stupid.'　The stupidity of the ordinary man　Is
determined by his (natural) defects.　The stupidity
of the wise man　Is from his doing violence (to
his ·proper character).

What is most powerful is the being the man [1];—

---

[1] Wû writes as the marquis of Wei, the ruler of a state; but
what he says is susceptible of universal application. In every
smaller sphere, and in the largest, 'being the man,' displaying,
that is, the proper qualities of humanity, will be appreciated and
felt.

414   In all quarters (of the state) men are influenced by
it. To an upright virtuous conduct All in the four
quarters of the state render obedient homage. With
great counsels and determinate orders, With far-
reaching plans and timely announcements, And with
reverent care of his outward demeanour, One will
become the pattern of the people.

As for the circumstances of the present time,
You are bent on error and confusion in your government. Your virtue is subverted; You are besotted
by drink¹. Although you thus pursue nothing but
pleasure, How is it you do not think of your relation to the past, And do not widely study the
former kings, That you might hold fast their wise
laws ?

Shall not those whom great Heaven does not
approve of, Surely as the waters flow from a spring,
Sink down together in ruin ? Rise early and go
to bed late, Sprinkle and sweep your courtyard;—
So as to be a pattern to the people². Have in good
order your chariots and horses, Your bows and
arrows, and (other) weapons of war;—To be prepared for warlike action, To keep at a distance
(the hordes of) the south.

Perfect what concerns your officers and people;

---

¹ Han Ying (who has been mentioned in the Introduction) says
that Wû made the sixth ode of the seventh decade of the former
Part against drunkenness, when he was repenting of his own giving
way to that vice. His mention of the habit here, at the age of
ninety-five, must be understood as a warning to other rulers.

² Line 3 describes things important to the cultivation of one's
self ; and line 4, things important to the regulation of one's family.
They may seem unimportant, it is said, as compared with the
defence of the state, spoken of in the last four lines of the stanza;
but the ruler ought not to neglect them.

Be careful of your duties as a prince (of the king-   415
dom). To be prepared for unforeseen dangers, Be
cautious of what you say; Be reverentially careful
of your outward behaviour; In all things be mild
and correct. A flaw in a mace of white jade May
be ground away; But for a flaw in speech Nothing
can be done.

Do not speak lightly; your words are your own[1].
Do not say, 'This is of little importance; No one
can hold my tongue for me.' Words are not to be
cast away. Every word finds its answer; Every
good deed has its recompense. If you are gracious
among your friends, And to the people, as if they
were your children, Your descendants will continue
in unbroken line, And all the people will surely
be obedient to you.

Looked at in friendly intercourse with superior
men, You make your countenance harmonious and
mild; Anxious not to do anything wrong. Looked
at in your chamber, You ought to be equally free
from shame before the light which shines in. Do
not say, 'This place is not public; No one can see
me here.' The approaches of spiritual beings
Cannot be calculated beforehand; But the more
should they not be slighted[2].

---

[1] And therefore every one is himself responsible for his words.

[2] *Kû* Hsî says that from the fourth line this stanza only speaks of
the constant care there should be in watching over one's thoughts;
but in saying so, he overlooks the consideration by which such
watchful care is enforced. Compare what is said of king Wăn in
the third stanza of the sixth ode of the first decade. King Wăn
and duke Wû were both influenced by the consideration that their
inmost thoughts, even when 'unseen by men,' were open to the
inspection of spiritual beings.

416   O prince, let your practice of virtue Be entirely good and admirable. Watch well over your behaviour, And allow nothing wrong in your demeanour. Committing no excess, doing nothing injurious, There are few who will not in such a case take you for their pattern. When one throws to me a peach, I return to him a plum [1]. To look for horns on a young ram Will only weary you, my son [2].

The tough and elastic wood Can be fitted with the silken string [3]. The mild and respectful man Possesses the foundation of virtue. There is a wise man;—I tell him good words, And he yields to them the practice of docile virtue. There is a stupid man;—He says on the contrary that my words are not true:—So different are people's minds.

Oh! my son, When you did not know what was good, and what was not good, Not only did I lead you by the hand, But I showed the difference between them by appealing to instances. Not (only) did I charge you face to face, But I held you by the ear [4]. And still perhaps you do not know, Although you have held a son in your arms. If people be not self-sufficient, Who comes to a late maturity after early instruction？

Great Heaven is very intelligent, And I pass

---

[1] That is, every deed, in fact, meets with its recompense.

[2] See the conclusion of duke Wû's ode against drunkenness. Horns grow as the young ram grows. Effects must not be expected where there have not been the conditions from which they naturally spring.

[3] Such wood is the proper material for a bow.

[4] That is, to secure your attention.

my life without pleasure. When I see you so dark   417
and stupid, My heart is full of pain. I taught you
with assiduous repetition, And you listened to
me with contempt. You would not consider me
as your teacher, But regarded me as trouble-
some. Still perhaps you do not know;—But you
are very old.

Oh! my son, I have told you the old ways. Hear
and follow my counsels:—Then shall you have no
cause for great regret. Heaven is now inflicting
calamities, And is destroying the state. My illustrations are not taken from things remote:—Great
Heaven makes no mistakes. If you go on to dete-
riorate in your virtue, You will bring the people to
great distress.

ODE 3, STANZAS 1, 2, 3, 4, AND 7. THE SANG ZÂU.

THE WRITER MOURNS OVER THE MISERY AND DISORDER OF THE TIMES,
WITH A VIEW TO REPREHEND THE MISGOVERNMENT OF KING LÎ,
APPEALING ALSO TO HEAVEN TO HAVE COMPASSION.

King Lî is not mentioned by name in the piece, but the second
line of stanza 7 can only be explained of him. He was driven
from the throne, in consequence of his misgovernment, in B.C. 842,
and only saved his life by flying to *K*ih, a place in the present
Ho *K*âu, department Phing-yang, Shan-hsî, where he remained
till his death in B.C. 828. The government in the meantime was
carried on by the dukes of Shâo and *K*âu, whose administration,
called the period of 'Mutual Harmony,' forms an important
chronological era in Chinese history. On the authority of
a reference in the *3*o Kwan, the piece is ascribed to an earl
of *Z*ui.

Luxuriant is that young mulberry tree, And
beneath it wide is the shade; But they will pluck
its leaves till it is quite destroyed[1]. The distress

---

[1] These three lines are metaphorical of the once flourishing
kingdom, which was now brought to the verge of ruin.

[1]   E e

418 inflicted on these (multitudes of the) people, Is an unceasing sorrow to my heart; My commiseration fills (my breast). O thou bright and great Heaven, Shouldest thou not have compassion on us ?

The four steeds (gallop about), eager and strong[1]; The tortoise-and-serpent and the falcon banners fly about. Disorder grows, and no peace can be secured. Every state is being ruined; There are no black heads among the people[2]. Everything is reduced to ashes by calamity. Oh! alas! The doom of the kingdom hurries on.

There is nothing to arrest the doom of the kingdom; Heaven does not nourish us. There is no place in which to stop securely; There is no place to which to go. Superior men are the bonds (of the social state)[3], Allowing no love of strife in their hearts. Who reared the steps of the dissatisfaction[4], Which has reached the present distress?

The grief of my heart is extreme, And I dwell on (the condition of) our land. I was born at an unhappy time, To meet with the severe anger of Heaven. From the west to the east, There is no quiet place of abiding. Many are the distresses I meet with; Very urgent is the trouble on our borders.

Heaven is sending down death and disorder, And

---

[1] That is, the war-chariots, each drawn by its team of four horses.

[2] The young and able-bodied of the people were slain or absent on distant expeditions, and only old and gray-headed men were to be seen.

[3] Intimating that no such men were now to be found in office.

[4] Meaning the king by his misgovernment and employment of bad men.

has put an end to our king. It is (now) sending down those devourers of the grain, So that the husbandry is all in evil case. Alas for our middle states [1]! All is in peril and going to ruin. I have no strength (to do anything), And think of (the Power in) the azure vault.

ODE 4. THE YUN HAN.

KING HSÜAN, ON OCCASION OF A GREAT DROUGHT, EXPOSTULATES WITH GOD AND ALL THE SPIRITS, WHO MIGHT BE EXPECTED TO HELP HIM AND HIS PEOPLE; ASKS THEM WHEREFORE THEY WERE CONTENDING WITH HIM; AND DETAILS THE MEASURES HE HAD TAKEN, AND WAS STILL TAKING, FOR THE REMOVAL OF THE CALAMITY.

King Hsüan does not occur by name in the ode, though the remarkable prayer which it relates is ascribed to a king in stanza 1. All critics have admitted the statement of the Preface that the piece was made, in admiration of king Hsüan, by *Z*ang Shû, a great officer, we may presume, of the court. The standard chronology places the commencement of the drought in B.C. 822, the sixth year of Hsüan's reign. How long it continued we cannot tell.

Bright was the milky way, Shining and revolving in the sky. The king said, 'Oh! What crime is chargeable on us now, That Heaven (thus) sends down death and disorder? Famine comes again and again. There is no spirit I have not sacrificed to [2]; There is no victim I have grudged; Our

---

[1] We must translate here in the plural, 'the middle states' meaning all the states subject to the sovereign of *K*âu.

[2] In the Official Book of *K*âu, among the duties of the Minister of Instruction, or, as Biot translates the title, 'the Director of the Multitudes,' it is stated that one of the things he has to do, on occurrences of famine, is 'to seek out the spirits,' that is, as explained by the commentators, to see that sacrifices are offered to all the spirits, even such as may have been discontinued. This rule had, no doubt, been acted on during the drought which this ode describes.

420　jade symbols, oblong and round, are exhausted [1] ; —
How is it that I am not heard?

'The drought is excessive; Its fervours become
more and more tormenting. I have not ceased
offering pure sacrifices; From the border altars
I have gone to the ancestral temple [2]. To the
(Powers) above and below I have presented my
offerings and then buried them [3] ;—There is no
spirit whom I have not honoured. Hâu-*kî* is not
equal to the occasion; God does not come to us.
This wasting and ruin of our country,—Would that
it fell (only) on me!

'The drought is excessive, And I may not try
to excuse myself. I am full of terror, and feel the
peril, Like the clap of thunder or the roll. Of the
remnant of *K*âu, among the black-haired people,
There will not be half a man left; Nor will God
from his great heaven exempt (even) me. Shall

---

[1] We have, in the sixth Book of the fifth Part of the Shû, an
instance of the use of the symbols here mentioned in sacrificing to
the spirits of departed kings. The Official Book, among the
duties of the Minister of Religion, mentions the use of these and
other symbols—in all six, of different shapes and colours—at the
different sacrifices.

[2] By 'the border altars' we are to understand the altars in the
suburbs of the capital, where Heaven and Earth were sacrificed
to ;—the great services at the solstices, and any other seasons.
The mention of Hâu-*kî* in the seventh line makes us think especially of the service in the spring, to pray for a good year, when
Hâu-*kî* was associated with God.

[3] 'The (Powers) above and below' are Heaven and Earth. The
offerings, during the progress of the service, were placed on the
ground, or on the altars, and buried in the earth at the close of it.
This explains what the king says in the first stanza about the
offerings of jade being exhausted.

we not mingle our fears together? (The sacrifices   421
to) my ancestors will be extinguished [1].

'The drought is excessive, And it cannot be
stopped. More fierce and fiery, It is leaving me
no place. My end is near;—I have none to look
up, none to look round, to. The many dukes and
their ministers of the past [2] Give me no help.
O ye parents and (nearer) ancestors [3], How can
ye bear to see me thus?

'The drought is excessive;—Parched are the
hills, and the streams are dried. The demon of
drought exercises his oppression, As if scattering
flames and fire [4] My heart is terrified with the
heat;—My sorrowing heart is as if on fire. The

---

[1] Equivalent to the extinction of the dynasty.

[2] The king had sacrificed to all the early lords of *K*'âu. 'The
many dukes' may comprehend kings Thâi and *K*'î. He had also
sacrificed to their ministers. Compare what Pan-kăng says in the
Shû, p. 109, about his predecessors and their ministers. Some
take 'the many dukes, and the ministers,' of all princes of states
who had signalised themselves by services to the people and
kingdom.

[3] The king could hardly hope that his father, the oppressive Lî,
would in his spirit-state give him any aid; but we need only find in
his words the expression of natural feeling. Probably it was the
consideration of the character of Lî which has made some critics
understand by 'parents' and 'ancestors' the same individuals,
namely, kings Wăn and Wû, 'the ancestors' of Hsüan, and who
had truly been 'the parents' of the people.

[4] Khung Ying-tâ, from 'the Book of Spirits and Marvels,' gives
the following account of 'the demon of drought:'—'In the southern
regions there is a man, two or three cubits in height, with the
upper part of his body bare, and his eyes in the top of his head.
He runs with the speed of the wind, and is named Po. In whatever state he appears, there ensues a great drought.' The Book
of Spirits and Marvels, however, as it now exists, cannot be older
than our fourth or fifth century.

422

many dukes and their ministers of the past Do not hear me. O God, from thy great heaven, Grant me the liberty to withdraw (into retirement[1]).

'The drought is excessive;—I struggle and fear to go away. How is it that I am afflicted with this drought? I cannot ascertain the cause of it. In praying for a good year I was abundantly early[2]. I was not late (in sacrificing) to (the spirits of) the four quarters and of the land[3]. God in great heaven Does not consider me. Reverent to the intelligent spirits, I ought not to be thus the object of their anger.

'The drought is excessive;—All is dispersion, and the bonds of government are relaxed. Reduced to extremities are the heads of departments; Full of distress are my chief ministers, The Master of the Horse, the Commander of the Guards,. The chief Cook[4], and my attendants. There is no one who has not (tried to) help (the people); They have not refrained on the ground of being unable. I look up to the great heaven;—Why am I plunged in this sorrow?

'I look up to the great heaven, But its stars sparkle bright. My great officers and excellent men, Ye have reverently drawn near (to Heaven) with all

---

[1] That is, to withdraw and give place to a more worthy sovereign.

[2] This was the border sacrifice to God, when Hâu-kî was associated with him. Some critics add a sacrifice in the first month of winter, for a blessing on the ensuing year, offered to 'the honoured ones of heaven,'—the sun, moon, and zodiacal constellations.

[3] See note 2 on p. 371.

[4] See note 1 on p. 356.

your powers. Death is approaching, But do not
cast away what you have done. You are seeking
not for me only, But to give rest to all our departments. I look up to the great heaven;—When
shall I be favoured with repose ? '

423

ODE 5, STANZAS 1, 2, AND 4. THE SUNG KÂO.

CELEBRATING THE APPOINTMENT BY KING HSÜAN OF A RELATIVE TO
BE THE MARQUIS OF SHĂN, AND DEFENDER OF THE SOUTHERN
BORDER OF THE KINGDOM, WITH THE ARRANGEMENTS MADE FOR
HIS ENTERING ON HIS CHARGE.

That the king who appears in this piece was king Hsüan is sufficiently established. He appears in it commissioning 'his great
uncle,' an elder brother, that is, of his mother, to go and rule, as
marquis of Shăn, and chief or president of the states in the
south of the kingdom, to defend the borders against the en-
croaching hordes of the south, headed by the princes of *Khû*,
whose lords had been rebellious against the middle states even
in the time of the Shang dynasty;—see the last of the Sacrificial
Odes of Shang.

Grandly lofty are the mountains, With their
large masses reaching to the heavens.. From those
mountains was sent down a spirit, Who produced
the birth of (the princes of) Fû and Shăn [1]. Fû and

---

[1] Shăn was a small marquisate, a part of what is the present
department of Nan-yang, Ho-nan. Fû, which was also called
Lü, was another small territory, not far from Shăn. The princes
of both were *K*iangs, descended from the chief minister of Yâo,
called in the first Book of the Shû, 'the Four Mountains.' Other
states were ruled by his descendants, particularly the great state of
*K*hî. When it is said here that a spirit was sent down from the
great mountains, and produced the birth of (the princes of) Fû and
Shăn, we have, probably, a legendary tradition concerning the
birth of Yao's minister, which was current among all his descendants; and with which we may compare the legends that have come
under our notice about the supernatural births of the ancestors of
the founders of the Houses of Shang and *K*âu. The character for

424   Shăn   Are   the   support   of   *K*âu,   Screens to all the states,   Diffusing (their influence) over the four quarters of the kingdom.

Full of activity is the chief of Shăn,   And the king would employ him to continue the services (of his fathers), With his capital in Hsieh [1], Where he should be a pattern to the states of the south. The king gave charge to the earl of Shâo,   To arrange all about the residence of the chief of Shăn,   Where he should do what was necessary for the regions of the south,   And where his posterity might maintain his merit.

Of the services of the chief of Shăn   The foundation was laid by the earl of Shâo,   Who first built the walls (of his city),   And then completed his ancestral temple [2]. When the temple was completed, wide and grand,   The king conferred on the chief of Shâo   Four noble steeds,   With the hooks for the trappings of the breast-bands, glittering bright [3].

'mountains' in lines 1 and 3 is the same that occurs in the title of Yâo's minister. On the statement about the mountains sending down a spirit, Hwang Hsün, a critic of the Sung dynasty, says that 'it is merely a personification of the poet, to show how high Heaven had a mind to revive the fortunes of *K*âu, and that we need not trouble ourselves about whether there was such a spirit or not.'

[1] Hsieh was in the present Făng *K*âu of the department of Nan-yang.

[2] Compare with this the account given, in ode 3 of the first decade, of the settling of 'the ancient duke Than-fû' in the plain of *K*âu. Here, as there, the great religious edifice, the ancestral temple, takes precedence of all other buildings in the new city.

[3] The steeds with their equipments were tokens of the royal favour, usually granted on occasions of investiture. The conferring of them was followed immediately by the departure of the newly-invested prince to his charge.

ODE 6, STANZAS 1 AND 7. THE *K*ĂNG MIN.   425

CELEBRATING THE VIRTUES OF *K*UNG SHAN-FÛ, WHO APPEARS TO HAVE
BEEN ONE OF THE PRINCIPAL MINISTERS OF KING HSÜAN, AND HIS
DESPATCH TO THE EAST, TO FORTIFY THE CAPITAL OF THE STATE
OF *KH*Î.

Heaven, in giving birth to the multitudes of the
people, To every faculty and relationship annexed
its law. The people possess this normal nature,
And they (consequently) love its normal virtue [1].
Heaven beheld the ruler of *K*âu, Brilliantly affecting it by his conduct below, And to maintain him,
its Son, Gave birth to *K*ung Shan-fû [2].

*K*ung Shan-fû went forth, having sacrificed to the
spirit of the road [3]. His four steeds were strong;

---

[1] We get an idea of the meaning which has been attached to
these four lines from a very early time by Mencius' quotation
of them (VI, i, ch. 6) in support of his doctrine of the goodness of
human nature, and the remark on the piece which he attributes
to Confucius, that 'the maker of it knew indeed the constitution
(of our nature).' Every faculty, bodily or mental, has its function
to fulfil, and every relationship its duty to be discharged. The function and the duty are the things which the human being has to
observe :—the seeing clearly, for instance, with the eyes, and hearing
distinctly with the ears; the maintenance of righteousness between
ruler and minister, and of affection between parent and child.
This is the 'normal nature,' and the 'normal virtue' is the nature
fulfilling the various laws of its constitution.

[2] The connexion between these four lines and those that precede is this:—that while Heaven produces all men with the good
nature there described, on occasions it produces others with virtue
and powers in a super-eminent degree. Such an occasion was
presented by the case of king Hsüan, and therefore, to mark its
appreciation of him, and for his help, it now produced *K*ung
Shan-fû.

[3] This was a special sacrifice at the commencement of a journey,
or of an expedition. See note 2 on p. 399.

426　His men were alert, He was always anxious lest he should not be equal to his commission; His steeds went on without stopping, To the tinkling of their eight bells. The king had given charge to *K*ung Shan-fû, To fortify the city there in the east.

ODE 7, STANZAS 1 AND PART OF 3. THE HAN YÎ.

CELEBRATING THE MARQUIS OF HAN:—HIS INVESTITURE, AND THE KING'S CHARGE TO HIM; THE GIFTS HE RECEIVED, AND THE PARTING FEAST AT THE COURT; HIS MARRIAGE; THE EXCELLENCE OF HIS TERRITORY; AND HIS SWAY OVER THE REGIONS OF THE NORTH.

Only one line—the first of stanza 3—in this interesting piece serves to illustrate the religious practices of the time, and needs no further note than what has been given on the first line of stanza 7 in the preceding ode. The name of the marquisate of Han remains in the district of Han-*kh*ǎng, department of Hsî-an, Shen-hsî, in which also is mount Liang.

Very grand is the mountain of Liang, Which was made cultivable by Yü. Bright is the way from it, (Along which came) the marquis of Han to receive investiture. The king in person gave the charge :— 'Continue the services of your ancestors; Let not my charge to you come to nought. Be diligent early and late, And reverently discharge your duties :— So shall my appointment of you not change. Be a support against those princes who do not come to court, Thus assisting your sovereign.'

When the marquis of Han left the court, he sacrificed to the spirit of the road. He went forth, and lodged for the night in Tû.

ODE 8, STANZAS 4 AND 5. THE *K*IANG HAN.

CELEBRATING AN EXPEDITION AGAINST THE SOUTHERN TRIBES OF THE
HWÂI, AND THE WORK DONE FOR THE KING IN THEIR COUNTRY, BY
HÛ, THE EARL OF SHÂO, WITH THE MANNER IN WHICH THE KING
REWARDED HIM, AND HE RESPONDED TO THE ROYAL FAVOUR.

Hû was probably the same earl of Shâo, who is mentioned in
ode 5, as building his capital of Hsieh for the new marquis of
Shăn. The lords of Shâo had been distinguished in the service
of *K*âu ever since the rise of the dynasty.

The king gave charge to Hû of Shâo :—' You
have everywhere made known (and carried out my
orders). When (the kings) Wăn and Wû received
their appointment, The duke of Shâo was their
strong support. You not (only) have a regard to
me the little child, But you try to resemble that
duke of Shâo. You have commenced and earnestly
displayed your merit ; And I will make you happy.

' I give you a large libation-cup of jade [1], And a
jar of herb-flavoured spirits from the black millet [2].
I have made announcement to the Accomplished
one [3], And confer on you hills, lands, and fields.
In (*Kh*î-)*k*âu shall you receive investiture, According as your ancestor received his.' Hû bowed with

---

[1] See note 2 on p. 386.

[2] The cup and the spirits would be used by the earl when
sacrificing in his ancestral temple. Compare the similar gift from
king *Kh*ăng to the duke of *K*âu, in the Shû, p. 194. More sub-
stantial gifts are immediately specified.

[3] 'The Accomplished one' is understood to be king Wăn (='the
Accomplished king'). He was the founder of the *K*âu dynasty.
To him the kingdom had first come by the appointment and gift
of Heaven. It was the duty therefore of his successors, in making
grants of territory to meritorious officers, to announce them to him
in *Kh*î-*k*âu, the old territory of the family, and obtain, as it were,
his leave for what they were doing.

428   his head to the ground (and said), 'May the Son
of Heaven live for ever!'

Ode 10, Stanzas 1, 5, 6, and 7. The *Kan Zang*.

THE WRITER DEPLORES, WITH AN APPEALING WAIL TO HEAVEN, THE
MISERY AND OPPRESSION THAT PREVAILED, AND INTIMATES THAT
THEY WERE CAUSED BY THE INTERFERENCE OF WOMEN AND EUNUCHS
IN THE GOVERNMENT.

The king addressed in this piece was most probably Yû. It suits
his character and reign.

I look up to great Heaven, But it shows us no
kindness. Very long have we been disquieted, And
these great calamities are sent down (upon us).
There is nothing settled in the country; Officers
and people are in distress. Through the insects
from without and from within, There is no peace
or limit (to our misery). The net of crime is not
taken up[1], And there is no peace nor cure (for
our state).

Why is it that Heaven is (thus) reproving (you)?
Why is it that Heaven is not blessing (you)? You
neglect your great barbarian (foes), And regard
me with hatred. You are regardless of the evil
omens (that abound[2]), And your demeanour is all
unseemly. (Good) men are going away, And the
country is sure to go to ruin.

Heaven is letting down its net, And many (are
the calamities in it). (Good) men are going away,
And my heart is sorrowful. Heaven is letting down

---

[1] By 'the net of crime' we are to understand the multitude of
penal laws, to whose doom people were exposed. In stanza 6,
Heaven is represented as letting it down.

[2] Compare ode 9 of the fourth decade in the former Part.

its net, And soon (all will be caught in it). (Good)   429
men are going away, And my heart is sad.

Right from the spring comes the water bubbling,
Revealing its depth. The sorrow of my heart,—Is
it (only) of to-day? Why were these things not
before me? Or why were they not after me? But
mysteriously great Heaven Is able to strengthen
anything. Do not disgrace your great ancestors :—
This will save your posterity [1].

ODE 11, STANZAS 1 AND 2. THE SHÂO MIN.

THE WRITER APPEALS TO HEAVEN, BEMOANING THE MISERY AND RUIN
WHICH WERE GOING ON, AND SHOWING HOW THEY WERE DUE TO THE
KING'S EMPLOYMENT OF MEAN AND WORTHLESS CREATURES.

Compassionate Heaven is arrayed in angry terrors.
Heaven is indeed sending down ruin, Afflicting us
with famine, So that the people are all wandering
fugitives. In the settled regions, and on the borders,
all is desolation.

Heaven sends down its net of crime ;—Devour-
ing insects, who weary and confuse men's minds,
Ignorant, oppressive, negligent, Breeders of confusion, utterly perverse :—These are the men
employed.

---

[1] The writer in these concluding lines ventures to summon the
king to repentance, and to hold out a hope that there might come
a change in their state. He does this, believing that all things are
possible with Heaven.

LESSONS FROM THE STATES.

Odes and Stanzas illustrating the Religious Views and Practices of the Writers and their Times.

It has been stated in the Introduction, p. 276, that the first Part of the Shih, called the Kwo Făng, or 'Lessons from the States,' consists of 160 pieces, descriptive of manners and events in several of the feudal states into which the kingdom of Kâu was divided. Nearly all of them are short; and the passages illustrating the religious views and practices of their times are comparatively few. What passages there are, however, of this nature will all be found below. The pieces are not arranged in decades, as in the Odes of the Kingdom, but in Books, under the names of the states in which they were produced.

Although the Kwo Făng form, as usually published, the first Part of the Shih, nearly all of them are more recent in their origin than the pieces of the other Parts. They bring us face to face with the states of the kingdom, and the ways of their officers and people for several centuries of the dynasty of Kâu.

Book II. The Odes of Shâo and the South.

The Shû and previous portions of the Shih have made us familiar with Shâo, the name of the appanage of Shih, one of the principal ministers at the court of Kâu in the first two reigns of the dynasty. The site of the city of Shâo was in the present department of Făng-khiang, Shen-hsî. The first possessor of it, along with the still more famous duke of Kâu, remained at court, to watch over the fortunes of the new dynasty. They were known as 'the highest dukes' and 'the two great chiefs,' the duke of Kâu having charge of the eastern portions of the kingdom, and the other of the western. The pieces in this Book are supposed to have been produced in Shâo, and the principalities south of it within his jurisdiction, by the duke.

ODE 2. THE *ZHÂI FAN*.

CELEBRATING THE INDUSTRY AND REVERENCE OF A PRINCE'S WIFE,
ASSISTING HIM IN SACRIFICING.

We must suppose the ladies of a harem, in one of the states of the
south, admiring and praising in these simple stanzas the way in
which their mistress discharged her duties. A view of the ode
maintained by many is that the lady gathered the southernwood,
not to use it in sacrificing, but in the nurture of the silkworms
under her care; but the evidence of the characters in the text is,
on the whole, in favour of the more common view. Constant
reference is made to the piece by Chinese moralists, to show that
the most trivial things are accepted in sacrifice, when there are
reverence and sincerity in the presenting of them.

One critic asked *K*û Hsî whether it was conceivable that the wife
of a prince did herself what is here related, and he replied that
the poet said so. Another has observed that if the lady ordered
and employed others, it was still her own doing. But that the
lady did it herself is not incredible, when we consider the sim-
plicity of those early times, in the twelfth century B.C.

She gathers the white southernwood, By the
ponds, on the islets. She employs it, In the
business of our prince.

She gathers the white southernwood, Along
the streams in the valleys. She employs it, In
the temple[1] of our prince.

---

[1] If the character here translated 'temple' had no other signification but that, there would be an end of the dispute about the
meaning of the piece. But while we find it often used of the
ancestral temple, it may also mean any building, especially one of
a large and public character, such as a palace or mansion; and
hence some contend that it should be interpreted here of 'the silk-
worm house.' We are to conceive of the lady, after having
gathered the materials for sacrificial use, then preparing them
according to rule, and while it is yet dark on the morning of the
sacrificial day, going with them into the temple, and setting them
forth in their proper vessels and places.

432   With head-dress reverently rising aloft,   Early, while yet it is night, she is in the prince's (temple). In her head-dress, slowly retiring,   She returns (to her own apartments).

ODE 4. THE *ZHÂI PIN*.

CELEBRATING THE DILIGENCE AND REVERENCE OF THE YOUNG WIFE OF AN OFFICER, DOING HER PART IN SACRIFICIAL OFFERINGS.

She gathers the large duckweed,   By the banks of the stream in the southern valley.   She gathers the pondweed,   In those pools left by the floods.

She deposits what she gathers,   In her square baskets and round ones.   She boils it,   In her tripods and pans.

She sets forth her preparations,   Under the window in the ancestral chamber[1].   Who superintends the business ?   It is (this) reverent young lady.

---

[1] 'The ancestral chamber' was a room behind the temple of the family, dedicated specially to the ancestor of the officer whose wife is the subject of the piece.   The princes of states were succeeded, as a rule, by the eldest son of the wife proper.   Their sons by other wives were called 'other sons.'   The eldest son by the wife proper of one of them became the 'great ancestor' of the clan descended from him, and 'the ancestral chamber' was an apartment dedicated to him.   Mâo and other interpreters, going on certain statements as to the training of daughters in the business of sacrificing in this apartment for three months previous to their marriage, contend that the lady spoken of here was not yet married, but was only undergoing this preparatory education. It is not necessary, however, to adopt this interpretation.   The lady appears doing the same duties as the wife in the former piece.

Book III.　The Odes of Phei.

433

Wʜᴇɴ king Wû overthrew the dynasty of Shang, the domain of its
kings was divided into three portions, the northern portion being
called Phei, the southern Yung, and the eastern Wei, the rulers
of which last in course of time absorbed the other two. It
is impossible to say why the old names were retained in the
arrangement of the odes in this Part of the Shih, for it is acknowledged on all hands that the pieces in Books iii and iv, as well
as those of Book v, are all odes of Wei.

Ode 4.　The Zäʜ Yüeh.

SUPPOSED TO BE THE COMPLAINT AND APPEAL OF *K*WANG *K*IANG, A
MARCHIONESS OF WEI, AGAINST THE BAD TREATMENT SHE RECEIVED
FROM HER HUSBAND.

All the Chinese critics give this interpretation of the piece. *K*wang
*K*iang was a daughter of the house of *K*hî, about the middle of
the eighth century ʙ.ᴄ., and was married to the marquis Yang,
known in history as 'duke *K*wang,' of Wei. She was a lady of
admirable character, and beautiful; but her husband proved
faithless and unkind. In this ode she makes her subdued moan,
appealing to the sun and moon, as if they could take cognizance
of the way in which she was treated. Possibly, however, the
addressing those bodies may simply be an instance of proso-
popoeia.

O sun, O moon, Which enlighten this lower
earth! Here is this man, Who treats me not according to the ancient rule. How can he get his
mind settled? Would he then not regard me?

O sun, O moon, Which overshadow this lower
earth! Here is this man, Who will not be friendly
with me. How can he get his mind settled? Would
he then not respond to me?

O sun, O moon, Which come forth from the
east! Here is this man, With virtuous words, but
really not good. How can he get his mind settled?
Would he then allow me to be forgotten?

[ɪ]　　　　　F f

434   O sun, O moon, From the east that come forth!
O father, O mother, There is no sequel to your
nourishing of me. How can he get his mind settled?
Would he then respond to me contrary to all reason?

Ode 15, Stanza 1. The Pei Măn.

AN OFFICER OF WEI SETS FORTH HIS HARD LOT, THROUGH DISTRESSES
AND THE BURDENS LAID UPON HIM, AND HIS SILENCE UNDER IT IN
SUBMISSION TO HEAVEN.

I go out at the north gate, With my heart full
of sorrow. Straitened am I and poor, And no one
takes knowledge of my distress. So it is! Heaven
has done it[1];—What then shall I say?

Book IV. The Odes of Yung.

See the preliminary note on p. 433.

Ode 1. The Pai *Kâu*.

PROTEST OF A WIDOW AGAINST BEING URGED TO MARRY AGAIN, AND
HER APPEAL TO HER MOTHER AND TO HEAVEN.

This piece, it is said, was made by Kung *K*iang, the widow of
Kung-po, son of the marquis Hsî of Wei (B.C. 855–814). Kung-
po having died an early death, her parents (who must have been
the marquis of *K*hî and his wife or one of the ladies of his harem)
wanted to force her to a second marriage, against which she
protests. The ode was preserved, no doubt, as an example of

---

[1] The 'Complete Digest of Comments on the Shih' warns its
readers not to take 'Heaven' here as synonymous with Ming,
'what is decreed or commanded.' The writer does not go on
to define the precise idea which he understood the character to
convey. This appears to be what we often mean by 'Providence,'
when we speak of anything permitted, rather than appointed, by
the supreme ruling Power.

what the Chinese have always considered a great virtue,—the refusal of a widow to marry again.

It floats about, that boat of cypress wood, There in the middle of the Ho[1]. With his two tufts of hair falling over his forehead[2], He was my mate; And I swear that till death I will have no other. O mother, O Heaven[3], Why will you not understand me?

It floats about, that boat of cypress wood, There by the side of the Ho. With his two tufts of hair falling over his forehead, He was my only one; And I swear that till death I will not do the evil thing. O mother, O Heaven; Why will you not understand me?

ODE 3, STANZA 2. THE *K*ÜN-ȜZE *K*IEH LÂO.

CONTRAST BETWEEN THE BEAUTY AND SPLENDOUR OF HSÜAN *K*IANG AND HER VICIOUSNESS.

Hsüan *K*iang was a princess of *K*hî, who, towards the close of the seventh century B.C., became wife to the marquis of Wei, known as duke Hsüan. She was beautiful and unfortunate, but various things are related of her indicative of the grossest immoralities prevailing in the court of Wei.

How rich and splendid Is her pheasant-figured

---

[1] These allusive lines, probably, indicate the speaker's widowhood, which left her like 'a boat floating about on the water.'

[2] Such was the mode in which the hair was kept, while a boy or young man's parents were alive, parted into two tufts from the pia mater, and brought down as low as the eyebrows on either side of the forehead.

[3] Mâo thought that the lady intended her father by 'Heaven;' while *K*û held that her father may have been dead, and that the mother is called Heaven, with reference to the kindness and protection that she ought to show. There seems rather to be in the term a wild, and not very intelligent, appeal to the supreme Power in heaven.

436 robe[1]! Her black hair in masses like clouds, No
false locks does she descend to. There are her ear-
plugs of jade, Her comb-pin of ivory, And her
high forehead, so white. She appears like a visitant
from heaven! She appears like a goddess[2].

ODE 6, STANZAS 1 AND 2. THE TING *K*IH FANG *K*UNG.

CELEBRATING THE PRAISE OF DUKE WĂN;—HIS DILIGENCE, FORESIGHT,
USE OF DIVINATION, AND OTHER QUALITIES.

The state of Wei was reduced to extremity by an irruption of some
northern hordes in B. C. 660, and had nearly disappeared from
among the states of *K*âu. Under the marquis Wei, known in
history as duke Wăn, its fortunes revived, and he became a sort
of second founder of the state.

When Ting culminated (at night-fall)[3], He
began to build the palace at *Kh*û[4], Determining

---

[1] The lady is introduced arrayed in the gorgeous robes worn by
the princess of a state in the ancestral temple.

[2] P. Lacharme translated these two concluding lines by ' Tu
primo aspectu coelos (pulchritudine), et imperatorem (majestate)
adaequas,' without any sanction of the Chinese critics ; and moreover there was no Tî (帝) in the sense of imperator then in
China. The sovereigns of *K*âu were wang or kings. *K*û Hsî
expands the lines thus :—' Such is the beauty of her robes and
appearance, that beholders are struck with awe, as if she were
a spiritual being.' Hsü *Kh*ien (Yüan dynasty) deals with them
thus:—' With such splendour of beauty and dress, how is it that she
is here? She has come down from heaven! She is a spiritual
being !'

[3] Ting is the name of a small space in the heavens, embracing
α Markab and another star of Pegasus. Its culminating at night-fall
was the signal that the labours of husbandry were over for the
year, and that building operations should be taken in hand. Great
as was the urgency for the building of his new capital, duke Wăn
would not take it in hand till the proper time for such a labour
was arrived.

[4] *Kh*û, or *Kh*û-*kh*iû, was the new capital of Wei, in the present district of *Kh*äng-wû, department 3*h*âo-*k*âu, Shan-tung.

its aspects by means of the sun. He built the   437
palace at *Kʰû*. He planted about it hazel and
chesnut trees, The Î, the T h u n g, the ᴣze, and the
varnish tree. Which, when cut down, might afford
materials for lutes.

He ascended those old walls, And thence surveyed (the site of) *Kʰû*. He surveyed *Kʰû* and
Thang [1], With the lofty hills and high elevations
about. He descended and examined the mulberry
trees. He then divined by the tortoise-shell, and
got a favourable response [2]; And thus the issue
has been truly good.

Book V. The Odes of Wei.

It has been said on the title of Book iii, that Wei at first was the
eastern portion of the old domain of the kings of Shang. With
this a brother of king Wû, called Khang-shû, was invested. The
principality was afterwards increased by the absorption of Phei
and Yung. It came to embrace portions of the present provinces of *Kʰ*ih-lî, Shan-tung, and Ho-nan. It outlasted the
dynasty of *Kʰ*âu itself, the last prince of Wei being reduced to
the ranks of the people only during the dynasty of *Kʰ*in.

Ode 4, Stanzas 1 and 2. The Măng.

AN UNFORTUNATE WOMAN, WHO HAD BEEN SEDUCED INTO AN IMPROPER
CONNEXION, NOW CAST OFF, RELATES AND BEMOANS HER SAD CASE.

An extract is given from the pathetic history here related, because
it shows how divination was used among the common people,
and entered generally into the ordinary affairs of life.

A simple-looking lad you were, Carrying cloth

---

[1] Thang was the name of a town, evidently not far from *Kʰû*.

[2] We have seen before how divination was resorted to on occasion of new undertakings, especially in proceeding to rear a city.

438 to exchange it for silk. (But) you came not so to purchase silk;—You came to make proposals to me. I convoyed you through the *Khî*[1], As far as Tun-*khiû*[2], 'It is not I,' (I said), 'who would protract the time; But you have had no good go-between. I pray you be not angry, And let autumn be the time.'

I ascended that ruinous wall, To look towards Fû-kwan[3]; And when I saw (you) not (coming from) it, My tears flowed in streams. When I did see (you coming from) Fû-kwan, I laughed and I spoke. You had consulted, (you said), the tortoise-shell and the divining stalks, And there was nothing unfavourable in their response[4]. 'Then come,' (I said), 'with your carriage, And I will remove with my goods.'

Book VI. The Odes of the Royal Domain.

King Wăn, it has been seen, had for his capital the city of Făng, from which his son, king Wû, moved the seat of government to Hâo. In the time of king *Kh*ăng, a city was built by the duke

---

[1] The *Khî* was a famous river of Wei.

[2] Tun-*khiû* was a well-known place —'the mound or height of Tun'—south of the Wei.

[3] Fû-kwan must have been the place where the man lived, according to *K*û. Rather, it must have been a pass (Fû-kwan may mean 'the gate or pass of Fû'), through which he would come, and was visible from near the residence of the woman.

[4] Ying-tâ observes that the man had never divined about the matter, and said that he had done so only to complete the process of seduction. The critics dwell on the inconsistency of divination being resorted to in such a case:—'Divination is proper only if used in reference to what is right and moral.'

of *K*âu, near the present Lo-yang, and called 'the eastern 　439
capital.' Meetings of the princes of the states assembled there;
but the court continued to be held at Hâo till the accession of
king Phing in B. C. 770. From that time, the kings of *K*âu sank
nearly to the level of the princes of the states, and the poems
collected in their domain were classed among the 'Lessons of
Manners from the States,' though still distinguished by the
epithet 'royal' prefixed to them.

ODE 1, STANZA 1. THE SHÛ LÎ.

AN OFFICER DESCRIBES HIS MELANCHOLY AND REFLECTIONS ON SEEING
THE DESOLATION OF THE OLD CAPITAL OF *K*ÂU, MAKING HIS MOAN
TO HEAVEN BECAUSE OF IT.

There is no specific mention of the old capital of *K*âu in the piece,
but the schools of Mâo and *K*û are agreed in this interpretation, which is much more likely than any of the others that have
been proposed.

There was the millet with its drooping heads;
There was the sacrificial millet coming into blade [1].
Slowly I moved about, In my heart all-agitated.
Those who knew me   Said I was sad at heart.
Those who did not know me,   Said I was seeking
for something. · O thou distant and azure Heaven [2]!
By what man was this (brought about) [3]?

---

　[1] That is, there where the ancestral temple and other grand
buildings of Hâo had once stood.
　[2] 'He cried out to Heaven,' says Yen *B*/an, 'and told (his distress), but he calls it distant in its azure brightness, lamenting that
his complaint was not heard.' This is, probably, the correct explanation of the language. The speaker would by it express his grief
that the dynasty of *K*âu and its people were abandoned and un-
cared for by Heaven.
　[3] Referring to king Yû, whose reckless course had led to the
destruction of Hâo by the *Z*ung, and in a minor degree to his
son, king Phing, who had subsequently removed to the eastern
capital.

440

Ode 9, Stanzas 1 and 3. The Tâ *Kü*.

A LADY EXCUSES HERSELF FOR NOT FLYING TO HER LOVER BY HER
FEAR OF A SEVERE AND VIRTUOUS MAGISTRATE, AND SWEARS TO HIM
THAT SHE IS SINCERE IN HER ATTACHMENT TO HIM.

His great carriage rolls along, And his robes of
rank glitter like the young sedge. Do I not think
of you? But I am afraid of this officer, and dare
not (fly to you).

While living we may have to occupy different
apartments; But, when dead, we shall share the
same grave. If you say that I am not sincere, By
the bright sun I swear that I am [1].

Book X. The Odes of Thang.

The odes of Thang were really the odes of 3in, the greatest of the
fiefs of *K*âu until the rise of *Kh*in. King *Kh*ăng, in B.C. 1107,
invested his younger brother, called Shû-yü, with the territory
where Yâo was supposed to have ruled anciently as the marquis
of Thang, in the present department of Thâi-yüan, Shan-hsî,
the fief retaining that ancient name. Subsequently the name of
the state was changed to 3in, from the river 3in in the southern
part of it.

Ode 8, Stanza 1. The Pâo Yü.

THE MEN OF 3IN, CALLED OUT TO WARFARE BY THE KING'S ORDER,
MOURN OVER THE CONSEQUENT SUFFERING OF THEIR PARENTS, AND
LONG FOR THEIR RETURN TO THEIR ORDINARY AGRICULTURAL PUR-
SUITS, MAKING THEIR APPEAL TO HEAVEN.

Sû-sû go the feathers of the wild geese, As

---

[1] In the 'Complete Digest' this oath is expanded in the following way:—' These words are from my heart. If you think that
they are not sincere, there is (a Power) above, like the bright sun,
observing me;—how should my words not be sincere?'

they settle on the bushy oaks [1]. The king's affairs   441
must not be slackly discharged, And (so) we cannot
plant our millets ;—What will our parents have to
rely on ? O thou distant and azure Heaven [2]!
When shall we be in our places again ?

ODE 11. THE KO SHĂNG.

A WIFE MOURNS THE DEATH OF HER HUSBAND, REFUSING TO BE COM-
FORTED, AND DECLARES THAT SHE WILL CHERISH HIS MEMORY TILL
HER OWN DEATH.

It is supposed that the husband whose death is bewailed in this
piece had died in one of the military expeditions of which duke
Hsien (B.C. 676–651) was fond. It may have been so, but there
is nothing in the piece to make us think of duke Hsien. I give
it a place in the volume, not because of the religious sentiment
in it, but because of the absence of that sentiment, where we
might expect it. The lady shows the grand virtue of a Chinese
widow, in that she will never marry again. And her grief would
not be assuaged. The days would all seem long summer days,
and the nights all long winter nights ; so that a hundred long
years would seem to drag their slow course. But there is not
any hope expressed of a re-union with her husband in another
state. The 'abode' and the 'chamber' of which she speaks are
to be understood of his grave ; and her thoughts do not appear
to go beyond it.

The dolichos grows, covering the thorn trees ;
The convolvulus spreads all over the waste [3]. The

---

[1] Trees are not the proper place for geese to rest on ; and the
attempt to do so is productive of much noise and trouble to the birds.
The lines would seem to allude to the hardships of the soldiers' lot,
called from their homes to go on a distant expedition.

[2] See note 2 on ode 1 of Book vi, where Heaven is appealed to
in the same language.

[3] These two lines are taken as allusive, the speaker being led
by the sight of the weak plants supported by the trees, shrubs, and
tombs, to think of her own desolate, unsupported condition. But
they may also be taken as narrative, and descriptive of the battle-
ground, where her husband had met his death.

442　man of my admiration is no more here;—With whom can I dwell? I abide alone.

The dolichos grows, covering the jujube trees; The convolvulus spreads all over the tombs. The man of my admiration is no more here;—With whom can I dwell? I rest alone.

How beautiful was the pillow of horn! How splendid was the embroidered coverlet[1]! The man of my admiration is no more here;—With whom can I dwell? Alone (I wait for) the morning.

Through the (long) days of summer, Through the (long) nights of winter (shall I be alone), Till the lapse of a hundred years, When I shall go home to his abode.

Through the (long) nights of winter, Through the (long) days of summer (shall I be alone), Till the lapse of a hundred years, When I shall go home to his chamber.

BOOK XI. THE ODES OF <i>KH</i>IN.

THE state of <i>KH</i>in took its name from its earliest principal city, in the present district of <i>KH</i>ing-shui, in <i>KH</i>in <i>K</i>âu, Kan-sû. Its chiefs claimed to be descended from Yî, who appears in the Shû as the forester of Shun, and the assistant of the great Yü in his labours on the flood of Yâo. The history of his descendants is very imperfectly related till we come to a Fei-ʒze, who had charge of the herds of horses belonging to king Hsiâo (B.C. 909–895), and in consequence of his good services was invested with

---

[1] These things had been ornaments of the bridal chamber; and as the widow thinks of them, her grief becomes more intense.

the small territory of *Kh*in, as an attached state. A descendant 443
of his, known as duke Hsiang, in consequence of his loyal services, when the capital was moved to the east in B.C. 770, was
raised to the dignity of an earl, and took his place among the
great feudal princes of the kingdom, receiving also a large
portion of territory, which included the ancient capital of the
House of *K*âu. In course of time *Kh*in, as is well known, superseded the dynasty of *K*âu, having gradually moved its capital
more and more to the east. The people of *Kh*in were, no doubt,
mainly composed of the wild tribes of the west.

ODE 6, STANZA 1. THE HWANG NIÂO.

LAMENT FOR THREE WORTHIES OF *KH*IN, WHO WERE BURIED IN THE
SAME GRAVE WITH DUKE MÛ.

There is no difficulty or difference in the interpretation of this
piece; and it brings us down to B.C. 621. Then died duke Mû,
after playing an important part in the north-west of China for
thirty-nine years. The 3o *K*wan, under the sixth year of duke
Wăn, makes mention of Mû's requiring that the three brothers
here celebrated should be buried with him, and of the composition of this piece in consequence. Sze-mâ *Kh*ien says that
this barbarous practice began with Mû's predecessor, with whom
sixty-six persons were buried alive, and that one hundred and
seventy-seven in all were buried with Mû. The death of the last
distinguished man of the House of *Kh*in, the emperor I, was subsequently celebrated by the entombment with him of all the
inmates of his harem.

They flit about, the yellow birds, And rest upon
the jujube trees[1]. Who followed duke Mû in the
grave? 3ze-*k*ü Yen-hsî. And this Yen-hsî Was
a man above a hundred. When he came to the

---

[1] It is difficult to see the relation between these two allusive
lines and the rest of the stanza. Some say that it is this,—that the
people loved the three victims as they liked the birds; others that
the birds among the trees were in their proper place,—very different
from the brothers in the grave of duke Mû.

444   grave, He looked terrified and trembled. Thou azure Heaven there! Could he have been redeemed, We would have given a hundred (ordinary) men for him [1].

Book XV. The Odes of Pin.

Duke Liû, an ancestor of the *K*âu family, made a settlement, according to its traditions, in B.C. 1797, in Pin, the site of which is pointed out, 90 lî to the west of the present district city of San-shui, in Pin *K*âu, Shen-hsî, where the tribe remained till the movement eastwards of Than-fû, celebrated in the first decade of the Major Odes of the Kingdom, ode 3. The duke of *K*âu, during the minority of king *Kh*ăng, made, it is supposed, the first of the pieces in this Book, describing for the instruction of the young monarch, the ancient ways of their fathers in Pin ; and subsequently some one compiled other odes made by the duke, and others also about him, and brought them together under the common name of ' the Odes of Pin.'

Ode 1, Stanza 8. The *Kh*î Yüeh.

DESCRIBING LIFE IN PIN IN THE OLDEN TIME ; THE PROVIDENT ARRANGE-MENTS THERE TO SECURE THE CONSTANT SUPPLY OF FOOD AND RAIMENT,—WHATEVER WAS NECESSARY FOR THE SUPPORT AND COM-FORT OF THE PEOPLE.

If the piece was made, as the Chinese critics all suppose, by the duke of *K*âu, we must still suppose that he writes in the person of an old farmer or yeoman of Pin. The picture which it gives of the manners of the Chinese people, their thrifty, provident ways, their agriculture and weaving, nearly 3,700 years ago, is

---

[1] This appeal to Heaven is like what we met with in the first of the Odes of the Royal Domain, and the eighth of those of Thang.

full of interest; but it is not till we come to the concluding stanza   445
that we find anything bearing on their religious practices.

In the days of (our) second month, they hew out
the ice with· harmonious blows [1]; And in those of
(our) third month, they convey it to the ice-houses,
(Which they open) in those of (our) fourth, early in
the morning A lamb having been offered in sacrifice with scallions [2]. In the ninth month, it is cold,
with frost. In the tenth month, they sweep clean
their stack-sites. (Taking) the two bottles of spirits
to be offered to their ruler, And having killed their
lambs and sheep, They go to his hall, And raising

---

[1] They went for the ice to the deep recesses of the hills, and
wherever it was to be found in the best condition.

[2] It is said in the last chapter of 'the Great Learning,' that 'the
family which keeps its stores of ice does not rear cattle or sheep,'
meaning that the possessor of an ice-house must be supposed to
be very wealthy, and above the necessity of increasing his means
in the way described. Probably, the having ice-houses by high
ministers and heads of clans was an innovation on the earlier custom, according to which such a distinction was proper only to the
king, or the princes of states, on whom it devolved as 'the fathers
of the people,' to impart from their stores in the hot season as
might be necessary. The third and fourth lines of this stanza are
to be understood of what was done by the orders of the ruler of
the tribe of *K*âu in Pin. In the Official Book of *K*âu, Part I,
ch. 5, we have a description of the duties of 'the Providers of Ice,'
and the same subject is treated in the sixth Book of 'the Record
of Rites,' sections 2 and 6. The ice having been collected and
stored in winter, the ice-houses were solemnly opened in the spring.
A sacrifice was offered to 'the Ruler of Cold, the Spirit of the
Ice,' and of the first ice brought forth an offering was set out in
the apartment behind the principal hall of the ancestral temple.
A sacrifice to the same Ruler of Cold, it is said, had also been
offered when the ice began to be collected. The ceremony may be
taken as an illustration of the manner in which religious services
entered into the life of the ancient Chinese.

446 　　the cup of rhinoceros horn, Wish him long life,—
that he may live for ever[1].

---

[1] The custom described in the five concluding lines is mentioned
to show the good and loyal feeling of the people of Pin towards
their chief.　Having finished all the agricultural labours of the
year, and being now prepared to enjoy the results of their industry,
the first thing they do is to hasten to the hall of their ruler, and
ask him to share in their joy, and express their loyal wishes for his
happiness.

THE HSIÂO KING

OR

CLASSIC OF FILIAL PIETY.

THE HSIÂO KING

OR

CLASSIC OF FILIAL PIETY.

INTRODUCTION.

CHAPTER I.

THE NAME OF THE CLASSIC; ITS EXISTENCE BEFORE THE HAN DYNASTY; ITS CONTENTS, AND BY WHOM IT WAS WRITTEN.

1. The Chinese character pronounced Hsiâo, which we translate by 'Filial Piety,' and which may also perform the part of an adjective, 'filial,' of a verb, 'to be filial,' or of an adverb, 'filially,' is one of the composite characters whose meaning is suggested by the meanings of their constituent parts combined together. It is made up of two others,—one signifying 'an old man' or 'old age,' and beneath it the character signifying 'a son.' It thus, according to the Shwo Wăn, the oldest Chinese dictionary (A.D. 100), presents to the eye 'a son bearing up an old man,' that is, a child supporting his parent. Hsiâo also enters as their phonetical element into at least twenty other characters, so that it must be put down as of very early formation. The character King has been explained in the Introduction to the Shû King, p. 2; and the title, Hsiâo King, means 'the Classic of Filial Piety.'

Meaning of the character Hsiâo.

2. Many Chinese critics contend that this brief treatise was thus designated by Confucius himself, and that it received the distinction of being styled a King before

[1]   G g

450 any of the older and more important classics. For the preservation of the text as we now have it, we

Was the treatise called the Hsiâo King by Confucius?

are indebted to Hsüan 3ung (A. D. 713–755), one of the emperors of the Thang dynasty. In the preface to his commentary on it there occurs this sentence :—' The Master said, "My aim is seen in the *Kh*un *Kh*iû; my (rule of) conduct is in the Hsiâo King."' The imperial author quotes the saying, as if it were universally acknowledged to have come from the sage. It is found at a much earlier date in the preface of Ho Hsiû (A. D. 129–182) to his commentary on the *Kh*un *Kh*iû as transmitted and annotated by Kung-yang. The industry of scholars has traced it still farther back, and in a more extended form, to a work called Hsiâo King *K*ü-ming *K*üeh,—a production, probably, of the first century of our era, or of the century before it. It was one of a class of writings on the classical books, full of mysterious and useless speculations, that never took rank among the acknowledged expositions. Most of them soon disappeared, but this subsisted down to the Sui dynasty (A. D. 581–618), for there was a copy of it then in the Imperial Library. It is now lost, but a few passages of it have been collected from quotations in the Han writers. Among them is this :— ' Confucius said, "If you wish to see my aim in dispensing praise or blame to the feudal lords, it is to be found in the *Kh*un *Kh*iû; the courses by which I would exalt the social relations are in the Hsiâo King."' The words thus ascribed to Confucius were condensed, it is supposed, into the form in which we have them,—first from Ho Hsiû, and afterwards from the emperor Hsüan 3ung. Whether they were really used by the sage or not, they were attributed to him as early as the beginning of our Christian era, and it was then believed that he had given to our classic the honourable name of a K i n g.

3. But the existence of the Hsiâo King can be traced several hundred years farther back ;—to within less than a century after the death of Confucius. Sze-mâ

The Hsiâo King existed before the Han dynasty.

*Kh*ien, in his history of the House of Wei, one of the three marquisates into which the

great state of *K*in was broken up in the fifth century B. C.,   451
tells us that the marquis Wǎn received, in B. C. 407, the
classical books from Pû 3ze-hsiâ, and mentions the names
of two other disciples of Confucius, with whom he was on
intimate terms of friendship. There remains the title of
a commentary on the Hsiâo King by this marquis Wǎn;
and the book was existing in the time of 3hâi Yung (A. D.
133–192), who gives a short extract from it in one of his
treatises.

4. The recovery of our classic after the fires of *Kh*in will
be related in the next chapter. Assuming here that it was

The contents of the classic, and by whom it was written. recovered, we look into it, and find a conversation, or memoranda, perhaps, of several conversations, between Confucius and his disciple 3ǎng-ʒze. The latter, however, is little
more than a listener, to whom the sage delivers his views
on Filial Piety in its various relations. There are two
recensions of the text;—one in eighteen chapters, and the
other in twenty-two. As edited in eighteen chapters, each
of them has a very brief descriptive heading. I have given
this in the subjoined translation, but the headings cannot
be traced back beyond the commentary of the emperor
Hsüan.

The saying attributed by Ho Hsiû and others to Confucius would seem to indicate that he had himself composed
the work, but the reader of it sees at once that it could not
have proceeded from him. Nor do the style and method
of the treatise suggest a view which has had many advocates,—that it was written by 3ǎng-ʒze, under the direction
of the master. There is no reason, however, why we should
not accept the still more common account,—that the Hsiâo
came from the school of 3ǎng-ʒze. To use the words of
Hû Yin, an author of the first half of our twelfth century:—'The Classic of Filial Piety was not made by
3ǎng-ʒze himself. When he retired from his conversation
(or conversations) with *K*ung-nî on the subject of Filial
Piety, he repeated to the disciples of his own school what
(the master) had said, and they classified the sayings, and
formed the treatise.'

G g 2

452   CHAPTER II.

THE RECOVERY OF THE HSIÂO KING UNDER THE HAN
DYNASTY, AND ITS PRESERVATION DOWN TO THE
PUBLICATION OF THE COMMENTARY OF THE THANG
EMPEROR HSÜAN ȝUNG.

1. The Hsiâo King suffered, like all the other Confucian
books except the Yî, from the fires of *K͟h*in. Its subsequent recovery was very like that of the Shû, described on
pp. 7, 8. We have in each case a shorter and a longer
copy, a modern text and an ancient text.

In the Catalogue of the Imperial Library, prepared by
Liû Hin immediately before the commencement of our
Recovery of the Christian era, there are two copies of the
  Hsiâo King. Hsiâo:—'the old text of the Khung family,'
which was in twenty-two chapters, according to a note by
Pan Kû (died A.D. 92), the compiler of the documents in
the records of the western Han; and another copy, which
was, according to the same authority, in eighteen chapters,
and was subsequently styled 'the modern text.' Immediately following the entry of these two copies, we find
'Expositions of the Hsiâo by four scholars,'—whose surnames were *K*ang-sun, *K*iang, Yî, and Hâu. 'They all,'
says Pan Kû, 'had laboured on the shorter text.'

The copy in eighteen chapters therefore, we must pre-
The shorter or sume, had been the first recovered; but of
  modern text. how this came about we have no account
till we come to the records of the Sui dynasty. There
it is said that, when the *K͟h*in edict for the destruction of
the books was issued, his copy of the Hsiâo was hidden
by a scholar called Yen *K*ih, a member, doubtless, of the
Yen family to which Confucius' favourite disciple Yen Hui
had belonged. When the edict was abrogated in a few
years, *K*ăn, a son of *K*ih, brought the copy from its hiding-
place. This must have been in the second century B.C.,
and the copy, transcribed, probably by *K*ăn, in the form
of the characters then used, would pass into the charge of
the board of 'great scholars' appointed to preserve the

ancient books, in the reigns of the emperors Wăn and *K*ing, B. C. 179–141.

The copy in the ancient text was derived from the tablets found in the wall of the Confucian house in the
The old or longer text. time of the emperor Wû (B. C. 140–87), and is commonly said to have been deciphered, as in the case of the tablets of the Shû, by Khung An-kwo. An-kwo wrote a commentary himself on the Hsiâo, which does not appear in Hin's Catalogue, just as no mention is made there of his commentary on the Shû. We find it entered, however, among the books in the Sui Library with the following note :—' The work of An-kwo disappeared during the troubles of the Liang dynasty (A. D. 502–556), and continued unknown till the time of Sui, when a copy was found in the capital, and came into the possession of a scholar called Liû Hsüan.' Hsüan made his treasure public, and ere long it was acknowledged by the court, while many scholars contended that it was a forgery of his own, and ascribed by him to An-kwo. Whatever opinion we may form on this matter, the discovery of the old text, and the production of a commentary on it by Khung An-kwo, can hardly be called in question.

It might be argued, indeed, that another copy in the old text was found in the first century B. C. In a memorial addressed about the Shwo Wăn dictionary to the emperor An, in A. D. 121, by Hsü *K*ung, a son of the author, he says
Was another copy in the old text discovered? that the Hsiâo King which his father used was a copy of that presented, by ' a very old man of Lû,' to the emperor *K*âo (B. C. 86–74)[1].
Many Chinese critics, and especially Wang Ying-lin

---

[1] The language of the memorial is :—' The Hsiâo King' (used by my father in the composition of his dictionary) ' was what San lâo of Lû presented in the time of the emperor *K*âo.' The San lâo most readily suggests to the reader the idea of ' three old men ;' but the characters may also mean, in harmony with Chinese idiom, ' the three classes of old men,' or ' an individual from those three classes.' The classical passage to explain the phrase is par. 18 in the first section of the sixth Book in the Lî *K*î, where it is said that king Wăn feasted the San lâo and Wû kang, ' the three classes of old men and five classes of men of experience,' in his royal college. The three classes of old men were such as were over 80, 90, and 100 years respectively. It was from a man of one of these classes that the emperor received the Hsiâo in the old

454

(better known as Wang Po-hâu, A. D. 1223–1296), say that this is a different account of the recovery of the old text from that with which the name of Khung An-kwo is connected. It is difficult to reconcile the two statements, as will be seen on a reference to the note below[1]; and yet it

---

text. According to the account given in the next note this man was Khung Ʒze-hui; and in the Books of Sui that is given as the name of the individual of the Khung family, who had hidden the tablets on the appearance of the *Khin* edict for the destruction of all the old books.

[1] The Catalogue Raisonné of the Imperial Libraries commences its account of the copies of the Hsiâo with a description of 'the Old Text of the Hsiâo, with the Commentary of Khung An-kwo,' obtained from Japan; but the editors give good reasons for doubting its genuineness. There is a copy of this work in the Chinese portion of the British Museum, an edition printed in Japan in 1732, which I have carefully examined, with the help of Professor R. K. Douglas and Mr. A. Wylie. It contains not only the commentary of Khung An-kwo, but what purports to be the original preface of that scholar. There it is said that the bamboo tablets of the copy in 'tadpole characters,' found in the wall of Confucius' old 'lecture hall, in a stone case,' were presented to the emperor by Khung Ʒze-hui, 'a very old man of Lû.' The emperor, it is added, caused two copies to be made in the current characters of the time by 'the great scholars,' one of which was given to Ʒze-hui, and the other to General Ho Kwang, a minister of war and favourite, who greatly valued it, and placed it among the archives of the empire, where it was jealously guarded.

This account makes the meaning of the phrase 'the San lâo of Lû' quite clear; but there are difficulties in the way of our believing that it proceeded from Khung An-kwo. No mention is made of him in it, whereas, according to the current narrations, the tablets with the tadpole characters were first deciphered by him; nor is the name of the emperor to whom Khung Ʒze-hui presented the tablets given. No doubt, however, this emperor was *Kâo*, with whom Ho Kwang was a favourite. If the preface were genuine, of course An-kwo was alive after Ʒze-hui went to court with the tablets. Now, the tablets were discovered in the period Thien-han, B. C. 100–97, and *Kâo* reigned from B. C. 86 to 74. An-kwo died at the age of sixty, but in what year we are not told. He had studied the Shih under Shǎn Kung, whose death can hardly be placed later than in B. C. 135. If An-kwo were born in B. C. 150, he would have been more than sixty years old—the age assigned to him at his death—at the accession of *Kâo*. I cannot believe, therefore, that the preface in the Japanese Hsiâo was written by him; and if we reject the preface, we must also reject the commentary before which it stands.

The text of the Hsiâo in the work is nearly identical with that of Sze-mâ Kwang, mentioned below on p. 458; but to the chapters there are prefixed the headings (which Kwang did not adopt), that cannot be traced farther back than the Thang dynasty. This might be got over, but the commentary throws no new light on the text. 'It is shallow and poor,' say the editors of the Catalogue Raisonné, 'and not in the style of the Han scholars.' I must think with them that Khung An-Kwo's commentary, purporting to have been preserved in Japan is a forgery.

is possible that the difficulty would disappear, if the details   455
of the discovery and the subsequent dealing with the tablets
had come down to us complete.

Certainly, in the first century B. C. there were two copies
of the Hsiâo King in the Imperial Library of Han. If those
copies, catalogued by Liû Hin, were the actual text, presented by Yen *K*ăn, and a faithful transcript in the current
Han characters of the ancient text discovered in the wall of
Confucius' old lecture hall, we should be able to say that
Can we rely the evidence for the recovery of the Hsiâo, as
fully on the it had existed during the *K*âu dynasty, was
copies cata-
logued by Liû as satisfactory as we could desire ; but there
Hin ? are some considerations that are in the way
of our doing so.

According to the records of Sui, after the old text came
into the possession of the court, and the differences between
it and the text earlier recovered were observed, Liû Hsiang
(B.C. 80–9), the father of Hin, was charged by the emperor
(*K*hăng, B.C. 32–7) to compare the two. The result of his
examination of them was that ' he removed from the modern
text what was excessive and erroneous, and fixed the number
of the chapters at eighteen.' It does not appear that previously there was any division of *K*ăn's copy into chapters.
What Hsiang did in the case of the old text we are not told.
A note by Yen Sze-kû of the Thang dynasty, appended
to Hin's Catalogue, quotes from him that ' one chapter of
the modern text was divided into two in the old, another
into three, and that the old had one chapter which did not
appear in the other.' This missing chapter, it is understood,
was the one beginning, 'Inside the smaller doors leading to
the inner apartments,' which I have appended, from the current old text, to my translation of the classic as published
by Hsüan Зung ; and yet the Sui account says that that
chapter was in the Hsiâo of *K*ang-sun, one of the four
early commentators on the modern text.

The copies catalogued by Hin were made after the examination and revision of the two texts by his father. There
are suspicious resemblances between the style and method
of the present classic and those of the original works of

456 Hsiang that have come down to us. It is impossible to say, from the want of information, what liberties he took with the documents put into his charge. The differences between the two texts as we now have them are trivial. I believe that the changes made in them by Hsiang were not important; but having them as they came from his revision, we have them at second hand, and this has afforded ground for the dealing with them by Kû Hsî and others in the manner which will be described in the next chapter.

2. I have said above (p. 450) that for the text of the classic,—the modern text, that is,—as we now have it, we are indebted to the labours of the emperor Hsüan 3ung of the Thang dynasty. Kû Î-tsun, of the Khien-lung period (1736–1795), in his work on the classics and the writings on them, has adduced the titles of eighty-six

From Khung An-kwo to the emperor Hsüan 3ung. different works on our classic, that appeared between Khung An-kwo and Hsüan 3ung. Not a single one of all these now survives; but the enumeration of them shows that the most distinguished scholars during the intervening centuries exercised their powers on the treatise, and would keep a watch on one another in the preservation of the text. Moreover, several of the works continued through the Thang dynasty, and on into that of Sung. The Catalogue of the Sui Library contains the titles of nineteen in its list.

The emperor Hsüan says, in his preface, that in the

Hsüan 3ung's work. making of his commentary he had freely used the commentaries of six earlier writers, whom he names. They were, Wei Kâo, Wang Sû, Yü Fan, and Liû Shâo, all of our second and third centuries; Liû Hsüan, of our sixth century, who laboured on the commentary of Khung An-kwo, which, as I have already stated, is said to have been discovered in his time and presented to him; and Lû Khang, rather earlier than Liû, who dealt critically with the commentary attributed to Kǎng Khang-khǎng. 'But,' says the imperial author, 'if a comment be right in reason, why need we enquire from whom it came? We have therefore taken those six writers, considered wherein

they agreed and differed, and decided between their inter-　457
pretations by reference to the general scope of the five
(great) King. In compendious style, but with extensive
examination of the subject, we have made the meaning of
the classic clear.'

The emperor says nothing himself about the differences
between the ancient and modern texts, though we know
that that subject was vehemently agitated among the
scholars of his court. The text as commented on by him
is in eighteen chapters, which do not include the chapter
to which I have referred on p. 455 as having been in the
copy of *K*ang-sun in the first century B.C. It is said,
and on sufficient authority, that this chapter was excluded
through the influence of the scholar and minister Sze-mâ
*K*ăn. To each of his chapters the emperor prefixed a brief
heading or argument, which I have retained in the translation. These headings, probably, were selected by him from
a variety proposed by the scholars about the court.

The text employed in this imperial commentary might
now be considered as sufficiently secured. It was engraved,
in less than a century after, on the stone tablets of Thang,
which were completed in the year 837, and set up in Hsî-an,
the Thang capital, where they remain, very little damaged,
to this day[1]. And not only so. The emperor was so
pleased with the commentary which he had made, that
he caused the whole of it to be engraved on four large
tablets or pillars of stone in 745. They are still to be
seen at Hsî-an, in front of the Confucian College.

---

[1] These tablets are commonly said to contain the thirteen classics (Shih-san
King). They, contained, however, only twelve different works,—the Yî, the
Shû, the Shih, the *K*âu Lî, the Î Lî, the Lî *K*î, and the amplifications of the
*K*hun *K*hiu,—by 3o *K*hiû-ming, by Kung-yang, and by Kû-liang. These form
' the nine King.' In addition to these there were the Lun Yü, the Hsiâo King,
and the R Yâ. According to Kû Yen-wû (1613-1682), the characters on the
tablets were in all 650,252. Mr. T. W. Rhys Davids (Buddhism, p. 19) esti-
mates that our English Bible contains between 900,000 and 950,000 words.
The first Psalm, in what is called the Delegates' version, very good and concise, contains 100 Chinese characters, and in our English version 130 words.
The classics of the Thang tablets, if the translator were a master of both languages, might be rendered in English so as to form a volume not quite so large
as our Bible.

458　　　It is hardly necessary to say more on the preservation
The work of　of the Hsiâo King. In A. D. 996 the second
Hsing Ping. emperor of the Sung dynasty gave orders
for an annotated edition of it to be prepared. This was
finally completed in 1001, under the superintendence of
Hsing Ping (932–1010), with a large critical apparatus, and
a lengthened exposition, both of the text and of Hsüan
Зung's explanation. This work has ever since been current
in China.

CHAPTER III.

CRITICISM OF THE HSIÂO SINCE THE THANG DYNASTY.

1. Notwithstanding the difficulty about one chapter
which has been pointed out on p. 455, Hsüan Зung's text
was generally accepted as the representative of that in
modern characters, recovered in the second century B. C.
There were still those, however, who continued to advo-
Works on the cate the claims of 'the old text.' Sze-mâ
old text by Kwang, a distinguished minister and scholar
Sze-mâ Kwang
and Fan of the Sung dynasty (1009–1086), presented
Зû-yü. to the court in 1054 his ' Explanations of the
Hsiâo King according to the Old Text,' arguing, in his
preface and in various memorials, for the correctness of that
text, as recovered by Liû Hsüan in the sixth century.
Fan Зû-yü (1041–1098), a scholar of the same century,
and in other things a collaborateur of Kwang, produced,
towards the end of his life, an ' Exposition of the Hsiâo
King according to the Old Text.' He says in his preface :—
' Though the agreement between the ancient and modern
texts is great, and the difference small, yet the ancient
deserves to be preferred, and my labour upon it may not
be without some little value[1].'

---

[1] In the Hsiâo King, as now frequently published in China, either separately
by itself, or bound up with Kû Hsî's Hsiâo Hsio, ' the Teaching for the
Young,' we find the old text, without distinction of chapters. The commentaries of Hsüan Зung and Sze-mâ Kwang, and the exposition of Fan Зû-yü,
however, follow one another at the end of the several clauses and paragraphs.

2. But our classic had still to pass the ordeal of the sceptical criticism that set in during the Sung
dynasty. The most notable result of this
was 'the Hsiâo King Expurgated,' pub-
lished by *Kû* Hsî in 1186. He tells us that when he first
saw a statement by Hû Hung (a minister in the reign of
Kâo Bung, 1127–1162), that the quotations from the Book
of Poetry in the Hsiâo were probably of later introduction
into the text, he was terror-struck. Prolonged examination, however, satisfied him that there were good grounds
for Hû's statement, and that other portions of the text
were also open to suspicion. He found, moreover, that
another earlier writer, Wang Ying-*khă*n, in the reign of
Hsiâo Bung (1163–1189), had come to the conclusion that
much of the Hsiâo had been fabricated or interpolated in
the Han dynasty. The way was open for him to give
expression to his convictions, without incurring the charge
of being the first to impugn the accepted text.

The fact was, as pointed out by the editors of the Catalogue Raisonné of the Imperial Library of the present dynasty,
that *Kû* had long entertained the views which he indicated
in his expurgated edition of the Hsiâo, and his references
to Hû and Wang were simply to shield his own boldness.
He divided the treatise into one chapter of classical text,
and fourteen chapters of illustration and commentary.
But both parts were freely expurgated. His classical text
embraces the first six chapters in my translation, and is
supposed by him to form one continuous discourse by Confucius. The rest of the treatise should not be attributed
to the sage at all. The bulk of it may have come from
Băng-ʒze, or from members of his school, but large inter-
polations were made by the Han scholars. Adopting the
old text, *Kû* discarded from it altogether 223 characters.

Attention will be called, under the several chapters, to

*Sceptical criti-
cism. Views
of Kû Hsî.*

459

Some portions also are in a different order from the arrangement of Hsüan
Bung and Hsing Ping, which I have followed in my translation. As has been
already said, the difference between its text and that of the Thang emperor is
slight,—hardly greater than the variations in the different recensions of our
Gospels and the other books of the New Testament.

460   some of the passages which he suppressed, and to the reasons, generally satisfactory, which he advanced for his procedure. Evidently he was influenced considerably by the way in which *Kḥ*ăng Î (1033–1107), whom he called 'his master,' had dealt with the old text of 'the Great Learning;' but he made his innovations with a bolder pencil and on a more extensive plan, not merely altering the arrangement of paragraphs, and supplementing what was plainly defective, but challenging the genuineness of large portions of the treatise, and removing them without scruple.

Under the Yüan dynasty, Wû *Kḥ*ăng (1249–1333), the
Views of   greatest of its scholars, followed in the wake
Wû *Kḥăng.*   of *K*û Hsî, yet with the independence charac-
teristic of himself. As *K*û had preferred the old text, Wû decided—and, I believe, more correctly—in favour of the modern, arguing that the copy of Khung An-kwo's text and commentary, said to have been recovered and published in the sixth century by Liû Hsüan, was a fabrication. He adopted, therefore, Hsüan ʒung's text as the basis of his revision, which appeared with the title of 'the Hsiâo King, in paragraphs and sentences[1].' He adopted *K*û's division of the treatise into classical text and commentary. The chapter of classical text is the same as *K*û's; the chapters of commentary are only twelve. He discarded, of course, the chapter peculiar to the old text, which has been referred to more than once, united Hsüan ʒung's eleventh chapter with another, and arranged the other chapters differently from *K*û. His revision altogether had 246 characters fewer than the old text.

3. *K*û Î-tsun gives the titles of nearly 120 works on our classic that appeared after the volume of Wû *Kḥ*ăng,
Later works   bringing its literary history down to the end
on the Hsiâo.   of the Ming dynasty. The scholars of the present dynasty have not been less abundant in their labours on it than their predecessors. Among the col-

---

[1] The title of this work in the Catalogue of the Imperial Libraries is 'Settlement of the Text of the Hsiâo King.'

lected works of Mâo *Khî*-ling (1623–1713) is one called
'Questions about the Hsiâo King,' in which, with his usual
ability, and, it must be added, his usual acrimony, he
defends the received text. He asserts—and in this he is
correct—that there is no difference of any importance
between the ancient and modern texts; when he asserts
further that there never was any such difference, what he
affirms is incapable of proof. He pours scorn on *K*û Hsî
and Wû *Kh*ăng; but he is not so successful in defending
the integrity of the Hsiâo as I have allowed him to be in
vindicating the portions of the Shû that we owe to Khung
An-kwo.

461

The Hsiâo King has always been a favourite with the
emperors of China. Before Hsüan Зung took it in hand,
the first and eighth emperors of the eastern *K*in dynasty
(317–419), the first and third of the Liang (502–556), and the
ninth of the northern Wei (386–534) had published their
labours upon it. The Manchâu rulers of the present dynasty
have signalised themselves in this department. In 1656 the
first emperor produced in one chapter his ' Imperial Commentary on the Hsiâo King,' and in 1728 the third published a ' Collection of Comments' on it. Between them was
the long reign known to us as the Khang-hsî period (1662–
1722), during which there appeared under the direction of
the second emperor, the most distinguished of his line,
his ' Extensive Explanation of the Hsiâo King,' in 100
chapters. The only portion of the text which it gives in
full is *K*û Hsî's chapter of Confucian text; but most of
the topics touched on in *K*û's supplementary chapters,
added, as he supposed, by some later hand, are dealt with
in the course of the work, the whole of which will amply
repay a careful study.

4. It will have been seen that the two great scholars, *K*û

Conclusion
regarding the
genuineness
and integrity
of the Hsiâo.

Hsî and Wû *Kh*ăng, who have taken the
greatest liberties with the text of our classic,
allow that there is a Confucian element in it,
and that more than a fifth part of the whole,
containing, even as expurgated by *K*û, about 400 characters,
may be correctly ascribed to the sage. I agree with them

462   in this. All the rest of the treatise, to whomsoever it may
be ascribed, from Ȝăng-ȝze, the immediate disciple of Confucius, down to Liû Hsiang (B. C. 80-9), took its present form
in the first century before our Christian era. The reader
will fail to see in it a close connexion between the different chapters, and think that the author or authors try
to make more of Filial Piety than can be made of it. The
whole, however, is a valuable monument of antiquity, and
an exhibition of the virtue which Chinese moralists and
rulers, from the most ancient times, have delighted to celebrate as the fundamental principle of human virtue, the
great source of social happiness, and the bond of national
strength and stability.

Note on the Translation.

In preparing the translation of the Hsiâo King for the
present work, I have made frequent reference to four
earlier translations.

Two of them were made by myself;—the one about
thirty years ago, simply as an exercise for my own improvement in Chinese; the other four years ago, when
I was anxious to understand fully the Confucian teaching
on the subject of Filial Piety, but without reference to my
earlier version.

The third is a translation in the fourth volume of the
Chinese Repository, pp. 345–353 (1835), for the accuracy
of which much cannot be said. Very few notes are appended to it. The fourth is in the 'Mémoires concernant
les Chinois' (Paris, 1779), being part of a long treatise on
the 'Ancient and Modern Doctrine of the Chinese about
Filial Piety,' by P. Cibot. In a preliminary notice to his
version of our classic, he says:—' P. Noël formerly translated the Hsiâo King into Latin. Our translation will
necessarily be different from his. He laboured on the
old text, and we on the new, which the scholars of the
Imperial College have adopted. Besides this, he has

launched out into paraphrase, and we have made it our 463
business to present the text in French such as it is in
Chinese.' I have not been able to refer to P. Noël's translation in preparing that now given to the public; but I had
his work before me when writing out my earliest version.
The difference between the old and modern texts is too
slight to affect the character of translations of them, but
P. Noël's version is decidedly periphrastic. The title of
his work is: — ' SINENSIS IMPERII LIBRI CLASSICI SEX,
nimirum Adultorum Schola, Immutabile Medium, Liber
sententiarum, Mencius, Filialis Observantia, Parvulorum
Schola, e Sinico idiomate in Latinum traducti à P. Fr.
Noël, S. J. (Prague, 1711).' The present version, I believe,
gives the text in English, such as it is in Chinese, more
accurately and closely than P. Cibot's does in French.

CHAPTER I.

THE SCOPE AND MEANING OF THE TREATISE.

(ONCE), when *K*ung-nî[1] was unoccupied, and his disciple ӡăng[2] was sitting by in attendance on him, the Master said, ' Shăn, the ancient kings had a perfect virtue and all-embracing rule of conduct, through which they were in accord with all under heaven. By the practice of it the people were brought to live in peace and harmony, and there was no ill-will between superiors and inferiors. Do you know what it was[3]?' ӡăng rose from his mat, and said, ' How

---

[1] *K*ung-nî was the designation or marriage-name of Confucius. We find it twice in the Doctrine of the Mean (chh. 2 and 30), applied to the sage by ӡze-sze, his grandson, the reputed author of that treatise. By his designation, it is said, a grandson might speak of his grandfather, and therefore some scholars contend that the Classic of Filial Piety should also be ascribed to ӡze-sze ; but such a canon cannot be considered as sufficiently established. On the authorship of the Classic, see the Introduction, p. 451.

[2] ӡăng-ӡze, named Shăn, and styled ӡze-yü, was one of the most distinguished of the disciples of Confucius. He was a favourite with the sage, and himself a voluminous writer. Many incidents and sayings are related, illustrative of his filial piety, so that it was natural for the master to enter with him on the discussion of that virtue. He shares in the honour and worship still paid to Confucius, and is one of his ' Four Assessors' in his temples.

[3] Both the translator in the Chinese Repository and P. Cibot have rendered this opening address of Confucius very imperfectly.

[1]   H h

466　　should I, Shǎn, who am so devoid of intelligence, be able to know this?' The Master said, '(It was filial piety). Now filial piety is the root of (all) virtue[1], and (the stem) out of which grows (all moral) teaching. Sit down again, and I will explain the subject to you. Our bodies—to every hair and bit of skin—are received by us from our parents, and we must not presume to injure or wound them :—this is the beginning of filial piety. When we have established our character by the practice of the (filial) course, so as to make our name famous in future ages, and thereby glorify our parents :—this is the end of filial piety. It commences with the service

---

The former has :—' Do you understand how the ancient kings, who possessed the greatest virtue and the best moral principles, rendered the whole empire so obedient that the people lived in peace and harmony, and no ill-will existed between superiors and inferiors?' The other :—' Do you know what was the pre-eminent virtue and the essential doctrine which our ancient monarchs taught to all the empire, to maintain concord among their subjects, and banish all dissatisfaction between superiors and inferiors?' P. Cibot comes the nearer to the meaning of the text, but he has neglected the characters corresponding to ' through which they were in accord with all under heaven,' that are expounded clearly enough by Hsüan ǯung. The sentiment of the sage is, as he has tersely expressed it in the Doctrine of the Mean (ch. 13), that the ancient kings ' governed men, according to their nature, with what is proper to them.'

[1] ' All virtue' means the five virtuous principles, the constituents of humanity, ' benevolence, righteousness, propriety, knowledge, and fidelity.' Of these, benevolence is the chief and fundamental, so that Mencius says (VII, ii, ch. 16), ' Benevolence is man.' In man's nature, therefore, benevolence is the root of filial piety ; while in practice filial piety is the root of benevolence. Such is the way in which Kû Hsî and other critical scholars reconcile the statements of the text here and elsewhere with their theory as to the constituents of humanity.

of parents; it proceeds to the service of the 467
ruler; it is completed by the establishment of
the character.

'It is said in the Major Odes of the Kingdom,
    "Ever think of your ancestor,
    Cultivating your virtue¹."'

CHAPTER II.

FILIAL PIETY IN THE SON OF HEAVEN.

He who loves his parents will not dare (to incur
the risk of) being hated by any man, and he who
reveres his parents will not dare (to incur the risk of)
being contemned by any man². When the love and
reverence (of the Son of Heaven) are thus carried to
the utmost in the service of his parents, the lessons
of his virtue affect all the people, and he becomes

---

¹ See the Shih King, III, i, ode 2, stanza 4. *K*û Hsî commences
his expurgation of our classic with casting out this concluding paragraph; and rightly so. Such quotations of the odes and other passages in the ancient classics are not after the manner of Confucius.
The application made of them, moreover, is often far-fetched, and
away from their proper meaning.

² The thing thus generally stated must be understood specially
of the sovereign, and only he who stands related to all other men
can give its full manifestation. Previous translators have missed
the peculiarity of the construction in each of the clauses. Thus
P. Cibot gives:—'He who loves his parents will not dare to hate
any one,' &c. But in the second member we have a well-known
form in Chinese to give the force of the passive voice. Attention
is called to this in the Extensive Explanation of the
Hsiâo (see p. 461):—'Wû yü *z*ăn does not mean merely to
hate men; it indicates an anxious apprehension lest the hatred
of men should light on me, and my parents thereby be involved
in it.'

468   a pattern to (all within) the four seas[1]:—this is the filial piety of the Son of Heaven[2].

It is said in (the Marquis of) Fû on Punishments[3], 'The One man will have felicity, and the millions of the people will depend on (what ensures his happiness).'

CHAPTER III.

FILIAL PIETY IN THE PRINCES OF STATES.

Above others, and yet free from pride, they dwell on high, without peril; adhering to economy, and carefully observant of the rules and laws, they are full, without overflowing. To dwell on high without peril is the way long to preserve nobility; to be full without overflowing is the way long to preserve riches. When their riches and nobility do not leave their persons, then they are able to preserve the altars of their land and grain, and to secure the harmony of their people and men in office[4]:—this is the filial piety of the princes of states.

---

[1] Chinese scholars make 'the people' to be the subjects of the king, and 'all within the four seas' to be the barbarous tribes outside the four borders of the kingdom, between them and the seas or oceans within which the habitable earth was contained—according to the earliest geographical conceptions. All we have to find in the language is the unbounded, the universal, influence of 'the Son of Heaven.'

[2] The appellation 'Son of Heaven' for the sovereign was unknown in the earliest times of the Chinese nation. It cannot be traced beyond the Shang dynasty.

[3] See the Shû, V, xxvii, 4, and the note on the name of that Book, p. 254.

[4] In the Chinese Repository we have for this:—'They will be able to protect their ancestral possessions with the produce of their lands;' 'They will make sure the supreme rank to their

It is said in the Book of Poetry [1],   469
'Be apprehensive, be cautious,
As if on the brink of a deep abyss,
As if treading on thin ice.'

CHAPTER IV. FILIAL PIETY IN HIGH MINISTERS
AND GREAT OFFICERS.

They do not presume to wear robes other than
those appointed by the laws of the ancient kings [2];
nor to speak words other than those sanctioned by
their speech ; nor to exhibit conduct other than that
exemplified by their virtuous ways. Thus none of
their words being contrary to those sanctions, and
none of their actions contrary to the (right) way,

---

families.' But it is better to retain the style of the original. The
king had a great altar to the spirit (or spirits) presiding over the
land. The colour of the earth in the centre of it was yellow;
that on each of its four sides differed according to the colours
assigned to the four quarters of the sky. A portion of this earth
was cut away, and formed the nucleus of a corresponding altar
in each feudal state, according to their position relative to the
capital. The prince of the state had the prerogative of sacrificing
there. A similar rule prevailed for the altars to the spirits presiding over the grain. So long as a family ruled in a state, so
long its chief offered those sacrifices; and the extinction of the
sacrifices was an emphatic way of describing the ruin and extinction of the ruling House.

[1] See the Shih, II, v, ode 1, stanza 6.

[2] The articles of dress, to be worn by individuals according to
their rank, from the sovereign downwards, in their ordinary attire,
and on special occasions, were the subject of attention and enactment in China from the earliest times. We find references to them
in the earliest books of the Shû (Part II, Books iii, iv). The words
to be spoken, and conduct to be exhibited, on every varying
occasion, could not be so particularly described; but the example
of the ancient kings would suffice for these, as their enactments
for the dress.

470 from their mouths there comes no exceptionable speech, and in their conduct there are found no exceptionable actions. Their words may fill all under heaven, and no error of speech will be found in them. Their actions may fill all under heaven, and no dissatisfaction or dislike will be awakened by them. When these three things—(their robes, their words, and their conduct)—are all complete as they should be, they can then preserve their ancestral temples[1]:—this is the filial piety of high ministers and great officers.

It is said in the Book of Poetry[2],

'He is never idle, day or night,
In the service of the One man.'

CHAPTER V. FILIAL PIETY IN INFERIOR OFFICERS.

As they serve their fathers, so they serve their mothers, and they love them equally. As they serve their fathers, so they serve their rulers, and they reverence them equally. Hence love is what is chiefly rendered to the mother, and reverence is what is chiefly rendered to the ruler, while both of these things are given to the father. Therefore when they serve their ruler with filial piety they are loyal; when they serve their superiors with reverence they are obedient. Not failing in this loyalty

---

[1] Their ancestral temples were to the ministers and grand officers what the altars of their land and grain were to the feudal lords. Every great officer had three temples or shrines, in which he sacrificed to the first chief of his family or clan; to his grandfather, and to his father. While these remained, the family remained, and its honours were perpetuated.

[2] See the Shih, III, iii, ode 6, stanza 4.

and obedience in serving those above them, they 471
are then able to preserve their emoluments and
positions, and to maintain their sacrifices [1]:—this is
the filial piety of inferior officers [2].

It is said in the Book of Poetry [3],
'Rising early and going to sleep late,
Do not disgrace those who gave you birth.'

CHAPTER VI.

FILIAL PIETY IN THE COMMON PEOPLE.

They follow the course of heaven (in the revolving seasons); they distinguish the advantages

---

[1] These officers had their 'positions' or places, and their pay.
They had also their sacrifices, but such as were private or personal to themselves, so that we have not much information about
them.

[2] The Chinese Repository has here, 'Such is the influence of
filial duty when performed by scholars;' and P. Cibot, 'Voilà
sommairement ce qui caractérise la Piété Filiale du Lettré.' But
to use the term 'scholar' here is to translate from the standpoint
of modern China, and not from that of the time of Confucius. The
Shih of feudal China were the younger sons of the higher classes,
and men that by their ability were rising out of the lower, and who
were all in inferior situations, and looking forward to offices of
trust in the service of the royal court, or of their several states.
Below the 'great officers' of ch. 4, three classes of Shih—the
highest, middle, lowest — were recognised, all intended in this
chapter. When the feudal system had passed away, the class of
'scholars' gradually took their place. Shih (士) is one of the
oldest characters in Chinese, but the idea expressed in its formation
is not known. Confucius is quoted in the Shwo Wǎn as making
it to be from the characters for one (一) and ten (十). A very
old definition of it is—'The denomination of one entrusted with
affairs.'

[3] See the Shih, II, iii, ode 2, stanza 6.

afforded by (different) soils[1]; they are careful of their conduct and economical in their expenditure;—in order to nourish their parents:—this is the filial piety of the common people.

Therefore from the Son of Heaven down to the common people, there never has been one whose filial piety was without its beginning and end on whom calamity did not come.

CHAPTER VII.

FILIAL PIETY IN RELATION TO THE THREE POWERS[2].

The disciple 3ăng said, ' Immense indeed is the greatness of filial piety!' The Master replied[3],

---

[1] These two sentences describe the attention of the people to the various processes of agriculture, as conditioned by the seasons and the qualities of different soils.

With this chapter there ends what *K*û Hsî regarded as the only portion of the H siâo in which we can rest as having come from Confucius. So far, it is with him a continuous discourse that proceeded from the sage. And there is, in this portion, especially when we admit *K*û's expurgations, a certain sequence and progress, without logical connexion, in the exhibition of the subject which we fail to find in the chapters that follow.

[2] 'The Three Powers' is a phrase which is first found in two of the Appendixes to the Yî King, denoting Heaven, Earth, and Man, as the three great agents or agencies in nature, or the circle of being.

[3] The whole of the reply of Confucius here, down to ' the advantages afforded by earth,' is found in a narrative in the 3o *K*wan, under the twenty-fifth year of duke *Kh*âo (B.C. 517), with the important difference that the discourse is there about 'ceremonies,' and not about filial piety. Plainly, it is an interpolation in the Hsiâo, and is rightly thrown out by *K*û and Wû *Kh*ăng. To my own mind it was a relief to find that the passage was not genuine, and had not come from Confucius. The discourse in the 3o *K*wan, which is quite lengthy, these sentences being only the com-

'Yes, filial piety is the constant (method) of Heaven, 473
the righteousness of Earth, and the practical duty of
Man [1]. Heaven and earth invariably pursue the
course (that may be thus described), and the people
take it as their pattern. (The ancient kings) imitated the brilliant luminaries of heaven, and acted
in accordance with the (varying) advantages afforded
by earth, so that they were in accord with all under
heaven; and in consequence their teachings, without
being severe, were successful, and their government,
without being rigorous, secured perfect order.

---

mencement of it, is more than sufficiently fanciful; but it is conceivable that what is here predicated of filial piety might be spoken
of ceremonies, while I never could see what it could have to do
with filial piety, or filial piety with it. After the long discourse in
the Ꝫo Kwan one of the interlocutors in it exclaims, 'Immense,
indeed, is the greatness of ceremonies!'—the same terms with
which Ꝫăng-ɜze is made to commence this chapter, saving that we
have 'ceremonies' instead of 'filial piety.' There can be no doubt
that the passage is interpolated; and yet the first part of it is
quoted by Pan Kû (in our first century), in a note to Liû Hin's
Catalogue, and also in the Amplification of the First Precept of the
Khang-hsî Sacred Edict (in our eighteenth century). Pan Kû may
not have been sufficiently acquainted with the Ꝫo Kwan to detect the
forgery; that Chinese scholars should still quote the description as
applicable to filial piety shows how liable they are to be carried
away by fine-sounding terms and mysterious utterances.

P. Cibot gives a correct translation of the first part in a note, but
adds that it carries the sense of the text much too high, and would
bring it into collision with the prejudices of the west, and he has
preferred to hold to the more common explanation:—'Ce qu'est
la régularité des monuments des astres pour le firmament, la fer-
tilité des campagnes pour la terre, la Piété Filiale l'est constam-
ment pour les peuples!'

[1] An amusing translation of this sentence is found in Samuel
Johnson's 'Oriental Religions, China,' p. 208, beginning, 'Filial
Piety is the Book of Heaven!' Mr. Johnson does not say where
he got this version.

474

'The ancient kings, seeing how their teachings [1] could transform the people, set before them therefore an example of the most extended love, and none of the people neglected their parents; they set forth to them (the nature of) virtue and righteousness, and the people roused themselves to the practice of them; they went before them with reverence and yielding courtesy, and the people had no contentions; they led them on by the rules of propriety and by music, and the people were harmonious and benignant; they showed them what they loved and what they disliked, and the people understood their prohibitions.

'It is said in the Book of Poetry[2],

"Awe-inspiring are you, O Grand-Master Yin,
And the people all look up to you."'

CHAPTER VIII. FILIAL PIETY IN GOVERNMENT.

The Master said, 'Anciently, when the intelligent kings by means of filial piety ruled all under heaven, they did not dare to receive with disrespect the ministers of small states;—how much less would they do so to the dukes, marquises, counts, and barons!' Thus it was that they got (the princes of) the myriad states with joyful hearts (to assist them) in the (sacrificial) services to their royal predecessors[3].

---

[1] Sze-mâ Kwang changes the character for 'teachings' here into that for 'filial piety.' There is no external evidence for such a reading; and the texture of the whole treatise is so loose that we cannot insist on internal evidence.

[2] See the Shih, II, iv, ode 7, stanza 1.

[3] Under the Kâu dynasty there were five orders of nobility, and the states belonging to their rulers varied proportionally in size.

'The rulers of states did not dare to slight wife- 475
less men and widows;—how much less would they
slight their officers and the people! Thus it was
that they got all their people with joyful hearts
(to assist them) in serving the rulers, their predecessors [1].

'The heads of clans did not dare to slight their
servants and concubines;—how much less would
they slight their wives and sons! Thus it was that
they got their men with joyful hearts (to assist them)
in the service of their parents.

'In such a state of things, while alive, parents
reposed in (the glory of) their sons; and, when sacrificed to, their disembodied spirits enjoyed their
offerings [2]. Therefore all under heaven peace and
harmony prevailed; disasters and calamities did not
occur; misfortunes and rebellions did not arise.

'It is said in the Book of Poetry [3],

" To an upright, virtuous conduct
All in the four quarters of the state render obedient
      homage." '

There were besides many smaller states attached to these. The
feudal lords at stated times appeared at the royal court, and one
important duty which then devolved on them was to take part in
the sacrificial services of the sovereign in the ancestral temple.

[1] These services were also the sacrifices in the ancestral temples
of the rulers of the states and of the chiefs of clans,—the feudal
princes and the ministers and great officers of chapters 3 and 4.

[2] In the Chinese Repository we read here :—'Parents enjoyed
tranquillity while they lived, and after their decease sacrifices were
offered to their disembodied spirits.' To the same effect P. Cibot :—
' Les pères et mères étoient heureux pendant la vie, et après leur
mort leurs âmes étoient consolées par des Tsî (sacrifices).' I believe that I have caught the meaning more exactly.

[3] See the Shih, III, iii, ode 2, stanza 2.

476　CHAPTER IX. THE GOVERNMENT OF THE SAGES[1].

The disciple 3ǎng said, 'I venture to ask whether in the virtue of the sages there was not something greater than filial piety.' The Master replied, ' Of all (creatures with their different) natures produced by Heaven and Earth, man is the noblest. Of all the actions of man there is none greater than filial piety. In filial piety there is nothing greater than the reverential awe of one's father. In the reverential awe shown to one's father there is nothing greater than the making him the correlate of Heaven[2]. The duke of Kâu was the man who (first) did this[3].

---

[1] ' The sages' here must mean the sage sovereigns of antiquity, who had at once the highest wisdom and the highest place.

[2] See a note on p. 99 on the meaning of the phrase ' the fellow of God,' which is the same as that in this chapter, translated ' the correlate of God.' P. Cibot goes at length into a discussion of the idea conveyed by the Chinese character P'ei, but without coming to any definite conclusion ; and indeed Tâi Thung, author of the dictionary Liû Shû Kû, says that ' its original significancy has baffled investigation, while its classical usage is in the sense of " mate," " fellow." ' The meaning here is the second assigned to it on p. 99. In the Chinese Repository we find :—' As a mark of reverence there is nothing more important than to place the father on an equality with heaven ;' which is by no means the idea, while the author further distorts the meaning by the following note :— ' T'ien, " Heaven," and Shang Tî, the " Supreme Ruler," seem to be perfectly synonymous ; and whatever ideas the Chinese attach to them, it is evident that the noble lord of Kâu regarded his ancestors, immediate and remote, as their equals, and paid to the one the same homage as the other. In thus elevating mortals to an equality with the Supreme Ruler, he is upheld and approved by Confucius, and has been imitated by myriads of every generation of his countrymen down to the present day.'

[3] It is difficult to say in what the innovation of the duke of Kâu

'Formerly the duke of *K*âu at the border altar　477
sacrificed to Hâu-*k*î as the correlate of Heaven,
and in the Brilliant Hall he honoured king Wăn,
and sacrificed to him as the correlate of God [1].　The

consisted.　The editors of the **Extensive Explanation of the
Hsiâo** say :—' According to commentators on our classic, Shun
thinking only of the virtue of his ancestor did not sacrifice to him at
the border altar.　The sovereigns of Hsiâ and Yin were the first to
sacrifice there to their ancestors ; but they had not the ceremony of
sacrificing to their fathers as the correlates of Heaven.　This began
with the duke of *K*âu.''　To this explanation of the text the editors
demur, and consider that the noun ' father' in the previous sentence should be taken, in the case of the duke of *K*âu, both of
Hâu-*k*î and king Wăn.

[1] The reader of the translations from the **Shih** must be familiar
with Hâu-*k*î, as the ancestor to whom the kings of *K*âu traced
their lineage, and with king Wăn, as the acknowledged founder of
their dynasty in connexion with his son, king Wû.　Was any greater
honour done to Hâu-*k*î in making him the correlate of Heaven
than to king Wăn in making him the correlate of God ?　We must
say, No.　As is said in the **Extensive Explanation**, 'The words
Heaven and **God** are different, but their meaning is one and the
same.'　The question is susceptible of easy determination.　Let
me refer the reader to the translations from the Shih on pp. 317
and 329.　The tenth piece on the latter was sung, at the border
sacrifice to Heaven, in honour of Hâu-*k*î ; and the first four lines
of it are to the effect—

> 'O thou, accomplished, great Hâu-*k*î !
>> To thee alone 'twas given
>> To be, by what we trace to thee,
>> The correlate of Heaven ;'

while the fifth and sixth lines are—

>> 'God had the wheat and barley meant
>> To nourish all mankind.
> None would have fathomed His intent,
>> But for thy guiding mind.'

The seventh piece on the former page was used at the sacrifice, in
the Brilliant Hall, to king Wăn, as 'the correlate of God.'　The
first three lines have been versified by—

478　consequence was that from (all the states) within the four seas, every (prince) came in the discharge of his duty to (assist in those) sacrifices. In the virtue of the sages what besides was there greater than filial piety ?

'Now the feeling of affection grows up at the parents' knees, and as (the duty of) nourishing those parents is exercised, the affection daily merges in awe. The sages proceeded from the (feeling of) awe to teach (the duties of) reverence, and from (that of) affection to teach (those of) love. The teachings of the sages, without being severe, were successful, and their government, without being rigo-

---

'My offerings here are given,
　　A ram, a bull.
Accept them, mighty Heaven,
　　All-bountiful;'

and the sixth and seventh lines by—

'From Wăn comes blessing rich;
　　Now on the right　　_
He owns those gifts to which
　　Him I invite.'

Since 'Heaven' and 'God' have the same reference, why are they used here as if there were some opposition between them ? The nearest approach to an answer to this is found also in the Extensive Explanation, derived mainly from *Kh*ăn Hsiang-tâo, of the Sung dynasty, and to the following effect :—' Heaven (Tien) just is God (Tî). Heaven is a term specially expressive of honour, and Hâu-*kî* was made the correlate of Heaven, because he was remote, far distant from the worshipper. God is a term expressive of affection, and king Wăn was made the correlate of God, because he was nearer to, the father of, the duke of *K*âu.' Hsiang-tâo concludes by saying that the sacrifice at the border altar was an old institution, while that in the Brilliant Hall was first appointed by the duke of *K*âu. According to this view, Heaven would approximate to the name for Deity in the absolute,—Jehovah, as explained in Exodus xv. 14; while Tî is God, 'our Father in heaven.'

rous, was effective.　What they proceeded from was the root (of filial piety implanted by Heaven).

'The relation and duties between father and son, (thus belonging to) the Heaven-conferred nature, (contain in them the principle of) righteousness between ruler and subject[1].　The son derives his life from his parents, and no greater gift could possibly be transmitted; his ruler and parent (in one), his father deals with him accordingly, and no generosity could be greater than this.　Hence, he who does not love his parents, but loves other men, is called a rebel against virtue; and he who does not revere his parents, but reveres other men, is called a rebel against propriety.　When (the ruler) himself thus acts contrary to (the principles) which should place him in accord (with all men), he presents nothing for the people to imitate.　He has nothing to do with what is good, but entirely and only with what is injurious to virtue.　Though he may get (his will, and be above others), the superior man does not give him his approval.

---

[1] We find for this in the Chinese Repository :—'The feelings which ought to characterise the intercourse between father and son are of a heavenly nature, resembling the bonds which exist between a prince and his ministers.'　P. Cibot gives :—' Les rapports immuable de père et de fils découlent de l'essence même du T i e n, et offrent la première idée de prince et de sujet;' adding on the former clause this note :—' Les commentateurs ne disent que des mots sur ces paroles; mais comment pourroient ils les bien expliquer, puisqu'ils ne sauroient en entrevoir le sens supreme et ineffable? Quelques-uns ont pris le parti de citer le texte de T â o-teh K i n g (ch. 42), "Le T â o est vie et unité; le premier a engendré le second; les deux ont produit le troisième; le trois ont fait toutes choses;" c'est-à-dire, qu'ils ont tâché d'expliquer un texte qui les passe, par un autre où ils ne comprennent rien.'　But there is neither difficulty in the construction of the text here, nor mystery in its meaning.

480   'It is not so with the superior man. He speaks, having thought whether the words should be spoken ; he acts, having thought whether his actions are sure to give pleasure. His virtue and righteousness are such as will be honoured ; what he initiates and does is fit to be imitated; his deportment is worthy of contemplation; his movements in advancing or retiring are all according to the proper rule. In this way does he present himself to the people, who both revere and love him, imitate and become like him. Thus he is able to make his teaching of virtue successful, and his government and orders to be carried into effect [1].

'It is said in the Book of Poetry [2],

"The virtuous man, the princely one,
Has nothing wrong in his deportment."'

Chapter X. An Orderly Description of the Acts of Filial Piety.

The Master said, 'The service which a filial son does to his parents is as follows :—In his general conduct to them, he manifests the utmost reverence ; in his nourishing of them, his endeavour is to give them the utmost pleasure ; when they are ill, he feels the greatest anxiety ; in mourning for them (dead), he exhibits every demonstration of grief ; in sacrificing to them, he displays the utmost solemnity. When a son is complete in these five things (he may be pronounced) able to serve his parents.

---

[1] This paragraph may be called a mosaic, formed by piecing together passages from the Ȝo *K*wan.

[2] See the Shih, I, xiv, ode 3, stanza 3.

'He who (thus) serves his parents, in a high 481 situation, will be free from pride; in a low situation, will be free from insubordination; and among his equals, will not be quarrelsome. In a high situation pride leads to ruin; in a low situation insubordination leads to punishment; among equals quarrelsomeness leads to the wielding of weapons.

'If those three things be not put away, though a son every day contribute beef, mutton, and pork[1] to nourish his parents, he is not filial.'

CHAPTER XI. FILIAL PIETY IN RELATION TO THE FIVE PUNISHMENTS.

The Master said, 'There are three thousand offences against which the five punishments are directed[2], and there is not one of them greater than being unfilial.

'When constraint is put upon a ruler, that is the disowning of his superiority; when the authority of the sages is disallowed, that is the disowning of (all) law; when filial piety is put aside, that is the disowning of the principle of affection. These (three things) pave the way to anarchy.'

CHAPTER XII. AMPLIFICATION OF 'THE ALL-EMBRACING RULE OF CONDUCT' IN CHAPTER I.

The Master said, 'For teaching the people to be affectionate and loving there is nothing better than Filial Piety; for teaching them (the observance of) propriety and submissiveness there is nothing better than Fraternal Duty; for changing their manners

---

[1] Compare with this the Confucian Analects, II, vii.
[2] See the Shû, p. 43, and especially pp. 255, 256.

482   and altering their customs there is nothing better than Music; for securing the repose of superiors and the good order of the people there is nothing better than the Rules of Propriety.

'The Rules of Propriety are simply (the development of) the principle of Reverence. Therefore the reverence paid to a father makes (all) sons pleased; the reverence paid to an elder brother makes (all) younger brothers pleased; the reverence paid to a ruler makes (all) subjects pleased[1]. The reverence paid to one man makes thousands and myriads of men pleased. The reverence is paid to a few, and the pleasure extends to many;—this is what is meant by an "All-embracing Rule of Conduct."'

CHAPTER XIII. AMPLIFICATION OF 'THE PERFECT VIRTUE' IN CHAPTER I.

The Master said, 'The teaching of filial piety by the superior man[2] does not require that he should go to family after family, and daily see the members of each. His teaching of filial piety is a tribute of reverence to all the fathers under heaven; his teaching of fraternal submission is a tribute of reverence to all the elder brothers under heaven; his teaching of the duty of a subject is a tribute of reverence to all the rulers under heaven.

---

[1] We must understand that the 'reverence' here is to be understood as paid by the sovereign. In reverencing his father (or an uncle may also in Chinese usage be so styled), he reverences the idea of fatherhood, and being 'in accord with the minds of all under heaven,' his example is universally powerful. And we may reason similarly of the other two cases of reverence specified.

[2] The *Kün-ʒze*, or 'superior man,' here must be taken of the sovereign. P. Cibot translates it by ' un prince.'

' It is said in the Book of Poetry[1],   483
    " The happy and courteous sovereign
        Is the parent of the people."
' If it were not a perfect virtue, how could it be
recognised as in accordance with their nature by the
people so extensively as this ? '

CHAPTER XIV. AMPLIFICATION OF 'MAKING OUR NAME FAMOUS' IN CHAPTER I.

The Master said, ' The filial piety with which the
superior man serves his parents may be transferred
as loyalty to the ruler ; the fraternal duty with which
he serves his elder brother may be transferred as
submissive deference to elders; his regulation of
his family may be transferred as good government
in any official position. Therefore, when his conduct
is thus successful in his inner (private) circle, his
name will be established (and transmitted) to future
generations.'

CHAPTER XV. FILIAL PIETY IN RELATION TO REPROOF AND REMONSTRANCE.

The disciple 3ǎng said, ' I have heard your instructions on the affection of love, on respect and
reverence, on giving repose to (the minds of) our
parents, and on making our name famous ;—I would
venture to ask if (simple) obedience to the orders of
one's father can be pronounced filial piety.' The
Master replied, ' What words are these ! what words
are these ! Anciently, if the Son of Heaven had
seven ministers who would remonstrate with him,

---

[1] See the Shih, III, ii, ode 7, stanza 1. The two lines of the
Shih here are, possibly, not an interpolation.

484 although he had not right methods of government, he would not lose his possession of the kingdom; if the prince of a state had five such ministers, though his measures might be equally wrong, he would not lose his state; if a great officer had three, he would not, in a similar case, lose (the headship of) his clan; if an inferior officer had a friend who would remonstrate with him, a good name would not cease to be connected with his character; and the father who had a son that would remonstrate with him would not sink into the gulf of unrighteous deeds[1]. Therefore when a case of unrighteous conduct is concerned, a son must by no means keep from remonstrating with his father, nor a minister from remonstrating with his ruler. Hence, since remonstrance is required in the case of unrighteous conduct, how can (simple) obedience to the orders of a father be accounted filial piety[2]?'

CHAPTER XVI. THE INFLUENCE OF FILIAL PIETY AND THE RESPONSE TO IT.

The Master said, 'Anciently, the intelligent kings served their fathers with filial piety, and therefore they served Heaven with intelligence; they served their mothers with filial piety, and therefore they served Earth with discrimination[3]. They pursued

---

[1] The numbers 7, 5, 3, 1 cannot be illustrated by examples, nor should they be insisted on. The higher the dignity, the greater would be the risk, and the stronger must be the support that was needed.

[2] Compare the Analects, IV, xviii, and the Lî Kî, X, i, 15.

[3] This chapter is as difficult to grasp as the seventh, which treated of Filial Piety in Relation to 'the Three Powers.' It is indeed a sequel to that. Heaven and Earth appear as two Powers, or as

the right course with reference to their (own) seniors and juniors, and therefore they secured the regulation of the relations between superiors and inferiors (throughout the kingdom).

'When Heaven and Earth were served with intelligence and discrimination, the spiritual intelligences displayed (their retributive power [1]).

'Therefore even the Son of Heaven must have some whom he honours ; that is, he has his uncles of his surname. He must have some to whom he concedes the precedence ; that is, he has his cousins, who bear the same surname, and are older than himself. In the ancestral temple he manifests the utmost reverence, showing that he does not forget his parents ; he cultivates his person and is careful of his conduct, fearing lest he should disgrace his predecessors.

'When in the ancestral temple he exhibits the

---

a dual Power, taking the place of Heaven or God. We can in a degree follow the treatise in transferring the reverence paid by a son to his father to loyalty shown by him to his ruler ; but it is more difficult to understand the development of filial piety into religion that is here assumed and described. Was it not the pressing of this virtue too far, the making more of it than can be made, that tended to deprave religion during the *Kâu* dynasty, and to mingle with the earlier monotheism a form of nature-worship ?

Hsing Ping, in his 'Correct Meaning,' makes the 'discrimination' here to be 'an ability to distinguish the advantages of the earth ;'— showing how he had the sixth and seventh chapters in his mind.

[1] 'The Spiritual Intelligences' here are Heaven and Earth conceived of as Spiritual Beings. They responded to the sincere service of the intelligent kings, as Hsing Ping says, with 'the harmony of the active and passive principles of nature, seasonable winds and rain, the absence of epidemic sickness and plague, and the repose of all under heaven.' Compare with this what is said in 'the Great Plan' of the Shû, pp. 147, 148.

486   utmost reverence, the spirits of the departed manifest themselves [1].   Perfect filial piety and fraternal
duty reach to (and move) the spiritual intelligences,
and diffuse their light on all within the four seas ;—
they penetrate everywhere.

'It is said in the Book of Poetry [2],
" From the west to the east,
From the south to the north,
There was not a thought but did him homage." '

Chapter XVII. The Service of the Ruler.

The Master said, 'The superior man [3] serves his
ruler in such a way, that when at court in his presence his thought is how to discharge his loyal duty
to the utmost ; and when he retires from it, his
thought is how to amend his errors.   He carries
out with deference the measures springing from his
excellent qualities, and rectifies him (only) to save
him from what are evil.   Hence, as the superior
and inferior, they are able to have an affection for
each other.

'It is said in the Book of Poetry [4],
" In my heart I love him ;
And why should I not say so ?
In the core of my heart I keep him,
And never will forget him." '

---

[1] The reader will have noticed many instances of this, or what
were intended to be instances of it, in the translations from the
Shih, pp. 365–368, &c.

[2] See the Shih, III, i, ode 10, stanza 6.

[3] 'The superior man' here can only be the good and intelligent
officer in the royal domain or at a feudal court.

[4] See the Shih, II, viii, ode 4, stanza 4.

Chapter XVIII.

487

Filial Piety in Mourning for Parents.

The Master said, 'When a filial son is mourning for a parent, he wails, but not with a prolonged sobbing; in the movements of ceremony he pays no attention to his appearance; his words are without elegance of phrase; he cannot bear to wear fine clothes; when he hears music, he feels no delight; when he eats a delicacy, he is not conscious of its flavour :—such is the nature of grief and sorrow.

'After three days he may partake of food; for thus the people are taught that the living should not be injured on account of the dead, and that emaciation must not be carried to the extinction of life :—such is the rule of the sages. The period of mourning does not go beyond three years, to show the people that it must have an end.

'An inner and outer coffin are made; the grave-clothes also are put on, and the shroud; and (the body) is lifted (into the coffin). The sacrificial vessels, round and square, are (regularly) set forth, and (the sight of them) fills (the mourners) with (fresh) distress [1]. The women beat their breasts, and the men stamp with their feet, wailing and weeping, while they sorrowfully escort the coffin to the grave. They consult the tortoise-shell to determine the grave and the ground about it, and

---

[1] These vessels were arranged every day by the coffin, while it continued in the house, after the corpse was put into it. The practice was a serving of the dead as the living had been served. It is not thought necessary to give any details as to the other different rites of mourning which are mentioned. They will be found, with others, in the translations from the Lî Kî.

488 there they lay the body in peace. They prepare the ancestral temple (to receive the tablet of the departed), and there present offerings to the disembodied spirit. In spring and autumn they offer sacrifices, thinking of the deceased as the seasons come round.

'The services of love and reverence to parents when alive, and those of grief and sorrow to them when dead :—these completely discharge the fundamental duty of living men. The righteous claims of life and death are all satisfied, and the filial son's service of his parents is completed.'

The above is the Classic of Filial Piety, as published by the emperor Hsüan in A.D. 722, with the headings then prefixed to the eighteen chapters. Subsequently, in the eleventh century, Sze-mâ Kwang (A.D. 1009–1086), a famous statesman and historian, published what he thought was the more ancient text of the Classic in twenty-two chapters, with 'Explanations' by himself, without indicating, however, the different chapters, and of course without headings to them. This work is commonly published along with an 'Exposition' of his views, by Fan Bû-yü, one of his contemporaries and friends. The differences between his text and that of the Thang emperor are insignificant. He gives, however, one additional chapter, which would be the nineteenth of his arrangement. It is as follows :—' Inside the smaller doors leading to the inner apartments are to be found all the rules (of government). There is awe for the father, and also for the elder brother. Wife and children, servants and concubines are like the common people, serfs, and underlings.'

TRANSLITERATION OF ORIENTAL ALPHABETS ADOPTED FOR THE TRANSLATIONS OF THE SACRED BOOKS OF THE EAST.

CONSONANTS.	MISSIONARY ALPHABET.			Sanskrit.	Zend.	Pehlevi.	Persian.	Arabic.	Hebrew.	Chinese.
	I Class.	II Class.	III Class.							
Gutturales.										
1 Tenuis	k			क	۹	۹	ۇ	ۇ	כ	k
2 „ aspirata	kh			ख	ۻ	ۓ			ה	kh
3 Media	g			ग	ۻ	ۓ			ר	
4 „ aspirata	gh			घ	۲	۹۲	ڭ	ڭ	ה ק	
5 Gutturo-labialis	q			ॿ						
6 Nasalis	ṅ (ng)			ङ	३ (ng) / ड़ (n)					h, hs
7 Spiritus asper	h			ह	ﻭ (ﻭ hv)	ﻭ	ﻭ	ﻭ	כ	
8 „ lenis	’						ﻭ	ﻭ	ז	
9 „ asper faucalis	ʿh						ﻭ	ﻭ	כ	
10 „ lenis faucalis	ʿh						ﻭ	ﻭ	ה	
11 „ asper fricatus		ʿh							ק	
12 „ lenis fricatus		ʿh								
Gutturales modificatae (palatales, &c.)										
13 Tenuis		k		च		۹	ۇ	ۇ		k
14 „ aspirata		kh		छ		۹۲	ۇ·۽	ۇ·۽		kh
15 Media		g		ज		۹۲				
16 „ aspirata		gh		झ						
17 „ Nasalis	ñ			ञ						

[1]

K k

Comparative alphabet table (rotated on page).

	CONSONANTS (continued).	MISSIONARY ALPHABET. I Class.	II Class.	III Class.	Sanskrit.	Zend.	Pehlevi.	Persian.	Arabic.	Hebrew.	Chinese.
18	Semivocalis	y	...	...	य	ॐ (init.)	و	ى	ى	י	y
19	Spiritus asper	...	(y)	...	...	...	...	...	...	...	...
20	„ lenis	...	(j)	...	...	...	...	...	...	...	...
21	„ asper assibilatus	...	s	...	श	...	...	...	...	...	z
22	„ lenis assibilatus	...	z	...	...	...	...	...	...	...	...
	Dentales.										
23	Tenuis	t	...	...	त	...	...	...	...	...	t
24	„ aspirata	th	...	TH	थ	...	...	...	...	...	th
25	„ assibilata	...	...	...	...	...	...	...	...	...	...
26	Media	d	...	...	द	...	...	...	...	...	...
27	„ aspirata	dh	...	DH	ध	...	...	...	...	...	...
28	„ assibilata	...	...	...	...	...	...	...	...	...	...
29	Nasalis	n	ř	...	न	...	...	...	...	...	n
30	Semivocalis	l	...	L	ल	...	...	...	...	...	l
31	„ mollis 1	...	...	...	...	...	...	...	...	...	...
32	„ mollis 2	...	...	...	...	...	...	...	...	...	...
33	Spiritus asper 1	s	...	S	स	...	...	...	...	...	s
34	„ asper 2	...	...	s	...	...	...	...	...	...	...
35	„ lenis	z	...	...	...	...	...	...	...	...	z
36	„ asperrimus 1	...	...	z (ž)	...	...	...	...	...	...	...
37	„ asperrimus 2	...	...	ž (ż)	...	...	...	...	...	...	ḍh

Dentales modificatae (linguales, &c.)									
38 Tenuis								*t*	
39 „ aspirata								*th*	
40 Media								*d*	
41 „ aspirata								*dh*	
42 Nasalis								*n*	
43 Semivocalis									r
44 „ fricata								*r*	
45 „ diacritica							R		
46 Spiritus asper									sh
47 „ lenis									zh
Labiales.									
48 Tenuis								*p*	p
49 „ aspirata									ph
50 Media									b
51 „ aspirata									bh
52 Tenuissima									m
53 Nasalis									m
54 Semivocalis									w
55 „ aspirata									hw
56 Spiritus asper									f
57 „ lenis									v
58 Anusvâra								*m*	
59 Visarga								*h*	

VOWELS.	MISSIONARY ALPHABET. I Class.	II Class.	III Class.	Sanskrit.	Zend.	Pehlevi.	Persian.	Arabic.	Hebrew.	Chinese.
1 Neutralis	0									ă
2 Laryngo-palatalis	ĕ					٠ fin.				
3 „ labialis	ŏ					٠ init.				
4 Gutturalis brevis	a			अ	११	١	١	١		a
5 „ longa	â	(a)		आ	१	٢	٢			â
6 Palatalis brevis	i			इ	٣					i
7 „ longa	î	(e)		ई						î
8 Dentalis brevis	ŭ			ऋ						
9 „ longa	ū			ॠ						
10 Linugualis brevis	ṛ			ऌ						
11 „ longa	ṝ			ॡ						
12 Labialis brevis	u			उ						u
13 „ longa	û	(u)		ऊ						ô
14 Gutturo-palatalis brevis	e	(e)		ए	ε(e) ε(e)					e
15 „ longa	ê (ai)	(e)		ऐ	ख, ख					ĕ
16 Diphthongus gutturo-palatalis	ai	(ai)								ăi
17 „ „	ei (ëi)									ei, ĕi
18 „ „	oi (ŏu)									
19 Gutturo-labialis brevis	o	(o)		ओ						o
20 „ longa	ô (au)	(au)		औ						
21 Diphthongus gutturo-labialis	âu				au (au)					âu
22 „ „	eu (ëu)									
23 „ „	ou (ŏu)									
24 Gutturalis fracta	ä									
25 Palatalis fracta	ï									
26 Labialis fracta	ü									ü
27 Gutturo-labialis fracta	ö									

索　引*

（索引中的页码为原书页码，即本书边码）

一、所引中文作品和评注者

---

*　本索引由费乐仁制作。——编者

（二）评注作品（没有提及作者）

（三）评注者（按中文人名音序排）

---

① 1871 年理雅各的拼写是 "Ch'un"，1879 年改为了 "Hsün"，但 "Ch'un" 似乎是正确的读音。参见《中国经典》第四卷，第 536 页。

② 这一拼写是根据其粤语发音。

③ "欧" 的拼写应该是 "Ou"，这里的拼写是根据其粤语发音。

二、所引西方作品和相关研究者

（一）西文作品

（二）相关研究者

图书在版编目（CIP）数据

理雅各文集 . 第 1 卷, 中国圣书 . 一, 书经、诗经、孝经 /（英）理雅各译注；丁大刚，潘琳主编 . --北京：商务印书馆, 2025. --ISBN 978-7-100-24274-5

Ⅰ．K207.8-53

中国国家版本馆 CIP 数据核字第 2024M3D356 号

总主编：张西平　〔美〕费乐仁

理雅各文集

第 1 卷

中国圣书（一）

书经、诗经、孝经

〔英〕理雅各　译注

丁大刚　潘琳　主编

商 务 印 书 馆 出 版
（北京王府井大街 36 号　邮政编码 100710）
商 务 印 书 馆 发 行
北京市艺辉印刷有限公司印刷
ISBN 978 - 7 - 100 - 24274 - 5

2025 年 1 月第 1 版　　　　开本 880×1240　1/32
2025 年 1 月北京第 1 次印刷　印张 23⅝　插页 1
定价：120.00 元